The Twentieth-Century West

EDITED BY
Gerald D. Nash
Richard W. Etulain

University of New Mexico Press

Albuquerque

The Twentieth-Century West

Historical Interpretations

Library of Congress Cataloging-in-Publication Data

The Twentieth century West: historical interpretations / edited by
Gerald D. Nash, Richard W. Etulain. — 1st ed.
   p.   cm.
  Bibliography: p.
  Includes index.
  ISBN 0-8263-1116-4
  1. West (U.S.)—Civilization—20th century.
I. Nash, Gerald D.
II. Etulain, Richard W.
F595.T9 1989
978'.03—dc19
                    88-7565

© *1989 by the University of New Mexico Press. All rights reserved.*
First edition.

Contents

Preface — xi

Prologue: The Twentieth-Century West
A New Historiographical Frontier
Richard W. Etulain — 1

Part One: People of the Twentieth-Century West — 33

1. *The People of the West since 1890*
   Walter Nugent — 35

2. *The Metropolitan Region*
   Western Cities in the New Urban Era
   Carl Abbott — 71

3. *Western Women*
   The Twentieth-Century Experience
   Karen Anderson — 99

4. *Mexican Americans in the New West*
   Ricardo Romo — 123

5. *Indians of the Modern West*
   Donald L. Parman — 147

CONTENTS

Part Two: Economy of the Twentieth-Century West   173

6   Comparing Depressions
    The Great Plains and Canadian Prairie Experiences, 1929–1941
    Howard R. Lamar   175

Part Three: Environment of the Twentieth-Century West   207

7   Environmental History in the West
    John Opie   209

8   The Western Lumber Industry
    A Twentieth-Century Perspective
    William G. Robbins   233

9   The Irrigation District and the Federal Relationship
    Neglected Aspects of Water History
    Donald J. Pisani   257

Part Four: Politics of the Twentieth-Century West   293

10 Politics without Parties
    The Western States, 1900–1984
    Paul Kleppner   295

11 The West as Laboratory and Mirror of Reform
    William D. Rowley   339

Part Five: Culture of the Twentieth-Century West   359

12 The Changing Face of Western Literary Regionalism
    Fred Erisman   361

13 Main Currents in Twentieth-Century Western Art
    H. Wayne Morgan   383

    Epilogue: Sharpening the Image
    Gerald D. Nash   407

    Selective Bibliography
    Richard W. Etulain   421

Contents

Contributors 447

Index 451

Illustrations

Figures

1.1	Population of the United States, 1890	38
1.2	Population by counties, 1920	56
1.3	Population by counties, 1950	57
2.1	Metropolitan growth in the West	78
2.2	Growth regions in the West	79
2.3	Metropolitan-centered subregions in the West	81

Tables

1.1	Aggregate trends, 1890–1920	41
1.2	Population and growth rates by states, 1890–1920	43
1.3	Nevada and Utah contrasted	47
1.4	Los Angeles city and county population	52
1.5	Population and growth rates of states, 1920–1950	54
1.6	Population and growth rates of states, 1950–1985	62
2.1	Metropolitan growth, 1940–1980	73
2.2	State growth rates in excess of the U.S. growth rate	77
8.1	Western lumber production, 1940–1979	247
10.1	Patterns of partisan strength, 1900–1984	297
10.2	Partisan leads at the state level, 1900–1984	298
10.3	Estimates of party-vote consistency	301
10.4	Normal vote analysis	302

ILLUSTRATIONS

10.5	Components of the electorate	*304*
10.6	The social instability of partisan choice	*307*
10.7	Progressive voters, 1912 and 1924: origins and destination	*309*
10.8	Mobilizing an economic coalition in the West	*311*
10.9	Forging the Roosevelt Coalition	*314*
10.10	The economic base of voting support, 1932–1944	*316*
10.11	Partisan support for public utility initiatives, Washington	*320*
10.12	Partisan support for public utility initiatives, Oregon	*322*
10.13	Demobilizing an economic coalition, 1948–1984	*326*
10.14	Employment and medical care	*331*
11.1	Urban population increase, 1900–1910	*343*

Preface

As the twentieth century draws to a close, Americans are beginning to reflect on various aspects of their national experience, from the discovery of America, to the Bicentennial of the Revolution and the Constitution, and also to the centennial of the supposed closing of the frontier in 1890. All of these events are significant milestones in the historical development of the United States and left a deep imprint on its institutions as well as on the consciousness and character of its people. But while much has been written about each of these subjects, the aftermath of the frontier experience still remains somewhat blurred. What happened to the American West—the region west of the 98th meridian—after the frontier was no more? That section was not really developed until the twentieth century, unlike the North and South. In many ways, the one hundred years after 1890 were the most significant era in the West's history, and witnessed the largest increase of population growth that it had yet experienced. But the process whereby the West matured so rapidly in the twentieth century is still imperfectly understood. To some extent this has been due to the fixation of Americans on the movement of people to earlier Wests before 1890. This romantic attachment has deep roots in national mythology and is likely to persist. Yet it should not preclude a closer examination of reality, particularly of the phenomenal growth of the West in the one hundred years since 1890.

A primary goal of this volume is to delineate major trends and approaches that will contribute to a clearer image of the twentieth-century West. The public perception of the West before 1890 is quite clear, in contrast to the years thereafter. That may be due in part to the fact that such perceptions are grounded as much in myth as in reality. Americans living in the highly urbanized industrial society of the twentieth century looked back with nostalgia to a simpler rural age when fur trappers and mountain men, miners, ranchers, and cowboys, and a declining number of Indians roamed the sparsely populated wilderness that was the West. These symbolic figures reflected virtues dear to the American mind, and the Protestant ethic, virtues such as individualism, self-reliance, and freedom from restraints. That image of the West has had a strong hold on the imaginations not only of Americans but on people around the globe, and was strongly reinforced by the mass media in the course of the twentieth century. By contrast, the image of the West since 1890 is not at all clear to Americans, nor as romantic. Clearly, it does not serve the same psychic purpose as the Old West in providing an escape from the problems and complexities of modernity.

But the advent of the twenty-first century forces Americans to confront their more recent past as well, and to reflect on the last one hundred years of western history. Obviously, the West before 1890 cannot forever be enshrined in our imaginations, frozen in time as if it were a museum piece rather than part of an ongoing historical process. The past century has witnessed dynamic growth and demands to be recorded and remembered, no less than earlier eras. During the last decade historians and other scholars have begun to examine elements of the West's development since 1890, using a variety of approaches and identifying some of the major influences that shaped the region. This volume provides illustrative examples of such work in progress and demonstrates how seemingly disparate efforts coalesce to contribute to a larger vision of the West. Collectively the essays contribute to an emerging image of the twentieth-century West and focus on elements that are now of concern to students of the region. Much of the literature on the West after 1890 has been impressionistic. By contrast, the authors in this book reflect research in depth. Broad overviews certainly have a place, but only research in archives and manuscript collections can provide solid foundations for truly creative synthesis.

It is our hope that these essays will provide ingredients necessary for the development of a sharper image of the twentieth-century West. In the first place, they focus on some of the major influences that have shaped the region since 1890. It is highly unlikely that scholars in the 1990s will develop an all-encompassing hypothesis like the Turner Thesis with one or two simple themes. Rather, the concepts now being developed are sensitive to diversity and complexity and emphasize multiple causation. In addition to identifying major influences that formed the twentieth-century West, scholars in the last decade have also done a great deal to develop various fruitful approaches or conceptual frameworks to facilitate study of the region. No single framework has emerged as dominant, but as these

Preface

essays demonstrate an impressive array of perspectives is at hand from which to approach the subject.

Within this context the book should contribute to the development of some form or structure for the emerging field of twentieth-century western history. Until now, writings about the region have tended to be diffuse. In contrast to works about the West before 1890 that have often fallen into a Turnerian framework, those dealing with the more recent period have ranged widely without a particular sense of direction with respect to the West as a larger whole. It may well be that the absence of a broad framework has inhibited research in the field. Although we make no claims to creating such a needed conceptual structure in this volume, it is our hope that it will make a modest contribution toward the development of such a framework in the future.

Finally, general guidelines for the authors provided that they survey the literature of the subject, identify research needs, and make suggestions concerning research opportunities in the special spheres of their respective fields. In addition, Richard Etulain's bibliography at the end of the book provides suggestions as to studies that can serve as tools for delving further into this aspect of the western American experience.

We have grouped the essays in five major categories. These encompass the people of the twentieth-century West, its economy, environment, political life, and culture. Part One opens with Walter Nugent's account of demographic changes in the West. Carl Abbott's broad essay on the urban dimension of the twentieth-century West highlights a central theme in the region's growth after 1890. Related essays in this part deal with particular groups within the enormous expansion of urban population outlined by Abbott. Karen Anderson focusses on women, Ricardo Romo on Chicanos, and Donald Parman on Indians. Part Two includes Howard Lamar's suggestive essay comparing American and Canadian responses to the Great Depression of the 1930s. Part Three touches on the persistent impact of environment in the West. John Opie explores the wide range of environmental influences even in the twentieth century when such conditions possibly had a lesser impact than in earlier years. A more detailed analysis of some of the West's main resources is provided by two of the contributors to this section. William Robbins discusses the changing fortunes of the lumber industry in the Pacific Northwest and how they profoundly affected the historical development of this subregion. And Donald Pisani demonstrates just how dependent the semiarid West has been on water and how vicissitudes of water supply affected many different dimensions in the region's life.

Part Four concerns the political life of the West. In his pathbreaking piece Paul Kleppner uses computer analysis of voting patterns in the West to provide suggestive explanations of the weakness of party affiliation in the region during the last one hundred years. The topics he uncovers have been barely touched by historians while his framework for analysis should provide much food for thought. William Rowley undertakes a sweeping view of political reform in the West, providing another dimension to the underdeveloped field of western politics.

Part Five deals with selected aspects of the region's cultural life. Fred Erisman underlines the importance of literature, especially fictional accounts, in shaping the image of the West since the assumed closing of the frontier. H. Wayne Morgan pursues a similar theme, but from a different perspective. He emphasizes the role that artists played in conveying impressions of time and place in the twentieth-century West. Most Americans were profoundly impressed by the artistic works painted by Frederic Remington and Charles Russell who fastened sharp images of the nineteenth-century West on their own, and successive generations who had never seen the region in their own lifetime.

The Epilogue by Gerald Nash attempts to draw the essays together and to assess their collective significance. In this endeavor it addresses two issues. First, it seeks to identify distinctive characteristics of the twentieth-century West as these contribute to an emerging image of the region. Second, it surveys approaches that have been used by scholars in their analyses of the western experience in the last century. These can provide structure for the field and suggest alternate pathways for future research.

In the preparation of this volume our primary thanks must go to our contributors. As editors we have collaborated closely on every aspect of the book. But there has been some division of labor. Richard Etulain provided much of the editorial form for the essays and prepared the opening historiographical essay and the closing bibliography. Gerald Nash wrote the Preface, Introductions, and the Epilogue. As we ponder the phenomenal growth of the West since 1890 we are aware that this volume is a reflection of the increasing consciousness of the modern West. That West did not disappear in 1890 but underwent a transformation to an urban civilization whose image deserves to be clarified.

Gerald D. Nash
Richard W. Etulain

Prologue
A New Historiographical Frontier

THE TWENTIETH-CENTURY WEST*

Richard W. Etulain

This historiographical overview by Richard W. Etulain shows that although writers have been slow to deal with the twentieth-century West, several authors—particularly historians and journalists—have begun since 1960 to treat the post-1900 West. Building on or diverging from earlier comments by such scholars as Frederick Jackson Turner, Walter Prescott Webb, and James Malin, these later writers have frequently defined the modern West as colony, region, or pacesetter. Historians Earl Pomeroy, Gerald D. Nash, Gene M. Gressley, and Richard Lowitt and journalists Carey McWilliams, Neil Morgan, and Neal R. Peirce have made particularly notable contributions to the historiography of the new West. As the present century draws to a close, these accomplishments in historical writing will not only aid students and scholars in understanding the modern West but will also provide a generation of new writers solid bases from which to launch their own interpretations of the twentieth-century West.

*An abbreviated version of this essay was presented at a conference of the Western History Association, Sacramento, California, October 1985. I have limited discussion primarily to book-length general studies because commentaries on numerous additional monographs would double the length of the essay. Full citations of most of the items mentioned in the text are included in the selective bibliography at the end of this volume. I am indebted to Martin Ridge, William G. Robbins, Elliott West, Michael P. Malone, Gerald D. Nash, and Earl Pomeroy for their readings of earlier drafts of this essay. Professor Pomeroy has particularly helped me to rethink my comments on Frederick Jackson Turner and his writings.

When Gerald D. Nash's *The West in the Twentieth Century* appeared in 1973, historians were treated to the first full-scale scholarly discussion of the new West. For a variety of reasons, but especially in their stress on the westward movement ("to-the-West" historiography) and in their neglect of western institution-building ("in-the-West" historiography), academics had been reluctant to deal with the modern West, and thus nearly three quarters of the twentieth century had elapsed before the publication of Nash's overview synthesis. The gradual discovery of the contemporary West and its treatment in a growing number of popular accounts and monographs are a revealing story of a new frontier in western historiography.[1]

With a few exceptions and some overlapping edges, the major trends in the historiography of the twentieth-century West fall into three periods. In the first three or four decades of the present century, major historians such as Frederick Jackson Turner and Frederic Logan Paxson dealt with the frontier West but avoided stressing the new West. The publication of *The Great Plains* by Walter Prescott Webb in 1931, however, signaled the possibility of a novel direction in this new field of study. Next, a group of journalists and economists such as Bernard De Voto, William Allen White, Carey McWilliams, and Morris E. Garnsey between 1930 and 1960 provided some of the first portraits of the American twentieth-century West. Finally professional historians, led by scholars like Earl Pomeroy, Gerald Nash, and Gene Gressley, have produced major, influential interpretations of the recent West in the last generation while at the same time journalists and nonprofessionals like Neil Morgan and Neal R. Peirce have continued to deal with the contemporary West.[2]

In the earliest years of the twentieth century, western historians rarely dealt with the post-1890 West, and when they did they most often followed a truncated version of the writings of Frederick Jackson Turner. While Turner viewed the frontier as both place and process, few historians moved beyond his emphasis on the westward movement (to-the-West historiography) to utilize his equally stimulating stress on the development of western social institutions (in-the-West historiography). To Turner's further credit, he was interested in and even wrote essays on and devoted sections of his books to the West as a postfrontier section, but historians who followed him were much less curious and venturesome than he. Indeed so pervasive was subsequent emphasis on the westward movement—and such minor stress on the rise of frontier social institutions and on the West as a developing section—that not until nearly thirty years into the century did a few historians and other writers move beyond the to-the-West perspective. Clearly, one of the reasons historical accounts of the

Prologue

modern West were so slow in developing was the too-close attachment of most western historians to Turner's discussions of the movements west and their inadequate concentration on his discussions of social institutions and the West as section.[3]

Had these historians been more acquainted with the full corpus of Turner's work, they would have realized that he was also intrigued, particularly from the 1920s on, with the modern history of the United States. In several of his essays, in his western history courses, and in his private correspondence, Turner dealt with this recent era. Although most of his published writings centered on the pre–Civil War era and his two monographs discussed the first half of the nineteenth century (not without providing models for studying western institutions and sectionalism, however), he ventured on a few occasions into the twentieth century with his research and writing. In fact, when Turner was offered handsome honoraria for lecturing or writing—enticements he rarely succeeded in rejecting—he moved past the nearly uncrossable Rubicon of the 1890s.

In 1916, for example, six years after he left Wisconsin for Harvard, Turner was invited to speak before students in the social sciences at the University of Chicago. In his address, entitled, "The Last Quarter-Century," and in a major address at Clark University several years later, "Since the Foundation," Turner focused on the problems that faced the United States in a postfrontier era. In the middle 1920s he also published a brief summary of a half-century of western development in "The West—1876 and 1926."[4]

Much of the image that emerged from Turner's earliest portraits of a frontierless United States was negative. In addition to mentioning immigration restrictions, higher costs of living, and a lessening birth rate, Turner pointed to monopolies gobbling up natural resources, encroaching government control of private business, and an increasingly evident class structure as illustrations of a nation falling on evil times. All these trends—and a loss of optimism about the future—Turner partially attributed to a frontierless world.[5]

But Turner later changed his mind. In the 1920s, as he worked on his second monograph, *The United States 1830–1850* (published posthumously in 1935), he discovered numerous parallels between the period from 1830 to 1850 and his own times. On several occasions Turner's preoccupation with these parallels provided an escape from an unfinished book that threatened to become an ever-present albatross. Indeed, the more Turner studied issues of the 1920s the more he was convinced that a new, vibrant regionalism characterized American life. Excited about what he considered to be this new sectional surge, Turner pulled together his notes, presented papers before several audiences in 1922, and later published the completed essay, "Sections and Nation," in the *Yale Review*.[6]

Here Turner described each of the sections of the United States, pointing out their unique qualities. While differences among these sections were not as momentous as those separating European nations—in part because U.S. sections shared the same language and political parties—still, varying geographic, economic, and other experiences divided the United States into "a federation of sections rather than of states." Moreover, Turner was convinced that a comprehension of the full range of sociocultural differences separating regions was necessary before one could understand the U.S. in the 1920s. Sectionalism, he concluded, was a key to understanding the modern U.S., and, one might add, a key to comprehending Turner's ideas about twentieth-century America.[7]

In addition to these guest lectures and essays Turner also moved past 1890 in his classroom lectures and in bibliographies he prepared for his classes. Ever the curious historian, Turner decided to teach a course on "The History of the United States, 1880–1920" in his last semester in 1924 before retiring from Harvard. He told his students they must understand recent America even if the bewildering complexities of public affairs and the lack of access to necessary manuscript materials made their research difficult. He also wanted to teach the course because he knew "too little of the period" and "wished to know more."[8]

Historians early in the new century did not follow Turner's lead into studying the modern West. While seeming to acknowledge his leadership in to-the-West historiography and its stress on immigration to the trans-Mississippi West, they were not captivated with in-the-West history—that is, with Turner's research and writing on the social institutions arising in this new frontier and region. For whatever reasons, most other specialists on the frontier and West were not much interested in the varied societies and cultures, the communities, that emerged after settlers had lived for a generation or two at the end of the trail.

This stress on the to-the-West movement of westward pioneers is evident in the writings of Frederic Logan Paxson, the western historian who replaced Turner at Madison when he left for Harvard in 1910. While Paxson's first book dealt with U.S.-Latin American diplomacy, he began publishing essays on the West before 1910 and continued writing scattered pieces about the West well into the 1940s, although in the late teens he moved increasingly toward an emphasis on contemporary U.S. history.[9] In his later histories of the post–Civil War era and the twentieth-century U.S., Paxson dealt with western topics but rarely treated them as examples of regional history. His first book on the West, *The Last American Frontier* (1910), covering the era from 1820 to 1885 and his second, *History of the American Frontier 1763–1893* (1924), which won the Pulitzer Prize, follow closely what Paxson considered Turner's major themes and conclusions.

Prologue

Even when Paxson hinted that he might break away from the to-the-West emphases in his writings about the frontier, he rarely did so, although he was convinced he was not imitating Turner. In 1929 when Paxson gave the Colver Lectures at Brown University entitled *When the West is Gone*, he did not focus on the postfrontier West, but, instead, devoted two lectures to early western frontiers and speculated in the final lecture on what a vanished frontier would mean to the future of the United States. Here and in "A Generation of the Frontier Hypothesis: 1893–1932" (1933) Paxson argued that Turner's frontier thesis "stands today as easily to be accepted as it was when launched."

In reviewing Paxson's prize-winning frontier volume, Walter Prescott Webb, six years before publishing his own *Great Plains*, astutely observed that though Paxson intended to write about the frontier, much of his volume was "conventional American history," and sometimes Webb was "not fully convinced," that in Paxson's account one was "reading frontier history." The reviewer continued: "Perhaps a certain amount of old wine must go into the new bottle, but the fact that the bottle is new should not obscure the nature of the contents." Webb's perceptive comments not only pointed to Paxson's tendency to follow well-known historiographic paths but also his hesitation to strike out on new interpretative trails.[10]

A less well-known historian than Paxson, John Carl Parish, who had moved to the West Coast in the early 1920s, agreed with much of what Paxson and Turner had written about the West as frontier, but he also stressed—in contrast to his two predecessors—that the westward movement had not ended in the 1890s but continued well into the twentieth century. Many disciples of Turner, Parish noted, were misleading in equating the westward movement primarily with the experiences of agriculturists. Parish, on the other hand, was convinced that economic and aesthetic developments followed settlers west and that these "frontiers" were still in their formative stages in the early twentieth century.[11]

At the same time Parish pointed to strong continuities existing between eastern society and culture and western experiences. While the frontier and later West may have redirected some incoming institutions and ideas, newcomers worked long and hard to replicate in the West what they had known in the East. Parish, like Earl Pomeroy thirty years later, concluded that continuities bulked as large as innovations in the West. Here too Parish was swimming upstream against the dominant currents in western historiography, which stressed the powerful, innovating forces of the frontier environment in changing the notions and institutions of migrants.

In dealing with the waves of settlers and the civilization they brought west, Parish was not so much breaking with traditional views of the West as adding new stages to those that Turner's hypothetical seers viewed at Cumberland Gap and South Pass. Since new industrial and cultural developments were still very much under way in the 1920s, the westward movement, Parish concluded, was incomplete. Unlike most western historians of the early twentieth century, Parish was not an entirely to-the-West historian. To the contrary, he urged historians to reexamine such developments as manufacturing, new forms of farming, conservation and reclamation, the establishment of schools, novel architecture and music, and recent literary movements as strong evidence that the westward movement was still in operation.

Another historian who began writing in the 1920s, James C. Malin, was even more unusual in his interpretations. Indeed, next to Turner and Walter Prescott Webb, Malin may have been the most bold and imaginative western historian in the first half of the twentieth century. Yet his influence on other writers seems limited because his turgid prose was difficult to follow, he chose to publish privately many of his major works, and he was reluctant to take part in professional meetings and exchanges. Indeed, he seemed to relish his status as the isolated curmudgeon of the Kansas grasslands. Clearly, however, he was much more than a historiographical oddity, and few western historians can compete with the depth of his research and the audacity of his conclusions.[12]

Early on Malin disagreed with what he called the "closed-space doctrine" of Turner and many of his followers. He opposed the concept of a closing frontier and instead argued for viewing time and space as fluid since they resulted primarily from the ingenuity of men's minds and since the application of these intellectual powers was the major reason for the shifting tides of sociocultural activity. Malin was certain, in short, that the 1890s were not the end of a frontier but merely another stage—and not a particularly dramatic one—in the history of the West. A believer in an open-ended world shaped more by the endeavors of mankind than the forces of a natural environment and thus an opponent of much that Turner and Webb believed, Malin called for a more holistic view of ecology and history than other contemporary western historians promulgated.

Since Malin saw little reason to divide western history into specific time periods, he was less reluctant than his contemporaries to deal with patterns of western experiences that bridged the uncrossable chasm of the 1890s. Indeed, in his demographic and other statistical studies, Malin moved easily from the last half of the nineteenth century into the twentieth. As a man who viewed history as something of a seamless web, Malin was much more at home with transitions between the nineteenth and twentieth centuries than other western historians. In his most notable works on the American West—*The Grassland of North America* (1947), *Grassland Historical Studies* (1950), and in a host of essays—he argued that looking for the beginnings and endings of historical eras, castigating

Prologue

pioneers for being too exploitative, and seeing governmental planning as a new panacea were fruitless activities. Instead, a historian, drawing upon his own field and the findings of natural scientists, should strive to understand rather than judge the multifaceted and ongoing human endeavors that shaped the past.

In his studies of Kansas and grasslands history, Malin provided a model of interdisciplinary history akin to that of the *Annales* school in France. Although not an advocate of a specific historiographical perspective, Malin called for a holistic view of links between people and their natural environment. He argued that historians needed to know geology, biology, ecology, and geography as well as census and manuscript records to understand the adjustments and adaptations plains farmers had made. Drawing on these and other disciplines, a historian could demonstrate that pioneer agriculturalists had changed crops as well as varieties of wheat to adapt to new or shifting demands of terrain, climate, and rainfall. And a comprehension of this past would show that the future depended not so much on nature and natural resources as upon humankind's abilities to use varied environments and resources.

While Malin's contemporaries and more recent historians testify to the provocative quality of his arguments, neither his ideas nor his research approaches seem to have influenced a large number of western historians. Although the works of such notable western historians as Paul Gates, Allan Bogue, and Robert Swierenga—and others particularly working in midwestern or agricultural history—bear the stamp of Malin's views, the Kansas historian has not reshaped the thinking of many others.[13] Much more influential, however, have been the provocative ideas and books of Walter Prescott Webb.

Indeed, the publication of Webb's *The Great Plains* in 1931 was a dividing point in western historiography, and if western historians had been inclined to do so, they could have utilized Webb's book as a paradigm for a new kind of historical writing. To his credit, Paxson was aware of the pathmaking quality of Webb's study, calling it "the most useful book on the West that has appeared in many years." Moreover, Paxson was just right in adding that *The Great Plains* did for one of Turner's "sections or provinces what no writer has yet done for any other."[14] What Webb had achieved was the first full-scale example of in-the-West historiography. Like an observant cultural geographer—and geographers and anthropologists influenced Webb a great deal—he provided an analysis of successive cultural landscapes being laminated into the Great Plains experience. Webb accomplished what no previous historian had attempted; he had analyzed the historical development of a regional culture rather than merely describing a series of movements into the region. To illustrate this newly formulated regional culture, Webb summarized and analyzed the

7

literature of the Great Plains in his penultimate chapter, implying that the plains were truly a separate, identifiable region when they produced their own literature.[15]

In essence, Webb agreed with the environmentalist interpretations of Turner and Malin. He asserted that a line running roughly parallel to the 98° from the Dakotas to Texas had forced pioneers to adapt to new kinds of landscape, climate, vegetation, and Indians before they could wrest a living from the plains. By utilizing novel weapons, implements, and farming techniques, Americans learned to control the fearful power of the new semiarid region. Through adaptation and application of new technology, these newcomers prepared the way for successful settlement of the Great Plains. A generation later in his key essay in *Harper's Magazine*, "The American West, Perpetual Mirage," Webb reiterated the importance of Westerners understanding aridity and adjusting their lives to this all-encompassing fact of the region's environment. Although Webb's emphases on the desertlike qualities of the interior West angered many regional boosters, his views have influenced increasing numbers of historians and other serious students of the West.

Webb's notable historical writings of the 1920s and 30s were part and parcel of a widespread interest in regionalism that swept through the United States during that period but a movement particularly apparent in the South and West. Although most Westerners were less defensive in their regionalism than were Southerners who produced *I'll Take My Stand* (1930), several editors, a clutch of authors, and a few cultural historians took up the cudgels for western regionalism.[16]

This shifting stance away from frontier and toward region—or at least the development of a regional interpretation to accompany the older frontier view—provided a new opportunity for commentators to deal with the modern West, for, like Webb, if they essayed the development of a western regional culture, they were forced to carry their stories into the twentieth century. Or, again like Webb, they dealt with a West that had already passed through its pioneer stages and treated the West as an established region, as he did in *Divided We Stand* (1937).

In the half dozen years following the publication of *The Great Plains*, Webb continued to demonstrate his strong commitments to a regional interpretation of western history in *The Texas Rangers: A Century of Frontier Defense* (1935) and particularly in *Divided We Stand: The Crisis of a Frontierless Democracy* (1937). Especially in the later volume, Webb—like Bernard De Voto in his first essays—prefigured the attitudes of later historians critical of the North (or East) for what they considered that region's economic domination of the South and West. (This attack on the East was not new, of course, since many earlier frontiersmen and historians had followed the same critical vein.) Webb argued at length that the

Prologue

West and the South were colonies, that they lagged behind the North because that region used the tariff, Civil War pensions, and patent monopolies to strangle regional competition. More outspoken and vociferous—and perhaps more defensive—than most other western regionalists, Webb asserted that the economic depression of the West and South resulted in large part from a century-long domination by outside (that is northern) interests. Like the southern Agrarians, the most notable regionalists of that section, Webb called for first an understanding of and then the defeat of these alien influences.[17]

Even as Webb continued to deal with the American West as a separate region with unique characteristics as he had in *The Great Plains* and *Divided We Stand*, other writers, particularly a talented group of journalists and nonhistorians, were beginning to write about the modern West. No one could argue that Webb or the new group of nonprofessionals dominated the field of western historiography—they did not; to-the-West historians still held sway—but in the generation from the 1930s until well into the 1950s they provided several new approaches and views of the modern West that became increasingly important points of embarkation for later historians treating the twentieth-century West.

The essays Bernard De Voto wrote about the West from the 1930s into the 1940s signaled a second period of historical writing about the modern West. Or, at least, his writings shared that role with Webb's *Divided We Stand*, which differed from De Voto's essays in approach and conclusions but which was also widely influential between the Depression and the late 1950s. What Webb and De Voto did share was the pronounced conviction that most Westerners—as well as many other Americans—little understood the recent West and the pressures on it, and they were certain that they should provide their countrymen much-needed information and instruction on the dilemmas of the contemporary West.

Utah-born De Voto wielded his lively and pugnacious pen in such journals as the *Saturday Review of Literature* and *Harper's* for more than a generation, taking cattlemen, legislators, and Easterners to task for not protecting the West from grasping corporations and politicians. Nowhere was his point of view clearer than in his notable essay "The West: A Plundered Province" (1934). Portraying the frontier West as a victim of selfish investors and insipid policy-makers, De Voto argued for the West-as-colony-of-the-East theme so prominent in later writings about the West. Like Webb in *Divided We Stand*, De Voto was convinced that the East (for Webb, the North) so dominated the West that it plundered the newer region, exploiting its natural resources, passing inapplicable land legislation for its arid lands, and generally caring little about the future of the West. But De Voto also noted that the West had learned valuable lessons from its demanding experiences: individualism did not work in the West; cooperation and careful planning were necessary to overcome the difficult barriers Westerners faced. These lessons, De Voto asserted, Easterners and many legislators had not learned, but the West could and must teach them.

As De Voto continued to write about the contemporary West, he gradually turned his attention to a new foe—to greedy interests within the West itself. His earlier criticisms of eastern investors and bureaucrats were as light jabs as compared to the knockout blows he aimed at western livestockmen and politicos who, he was convinced, were willing to sell off the western domain and relentlessly exploit its resources. In short, the "West Against Itself," the western paradox, encompassed the conflicting tendencies of Westerners who called for less eastern domination and yet displayed a pronounced willingness to trade their resource birthright for a brief and uncertain future. If Westerners were unwilling to protect their land, lumber, and wilderness areas, De Voto vowed, others would have to do so.[18]

De Voto's comments during the 1930s and 1940s markedly influenced his contemporaries and have continued to shape the opinions of such writers as Wallace Stegner, Robert Edson Lee, and Gene Gressley down to the present. From the lofty position of his *Harper's* Easy Chair, De Voto depicted the colonialism he thought had dominated the West for nearly a century and also made explicit what historian Gene Gressley has termed "western particularism,"[19] the tendency of the West to call for government support and its simultaneous, forthright condemnation of national bureaucratic control; its love of aid from Washington, D.C., on the one hand, but its concomitant hatred of threats to its freedom and individualism on the other.

Several of De Voto's contemporaries were attracted to issues and plans that fired his imagination. Notable among these was William Allen White in his slim volume, *The Changing West: An Economic Theory About Our Golden Age* (1939). One of the first writers to deal with the prospects of the modern West as part and parcel of the future of the country, the noted journalist and pundit of Kansas drew upon his commitments to capitalism, democracy, and his attachments to the Sermon on the Mount to call for continuing support of these ideas as keys to the future of America. He added that the West would have to produce more, especially its farmers, to survive and must avoid falling victim to the demands of alien regions on the West. In his calling for economic answers to problems facing a Depression-plagued West and in his plea for severing colonial ties to the East, the Sage of Emporia reminds one of De Voto and Webb, and his views also foreshadow the comments of several other writers in the 1940s and 50s.

Prologue

Another volume that illustrates the contentions of Webb and De Voto about a beleaguered West is A. G. Mezerik's *The Revolt of the South and West* (1946). Explicitly following the colonial interpretation of the new West, journalist Mezerik notes in his introduction that recent evidence of "renewed aggression by the Eastern corporate oligarchy" is but "the latest in a very long list of invasions by the East into the plundered provinces of our South and West" (pp. xii–xiii). But the author is hopeful that the winds of change blowing across the Mississippi during World War II will destroy the colonial economic relationships the East has forced upon the South and West.

The major point of Mezerik's volume, seemingly based more on emotion and personal conviction than on thorough research, is that the South and West are on the verge of revolt. Experiencing new economic freedoms and successes during the recent war, the two regions are ready to join in an assault on the exploitative East. The South and West want, Mezerik writes, "democracy in all departments—in suffrage, in social values, in education, and in economic opportunity" (p. 289). Since these sections of the country have recently profited from "decentralization forced by the atomic bomb, TVA, war-built plants, new political power, new skills and knowledge," they are optimistic and confident of the future. While the South and East are willing to work with more constructive and less greedy interests in the East, Mezerik implies that they are just as willing to go their own ways now that they are gaining the power and freedom they desire.[20]

Several of the same points are expressed in *America's New Frontier: The Mountain West* (1950) by economist Morris E. Garnsey, who details the economic problems facing that region and lays out a plan for the future. Straightforward in approach and didactic in manner, *America's New Frontier* now seems a curious period piece, although at the time of publication its call for government planning of resources management might have sounded radical and controversial, particularly to many conservatives of the mountain region. Garnsey urges on his readers a Missouri Valley Authority, a plan reminiscent of New Deal regional planning, but he also argues that residents of the mountain states will have "to recapture the venturesome spirit of an earlier day and overcome the timidity of government bureaus and opposition of pressure groups" to gain necessary economic experience and control and much-needed conservation of resources in the region. If they are able to achieve these goals, the mountain area will become the "new frontier" of American experience.

Garnsey's call for better planning—for planning based on knowledge of the past and a hard-headed look at the present and future—is but one of several books like his in the 1940s and 50s dealing with the economic possibilities of western subregions. Such a work is *The Great Plains in*

Transition (1955) by sociologist Carl Frederick Kraenzel. Like De Voto and Webb, Kraenzel is convinced that residents of the region are "at the mercy of forces outside the region" (p. 7), and thus he has written a book to show those residents how they might free themselves from these alien forces. Following an approach similar to Webb's in *The Great Plains*, the author provides a narrative of the stages of exploration and settlement in the region and elucidates sociocultural experiences resulting from these previous experiences. Although sometimes discursive, Kraenzel's book is an important document for understanding the point of view of many nonhistorians of his time in treating the new West. Prescriptive and realistic in tone, *The Great Plains in Transition* offered readers and residents of the Great Plains a plan for the middle 1950s. If they could accept and work toward his goal of a democratic and pragmatic regionalism, he assures them that the West will no longer be a plundered economic province nor a social or cultural colony. Planning, community-mindedness, and a healthy democratic participation are the keys to the future. If people of the Great Plains can learn from their past—if they can elevate experience into principle—they can establish a showcase region and thereby demonstrate social and economic equality to onlookers. Kraenzel is certain that this is needed for survival in the Plains but also to make the region an example for others—nationally and internationally—who need paradigms to emulate.

Although written at the same time as several of the works that advance a colonial interpretation of the West, Carey McWilliams's *Southern California Country: An Island on the Land* (1946) takes a different tack. Indeed, this notable volume is but one of the several important works that McWilliams, a brilliant lawyer and journalist, turned out in the 1930s and 40s. Unlike several other volumes on the West in the American Folkways series, which Erskine Caldwell edited, *Southern California Country* is a solidly researched, richly interpretative work of memorable insights and sharply etched vignettes.

The approach of McWilliams is similar to that of a regional geographer or historian. After providing background chapters on physical and early sociocultural landscapes, McWilliams elaborates on the myths of southern California that had emerged by the beginning of the twentieth century. More than half of his nearly 400 page book deals with the first forty-five years of the twentieth century, with heavy emphasis on social and cultural life. At the same time, McWilliams aptly uses statistics to demonstrate population shifts and the impact of these demographic changes on life in the region. The author's probing sections on political, religious, and utopian leaders, on notable social and economic happenings, and on migrant groups convinces one that, as McWilliams writes in a remarkable chapter "The Cultural Landscape," southern California, "is a sharply

Prologue

defined region, not merely in the geographic sense, but in the sense that it is made up of people bound together by mutual dependencies from common interests" (p. 138). Like Josiah Royce and Webb before him, McWilliams is interested in the characteristics of community- or region-building, the layers of experience, that, once laminated, create a community or regional society and cultural. In *Southern California Country,* he sets a high mark for those wanting a probing, analytical history of the modern West or one of its subregions, and in doing so he produces one of the memorable books about the recent West.[21]

Although the most significant works dealing with the twentieth-century West and published between the Depression and 1960 were written by journalists and nonhistorians, some devotees to Clio were beginning to discover the new West, particularly in works that attempted to cover both the frontier and post-1890s eras. Before a discussion of these books is undertaken, however, it should be noted that western history texts published in the 1930s followed, by and large, the to-the-West framework and, like Paxson had in his pioneering texts, did not push past 1890. For example, Robert Riegel, a student of Paxson, ends his *America Moves West* (1930) with chapters on "The Disappearance of the Frontier" and "Where Has the Frontier Gone," which devote a few paragraphs to fictional and cinematic treatments of the Old West but which do not treat other events between the 1890s and 1930. His revised edition published nearly two decades later is largely rewritten and includes a closing chapter on Turner, his critics, and the meaning of the frontier, although Riegel chooses not to include comment on the twentieth-century West. Dan Elbert Clark also ends with the 1890s in his *The West in American History* (1937), concluding that Paxson's views in his historiographical essay on Turner and *When the West is Gone* are essentially correct.

Western America: The Exploration, Settlement, and Development of the Region Beyond the Mississippi (1941), authored by LeRoy R. Hafen and Carl Coke Rister and dedicated to their mentor Herbert Eugene Bolton, is equally hesitant to move beyond the frontier period of western history. Dedicated to the conviction that the western experience has reshaped eastern immigrants and made them into Westerners, who have become regionalists, "not superior perhaps to any other of the nation, but certainly distinctive" (p. vii), the two authors elect not to use the twentieth-century West to support their interpretation. They devote but a few scattered paragraphs to natural resources, agrarian unrest, and the development of schools and literature in the period after 1900.

Another of Bolton's students, John Walton Caughey, was more interested in the twentieth century, however. His *History of the Pacific Coast* (1933) is a useful survey of the Pacific Slope area from early Spanish exploration to the early 1900s and places major emphasis on the borderlands and pioneer eras, but nearly a decade later in the first edition of his important text on California (1940), Caughey succeeds in giving "more generous treatment of recent decades" (p. vii). *California,* which one recent historian has called "the most successful college text in California history at the time—and for several decades thereafter," devotes several chapters to the post-1890s. Although more summary than analysis, the volume provides an early framework for those who wish to see the development of the state into the modern period, and Caughey's comments on California literature in this and later editions of his text are still unsurpassed.[22]

Other historians dealing with the development of western subregions were also willing to move into the twentieth century in their regional histories. Such is the case with two volumes written about the Pacific Northwest. In *The Great Northwest: A History* (1947), Oscar Osburn Winther, who spent most of his early years in Oregon, provides a workmanlike narrative of the region, with about one-fifth of the book (pp. 273–345) treating the twentieth century. Three years later in a second, revised edition, Winther adds a good deal on the political, social, and cultural history of the modern Pacific Northwest but agrees with another regional historian that not enough "spadework" has been carried out for him to give "adequate insight into recent trends" (p. v). Although Winther—a specialist in western transportation history—provides a readable and straightforward account, he is notably nonconceptual and unanalytical and skips over most cultural activities in both editions of his volume. Still, in the second edition, he divides his book at 1883 (the completion of the Northern Pacific Railroad), giving more coverage of the post-1880 West than most of his contemporaries.

Appearing a decade after the publication of the first edition of Winther's volume, *Empire of the Columbia: A History of the Pacific Northwest* (1957) by Dorothy O. Johansen and Charles M. Gates devotes even more pages than Winther to the modern Northwest. This section of the volume, written by Professor Gates, is particularly strong on economic and urban developments, two of Gates's areas of speciality. While the authors view their topic in national circumference, the colonialism theme so popular in the writings of many nonhistorians in the 1930s through the 1950s is not apparent here, as it was not in many regional and state histories that historians turned out in the 1950s.

In fact, toward the end of the 1950s emphases on the West as colony began to diminish. Not that the theme disappeared from western historiography, for it continues into the 1980s; but western historians became interested in other themes after the 1930s and 1940s. Historian John Higham has suggested that the rise of consensus historiography of the 1950s undercut the regional competition that fostered the earlier colonial interpretation.[23] Perhaps, although just as reasonable as a cause for lessened regional defensiveness was the growing self-confidence of the West, realizing it could compete with the East and had less reason to take a backseat to competitors. At any rate, the Webb–De Voto emphasis on colonialism seemed less important to western historians as the 1950s came to a close.

At the same time that the theme of colonialism became less popular, Earl Pomeroy made explicit an interpretation that he had introduced in his earlier writings. Drawing upon his studies of territorial government, trans-Mississippi institutions, and his reading in American colonial history and historiography, Pomeroy argued in the most notable essay on western history since Turner—"Toward a Reorientation of Western History: Continuity and Environment" (1955)—that continuities from eastern U.S. society and culture bulked as large as institutions and ideas arising from the novel environment of the frontier.[24] In putting more stress on replication of previous experiences, Pomeroy was making a sharp break with previous historiography, which stressed the radical, innovative powers of new frontiers. Although Pomeroy's essay appeared in 1955, the impact of its pathbreaking interpretation was slow in coming, and not until a decade or so later did historians begin to test the validity of his continuity thesis. As we shall see, however, in the last generation this theme has been a major focus of several historians studying the modern West.

If historians by and large were reluctant to deal with the modern West in the period between the Depression and 1960, that hesitation seems to have dissolved in the last quarter century. Indeed, several historians—as well as many popular writers—have turned to the twentieth-century West for numerous recent studies. So pronounced has been this tendency that one no longer can say that the topic is overlooked. Instead, judging from the publications of the last decade or so and from projects currently underway, one might argue that twentieth-century western historiography is coming into its own and is a new frontier rapidly becoming explored and settled.

One indication of this increased interest in the recent West is the publication between 1960 and 1965 of three notable regional histories by well-known western historians who moved well into the twentieth century in covering their respective subregions. The first of the triumvirate is Robert Athearn's *High Country Empire* (1960), which treats the upper mountain and plains states. Avoiding a state-by-state approach in this volume dedicated to the author's mentor, Ernest Staples Osgood, Athearn instead explores the broad, general development of this region drained by the Missouri and its tributaries. Narrative and ancedotal in nature, *High Country Empire* is a well-written overview, based primarily on secondary sources. The author does not test major interpretations of the West nor point to new ones of his own, but his engaging style, his eye for detail, and his humor and witty turn of phrase combine to make the volume useful for students and scholars.

In the fourth and final section of his volume, "Vintage Years" (pp. 255–334), Athearn treats the twentieth century. Here the author emphasizes agriculture and mining, other economic topics, and relationships between the region and the federal government. He also includes extensive commentary on the environmental impact of the high plains on incoming peoples. In his concluding pages Athearn calls upon people in the region to take a new, realistic view of their future, to stop believing in never-ending abundance and other myths of the past, and "to make the necessary adjustments." Here the author is more explicit than in any other section of his readable synthesis. Altogether, Athearn's well-written volume is enjoyable reading even if short on analysis and interpretation. While he eschews conceptualization, his volume, studded with appealing vignettes and anecdotes, remains the best introduction to the region covered.

Shortly before his death in 1983, Athearn had nearly completed a sociocultural history of the modern high country empire. Completed and edited by Athearn's student Elliott West, *The Mythic West in Twentieth-Century America* (1986) illustrates its creator's first-rank synthetic abilities. Based on his wide and close reading of hundreds of primary and secondary sources, Athearn's final volume follows in the tradition of Henry Nash Smith, whose *Virgin Land: The American West in Symbol and Myth* (1950) has inspired two generations of revisionist interpretations of the American West. Like all of his early regional histories, Athearn's last book sparkles with appealing writing and telling vignettes.[25]

The second of the three notable regional histories is W. Eugene Hollon's *The Southwest: Old and New* (1961), also dedicated to the author's mentor Walter Prescott Webb. Hollon's volume is at once similar to and different from the works of Webb, Athearn, and Earl Pomeroy. In treating Texas, Oklahoma, New Mexico, and Arizona, Hollon follows Athearn's format of lively narrative history powered by appealing pen portraits of well-known regional figures and apt anecdotes and quotations. Hollon is less interested than Pomeroy in testing major historiographical themes of western history, however, and more inclined to base his story on published sources.

Less than half of Hollon's long book deals with the twentieth century, but, like Webb in *The Great Plains*, Hollon places a man–landscape theme at the center of his volume, a theme that becomes even more explicit in Hollon's later *The Great American Desert* (1966). One chapter in the earlier volume, "Desert and Oasis," provides a model of Hollon's point of view and approach in which aridity and other aspects of southwestern climate are described as the shaping forces on regional society and culture. Only careful planning and renewed pioneer determination, Hollon argues, will keep the region ahead of its pressing problems of inadequate rainfall and water supply for immigrants moving into the Southwest.

Probably before the publication of Gerald Nash's *The American West in the Twentieth Century* (1973), no book has been cited more often for its innovative approaches to the modern Far West than the third volume of the regional triplex, Earl Pomeroy's *The Pacific Slope: A History of California, Oregon, Washington, Idaho, Utah, and Nevada* (1965). While intended for the same series as Athearn's *High Country Empire* and Hollon's *The Southwest: Old and New,* Pomeroy's is a far different kind of volume. Indeed, in the nearly twenty-five years since its appearance, *The Pacific Slope* has continually impressed readers because of its pathbreaking interpretations, its notable emphases on western urbanization, and its stress on the twentieth century.

As he had in his earlier writings, Pomeroy emphasizes eastern influences on western economic and sociocultural developments in *The Pacific Slope.* Repeatedly noting continuities rather than interruptions between eastern urban, economic, and social experiences and western community-building, Pomeroy breaks with the dominant western historiographical paradigm that stressed frontier innovations. Moreover, in the longest and perhaps most provocative chapter in the volume, "The Power of the Metropolis," the author traces the rise of major far-western cities from their origins into the twentieth century, thereby avoiding the traditional view of the 1890s as a closing frontier and preparing readers for his urban emphases in discussing late-nineteenth and early twentieth-century economic and political questions.

If Pomeroy's emphasis on eastern influences upon the West and western urbanization breaks new ground, so does his emphasis on the modern West. More than half of his long book deals with economic, social, and political dimensions of the twentieth-century Pacific Slope. As the author notes in his introduction, many western historians are predisposed to treat far-western beginnings at length and to skip over recent happenings. On the other hand, Pomeroy is convinced that "the early years need not lose meaning if we traverse them at more than the speed of an immigrant's oxcart, the later years at less than the speed of a jet-propelled aircraft" (p. v). Nearly a decade later in writing a new preface for his book Pomeroy was still persuaded that his major emphases on cities and the modern West are valid for those wishing a general, interpretive introduction to the region.

Finally, *The Pacific Slope* avoids romantic or nostalgic narrative history of the West and, instead, demonstrates that western history can be conceptual and interpretative. In addition, the history of the region is not viewed in a vacuum, but the shaping influences of other regions and the nation—indeed international ones—are pictured throughout the volume. Pomeroy's most significant volume to date, *The Pacific Slope* is a benchmark in the historiography of the modern West. Its provocative, conceptual quality continues to whet one's appetite for his nearly completed history of the twentieth-century West.[26]

Meanwhile, Pomeroy's best-known student Gene Gressley has also produced several notable essays and books about western historiography and economic relationships between East and West. In addition to a perceptive historiographical overview of Turner and his frontier thesis, Gressley in his doctoral dissertation—later published as *Bankers and Cattlemen* (1966)—follows his mentor's call for a study of eastern influences on the West and concludes that eastern bankers played major roles in financing the cattle industry of the Rocky Mountain West. A few years later Gressley produced the best brief overview of colonialist interpretations of the West in his essay "Colonialism: A Western Complaint." Since that time Gressley has written a number of stimulating essays, many of which deal with the twentieth-century West and its economic relationships with the East and the rest of the world. Several of these essays have been gathered in *The Twentieth Century West: A Potpourri* (1977). Following Pomeroy, Gressley continues to call for a reorientation of western history that is less narrative, less provincial, more analytical, and more inclined to see the impact of outside influences on the region. These important essays and books place Gressley solidly among the in-the-West scholars of western historiography.[27]

If the works of Earl Pomeroy and Gene Gressley lay out paradigms for subsequent studies of the modern West, the writings of Gerald D. Nash, particularly his most recent articles and books, establish him as one of the two or three leading interpreters of the modern West. In his first book, *State Government and Economic Development: A History of Administrative Policies in California 1849–1933* (1964), which originated as a dissertation for John D. Hicks, in his later *U.S. Oil Policy, 1890–1964* (1968), and in several essays, Nash deals with various aspects of modern western history. But in his *The West in the Twentieth Century: A History of an Urban Oasis* (1973) Nash contributes the first and only scholarly overview of the contemporary West. Nash not only provides a summary of the period from 1900 to 1970, he also indicates the major turning points of the twentieth-century West and devotes much attention to the shifting relationships between East and West as well as between the West and the federal government. Judging from his training and his earlier publications, it is not surprising that Nash's treatments of economic and political trends are particularly thorough.[28]

In dividing his volume into two major parts, Nash places major stress on the two world wars and the Depression and New Deal as helping to foster notable changes in the twentieth-century West. In fact, Nash argues that the West, primarily colonial in its relationships with the East and Wall Street in the first decades of the century, changed rapidly and radically under the giant infusion of federal capital and control in the 1930s and during World War II. He sums up these changes in noting that "in the three decades after 1941, Pennsylvania Avenue displaced Wall Street as a headquarters for charting many directions for the future of the region's growth" (p. 186).

In the dozen years since its publication *The West in the Twentieth Century* has proven to be an admirable synthesis of the contemporary West. Scholars in political, economic, and cultural history, especially, have found Nash's periodization helpful in dealing with their own subjects in the present century. In addition, Nash's division of the West into colonial and pace-setting eras provides one of the few interpretations of the modern region, one that deserves additional testing in many subject areas.

Still another indication of the increasing attention historians are devoting to the recent West is the additional treatment given the topic in new or newly revised western history texts. Although the most widely read and adopted text, Ray Billington's *Westward Expansion,* which appeared first in 1949, stops in the 1890s in all of its five editions (Martin Ridge helped prepare the fifth edition), its extensive bibliography cites recent works on several twentieth-century topics. Trained in western history as an undergraduate under Paxson at Wisconsin and as a graduate student with Frederick Merk at Harvard (although A. M. Schlesinger, Sr., directed his dissertation), Billington remained convinced of the persuasiveness of Turner's frontier thesis and, conversely, the inapplicability of Turner's theory on section. Perhaps a higher regard for the sectional thesis might have urged Billington into a consideration of the modern West.

On the other hand, Merk, a student of Turner at Wisconsin and Harvard and his successor at Cambridge, ventured past 1900 in his posthumously published text *History of the Westward Movement* (1978). While all of Merk's major publications dealt with pre-1900 topics, his text of 64 chapters includes more than a dozen chapters—about 100 of 600 pages—on the modern West. Nearly all these sections discuss economic or bureaucratic topics, with Merk providing a few pages on Indians and skipping over nearly all other social and cultural topics. When Merk proceeds past 1900 he sees adaptation and the use of science and technology as keys to understanding the modern West. Unlike Turner and Paxson, to whom in many other ways he seems akin, Merk views the Populists of the 1890s as

Janus figures, looking back to the individualism of the western frontier and yet leaning toward an era of increased government involvement in economic affairs. With additional years of hindsight, Merk is able to see the famous campaign of 1896 as much a prologue to the future as a symbol of the past.

Much less extensive are the three chapters that Arrell Gibson devotes to the twentieth-century West in his text *The West in the Life of the Nation* (1976). Providing brief chapters on economic, social, and political affairs of the modern West and drawing heavily on the facts—but not the interpretations—of several historians mentioned here, Gibson allots about 45 of 620 pages to the recent West. Another historian, Robert Hine, in the second edition of his smoothly written *The American West: An Interpretive History* (1973, 1984), adds a brief section on the modern West, utilizing a series of lively biographical vignettes on which to build his chapter. As he had in his first edition on the frontier West, Hine emphasizes noted social and cultural figures to illustrate trends in the modern West.

The most extensive additions on the recent West in a previously published text are those incorporated into the second and third editions of *Western America* (1950, 1971) by C. C. Rister, LeRoy R. Hafen, and W. Eugene Hollon. Drawing upon the authors' new research on the modern West, the text of these two editions includes more than 100 pages on the new West not contained in the first edition (1941). In addition to a brief chapter on recent Hawaii and Alaska, the authors add sections on agriculture, industry, natural resources, urbanization, and culture and recreation in the new West. The largest chapter on western urbanization contains more information on that topic, including miniportraits of more than a dozen cities, than has appeared in any other western text. While the chapter does not test Richard Wade's or Earl Pomeroy's theories on frontier and western urbanization, it contains much material helpful to students and general readers.[29]

Expanded coverage of the twentieth-century West is also apparent in several recent western state histories. Volumes in the University of Nebraska Press series—those by James C. Olson on Nebraska (1955, 1966), Herbert S. Schell on South Dakota (1961, 1975), Elwyn B. Robinson on North Dakota (1966), T. A. Larson on Wyoming (1967, 1978), and Russell R. Elliott on Nevada (1973)—have devoted extensive sections to the modern West, particularly in chapters dealing with political and economic subjects. The books by Robinson, Larson, and Elliott have notably thorough sections on the modern West.[30]

This increasing emphasis on the post-1900 years is likewise evident in Walton Bean's *California: An Interpretive History* (1968, 1973, 1978 [1983, with James J. Rawls]). Bean also provides more extensive coverage

Prologue

of sociocultural topics than most writers of western texts without overlooking political and economic topics. Even more extensive treatment is given to the new West in Michael P. Malone and Richard B. Roeder's first-rate text *Montana: A History of Two Centuries* (1976). Particularly interested in supplying "the first book to study the state's general development since the 1920s" and in focusing "upon those historical trends and personalities that proved vital to the shaping of present-day Montana," Malone and Roeder have produced a model text, comprehensive and factual and yet interpretive and well-written.[31]

Another indication of the enlarged interest among historians in the modern West is illustrated in the individual volumes in the bicentennial State and Nation Series (1976–81). Most of the books (two thirds of which are by professional historians) dealing with states west of the 98th meridian devote an average of about 40 percent of their texts to the twentieth-century West, with notable emphases on economic and political history. The volumes by Norman H. Clark (Washington), Charles S. Peterson (Utah), and Robert P. and Wynona H. Wilkins (North Dakota) dedicate nearly half of their space to the modern West while those by Dorothy W. Creigh (Nebraska), Marc Simmons (New Mexico), Joe B. Frantz (Texas), and Kenneth S. Davis (Kansas) are notably brief on contemporary topics.

Nonhistorians have also contributed many important recent studies of the modern West. For example, Neil Morgan's *Westward Tilt* (1963), written in the atmosphere of California's becoming the most populous state in the union and the general emergence of the Far West as part of the power shift west, remains one of the half dozen or so most useful books about the modern West. Following in the vein of Carey McWilliams's earlier volume, and like the many volumes of Neal Peirce on subregions of the United States—what might be called journalistic "thick description," to abuse the apt phrase of anthropologist Clifford Geertz—Morgan's volume remains a thorough, stimulating overview despite its being a generation old.

The approach in *Westward Tilt* is also similar to that in the "inside" books of John Gunther and the format utilized more recently in the volumes of Joel Garreau, Richard Lamm and Michael McCarthy, and Peter Wiley and Robert Gottlieb. Following a clutch of chapters summarizing social and cultural affairs, ecological efforts, and western lifestyles, Morgan devotes four probing chapters to California, after which he contributes extensive sections on each of the other ten far-western states.

Like McWilliams, Morgan does his homework, utilizing statistics, oral interviews, and wide reading in obscure as well as well-known sources to piece together a more-than-impressionistic account of the new West. He understands the spirit and mobility of the region, its urbanness, its rapid changes, and its becoming the pacesetter for much of the nation. At the same time he urges outsiders—and insiders—to pay more attention to the contemporary West and not to be so fixed on the frontier period of the region. If Morgan is hopeful about the future of the West, his hopefulness is based, in part, on a large understanding of the West, its uniquenesses, and its ties to previous societies and cultures. Because of its insights, its readableness, and its solid research, *Westward Tilt* belongs on the top shelf of books written about the modern West.

Unfortunately, one can not say the same about Wiley and Gottlieb's *Empires in the Sun: The Rise of the New American West* (1982). If the volume is lively, up-to-date, and easy reading, it is also much less substantial than the works of either Neil Morgan or Carey McWilliams, the latter one of the authors to whom the book is dedicated. While knowledgeable about the recent shifts in political and corporate power—perhaps their major theme—the authors are inadequately grounded in the western historical trends and influences of the nineteenth and early twentieth centuries that helped mark the period they cover. Indeed, their story seems truncated, with so much emphasis on contemporary political-economic topics and so little mention of earlier or more recent sociocultural affairs that one emerges from their volume with numerous interesting stories and a plethora of facts but too little understanding of the earlier events of western history that continue to influence the region as much or more so than the changes the authors chronicle.

Nor do the authors seem willing to test any of the several themes academic historians and other scholars have raised about the nature of the modern West. Unlike McWilliams and Neil Morgan, they seem unacquainted with these important historiographical themes; more extensive reading in published essays and monographs would have given the authors much-needed perspective and additional depth. Finally, while Wiley and Gottlieb contribute heavy doses of information on resources, power, and conflict, they are light on the human side of their story—that is, on individuals in this new society and culture. The power of the purse, corporate rooms, and city centers dominate their story—nearly exclusively so.[32]

While using an approach similar to that of Wiley and Gottlieb—part history and part journalism with major emphasis on the recent West—Neal R. Peirce, a Washington-based political writer, ranges farther and probes deeper than they in his extensive writings on modern America. In his *The Megastates of America* (including treatment of California and Texas), *The Great Plains States of America*, *The Mountain States of America*, *The Pacific States of America*, and more recently his jointly authored (with Jerry Hagstrom) *The Book of America: Inside 50 States Today* (1983), Peirce is also much interested in "politics and power"—as the subtitles of his volumes indicate—but he has done much more than other recent general writers to deal with persons involved in these bureaucratic power struggles and decisions. In researching fairly extensively newspapers, popular magazines, and a variety of other printed historical sources and in interviewing a large number of citizens and leaders, Peirce provides broader coverage in his popular histories. Moreover, he pays more attention to sociocultural details and events than Wiley and Gottlieb, thereby giving more variety to his findings. Now more than fifteen years old—except for *The Book of America*—Peirce's volumes are still useful for scholars and students attempting to understand the modern West.

Although several academics and journalists have provided general overviews of the modern West during the last generation, two scholars—Richard Lowitt and Gerald Nash—in the last five years have contributed the first in-depth monographs on specific periods of the modern West. Lowitt's *The New Deal and the West* (1984) is particularly thorough in tracing the impact of the policies of the departments of Interior and Agriculture on the West from 1932 to 1940. Agreeing with the earlier conclusions of such scholars as Leonard Arrington and Nash, Lowitt depicts New Deal policies as transforming the West, lifting the region by the end of the 1930s from the despair and economic dilemmas of the Depression to a new, more informed view of the possibilities of economic planning. Westerners, the author contends, realized by 1940 that frontier individualism was a thing of the past; the future necessitated better and more systematic organization in dealing with natural resources, conservation, and public power—better planning that would involve the federal government in projects beyond the realization of persons and powers merely within the region.

The New Deal in the West belongs squarely in the recent historiographical trend of bureaucratic studies that has characterized the historiography of twentieth-century U.S. history. Lowitt has clearly focused on the functioning of New Deal policies in the region and thus is not so much interested in depicting the West during the New Deal as in showing what happened to New Deal ideas once they were applied to the West. Utilizing a regional approach, Lowitt traces the impact of these policies as they influenced the Great Plains, the Pacific Northwest, California, and the Southwest. He is most intrigued with economic and social transformations, much less so with political and cultural shifts. Altogether, Lowitt's volume, the first on its subject, is clearly from the Washington, D.C., focus and leaves to other scholars companion studies of the West during the New Deal.

The other recent study dealing with a specific period in the modern West is Nash's *The American West Transformed: The Impact of the Second*

World War (1985). In this new monograph, which builds on Nash's earlier work on the modern West, he boldly asserts that the four years from 1941 to 1945 transformed the Far West from "an area with a self-image that emphasized colonialism into one boosting self-sufficiency and innovation" (p. vii). Devoting six chapters to the moving social changes that war brought to the West, Nash also treats science and Hollywood during the 1940s. In addition he sketches in broad backgrounds and economic changes, the latter of which will be treated in a soon-to-be-published study of the economic impact of the war on the West.

Nash's study is particularly helpful for understanding the population shifts that remade western cities and that disrupted the lives of such ethnic groups as Blacks, Hispanics, Indians, and Japanese Americans. While Nash does not treat the traumas of women during these disruptions, he correctly notes that this notable topic deserves book-length treatment. Drawing upon the generalizations presented in his several volumes on the recent West, Nash stresses the manner in which the Second World War impelled the West away from its earlier colonial status toward becoming a much more independent region. As he had earlier, Nash adds that Turner's frontier thesis, with its strong environmental emphasis, is of little use in understanding the modern West, especially in evaluating the dramatic changes that occurred in the early 1940s. Finally, in his stress on the impact of government aid and policies, Nash places his work among the new organizational-bureaucratic interpretations that one historiographer calls the major trend in recent interpretations of modern American history.[33]

In addition to the recent volumes mentioned previously, other multi-volume series and individual studies now under way promise to cover topics and periods not yet dealt with in book-length studies. Volumes on modern Mormonism, western energy and natural resources, and other topics stressing the impact of national and governmental influences on the West are planned in Martin Ridge's series for Indiana University Press, The West in the Twentieth Century, of which Lowitt's *The New Deal and the West* is the notable first volume. Gerald Nash will also edit a series on the modern West for the University of Arizona Press, and the University of Nebraska Press has recently announced a series dealing with the twentieth-century West to be edited by Howard R. Lamar, Michael P. Malone, and Earl Pomeroy. In addition, the University of New Mexico Press plans to publish books that will treat, in part, the modern West in its well-known frontier series. And a forthcoming set of western biographies from the University of Oklahoma Press, edited by Richard W. Etulain, will include lifestories of several contemporary western figures. Finally, a brief overview synthesis of the new West, authored by Malone and Etulain and forthcoming from the University of Nebraksa Press, is based on much of the research published in the past generation.

While these noteworthy projects should fill many of the apparent gaps in the historiography of the twentieth-century West, numerous other projects are needed, as even a casual observer will see. For example, no comprehensive studies of comparative regions—of the West and the Canadian West, of the West and the American South—are available, although several comparative frontier studies have been published. Moreover, if more work on East-West differences is needed, so is more research and writing that bridges 1900, that plots out changes or continuities across the traditional breaking point in western history. As Patricia Nelson Limerick notes in her provocative volume, *The Legacy of Conquest: The Unbroken Past of the American West* (1987), historians must see the West whole, must recognize that many of the central themes of the nineteenth century have occupied Westerners in the present century. As a synthesis of pertinent secondary sources, Limerick's volume asks large questions about western history that other historians should heed and address in even more detail.

Fertile possibilities are apparent in still other areas. Nash has argued that California—and others have pointed to Texas—has emerged as something of a pacesetter for national trends. Extensive, careful study of this intriguing theme is lacking. Or, to cite two other topics, urbanization and women's experiences are considered "hot" subjects in western historiography, but nothing like Gunther Barth's *Instant Cities* is available for the new West, and interpretations of women in the modern West are even less thorough and extensive than those on western cities. Further studies of the large and lasting impact of technology on the West must also be undertaken. In this regard, Donald Worster has recently argued that attempts to overcome the West's aridity through gigantic reclamation and irrigation projects threaten the future of the region, an argument he elaborates in his well-written and pointed volume *Rivers of Empire: Water, Aridity, and the Growth of the American West* (1986). Not all readers will agree with Worster's impassioned book, but all should profit from his attempt to see the region in large perspective.

In the varied fields of social history, much also remains to be undertaken. For example, while social historians have done—or are beginning to do—a great deal with Chicano and Indian experiences in the twentieth century, no current overview synthesizes minority experiences and provides valuable comparative perspectives. The situation is much the same in family history. Although such scholars as Joan M. Jensen, Karen Anderson, Susan Armitage, and Julia Kirk Blackwelder have contributed useful essays or monographs on women's experiences in the modern West, general overviews of women or families in the twentieth-century West are lacking.

The needs in the field of cultural-intellectual history are even more pressing. This general area lags far behind, as it does in U.S. historiography, the number and thoroughness of recent treatments of economic and social history. Except for the field of literary history, the cultural history of the modern West is almost that of another country—unknown and instudied.[34] Henry Nash Smith provided a richly rewarding analysis of the mythic West in his classic *Virgin Land* (1950), but he and others like Richard Slotkin stopped with the nineteenth century. Scholars have not yet produced such provocative and synthetic volumes for the twentieth century, the kind of well-researched and well-written work appearing in Franklin Walker's *A Literary History of Southern California* (1950) and in Kevin Starr's two volumes (*Americans and the California Dream 1850–1915* [1973] and *Inventing the Dream: California through the Progressive Era* [1985]), both of which nudge into modern California. If Smith and others have provided image studies of the West, no one has done *western* image studies of the West or of other regions. It is time for such works.

The list is endless, the possibilities numberless. Thus if historians have made major strides in the last decade or two in treating some of the major subjects, periods, themes, and persons of the twentieth-century West, one is also correct in suggesting that even more remains to be done—in just about any area to which one wishes to point.[35]

Notes

1. The beginning place for the study of western historiography is Michael P. Malone, ed. *Historians and the American West* (Lincoln: University of Nebraska Press, 1983). Another collection of useful historiographical essays that focuses on the pioneer West is Roger L. Nichols, ed., *American Frontier and Western Issues: A Historiographical Review* (Westport, Conn.: Greenwood Press, 1986). For a convenient overview, also see Rodman W. Paul and Michael P. Malone, "Tradition and Challenge in Western Historiography," *Western Historical Quarterly* (16 (January 1985): 27–53.

2. Jack L. August, Jr., summarizes and evaluates the work of Pomeroy, Nash, and Gressley in his "The Future of Western History: The Third Wave," *Journal of Arizona History* 27 (Summer 1986): 229–44.

3. Ray Allen Billington deals with Turner's interests in the twentieth-century West in his brilliant biography, *Frederick Jackson Turner: Historian, Scholar, Teacher* (New York: Oxford University Press, 1973). Turner's tendency to side with the negative ideas of the "alarmists" is detailed in Billington, "Frederick

Prologue

Jackson Turner and the Closing Frontier" in *Essays in Western History in Honor of T. A. Larson,* ed. Roger Daniels, *University of Wyoming Publications* 37 (October 1971): 45–56.

4. Billington, *Frederick Jackson Turner,* p. 367; Turner, "The West—1876 and 1926," *The World's Work* 52 (July 1926): 319–27.

5. Billington, "Turner and the Closing Frontier."

6. Turner, "Section and Nation," *Yale Review* 12 (October 1922): 1–21.

7. Turner, "The Significance of the Section in American History," *Wisconsin Magazine of History* 13 (March 1925): 255–80. For a very useful analysis of Turner's ideas on section and region, see Michael C. Steiner, "The Significance of Turner's Sectional Thesis," *Western Historical Quarterly* 10 (October 1979): 437–66.

8. Billington, *Frederick Jackson Turner,* 388. Turner as a frontier historian is discerningly treated in William Cronon, "Revisiting the Vanishing Frontier: The Legacy of Frederick Jackson Turner," *Western Historical Quarterly* 19 (January 1988): 5–20. Martin Ridge elaborates on Billington's important role in western historiography in his, "Ray Allen Billington, Western History, and American Exceptionalism," *Pacific Historical Review* 56 (November 1987): 495–511.

9. While the life and historical writings of Turner, Walter Prescott Webb, Herbert Eugene Bolton, and James Malin have been treated in biographical and analytical studies, only Earl Pomeroy, a Paxson student, has dealt with his mentor's research methods in "Frederic L. Paxson and His Approach to History," *Mississippi Valley Historical Review* 39 (March 1953): 673–92. Paxson's important roles as author of general surveys of western and U.S. history and as teacher of dozens of graduate students deserve further attention. A full listing of Paxson's essays, books, and most of his reviews is available in *The Great Demobilization and Other Essays* (Madison: University of Wisconsin Press, 1941).

10. Webb, a review of Paxson, *History of the American Frontier—1763–1893, Southwestern Historical Quarterly* 28 (January 1925): 247–52.

11. The two notable essays Parish wrote on the continuation of the westward movement into the twentieth century are included in John Carl Parish, *The Persistence of the Westward Movement and Other Essays* (Berkeley: University of California Press, 1943).

12. For a recent, well-edited anthology of Malin's writings, consult Robert P. Swierenga, ed. *James C. Malin, History & Ecology: Studies of the Grassland* (Lincoln: University of Nebraska Press, 1984).

13. Useful commentaries on Malin and his influences on other historians are included in Swierenga's introduction to *James C. Malin,* xiii–xxix; Allan G. Bogue, "The Heirs of James C. Malin: A Grassland Historiography," *Great Plains Quarterly* 1 (Spring 1981): 105–31: and Robert G. Bell, "James C. Malin and the Grasslands of North America," *Agricultural History* 46 (July 1972): 414–24. These writers argue for a larger influence of Malin and his writings on western historians than this writer does.

14. Frederic L. Paxson, review of Webb, *The Great Plains, American Historical Review* 37 (January 1932): 359–60.

15. The best discussion of Webb and *The Great Plains* is in Gregory M. Tobin, *The Making of a History: Walter Prescott Webb and The Great Plains* (Austin:

University of Texas Press, 1976); also see Necah Stewart Furman, *Walter Prescott Webb: His Life and Impact* (Albuquerque: University of New Mexico Press, 1976). Several of Webb's key ideas are briefly summarized in his later essay: "The American West, Perpetual Mirage," *Harper's* 214 (May 1957): 25–31. The other major western historian of the early twentieth century, Herbert Eugene Bolton, was not much interested in writing about the modern West. On a few occasions Bolton briefly mentions the legacies Spanish society and culture bequeathed to Americans and Latin Americans, but these discussions—for example in four of his best-known essays collected in *Wider Horizons of American History* (Notre Dame: University of Notre Dame Press, 1967)—are brief and sketchy. Bolton is intrigued most with the beginning settlements and influences of the Spanish in the New World, and thus his comments rarely deal with the twentieth-century American West. For a narrative overview of Bolton's life and writings, see John Francis Bannon, *Herbert Eugene Bolton: The Historian and the Man* (Tucson: University of Arizona Press, 1978). David J. Weber evaluates the ties of Bolton and Borderlands scholars to the ideas of Turner in "Turner, the Boltonians, and the Borderlands," *American Historical Review* 91 (February 1986): 66–81.

16. The best summary of regionalistic thought in modern America is Richard Maxwell Brown, "The New Regionalism in America, 1970–1981," in William G. Robbins, Robert J. Frank, and Richard E. Ross, eds. *Regionalism and the Pacific Northwest* (Corvallis: Oregon State University Press, 1983): 37–96. A helpful survey of southern regionalism in the 1920s and 1930s is contained in George B. Tindall, *The Emergence of the New South 1913–1945* (Baton Rouge: Louisiana State University Press, 1967), 575–606. The discussions on southern literary regionalism in Louis D. Rubin, et al., eds., *The History of Southern Literature* (Baton Rouge: Louisiana University Press, 1985), are very useful. Also see Michael C. Steiner, "Regionalism in the Great Depression," *Geographical Review* 73 (October 1983): 430–46. The most recent call for the study of the West as region is Donald Worster, "New West, True West: Interpreting the Region's History," *Western Historical Quarterly* 18 (April 1987): 141–56. Warren I. Susman, in his "The Useless Past: American Intellectuals and the Frontier Thesis: 1910–1930," *Bucknell Review* 11 (March 1963): 1–20, argues that many intellectuals (but not historians) abandoned the frontier thesis because of its overly sympathetic view of the pioneer past.

17. In addition to the materials mentioned above in note 15, Walter Rundell, Jr., provides interesting commentary in "W. P. Webb's *Divided We Stand*: A Publishing Crisis," *Western Historical Quarterly* 13 (October 1982): 391–407.

18. Wallace Stegner elucidates De Voto's stances on the West in *The Uneasy Chair: A Biography of Bernard DeVoto* (Garden City, N.Y.: Doubleday and Company, 1974); and in Stegner and Richard W. Etulain, *Conversations with Wallace Stegner on Western History and Literature* (Salt Lake City: University of Utah Press, 1983). William G. Robbins retests the De Voto thesis as an explanation of the modern West in his stimulating essay "The 'Plundered Province' Thesis and Recent Historiography of the American West," *Pacific Historical Review* 55 (November 1986): 577–97.

19. Gressley, "James G. Blaine, 'Alferd' E. Packer and Western Particularism," *Historian* 44 (May 1982): 364–81. Those acquainted with Gressley's *The Twen-*

tieth-Century American West: A Potpourri (Columbia: University of Missouri Press, 1977) will realize my indebtedness here to him, especially to his "Preface," and "Colonialism and the West," pp. 1–47.

20. For other books with points of view similar to those of Mezerik and Garnsey, see Wendell Berge, *Economic Freedom for the West* (Lincoln: University of Nebraska Press, 1946); Rufus Terral, *The Missouri Valley: Land of Drouth, Flood, and Promise* (New Haven: Yale University Press, 1947): and Joseph Kinsey Howard, *Montana: High, Wide and Handsome* (New Haven: Yale University Press, 1943). George B. Tindall traces similar colonial experiences and interpretations of those experiences in the South in *The Emergence of the New South 1913–1945*, 433–72, 575–606.

21. Other notable works by McWilliams include *The New Regionalism in American Literature* (Seattle: University of Washington Book Store, 1930): *North from Mexico: The Spanish-Speaking People of the United States* (Philadelphia: J. B. Lippincott, 1949); *Factories in the Field* (Boston: Little, Brown and Company, 1939). Josiah Royce provided an early regionalistic interpretation of California in *California, from the Conquest in 1846 to the Second Vigilance Committee in San Francisco: A Study in American Character* (Boston: Houghton, Mifflin and Company, 1886).

22. Caughey has displayed an increasing interest in the West as region. See his *The American West: Frontier and Region*, edited with Introduction by Norris Hundley, Jr., and John A. Schutz (Los Angeles: Ward Ritchie Press, 1969). Also see his presidential address before the Western History Association in 1973—"The Insignificance of the Frontier in American History or 'Once Upon a Time There Was an American West,'" *Western Historical Quarterly* 5 (January 1974): 5–16. For a convenient, sympathetic summary of Caughey's career, see Stephen Dow Beckham, "John Walton Caughey, Historian and Civil Libertarian," *Pacific Historical Review* 56 (November 1987): 481–93. The presidential address of the previous year also dealt with the modern West: Howard R. Lamar, "Persistent Frontier: The West in the Twentieth Century," *Western Historical Quarterly* 4 (January 1973): 5–25, which contains a useful selective bibliography. The evaluation of Caughey's *California* is contained in Gerald D. Nash, "California and Its Historians: An Appraisal of the Histories of the State," *Pacific Historical Review* 50 (November 1981): 402.

23. John Higham, *History: The Development of Historical Studies in the United States* (Englewood Cliffs, N.J.: Prentice-Hall, 1965), 214–15.

24. Earl Pomeroy, "Toward a Reorientation of Western History: Continuity and Environment," *Mississippi Valley Historical Review* 41 (March 1955): 579–600; Pomeroy, *The Territories and the United States 1861–1890: Studies in Colonial Administration* (Philadelphia: University of Pennsylvania Press, 1947); Pomeroy, "What Remains of the West?" *Utah Historical Quarterly* 35 (Winter 1967): 37–55; Pomeroy to R. W. Etulain, September 22, 1984; interview with Pomeroy, November 2, 1985, Eugene, Oregon. For a fine overview of Pomeroy's ideas and major publications, see Howard R. Lamar, "Earl Pomeroy, Historian's Historian," *Pacific Historical Review* 56 (November 1987): 547–60.

25. Athearn deals informally with his philosophy of history in "A View from the High Country," *Western Historical Quarterly* 2 (April 1971): 125–32.

26. Except for the works of Turner and Webb, the writings of Earl Pomeroy are mentioned more often than those of any other western historian in Malone, *Historians and the American West.*

27. Gressley, "The Turner Thesis—A Problem in Historiography," *Agricultural History* 32 (October 1958): 227–49: editor, *The American West: A Reorientation* (Laramie: University of Wyoming, 1966): "Regionalism and the Twentieth-Century West," in Jerome O. Steffen, ed., *The American West: New Perspectives, New Dimensions* (Norman: University of Oklahoma Press, 1979), 197–234: and "Whither Western American History? Speculations on a Direction," *Pacific Historical Review* 53 (November 1984): 493–501; and "The West: Past, Present, and Future," *Western Historical Quarterly* 17 (January 1986): 5–23.

28. Also see Nash, "The Twentieth-Century West," *Western Historical Quarterly* 13 (April 1982): 179–81; and "Mirror for the Future: The Historical Past of the Twentieth-Century West," in Thomas G. Alexander and John F. Bluth, eds. *The Twentieth Century American West,* Charles Redd Monographs in Western History No. 12 (Provo, Utah: Charles Redd Center for Western Studies, 1983), 1–27; and "Where Is the West?" *The Historian* 49 (November 1986): 1–9.

29. Richard C. Wade, *The Urban Frontier* . . . (Chicago: University of Chicago Press, 1959): Pomeroy, "The Urban Frontier of the Far West," in John G. Clark, ed. *The Frontier Challenge: Responses to the Trans-Mississippi West* (Lawrence: University Press of Kansas, 1971), 7–29.

30. For very useful evaluations of far-western state histories, see the collection of essays by several authors in "Western State Historiography: A Status Report," *Pacific Historical Review* 50 (November 1981): 387–525.

31. Bean's major competitor among California history texts—John W. Caughey with Norris Hundley, Jr., *California: History of a Remarkable State,* 4th ed. (Englewoods Cliffs, N.J.: Prentice-Hall, 1982)—treats the modern West in about 150 of its 433 pages. K. Ross Toole's *Twentieth-Century Montana: A State of Extremes* (Norman: University of Oklahoma Press, 1972) is misnamed since it skims over the state's history after the 1920s. For a well-written, impressionistic (and now dated) treatment of modern Texas, see Frank Goodwyn, *Lone-Star Land: Twentieth-Century Texas in Perspective* (New York: Alfred A. Knopf, 1955).

32. An even less successful popular account of the modern West is Richard D. Lamm and Michael McCarthy, *The Angry West: A Vulnerable Land and Its Future* (Boston: Houghton Mifflin Company, 1982), which is much too simplistic and sentimental. It belongs to the colonial tradition in western historiography, as does K. Ross Toole, *The Rape of the Great Plains: Northwestern America, Cattle and Coal* (Boston: Little, Brown, and Company, 1976).

33. Useful historiographical essays on the organizational-bureaucratic school of historians include Alan Brinkley, "Writing the History of Contemporary America: Dilemmas and Challenges." *Daedalus* 113 (Summer 1984): 121–41: and Robert F. Berkhofer, Jr. "The Organizational Interpretation of American History: A New Synthesis," in Jack S. Salzman, ed. *Prospects: An Annual of American Cultural Studies* 4 (New York: Burt Franklin and Company, 1979), 611–29. For a discussion of Nash's attachments to the organizational school of historians, see his *The*

Prologue

Great Depression and World War II: Organizing America, 1933–1945 (New York: St. Martin's Press, 1979), v–vii.

34. Recent trends and remaining gaps in western literary and cultural historiography are summarized in Richard W. Etulain, "The American Literary West and Its Interpreters: The Rise of a New Historiography," *Pacific Historical Review* 45 (August 1976): 311–48; "Frontier, Region, and Myth: Changing Interpretations of Western American Culture," *Journal of American Culture* 3 (Summer 1980): 268–84; "Shifting Interpretations of Western American Cultural History," in Malone, *Historians and the American West*, 414–32; and "Contours of Culture in Arizona and the Modern West," in Beth Luey and Noel J. Stowe, eds., *Arizona at Seventy-Five: The Next Twenty-Five Years* (Tempe: Arizona State University Public History Program; Tucson: Arizona Historical Society, 1987), 11–53.

35. For a very useful review of Malone's volume and for a list of research needs in western history, some of which deal with the twentieth century, see Walter Nugent, "Western History: Stocktakings and New Crops," *Reviews in American History* 13 (September 1985): 319–29. Elliott West covers some of the newer interpretations of the modern West in his lively essay "Cowboys and Indians and Artists and Liars and Schoolmarms and Tom Mix: New Ways to Teach the American West," in Dennis Reinhartz and Stephen E. Maizlish, eds. *Essays on Walter Prescott Webb and the Teaching of History* (College Station: Texas A & M University Press, 1985), 36–60.

I

People of the Twentieth-Century West

Throughout its history the American West has attracted a wide range of ethnic and racial groups from around the world. This was even more pronounced in the years after 1890 when the West developed a truly multicultural society. As Walter Nugent indicates in his essay, the demographic trends of the twentieth-century West were not unique but clearly reflected national patterns, especially the spectacular growth of towns and cities. Although the majority of migrants in the nineteenth century settled on farms and in rural areas, the overwhelming majority of migrants a century later streamed into urban centers. Carl Abbott provides a concise analysis of the characteristics that these new metropolitan centers acquired after 1890. The composition of the population in the metropolises of the West differed sharply from that in the nineteenth century. Then the West had been primarily a male-oriented society, settled by a majority of young men under twenty-five years of age and only a small percentage of women. By contrast, the twentieth-century West was settled by families rather than single individuals and reflected a greater balance in ratios between the sexes. Karen Anderson in her essay sketches some of the parameters of this demographic change. In addition, the ethnic and racial composition of the West differed appreciably. In the nineteenth century the ethnic and racial character of the region was largely set by native-born Americans and immigrants from northern and central Europe as well as the British Isles. But the twentieth-century West counted increasing numbers of Hispanic Americans, black Americans, Asian Americans and immigrants from southern and eastern Europe. And a growing number of American Indians were moving from reservations to towns and cities. The selections by Ricardo Romo and Donald Parman touch on these significant changes. The varied essays in this section point to an emerging image of a West characterized by an urban, multicultural, multiracial, and multiethnic society reflecting great diversity.

1

The People of the West since 1890

Walter Nugent

In this suggestive essay Walter Nugent utilizes insights drawn from demography to explain major changes in the West's population patterns after 1890. It was in the West, he argues, that two major transformations in American life manifested themselves, but more dramatically than elsewhere. One was the decline of the traditional rural frontier pattern of settlement; the other was the emerging metropolitan mode of settlement—to become increasingly dominant in the course of the twentieth century. The enormous influx of newcomers to the West after 1890—when the West was still an underpopulated region—paced the nation. It symbolized the profound change in America from an agrarian to an industrial nation, a process traced by Professor Nugent with special reference to western population trends.

The West in this essay is the Census Bureau's West. The region includes the two census divisions of Mountain and Pacific, which covers the eleven states of Montana, Wyoming, Colorado, and New Mexico on the east as well as Arizona, Utah, Idaho, Nevada in the Great Basin, and the Pacific states of Washington, Oregon, and California. (Hawaii and Alaska became part of the region when they were admitted as states in 1959, but since they were such recent entrants and, more importantly, so different from the other eleven, they will receive only brief attention.) One can argue, quite properly, that at least the western portions of the Great Plains should be included. The area west of the hundredth meridian is as western ecologically and economically as many parts of the Mountain states. John Wesley Powell included it in the "Arid Region" in his famous report of 1879;[1] and it is big-sky and big-acreage territory. But to include another several hundred counties from North Dakota to Texas would make this essay too cumbersome and, more to the point, less useful for comparative or analytical purposes.

The *twentieth century* in this essay begins with 1890. The census taken in that year revealed the absence of a meaningful frontier line, or edge of western settlement, for the first time in American history: "at present the unsettled area has been so broken into by isolated bodies of settlement that there can hardly be said to be a frontier line"[2] (see fig. 1.1). On that observation Frederick Jackson Turner based his two-stage periodization of all American history—a past when the United States was dominated by the frontier process and a future when it would not be. Turner was well aware, as his later writings show, that the frontier "did not end 'with a bang'" in 1890 but persisted in certain areas for several decades.[3] I have argued elsewhere that 1920 is a better date to mark the conclusion of the frontier or, more accurately, of "Type I," traditional, agricultural, high-fertility, frontier processes.[4] Looked at in terms of deep social structures as evidenced by demographic events, the history of the United States was remarkable in the years from 1890 to 1920 for a competing overlap of two different patterns of population behavior, geographic and economic expansion, and modes of social existence. The traditional frontier-rural mode was then in its death throes nationally but remained vigorous on the Great Plains and the arable parts of the Pacific states. The newer metropolitan mode, which first appeared in the Northeast in the middle of the nineteenth century, surged forward with its cities, industries, and immigrants and, after 1920, became *the* American mode of life. The American West is especially significant in the 1890–1920 period, therefore, since it is the region where the great struggle between those modes took place. Thus 1890 provides a convenient start, 1920 an important punctuation, and 1950 (for reasons to be seen) another stopping point.

Demography as used here refers generally to what the United States Census and a few other sources relate. While the census does not answer every demographic question, it does speak to some: the size of the western population, in itself and within the nation; the changing age and sex composition of the West; its races and ethnicities; where people came from and where they went; the appearance (and where and when) of towns, cities, and metropolises; changes in agricultural settlement; and a few other facts and trends. Census data permit, therefore, an accurate basic description of the West's population changes, the basic substrata of the rest of its history.

The West and the United States: Size and Growth

Since 1890 the West has been growing faster in population than the other three regions of the United States (South, North Central, and Northeast).

Americans have become inured to this fact without reflecting that the United States' rate of growth outran that of any of the other industrialized or New World countries. Thus the expansion of the West as a region has been unusual in structure and unique in size. While the United States expanded from 63 million in 1890 to 226 million in 1980, the West rose during the same period from 3 million to 43 million, from 5 percent of the whole nation to nearly 20 percent. In each decade except the 1890s and 1960s, the western growth rate was more than twice, occasionally three times, the rate for the United States in general. While eighteenth- and nineteenth-century "wests"—wherever they happened to be at a given time—always grew faster than the whole United States, they never accounted for such a large part of the total numbers as the West has in the twentieth century. By the 1970s the West accounted for more than a third of the entire population increase of the United States.

Cast in the context of United States population patterns since their seventeenth-century beginnings, the growth of the western region since 1890 presents some unusual features. Total American population growth during much of the eighteenth and nineteenth centuries held steady at the very high rate of about 35 percent per decade. But it fell abruptly to around 26 percent from the 1860s to the 1890s and then to about 21 percent from the 1890s to just before the 1920s, when it fell abruptly a second time to approximately 13 percent per decade, where it has remained ever since (averaging out the aberrations of the Great Depression and the Baby Boom). The rapid growth of the long, early period was almost entirely rural and took place largely on or near frontiers. As society urbanized, the growth rate slowed. Although all the causal relationships are not obvious, or even known, it is no coincidence that the post-1920 period with its relatively slow growth has also been the period when the majority of the American population became metropolitan in the social as well as geographical sense.

The West presents different patterns. The region's growth of 24 percent in each of the decades of the 1960s and 1970s roughly matches the rate for the whole United States a century earlier. The West's increases of about 40 percent in each of the baby-boom decades of the 1940s and 1950s exceeded the rate for the United States during its purest and fastest frontier-rural expansion. Yet the most remarkable feature of western growth since 1890 is that much of it has been urban. Ever since 1890, in fact, the western region has had a larger proportion of urban population than the whole United States (38 percent urban compared to 35 percent then, and in the 1980s, 84 percent against 74 percent). Decade by decade the West's rate of urbanization has been higher, often much higher, than the national rate. Rural population also increased in the West, except during the 1960s, while it steadily decreased elsewhere. But urban growth was the

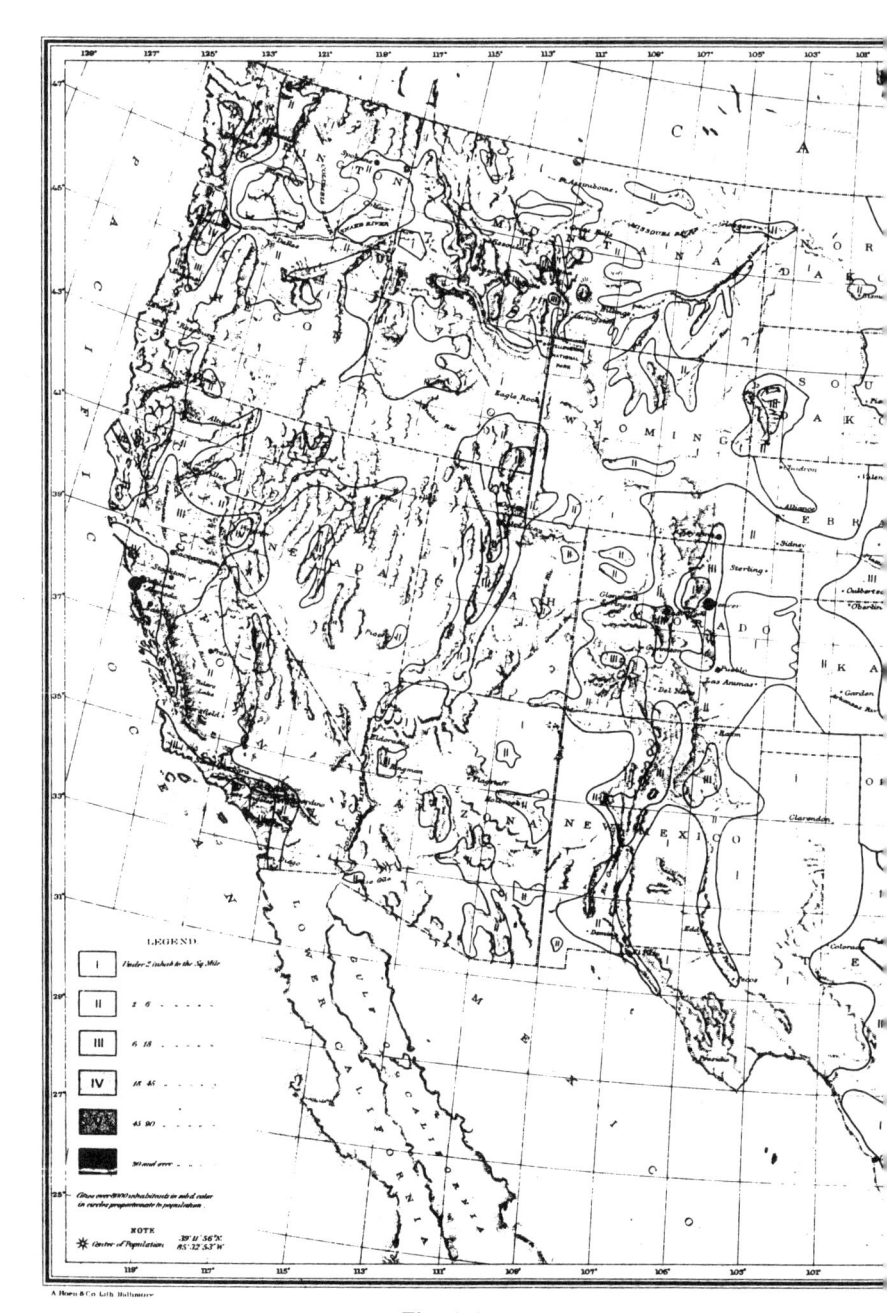

Fig. 1.1
Population of the United States, 1890
(*Eleventh Census of the United States*)

The People of the West

main show; rural growth provided only a mild assist over the past century. Thus while the West has been the fastest-growing region of the country, it has been unusually urban and is now heavily so. This phenomenon, contradicting past national experience, is compounded by the fact that increasingly urban California accounted for about 34 percent of the West in 1900 but by 1950 included over 50 percent and still does.

The history of population in the West since 1890, then, has differed from the rapid frontier-rural expansion of earlier American history. But it has also differed from the sluggish performance of much of metropolitan America elsewhere. The only near-parallel, historically speaking, is the way in which large- and medium-sized cities expanded in the Northeast and Great Lakes states in the late-nineteenth and early-twentieth centuries. They have recently slowed or fallen back, while the West, especially California, sped on. When, or even whether, the West will eventually resemble the patterns of the older regions is an open question.

The End of Old Frontiers, 1890–1920[5]

Three million people or one of twenty Americans lived in the western region in 1890; in 1920, nine million or about one in twelve lived there (table 1.1). The growth during these three decades was uneven in time and place. The West's most rapid expansion—in total numbers, percent overall increase, and percent urban increase—took place between 1900 and 1910. But in all three decades the rise in numbers is impressive.

Beyond these numbers lay a chaotic array of facts and events suggesting that western growth in this period was unusually and perhaps uniquely complex. It included several different types at the same time. A quick comparison to other areas in their times of rapid expansion reveals occasionally two, usually only one, dominant social-demographic process. For example, Kansas boomed in the 1870s and 1880s but almost wholly as a traditional agricultural frontier; the same can be said for Indiana in the 1830s through the 1850s, or Kentucky and Tennessee from 1790 to 1810. New York grew rapidly in the 1790s mostly because of a boom in frontier farms, and its later boom in the 1880s came almost entirely from industrial cities across the state while its farm frontier had long since disappeared.

In the West from 1890 to 1920, and especially in California (California is always "especially" in this story), growth was manifest in at least six ways, each involving a different cluster of demographic, social, and economic characteristics. The traditional family-farm frontier process was happening in nearly all western states except the desert Southwest. Second, large-scale, mechanized, fully commercial, often irrigated agriculture

The People of the West

Table 1.1
Aggregate Trends, 1890–1920

	1890	1900	1910	1920
West, total people (millions)	3.1	4.3	7.1	9.2
Increase during preceding decade		1.2	2.8	2.1
Pct. increase, preceding decade	74.0	37.5	64.4	30.1
Pct. urban increase, prec. decade		48.0	97.4	40.8
Pct. rural increase, prec. decade		31.3	42.5	20.3
Pct. of region's pop. that was urban, in year indicated	38.3	39.9	47.9	51.8

Source: *Historical Statistics of the United States*, 1975, series A172, A178, A179. "Urban" means people living in incorporated places of 2,500 or more, the traditional census definition before 1950.

began appearing in California and the drainage areas of major rivers. Third, traditional, exploitative, root-hog-or-die prospecting and placer mining, though fading, still popped up unpredictably and sporadically as the cork of opportunity on the vast surface of the West. Fourth, hard-rock mining, requiring capital as well as labor, became important and often dominant in the economies of states like Arizona, Colorado, and Idaho, changing the demography because miners who were really industrial workers had wives and children, whereas gold-rush-type miners operating as lone gamblers did not. Fifth, central cities, large or small, expanded or appeared for the first time, replicating the urbanization that was by then the dominant form of social life in the Northeast and Great Lakes states. Sixth, built-up areas, the suburbs and fringes that were the first suggestions of the urban sprawl to become typical later in the century, especially in southern California, began to appear. While Chicago and New York would always be central cores with suburbs, Los Angeles was many-centered even in the early twentieth century. Western suburbanization differed from northeastern.

In numerous ways the 1890–1920 years were decisive in changing the West and setting it on its paths of unusually high urbanization and peculiar suburbanization. Yet in 1890 the West was still the "Old West" of legend and stereotype, of cowboys and Indians, prospectors and magnates. The OK Corral fracas at Tombstone was only nine years in the past; Geronimo surrendered near the Arizona-Mexico border as recently as 1886; the Wounded Knee episode took place at the end of 1890; and the Johnson County "war" was still ahead, to disturb north-central Wyoming in 1892. The great bulk of western acreage was unoccupied by American citizens. The sooner-boomer land rush into Oklahoma began in 1889 and would continue as further slices of the Indian reserves were opened to homesteaders. These and other events were extensions of the two principal types of frontiers prevalent in the United States in the eighteenth and nineteenth centuries. Type I was the agricultural frontier, accounting for the great mass of western settlers, who normally took up land and cultivated it as families—usually two young parents with proliferating broods, and hence in demographers' terms, fairly balanced sex ratios, high fertility, normally distributed age pyramids, and high mobility as the children reached adulthood and sought better life chances in yet another "west" where land was still cheap. Type II included the get-in-and-get-out exploiters, the placer miners, the cattlemen of the long drives, the jobseekers and drifters—a population of young men without wives and children, volatile and transient. The two types did not die out after 1920, and more than a trace continued in fictional form in John Steinbeck's Tom Joad in the 1930s and in the ill-starred motorcycle jockeys of "Easy Rider" in the 1960s. The West of the 1890s was filled with these traditional figures, and more.

Enough people lived in Montana, Wyoming, Washington, and even Idaho (stretching the rules) to admit them as states in 1889 and 1890. Utah, after the Mormon Church formally foreswore plural marriage in 1890, entered the Union in 1896. Arizona and New Mexico had large enough populations, although politics delayed their admissions until 1912. Beyond these legal signs of maturity, the West displayed respectable signs of urbanization by the 1890s. Puget Sound, Portland, and southern California were joined to the rest of the country by transcontinental railroads as San Francisco had been in 1869. San Francisco's population had passed the 100,000 mark in 1870, and Denver's did so in 1890. Los Angeles in 1890 had 50,000 residents and was, in one historian's words, "a real estate boom waiting to happen." During the 1880s Portland's population reached 46,000, while Seattle's hit 43,000 by 1890 and continued to soar. Smaller cities developed as mining became big business, as farms were connected to distant markets, or as second- or third-generation Mormons spun colonies outward from Utah into Idaho, Arizona, Colorado, and beyond. These growing centers were in large part filled with families, and the western sex ratio and age structure, recently so heavily male and youthful, evened toward normal balance. The Indian and Hispanic populations began rising from low points about 1890, while the West's ethnic complexity, always higher than the national average in foreign-born and foreign-stock, intensified. From a demographic standpoint, the region was kaleidoscopic, at once frontier-agricultural, exploitative, and newly urban.

In most of the western states, the first decade of the twentieth century brought the greatest percentage gains of the 1890–1920 period (table

Table 1.2
Population and Growth Rates of States, 1890–1920

	Population (000s)				% Increase		
	1890	1900	1910	1920	90–00	00–10	10–20
Arizona	88	123	204	334	39	66	64
Colorado	413	540	799	940	31	48	18
Idaho	89	162	326	432	83	101	33
Montana	143	243	376	549	71	55	46
Nevada	47	42	82	77	−11	42	−6
New Mexico	160	195	327	360	22	68	10
Utah	211	277	373	449	31	35	20
Wyoming	63	93	146	194	48	57	33
California	1213	1485	2378	3427	22	60	44
Oregon	318	414	673	783	30	63	13
Washington	357	518	1142	1357	45	120	19

Source: *Hist. Stat. U.S.*, 1975, series A195–A209.

1.2). The second, 1910–1920 decade, brought somewhat lower percentage rises as well as smaller additional numbers except in California, Arizona, and Montana. In every state except Colorado and Montana, city dwellers became a larger proportion of the population, and in 1920, California (the most urban of the eleven states) had 68 percent of its people living in cities. By 1920 California included 3.4 million of the nation's 106 million, thanks to the addition of over a million since 1910, and Washington had 1.4 million, with the rest of the region ranging downward from Colorado's 940,000 to Nevada's 77,000.

A state-by-state glance at the 401 counties that composed the western region by 1920 reveals many local and regional patterns of growth and some of decline. Although Montana's development, both rural and urban, was rapid through the whole period, beneath the seemingly placid state averages lurked a few blips and dips. Of its fifty-one counties in 1920, thirty-five did not exist in 1890. Most of these were organized on or near the Canadian border, the North and South Dakota lines, or around Billings, reflecting the farmers' (or stockmen's) last frontier in the northern Great Plains. Such settlement extended northward into southern Alberta and Saskatchewan in the early twentieth century. A rural movement as vigorous as this was rare for the West in this period. By 1920 thirty-five of the state's counties had no urban population at all—no town as large as 2,500.

In 1890 Montana had only two counties, Custer and Dawson, bordering the Dakotas. In them were 7,400 people. By 1910 they had become four counties with 48,400 people, and ten years later the same area included all or parts of sixteen counties with 117,700 people. Miles City and Glendive were the only sizeable towns by 1920, with 7,937 and 3,816 respectively. Similar rural expansion took place along the Canadian border, some of the central counties (the highest Plains in the lee of the Rockies), and around Billings, the metropolis of Plains Montana as it rose from 836 people in 1890 to over 15,000 in 1920. The mountain and mining parts of the state—places such as Anaconda, Bozeman, Helena, Livingston, Deer Lodge, and Butte—expanded through the period, though not as rapidly as the Plains counties. Although the mining area had been opened up earlier, it grew more slowly than the new farm and ranch country. Some booms, however, did occur: for example, Anaconda expanded from 4,000 to 9,500 and Butte from 10,700 to 30,500 in the 1890s; Missoula from 4,300 to 12,900 in the 1900s; Great Falls from 13,900 to 24,100 in the 1910s. But prior to 1920 the mining and mountain area developed as a rule more erratically and slowly than the farm and stock counties.

Through the 1890–1920 period, Montana, like all western states, was a net receiver of migrants from elsewhere. During the 1890s and 1900s roughly two-thirds of its new people were immigrants, and during the farm boom of the 1910s almost as many. Virtually none of the in-migrants was black; the majority were foreign-born from 1890 to 1910, but only one-fifth of them after that. Farms averaged just over 600 acres, well above the national average.

Wyoming, vast and empty, squeaked into statehood with 63,000 people in 1890 but more than tripled by 1920. The urban proportion remained stable at about 30 percent, but beneath this bland average lay moderate declines in Cheyenne and Laramie and a boom in Casper from 2,600 to 11,400 between 1910 and 1920. With little of the mining that buoyed neighboring Montana and Colorado, Wyoming's expansion in this period resulted from the developing stock-raising areas. Farms averaged 750 acres, but there were few towns within the state. Only Cheyenne and Casper exceeded 10,000 by 1920, when Laramie, Sheridan, and Evanston were the only other places that could be called urban at all. Half to two-thirds of Wyoming's increase came from migrants into it, of whom the great majority were native-born whites.

Colorado included Denver, at 107,000 the only western metropolis other than San Francisco in 1890. Colorado's population also lived in the mining areas of the Rockies, and the farm and stock counties of the high Plains, east of the front range. Denver reached 257,000 in 1920, and nearby cities such as Aurora and Englewood, essentially suburbs or satellites of Denver, began taking off after 1910. Aside from its metropolis, however, Colorado had few urban centers, and those were mining or mine-processing towns.

Despite Denver's expansion, the urban proportion in the Colorado population remained stable at about 48 percent through the 1890–1920 period. This can be explained by equivalent growth in the rural eastern counties and certain not-too-mountainous far-western counties. The northeast, especially around Sterling, Fort Morgan, and Greeley, doubled or tripled in the 1900s and kept rising rapidly between 1910 and 1920. Certain west-central counties such as Mesa (Grand Junction) and Montrose also blossomed in the 1900s. As in Montana, Wyoming, and elsewhere on the high Plains, these Colorado counties were part of the farmers' last frontier—or the stockmen's; the average size of a Colorado ranch or farm in 1920 was 408 acres. With the so-called rationalizing of farming and stockraising after the disastrous shake-outs of the late 1880s, the number of farm enterprises in this state rose from 25,000 in 1900 to 60,000 in 1920—a boom of questionable rationality itself.

Colorado's mountain areas, meanwhile, demonstrated the instability of the mining frontier. Very few places, Leadville and Telluride among them, did well in the 1890s. Aspen, Ouray, and Cripple Creek (despite its will-o'-the-wisp boom in 1893) lost people in each decade between 1890 and 1920, as the drama of Horace Tabor and Baby Doe was played out on a smaller scale in many settlements. Some communities based on mining, such as Pueblo and Golden, revived in the 1900s, but most others declined and continued to do so in 1910–1920. In sum, the Colorado story mirrored the continuing growth of Denver and its environs, the attraction of people to agriculture, and the decrease of people in mining. As in most of the western states, Colorado's best decade for growth was 1900–1910. After that, all of the larger eastern farming counties grew much more slowly. Net migration into the state dropped from 160,000 in 1900–1910 to 40,000 in 1910–1920. A trend downward was beginning on the Great Plains by 1920, but it would not be seen clearly until the figures actually became negative later on.

New Mexico's overall pattern resembled Colorado's, as it gained 22 percent in the 1890s, 68 percent in the 1900s, but only 10 percent in the 1910s. New Mexico's actual numbers were much smaller since it had no Denver or other large city (Albuquerque reached only 15,000 by 1920); and New Mexico's eastern counties, which were extensions of the high Plains of the Oklahoma and Texas panhandles, were very unstable. These counties all showed some increases in the 1890s and then soared in the 1900s—for example, Chaves (Roswell) and Eddy (Carlsbad, Artesia) counties in the southeast rose over 250 percent; but they lost a quarter of their people in 1910–1920. The northeast fared better—Colfax (Raton) and Union (Clayton), just west of the Oklahoma panhandle, continued to gain after 1910. But their days of woe were ahead. Southwestern New Mexico, however, from Las Cruces through Deming and Silver City to the Arizona line, a developing area of hard-rock mining, increased in all three decades (particularly between 1910 and 1920) as did Gallup and the northwest. The considerable Indian population, surpassed in 1920 only by Arizona and Oklahoma, stabilized after 1910 at around 20,000. New Mexico was the first western state other than Nevada to suffer a net loss through migration, some 20,000 during the 1910-1920 decade—actually 32,000 native-born whites who were partially offset by an inflow of 8,000 foreign-born, many from Mexico. With its unique mixture of Indian, Hispanic, and Anglo cultures, New Mexico has had a special demographic history. But before 1920 the numbers were small, and the urban proportion the lowest (18 percent in 1920) in the West.

Arizona was almost as bereft of towns as New Mexico in 1890, when Tucson had 7,500 people and Phoenix 5,500. But by 1920 Arizona was 35 percent urban. This shift was due in part to Phoenix reaching 29,000 and Tucson 20,000, but also to the establishment after 1900 of Bisbee, Douglas, and other mining settlements in the extreme southeastern county of Cochise, which held 47,000 in 1920, and in east central Gila county, which rose from 2,000 to 26,000 in those thirty years. Around Phoenix, the towns of Glendale, Tempe, and Mesa—virtually nonexistent in 1890—each included 2,000 to 3,000 people by 1920, and together with Phoenix they made Maricopa by far the largest county with 90,000. On the lower Colorado River, Yuma made its appearance by 1910. But there and across the state only 10,000 farm enterprises operated in 1920. Although this represented a tenfold rise in farms since 1890, Arizona had the fewest farms of any state in the West except Nevada. Thus Arizona's demographic pattern showed impressive rises in the future metropolises of Phoenix and Tucson as well as in the first satellite-suburbs around Phoenix and in the rapid development of hard-rock mining in one or two counties. The state also included 33,000 Indians in 1920, up from 26,000 in 1900.[6]

Utah, with a steadier rate of increase than the rest of the West, experienced abnormally low in-migration and an unspectacular, gradual increase in farms from 11,000 to 26,000 over thirty years. These characteristics plus the fact that the farms averaged 197 acres, the lowest in the West except for California and matched only by neighboring Idaho, reflected the expansion of rural and small-town Mormon communities from St. George in the extreme southwest, along the valley just west of the Wasatch range, through Utah (Provo), Salt Lake, and Weber (Ogden) counties into the Cache Valley in the north. All underwent steady and rapid natural increase.[7] Towns like Moroni, Nephi, Kanab, and Provo were typical in that they were not large but were growing in a continuing, close-knit way. Places such as Price, Green River, Moab, or the moun-

The People of the West

tainous Wasatch county in north central Utah above Provo provided a sharp contrast. Wasatch, for example, rose 27 percent in the 1890s, 88 percent in the 1900s, but lost 48 percent in 1910–1920. As in other states, the mining areas of Utah were demographically unstable. The western desert counties of Tooele and Juab, stretching to the Nevada line, nearly doubled in the 1890s but gained almost nothing or lost a few people after 1900. Salt Lake City, the Mormon capital but home to others as well, included 45,000 in 1890, reached 54,000 in 1900, then boomed to 93,000 in 1910, and attained metropolitan size at 118,000 in 1920. Much the largest city, it was followed then by Ogden with 33,000 and Provo with 10,000. Utah's urban population lagged behind the regional norm and was much below it outside of Salt Lake City.

Nevada, virtually without agriculture and with a notoriously unstable mining force, had little reason except the exigencies of Republican politics in 1864 to have become a state at all, and it fell in population in the late-nineteenth century. In 1900 it had one-third of the population of Arizona and one-fourth of New Mexico's, but those were not admitted to statehood for another twelve years. As is evident in table 1.3 the contrast is stark between Type II Nevada, the purest example of a long-lived mining frontier, and neighboring Utah, a Type I frontier with its large frequency of solidly growing Mormon communities. Since the first Mormon migrations in the late 1840s, Utah had a sex ratio and age structure unlike most frontier areas, even agricultural frontiers in the Mississippi and Missouri Valleys, because its settlers arrived in family groups. Nevada, like mining frontiers generally (California in the 1850s was a severe case) had a preponderance of unattached young men, the obverse of which is few women, children, or older people. With its economy and population so

Table 1.3
Nevada and Utah Contrasted

	1890	1900	1910	1920
Utah, total pop. (000s)	211	277	373	449
Nevada, total pop. (000s)	47	42	82	77
Utah, pct. increase previous decade		31	35	20
Nevada, same		−11	93	−6
Utah, pct. male	53.0	51.3	52.8	51.7
Nevada, same	63.8	61.9	64.6	59.7
Utah, pct. under 14 or 45+	54.0	55.2	52.3	54.3
Nevada, same	46.8	46.8	41.5	48.1

Source: *Hist. Stat. U.S.*, 1975, series A195, A197, A204–A209.

heavily concentrated in mining and mining-dependent occupations from its founding until well into the twentieth century, Nevada had to be abnormal and explosive. Only in the 1900–1910 decade did it attract people (a net 33,000) based on Reno's jump of 141 percent and pickups in south central counties, mostly from mining ventures, including Esmeralda with 375 percent and Nye with 559 percent. But those counties had huge acreage and very few people, and they—indeed all other Nevada counties except Washoe, containing Reno and its satellite Sparks—had no urban places. Carson City, whose 4,000 in 1890 made it larger than Reno, fell to 1,685 in 1920. By then Reno-Sparks, the "greater Reno" with over 15,000 people, was the largest place in the state and held about 24 percent of its people. Not until 1920 did Las Vegas, with 2,304, even appear in the census. Once-booming Storey county (Virginia City) lost people in every decade. Nevada's demography in 1920 was as small and stormy as it had always been.

Idaho's population growth in this period resembled Montana's except that Idaho developed faster. It roughly doubled in the 1890s and again in the 1900s and rose by another third in the 1910s. In 1900–1910 alone, urban places soared 599 percent—all from northern mining towns like Coeur d'Alene, Kellogg, and Wallace; the West central cities of Boise, Nampa, and Caldwell; and the southeastern towns farther up the Snake River Valley or near the Utah line. Growth in southeastern Idaho was also agricultural, since it was largely an extension of Mormon Utah. As Utah itself or the contrast between Utah and Nevada shows, clear differences appeared between the north, whose counties nearly all fell in population between 1910 and 1920 after earlier surges, and the steadier southeast and south central counties. Mining versus farming, transiency versus permanent settlement, accounted for these differences. With 42,000 farms in 1920 (up from 7,000 in 1890) and with an average acreage of 199 (much like Utah's), Idaho exhibited the two classic frontier types. It also began to show signs of urbanism with Boise at 21,000 and Pocatello at 15,000 in 1920.

On the Pacific Coast, Washington was a demographic success second only to California in the western region. From 75,000 in 1880, Washington boomed to 357,000 and statehood by 1890. The arrival of the Northern Pacific Railroad in 1887 and the Great Northern Railroad in 1893 tied the marvelous harbors of Puget Sound to the Midwest and beyond. Eighty thousand newcomers arrived during the 1890s, nearly a half-million in the 1900s, and another 100,000 in the 1910s. As a result of immigration and natural increase, Washington grew by exactly a million people in thirty years. By 1920 its 1,357,000 people included 30 percent who had been born there, 49 percent born elsewhere in the United States, and about 20 percent born in other countries. The latter included 17,000

The People of the West

Japanese (second only to California's 72,000), and large contingents of Germans and Austrians, Scandinavians, and Canadians; but only 7,000 blacks. The sex ratio, frontier-like in 1900 at 142 males per 100 females in 1890, dropped to 118 per 100 in 1920, as a result of family farming and more mature cities. The 1920 ratio was similar to Idaho's and Montana's and close to California's, by then nearly even at 112 males per 100 females.[8]

Puget Sound, and especially Seattle, led the state's growth. Seattle rose from 43,000 in 1890 to 81,000 in 1900, then 237,000 in 1910, and 315,000 in 1920. By 1920, Tacoma verged on metropolitan size at 97,000. Spokane soared from 20,000 in 1890 to 104,000 in 1910, but then remained stable for the next decade. The numbers demonstrate the continued growth of the Puget Sound counties throughout the period (although, like most of the West, slower between 1910 and 1920). The central and eastern parts of the state, however, stabilized after agriculture developed early in the century and then closed another segment of the farmers' last frontier by 1912 or 1915.

King, Pierce, Thurston, and Kitsap counties, forming a "U" around the southern reaches of Puget Sound from Seattle, sustained their growth throughout the period and began to appear as a unified conurbation by 1920. Clark county (Vancouver), across the Columbia River from Portland, was linked to that city and kept growing, unlike its neighbors along the Washington side of the river, all of which lost people during the 1910s. So too did much of the Columbia Plain, after big gains in the 1890s and 1900s. In that part of the state, only Yakima county kept growing and did so both in towns and in the countryside. As wheat markets tightened, the grain-growing counties of the basin between the Columbia and Snake Rivers shrank in numbers.[9] Spokane, nearby and dependent, languished as a result. Growth rates remained high in smaller outlying areas such as Aberdeen on the Pacific and Okanogan county on the Canadian border, later to become a wine-making region. To summarize: Washington demonstrated the West's propensity for urbanization. With Seattle leading a number of nearly smaller cities, a combination of fine natural harbors, railroads to the east and south, temperate climate, and attractiveness to manufacturing and primary processing industries allowed the Puget Sound region to develop from a glorified trading post to an economically complex metropolis. East of the Cascades, following an earlier rush of farmers and stockraisers, growth after 1910 was slow or nonexistent.

Oregon reflected similar patterns less dramatically. Its population was 89 percent as large as Washington's in 1890 but only 58 percent as large in 1920. Oregon grew and urbanized, to be sure, but more hesitantly. Portland was slightly larger than Seattle in 1890 and 1900, but fell behind in the early twentieth century, reaching 258,000 in 1920. Although Portland was becoming a major seaport, the surrounding area was not as well-favored with harbors as Puget Sound was, and the counties and towns near Portland contained few people by 1920. To the south, Eugene and Salem doubled or tripled in the 1900s; but the general growth of the long-settled Willamette Valley, while steady, was slower than Portland's and the state's. The eastern stockraising counties from Umatilla (Pendleton) southward showed large increases in the 1890s and further substantial growth in the 1900s. But except for Umatilla, and Malheur in the extreme southeast, most of these counties lost people after 1910, like parts of Washington's Columbia Basin. Crook and Lake counties east of the Cascades and Josephine and Jackson counties in the southwest lost several thousand people in the 1910s. In general, Oregon and Washington east of the Cascades exhibited a boom in farming and stockraising in the 1900s, which was followed in the 1910s by stability or decline. At the same time the two states throve—spectacularly around Seattle and respectably in Portland—throughout the thirty-year period from the complex, large-scale urbanization they both experienced.

Finally, there is California. At 1.2 million and 39 percent of the entire West in 1890 (34 percent in 1900, but never again lower), it rose to 3.4 million and 37 percent of the West in 1920. California displayed virtually all of the patterns of population development that were taking place elsewhere in the region: the shakiness of mining, agricultural boom early in the century and slowdown after 1910 (though less than in the Columbia Basin or the Great Plains), heavy in-migration, normalizing of the sex and age structures, and rapid, complex urbanization. California shared with other parts of the West—but in a more clearly-defined way—the disappearance of typically nineteenth-century frontier modes of life and the emergence of recognizably twentieth-century metropolitan modes.

To make sense of California's size and diversity throughout the period, one can think of it as including eight zones: Zone 1, *the North*—Mendocino, Lake, Colusa, Sutter, Yuba, and Sierra counties and everything north of them (17 counties in all); 2, *the Bay Area*—Marin, Napa, Sonoma, Contra Costa, Alameda (Oakland, Berkeley), Santa Clara (San Jose), San Mateo, and San Francisco (8 counties); 3, *the Sacramento Valley*—Yolo, Solano, and Sacramento; 4, *the Sierras*—Nevada, Placer, El Dorado, Amador, Calaveras, Alpine, Tuolumne, Mariposa, Mono, and Inyo (10 counties); 5, *the Central Valley*—San Joaquin (Stockton), Stanislaus (Modesto), Merced, Madera, Fresno, San Benito, Kings, Tulare (Visalia), and Kern (Bakersfield) (9 counties); 6, *the Central Coast*—Santa Cruz, Monterey, San Luis Obispo, and Santa Barbara counties; 7, *the Los Angeles Basin*—Los Angeles, Ventura, and Orange counties; 8, *the Desert and South*—San Bernardino, Riverside, Imperial, and San Diego. Some counties, such as Napa and Sonoma, Ventura, or San Diego, might arguably be placed in different zones from those indicated, but these assignments are workable.[10]

California as a state increased 22 percent in the 1890s, 60 percent in the 1900s, and 44 percent in the 1910s. Thus it shared with most of the region the unusually high *rate* of 1900–1910. In California's case, however, the actual numbers rose about 900,000 in 1900–1910 but 1.1 million in 1910–1920. In-migrants accounted for about 700,000 in the first decade and 800,000 in the second.[11] The state was 40 percent urban in 1890 and rose to 68 percent urban in 1920. Hence urban growth was much faster than rural, especially in the 1900s. Yet the number of farms rose healthily, but later than in Washington and Oregon, in that twice as many new farms appeared during the 1910s (30,000) as during the 1900s (15,000). By 1920 California had 118,000 farming establishments, averaging 250 acres.[12] Irrigation in the Central and Imperial Valleys contributed substantially to this expansion.

The seventeen counties in the North grew in population in this period but well below the state rate. Some lost people, as the Chico area did in the 1890s, Yuba county (Marysville) in the 1900s, and Shasta (Redding) and Mendocino counties in the 1910s. The North remained the most rural part of the state except for the Sierras.

In the Bay Area the greatest gain took place in San Francisco, though it fell from 25 percent of the entire state's population in 1890 to 15 percent in 1920. Rising at a relatively sedate 22 percent in both the 1900s and 1910s, San Francisco managed to reach 507,000 in 1920. By then, however, Los Angeles had passed it (at 577,000), and San Francisco was no longer the preeminent metropolis of the West as it had been in 1890 and indeed long before. Yet it remained the economic and cultural leader, reinforced by the faster population rises of nearby Contra Costa, San Mateo, Santa Clara, and especially Alameda counties. With no Golden Gate Bridge as yet, Marin and the other north bay counties remained sparse.

The area around Sacramento (zone 3) increased at roughly the state average. Yolo and Solano remained largely rural, but Sacramento county grew from 40,000 to 91,000, and the city from 26,000 to 66,000 between 1890 and 1920. The Sierras (zone 4), reflecting the uncertainties of mining, lost population during most of this period, and were sparse at any rate, ranging from Placer county's 19,000 down to Alpine's 200 in 1920. The Central Valley (zone 5) presented a different picture. From San Joaquin in its north to Kern in its south, the nine counties all grew in all three decades (except for Tulare and Stanislaus in the 1890s) faster than the state average. None had an urban majority by 1920 except San Joaquin, where Stockton reached 40,000, and most were heavily rural. The great boom in California agriculture, the start of the "hydraulic society," had happened.[13] Each county along the Central Coast (zone 6) from Monterey Bay southward past Santa Barbara developed more slowly than the state average. Santa Barbara was the largest town, with 7,000 in 1890 rising to 19,000 in 1920.

As is seen in table 1.4 the Los Angeles Basin (zone 7), especially the city and county of Los Angeles, was the fastest-growing place in the West. By 1920, several other of the state's larger municipalities were in the county, including Glendale (nothing in 1890 to 14,000 in 1920), Long Beach (2,000 to 56,000), Pasadena (9,000 to 45,000), Pomona (6,000 to 14,000), Santa Monica (3,000 to 15,000), and Venice (nothing to 10,000). As for Ventura and Orange counties on its borders, Ventura grew at the slower rate of Santa Barbara and the rest of the Central Coast, while Orange, though rising faster (from 14,000 to 61,000), was only hinting at its later development and still had a slight rural majority in 1920. By then, however, Los Angeles county was 84 percent urban, clearly taking shape as the sprawling complex of the future, feeding on Henry E. Huntington's street railways and William Mulholland's water aqueduct from the Owens Valley east of the distant Sierras.

Zone 8 underwent rapid growth, notably in the 1900s in San Bernardino and Riverside counties and in 1910–1920 in Imperial, carved just then out of the eastern half of San Diego county. The city of San Diego, reinforced by a dependable water supply and a naval base, climbed to 75,000 by 1920 and became the state's fourth largest city behind Los Angeles, San Francisco, and Oakland.

In sum, the fastest-growing zones in this rapidly expanding state were the Los Angeles Basin, the Bay Area, the Central Valley, and the smaller Imperial Valley. Average rates characterized Sacramento and much of zone 8. Slowest were the Central Coast, the North, and the Sierras. California's economic and demographic development ceased during this period to depend in any significant way on mining. Agriculture and oil, both capital-intensive, were its main extractive industries by 1920. By then it also contained myriad activities associated with large-scale urbanism.

Table 1.4
Los Angeles City and County Population (000s)

	1850	1860	1870	1880	1890	1900	1910	1920
County	3.5	11	15	33	101	170	504	936
City	1.6	4	6	11	50	102	319	577

Source: 1900 *Census*, v. I:1, 439; 1920 *Census*, v. I:1, 78.

Between 1890 and 1920 the population of the West not only grew through natural increase and in-migration, but also truly became urban and often metropolitan. The frontier of small family farms made its final appearance on the high Plains, the basin between the Cascades and the northern Rockies, and a few other places, most markedly in 1900–1910, after which it stabilized and declined. After 1910 the cutting edge of agricultural expansion was in large and often capital-intensive operations, most notably in the irrigated valleys of California. Placer mining had given way almost entirely to hard-rock, as shown by the change from the old-style mining of the Cripple Creek gold rush of 1893 to the new industrial style of Bisbee, Anaconda, or Coeur d'Alene ten or twenty years later. With its planned growth, mix of farms and villages, and irrigation, Mormon Utah flourished and spilled over into Idaho and other adjacent states. Finally, urban agglomerations with core cities, suburbs, and satellites were centered in Seattle, Portland, the Bay Area, and Los Angeles, with smaller but true metropolises at Denver and Salt Lake City, in contrast to the much less populated and more solitary cities of 1890. Important corners were turned in the 1890–1920 period. After 1920, expansion continued, but often in patterns already formed.

From Isolation Through the War: 1920–1950[14]

Still set apart from the rest of the country by distance, sparseness, and several lingering signs of its recent frontier past, the West closed the gaps by 1950 and approached national norms in all major demographic ways. It continued to grow, especially the Pacific states, and most especially California, even in the Depression of the 1930s (table 1.5). California was its engine, rising from 37 percent of the region's population in 1920 to 52 percent in 1950, and its in-migration during the 1940s of 2.3 million people accounted for 77 percent of the region's. Of that number over 259,000 were black. For the first time a western state participated in the black migration out of the South to the three other regions, a significant demographic shift that had been swelling the Northeast and North Central regions since about 1915.

Given the West's wide open spaces, it may seem strange that the region has been, since the late nineteenth century, more urban than the rest of the country. But the deserts and mountains supported few people compared to the fertile farmlands of the East, Midwest, and South. The West's urbanization accelerated from the 1920s to 1950 not only from urban growth itself but also as a result of stable or falling rural numbers. California, already 68 percent urban in 1920, reached 81 percent in 1950, following the new census definition that included built-up though unin-

Table 1.5
Population and Growth Rates of States, 1920–1950

	Pop. (000s)				% Incr		
	1920	1930	1940	1950	20–30	30–40	40–50
Arizona	334	436	499	750	31	14	50
Colorado	940	1036	1123	1325	10	8	18
Idaho	432	445	525	589	3	15	12
Montana	549	538	559	591	−2	4	6
Nevada	77	91	110	160	18	21	46
New Mexico	360	423	532	681	18	26	28
Utah	449	508	550	689	13	8	25
Wyoming	194	226	251	291	17	11	16
California	3427	5677	6907	10586	66	22	53
Oregon	783	954	1090	1521	22	14	40
Washington	1357	1563	1736	2379	15	11	37

Source: *Hist. Stat. U.S.*, 1975, series A195–A209.

corporated fringe areas around larger cities. The age structure of western states changed gradually to include more children and older people and a smaller proportion in the prime working years of fifteen to forty-four. Only Wyoming and anomalous Nevada included more than half of their populations in that group and only before 1930. All western states took part in the baby boom, showing in the 1940s a jump in the proportion of children. The sex ratio evened out. Although no western state had a female majority by 1950, as some states farther east had, all were close to an even ratio.

The front range states shared certain experiences, but their development quickened toward the south. Montana lost 2 percent in the 1920s—the first western state other than Nevada ever to suffer a net loss in a decade—and increased only 4 and 6 percent in the 1930s and 1940s. Its western and mining counties, and the Billings area, were consistent gainers, but the interior farming counties lost heavily throughout (more in the 1920s than later), reflecting over-optimistic exploitation of the high Plains earlier in the century. The farmers' last frontier not only ended, it went into reverse. Wyoming's growth was faster, though moderate by regional standards, and it remained sparsely settled—the most sizeable places being Cheyenne, which rose from 14,000 to 32,000 from 1920 to 1950, and Casper, which reached 24,000 in 1950. Some farming and stockraising counties made reasonable gains except those on the South Dakota and Nebraska lines, which lost heavily. People were still moving into northwestern

The People of the West

Wyoming, between Casper and Yellowstone Park, though the numbers were small (figs. 1.2 and 1.3).

The Colorado story centered on its metropolis, including Denver itself but increasingly the adjacent counties of Adams, Arapahoe, Boulder, and Jefferson. Here was a case of metropolitan development, a core city with a faster-growing suburban fringe. The five-county Denver area rose from 331,000 in 1920 to 612,000 in 1950, with the fringe increasing 73 percent in the 1940s against the core's 29 percent. Colorado Springs and Pueblo also grew well above the state average. The mining areas of Colorado continued to be highly volatile, with several important counties losing people in the 1920s, winning some back in the 1930s, but losing again in the 1940s. The stretch from Idaho Springs through Leadville and Aspen as well as Ouray and San Miguel counties farther southwest were part of this process. In some instances farming and stockraising counties starting losing population in the 1920s (Bent and Las Animas counties, for example, in southeastern Colorado) and were joined in decline by the northeastern counties along the South Platte River in the 1930s; but they held their size in the 1940s. An exception was the growth of the Alamosa area and the valley between the Sangre de Cristo and San Juan ranges in south central Colorado where a substantial Mormon component lived.

New Mexico, sleepy before 1920, expanded beyond the regional norm through most of the 1920–1950 period. The greatest growth was in Bernalillo county (Albuquerque), which gained 52 percent in the 1920s, another 53 percent in the 1930s, and 110 percent in the 1940s, reaching 146,000. Clear signs of the impact of the federal government appeared in the 1940s. Los Alamos county was carved out of Santa Fe and Sandoval to give nuclear researchers their own municipality, and Alamogordo and the rest of southeastern New Mexico swelled from air and weapons activity. Except for Albuquerque and Denver, New Mexico's southeastern counties including the cities of Carlsbad, Artesia, and Roswell made the greatest gains anywhere in the front range states. Reversing the overexpansion of 1900 to 1920, New Mexico's farming counties on the edge of the Dust Bowl declined in the 1930s just as the high Plains counties of Colorado, Wyoming, and Montana (as well as Kansas and Oklahoma) did. The average size of a New Mexico farm rose from about 800 acres in 1920 to over 2,000 in 1950, not unlike what was happening to the north. The Indian counties in the northwestern part of the state nearly all gained in every decade. And the band of mining settlements, from Dona Ana (Las Cruces) to the Arizona line, held stable during the Depression and made respectable gains in the 1940s.

With a 50 percent rise in the 1940s to reach 750,000, Arizona grew even faster than New Mexico. In the four Great Basin states (Arizona, Nevada, Utah, and Idaho), southern expansion outsped northern, and thus within

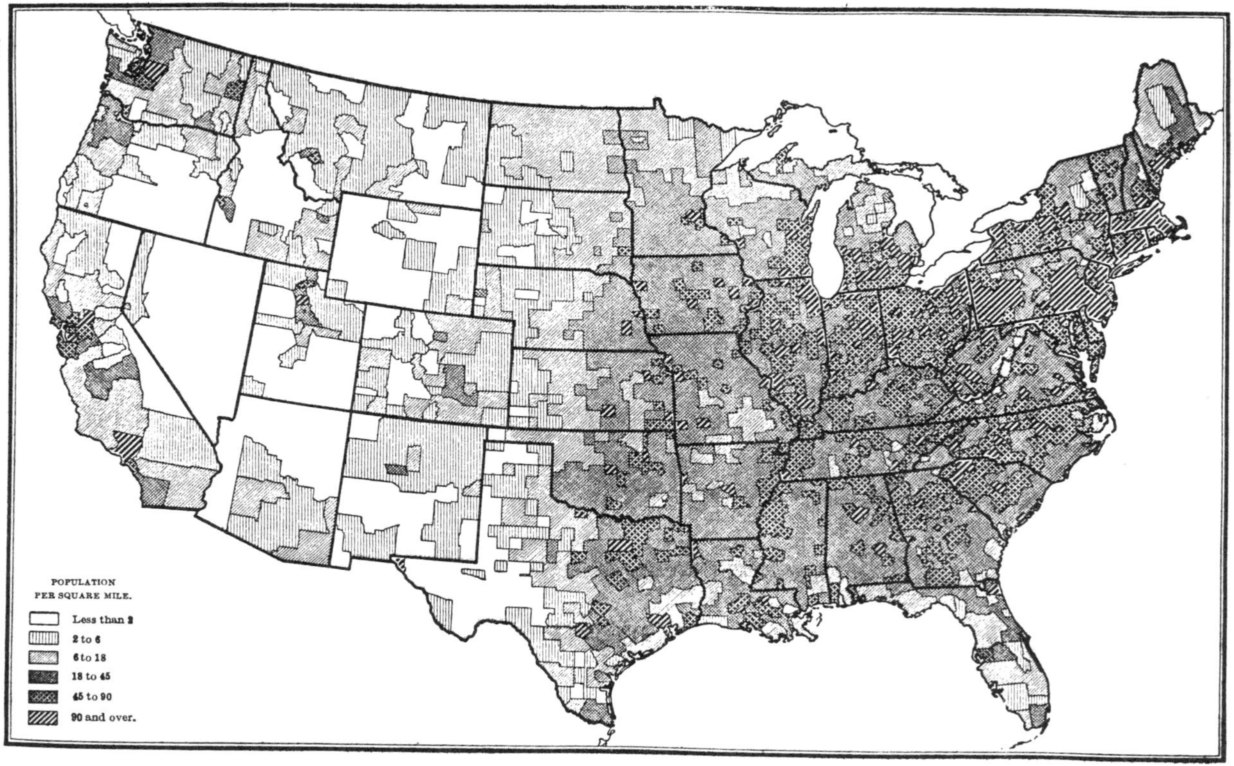

Fig. 1.2 Population by Counties, 1920 (*Fourteenth Census of the United States*)

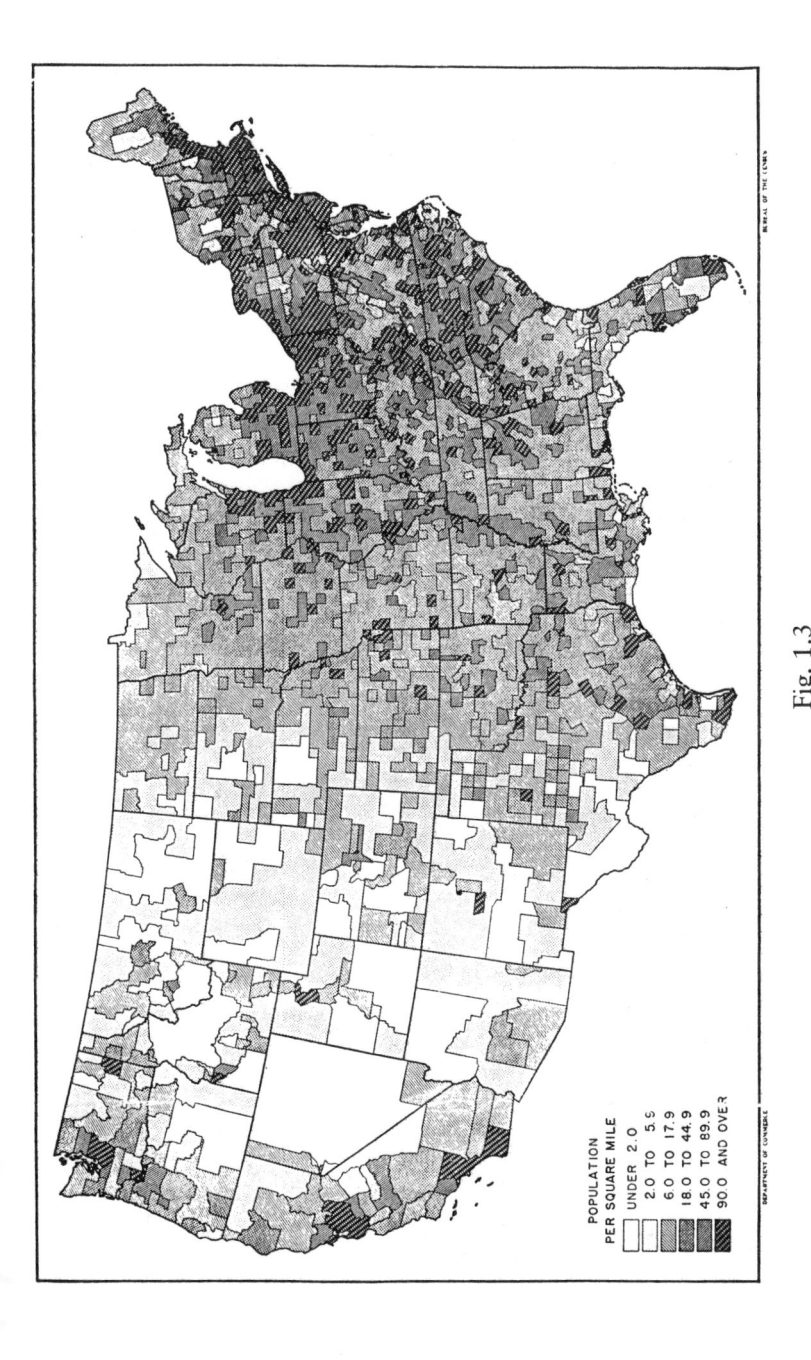

Fig. 1.3
Population by Counties, 1950 (*Seventeenth Census of the United States*)

the Mountain states the snowbelt-to-sunbelt phenomenon so evident after 1970 was already embryonically present. Arizona's principal growth from 1920 to 1950 took place in Maricopa county (Phoenix), Pima county (Tucson), and in the late 1930s and the 1940s, Pinal county between them. Phoenix's smaller neighbors—Tempe, Glendale, and Mesa—more than doubled during the 1940s, forming a core city with satellites. By 1950, Phoenix reached 107,000, but Maricopa county, 332,000. The most striking decline took place in the mining southeast, as Cochise and Santa Cruz counties lost people in each of the three decades; the mining town of Bisbee fell from 9,200 in 1920 to 3,800 in 1950. Only nearby (and smaller) Greenlee gained in the 1940s, like the adjacent counties in southwestern New Mexico. Arizona's northeastern Indian counties (Apache, Navajo, and part of Coconino) surged throughout the period, while irrigated Yuma in the southwest edged upward from 14,900 in 1920 to about 28,000 in 1950. Natural increase accounted for most of Arizona's growth in the 1920s and 1930s, but in the 1940s the state attracted nearly 100,000 native-born whites and 20,000 blacks and foreign-born, the start of its postwar boom.

Utah grew in all three decades well below the regional rate. Much of the increase happened in the urban north-central counties of Utah, Salt Lake, Davis, and Weber; Davis had the highest rates (96 percent in the 1940s) and Salt Lake the largest numbers. The four counties held 57 percent of Utah's people in 1920, and 68 percent in 1950. To the south and east, counties based on mining and/or farming such as Summit, Sanpete, and Emery generally declined (notably in the 1940s), although the mining area around Price expanded. About 30,000 whites (net) left the state in the 1920s and another 30,000 did so in the 1930s. After that, net migration was slightly positive. But Utah's growth resulted almost entirely from natural increase, in decided contrast to the Pacific states.

Nevada grew faster than the region in all three decades, mostly in two urban areas. While its mining counties (Storey, Esmeralda, etc.) were volatile and never held many people, the Reno-Sparks area expanded about 50 percent in the 1920s and again in the 1940s, reaching 40,000 by 1950, while Las Vegas, a speck on the map in 1920, passed 8,000 in 1940 as Hoover Dam was completed nearby, and jumped to about 25,000 in 1950. After World War II, Nevada ceased to be its historic self, a desert with a few boom-to-bust mining towns, and began its rapid modern expansion as a playground for California and increasingly, the rest of the country.

In almost complete contrast, Idaho was the slowest-growing state in the West except for Montana, adding only 12 percent in the 1940s. It underwent net outmigration in each decade. The farming counties in the southeast, on or near the Utah border, lost people. The "urban" counties led by Ada (Boise) and nearby Payette and Canyon (Nampa, Caldwell) were the state's major gainers in both the 1930s and 1940s, but that still left Boise with only 34,000 and Pocatello with 26,000 in 1950. The mining counties in the north showed small gains throughout the period, as Idaho remained a, sometimes the, leading producer of silver, lead, and zinc among the forty-eight states.[15]

The Pacific states each attracted many thousands from other places in each decade. In the 1940s, Washington's net influx was 351,000, Oregon's 223,000, and California's 1,875,000. In Washington all of the counties around Puget Sound, with very minor exceptions, expanded between 1920 and 1950; King, Pierce, and Thurston held 41 percent of the state's people in 1920 and 44 percent in 1950. Seattle and Tacoma rose only about 2,000 each in the depressed 1930s, but during and after World War II they boomed, Seattle adding 100,000 in the 1950s to reach 468,000. Spokane, held stable for years by the stagnant farm region around it, leaped to 162,000 in 1950. The Columbia Plateau fell badly in the 1920s, continuing the agrarian shakeout of the previous decade, and remained generally level through the Depression and into the 1940s, when Grant, Walla Walla, and Yakima counties started growing again. Clark and Cowlitz counties across the Columbia River from Portland added substantial numbers throughout the period, but nearby rural counties such as Klickitat and Skamania generally did not. Grant county, with Grand Coulee Dam rising in its northeastern tip, expanded 158 percent in the 1930s and 66 percent in the 1940s, an example of how federal impact, first from public works and then from defense industries, swelled Washington's population in those two decades.

In Oregon, growth rates were slightly below the regional average, yet strong. Portland and Multnomah county resembled the pattern of Seattle and Tacoma in growing respectably in the 1920s, hardly at all in the 1930s, and then very rapidly in the 1940s, when Portland increased from 305,000 to 374,000. But unlike the Puget Sound metropolises, Portland slowly declined in the state context from 33 percent of Oregon's people in 1920 to 25 percent in 1950. The reason was steady and sometimes sudden growth southward through the Williamette Valley to the California border, led by 112 percent growth in Douglas county and 82 percent in Lane (Eugene) in the 1940s, with most others in western Oregon increasing nearly as fast. Elsewhere it was a mixed bag: virtually every county along the Columbia east of Portland, except Umatilla in the 1940s, lost people, sharing the experience of rural counties in central Washington. A few places east of the Cascades attracted people from time to time, but a pattern clarified in the 1940s to reveal that about a third of Oregon's people were living in Portland and Multnomah county, and another 40 percent in the ten counties south to California, which contained a string of cities ranging from Salem's 43,000 on downward.

California's almost infinite variety may be summed up as abnormal growth, from natural increase and in-migration; urbanization, especially in the Los Angeles basin, the San Francisco Bay area, and San Diego most swiftly in the 1920s and 1940s but even to some extent in the 1930s; and almost equally rapid gains (though smaller numbers) in the Central Valley. Slower but still positive growth rates were evident in the southern desert counties (the fastest), around Sacramento, the Central Coast, the North, and the Sierras (the slowest). Negative rates appeared in the 1920s only in some Sierra and northern counties; in the 1930s only in Imperial county (a 2 percent loss); and in the 1940s in scattered parts of the Sierras again. Otherwise it was all gain everywhere. With state-wide increases of 66, 22, and 53 percent in the three decades between 1920 and 1950, California led the region in both rates and numbers.

Many people came from outside the state. Of California's net growth between 1920 and 1950, about 2.1 million came from natural increase but 5 million from in-migration. The migrants were largely native-born whites, but roughly 700,000 were foreign-born (often Mexican), and about 330,000 were black, arriving during and after World War II.

In the Bay Area, the twin cores of San Francisco and Oakland kept growing (though not much in the 1930s) but more rapid development took place in the surrounding counties, notably San Mateo just south of San Francisco with increases of about 110 percent in the 1920s and again in the 1940s, and Contra Costa, north of Oakland and Berkeley, at about 200 percent in the 1940s. Shipyards and munitions were the chief causes. Except for San Francisco and Alameda counties, the Bay Area expanded well beyond the state average through most of the period.

Something similar was happening in the Los Angeles basin. Although the huge increases in numbers disguised the trend, the core city was slowing down, with the fastest growth (especially in the 1940s) outside it and even outside the county. In that decade, when the state-wide growth was 53 percent, the city of Los Angeles grew 31 percent, the county 49 percent, but the outlying counties of Ventura, Orange, San Bernardino and Riverside from 60 to 75 percent. Similarly, farther south, San Diego county increased 93 percent but the city "only" 65 percent in the 1940s. The sprawling, typically southern Californian conurbations, spurred greatly by World War II and continuing booms in entertainment, oil, aircraft, autos, shipping, and other industries, were clearly evident. Between the Bay Area and Los Angeles, the great agricultural factory of the Central Valley attracted people to farms and farm-related enterprises and jobs, growing 65 percent during the 1940s alone to over 1,150,000 in its nine counties, more people than in eight of the West's eleven states.

Between 1920 and 1950, then, the West's population development reflected the force of national events: the urban-industrial prosperity but shaky agricultural conditions of the 1920s, the Great Depression of the 1930s, and World War II and the onset of the baby boom in the 1940s. The region grew faster than the nation, the Pacific states faster than the Mountain states, California and especially southern California fastest of all. Defense and national security stimulated selected areas such as southeastern and north central New Mexico, Puget Sound, the east Bay Area, and the Los Angeles basin. The requirements of national and regional markets upheld mining in the Mountain states, timber and paper-making in the Pacific Northwest, and oil development in California. Fed by an intricate and massive aqueduct system, mass-production agriculture flourished in California's Central Valley and on a lesser scale elsewhere. The West was no longer frontier country, no longer remote. With over one-eighth of the nation's people by 1950, its continuing expansion was an easy prediction.

The Metropolitan West, 1950–1980s[16]

In the years since 1950, the West participated in most of the important population developments experienced by the nation at large (table 1.6). These included the recession of rural population and farm workers from the high Plains and elsewhere, the north-to-south or "snowbelt to sunbelt" shift, and the concentration of population in large metropolitan areas, though their core cities were usually shrinking. The West also did its share to create the baby boom, though it also expanded from net in-migration. As the historic exodus of blacks out of the South continued into the late 1960s, Los Angeles received several hundred thousand, though other parts of the West received few. In the 1970s, Asian and Hispanic peoples arrived in the United States in unprecedented numbers, and again California was the chief beneficiary.

For these reasons, the West's demographic history after 1950 differed markedly from what it had been earlier in the century. The previous arrangement of the western states into front range, Great Basin, and Pacific groups is less appropriate than the following, which roughly combines climate, size, and growth rates: (1) the interior northwest, including much of Joel Garreau's "empty quarter":[17] Montana, Wyoming, Idaho, Utah, and Colorado; (2) the desert states of New Mexico, Arizona, and Nevada; (3) the Pacific Northwest of Washington and Oregon; (4) the

THE TWENTIETH-CENTURY WEST

Table 1.6
Population and Growth Rates of States, 1950–1985

	Pop. (000s)					% Incr			
	1950	1960	1970	1980	1985	50s	60s	70s	80s
Arizona	750	1302	1775	2718	3187	74	36	53	35
Colorado	1325	1754	2210	2890	3231	32	26	31	24
Idaho	589	667	713	944	1005	13	7	32	13
Montana	591	675	694	787	826	14	3	13	10
Nevada	160	285	489	800	936	78	71	64	34
New Mexico	681	951	1017	1303	1450	40	7	28	23
Utah	689	891	1059	1461	1645	29	19	38	25
Wyoming	291	330	332	470	509	14	1	43	17
California	10586	15717	19971	23668	26365	49	27	19	23
Oregon	1521	1769	2092	2633	2687	16	18	26	4
Washington	2379	2853	3413	4132	4409	20	20	21	13
Alaska	129	226	303	402	521	76	34	33	59
Hawaii	500	633	770	965	1054	27	22	25	18

Sources: *Hist. Stat. U.S.*, 1975, series A195–A209; 1980 Census, *United States Summary*, 1:63–98 (Table 17); *New York Times*, December 30, 1985. The period covered in the "80s" is from mid-1980 to July 1, 1985; the percentage rate is the five-year increment multiplied by two to produce a decadal rate comparable to those given for the 1950s, 1960s, and 1970s.

offshore states of Alaska and Hawaii; (5) California, with 52 to 57 percent of the entire region's people after 1950.

The interior northwest grew more slowly than the rest of the region in the 1950s and 1960s, exceeded the regional rate in the 1970s, and closely matched it from 1980 to 1985. The search for fossil fuels helps explain the 1970s bulge, led by Wyoming's jump of 43 percent in that decade. Otherwise the marked features were thickenings of central Colorado and north central Utah (despite declines in Denver and Salt Lake City themselves) and the growth of smaller cities in all five states, while rural areas were stable or falling. A counter-trend toward rural counties appeared in Colorado, Montana, and Idaho in the 1970s from a combination of exurbanites, nature-seekers, and resort people (both buying and selling). Montana, Wyoming, and Idaho lost a net 85,000 in the 1960s and 139,000 in the 1970s from out-migration, while Colorado attracted a net 164,000 and 215,000, and Utah neither gained nor lost appreciably; with a birthrate about twice the national average, Utah produced its own gains. Montana's eastern farm and stock counties lost population although some towns continued to grow, Billings reaching 67,000 in 1980 to become Montana's largest city. Mining counties, especially Deer Lodge and Silver Bow (containing the cities of Anaconda and Butte) were ravaged by the close-out of copper mining. But in the 1950s, and even more in the 1970s,

The People of the West

expansion from various causes marked certain counties in and just east of the Rockies, notably those including the cities of Great Falls, Missoula, and Bozeman. By 1980, of 328,000 Montanans with jobs, only 30,000 were farming and 9,000 in mining. The Idaho picture was similar, with 34,000 farmers and 5,000 miners among 384,000 employed. Many counties, especially in the south and east, lost people, but along the Snake River the larger towns from Idaho Falls through Pocatello, westward to Twin Falls and the Boise area, rose in size, especially Boise with its surge from 34,000 in 1950 to 102,000 in 1980.

Wyoming's eastern farm counties also stabilized or declined in the 1950s and 1960s, but west and northwest from Casper to the mountains, population rose in the 1970s, as in similar parts of Montana. With coal production up following the 1973 oil crisis, Wyoming found itself with several small boom towns, and 32,000 jobs in mining in a work force of 217,000 by 1980. Casper then reached 51,000 and Cheyenne 47,000; not a single county lost people during the 1970s.

In Colorado the good news was not in mining but in 403,000 service and 237,000 retail jobs, some in old mining towns being converted into resorts and condominium villages in the Rockies. Denver, after modest increases in the 1950s and 1960s, lost 4 percent in the 1970s, but neighboring Adams (up 200 percent in the 1950s), Jefferson (85 percent in the 1960s), and Arapahoe (81 percent in the 1970s), and others farther from the core such as Douglas, Clear Creek, and Gilpin, made the Denver area truly metropolitan (including smog and a congested airport). In the 1960s, Colorado became the third most populated state in the West, behind California and Washington, and in 1980 was second to California in black population with 106,000.

Utah did not grow quite as fast but was even more metropolitanized; Salt Lake City fell in population but the four north central counties from Provo to Ogden (Utah, Salt Lake, Davis, and Weber) included 68 percent of the state's people in 1950, rising to 77 percent in 1980. Several other outlying Mormon counties such as Cache (Logan) in the northeast and Washington (St. George) in the extreme southwest expanded rapidly in the 1970s. The mountain counties, from Summit southward to the Arizona line, lost people in the 1950s and 1960s but boomed in the 1970s from ski resorts, tourism, the natural increase of Mormon families, energy seekers, and even some remaining mining. Depressed since the 1920s, these counties expanded at rates ranging from Sanpete's 33 percent on up to Emery's 123 percent. Their numbers, however, were small compared to the Salt Lake area.

The desert states were rapid gainers, with New Mexico at roughly the regional average, Arizona well above it, and Nevada fastest in the West. In New Mexico, Albuquerque and Bernalillo county did not quite match, after 1960, their explosive growth rates of the 1940s (110 percent) and 1950s (79 percent), but they did continue to expand from 100,000 in the county just after World War II to 420,000 in 1980. Farmington and the rest of northwestern New Mexico battened on tourism and searches for fossil fuels in the 1970s, and Dona Ana county (Las Cruces) rose rapidly, in part because of its proximity to booming El Paso, Texas. Meanwhile the southeast prolonged its wartime boom into the 1950s—Otero county (Alamogordo) rose 147 percent—and then stabilized. The northeastern high Plains steadily lost people, and in 1980 fewer people lived there than in 1920 or even 1900. Despite the expansion of Albuquerque, Las Cruces, and the northwestern corner, New Mexico lost a net 130,000 out-migrants during the 1970s.

Arizona, on the other hand, attracted more than half a million between 1960 and 1980, which together with natural increase lifted the state above three million by 1985. Virtually every county gained population in every decade after 1950, even the one-time mining areas. But a resurgence of mining was not the reason; of Arizona's 1.1 million employed in 1980, only 27,000 worked in mining, while 202,000 worked in retail trade and 332,000 in various services. Bisbee, the state's third city in 1920 with 9,000, when Phoenix had 29,000, contained only 7,000 in 1980. But Phoenix by then had 765,000 and together with its many suburbs and satellites gave Maricopa county 1.5 million. Maricopa and Pima county (Tucson), at 531,000 by 1980, formed two metropolises with 75 percent of Arizona's people, up from 46 percent in 1950. So the main story in Arizona was metropolitan development. But leitmotifs existed, for example, in Mohave county in the northwest corner. Stagnant in the 1940s and dropping 10 percent in the 1950s to 7,700, it exploded by 234 percent in the 1960s, another 116 percent in the 1970s, to 56,000 in 1980. Part of the reason was Lake Havasu City, a retirement community that did not exist in 1960 but held almost 16,000 in 1980. In-migrating "senior citizens" also explain partially the growth of Tucson and Phoenix. Climate, scenery, air conditioning, and (for the moment at least) adequate water, enticed crowds of pensioners from less clement parts of the country.

Nevada grew even a little faster than Arizona, and its expansion also took place in two metropolitan areas: the strip from Reno-Sparks southward a few miles to Carson City and Lake Tahoe, and the growth of Clark county (Las Vegas) by more than tenfold, to touch a half million after 1980. By then, 86 percent of Nevadans lived around Las Vegas, Carson City, and Reno. The volatile, unpredictable silver and gold mines of frontier days had been replaced by the permanent goldmine of casinos and resorts. Of Nevada's 400,000 jobholders in 1980, only 5,000 were in mining and 23,000 in manufacturing, but 36,000 were in entertainment and recreation and another 66,000 in "other services."

The People of the West

Washington and Oregon contrasted with the southwestern states, of course, in climate and water resources, but also in having much lower growth rates between 1950 and 1980, about 20 percent per decade on average. In the first half of the 1980s, with agriculture flat, manufacturing and construction slow, and the lumber industry badly depressed, Washington eased forward at a 13 percent decadal rate and Oregon at only 4 percent. Many of the gains through the period were, as elsewhere, around large cities. In both states, the phenomenon of slow or negatively growing core cities amidst still-booming surroundings were present: Seattle and Portland lost people after 1970, but their metropolitan areas kept rising. In the Northwest the concentration was not as severe as in Arizona or Nevada; the three Oregon counties around and including Portland stayed at about 40 percent of Oregonians through the period because of the equally fast growth of Salem, Eugene, and the rest of the valley southward through Medford to the California line.

In Washington, suburbs and satellites spread out from the major urban areas of Seattle and Tacoma into Kitsap county (Bremerton), Island, and Snohomish (Everett) counties to include roughly 60 percent of the state's people, up moderately from 1950. Meanwhile, with few exceptions, the open spaces east of the Cascades in both states stabilized or lost people in the 1960s and regained only a few in the 1970s. Both states attracted newcomers, especially Washington in the 1970s with about 250,000 net in-migration (which accounted for a high 35 percent of its total increase). In 1980 Washington (mostly Seattle itself) included 102,000 blacks, about 130,000 American Indians on and off reservations, 26,000 Japanese, 24,000 Filipinos, and others, as well as nearly 200,000 whites of Scandinavian descent, making the state something of a melting pot unusual for the nondesert West.

Chilly Alaska and warm Hawaii have little in common except that they are offshore, became states of the Union in 1959, and expanded rapidly between 1950 and 1985: Alaska from 129,000 to 521,000 (304 percent), and Hawaii from 500,000 to 1,054,000 (111 percent). In the first half of the 1980s, Hawaii slowed and Alaska, with its new north-south oil pipeline, sped up. In the process Alaska became more urban, particularly around Anchorage, which was a village of 3,500 in 1940 but a metropolis of 174,000 in 1980. By then Eskimos and Aleuts made up about 10 percent of the state's population, and American Indians another 5 percent; the great majority of Alaskans were native-born whites. Hawaii, however, was the only American state where whites were a minority (33 percent in 1980), because of the presence of Japanese (240,000), Filipinos (134,000), Hawaiians (115,000), Chinese (56,000) and other Asian and Pacific peoples. Honolulu county (Oahu) was the major gainer in the 1940s and 1950s, while Hawaii county (the big island) and Maui lost people. But after 1960, and even more in the 1970s, Hawaii and Maui expanded very rapidly. Oahu grew more slowly, but it still accounted for 79 percent of Hawaii's people in 1980.

California, after the great influx of the World War II years, held over half the people of the entire West by 1950, and continued to do so ever since; in 1985 it held 55 percent. It attracted (net) over 3 million people in the 1960s and over 2 million in the 1970s, greater than its natural increase of 1.1 and 1.6 million. Of the in-migrants, over a quarter-million blacks arrived in the 1960s and 272,000 in the 1970s, after black in-migration had stopped or reversed in the North Central and Northeast regions. Aside from Hawaii, California was the West's most multiracial, multi-ethnic state, including in 1980, besides 18 million nonHispanic whites of (in descending order) English, German, Irish, Italian, Russian, Portuguese, Polish, Swedish, Norwegian, and other stocks, nearly 2.4 million Hispanics, 1.8 million blacks, 357,000 Filipinos, 322,000 Chinese, 262,000 Japanese, 104,000 Koreans, 90,000 Vietnamese (mostly arriving after 1973), 58,000 from India, and about 200,000 American Indians.

This huge population created new metropolises and swelled existing ones from the Sacramento and Bay areas southward through the Central Valley to the Los Angeles basin and San Diego, leaving only the North, the Sierras, and the southeastern desert thinly populated, although even those zones gained considerably. One cannot usefully speak of counties or zones that gained or lost people, because—except for the city-county of San Francisco—virtually none lost. Instead one can speak of areas whose increases were faster or slower than the whole state's, remembering that state growth considerably exceeded the nation's. In the 1950s, the Sierras began at last to gain steadily, beginning with El Dorado county (the resort area around South Lake Tahoe), and by the 1970s several counties were doubling, though of course actual numbers were in the tens, not hundreds, of thousands as elsewhere in California. The previously underpopulated North likewise attracted exurbanites or small-business people, especially in and around Chico and Redding. The city of Sacramento doubled between 1950 and 1980, as befitted the capital of such a state, and the three-county zone grew somewhat faster than the state. The Central Valley remained attractive, with Fresno and Stockton passing 100,000 by 1970 and Modesto and Bakersfield doing so by 1980. Yet this zone was outpaced by others. The Central Coast from Santa Cruz to Santa Barbara jumped swiftly in the 1950s and 1960s, after which Monterey and Santa Barbara counties slowed considerably while the thinner-populated San Luis Obispo and Santa Cruz counties rose 47 and 52 percent. Imperial county, the southeastern desert, increased very little before 1970 but then expanded 24 percent in the 1980s.

The remaining zones experienced the bulk of California's expansion:

The People of the West

the Bay Area, Los Angeles and nearby counties, and San Diego. In the Bay Area, San Francisco and Oakland stabilized and then shrank, but growth in other parts was fast in the 1960s and close to the state average in the 1970s. San Jose and Santa Clara county made the greatest gains: from 95,000 in 1950, San Jose rose to 629,000 in 1980 and in the early 1980s passed San Francisco to become the state's third largest city behind Los Angeles and San Diego. Los Angeles, contrary to the national trend of core-city slippage, grew in the 1970s, but only by 6 percent (as did Los Angeles county), but Ventura, Riverside, San Bernardino and especially Orange counties made high double-digit, even triple-digit, percentage gains in each decade, as the entire conurbation kept spreading. Rising real estate prices braked growth in the center of the area in the late 1970s, but outlying parts with lower prices found buyers; the limits of distance were yet to be reached in 1985. The 1980 Census revealed that 12 California cities passed 100,000 during the 1970s, and except for Modesto and Bakersfield, all were in the Bay Area or near Los Angeles: Concord, Fremont, and Sunnyvale near the Bay, and Anaheim, East Los Angeles, Fullerton, Garden Grove, Huntington Beach, Oxnard, and Torrance in the south. San Diego city and county has grown well above the state average ever since World War II. The three major conurbations, plus the Central Valley, all with tolerable to highly desirable climates, excellent highway networks, and an exceptionally diverse and balanced economic life, displayed the most rapid and sizeable population development in the industrialized world from World War II to the 1980s.

The Mid-1980s and Beyond

Never quiescent, western population continued to move in unexpected directions in the first half of the 1980s, led by forces as diverse as international oil price fluctuations, the aging of the American population, and local real estate markets. In the Rocky Mountain states, according to the *New York Times,* "the region's copper industry is at its lowest point in a half century; development of coal mines has all but stopped, timber cutting is depressed by low prices and low demand, and the other boom of the turn of the decade, oil and gas development [including shale oil], is in as severe a recession as any of the others."[18] Jobs in mining and smelting dropped from 94,000 to 24,000 between 1981 and late 1985. The one-time mining town of Jerome, in Arizona's once-booming Yavapai county, was getting publicity (and prosecution) as a producer of marijuana rather than metal ores, and in some of California's bucolic North, marijuana was reputed to be the main cash crop.[19] Oregon lost 43,000 people from net migration between 1980 and 1984, while Montana and Idaho scarcely expanded beyond natural increase. San Francisco and much of Los Angeles priced all but the wealthy out of residential real estate.

Yet the West continued to outstrip the other three regions in growth rates during the early 1980s. If prices were high in the largest cities, people moved to the Central Valley or the edge of the desert, so that "for the first time the population in a 600-mile spine in the interior of [California] is growing faster than the narrow strip beside the Pacific Coast."[20] The West attracted a net 1.6 million in-migrants between 1980 and 1984, 950,000 of them to California. Continual since 1890, almost explosive since World War II, demographic expansion in the West led the nation, changing through a multitude of local disruptions and booms from frontier to metropolitan region.

Notes

1. John Wesley Powell, *Report on the Lands of the Arid Region of the United States* (Facsimile of the 1879 edition; Harvard and Boston: The Harvard Common Press, 1983).

2. Robert P. Porter, Henry Gannett, and William C. Hunt, "Progress of the Nation 1790 to 1890," in United States Department of the Interior, Census Office, *Report on the Population of the United States at the Eleventh Census: 1890* (Washington: Government Printing Office, 1895), I: xxxiv.

3. Frederick Jackson Turner to Frederick Merk, [probably San Marino, CA], January 9, 1931; Turner, draft of "Pasadena Lecture," February 20, 1928, in Turner Papers, TU Box 45 and Box 14B(11), Henry E. Huntington Library, San Marino, CA.

4. Walter Nugent, *Structures of American Social History* (Bloomington: Indiana University Press, 1981), 29, 110–20; "Frontiers and Empires in the Late Nineteenth Century," in Michael Heyd, et al., eds., *Religion, Ideology and Nationalism in Europe and America: Essays Presented in Honor of Yehoshua Arieli* (Jerusalem, 1986), 269–72. In this essay, frontiers are separated into Types I and II, with Type I including agricultural frontiers, populated by families, with balanced sex and age structures. Type II frontiers, in contrast, include mining camps, cattle towns, and other transient, exploitative settlements, which are peopled largely by young men and include few women, children, or older people. As for Type I, "its people were the colorless many"; as for Type II, "its people were the colorful few," p. 269. Type I frontiers are very rural, but Type II frontiers heavily urban, with numbers of unrelated persons densely clustered in confined areas.

5. Unless otherwise indicated, numerical data on states, counties, and municipalities in this section on 1890–1920 are taken from United States Department of the Interior, Census Office, *Report on the Population of the United States at the Twelfth Census: 1900*, vol. I:1, Table 8, 438–80; United States Department of

Commerce, Bureau of the Census, *Fourteenth Census of the United States taken in the Year 1920*, vol. I:1, Tables 49–51, 94–319. Data on sex ratios, age structures, migration, ethnicity and race are taken from United States Bureau of the Census, *Historical Statistics of the United States, Colonial Times to 1970* (Washington: Government Printing Office, 1975), series A172–A194, A195–A209, and from the Census, specifically 1900, I:1, Tables xli, xliii, li, and lxxii (pp. xcix–clxxiv), and 1920, I:2, Table 11 (p. 37), Tables 11–17 (pp. 618–39), Table 10 (pp. 722–26), Table 8 (pp. 921–25), and Table 14 (p. 963). For county boundaries and changes in them I am indebted to Thomas D. Rabenhorst and Carville V. Earle, eds., "Historical U.S. County Outline Map Collection 1840–1980," unpublished compilation by the Department of Geography, University of Maryland Baltimore County, 1983.

6. U.S. *Census,* 1920, I:2, Table 11, p. 37.

7. Dean L. May, "Two Western Towns: A Comparative View," and Charles M. Hatch, "Land, Inheritance and Family in the Formation of Mormon Towns," papers presented at the Western History Association, Salt Lake City, Utah, October 21, 1982.

8. U.S. *Census,* 1920, I:2, pp. 37, 114, 620, 924.

9. D. W. Meinig, *The Great Columbia Plain: A Historical Geography, 1805–1910* (Seattle: University of Washington, 1968), esp. chap. 14.

10. Of California's 58 counties, Madera, Kings, Riverside, and Imperial were organized between 1890 and 1920.

11. *Hist. Stats. U.S.,* 1975, series C73.

12. *Ibid.,* series K79.

13. Donald Worster, "Hydraulic Society in California: An Ecological Interpretation," *Agricultural History* 56 (July 1982): 503–15.

14. Unless otherwise indicated, numerical data for states, counties, and municipalities in this section on 1920–1950 are taken from the Censuses, specifically U.S. Department of Commerce, Bureau of the Census, *Fifteenth Census of the United States: 1930* (Washington: Government Printing Office, 1931), Table 3 for each state, "Area and Population of Counties 1890 to 1930," I:92–1210; *ibid.,* Tables 12–16 (populations of urban places), I:23–61; U.S. Department of Commerce, Bureau of the Census, *Census of Population: 1950* (Washington: Government Printing Office, 1952), I:1, Table 19, pp. 130–42; Table 24, pp. 48–64; Table 27, pp. 69–73. Also, on migration, *Hist. Stats. U.S.,* 1975, series C63–73, and on farms, K68–K79.

15. U.S. Department of Commerce, Bureau of the Census, *Statistical Abstract of the United States: 1950* (Washington: U.S. Government Printing Office, 1950), 700, 702–3).

16. Unless otherwise indicated, numerical data for states, counties, and municipalities in this section on 1950–1980 are taken from the 1950 Census, pages cited in note 14 above, and from U.S. Department of Commerce, Bureau of the Census, *1980 Census of Population* (Washington: Bureau of the Census, 1983), I ("Characteristics of the Population"), A ("Number of Inhabitants"), part 1 ("United States Summary"), Tables 8 (p. 43), 9 (p. 45), 11 (p. 47), 13 (pp. 50–58), 17 (pp. 63–98); *ibid.,* B ("General Population Characteristics"), Tables 50 (pp. 53–

54), 52 (p. 57), 62 (p. 125), 71 (pp. 300–303); *ibid.*, C ("General Social and Economic Characteristics"), Tables 234 (pp. 283–84), 235 (pp. 289–90), 242 (pp. 327–32).

17. Joel Garreau, *The Nine Nations of North America* (Boston: Houghton Mifflin Company, 1981), 287–327.

18. *New York Times,* February 4, 1986.

19. *Ibid.,* January 21, 1986.

20. *Ibid.,* January 16, 1986.

2

The Metropolitan Region

WESTERN CITIES IN THE NEW URBAN ERA

Carl Abbott

That the West in the twentieth century was primarily an urban region may seem self-evident to contemporaries. But it was not always thus, for the West in the nineteenth century had been overwhelmingly rural. The process unfolded so rapidly that its significance was not always readily apparent. In this essay, which traces the growth of new metropolitan centers, Carl Abbott scrutinizes this spectacular development, focussing particularly on the years since 1940 as the most dynamic period in the region's urban expansion. His essay provides a clear analysis of the process whereby the metropolitanization of the West was accomplished and how it came to be a major factor in shaping life in the region.

In the American West, the contemporary era in urban growth dates from 1940. From the southern plains to the Pacific Northwest, national mobilization for World War II triggered a surge of extraordinary growth that has lasted for nearly half a century. In the words of historian Earl Pomeroy, the war "brought probably the most drastic changes in the Far West since 1849."[1] The effects of mobilization were similar in the Rocky Mountain states and Southwest. The pace of change in Texas and Oklahoma matched the great turn-of-the-century oil booms.

Wartime growth and the decades of prosperity that have followed essentially involved the *urban* West. During the war itself, expansion of military bases at a cost of $4.3 billion and federal investment of another $4.1 billion in military production facilities revitalized cities that had stagnated with the agricultural and mining depressions of the 1920s and 1930s, transformed small communities into booming cities, and built entirely new towns on desert mesas and sagebrush flats. Migrating war workers gave cities like Portland, Seattle, and San Francisco their first substantial black ghettos and consequent social tensions. As Gerald Nash and other historians have detailed, local officials struggled to provide adequate public transportation, recreation, police protection, and housing for new and mobile populations.[2] Decent lodging was as scarce in Tonopah, Nevada, where the only hotel booked its rooms two years in advance, as in Seattle, where war workers in 1942 made do with tourist courts, trailer camps, tents, offices, and chicken coops.[3]

The extraordinary growth of the early 1940s initiated basic changes in the economic functions of western cities and their roles within the national urban system. During postwar "G. I. booms" and the Cold War, high rates of metropolitan population growth were sustained and provided markets for local manufacturing and services. In the same decades, western cities captured major shares of several emerging growth sectors in the American economy and found new national and international markets. In significant measure, the "colonial" dependence that writers such as Walter Prescott Webb, Wendell Berge, and Morris Garnsey described and lamented in the 1930s and 1940s was reversed by growing economic independence, cultural influence, and political weight. By the 1970s, popular writers probed the national "power shift" to the booming metropolitan centers of the West.[4]

The result has been a coming of age that has transformed western cities and their region. In 1940, 43 percent of the population in the nineteen states and territories from Texas and the Great Plains to the Pacific lived within metropolitan districts. In 1980, 78 percent of all westerners lived in metropolitan areas, defined as major central cities with populations of 50,000 or more plus their adjacent suburban counties.[5] The shift outpaced that in the rest of the United States, where the metropolitan share of total population moved from 55 percent to 74 percent. In absolute numbers, the West added 39,121,000 metropolitan residents, or 1.4 times its entire regional population in 1940 (table 2.1).

The "metropolitanization" of the West since 1940 has matched the dual process described in Hope Tisdale's standard definition of urbanization.[6] The number of points of metropolitan concentration has more than tripled, accounting for 23 percent of metropolitan areas in 1940 and 31 percent by 1982. At the same time, the average size of western metropolitan areas increased more rapidly than that of southern and eastern areas. The average western metropolis was substantially smaller than its counterpart east of the 95th meridian in 1940. It was effectively equal in size by 1980. Overall, the metropolitan West accounted for 9 percent of the nation's residents in 1940 and 23 percent by 1980.

As the nation struggled to come to terms with its urban character in the years after World War II, the boom cities of the West provided some of the

The Metropolitan Region

Table 2.1
Metropolitan Growth: West and Other United States

		1940	1960	1980
Metropolitan population	West	11,791	28,723	50,912
(000s)	Other U.S.	57,746	84,095	118,519
Metropolitan population	West	8.9%	16.0%	22.5%
as % U.S. population	Other U.S.	43.8%	46.9%	52.3%
Metropolitan population	West	42.8%	64.0%	77.5%
as % regional population	Other U.S.	55.2%	62.5%	73.7%
Number of metropolitan areas*	West	33	60	95
	Other U.S.	107	142	217
Proportion of all metro areas	West	24%	28%	31%
	Other U.S.	76%	72%	69%

*Metropolitan districts in 1940.

most popular symbols of the new urban realities. When the editors of *Fortune* magazine wanted an "exploding metropolis" in 1957, they flew to San Jose. In the 1950s and 1960s, Los Angeles was a frequent example of the "ultimate city" where New York journalists could ponder the future of American civilization. By the 1970s, a procession of journalists decided instead that Houston was "the last word in American cities."[7] Los Angeles, Houston, Phoenix, and similar western cities mirrored the basic American ambiguity about our urban experience. Ugly but thriving, unmanageable but still livable and exciting, western cities seemed to be successful in spite of themselves.

Certainly by 1980, objective measures as well as popular imagery showed a West that was well on the way to becoming *the* urban region in the United States. Los Angeles-Anaheim formed the nation's second largest urban complex, the Bay Area conurbation ranked fifth, Houston-Galveston eighth, and Dallas-Fort Worth ninth. Fourteen of the twenty metropolitan areas with the largest absolute population increases for 1970–80 were western, as were five of the ten fastest growing standard metropolitan statistical areas (SMSAs).[8]

In the following pages, I hope to accomplish two aims. The first is to outline an interpretive framework for understanding the metropolitan explosion in the West and its impacts on regional growth and the character of urban life. The approach assumes that cities themselves are important units of analysis as economic entities, as arenas for economic change, and as objects of public policy. It therefore gives primary attention to the facts and sources of metropolitan growth—the basic questions of what, where, and why. The parallel goal is to review the existing literature that contributes to the interpretation and to suggest broad needs for new research.

Urban History and the New West

Historians are a cautious breed who usually allow new phenomena to season for a respectable two or three decades in the hands of other social scientists. In the present instance, historians began to turn concerted attention to the West's great metropolitan surge only in the 1970s. The most basic building blocks for urban history are comprehensive narratives or "urban biographies" that summarize and organize the experience of individual cities and provide the context for detailed studies. Apart from two pages on postwar Wichita and four pages on postwar Seattle in Constance Green's collection of narrative essays in *American Cities in the Growth of the Nation* (1957), the first full scale biography of a western city that reached significantly past 1940 was David McComb's 1969 study of Houston. Since 1975, however, the list has grown with individual books on Seattle by Roger Sale, Denver by Lyle Dorsett, Salt Lake City by co-authors Thomas Alexander and James Allen, Portland by E. Kimbark MacColl and by myself, and Tucson by C. L. Sonnichsen. Bradford Luckingham has added a combined "profile history" of Albuquerque, El Paso, Phoenix, and Tucson that can be supplemented with recent summary articles by Howard Rabinowitz on Albuquerque and Michael Konig on Phoenix.[9]

In varying degrees, each of these historians has defined his central theme as the public life of metropolitan centers. They examine the politics and policies of local governmental units, the role of business and reform organizations, and the provision of public services. Although urban biographers try to encompass the full variety of trends and issues in metropolitan development, they look at cities primarily as entities to which residents give a degree of loyalty and about which they make direct or indirect decisions. Internal divisions by class, occupation, ethnic group, and geography—the core of urban social history—are considered largely as they affect and result from such decisions. Both by intent and practical necessity, the key sources are metropolitan and specialized newspapers, local interest magazines, interviews with key politicians, businessmen, and bureaucrats, planning reports, and other government documents.

Perhaps because of their intimidating size, the conurbations of southern California and San Francisco Bay have not attracted the same sorts of comprehensive biography. However, an especially rich literature from related disciplines is available as source material to historians interested in specific aspects of postwar growth. For greater Los Angeles, the most popular topic has been the physical form of the metropolis, with studies of urban design, planning, and social geography.[10] The Bay area, in contrast, has generated detailed analysis of the process and politics of decisions about transportation, housing, redevelopment, and similar public sector activities.[11] Some smaller cities have also attracted comparable work on local government and geography that has yet to be digested in general narratives. A good example is the cluster of studies dealing with power structure and group interests in San Antonio.[12] Another is work on ethnic patterns and relations in Denver.[13]

Both the urban biographies and the related social science literature are rich sources of information about urban growth and its problems, but they contribute relatively little to the history of the American West as a changing region. By basic intent, this body of work has little interest in regional patterns. Instead, the major concern is to test particular city experiences against the broad issues and trends in *national* urban development. We can therefore learn about Portland as an arena for the development of professional planning, about metropolitan structure in Albuquerque, and about the professionalization of public services in Salt Lake, but not about the roles of each city within a larger regional context. This characterization is not a criticism of quality, but a description of scholarly intention. Essentially, each author takes his city as a self-contained subject and regional growth as a given. As a result, the studies deal more with history *in* the West than they do with the history *of* the West.

We find a parallel situation with comparative studies of cities within various of the West's economic or physical subregions. As with urban biographies, there has been an intellectual population explosion in the last half dozen years. For the first two decades after the war, Ray B. West's edited volume on *Rocky Mountain Cities* (1949) stood alone as a source of information on the middle-sized cities of the western interior since the 1920s.[14] In the middle 1960s, Earl Pomeroy added a chapter on postwar urban trends on the Pacific Slope, Eugene Hollon described "Desert Cities on the March," and Leonard Goodall edited original essays on politics in eleven cities of a "Southwest" that extended from Phoenix to Wichita.[15] The 1980s, in contrast, have brought a spate of books and articles dealing with the recent past and present of Texas oil towns, Great Plains cities, border cities, Sunbelt cities, and the cities of both a "lesser" and "greater" Southwest.[16]

Each of these studies covers a different subregion and a different set of cities. With the partial exception of books dealing with the Sunbelt, which attempt to derive and justify their regional coverage, each author or editor has tended to view urban development as a response to conditions within one of the traditionally defined subareas of the West, giving considerable emphasis to the peculiarities induced by such locales as desert, plains, or

Mexican border. As with individual city narratives, these subregional studies provide rich information and suggestive insights. However, they pay limited attention to urban growth itself as a causative factor in regional development and offer little comparative context that relates urban development in each subregion to the overall growth of the West.

By the nature of their concerns, in short, historians and other social scientists who have studied cities in the contemporary West have bypassed several basic questions. Urban history can make a fundamental contribution to modern western history by asking (1) *where* metropolitan growth has occurred within the West, (2) *why* the West and certain of its subregions have experienced this extraordinary growth, and (3) *what consequences* this growth has had for the West as a region. Answers to each of these questions can help to explain how and why the West may differ from the rest of the nation and within itself. The resulting framework can also provide a context and rationale for comparing the experience of individual cities, smaller sets of cities, and groups within metropolitan areas.

Patterns of Metropolitan Growth

The first step in an urban approach to recent western history is to explore the differential impacts of the region's metropolitan explosion—the "where" question mentioned above. Rates of metropolitan growth and demographic change can be used to define western subregions with results that are substantially different from the familiar areas based on rainfall, altitude, and settlement history.

In absolute terms, metropolitan growth concentrated in the region's western and southern corners. Seven states recorded metropolitan population increments of more than 1 million from 1940 to 1980. California topped the list with 17 million new metropolitan residents, Texas added 9 million, and Washington 2.5 million, followed by Oregon, Arizona, Colorado, and Oklahoma. The fourteen individual metropolitan areas whose increments of 180,000 or more for the 1970s put them in the national top twenty were located in the same seven states plus Nevada and Utah (fig. 2.1).

Analysis of growth rates of metropolitan and total population by states further confirms that uneven distribution of metropolitan development created distinct regions within the West (table 2.2 and fig. 2.2). Seven states exceeded the national average in rate of growth of metropolitan population and total population for every decade between 1940 and 1980. Use of urban growth rates for earlier decades in which states lacked defined metropolitan areas adds Nevada and Alaska, while New Mexico

The Metropolitan Region

Table 2.2
State Growth Rates in Excess of United States Growth

	Metropolitan Population				Total Population			
	1940s	1950s	1960s	1970s	1940s	1950s	1960s	1970s
Alaska	+	+	+	+	+	+	+	+
Hawaii	+	+	+	+	+	+	+	+
Washington	+	+	+	+	+	+	+	+
California	+	+	+	+	+	+	+	+
Nevada	+	+	+	+	+	+	+	+
Utah	+	+	+	+	+	+	+	+
Arizona	+	+	+	+	+	+	+	+
Colorado	+	+	+	+	+	+	+	+
Texas	+	+	+	+	+	+	+	+
New Mexico	+	+	+	+	+	+		+
Oregon	+		+	+	+		+	+
Oklahoma	+	+	+	+				+
Wyoming	+			+	+			+
Idaho	+		+	+				+
Montana		+		+				
North Dakota				+				
South Dakota	+			+				
Nebraska		+	+					
Kansas	+	+						

Several states had no officially defined metropolitan areas until well into the postwar era. Rather than comparing metropolitan growth rates for these cases, the first panel of the table therefore compares state *urban* population growth to national urban growth for the following: Nevada, Montana, and North Dakota, 1940–50; Alaska and Idaho, 1940–60; Wyoming, 1940–70.

lagged behind the national average in only one of the eight possible instances. Oregon lagged in both total and metropolitan growth in the 1950s, but its overall rates were comparable to Washington and Colorado. Oklahoma showed the slow growth in total population characteristic of the plains states but posted four decades of above average metropolitan growth like its neighboring states to the south and west. Combining all twelve of these states gives a Pacific-Southwest rim region that closely matches the distribution of absolute metropolitan growth.

The remaining seven states fall into three smaller subregions on the basis of their growth experience. Kansas and Nebraska are "metropolitan dropouts" that combine slow overall growth with the relative decline of metropolitan growth in recent decades. The states of the upper Rockies, in contrast, showed an uneven pattern in the earlier decades but shared a surge of growth in the 1970s, responding in particular to rapid expansion in the energy and recreation industries. The Dakotas recorded the same metropolitan boom in the 1970s without the supportive market expansion provided by above average overall growth.

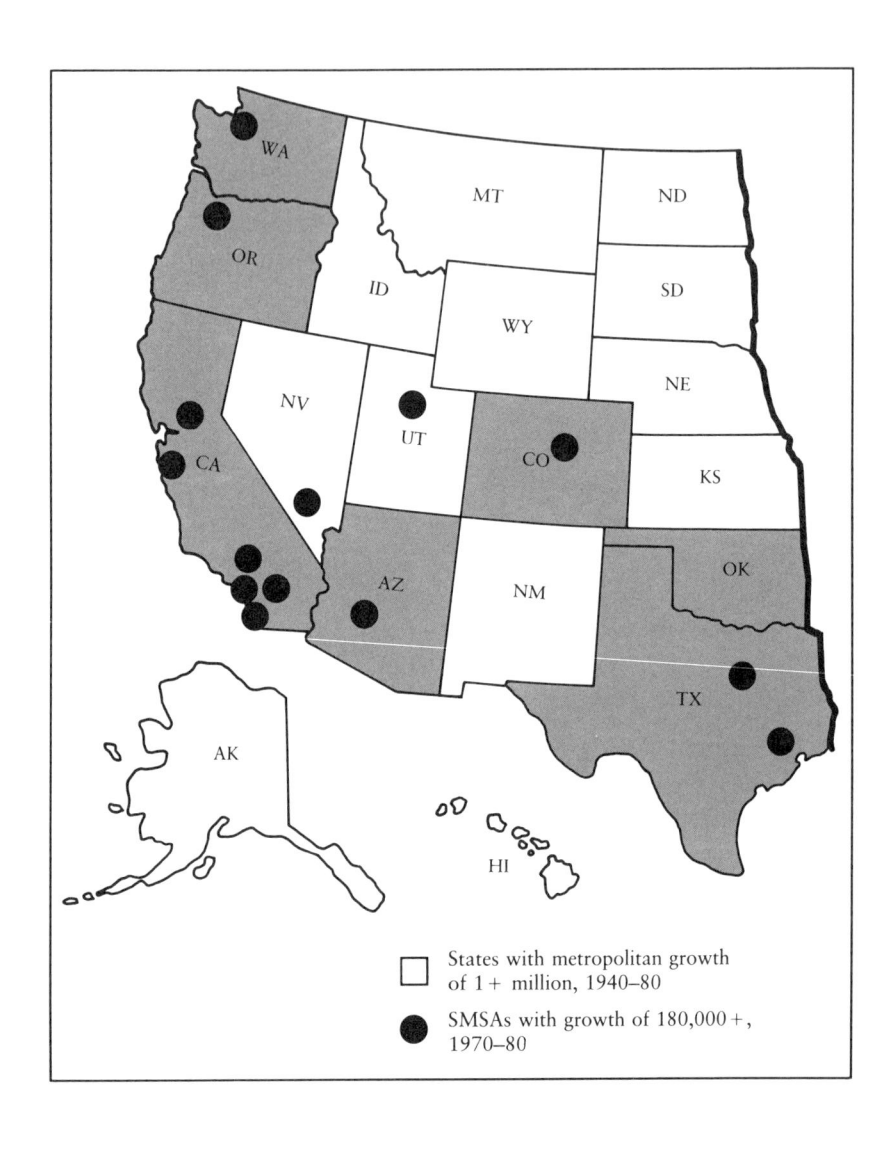

Fig. 2.1
Metropolitan Growth in the West

The Metropolitan Region

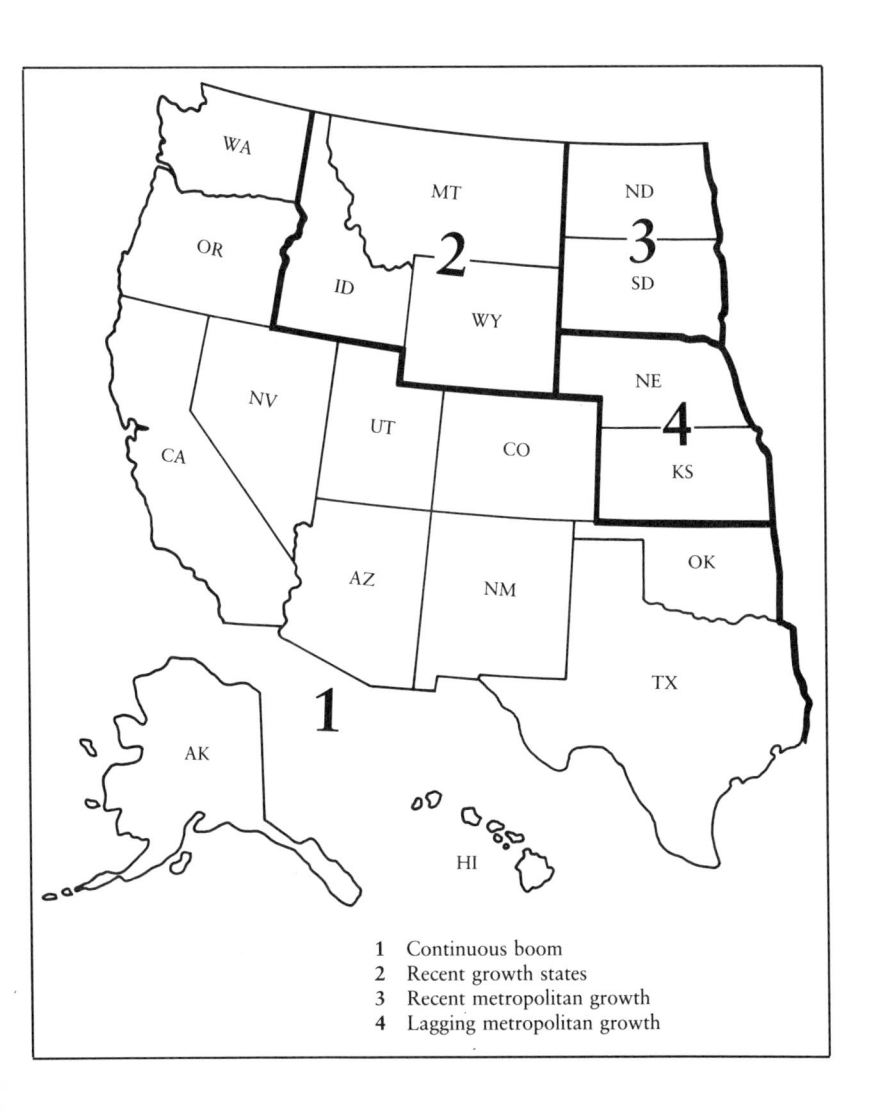

Fig. 2.2
Growth Regions in the West

To a substantial extent, the differentiation of the Pacific-Southwest rim can also be viewed in terms of the expansion and intensification of the regional influence of California and Texas. San Francisco, Los Angeles, Houston, and Dallas-Fort Worth have acted as dynamic organizing forces that have helped to tilt the entire West toward its southern and western margins.

"Imperial Texas" as an economic region has long included the grazing country of New Mexico and the oil country of Oklahoma, with many key decisions made in Dallas banks and board rooms.[17] The same area is linked by high volumes of highway traffic and constitutes the core of a "southern-western" culture region defined by speech, religion, musical taste, and political culture. After World War II, the Dallas-Houston influence extended increasingly into Colorado and the central Rockies through real estate investment, recreational use, and the growth of both investment and employment in the Colorado and Wyoming oil business. At the same time, San Antonio and El Paso have been the staging points for most of the Hispanic migrant workers employed in the Rocky Mountain and plains states.[18]

California cities have played the same role on the Pacific Slope. Nevada's historical status as a California colony has been well documented from the development of the Comstock Lode to the rise of Reno and Las Vegas as distant weekend suburbs of San Francisco and Los Angeles. Arizona, Hawaii, Oregon, and parts of Idaho have had a similar dependence on the money and markets of California's supercities.[19] Patterns of recreational travel, seasonal and permanent migration run predominantly north-south among the six states, bringing Oregonians to vacation in Anaheim, Honolulu, and Reno, Mexican workers from Los Angeles to the Willamette and Yakima valleys, and California retirees to Oregon or Arizona. The area's core of southern and central California, Nevada, and Arizona constitute a sort of uniform "TV country" that furnishes the settings for the majority of television shows.[20]

In broadest terms, the supermetropolitan influence of the Texas and California supercities *may* be slowly reorienting the West's regional grain (fig. 2.3). The transcontinental railroads and economic dependence of the nineteenth-century West on eastern markets and suppliers established a basic pattern of east-west hinterlands and connections, with Dallas and Albuquerque linked to St. Louis, Denver to Chicago, and Seattle to Minneapolis.[21] Except along the northern tier, where northern Idaho and Montana still look to Seattle and the Dakotas to the Twin Cities, recent patterns of travel, migration, and financial control appear to be creating a substantial north-south orientation that cuts across the old grain and draws the West away from the old national core.[22]

The Metropolitan Region

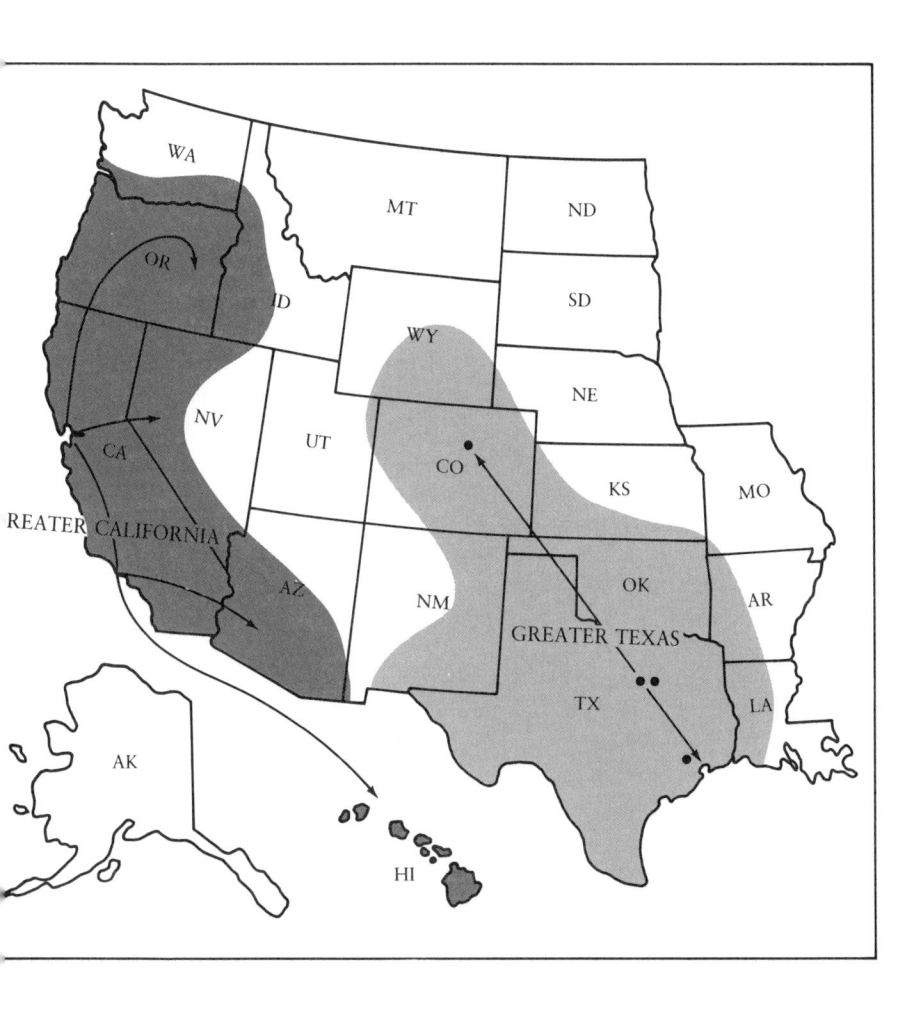

Fig. 2.3
Metropolitan-Centered Subregions in the West

Sources of Metropolitan Growth

The West's metropolitan explosion is a result of basic changes in the structure of the American economy and in the comparative advantage of regions. The interlocking economic and demographic trends can most easily be understood in terms of "basic" and "nonbasic" economic sectors. Basic activities involve the sale or export of regional goods and services to outside users and thereby increase regional income. Nonbasic or "residentiary" activities supply the needs of the region's own residents and businesses. Their growth depends on the size of regional markets and the economic interconnections that are facilitated by an increasingly diversified economy.

Since 1940, the American West has claimed a disproportionate share of new jobs and investment from three fundamental changes in the national economy: (1) the expansion of the defense establishment and its industrial allies, (2) the internationalization of the American economy, and (3) the rise of a leisure society. In some specific categories within these sweeping trends, western cities have benefitted from obvious advantages such as sunshine for air bases, convenient ports for trade with Japan, and amenities for retirees. In other cases, the West's edge can be traced to accidents of innovation, entrepreneurship, and political influence, with examples in such industries as electronics and aerospace research and development. In addition, the nation's economic and geopolitical tilt toward Asia has been an exogeneous factor that has favored western over eastern cities.[23]

National defense has been one of the nation's growth industries since 1940, and one whose effects have been felt disproportionately in western cities. The massive mobilization from 1941 to 1945 was a spectacular preview of continued defense activity during the Cold War. In 1967, James Clayton defined Alaska, Hawaii, California, Utah, Colorado, New Mexico, and Arizona as heavily dependent on defense spending and Washington, Nevada, Wyoming, and Montana as moderately dependent. Echoing Pomeroy's evaluation of World War II, he argued that "it is entirely possible that defense spending will loom as the single most important economic and demographic factor in the history of the West during the past two decades."[24]

By the end of the 1970s, a variety of indicators supported Clayton's generalization. In relation to total population, the West received more than its share of federal spending on defense, science, and space industries. Six of the ten United States metropolitan areas with the highest numbers of civilian Department of Defense employees were western—San Antonio, Salt Lake City, San Diego, San Francisco, Sacramento, and Honolulu. Half of the metropolitan areas in the West are net gainers from the defense budget, receiving more from federal defense spending than they pay in tax contributions for defense. The comparative proportion for the rest of the United States is less than 30 percent.[25]

For historians of the modern West, decisions about the location of defense facilities are the recent equivalent of nineteenth-century railroad competitions and county seat wars. Gilbert Guinn has identified the earliest use of the term "sunshine belt" by Army Air Force planners in 1944, describing a policy of locating new training facilities south of the 37th parallel. Other historians have looked at the interaction of local promotional efforts, local political influence, and bureaucratic criteria in decisions to build such facilities as Tinker Air Force Base (AFB) at Oklahoma City and Hill AFB and Clearfield Naval Depot near Ogden.[26]

The aerospace and electronics industries, which have found the Pentagon their single best customer, have also been weighted toward the West. A general study of the aircraft industry in 1950 found that airframe production was heavily concentrated in the six cities of Wichita, Dallas, Fort Worth, San Diego, Los Angeles, and Seattle, although the production lines used engines built in the Northeast. Martin Schiesl, James Clayton, and David Clarke have looked in more detail at the growth of the aerospace business in Los Angeles, while Stephen Oates chronicled the origins, planning, and initial impacts of NASA's Houston space center.[27]

For a broader definition of the nation's "high tech" sector, a recent study in the *Monthly Labor Review* identified six industries in which the ratio of research and development (R and D) spending to net sales was twice that for all industries—aircraft, guided missiles and space vehicles, drugs, computing machines, communication equipment, and electronic components. Arizona, California, Washington, Kansas, Utah, and Colorado all ranked among the top ten states when high tech jobs are measured as a percentage of total nonagricultural employment. When *growth* in high tech jobs from 1972 to 1982 compared to growth in all nonagricultural jobs is measured, Arizona, Oregon, California, Washington, and South Dakota make the top ten.[28]

There has been a similar concentration of general research and development spending within the Pacific-Southwest rim. Los Angeles was far and away the leading metropolitan area for federal R and D funds in 1977, with twice the contract volume of number two Washington and number three San Francisco. Other western SMSAs in the top twenty were Seattle, Albuquerque, San Diego, Dallas, Salt Lake, and the nuclear city of Richland, Washington. Federal R and D dollars at universities can also be measured on a per capita basis by states, with Alaska, Utah, Hawaii, New Mexico, Washington, California, Colorado, and Wyoming among the seventeen states exceeding the national average.[29]

In a second broad growth sector, western cities have led and benefitted from the increasing internationalization of the United States during the

1960s and 1970s. Substantial amendments to the Immigration and Nationality Act in 1965 led to steady upturn in documented immigration, with levels by the late 1970s nearly 2.5 times those of the 1950s. More than half of this new wave of international migration is entering through and settling in the cities of the West. Koreans, Taiwanese, Filipinos, Indo-Chinese, Mexicans, and Central Americans have settled disproportionately in the Pacific and southwestern states. Los Angeles, designated the "new Ellis Island" by *Time* magazine, was 6 percent Asian and 29 percent Hispanic by 1980. Seattle was 4 percent Asian, San Francisco 10 percent, and Honolulu 60 percent. Since a high proportion of Asian immigrants are managers and professionals, their effects on metropolitan growth are both directly and indirectly positive.[30] Hispanic populations of more than 100,000 were found in twenty western SMSAs in 1980 compared to seven elsewhere.

The importance of foreign trade for the American economy has grown in parallel with immigration, rising from 3 percent of GNP in 1965 to 9 percent in 1979.[31] During the 1970s, the proportion of American trade carried in and out of west coast ports jumped from 15 to 23 percent of the national total, and Texas trade rose from 10 to 15 percent.[32] The evolution of local port agencies and port facilities that have served this western trade has been described in Marilyn Sibley's history of the Port of Houston, Padraic Burke's history of the Port of Seattle, and James Hitchman's history of the smaller port of Bellingham, Washington.[33] Each author depicts a situation in which local business leaders have used the port authority to implement longterm economic development strategies. Examples of topics that invite more detailed comparative study include the local response to technological changes such as cargo containerization, the development of landside connections, and the accommodation of port land needs within the city planning process.[34]

A third factor that has fueled the rapid growth of western cities has been the temporary and permanent population movements of tourists and retirees. Demographic data, for example, confirm the popular impression of a retirement migration to the Southwest, particularly from the states of the Middle West. Military retirees, an easily identifiable subgroup, make up at least 1 percent of the total population of Washington, Hawaii, Nevada, Arizona, Colorado, and New Mexico. They constitute a major continuing military presence in military base cities such as Denver, Phoenix, San Diego, Honolulu, and San Antonio.[35]

Although a number of western states proudly claim that tourism is their second or third largest industry, relatively little information is available on its promotion by and effects on metropolitan areas over the last several decades. It would be valuable to build on scattered studies such as Perry Kaufman's analysis of Las Vegas efforts to make tourism a major industry after World War II, Mark Foster's description of Denver's contrasting rejection of the 1976 Winter Olympics, and Bryan Farrell's brief description of the effects of tourism on Hilo and Honolulu.[36] A specific topic might be the role of local government and business organizations in the promotion of western cities as convention centers through the construction of arenas, meeting halls, and hotels and the expansion of airports.[37] It would also be valuable to put the modern world's fairs in Seattle (1962), San Antonio (1968), Spokane (1974), and Vancouver, British Columbia (1986) in comparative perspective as booster events, tourist attractions, and land development schemes. In larger context, development of convention and tourist facilities can be compared with parallel efforts to expand maritime terminals or secure defense facilities.

Rapid growth of these leading sectors supported broader expansion within each metropolitan economy. Booming cities required greater volumes and variety of goods, services, and management functions to meet the needs of growing populations and business markets. At the same time, the increasing variety of producer services, industrial suppliers, and transportation facilities reduced costs in previously isolated western cities through the economies of agglomeration. The expanding social infrastructure of universities and urban services in the larger cities also supported economic concentration, leading to local production of previously imported goods in a self-reinforcing growth cycle.[38]

The process was apparent in the first decade after the war. Cities such as Denver and Salt Lake attracted smaller manufacturing operations to serve local markets, while accessibility to the entire West brought them a number of larger firms. The number of new or expanded manufacturing plants in Los Angeles was 50 percent higher for the 1945–48 period than for the war years 1942–44. The Pacific, mountain, and southwestern states all received a disproportionate share of new manufacturing investment as judged against prewar industrial capacity, with especially marked increases in Texas and Oklahoma.[39]

The role of western cities as distribution centers also grew with the size of regional markets, the increasing variety of local products, and a shift in the national economy toward such industries as petroleum and electronics. Data for the three decades from 1948 to 1977 show particularly rapid growth of wholesaling in Dallas-Fort Worth, Houston, Denver, Phoenix, and Portland.[40]

The growth of management functions in the major western cities reflected both the enhancement of their national roles and the need for greater depth in regional services. Federal civilian employment topped 20,000 in a dozen western cities by 1980, compared with a total of thirteen cities for the much more populous South, East, and Middle West.[41] The drift of corporate headquarters to the major cities of California, Texas, and the southern Rockies has been documented for both corporate giants (the *Fortune* 500) and for a much larger sample of middle-sized firms (the 35,000 companies rated by Standard and Poor's). Acceleration of the shift in the 1970s provided journalists with instant evidence of the rise of the Sunbelt.[42]

Overall, analysis of the sources of the western metropolitan explosion suggests the need to modify the "staple export" and "boom stage" models of regional development appropriate to the nineteenth century, when western cities served as gateways between the industrializing East and market-oriented resource regions in the West.[43] By the latter decades of the twentieth century, western cities are much more than funnels that supply locally produced goods to outside markets and distribute manufactured goods imported from outside. As geographer Allan Pred has detailed in a study of "multi-locational" corporations headquartered in San Francisco, San Diego, Honolulu, Phoenix, Portland, Seattle, and Boise, the region's major cities now connect in complex ways not only to local hinterlands but throughout the continental and world economies.[44] Although parts of the West still retain a measure of the dependence that characterized its earlier history (especially in relation to federal land and resource bureaucracies), the themes of self-sufficiency, economic control, and cultural independence now deserve equal attention. Greater Los Angeles, greater San Francisco, and greater Houston have emerged as international decision centers in their own right, with major roles in finance and trade. Such measures as wholesaling volume, air traffic, and bank capital indicate that Dallas-Fort Worth matches Houston as a domestic decision center.[45]

At the other end of the metropolitan scale, the same perspectives can help explain how several dozen small western communities have evolved during the last generation into new metropolitan centers, while others have remained stranded as energy and agricultural resource towns. In Grand Junction, Colorado, for example, the keys to long-term growth have been regional services, distribution, recreation, and diversified small manufacturing, with uranium and oil shale booms as perturbations of a basic growth trend. William Robbins's study of Coos Bay, Oregon, documents a contrasting situation in which the persistence of external control and physical limits on accessible markets have left the community at the mercy of the timber production cycle.[46]

Examination of growth sources can thus help to explain regional patterns and variations in metropolitan growth, answering the paired questions of why western cities have grown faster than eastern and why metropolitan growth has been most pronounced within certain parts of the West. The incidence of military facilities, defense procurement, related high tech production and research, foreign trade, Latin American and

The Metropolitan Region

Asian immigration, and resort and retirement activities have all favored the established metropolitan centers of the Pacific-Southwest rim. The advantages of agglomeration have helped the big get bigger. At the broadest scale, finally, the analysis confirms the importance of the West's supercities of Houston, Dallas-Fort Worth, Los Angeles, and San Francisco-Oakland as driving forces whose financial, industrial, and business service resources can control vast western regions and support both regional and national growth.

Metropolitan Growth and Western Life

Discussion of causative factors in the metropolitan explosion leads directly to consideration of its effects on the fabric and character of life in the urbanized West. The implied research strategy is to approach political and social change in individual cities through comparative history organized around the basic dimensions of metropolitan development and functions. Contextual variables such as metropolitan size, age, growth history, economic base, and location can help to explain differences and similarities among western cities as human environments.

One fruitful field for further research may be variations in the goals and outcomes of urban politics and policy. In examining postwar metropolitan politics in the West or Sunbelt, John Mollenkopf, Bradley Rice and Richard Bernard, and I have independently described two broadly similar stages.[47] The two decades after 1945 were an era of "businessmen's government" in cities such as San Antonio, Dallas, Denver, Albuquerque, Phoenix, Oklahoma City, San Francisco, and Seattle. The business agendas placed heavy emphasis on economic restructuring to take advantage of postwar growth opportunities. The most obvious manifestations were big capital projects—urban renewal, freeways, central office buildings, sports facilities, airports, convention centers. Vigorous annexation drives frequently accompanied the physical reconstruction. In the later 1960s and early 1970s, many of these business coalitions weakened or collapsed, partly because of pressures from growing suburbs over the division of public investments and even more because of neighborhood-focused reactions based on activism by minorities and the professional middle class.

As these brief descriptions suggest, the several political stages are related to the growth histories of western cities. The first members of the 1940s baby boom (which was intensified in the West by the extraordinary wartime and postwar migration of people in their twenties and thirties) reached voting age in the 1960s. Reduction in the average age of the urban electorate brought pressures for younger leadership and changes in service demands, such as an increased emphasis on urban environmental amenities. Rapid expansion of downtown professional and managerial employment supported new attention to preservation of older centrally located neighborhoods for the middle class at the same time that downtown expansion was displacing minority groups from poorer, inner-ring communities. Variations in these sorts of land use and demographic dynamics may help to explain significant differences in the transition from one political stage to the next.

The same type of analysis can account for the apparent emergence in recent years of a third stage marked by renewed interest in "businesslike," growth-oriented local government. The reaction may be a response to the depression of the early 1980s in the resource-extraction industries. It can also be seen as a logical synthesis of postwar political trends as newly empowered minorities press for a share of an expanded pie and quality-of-life liberals mature into middle-aged consumers. Examples include Seattle, Portland, San Diego, Oklahoma City, Houston, Albuquerque, Denver, and San Antonio.

Political evolution provides a framework for analysis of urban development policy. Urban historians have available a number of case studies of the location and growth of individual industries or facilities. Social scientists interested in regional growth have also digested a wide range of aggregate economic data by states or metropolitan areas.[48] However, the need remains to link the specific and general in comparative studies that examine the local origins and support for growth strategies, the dimensions of interurban competition, and the effects of success or failure on society and politics. A useful model is Roger Lotchin's work on California cities and the military during the 1920s and 1930s.[49] For the postwar decades, Mollenkopf's comparison of San Francisco and Boston and my own work on Portland, Denver, and San Antonio look at the first and third concerns but not the second, while Peter Wiley and Robert Gottlieb focus their account of the rise of "centers of power" in the Southwest on colorful characters and back-room deals.[50]

Cities, of course, are social and residential environments as well as markets and production centers. Within the traditional division of the United States between an eastern core and a western periphery, cities functioned historically as agents of national culture. A distinguished series of historians have described western towns and cities as civilizing forces that provided conducive settings for reproducing the values and way of life of the core.[51] A similar nationalizing process has been apparent at a variety of levels in the mid-twentieth century as the maturing of the western urban system has brought more and larger points of population concentration.

In specific, urban historians may want to examine the changing roles of submetropolitan centers, especially with the reversal of nonmetropolitan population decline in the 1960s. A generation ago, Carey McWilliams commented that many western cities that are small in population are still "big in relation to the territories they serve, big in relation to total state population, big in relation to the functions they discharge." Geographers Dean Rugg and Donald Rundquist have similarly argued that many Great Plains towns of 20,000 or 30,000 residents are effectively metropolitan centers for their sparsely settled region, offering Bozeman, Grand Island, and Rapid City as examples.[52] Preliminary impressions suggest that the influence of regional towns may have peaked in the 1920s, declined from the 1930s through the 1960s as automobiles and improved highways centralized retailing and services, and begun to expand again in the 1970s. In my section of the West, the architectural symbol of the ambitious 1920s is a series of mid-rise hotels in communities as improbable as Walla Walla, Pendleton, Baker, and Astoria. The comparable symbol of the 1970s and 1980s, of course, is store front restoration and rehabilitation along the old main streets.

At the same time, a central concern of urban historians remains the deepening influence of metropolitan centers throughout their entire hinterlands. Benchmark definitions of hinterland boundaries as measured by flows of goods and business information were provided by Robert Park and Charles Newcomb in 1929 and by John Borchert in 1972. As Borchert's data also indicate, economic hinterlands overlap with the intensely personal dimension of urban migration fields. Detailed analysis of states of origin of war workers and postwar migrants, utilizing available data, would provide additional understanding of intermetropolitan variations in political goals and behavior.[53]

Metropolitan areas set in motion intermittent or short-term flows of population as well as permanent migrations. The same westerners who adamantly refuse to *live* in major cities make 150- or 200-mile shopping trips from Kemmerer, Wyoming, to Salt Lake City, from Pasco, Washington, to Portland, or from Baggs, Wyoming, to Grand Junction.[54] The reciprocal relationship may be the growth of weekend recreation zones that are located beyond the range of daily commuting but clearly serve as parttime annexes to the metropolitan field. Richard White's insightful study of the nineteenth- and early-twentieth-century development of Whidbey Island, Washington, which lies thirty to eighty miles from Seattle, provides a model for exploring the impact of such recreation use on agriculture, land ownership, and community characteristics.[55]

A related research concern that touches the established subject matter of urban social history is the continuing process of community formation within major metropolitan areas. The second of the postwar political stages outlined above implies a growth in the size and political coherence of black and Hispanic populations. Such political influence has been both product and cause of group consciousness and community organization. Formal recognition of minority power since 1970 has frequently taken the form of a shift from at-large to district elections for city councils.[56] The related emergence of neighborhood associations and civic leagues as important political factors has been set in historical perspective for Portland and Houston.[57] West coast cities also invite attention to the articulation and evolution of ethnic group identity and institutions among recent Asian and Latin American immigrants.[58]

Conclusion

The preceding discussion has been designed to explore and illustrate the value of two complementary approaches to the history of cities in the twentieth-century West.

The first assumption is that the American West in the latter half of the twentieth century can best be understood in terms of regional growth and subregional differentiation driven by metropolitan development. Cities have led the West to a new role in the national and international economies; they have organized commercial and cultural hinterlands; and they have extended metropolitan connections to communities as superficially isolated as Sandpoint, Idaho, and Parachute, Colorado. In the process, the West and its cities have emerged as new centers for American life. The former "colony" may now enjoy the same advantages of market size, market access, and industrial innovation that led to the self-reinforcing growth of the northeastern industrial belt a century ago. Los Angeles is now the nation's "second city." The San Francisco Bay region matches the commercial and cultural influence of Chicago. Houston rivals Detroit as an industrial capital, and the twin cities of Seattle-Tacoma match their older counterparts of Minneapolis-St. Paul.[59]

In addition, this discussion assumes that "external" history of cities can provide an effective context for "internal" history. Rates of growth, size, changing economic roles, and regional connections create particular issues for public attention and for action through formal entities such as local governments. The same factors set the conditions within which urban residents create and modify the informal social structure and networks that are the components of local and metropolitan communities.[60] Narrative and comparative history that deals directly with the central problems of how and why cities have grown, how urbanites have made decisions about their cities, and how cities as social and economic environments affect their citizens speaks to the interests of both scholars and the nonacademic public. The metropolitanization of the West has been a process in which ambitious or concerned citizens have utilized and modified broad economic and demographic trends. The more clearly that process is understood, the more effectively those same citizens can build prosperous and humane communities.

Notes

1. Earl Pomeroy, *The Pacific Slope* (New York: Alfred A. Knopf, 1965), 297.
2. The following deal with the general impacts of the war: Gerald D. Nash, *The American West Transformed: The Impact of the Second World War* (Bloomington: Indiana University Press, 1985); Carl Abbott, *The New Urban America: Growth and Politics in Sunbelt Cities* (Chapel Hill: University of North Carolina Press, 1981), 98–119; Leonard J. Arrington and Anthony Cluff, *Federally Financed Industrial Plants Constructed in Utah during World War II* (Logan: Utah State University, 1969); Pomeroy, *Pacific Slope*, 297–301. Data on federal investment from U. S. Bureau of the Census, *County and City Data Book* (Washington: Government Printing Office, 1947). Specifically focused on the responses of local governments are Martin Schiesl, "City Planning and the Federal Government in World War II: The Los Angeles Experience," *California History* 58 (April 1979): 127–43; Philip J. Funigiello, *The Challenge to Urban Liberalism: Federal-City Relations during World War II* (Knoxville: University of Tennessee Press, 1978); Carl Abbott, "Planning for the Home Front in Seattle and Portland, 1940–45," in Roger Lotchin, ed., *The Martial Metropolis* (New York: Praeger Publishers, 1984), 163–90; Gerald Nash, "Planning for the Postwar City: The Urban West in World War II," *Arizona and the West* 27 (Summer 1985): 99–112.
3. Calvin F. Schmid, *Social Trends in Seattle* (Seattle: University of Washington Press, 1944); unattributed letter, August 27, 1944, from military wife in Tonopah, Nevada, to family in Craig, Colorado, in possession of author.
4. Walter Prescott Webb, *Divided We Stand* (New York: Farrar and Rinehart, 1937); Joseph K. Howard, *Montana: High, Wide and Handsome* (New Haven: Yale University Press, 1943); Wendell Berge, *Economic Freedom for the West* (Lincoln: University of Nebraska Press, 1946); Morris Garnsey, *America's New Frontier: The Mountain West* (New York: Alfred A. Knopf, 1950). This literature is discussed in Nash, *American West Transformed*, 208–13. Positive evaluations of the West's relative status begin with Neil Morgan, *Westward Tilt: The American West Today* (New York: Random House, 1963) and include Kirkpatrick Sale, *Power Shift: The Rise of the Southern Rim and Its Challenge to the Eastern Establishment* (New York: Random House, 1975); Peter Wiley and Robert Gottlieb, *Empires in the Sun* (New York: Putnam, 1982); Richard D. Lamm and Michael McCarthy, *The Angry West: A Vulnerable Land and Its Future* (Boston: Houghton Mifflin, 1982).
5. This essay examines the "historians' West" that includes the five-state Pacific census region, the eight-state Mountain census region, and the plains states of North Dakota, South Dakota, Nebraska, Kansas, Oklahoma, and Texas—"Gun-

smoke country" as well as "Bonanza country." The discussion cites metropolitan population (large cities and their suburban rings) rather than urban population (all cities and towns of 2,500+ residents) because the former gives a better measure of the concentration of Westerners in a few major centers.

6. Hope Tisdale, "The Process of Urbanization," *Social Forces* 20 (March 1942): 311–16.

7. William H. Whyte, Jr., "Urban Sprawl," *Fortune* 57 (January 1958): 103–9, 194–200; Christopher Rand, *Los Angeles: The Ultimate City* (New York: Oxford University Press, 1967); Richard Elman, *Ill-at Ease in Compton* (New York: Pantheon, 1967); Theodore Roszak, "Life in the Instant Cities," in Carey McWilliams, ed., *The California Revolution* (New York: Grossman Publishers, 1969), 53–83; William Hale Thompson, *At the Edge of History* (New York: Harper and Row, 1971); Lynn Ashby, "The Supercities: Houston," *Saturday Review* 3 n.s. (September 4, 1976): 16–19; "New No. 1 City in the Southwest," *Business Week* (June 12, 1971): 82–86; Larry King, "Bright Lights, Big Cities," *Atlantic* 235 (March 1975): 84–88; *New York Times*, February 9, 15, 1976.

8. The fourteen SMSAs, in descending order of metropolitan population increments, were Houston, Dallas-Fort Worth, Phoenix, San Diego, Anaheim, Los Angeles, Riverside, Denver, Portland, San Jose, Salt Lake City, Sacramento, Las Vegas, and Seattle. The five very fast growing metropolitan areas were Olympia, Reno, Las Vegas, Fort Collins, and Bryan-College Station.

9. Constance McLaughlin Green, *American Cities in the Growth of the Nation* (London: Athlone Press, 1957); David McComb, *Houston: The Bayou City* (Austin: University of Texas Press, 1969); Roger Sale, *Seattle: Past to Present* (Seattle: University of Washington Press, 1976); Lyle Dorsett, *The Queen City: A History of Denver* (Boulder: Pruett Publishing Co., 1977); Thomas G. Alexander and James B. Allen, *Mormons and Gentiles: A History of Salt Lake City* (Boulder: Pruett Publishing Co., 1984); E. Kimbark MacColl, *The Growth of a City: Power and Politics in Portland, Oregon, 1915 to 1950* (Portland: Georgian Press, 1979); Carl Abbott, *Portland: Politics, Planning and Growth in a Twentieth Century City* (Lincoln: University of Nebraska Press, 1983); C. L. Sonnichsen, *Tucson: The Life and Times of an American City* (Norman: University of Oklahoma Press, 1982); Bradford Luckingham, *The Urban Southwest: A Profile History of Albuquerque—El Paso—Phoenix—Tucson* (El Paso: Texas Western Press, 1982); Howard N. Rabinowitz, "Growth Trends in the Albuquerque SMSA, 1940–1978," *Journal of the West* 18 (July 1979): 62–74; and "Albuquerque: City at a Crossroads," in Richard Bernard and Bradley Rice, eds., *Sunbelt Cities: Politics and Growth since World War Two* (Austin: University of Texas Press, 1983), 255–67; Michael Konig, "Phoenix in the 1950s," *Arizona and the West* 24 (Spring 1982): 19–38.

10. Rayner Banham, *Los Angeles: The Architecture of the Four Ecologies* (New York: Harper and Row, 1971); Howard J. Nelson and William A. V. Clark, *Los Angeles: The Metropolitan Experience* (Cambridge, MA: Ballinger Publishing Co., 1976); Sam B. Warner, Jr., *The Urban Wilderness* (New York: Harper and Row, 1972), 113–49; Stephan Thernstrom, "The Growth of Los Angeles in Historical Perspective: Myth and Reality," in Werner Z. Hirsch, ed., *Los Angeles: Viability and Prospects for Metropolitan Leadership* (New York: Praeger, 1971), 3–19; Derek Walker, ed., *Los Angeles* (London: Architectural Design, 1981);

The Metropolitan Region

David Brodsly, *Los Angeles Freeway: An Appreciative Essay* (Berkeley: University of California Press, 1981).

11. Frederick Wirt, *Power in the City* (Berkeley: University of California Press, 1975); Mel Scott, *The San Francisco Bay Area: A Metropolis in Perspective* (Berkeley: University of California Press, 1959); Chester Hartman, *Yerba Buena: Land Grab and Community Resistance in San Francisco* (Berkeley: National Housing and Economic Development Law Institute, Earl Warren Legal Institute, University of California, 1974), and *The Transformation of San Francisco* (Totowa, NJ: Rowman and Allenheld, 1984); John H. Mollenkopf, *The Contested City* (Princeton: Princeton University Press, 1983); Aaron Wildavsky and Jeffrey Pressman, *Implementation* (Berkeley: University of California Press, 1973); Frank Levy, Arnold J. Meltsner, and Aaron Wildavsky, *Urban Outcomes: Schools, Streets, and Libraries* (Berkeley: University of California Press, 1974); Philip J. Trounstine and Terry Christensen, *Movers and Shakers: The Study of Community Power* (New York: St. Martin's Press, 1982); Susan S. Fainstein, Norman I. Fainstein, and P. Jefferson Armistead, "San Francisco: Urban Transformation and the Local State," in Susan Fainstein, et al., *Restructuring the City: The Political Economy of Urban Redevelopment* (New York: Longman, 1983), 202–44.

12. David R. Johnson, John A. Booth, and Richard J. Harris, eds., *The Politics of San Antonio: Community, Progress, and Power* (Lincoln: University of Nebraska Press, 1983); Robert L. Lineberry, *Equality and Urban Policy: The Distribution of Municipal Services* (Beverly Hills: Sage Publications, 1977); Charles L. Cotrell, *Municipal Services Equalization in San Antonio, Texas: Explorations in Chinatown* (San Antonio: St. Mary's University, Department of Urban Studies, 1976); Arnold Fleischman, "Sunbelt Boosterism: The Politics of Postwar Growth and Annexation in San Antonio," in David C. Perry and Alfred J. Watkins, eds., *The Rise of the Sunbelt Cities* (Beverly Hills: Sage Publications, 1977), 151–68; Wayt T. Watterson and Roberta T. Watterson, *The Politics of New Communities: A Case Study of San Antonio Ranch* (New York: Praeger Publishers, 1975); Charles Cotrell and R. Michael Stevens, "The 1975 Voting Rights Act and San Antonio, Texas," *Publius* 8 (Winter 1978): 79–100; Bill Crane, "San Antonio: Pluralistic City and Monolithic Government," in Leonard Goodall, ed., *Urban Politics in the Southwest* (Tempe: Arizona State University Institute of Public Administration, 1967), 127–42.

13. George Bardwell, *Characteristics of Negro Residents in Park Hill Area of Denver, Colorado* (Denver: Commission on Community Relations, 1966); Daniel Doeppers, "The Globeville Neighborhood in Denver," *Geographical Review* 57 (October 1967): 506–22; Harold E. Jackson, "Discrimination and Busing: The Denver School Board Election of May, 1969," *Rocky Mountain Social Science Journal* 8 (October 1971): 101–8; Nicholas P. Loverrich, Jr., and Otwin Marenin, "A Comparison of Black and Mexican-American Voters in Denver," *Western Political Quarterly* 29 (June 1976): 284–94; Franklin J. James, *Minorities in the Sunbelt* (New Brunswick, NJ: Center for Urban Policy Research, Rutgers University, 1984).

14. Ray B. West, ed., *Rocky Mountain Cities* (New York: W. W. Norton, 1949). The chapter on "The Rise of Western Cities" in Leroy Hafen and Carl Coke Rister. *Western America* (Englewood Cliffs, NJ: Prentice-Hall, 1950) has extensive dis-

cussion of nineteenth-century growth and brief mention of twentieth-century developments.

15. Pomeroy, *Pacific Slope*, 302–15; W. Eugene Hollon, *The Great American Desert* (New York: Oxford University Press, 1966), 217–37; Goodall, ed., *Urban Politics in the Southwest*.

16. Niles Hansen, *The Border Economy: Regional Development in the Southwest* (Austin: University of Texas Press, 1981); Roger Olien and Diana Davids Olien, *Oil Booms: Social Change in Five Texas Towns* (Lincoln: University of Nebraska Press, 1982); Dean S. Rugg and Donald C. Rundquist, "Urbanization in the Great Plains: Trends and Prospects," in Merlin P. Lawson and Maurice E. Baker, eds., *The Great Plains: Perspectives and Prospects* (Lincoln: University of Nebraska Press, 1981); Abbott, *New Urban America*; Bernard and Rice, *Sunbelt Cities*; Luckingham, *The Urban Southwest*; Wiley and Gottlieb, *Empires in the Sun*.

17. Donald Meinig, *Imperial Texas: An Interpretive Essay in Cultural Geography* (Austin: University of Texas Press, 1969); Rupert Vance and Sara Smith, "Metropolitan Dominance and Integration," in Rupert Vance and Nicholas Demerath, eds., *The Urban South* (Chapel Hill: University of North Carolina Press, 1954), 114–34.

18. U.S. Geological Survey, *National Atlas of the United States* (Washington: Government Printing Office, 1970), 227; Daniel J. Elazar, "Political Culture on the Plains," *Western Historical Quarterly* 11 (July 1980): 261–83; John F. Rooney, Jr., Wilbur Zelinsky, and Dean R. Louder, *This Remarkable Continent: An Atlas of United States and Canadian Society and Culture* (College Station: Texas A&M University Press, 1982), 107, 126, 188, 209, 239.

19. Rodman Paul, *Mining Frontiers of the Far West, 1848–1880* (New York: Holt, Rinehart, Winston, 1963); Gilman Ostrander, *Nevada: The Great Rotten Borough, 1859–1964* (New York: Alfred A. Knopf, 1966); Raymond Gastil, *Cultural Regions of the United States* (Seattle: University of Washington Press, 1975).

20. Geological Survey, *National Atlas*, 227; Rooney, Zelinsky, and Louder, eds., *Remarkable Continent*, 107, 289.

21. For example, see Mildred Hartsough, *The Twin Cities as a Metropolitan Market* (Minneapolis: University of Minnesota Studies in Social Science, No. 18, 1925).

22. Growth of the wholesaling and distribution functions of Los Angeles and Dallas provides an example of this change. J. Dennis Lord, "Shifts in the Wholesale Trade Status of United States Metropolitan Areas," *Professional Geographer* 36 (February 1984): 51–63.

23. The same explanatory model for the rise of the Sunbelt is suggested in Alfred Watkins and David Perry, "Regional Change and the Impact of Uneven Urban Development," in Perry and Watkins, eds., *Sunbelt Cities*, 19–54, and in Mollenkopf, *Contested City*, 26–41, 232–42.

24. James L. Clayton, "The Impact of the Cold War on the Economies of California and Utah, 1946–1965," *Pacific Historical Review* 36 (November 1967): 449–73.

25. U.S. Office of Personnel Management, *Federal Civilian Labor Force Statis-*

tics: Annual Report of Employment by Geographic Area, December 31, 1980 (Washington: Government Printing Office, 1981); James Anderson, *Bankrupting American Cities* (Lansing, MI: Employment Research Associates, 1982); Clyde E. Browning, "The Effect of Federal Spending on Regional Development," *Texas Business Review* 55 (September-October 1981): 214.

26. Gilbert S. Guinn, "A Different Frontier: Aviation, the Army Air Force, and the Evolution of the Sunshine Belt," *Aerospace Historian* 29 (March 1982): 34–45; James Eastman, "Location and Growth of Tinker Air Force Base and Oklahoma City Air Material Area," *Chronicles of Oklahoma* 50 (Autumn 1972): 326–46; Leonard J. Arrington and Archer L. Durham, "Anchors Aweigh in Utah: The U.S. Naval Supply Depot at Clearfield, 1942–62," *Utah Historical Quarterly* 31 (September 1963): 109–26; Leonard J. Arrington, Thomas G. Alexander, and Eugene H. Erb, Jr., "Utah's Biggest Business: Ogden Air Material Area at Hill Air Force Base," *Utah Historical Quarterly* 33 (Winter 1965): 9–33; Thomas G. Alexander, "Ogden: A Federal Colony in Utah," *Utah Historical Quarterly* 47 (Summer 1979): 291–309.

27. William Glenn Cunningham, *The Aircraft Industry: A Study in Industrial Location* (Los Angeles: Lorrin L. Morrison, 1951); Martin Schiesl, "Airplanes to Aerospace: Defense Spending and Economic Growth in the Los Angeles Region, 1945–60," in Lotchin, ed., *Martial Metropolis*, 135–50; David L. Clark, "Improbable Los Angeles," in Bernard and Rice, eds., *Sunbelt Cities*, 282–88; Clayton, "Cold War"; Stephen B. Oates, "NASA's Manned Spacecraft Center at Houston, Texas," *Southwestern Historical Quarterly* 67 (January 1964): 350–75; Amy Glasmeier, "Innovative Manufacturing Industries: Spatial Incidence in the United States," in Manuel Castells, ed., *High Technology, Space, and Society* (Beverly Hills: Sage Publications, 1985), 55–80.

28. Richard Riche, Daniel Hecker, and John Burgan, "High Technology Today and Tomorrow," *Monthly Labor Review* 106 (November 1983): 50–59.

29. Edward J. Malecki, "Federal R and D Spending in the United States of America: Some Impacts on Metropolitan Economies," *Regional Studies* 16 (February 1982): 19–35, and "High Technology and Local Economic Development," *Journal of the Association of American Planners* 50 (Summer 1984): 267; Annalee Saxenian, "Silicon Valley and Route 128: Regional Prototypes or Historic Exceptions," in Castells, ed., *High Technology*, 81–105.

30. Bryant Robey, "America's Asians," *American Demographics* 7 (May 1985): 22–29.

31. Ronald P. Wilder, "Foreign Trade and the Increasing Importance of Southern Ports," *Texas Business Review* 55 (May-June 1981): 96.

32. U.S. Bureau of the Census, *Highlights of U.S. Export and Import Trade*, monthly series.

33. Marilyn Sibley, *The Port of Houston: A History* (Austin: University of Texas Press, 1968); Padraic Burke, *A History of the Port of Seattle* (Seattle: Port of Seattle, 1976); James H. Hitchman, "The Bellingham Port Commission, 1920–1970," *Journal of the West* 20 (July 1981): 57–64.

34. Richard W. Barsness, "Maritime Activity and Port Development in the United States since 1900: A Survey," *Journal of Transport History* 11 (February 1974): 174–79.

35. C. Taylor Barnes and Curtis C. Roseman, "The Effect of Military Retirement on Population Redistribution," *Texas Business Review* 55 (May-June 1981): 100–104.

36. Perry Kaufman, "City Boosters, Las Vegas Style," *Journal of the West* 13 (1974): 46–60; Mark S. Foster, "Colorado's Defeat of the 1976 Winter Olympics," *The Colorado Magazine* 53 (Spring 1976): 163–86; Bryan H. Farrell, *Hawaii: The Legend that Sells* (Honolulu: University Press of Hawaii, 1982).

37. For examples, see the brief discussion of airport development in Konig, "Phoenix," and Dennis Judd's discussion of the national convention business in *The Politics of American Cities: Private Power and Public Responsibility* (Boston: Little, Brown, 1979), 373–83.

38. Wilbur Thompson, *A Preface to Urban Economics* (Baltimore: The Johns Hopkins Press, 1965), 21–24, develops the idea of an urban "size ratchet" through which growth itself induces further growth. "Import substitution" as the engine of urban growth is the central theme of Jane Jacobs, *The Economy of Cities* (New York: Random House, 1969).

39. John D. Garwood, "An Analysis of Postwar Industrial Migration to Utah and Colorado," *Economic Geography* 29 (January 1953): 79–88; Mel Scott, *Metropolitan Los Angeles* (Los Angeles: The Haynes Foundation, 1949), 40; Pomeroy, *Pacific Slope*, 300–302; Calvin B. Hoover and B. U. Ratchford, *Economic Resources and Policies of the South* (New York: Macmillan Co., 1951), 130–32.

40. Lord, "Wholesale Trade."

41. Office of Personnel Management, *Federal Civilian Labor Force Statistics.*

42. R. Keith Semple, "Recent Trends in the Spatial Concentration of Corporate Headquarters," *Economic Geography* 49 (October 1973): 309–18; Stanley C. Vance, "The Sunshine Belt: A New Home for Corporate Headquarters," *Review of Regional Economics and Business* (April 1977): 5–10; John Rees, "Manufacturing Headquarters in a Post-Industrial Urban Context," *Economic Geography* 54 (1978): 337–54.

43. Charles Gates, "Boom Stages in American Expansion," *Business History Review* 33 (Spring 1959): 32–42.

44. Allan Pred, *City Systems in Advanced Economies* (New York: John Wiley, 1977), 127–66.

45. Thierry J. Noyelle and Thomas M. Stanback, Jr., *The Economic Transformation of American Cities* (Totowa, NJ: Rowman and Allanheld, 1983).

46. Hollon touches briefly on Great Falls as an emerging metropolis in *Great American Desert*, 229. Comments on Grand Junction are based on the author's interviews with local economic development officials, April 1985. Coos Bay is discussed in William G. Robbins, "Timber Town: Market Economics in Coos Bay, Oregon, 1850 to the Present," *Pacific Northwest Quarterly* 75 (October 1984): 146–55.

47. John Mollenkopf, *Contested City*, 139–212. Bradley R. Rice and Richard M. Bernard, "Introduction," in Bernard and Rice, eds., *Sunbelt Cities*, 20–26; Abbott, *New Urban America*, 120–256. Also see Trounstine and Christensen, *Movers and Shakers*, 184–93.

48. Most studies using aggregate data deal with the 1960s and 1970s, but it

would be possible to generate counterparts for the 1940s and 1950s using readily available data sources.

49. Roger Lotchin's articles on the "metropolitan-military complex" include "The City and the Sword: San Francisco and the Rise of the Metropolitan Military Complex, 1919–41," *Journal of American History* 65 (March 1979): 996–1020; "The Darwinian City: The Politics of Urbanization in San Francisco between the World Wars," *Pacific Historical Review* 48 (August 1979): 357–81; and "City and Sword in Metropolitan California, 1919–1941," *Urbanism Past and Present* 7 (Summer-Fall 1982): 1–16.

50. Mollenkopf, *Contested City;* Abbott, *New Urban America;* Wiley and Gottlieb, *Empires in the Sun.*

51. For examples, see Duane Smith, *Rocky Mountain Mining Camps: The Urban Frontier* (Bloomington: Indiana University Press, 1967); Robert R. Dykstra, *The Cattle Towns* (New York: Alfred A. Knopf, 1968); Lawrence H. Larsen, *The Urban West at the End of the Frontier* (Lawrence: The Regents Press of Kansas, 1978); John Reps, *Cities of the American West* (Princeton: Princeton University Press, 1979); Gunther Barth, *Instant Cities* (New York: Oxford University Press, 1975); Earl Pomeroy, "The Urban Frontier of the Far West," in John G. Clark, ed., *The Frontier Challenge: Responses to the Trans-Mississippi West* (Lawrence: University Press of Kansas, 1971), 7–29.

52. Carey McWilliams, "Introduction," in West, *Rocky Mountain Cities,* 9; Rugg and Rundquist, "Urbanization in the Great Plains," 228. These communities are "significant local business centers" in the commonly used Rand-McNally classification of market areas.

53. Robert E. Park and Charles Newcomb, "Newspaper Circulation and Metropolitan Regions," in Roderick McKenzie, *The Metropolitan Community* (New York: McGraw-Hill, 1933); John Borchert, "America's Changing Metropolitan Regions," *Annals of the Association of American Geographers* 62 (June 1972): 352–73. For WW II migration, see President's Committee for Congested Production Areas: Final Report (December 1944).

54. See Chilton Williamson, *Roughnecking It: Or, Life in the Overthrust* (New York: Simon and Schuster, 1982), on life in Kemmerer.

55. Richard White, *Land Use, Environment and Social Change: The Shaping of Island County, Washington* (Seattle: University of Washington Press, 1980).

56. Chandler Davidson and George Korbel, "At Large Elections and Minority Group Representation," *Journal of Politics* 43 (November 1981): 982–1005; Delbert Taebel, "Minority Representation on City Councils: The Impact of Structure on Blacks and Hispanics," *Social Science Quarterly* 59 (June 1978): 142–52.

57. Robert Fisher, *Let the People Decide: Neighborhood Organizing in America* (Boston: Twayne Publishers, 1984), 80–89, on Houston civic clubs, and Carl Abbott, *Portland,* 183–206, on Portland neighborhood associations.

58. To date, many historical studies have stopped with the 1940s, leaving geographers and sociologists to explore such issues as residential patterns, business entrepreneurship, and community institutions. Examples that provide historical as well as current perspectives includes James P. Allen, "Recent Immigration from the Philippines and Filipino Communities in the United States," *Geograph-*

ical Review 67 (April 1977): 195–208; and Edna Bonancich and John Modell, *The Economic Basis of Ethnic Solidarity: A Study of Japanese Americans* (Berkeley: University of California Press, 1980).

59. Noyelle and Stanback, *Economic Transformation.*

60. The distinction in the various social sciences between the external relations of cities and their internal structure and characteristics can be found in Richard Wade, "An Agenda for Urban History," in Herbert Bass, ed., *The State of American History* (Chicago: Quadrangle, 1970), and in the following essays in Philip Hauser and Leo Schnore, eds., *The Study of Urbanization* (New York: John Wiley and Sons, 1965); Harold Mayer, "A Survey of Urban Geography," 81–114, Wallace Sayre and Nelson Polsby, "American Political Science," 115–56, and Wilbur Thompson, "Urban Economic Growth and Development in a National System of Cities," 431–80.

3

Western Women

THE TWENTIETH-CENTURY EXPERIENCE

Karen Anderson

The metropolitanization of the West described by Abbott had such far-ranging effects that it transformed most aspects of life in the region, including the relationships between men and women. If the nineteenth-century frontier had a repressive impact on women in a male-dominated society, then the twentieth-century western city swept away some of the subordination and opened a wide range of new opportunities and life styles. In her essay about women's roles in the building of the West since 1890, Karen Anderson urges new methods of approach to the subject and suggests that they can provide new insights on other aspects of western development such as the emergence of a consumer society and the broker state.

In 1964 historian David Potter noted the androcentrism of Frederick Jackson Turner's frontier thesis, speculating that "for American women . . . opportunity began pretty much where the frontier left off." According to Potter, the modern city had provided the American woman with access to independent employment so that "the historic basis for her subordination had been swept away." More recently, women's historians have elaborated Potter's critique of Turner, noting that the Turnerian emphasis on individualism and public sphere activities has not provided a perspective that encouraged scholars to focus on women or one that elucidated women's experiences. In the absence of an appropriate framework, historians have often resorted to gender stereotypes that distort both women's and men's lives in the West. The Turnerian tendency to depict men as self-reliant individualists contrasts dramatically with the fact that feminine stereotypes often favored by historians inevitably see women in relation to men—whether as helpmeets or as harlots with a heart of gold. Taken as a whole, western history seems to be claiming that those relationships central to women's lives were tangential to men's—an assumption that reveals more about modern gender politics than about the western experience.[1]

More recent works, which concentrate on the modern period and focus especially on the West's economic and political development, have also failed to use gender as an analytical category or to take seriously women's experiences and activities. Carl Abbott's work on Sunbelt cities (which also looks at the South) provides no analysis of women's roles in metropolitan politics or of the implications of suburban independence for women's lives and status. Gerald Nash indicates the importance of women's history to an understanding of the West in the twentieth century, but omits it from his own recent study with the claim that the topic deserves a full-length monograph of its own. Although true enough, the absence of such a work does not justify the exclusion of women (or other social groups) from any book that claims to be comprehensive.[2]

This myopia persists even though several women's historians have offered alternative perspectives for understanding women's place in western history. Susan Armitage, for example, has provided a timely reminder that gender affects the everyday experiences of women and men in many ways. As a result, scholars cannot understand values, social relations, or institutional development in the West unless they take gender seriously as an analytical category. Neither can they adequately explain the formation of a western regional identity. Armitage's call for attention to the dynamics of a multicultural society echoes that of Joan Jensen and Darlis Miller in their important review essay of 1980. As they pointed out, a multiethnic perspective not only allows the historian to examine the complexities and diversities of western women's experiences, but also generates new insights on major topics in western history, including migration, crosscultural relations, and the development of the western political economy.[3]

Jensen and Miller also observed that gender has been central to the process of urbanization, as many western cities attracted disproportionate numbers of women. Did this occur, as Potter surmised, because the cities provided women economic opportunities and thus enabled them to secure access to resources, personal autonomy, and social power? Have the economic trends of the twentieth century operated to enhance women's status and power or merely to alter the mechanisms for women's subordination? Has the West differed from the rest of the nation in the historical evolution of its gender relations in the modern period?[4]

Although scholars have examined various aspects of these questions, the issues they raise have not received systematic attention. The historical literature on women in the twentieth-century West is, in fact, surprisingly sparse. As a result, no debates comparable to those engaging nineteenth-century western historians have emerged. This essay will offer suggestions for conceptualizing twentieth-century western women's history—focusing especially on the urban experience—and discuss those works whose information and analysis exemplify the possibilities in this field of historical inquiry. In order to do so, I will also survey the most important frameworks from other disciplines and indicate their utility for historians.

Scholars have suggested various perspectives on the implications of urbanization for women. Some have claimed that cities function as places of economic and social opportunity for women, while others have stressed the reproduction of structures of constraint in women's lives in an urban context. Partisans of the former approach focus on the greater variety of jobs and the higher pay levels offered to women in the cities compared to those of small towns and rural areas and the erosion of control over women by the institutions of church, family, and community. Proponents of the latter view tend to emphasize the continuation of the patriarchal form of household organization and the controls exercised by capitalist modes of production in the modern city.[5]

Such debates, however, obscure the diversities of women's experiences in American cities and elide women's agency in affecting their lives and shaping the urban environment. At its worst, each of these perspectives tends to view women as pawns at the mercy of forces they neither control, contest, nor understand. At their best, these interpretations allow one to understand cities as the intersections of various systems of power—based on *gender,* class, race, ethnicity, and region. The spatial division of function and property by and within cities allocates power and resources differentially to various social and economic groups. As a result, cities are contested terrain. Women have acted in various ways to claim the city as a place of empowerment for themselves, taking advantage of the very dynamism and diversity of cities to broaden their social power. As Laura Balbo has noted, women in industrial capitalist societies are "continuously caught between complying and resisting." Their resistance is sometimes individual and informal, sometimes in the form of aggregate behavior, and occasionally in the form of collective action to ameliorate or overturn the conditions that limit them. Whatever their forms, women's political actions are often most visible and successful in an urban setting.[6]

When assessing the influence of region on women, historians of the West must consider those attributes that make the West distinctive in its development. This approach involves an examination of the relationship between urban policies and structures and the economic bases of western cities; an attention to the demographics of western populations, including the importance of large migrations from Mexico and, more recently, Asia; the specific impact of technologies that have been particularly important in the West, including the automobile, air conditioning, and mass communications; the role of climate and topography; the metropolitan spread that has especially characterized the newer cities of the West; and the greater predominance of owner-occupied single family residences.[7]

Given the rise of the Sunbelt to economic and political power in recent decades, the West has perhaps become a locus for the shift into the post-industrial world. Analyzing that shift entails far more than tracing the regional movement of capital or investigating the effects of public policies on economic development. It requires a complex human story, one that relates the individual and family decisions regarding migration, work, residence, and public life to the political economy so as to reveal their interconnections. In such an enterprise, gender must become an essential explanatory variable, elucidating men's as well as women's experiences and providing a vantage point from which to examine historical processes more fully.

It is important to note, for example, that recent economic trends disproportionately involve the movement of capital to low-wage workers—especially women and minorities. Although the image of the new Sunbelt worker is an Anglo male engineer, that worker, in fact, is more likely to be a Hispanic woman in the rapidly expanding service sector or in low-wage production line jobs in computer-related enterprises or in traditional female-employing industries. In El Paso, for example, 90 percent of the growth in manufacturing employment from 1954 to 1968 was accounted for by expansion in the garment industry. In the "Silicon Valley" of Santa Clara County, California, many manufacturing jobs in high-tech fields have been feminized, with a corresponding decline in the relative wages paid to the workers involved.[8]

Such dynamics obviously relate to public policies in ways that do not usually draw the attention of scholars. They are predicated on the easy availability of immigrant workers (including illegals) and on the retention of welfare policies that make substandard wages more appealing than even more meager welfare allotments. The development of the Border Industries Program and the commuter worker program has accelerated this process and encouraged the migration of large numbers of Mexican women to the border area, thus ensuring the existence of a substantial labor surplus. The presence of many illegal aliens, especially in garment-making and service jobs in the Southwest, has made enforcement of minimum wage and other worker protections difficult and has depressed wages for many who are employed in this area.[9]

Although scholars must analyze social and economic dynamics, they should also take seriously the archetypal vision of the West as a masculine place. The lone vigilante figure who is "unfit" for and outside of the law or family life represents and encourages a denial of dependence on others that often entails an evasion of social responsibility as well. Ironically, then, the region of the country that has arguably been the most dependent on federal largesse and law for its economic development has become the symbol for self-made manhood and individualistic mobility tales. Whether this ironic situation has affected women's access to resources (including paid work, welfare, and child support and alimony) or has affected women's and men's political values remains unclear. That regional imagery has been important in modern gender ideology is quite obvious.[10]

Did these regional patterns and imagery in fact create a distinctive gender system in western cities, or is it more appropriate to stress the national and international dimensions of women's roles and statuses in the West? Scholarly answers to this question must of necessity be very tentative at this stage. They will vary, depending on the time, place, and groups under study. Moreover, the scholar's choice of theoretical perspectives will affect the barometers of status and power deemed significant and focus the inquiry on particular institutions, groups, and structural dynamics. Whatever interpretive frameworks are adopted, they must assess gender relations as a system of power that affects all women. As feminist scholars have noted, gender interacts with other systems of stratification to produce differences in status, roles, and material circumstances among women. Historical inquiry should account for both the commonalities and diversities of the female experience.[11]

All aspects of urban politics and urban structures derive from and affect the politics of gender—housing policies create the central workplace for many women; zoning, transportation, and development policies affect women's abilities to balance their responsibilities as workers, consumers, mothers, wives, and friends; welfare, educational, and other policies affect women's ability to perform effectively as mediators between the goods and services provided by the market and the state and the historically dynamic needs of their families.[12]

Within cities, divisions of power and resources are often expressed in the built environment. The central cities with their highrise monuments to patriarchal, capitalist power contrast with the suburbs whose privatized, enclosed spaces enscribe "woman's place." For those women who live on the margins of the system in the housing projects and ghettos of the inner cities, their occupancy of a place where sexuality is public and commercialized and where domesticity and maternity cannot be organized by middleclass standards leaves them vulnerable and exploited—visible symbols of the other countenance of Janus-faced womanhood. These patterns developed over time, a product of economic development patterns and political conflicts over zoning, race and class-based segregation, law enforcement, and related issues. Periods of rapid population growth and dramatic changes in economic structures, such as during World War II, might profitably be investigated for their impact on city landscapes and the gender implications of such changes.[13]

In an advanced, industrial society, women and men still do different kinds and amounts of work within the household and in the paid economy. The unequal allocation of power, money, and responsibility that derives from this gender division of labor constitutes the lynchpin for women's oppression in the modern world. As historians we must describe and analyze the means whereby gender stratification in occupation and pay is reproduced in the West and discuss the implications of these patterns for women of the region. The efforts of western politicians and economic planners to lure particular kinds of businesses to their localities has, in many cases, encouraged occupational segmentation, an important topic for further scholarly study. To what extent, for example, did the successful efforts of many western cities to lure defense establishments and industries enhance or limit women's economic position in their local economies? As has been indicated, western economies are particularly dependent on service and clerical workers. How have they managed to secure the tractable, low-wage labor force (largely female) required by these sectors?

The study of the West also offers the possibility for a careful examination of the dynamics of segmentation in a multicultural society entering the postindustrial era. Does the presence of large numbers of racial or ethnic men lower Anglo women's participation in certain service categories? Albert Szymanski found such patterns in the South; whether they have been replicated in the West or diminish in their importance in the latter region remains unclear. Kristin Nelson has documented the use of office location decisions in the San Francisco Bay Area as the means whereby employers shape the class, gender, and racial composition of their labor force. Her data reveals that these companies had relocated back office clerical work (which does not require much direct contact with customers or managers) to the suburbs. The concentration of large numbers of married, Anglo, middle class women in these areas enabled employers to avoid minority women and female heads of households whom they presumed to be less qualified and less manipulable. Is this pattern unusual? Is the West pioneering in new forms of occupational segregation? How does this possible change relate to prior patterns of segmentation and de-skilling in office work and to the integration of Hispanic and black women into some clerical categories in the period since World War II?[14]

A more complex understanding of the processes of segmentation will enable us to discuss more fully the sources of rising female labor force rates and their variations on the basis of class and ethnicity. As Patricia

Zavella has suggested, cultural interpretations of Chicanas' work patterns have to be qualified or rejected when the range and accessibility of jobs to women of various groups is taken into account. Not surprisingly, the development of aspirations in an industrial society is closely related to the structure of opportunity, as well as other variables. Urban historians can aid in this process by paying more attention to employer policies and public policies in the areas of transportation, commercial services, housing, day care, and the availability of birth control services. Labor force patterns in urban settings derive from a complex constellation of forces.[15]

Possibly patterns of occupational stratification in the West differ from those in other regions in some particulars. Micaela di Leonardo's study of Italian-American women in the San Francisco Bay area found that the labor force rates of women there were higher than those in Boston in 1950 and 1970 and that the level of ethnic stratification among European immigrants was less pronounced among women and men. Di Leonardo concludes that these white ethnic women achieved their greater mobility in part because Hispanic women occupied the lowest rungs, although she provides no data on Mexican-origin women in her tables and supplies no details on the economic structures of the area. As a result, it is impossible to determine whether differences in developmental dynamics, demographics, or the interactions between them might account for regional variations. To conclude from this study alone that the West constituted some kind of Promised Land (even if only for Anglo women) would be, to say the least, premature.[16]

A study by David Lee and Ronald Schultz provides more complete and general data by region to enable one to generalize with more confidence about some of the major barometers of women's status. When these authors measured income, education, and occupational distribution, they found that women advance their status with urbanization and that the West and Northeast offer women the greatest opportunities for work and education. The data also suggest, however, that the move to the cities and the West is even more beneficial to men, whose work choices and pay levels increase even more rapidly than is the case for women. Thus, women in western cities compare favorably in the circumstances of their lives to women elsewhere, but find that their status relative to men deteriorates with urbanization and western residence. This study does not indicate, however, whether women's occupational advantages in the West and Northeast derive from a different distribution of women workers within the female labor force, with more concentrated in white collar work, or from gains in previously male-dominated fields. My work on Seattle during World War II suggests that the former is more likely to be the case. That the Lee and Schultz study did not examine important forms of stratification other than gender obscured the fact that some groups of women benefit a great deal more than others in growth regions. Whether the West will remain a place where women's educational and occupational opportunities exceed those in some other regions, given that economic growth in the Sunbelt has been concentrated in very low-wage jobs in the female labor force, remains to be seen.[17]

Lee and Schultz also found that measures of absolute and relative status for women varied enormously within the West "with the largest concentration of below-average scores found in the Rocky Mountain and intermontane states of the West." They separated this area from their western data and labelled it the "Mormon Region." Moreover, public opinion poll data from the 1970s confirm the importance of this intraregional pattern, revealing that the plains and mountain states registered the lowest approval ratings in the nation for women working. The Pacific Coast states showed somewhat more favorable attitudes for the woman worker. This reminds us that the West is a diverse region that varies by religion, economic structures, and demographic composition; generalizations will have to be qualified and explicated so that such differences can be taken into account.[18]

As scholars of women's studies have long noted, the organization of work in the household and its relationship to other institutions and processes affect women's status and roles in complex ways. According to Dolores Hayden, contemporary Americans have institutionalized nineteenth-century ideals regarding the home as haven and the homemaker-breadwinner division of labor in the urban structures of the twentieth century. This arrangement derived from the dynamics of the American consumer society in its early stages. In order to expand the consumer market, American enterprises encouraged conspicuous display within the household and redundancy in purchasing for domestic activities (every woman uses her own washing machine, rather than a laundry in the neighborhood). The assumption that every household would include a homemaker with sufficient time to dedicate to consumption and to traversing the distances her various roles required was expressed in suburbanization itself. These arrangements, however, have become increasingly dysfunctional as many women have redefined their place in the world of consumption. The process of redefinition has included a marked shift into paid labor outside the home on the part of many women, who have redefined material need for their families in ways that mandate that shift. Even for those women who have remained homemakers, changes in the organization of consumption have increased the distances women must travel to do their shopping and have diminished the availability of delivery services.[19]

Because western cities grew later than those elsewhere in the nation, the spatial division between home (a workplace for virtually all women) and public institutions (whether their functions are economic, political, or recreational) is especially great. Moreover, the heavier reliance on the automobile, as opposed to public transportation systems, affects women in many ways. At this point, it is not even known what women's roles were in creating these patterns or exactly how these western patterns affected various groups of women in the past. Further investigation may show that women acted to support suburbanization and automobile transportation systems to create accessible and secure places for themselves in an urban world. As Virginia Scharff has suggested, women may have preferred automobiles in the 1910s and 1920s because they provided easy access to various forms of community activities "free from the surveillance of nosy neighbors" and because they enabled middle class women to carry out their multiple household tasks with greater convenience than public transportation. For the many carless women in the automobile culture of the West, however, the lack of mobility affected all aspects of their roles and status.[20]

Some middle class women may have found the movement to the suburbs initially appealing. The greater space and safety of these residences ease aspects of women's mothering role. When family quarters are less congested and children can play more safely outside, the emotional drain and work attendant to domesticity is eased. Moreover, the status-enhancing dimensions of middle class women's work is facilitated in various ways by suburban living. The point is not to romanticize suburban living, but rather to indicate that we cannot conclude that the suburban woman is the modern equivalent of the nineteenth-century frontier woman dragged West against her will and contrary to her best interests.[21]

Under certain historical circumstances, some women have promoted the organization of public spaces on the basis of gender. Galen Cranz's work on women's access to public parks indicates a shift from a late Victorian stress on shared access to recreational areas (with the understanding that women were to come with male escorts) to a gender-segregated system during the Progressive era. This change, which was legitimated partly as a means of ensuring safety, could represent a mechanism whereby women sought access to public recreation without the necessity of male companions and with less possibility of their being harassed as trespassers in men's public urban space. As Cranz makes clear, gender segregation had the effect of reinforcing traditional role divisions since men were excluded from "mother's corners" and such places as the Children's Building in San Francisco's Golden Gate Park.[22]

It is important also to consider the effect of marital status on women's experiences in the urban environment. For single women, cities have offered the possibility to create more autonomous lives. As Joanne Meyerowitz has shown in her study of Chicago, workingclass single women devised a variety of strategies to enable them to live outside of families despite the very low wages these women generally received. As the wages of women have increased over time, the material basis for new patterns has improved, although restrictive cultural expectations have sometimes operated to diminish the effects of labor force gains. During the 1950s, for example, cultural pressures on women to marry at a younger age reduced the number of single women in the society and, obviously, in the economy. So improvements in the numbers of white collar jobs available for women workers and a general context of economic growth did not promote dramatic alterations in women's access to power or their public activities and status.[23]

For middle class women reformers, the city has also provided a locus for associational activities and political activism. Whether regional differences in values or institutional structures made the West distinctive is not clear from the available scholarship. If Joseph Tripp's study of the campaign for a minimum wage law in Washington is any indication, the goals and strategies of women reformers in the West did not differ significantly from those in the East. The small number of women and child earners in the state of Washington may have made their reform goals easier to accomplish, however. The Washington State Federation of Women's Clubs, which was involved in politics by 1903, was especially important in lobbying the minimum wage law to an impressive victory. When the Industrial Welfare Commission created by that law was appointed, the first three members were women.[24]

Ronald Schaffer's evidence from the California woman suffrage movement indicates that the ideological appeals and organizational strategies employed in California mirrored those of the East, although he does not explicitly point this out or ask why suffragists succeeded earlier in that western state than in the East. His conclusion that male suffragists were less likely to use what he calls "personal feminism," the equivalent of Aileen Kraditor's argument from justice, and more likely to appeal to the idea of women as civilizers does enhance our understanding of the gender dimension of suffrage activism. On the other hand, his conclusion that rural women were harder to organize as suffragists, while hardly surprising, confirms the importance of cities in the leadership of the movement for the vote. According to Eleanor Flexner, however, the rural and small town vote accounted for the referendum victory in California.[25]

Ruth Barnes Moynihan's biography of Abigail Scott Duniway, pioneer suffragist of Oregon, reflects the influence of Frederick Jackson Turner among some women's historians. According to Moynihan, Duniway's frontier experiences and heritage accounted for the personal qualities that made her such an indefatigable fighter for her cause. Moynihan's study, however, provides no meaningful interpretation of the larger social and political bases for the eventual triumph of suffrage in Oregon in 1912. Although Moynihan states that Portland voters more than accounted for the defeat of the state referendum of 1906 on woman suffrage, she does not discuss the role of cities in the final victory. Neither does she place the struggle in the larger context of Oregon electoral politics, except to indicate the divisive effect of the temperance issue.[26]

On the other hand, Joan Jensen's work on the New Mexico suffrage movement more adequately documents the complexities of suffrage activism, in a multiethnic state. Not until the creation of an associational base in urban women's clubs did New Mexico women develop an effective suffrage movement. Their task was made enormously more difficult by the Constitution of 1910, which required that amendments to its suffrage provisions had to pass with a three-fourths vote. This measure was initially included in the Constitution in order that the enfranchisement of Hispanic males be protected from future Anglo maneuvers. This stipulation made state suffrage for women virtually impossible to secure and thus focused New Mexico suffragists' efforts on the campaign for a national amendment. Recognizing that their political base was almost entirely Anglo, New Mexico suffrage leaders sought the support of Hispanic women. As a result, Adelina Otero-Warren assumed a leadership position in the movement and became especially important to the success of the cause in the next few years. As was true of Anglos, Hispanic women in New Mexico tended to enter politics through family political networks.[27]

After women secured the vote in the West, their political roles were no more dramatically altered than elsewhere in the country. Many women's charitable, cultural, and reform associations were formed in western states prior to women's enfranchisement, and it is difficult to assess whether women activists became more effective in their goals as a result of suffrage. Although suffragists and their supporters in these states claimed that women voters helped to secure gambling prohibitions and other morals legislation, labor regulations, improved property rights for women, and the like, such assertions are hard to verify. The same proponents of suffrage were also likely to stress the "conservative character" of equal suffrage and to reassure eastern critics that women voted as their husbands did.[28]

The West's pioneering role in the extension of suffrage to women was not a prelude to the removal of other barriers to effective political power. When Wyoming women took seriously their "civilizer" role in jury duty in the immediate aftermath of suffrage, male legislators rethought their enthusiasm for women's moral vigilance and barred them from the jury box from 1871 to 1950. Although some states seem to have reserved the office of superintendent of public instruction for women (at least during the Progressive era), most western states held the line at according women substantial access to state legislatures, office holding, or the informal channels of power in state and local politics.[29]

As a result, women's political activism remained centered in various volunteer agencies and organizations, ranging from the charitable to the radical. In most cases, however, women's civic activities have served to provide important services to their community without dramatically altering social relations. During World War II, for example, women volunteers in Seattle contributed essential labor so that serious crises in housing, transportation, day care, civil defense, rationing, and in other areas could be managed. The understandable focus on war-related concerns probably diminished the ability of women activists to promote long-term improvements in women's status. In the postwar period, women's volunteerism may have been channeled even more directly into support for institutions whose policies and goals were defined by and for men. Cheryl Malone's study of hospital volunteers in Arizona in the postwar period demonstrates the extent to which their work derived from and reproduced existing class and gender relations. Women volunteers, for example, often did the same work that women service workers performed, indirectly undercutting the wage scales of those women.[30]

As was true elsewhere, western cities have also served as the basis for some forms of worker resistance to corporate control. Because scholarship in labor and community history has focused almost entirely on the East, our understanding of women's labor activism in the West is limited. Chicana history, however, has focused to a considerable extent on workplace politics. Although the intersection of women's culture and ethnic culture is often assumed to be conservative, this scholarship indicates that it has often served as a grounding for labor radicalism in the food processing and garment industries of the Southwest. For example, Vicki Ruiz's study of the United Cannery, Agricultural, Packing, and Allied Workers (UCAPAWA) during the 1930s and 1940s found that Chicanas were critical to that union's initial successes, as local leaders and as rank and file members. In addition, George Green's study of union activism among El Paso garment workers revealed that religious culture played an important role in symbolizing and promoting political stands taken in the workplace. Louise Lamphere's study of women workers in Albuquerque has demonstrated that women's culture is sometimes used by management to coopt workers and secure their loyalty to company practices and at other times provides women workers with an autonomous basis for challenges to corporate power.[31]

In recent decades, working class women and women who head families have faced increasing difficulties created by the structures of cities, especially if they live in areas of urban sprawl and low population density. The dispersion of commercial services, especially day care facilities, creates spatial limits on women's abilities to secure paid employment. The inadequacies and costs of public transportation exacerbate the economic and social disabilities these women experience, whether they live within cities or in the suburbs. As housing costs have escalated in the last decade, the spatial limitations on women job-seekers have worsened. For many women, the urban experience has meant making seriously constrained choices between the requirements of their various roles. As breadwinners, they must find work that pays decently and struggle to keep housing, transportation, food, and other costs down. As mothers, they need good schools, convenient day care with quality service, and some support network to enable them to cope with the emotional and practical difficulties that role overload created. Historians examining the roots of these difficulties must pay attention to the effects of an uncritically supported developmental imperative in some western cities. To what extent did city planners and corporate leaders make zoning, housing, transportation, plant location, and other decisions that promoted the feminization of poverty?[32]

Whatever the political debates of the past, many women today find that changes in their status and roles have necessitated a new political agenda. Women's rising labor force rates, the increase in female-headed families, and the increased community activism of many women have made urban structures anachronistic. As Ann Markusen has indicated, the process of gentrification in central cities may represent an attempt to reverse the decisions of the past and secure a place in the cities for middle class professional couples. For the employed woman, the improved access to urban activities, offices, transportation systems, and commercial services is essential to her career development and her ability to manage her other responsibilities. Scholars might profitably explore the relationship between urban political structures and policies and the demography of urban residential patterns, paying careful attention to the gender dimension of these dynamics.[33]

The study of cities as they reflect and shape the social organization of sexuality, reproduction, and women's social lives offers rich possibilities for urban historians. As Diane Sands' work on abortion in Montana indicates, cities have long served as centers for abortion (and birth control) services. Using oral histories, court records, and newspaper accounts, she has documented an extensive and socially tolerated business in illegal abortions in the period before the legalization of abortion in 1973. That women went to cities other than their place of residence to obtain abortions indicates the surreptitious and potentially dangerous aspect of access to reproductive control at this time. That the anonymity of urban life constituted an important component of access signifies abortion's status as a commonplace but officially deviant behavior. A similar examination of the geography of birth control services might reveal the complex interplay between social control and social liberation. A historical study of the organization, locations, and policies of Planned Parenthood clinics, for example, would elucidate a great deal regarding the values and practices surrounding reproduction and sexuality as they vary by class, ethnicity, and gender.[34]

Some scholars have claimed that western cities offered women more social freedoms than did their eastern counterparts in the early years of urban development. Such conclusions, which rely on a few anecdotal accounts for their evidence, need to be verified or revised through more careful attention to the issue. Mary Murphy's research on prostitutes in Butte, Montana indicates that women's access to the streets was variable. In the red light districts, every woman on the streets was assumed to be a prostitute and her dress, demeanor, and other activities became a subject for scrutiny and regulation by public officials. The "respectable" women who lived and walked in other areas of the town had their access to public spaces protected by customs and laws that proscribed behaviors that might be construed as demeaning to women. City ordinances forbade, for example, "lewd and dissolute female persons" from "improper, profane, or obscene" conduct within the sight or hearing of women (a category that seemingly excluded the former group). The cultural barriers between "good" and "bad" women were thus maintained and signified spatially and behaviorally. No such dichotomous view of manhood, however, entered the law books or social practice. According to Paula Petrik, prostitutes opened up spaces to twentieth-century women by confining "vice" to limited areas. As a result, "respectable women profited over the years from other women's willingness to trade in their bodies."[35]

Lewis Erenberg, in his work on New York City, has speculated that the increasing segregation of neighborhoods and social institutions on the basis of class, race, and ethnicity in American cities in the twentieth century has enabled middle class, white women to have more spatial access to the city by creating places and settings (where dress and other social requirements insure the "right" clientele) where women can engage in previously proscribed activities in public places. Whether this pattern is general or limited to the early twentieth century or whether different regional and local systems of the spatial control of sexual and social activities have developed has not yet been investigated.[36]

Women's spatial access and social activities in western cities also varied by class and ethnicity. Some of the literature on Mexican-American women suggests that traditional mores and apprehensiveness regarding Anglo, Protestant control of some institutions constrained women in their use of urban recreational and cultural resources. Ruth Tuck, for example, noted that women who allowed their daughters to engage in many of the social activities commonly available to Anglo girls were accused of being "alcahuetas" (or female panderers) and exposing their daughters to moral peril. The changing urban milieu of western cities did pose a challenge to Mexican mothers who had to cope with different cultural meanings attached to various activities and behaviors and equip their daughters to cope with the ambiguities inherent in the situation.[37]

Examining the history of women's access to public spaces offers scholars especially exciting possibilities. Clearly, for example, streets are often contested territory. The mechanisms for marking certain places as masculine turf vary over time, but they include violence, verbal and sexual harassment, economic control, visual symbolism, ideological control, and formal and informal barriers to admission. Scholars might discover the links between law and convention as tools of social control in women's lives by using court records and other historical documents of rape and assault cases where women are victims. To what extent did women's presence in certain places mark them for victimization by the judicial process itself? Such an approach also places the "Victory girl" of World War II in a new perspective. As a woman who had challenged the distinction between the prostitute and the good woman, the "khacky-wacky" was identified not so much through her actual transgression of sexual mores but rather through her violation of spatial limitations that functioned to enforce those divisions. By her actions, she put the whole system of boundaries into question. No longer could one distinguish between public and private spaces, commercialized and noncommercialized sexuality, "free" and (implicitly) "unfree" women. For all the official repression, however, women probably experienced as much safe, unescorted access to urban activities during World War II as they have in modern America. As wartime circumstances threatened the economic and social foundations of women's subordination, however, concern for the containment of such liberative possibilities also developed. In this regard, the West was no different from the rest of the nation, although women may have been more resistant to efforts to reassert the double standard of morality there. D'Ann Campbell's study of 1943 poll data found that women in the Pacific Coast states were more secular and less concerned with regulating women's morality than women in other regions. Whether men's views on these issues differed by region is not known.[38]

Women have fought against these limitations in various ways over time. Women's repeated efforts to limit or eliminate prostitution also constitute attempts to make more urban areas safe and comfortable for the use of most women. Their fights for public recreational areas, for safety in the streets, and for the establishment of women's centers and buildings also constitute an important component of this struggle. Much of these efforts remains undocumented. In Arizona in the 1930s, women's clubs from across the state organized to fight the parole of convicted rapists from the state penitentiary. In more recent years, women have organized in a multitude of ways in order to combat crime, to challenge social inequality in all its forms, to improve the urban environment, and to ensure that cities serve the needs of all of their citizens.[39]

The historical work done so far indicates that western women have not differed substantially from women elsewhere in the nation in their labor force status, political rights and roles, or family roles and status. We have not studied the role of settlement houses, public interest lobbies, or women's clubs in western cities sufficiently to understand whether women's contributions to Progressive era politics in the West distinguished them from their eastern counterparts, but the initial evidence does not indicate any important differences. During the New Deal, western women's national political influence may have diminished, given the centrality of the Eleanor Roosevelt network to women's political access at this time. In terms of their workplace and family status, the experiences of urban western women have differed in some ways from national trends, but seem generally to have typified or anticipated national developments. Given these preliminary conclusions, it seems likely that western history will be changed more by the inclusion of gender than women's history will be altered by a new regional perspective, but each will profit by a more inclusive approach to its subject matter.[40]

Writing the history of women in the modern West requires methodological innovations and a rethinking of conventional paradigms. For those who are willing to take gender politics and feminist frameworks seriously, the field offers rich possibilities. Western women's history offers a vantage point for analyzing the most important trends of the modern era—the development of a postindustrial consumer society, the military-industrial complex, the postnuclear family, and the broker state of the twentieth century. Until historians examine these and other historical processes as they are experienced, shaped and perceived by women, however, their conclusions will remain partial, simplistic, and distorted.

Notes

1. For the critique of the frameworks of Frederick Jackson Turner as they relate to women, see David M. Potter, "American Women and the American Character," in *The Woman Question in American History*, ed., Barbara Welter (Hinsdale, Ill.: The Dryden Press, 1973), 117–32; Joan M. Jensen and Darlis A. Miller, "The Gentle Tamers Revisited: New Approaches to the History of Women in the

American West," *Pacific Historical Review* 49 (May 1980): 173–213; Sandra L. Myres, "Women in the West," in Michael P. Malone, ed., *Historians and the American West* (Lincoln: University of Nebraska Press, 1983), 369–86; Susan Armitage, "Women and Men in Western History: A Stereoptical Vision," *Western Historical Quarterly* (October 1985): 381–91. Paula Petrik, however, sees promise in Turnerian frameworks. Paula Petrik, "The Gentle Tamers in Transition: Women in the Trans-Mississippi West (a Review Essay)," *Feminist Studies* 11 (Fall 1985): 677–94.

2. Gerald D. Nash, *The American West Transformed: The Impact of the Second World War* (Bloomington: Indiana University Press, 1985); Carl Abbott, *The New Urban America: Growth and Politics in Sunbelt Cities* (Chapel Hill: University of North Carolina Press, 1981). For a discussion of these and other recent works, see Richard W. Etulain, "The Twentieth-Century West: A New Historiographical Frontier," this volume.

3. Potter, "American Women and the American Character," in Welter, *The Woman Question*, 117–32; Jensen and Miller, "The Gentle Tamers Revisited," 173–213; Sandra Myres, "Women in the West," 369–86; Armitage, "Women and Men in Western History," 381–91; Petrik, "The Gentle Tamers in Transition," 677–94.

4. Jensen and Miller, "The Gentle Tamers Revisited," 193.

5. For optimistic appraisals of the implications of urbanization, see Carl Degler, "The Changing Place of Women in America," in Welter, *The Woman Question*, 133–46; Potter, "American Women and the American Character," in Welter, *The Woman Question*, 117–32. For interpretations that stress structural constraints, see Dolores Hayden, *Redesigning the American Dream: The Future of Housing, Work, and Family Life* (New York: W. W. Norton & Company, 1984); Leslie Kanes Weisman, "Women's Environmental Rights: A Manifesto," *Heresies II* (1981), 6–9; Sylvia F. Fava, "Women's Place in the New Suburbia," in Gerda R. Wekerle, Rebecca Peterson, and David Morley, eds., *New Space for Women* (Boulder, Colo.: Westview Press, 1980), 129–49. In the general historiography of cities, the idea of cities as a source of freedom has also been promoted (Ronald L. F. Davis, "Western Urban Development: A Critical Analysis," in Jerome O. Steffen, ed., *The American West: New Perspectives, New Dimensions* [Norman: University of Oklahoma Press, 1979], 175–96). Unfortunately, feminism is not among the new perspectives incorporated in this anthology.

6. Laura Balbo, "The Servicing Work of Women and the Capitalist State," *Political Power and Social Theory* 3 (1982): 251–70. Cross-disciplinary scholarship on women and cities offers an especially rich conceptual legacy for historians. See Wekerle, et. al., *New Space for Women*, and Catherine R. Stimpson, Elsa Dixler, Martha J. Nelson, and Kathryn B. Yatrakis, eds., *Women and the American City* (Chicago: University of Chicago Press, 1981). On the forms of women's resistance, see William Chafe, *American Women and Equality* (New York: Oxford University Press, 1981). The appeal of interpretations of women's status that stress only structural constraints derives from their compatibility with many conventional frameworks (whether liberal, conservative, or radical) and, in some cases, from the fact that they obviate and obscure women's agency in historical processes.

7. Abbott, *The New Urban America*, 60; Lawrence H. Larsen, *The Urban West at the End of the Frontier* (Lawrence: The Regents Press of Kansas, 1978), 49; Mark S. Foster, "The Western Response to Urban Transportation: A Tale of Three Cities, 1900–1945," *Journal of the West* (July 1979): 31–39; Roy A. Jordan and Tim R. Miller, "The Politics of a Cowboy Culture," *Annals of Wyoming* 52 (Spring 1980): 40–45. Air conditioning, for example, probably affected the domestic sphere dramatically in the Southwest, bringing cooking indoors and altering child-care techniques and patterns of neighborhood sociability.

8. Brian Scott Rungeling, "Impact of the Mexican Alien Commuter on the Apparel Industry of El Paso, Texas" (Ph.D. dissertation, University of Kentucky, 1969); George C. Kiser and Martha Woody Kiser, *Mexican Workers in the United States: Historical and Political Perspectives* (Albuquerque: University of New Mexico Press, 1979), 215, 227–31; Lamar B. Jones, "Mexican-American Labor Problems in Texas," (San Francisco: R and E Research Associates, 1971), reprint of University of Texas dissertation, 1965, 18–54; Sheldon L. Maram, *Hispanic Workers in the Garment and Restaurant Industries of Los Angeles County*, Working Papers in United States-Mexico Studies, 12, Program in United States-Mexico Studies, University of California at San Diego, 1980; Karen Anderson, "Conditions for the Woman Worker: From Factory Floor to Corporate Office," in *Women and the Arizona Economy*, Research Report prepared by the Southwest Institute for Research on Women/Women's Studies, University of Arizona, for the first Arizona Women's Town Hall (Tucson, 1986), 158–93; Susan Christopherson, *Parity or Poverty: The Spatial Dimension of Income Inequality*, Southwest Institute for Research on Women, Working Paper Number 20, 1985; Susan Christopherson, "Sweatshops and Suburbs: Women's Place in the Sunbelt," paper presented at the Sunbelt: A Region and Regionalism in the Making conference, Miami, 1985; Judith Stacey, "Post-Feminism and Post-Industrialism: Working Class Families in the Silicon Valley," paper presented at the University of Arizona, March 5, 1985; Louise Lamphere, "Bringing the Family to Work: Women's Culture on the Shop Floor," *Feminist Studies* 11 (Fall 1985): 519–40.

9. Anderson, "Conditions"; Kiser and Kiser, *Mexican Workers*, 215, 227–31; Jones, "Mexican-American Labor Problems in Texas," 18–54; Maram, *Hispanic Workers in the Garment and Restaurant Industries;* Christopherson, "Sweatshops and Suburbs"; Christopherson, *Parity or Poverty.* Scholarship on competition between cities for these jobs provides only a partial picture of Sunbelt development and often omits its implications for social relations because of the unexamined assumption that growth (especially in such a modern sector) is automatically positive and, implicitly, benefits all equally (Larry Sawers and William K. Tabb, eds., *Sunbelt/Snowbelt: Urban Development and Regional Restructuring* [New York: Oxford University Press, 1984]). Border cities like El Paso have been magnets for unmarried women migrants for decades, indicating the importance of family dynamics for patterns of economic development (Karen Anderson, "The Chicana in Transition, 1910–1950," paper presented at the Berkshire Conference of Women's History, Smith College, June 2, 1984).

10. Gerald D. Nash, *The American West Transformed;* Robert V. Hine, *The American West: An Interpretive History* (Boston: Little, Brown and Company,

1973), 136–38, 281, 324. Hine's observation that the cult of masculinity supported all forms of violence also requires that the study of violence in the West be expanded to include consideration of the gender dimension of violence and particularly to include that which was directed against women. Roger McGrath's naive and unpersuasive contention that nineteenth-century violence was contained within the bounds of a masculine culture (largely centered in bars) to the benefit of women dissolves once prostitutes are acknowledged to be women and other forms of evidence are investigated. Roger McGrath, "Old Myths, Some Not So Old Myths, and New Realities," paper presented at the conference of the Western History Association, Sacramento, October 10, 1985; Paula Petrik, " 'If She Be Content': The Development of Montana State Divorce Law, 1865–1907," paper presented at the conference of the Western History Association, Sacramento, October 11, 1985; Stacy King-Powers, " 'Till Death Do Us Part': Violence Against Women in Butte, Montana, 1895–1920," paper presented at the conference of the Western History Association, Sacramento, October 11, 1985; Roger W. Lotchin, "The Metropolitan-Military Complex in Comparative Perspective: San Francisco, Los Angeles, and San Diego, 1919–1941," *Journal of the West* (July 1979): 19–30. For regional aspects of gender ideology in the Freudian tradition, see Erik H. Erikson, *Childhood and Society*, 2nd. ed. (New York: W. W. Norton & Company, 1963), 292–95 (a very muddled argument), and Robert Coughlan, "Changing Roles in Modern Marriage: Psychiatrists Find In Them A Clue To Alarming Divorce Rise," *Life* 41 (December 1956): 108–18. It would be interesting to investigate whether the masculine flight from domestic responsibility described by Barbara Ehrenreich occurred earlier or more systematically in the West (Barbara Ehrenreich, *The Hearts of Men: American Dreams and the Flight from Commitment* [New York: Doubleday, 1983]). Records for the Arizona Department of Economic Security indicate a major problem with default on child support payments as early as the 1950s.

11. Vicki Ruiz, "Working for Wages: Mexican Women in the Southwest, 1930–1980," Working Paper Number 19, Southwest Institute for Research on Women. Ruiz, for example, presents data on ethnic and gender differences in occupational and income status in the Southwest, which indicate that stratification within the female labor force is diminishing, but that based on gender persists. For those women who head households, the economic situation is bleak across all ethnic lines, although better for Anglo women than others.

12. Balbo, "The Servicing Work of Women"; Wekerle, et. al., *New Space for Women;* Stimpson, et al., *Women and the American City*, especially Gerda R. Wekerle, "Women in the Urban Environment," 185–211. Balbo's important work on the necessary mediating work of women provides a basis for a critique of socialist and capitalist theoretical assumptions. She analyses the ways in which the structure of the American economy requires the unpaid work of women to provide a link between families and public institutions, including schools, government agencies, and the economy. She thus exposes the fallacies of human capital approaches that ignore such structural arrangements and assume that women can choose to take paid work instead of domestic tasks. This point of view fails to take into account that neither men in the home, the state, or the consumer economy can

or will readily assume the tasks that women undertake. Her implicit conclusion that this is characteristic of capitalist societies alone, however, overlooks the extent to which this mediating function is essential in all patriarchal, industrial bureaucratic societies. Moreover, her astute observation that contemporary "analysis of the economic impact of family production is inadequate, given that the value of the services provided within the family lies precisely in their affective qualities, which cannot be marketed and thus directly quantified in monetary terms" applies also in socialist nations and in relation to Marxist theory. Women's work entails the creation of interpersonal relations whose emotional saliency exposes the inadequacy of any purely economic interpretation.

13. E. Relph, *Place and Placelessness* (London: Pion Limited, 1976); Weisman, "Women's Environmental Rights"; Pat Therese Francis, " 'Where Do You live?' Women in the Landscape of Poverty," *Heresies II* (1981): 10–11. The "pornscapes" that mark many areas of the city provide the visual signification of the gender/class politics that underly the organization of work, sexuality, and family life (Relph, *Place and Placelessness,* 35, 95); Hayden, *Redesigning the American Dream,* 217–22.

14. The relationship between demographics, industries, and segmentation policies is a complex one. Scholars thus far have only examined pieces of the picture. See, for example, Karen Anderson, "Last Hired, First Fired: Black Women Workers During World War II," *Journal of American History* 69 (June 1982): 82–97; Albert Szymanski, "Racism and Sexism as Functional Substitutes in the Labor Market," *Sociological Quarterly* 17 (Winter 1976): 65–73; Dorothy Remy and Larry Sawers, "Urban Industrial Decline and the Dynamics of Sexual and Racial Oppression," in Sawers and Tabb, eds., *Sunbelt/Snowbelt: Urban Development and Regional Restructuring* 128–51; Kristin Nelson, "Female Labor Supply Characteristics and the Suburbanization of Low-Wage Office Work" in M. Storper and A. Scott, eds., *Production, Work, Territory* (London: Allen Unwin, 1986). Of these studies only Nelson focuses explicitly on the West. For the migration of garment work to the Southwest, see Rungeling, "Impact of the Mexican Alien Commuter." Julia Kirk Blackwelder, *Women of the Depression: Caste and Culture in San Antonio, 1929–1939* (College Station: Texas A&M University Press, 1984), provides evidence regarding discrimination in work and welfare based on gender and ethnicity, but does not locate that information in any useful theoretical framework. Her stress on caste as an explanation for ethnic discrimination requires a psychological, rather than a historical, framework. It obscures the institutional bases for such systems and offers little insight into the mechanisms for historical change in ethnic and gender relations.

15. Patricia Zavella, "The Impact of 'Sun Belt Industrialization' on Chicanas," *Frontiers* 8 (1984): 21–27. For a review of some of the class/culture debate, see Vicki Ruiz, "UCAPAWA, Chicanas, and the California Food Processing Industry, 1937–1950," (Ph.D. dissertation, Stanford University, 1982), 10–25. For the argument from culture, see Julia Kirk Blackwelder, "Women in the Work Force: Atlanta, New Orleans, and San Antonio, 1930–1940," *Journal of Urban History* 4 (May 1978): 331–58. For the argument on the basis of class, see Rosalinda Gonzalez, "Chicanas and Mexican Immigrant Families 1920–1940: Women's Subordination and Family Exploitation," in Lois Scharf and Joan Jensen, eds.,

Decades of Discontent (Westport, Ct.: Greenwood Press, 1983), 60–84. See also Mario T. García, "The Chicana in American History: The Mexican Women of El Paso, 1880–1920—A Case Study," *Pacific Historical Review* 49 (May 1980): 315–37; Albert Camarillo, *Chicanos in a Changing Society: From Mexican Pueblos to American Barrios in Santa Barbara and Southern California, 1848–1930* (Cambridge: Harvard University Press, 1979). Some scholarship, however, indicates the continuing importance of cultural values in constraining Chicanas' work rates, although that tendency has diminished over time (Anderson, "The Chicana in Transition"; Rosemary Cooney, "Changing Labor Force Participation of Mexican American Wives: A Comparison with Anglos and Blacks," *Social Science Quarterly* 56 [September 1975]: 252–61). Cooney found that education beyond high school changed Mexican-American women's labor force rates more than any other variable. That black women's rates have historically been higher than those of Mexican-American women also indicates that the structure of opportunity alone cannot account for working class women's labor force choices. To complicate matters further, Janice Webster's work on Scandinavian women in Seattle indicates that secure and adequate incomes for men can depress the labor force rates of women (Janice Reiff Webster, "Domestication and Americanization: Scandinavian Women in Seattle, 1888–1900," *Journal of Urban History* 4 [May 1978]: 275–90).

16. Micaela di Leonardo, *The Varieties of Ethnic Experience: Kinship, Class, and Gender Among California Italian-Americans* (Ithaca: Cornell University Press, 1984).

17. David Lee and Ronald Schultz, "Regional Patterns of Female Status in the United States," *Professional Geographer* 34 (1982): 32–41; Karen Anderson, *Wartime Women: Sex Roles, Family Relations, and the Status of Women During World War II* (Westport, Ct.: Greenwood Press, 1981); W. T. Bielby and J. N. Baron, "Women and Men at Work: Sex Segregation and Statistical Discrimination," n.p. Bielby and Baron have studied job distributions in "mixed sex" occupations (as indicated by aggregate data) in almost 300 California industries and have found that at the level of job title gender segregation is virtually complete. More than 96 percent of the women in their study would have to change jobs in order to create a random distribution of employees by gender in these occupations. Clearly, the West is not leading in the elimination of gender segregation, if California is a barometer.

18. *Ibid.*; Paul Burstein, *Discrimination, Jobs, and Politics: The Struggle for Equal Employment Opportunity in the United States since the New Deal* (Chicago: University of Chicago Press, 1985), 54. These findings indicate that cultural ideologies regarding women's proper roles, especially those deriving from religious belief, may shape behavior independently from economic structures in some instances.

19. Dolores Hayden, *The Grand Domestic Revolution: A History of Feminist Designs for American Homes, Neighborhoods, and Cities* (Cambridge, Ma.: MIT Press, 1982); Hayden, *Redesigning the American Dream*; Ruth Schwartz Cowan, *More Work For Mother: The Ironies of Household Technology From the Open Hearth to the Microwave* (New York: Basic Books, 1983); Susan Strasser, *Never Done: A History of American Housework* (New York: Pantheon Books, 1982);

Winifred Wandersee, *Women's Work and Family Values, 1920–1940* (Cambridge: Harvard University Press, 1981); Anderson, *Wartime Women*.

20. Susan Saegert, "Masculine Cities and Feminine Suburbs: Polarized Ideas, Contradictory Realities," in Stimpson, et al., *Women and the American City*, 93–108; Virginia Scharff, "Putting Women in the Driver's Seat: American Women and the Car Culture," paper presented at the conference of the National Women's Studies Association, Seattle, Washington, June 21, 1985. Scholars need to examine women's access to cars in terms of class, gender ideology, and education (specifically the rise of public school and private driver's education classes). They should also investigate whether characterizations of public transportation as "no place for a lady" affected women's mobility in urban settings. Virginia Joy Scharff, "Reinventing the Wheel: American Women and the Automobile in the Early Car Culture," Ph.D. dissertation, University of Arizona, 1987.

21. Jo Freeman, "Women and Urban Policy," in Stimpson, et al., *Women and the American City*, 1–19; Ann R. Markusen, "City Spatial Structure, Women's Household Work, and National Urban Policy" in Stimpson, et al., *Women and the American City*, 27; Saegert, "Masculine Cities and Feminine Suburbs," in Stimpson, et al., *Women and the American City*, 93–108. For a more complex view of the meaning of the frontier experience in women's lives, see Julie Roy Jeffrey, *Frontier Women: The Trans-Mississippi West, 1840–1880* (New York: Hill and Wang, 1979).

22. Galen Cranz, "Women in Urban Parks," in Stimpson, et al., *Women and the American City*, 76–92.

23. Joanne Meyerowitz, "Working Women's Alternatives to the Family Economy, Chicago, 1880–1930," paper presented at the Berkshire Conference on the History of Women, June 1984.

24. Joseph F. Tripp, "Toward an Efficient and Moral Society: Washington State Minimum-Wage Law, 1913–1925," *Pacific Northwest Quarterly* 67 (July 1976): 97–112.

25. Anne Firor and Andrew M. Scott, *One-Half the People: The Fight for Woman Suffrage* (Philadelphia: J. B. Lippincott Co., 1975); Ruth Barnes Moynihan, *Rebel for Rights: Abigail Scott Duniway* (New Haven, Ct.: Yale University Press, 1983); Sandra Myres, *Westering Women* (Albuquerque: University of New Mexico Press, 1982); Ronald Schaffer, "The Problem of Consciousness in the Woman Suffrage Movement: A California Perspective," *Pacific Historical Review* 45 (November 1976): 469–93; Eleanor Flexner, *Century of Struggle: The Woman's Rights Movement in the United States* (Cambridge, Ma.: The Belknap Press, 1975), 263–65; Aileen Kraditor, *The Ideas of the Woman Suffrage Movement: 1890–1920* (New York: Columbia University Press, 1965); T. A. Larson, "The Woman Suffrage Movement in Washington," *Pacific Northwest Quarterly* 67 (April 1976): 49–62. Larson attributes the surprisingly easy victory for suffrage in Washington to the "Progressive spirit."

26. Moynihan, *Rebel for Rights*, especially pp. 206–19.

27. Joan M. Jensen, "'Disfranchisement is a Disgrace': Women and Politics in New Mexico 1900–1940," in Joan M. Jensen and Darlis A. Miller, eds., *New Mexico Women: Intercultural Perspectives* (Albuquerque: University of New Mexico Press, 1986), 301–31.

28. T. A. Larson, "Idaho's Role in America's Woman Suffrage Crusade," *Idaho Yesterdays* 18 (Spring 1974): 2–17; Larson, "Wyoming's Contribution to the Regional and National Women's Rights Movement," *Annals of Wyoming* 52 (Spring 1980): 2–15; Reda Davis, *California Women: A Guide to Their Politics, 1885–1911* (San Francisco: California Scene, 1967). Most of the California women's organizations Davis lists were formed in the nineteenth century.

29. Jordan and Miller, "The Politics of a Cowboy Culture," 40–45; Larson, "Wyoming's Contribution," 9–11; Larson, "Idaho's Role," 4, 10–13. In Idaho, women voters could not even prevent Senator William Borah from opposing the woman suffrage amendment. Borah took his position on the grounds of states' rights (Flexner, *Century of Struggle,* 314–15). In New Mexico (as elsewhere) women also had to organize to remove many other legal inequities in the post-suffrage period (Joan M. Jensen, "The Campaign for Women's Community Property Rights in New Mexico, 1940–1960," in Jensen and Miller, 333–55).

30. Anderson, *Wartime Women,* 88–90; Cheryl Knott Malone, "Labor Without Pay: Women's Volunteer Work in Arizona Hospitals, 1945–1965" (M.A. Thesis, University of Arizona, 1985).

31. Vicki Lynn Ruiz, *Cannery Women, Cannery Lives: Mexican Women, Unionization, and the California Food Processing Industry, 1930–1950* (Albuquerque: University of New Mexico Press, 1987); George N. Green, "ILGWU in Texas," *Journal of Mexican-American History* 2 (Spring 1971): 144–69; Melissa Hield, "'Union-Minded': Women in the Texas ILGWU, 1933–1950," *Frontiers* 4 (1979): 59–70; Blackwelder, *Women of the Depression,* 130–51; Lamphere, "Bringing the Family to Work," 519–40; Patricia Zavella, "'Abnormal Intimacy': The Varying Work Networks of Chicana Cannery Workers," *Feminist Studies* 11 (Fall 1985): 541–57.

32. Donald N. Rothblatt, Daniel J. Garr, and Jo Sprague, *The Suburban Environment and Women* (New York: Praeger Publishers, 1979); Freeman, "Women and Urban Policy," in Stimpson, et al., *Women and the American City,* 9; Fava, "Women's Place in the New Suburbia," in Wekerle, et al., *New Space for Women,* 129–49; Saegert, "Masculine Cities and Feminine Suburbs," in Stimpson, et al., *Women and the American City,* 93–108. Clearly, urban renewal efforts have often destroyed community and kin networks critical to the well-being of minority group women. The city of Los Angeles, for example, destroyed hundreds of Hispanic homes between 1906 and 1913 during a slum clearance campaign and did the same in the 1950s, initially because of a planned public housing project (Pedro G. Castillo, "The Making of a Mexican Barrio: Los Angeles, 1890–1920" [Ph.D. dissertation, University of California at Santa Barbara, 1979], 104–5; Thomas S. Hines, "Housing, Baseball, and Creeping Socialism: The Battle of Chavez Ravine, Los Angeles, 1949–1959," *Journal of Urban History* 8 [February 1982]: 123–43).

33. Fava, "Women's Place in the New Suburbia," in Wekerle, et al., *New Space for Women,* 129–49; Saegert, "Masculine Cities and Feminine Suburbs," in Stimpson, et al., *Women and the American City,* 93–108.

34. Diane Sands, "Using Oral History to Chart the Course of Illegal Abortions in Montana," *Frontiers* 7 (1983): 32–37.

35. Gunther Barth, *Instant Cities: Urbanization and the Rise of San Francisco*

and Denver (New York: Oxford University Press, 1975), 175–76; Mary Murphy, "The Private Lives of Public Women: Prostitution in Butte, Montana, 1878–1917," *Frontiers* 7 (1984): 30–35. For a discussion of the importance of prostitution as a system of control that enforces marriage, see Marion Goldman, *Gold Diggers and Silver Miners: Prostitution and Social Control on the Comstock Lode* (Ann Arbor: University of Michigan Press, 1981). Paul Petrik, "Capitalists with Rooms: Prostitution in Helena, Montana, 1865–1900," *Montana, The Magazine of Western History* 31 (Spring 1981): 28–41; Lucie Cheng Hirata, "Chinese Immigrant Women in Nineteenth-Century America," in Carol Ruth Berkin and Mary Beth Norton, eds., *Women of America: A History* (Boston: Houghton Mifflin Company, 1979), 224–44.

36. Lewis Erenberg, "Everybody's Doing It: The Pre-World War I Dance Craze, The Castles, and the Modern American Girl," *Feminist Studies* I (Fall 1975): 158.

37. Ruth Tuck, *Not With the Fist: Mexican-Americans in a Southwestern City* (New York: Harcourt, Brace & Company, 1946), 127, 149–56. Mexican-American folklore and *corridos* provide interesting insights into Mexican immigrant reactions to American urban culture and its implications for gender relations (Maria Herrera-Sobek, "The Acculturation Process of the Chicana in the *Corrido*," *De Colores* [1982]: 7–16; Anderson, "The Chicana in Transition").

38. Anderson, *Wartime Women*, 103–11; D'Ann Campbell, "Was the West Different? Values and Attitudes of Young Women in 1943," *Pacific Historical Review* 42 (August 1978): 453–63; Relph, *Place and Placelessness*, 95; Hayden, *Redesigning the American Dream*, 217–22. John D'Emilio's work on the rise of lesbian communities in the post-World War II period provides an indication of the various barriers to the creation of urban spaces for women. He notes that lesbians had greater difficulty establishing a bar culture because they had less money and less time and freedom to travel within cities than gay men and were constrained by safety considerations and by domesticity if married or mothers (John D'Emilio, *Sexual Politics, Sexual Communities: The Making of a Homosexual Minority in the United States, 1940–1970* [Chicago: University of Chicago Press, 1983], 92–107).

39. Markusen, "City Spatial Structure," in Stimpson, et al., *Women and the American City,* 34–35; Governor's Meeting with Representatives of Women's Groups, February 17, 1939, Governor's Papers, Arizona State Archives, Box 13A.

40. Susan Ware, *Beyond Suffrage: Women in the New Deal* (Cambridge: Harvard University Press, 1981).

4

Mexican Americans in the New West

Ricardo Romo

Among minority groups in the twentieth-century West, Spanish-speaking Americans have come to be the most numerous. As Ricardo Romo points out, however, historical assessments of this migration have not kept pace with the rapid flow of Mexican Americans, particularly after the Second World War. Such studies as have appeared are often fragmented or deal with particular localities. Thus, the primary aim of his essay is to provide a broad overview of the major influences, whether political, social, or economic, that shaped the Mexican American community in the West, particularly in the last fifty years, and to assess its impact on the region.

Although the first historical studies of Mexican Americans appeared in the 1940s, the majority of publications on this topic are less than twenty years old and generally have emphasized social, political, and economic issues. The newness of the field is evidenced by the small number of journals dedicated to the history of Mexican-origin people, even though Mexican Americans have long been the second largest minority in this nation.[1] While historians have been hindered by the dearth of historical resources, they have benefitted from the growing availability of census data and other materials concerned with migration, assimilation, stratification, and inequality.[2] The purpose of this essay is to give readers a general overview of twentieth-century social, economic, and political forces that have shaped the Mexican American community in the West.

Carey McWilliams, one of the first interpreters of Mexican American history, advanced the idea that Mexican Americans constituted a unique minority group. What made Mexicans different, McWilliams argued, was that they had been "annexed by conquest, along with the territory they occupied, and, in effect, their cultural autonomy was guaranteed by a treaty."[3] McWilliams wrote that "unlike most European minorities in America, Mexicans have been rooted in space—in a particular region—over a long period of years."[4] More recently, Myron Weiner commented that "Mexican Americans are among dozens, possibly hundreds of peoples whose traditional homelands are divided by an international border."[5] When the United States conquered the West, it gave the Spanish-speaking people the right under international treaty to maintain their own culture. Arguably, then, Mexican Americans enjoy a unique status among minority groups in the United States.

McWilliams further suggested that the conquest of Mexicans in the West explained the harsh treatment that subsequent generations of Mexicans—both native and immigrants—experienced. McWilliams observed that "the tradition of dominance was interwoven into the fabric of the [Anglo] community; generations had been steeped in the Mexican stereotype. Almost by instinct, Anglo Americans equated Mexicans with Indians."[6] More recently, sociologist Rodolfo Alvarez has argued that the new wave of Mexicans entering the United States in the post-1900 era encountered a social situation very different from that of immigrants from other lands. Like McWilliams, Alvarez asserted that the experience of Mexicanos "upon entering the United States was predefined by the well established social position of pre-1900 Mexican Americans as a conquered people (politically, socially, culturally, economically, and in every other respect)."[7]

Various theories of colonialism have been repeated frequently since the early 1970s. Historian Rodolfo Acuña's central thesis for his monograph *Occupied America* is that "Mexicans in the United States are still a colonized people, but now the colonization is *internal*—it is occurring *within* the country rather than being imposed by an external power."[8] When Acuña prepared a second edition of *Occupied America*, he advised readers that he had "reevaluated the internal colonial model and set it aside as a useful paradigm relevant to the nineteenth century but not to the twentieth."[9] Although Acuña did not elaborate, he apparently thought that Mexicans were far too mobile and too active in labor organizations and political movements to conclude that they lived as a nearly separate nation within the United States.

As Acuña was preparing his revised edition of *Occupied America*, Mario Barrera undertook yet another examination of Mexican American history from the perspective of the "internal colonial" model. His study of southwest history, political economy, and power relations led him to proclaim that "the imperial expansion of the United States resulted in internal colonialism, a condition which Chicanos have shared with other racial minorities."[10] Barrera argued that the initial conquest immediately affected only certain parts of the Southwest and left other areas in a more or less peripheral state; but that economic penetration of railroads, construction projects, and mining in the late-nineteenth century eventually drew all parts of the area into the "internal colony."[11]

In a recent essay this writer and S. Dale McLemore acknowledge that "like the American Indians, the Mexican Americans became an American minority through the direct conquest of their homelands."[12] We point out, however, that scholars and students must recognize that the "conquered minority" perspective conflicts with the most common approach to studying the adjustment of American ethnic groups to the larger society—the three-generation analysis. First generational immigrants attempt to establish a base in the community. Clustering in ethnic neighborhoods, they struggle with language problems and new customs. Sons and daughters of this foreign-born cohort find adjustment somewhat easier. Most often they benefit from an American education, and their jobs are usually in the skilled or white-collar categories. Many attempt to assimilate, joining social groups that would have excluded their parents.

According to this model, the third generational group is nearly "indistinguishable" from the mainstream population. Most cannot communicate with their grandparents in the old world language. They also live in suburbs and have opportunites that were but dreams for their parents. Since this three-generation approach is a living reality for many Anglo-American families, it has intrigued many Mexican American scholars. However, the Mexican American community in the Southwest predates, for example, the Irish and German immigrant communities, and three generations is but a limited aspect of their experience. In addition, factors of geographic isolation, limited racial integration, and conflict over territory suggest that Mexican Americans are quite different from immigrant groups traditionally included in the three-generational model. This essay will assume that Mexican Americans should be studied by applying a combination of both perspectives—the colonial model and the generational approach. Fine distinctions can be made, but the larger story leads this writer to identify three principal stages of historical development in the twentieth century: the immigrant era, a period of transition, and the rise of new ethnicity.

The Migration Stage

In the immigrant era, the years roughly between 1900 and 1940, the most striking influences upon the Mexican American community in the West were mass migration and the rise of immigrant colonies. The presence of a porous border led to a population movement of significant proportions.

More than a million Mexicans, largely unskilled workers, moved into the West. These new immigrants retained a pronounced loyalty to Mexico, and while they despaired at the discrimination and segregation they encountered, they were unable to do much to combat them. The large urban barrios of the West are a consequence of this segregation and discrimination. While Spanish-language newspapers and patriotic societies flourished during this era, largely immigrant groups were seldom politically active.

Inadvertently, the United States government helped encourage mass migrations from Mexico to the American West. Western agricultural development took a pathbreaking turn in the summer of 1901 when thirty senators and representatives of the seventeen western states met at Cheyenne, Wyoming, to develop a program of dam construction and reclamation.[13] The resulting Newlands Reclamation Act (1902) helped to trigger an agricultural revolution in the American West with long-lasting economic consequences for Mexican communities. Thousands of unskilled Mexican laborers toiled in the reclamation of the "Great American Desert" and thereby contributed directly to the first modern wave of Mexican immigration.

The reclamation of the "American Desert" paralleled other important changes that were under way south of the United States border. The construction of a Mexican national railway system linking the interior of Mexico with the borderland states also promised to open new economic opportunities for both capitalists and workers. Unskilled workers who had been earning less than fifty cents a day in Mexico left their homeland when they learned similar work in the West paid double to triple that amount. The new rail linkage between the United States and Mexico, as well as the Mexican Republic's proximity to the American West, increased the probability of new migration patterns. In agricultural areas and in industrial sites in the New West where work was often seasonal and laboring conditions primitive, Mexican migrants remained on the job because the wages surpassed those in Mexico. In addition, proximity to Mexico meant that migration expenses were minimal. It cost Mexicanos as little as $30 to migrate from interior central states, and unlike other immigrants, many could return to their homeland after periods of seasonal work.[14]

In the aftermath of the Newlands Reclamation project, capital investments for agriculture, mining, and railroad expansion were readily available. Less certain, however, was the steady supply of cheap labor. Western labor contractors of an earlier generation had drawn upon Chinese and Japanese laborers, but Asians proved a problem for nativists and as a result their migration never reached significant proportions. Prior to the outbreak of World World I in Europe, Slavic, Greek, and Italian workers filled the labor vacuum for a time; however, southern European workers preferred work in mining and transportation industries. The reclamation project, nonetheless, opened America's southern door, and an army of Mexican workers flocked northward. Economist Victor S. Clark reported in 1908 that railroad construction had "carried the central Mexican villager a thousand miles from his home and to within a few miles of the border; and American employers, with a gold wage, . . . had little difficulty in attracting him across that not very formidable dividing line."[15] The northern Mexican mining industries had a similar problem with labor losses. According to one representative of mining properties in the state of Chihuahua, more than 8,000 workers brought to Chihuahua from the interior state of Zacatecas had left their jobs in Chihuahua for mining work in New Mexico and Arizona.[16]

As homogeneous as these immigrant laborers appeared to their employers, they were by no means one-dimensional individuals. Anthropologist Paul Friedrich's story of Primo Tapia, a Mexican agrarian rebel of the 1920s, reveals the varied experiences of these sojourners.[17] Tapia, a native of Naranja, a small village in Michoacan, immigrated to the United States in 1907. He arrived in Los Angeles during its heyday of political turmoil and labor unrest. Tapia's strong interest in labor organizing and socialism led to the formation of the Mexican Liberal Party (PLM), a group of exiled socialists and anarchists.[18] In Mexico and later in the United States, PLM members had waged a vocal campaign against the aging dictator, Porfirio Díaz, who had jailed the PLM's founder Ricardo Magon and other leaders.[19] Upon their release, Magon and numerous PLM members fled north, settling in Los Angeles. In southern California Tapia met the Magonistas, helping them to distribute a radical newspaper and assisting in the organization of mass meetings among the workers.[20]

During the World War I era, Mexican unskilled workers constituted the larger share of the unskilled day laborers employed in Los Angeles and other western urban centers. Workers like Tapia found employment in the railroad and urban railway systems, construction industries, street paving, lumber, and meat-packing companies. Like agriculture, these industries had their peak seasons, usually in the spring and summer, so many of the immigrant workers returned to their homeland over the winter months. Tapia returned to Mexico several times during his thirteen-year stay in the United States.[21]

Many commentators have argued that emigrants leaving the homeland represent the best of a nation's work force. Laborers "pushed" out of Mexico by chaotic social and political conditions there, or "pulled" to the United States by the promising economic situation in the New West between the years 1900 and 1930 clearly came from the most productive age group. For the first three decades of the twentieth century, the majority of the immigrants from Mexico were young males like Primo Tapia. The relative proximity of their Mexican villages to work places in the American West allowed many of these workers to postpone for long periods the decision to bring their families north.

Still, not all the immigrants who labored in the United States desired to abandon their homeland. Primo Tapia proved an exception to this rule, however. From 1916 to 1920 he worked as an organizer for the Industrial Workers of the World (IWW), enlisting unskilled miners and migrant harvest hands of the Rocky Mountains and wheat belt.[22] When government agents opened a campaign after the war to arrest or deport alleged radicals, Tapia chose to return to his village in Michoacan. There, he became the principal leader in the agrarian revolt movement of the 1920s. Subsequently, the region won important concessions in labor reform during Tapia's involvement. Tapia, like thousands of talented Mexicans who returned home after living as sojourners in the United States, used his wages and experiences to build a new life.

Sojourners like Primo Tapia immigrated to the United States with relative ease as a result of the transportation revolution begun under the administration of strongman Porfirio Díaz. The Díaz regime had constructed the railroad in northern Mexico in the late-nineteenth century to haul mineral and agriculture products north to United States refineries and processing plants. Between 1900 and 1920, however, the rail cars more often transported cargoes of immigrant workers and their families. In the years after World War I, three western cities, Los Angeles, San Antonio, and El Paso, emerged as principal distribution centers for Mexican workers, with the West becoming a safety valve for the underemployed and underpaid workers of Mexico.[23] Not all of the immigrants arrived on the border by train, however; thousands simply walked or rode their horses to the border where crossing was a simple matter. In the span of one year, more than 200,000 Mexicans arrived in San Antonio to await further transport to other regions of the West.[24] At a few designated points along the 2,000-mile border, immigration officials collected an $8 a head tax from the newcomers, which many considered too high and so instead waded across shallow sections of the Rio Grande distant from the port of entry. Still, so many immigrants passed through the official port of entry at Cuidad Juárez that on some days the international bridge resembled a giant turnstile. In El Paso, its streets dusty brown from dirt blowing from the Chihuahua desert and local smeltering plants, immigrants milled around employment agencies.[25]

Mexican immigrants who crossed the shallow waters of the Rio Grande in the second decade of the twentieth century dreamed not only of new economic opportunities but also of religious and political freedoms. The long and bloody Mexican Revolution failed to bring immediate relief for the Mexican working class. Wages, near subsistence levels before Francisco Madero took up the call of rebellion, improved but slightly during the 1920s; and when government forces in Jalisco and Michoacan went to battle with Catholic zealots to enforce new legislation calling for separation of church and state, thousands of persecuted families fled northward.[26] A mass migration that had begun at the turn of the century grew in significance during this decade as the American West experienced another economic boom.

Just as the Prohibition era differed from earlier economic periods, likewise, a sharp contrast existed between post–World War I Mexican immigrants and earlier migrants. The young, unskilled male laborers who migrated north during the turn of the century generally came alone and sought work in rural areas of the West; in contrast, the newcomers of the 1920s brought their families and settled in urban communities. One could witness the changing nature of Mexican immigration in the large, sprawling barrios of Los Angeles, Tucson, El Paso, and San Antonio. For example, the Mexican population in Los Angeles, jumped from 42,000 in 1920 to more than 100,000 by 1930.[27] San Antonio likewise experienced a population explosion as thousands of migrants took up residence in the area immediately west of the railroad yards.

In all these Spanish-speaking communities, the new immigrants created their own local institutions. Some of these, particularly ethnic newspapers and mutual-aid societies, eased the immigrants' adjustment to new experiences in the West. Other barrio institutions such as Spanish-language schools and labor associations arose in response to the class and racial prejudice in U.S. mainstream society. In large cities such as Los Angeles, San Antonio, and El Paso, the new wave of twentieth-century Mexican immigrants moved into European enclaves. In many western communities, however, newcomers as well as second and third generation Mexicans could neither send their children to "Anglo" schools, nor eat in most restaurants.[28]

The immigrant class that fled Mexico during the first third of the twentieth century contributed not only to the economic development of the West but also to the rise of *colonias* or immigrant colonies.[29] Of course, many of these immigrants settled in communities that their Spanish and Mexican ancestors had founded. Southwestern cities, such as Los Angeles and San Antonio, began in the eighteenth century. Anglo settlers who arrived in the mid-nineteenth century built new towns, mostly mining communities, but for the most part they settled where Spaniards and Mexicans had already built homes, churches, and schools. Over time, these frontier communities grew into large cities.[30] In all these western enclaves, Mexicans lived in isolation, maintaining little contact with the political and economic mainstream. Their isolation increased because of their desire to live near factories and construction yards. Industries such as mining and railroads promoted isolation by segregating workers in company-owned homes. However, segregation also resulted from restrictive housing covenants. When not excluded by legal policies, Mexicans found themselves restricted from housing outside of the barrio by threats of violence. In San Bernadino, California, for instance, Anglos opposed the opening of new tract home sites to Mexican residents so vehemently in 1909 that they proclaimed they were prepared "to give the newcomers a hot reception." One resident claimed he would "use a shotgun on these aliens if necessary."[31] Such intimidation kept Mexican American residents in enclaves long after European immigrants had begun integrating into American society.

During the late-nineteenth and early-twentieth centuries, Westerners expressed nativistic attitudes toward immigrant minorities in their treatment of Chinese and Japanese communities and in their support of immigration quotas for eastern and southern Europeans. That Mexicans were excluded from restrictive quotas resulted more from their economic value than from enlightened racial attitudes.[32] The Great Depression, however, eliminated thousands of unskilled jobs in the West, sending Mexicans and Anglos to unemployment lines. Unemployment and the related issue of relief stirred new nativist feelings toward Mexicanos, resulting in a massive deportation program that began in 1929 and lasted until 1939.

The downturn in the world economy in 1929 sent shock waves across America. Western farmers suffered particularly from the stock market collapse as tight money lessened demand for their products. Furthermore, many farmers had borrowed heavily in anticipation of continued world utilization of cotton and other agricultural products. With the demand gone and with mortgaged land and tractors sitting idle, the need for labor also dropped. Although many farmers eventually received relief from New Deal programs, particularly in the form of subsidies for not growing cotton, migrant workers were the forgotten people in Washington. Without work and transportation, many migrants remained in the communities they had so ably contributed to during good harvests.

Under the strain of unemployment compensation, community leaders in western towns began to consider alternative solutions. Charles P. Visel, the Los Angeles coordinator for unemployment relief, offered Washington officials a relatively simple answer to the unemployment and relief problem. Estimating that there were 400,000 "deportable aliens in the U.S.," he suggested "getting rid" of the Mexican workers.[33] Arguing that "we need their jobs for needy citizens," Visel initiated a massive round-up of Mexican immigrant families in southern California.[34]

Because the deportation of "aliens" occurred during a period of intense hostility and hysteria, it is not surprising that many civil rights violations occurred. Officials who participated in these raids often ignored the citizenship status of those whom they deported. Thousands of children born in the United States were taken to Mexico with parents who did not have citizenship even though their children were qualified to remain in the United States.[35] In Texas, where almost 50 percent of the half million deportees resided, one scholar found that the civil rights violations included "not permitting returnees to dispose of their property or to collect their wages, deporting many not legally subject to deportation because of their length of Texas residency, separating family, and deporting the infirm."[36] Communities that only a few years earlier praised the diligence of Mexican laborers turned their backs on them in needy times.

As civil rights violations reached an unprecedented level during the Great Depression years, the Mexican American communities of the West intensified efforts to achieve full equality and justice. While labor strikes constituted part of the struggle for equality for Mexican American women pecan shellers of San Antonio in the mid-1930s, in California 5,000 Mexican American laborers walked out of Imperial Valley cotton fields, protesting low wages and poor working conditions. Hundreds of other strikes involving Mexican Americans occurred during the turbulent Depression era when issues went beyond demands for higher wages.[37] Labor activity was but one form of opposing inequities. Mexican Americans also formed associations to challenge socioeconomic inequities.

Early twentieth-century demands for justice and equality had been channelled through the immigrant institutions in the community, notably the Mexican Consular offices and the immigrant press. However, in the late years of the immigrant era, challenges emanated from the community itself. The League of United Latin American Citizens (LULAC), founded by middle-class Texas-Mexicans in 1928 and highly critical of noncitizen elements within the barrios of the New West, illustrates how this political transition evolved. LULAC leaders expressed a strong loyalty to American values and declared their desire to "use their influence in all fields of social, economic, and political action in order to realize the greatest enjoyment possible of all the rights and privileges and prerogatives extended by the American Constitution."[38] In the 1930s, LULAC leadership challenged the segregation of Mexican American school children in Del Rio, Texas, on the basis that Mexican Americans were legally white and thereby entitled to equality in education. Eventually, LULAC attorneys lost the case, but the concession from the school authorities that the instruction of Mexican children in separate buildings had been only for instructional purposes and not based on racial considerations was a partial victory for the Mexican American community. These early protest efforts of the Depression years took on new dimensions when America went to war in 1941. The lessons of LULAC's struggle would not be lost on the larger

Mexican American population. However, the transitional generation of the 1940s and 1950s viewed their assigned status as second-class citizens more contemptuously than LULAC or the immigrant generation before them.

The Transitional Period

The transitional stage in twentieth-century Mexican American history lasted from 1940 to 1965. This quarter century is characterized by social and political regeneration. Changes in Mexican American barrios are best exemplified by the emergence of new political organizations and the creation of new alliances between existing barrio institutions and other ethnic associations. As a consequence, Mexican Americans experienced some success in challenging Jim Crow-type segregation. Other changes involved international affairs. For example, the United States government's establishment of a labor alliance with Mexico culminated in the Bracero Program, through which labor markets in most western communities were internationalized. Finally, the three wars of this era brought both pride and sorrow to the barrios: pride in that so many Spanish-surnamed men and women served with distinction; sorrow in that many Spanish-surnamed individuals gave their lives in Germany, Japan, Korea, and Vietnam.

World War II represented a decisive impetus for the transitional phase in the Mexican American community. This desire to foster a united front produced what Richard Polenberg has characterized as a "heightened interest in American history, tradition, and culture, a search for common roots that would provide a means for collective identification."[39] Americans found it more difficult than ever to rationalize the segregation of Blacks in military units, the internment of Japanese Americans at home, and prolonged racial riots on the homefront. As the men and women from Spanish-speaking barrios of the West went to war, Mexican American civilians began to envision a new era with a challenge to overturn Jim Crowism.[40]

Mexican Americans who lived in segregated barrios, attended segregated schools, and were denied use of many public facilities understood the broad ramifications of racism and discrimination. What frustrated Mexican American leaders in the town of Three Rivers, Texas, was that such abuse should be tolerated at the burial ceremony of a Mexican American war veteran. In Texas the case of Felix Longoria exemplified a form of second-class citizenship that pushed Mexican Americans into action.[41] Longoria had been killed in the Philippines during the war, but his body remained in that territory until 1949. When the U.S. Army informed his parents that his body would be shipped home, his mother attempted to contract the local funeral home to handle his burial in a local cemetery. The director of the funeral home refused to handle the veteran's body, claiming that they did not do business with Mexican clients. This refusal galvanized into action the American G.I. Forum, a newly formed Mexican American veterans organization based in Corpus Christi. Led by energetic and resourceful physician Dr. Hector Garcia, the veterans group arranged with the young Texas Senator Lyndon B. Johnson to have Longoria buried at the Arlington National Cemetery. The incident stung Texas officials who claimed that racial discrimination against Mexicans had been abolished during recent years.[42] The Longoria incident represented one of the first successful efforts of the Mexican American community in its battle against Jim Crow.

The Mexican American communities remained in transition status not simply because of civil rights issues, but also because of international labor agreements between the United States and Mexico. An agreement known as the Bracero Program introduced millions of Mexican laborers to the American West during the period from 1942 to 1964.[43] Americans who discriminated against Mexican Americans had no more respect for bracero workers. However, problems arose when Americans of Mexican descent were denied basic privileges such as education and health services on the assumption that they were bracero workers. This failure by some Americans to distinguish between the seasonal workers from Mexico and the citizens of Mexican descent created yet more tension in the Mexican American communities of the West.[44]

Bracero laborers proved extremely valuable to various western American industries that required large numbers of unskilled workers. The peak years for the recruitment of labor from Mexico came in 1944 and 1945. The braceros came as seasonal workers, generally under a six-month contract. The number employed in the U.S. during 1945 varied from 21,515 in February to 67,860 in the peak harvest month of August. In railroad industries, 135,283 workers came under contract for the last two years of the war. Overall, more than five million braceros worked in the U.S. during the twenty-year program.[45]

When the U.S. Congress allowed the Bracero Program to lapse briefly in 1948, Texas farmers scurried to fill the surplus labor pool. Texas farmers, long accustomed to using cheap, illegal labor, contrived an ingenious plan to insure that they would have a sufficient—if not a surplus—labor pool for the 1948 harvest. *Newsweek* reporters who visited Texas that year explained how this labor scheme functioned. Once Mexicans crossed into Texas, "they were placed under technical arrest, paroled to the Texas

Employment Commission, and loaded on trucks headed for the fields."[46] This work force saved the cotton harvest of that year, picking nearly 90 percent of the crops grown in the upper Rio Grande Valley. *Newsweek* concluded that the "wetback invasion had become so great that part of it was dryback."[47] Indeed, western farmers complained that they were at a loss without Braceros. Not surprisingly, they lobbied vigorously and successfully in the fall of 1948 for its return.

Opposition to the Bracero Program came from many quarters. Organized labor opposed the importation of foreign laborers, arguing that the use of such workers threatened unionization efforts and wage gains. Mexican American workers of the borderland states, where much of this labor was utilized, also opposed braceros largely because the practice cost them their jobs. Although the bracero agreement clearly prohibited the use of bracero labor in place of domestic workers, such restrictions did not prevent the wholesale displacement of domestic labor with bracero labor in the West. According to the National Farm Labor Union, California's Imperial and San Joaquin valleys could count on the availability of 60,000 to 80,000 native workers for harvesting the crops; but braceros were preferable, according to *Fortune Magazine,* because they worked for 60 cents an hour (20 cents less than the prevailing rate), plus board, "while the 'wetbacks' because they cannot protest, work at half the rate."[48]

The issue of discrimination directed at Mexican nationals and citizens of the United States of Mexican origin surfaced during the bracero years. Officials in Mexico City well understood that Americans discriminated against persons of Mexican descent. If, as citizens, Mexican Americans could not enjoy full privileges, it was no great surprise that seasonal labor would be ill-treated. Initially, the Mexican government raised the issue of discrimination when it refused to allow braceros to work in Texas because of the state's exemplary record in allowing overt discrimination against Mexicans to go unchecked. Although farmers pressured Texas officials to rescind the labor ban, not until the founding of the Texas Good Neighbor Commission after the war was it actually lifted. Nonetheless, the issue of discrimination attracted public scrutiny, and Mexican American leaders involved with the American G.I. Forum, the League of United Latin American Citizens, and the newly created American Council for Spanish-Speaking People (ACSSP) began to organize against Jim Crow laws affecting the Mexican American community.[49]

The war in Europe and the Bracero program at home heightened the level of emotional stress in Spanish-speaking communities. However, with much of the community leadership involved in the war effort, the challenges to legal and economic inequities were not undertaken until World War II ended. In the late 1940s, Mexican Americans began a drive to upgrade their social and political status. The leadership challenged segregation policies in public schools, residential neighborhoods, and public accommodations. The most successful challenge came in 1946 in the school desegregation drive in California where a federal district court found the segregation of school children a violation of rights protected by the Fourteenth Amendment.[50]

Another test case came in Texas when an all-white jury convicted Pete Hernandez of murder in Jackson County. LULAC, the American G.I. Forum, and the ACSSP decided to challenge the ruling because of jury exclusion of Mexican Americans. Two Mexican American attorneys who had worked closely with the ACSSP, law professors Carlos Cadena and Gus Garcia, took the case. On appeal, the Texas courts ruled that since Mexican Americans were white, and whites (Anglos) served on the jury in question, there was no discrimination against U.S. population of Mexican origin. In the factual brief that ACSSP head George I. Sanchez prepared, he argued that Mexican Americans in Texas "were recognized as a separate class—by the U.S. Bureau of the Census, by the public schools, and by the state government."[51]

On May 3, 1954, two weeks before the United States Supreme Court handed down its decision in *Brown v. Board of Education*, Chief Justice Earl Warren delivered the majority opinion in *Hernandez v. State*. Justice Warren noted that the petitioner's initial burden in substantiating his charge of group discrimination was to prove that persons of Mexican descent constituted a separate class in Jackson County distinct from "whites."[52] Verification cited included (1) the admission of responsible officials and citizens that residents of the community distinguished between "whites" and "Mexicans"; (2) the low or slight participation of persons of Mexican descent in business and community groups; (3) until recent time, the segregation of Mexican children; (4) the segregation of "Mexicans" in public places; (5) the presence in the courtyard of two men's toilets, one unmarked and the other marked "Colored Men and Hombres Aqui [Men Here]."[53] The court also commented that the absence of a Mexican American juror for twenty-five years in a county where that ethnic group comprised 14 percent of the population "bespeaks discrimination, whether or not it was a conscious decision on the part of any individual jury commissioner."[54]

For the Mexican American community, an important legal precedent was established when Chief Justice Warren asserted that "When the existence of a distinct class is demonstrated, and it is further shown that the laws, as written or as applied, single out that class for different treatment not based on some reasonable classification, the guarantees of the Constitution have been violated."[55] The transitional period produced some legal victories for Mexican Americans, but it was in the sixties, the era of "ethnicity," that Mexican American leaders engaged in a more active form of protest.

The New Ethnics

The last stage of development for the Mexican American community in the West extends from 1965 to the present and includes as principal features, a broad-based surge of ethnic activity and a militant demand for equality. The era's beginning corresponded with the Black civil rights movement and the protest against the Vietnam war. Characteristic of this Chicano militancy was the emergence of an ethnic political party, La Raza Unida, and the conflicts over nineteenth-century land titles in New Mexico. Chicanos and the more conservative Mexican Americans successfully challenged the old political structure and managed to elect several Spanish-speaking congressmen and governors; however, full political participation still eludes many barrio residents. Likewise, although there were numerous stories of successful economic integration, most Mexican Americans continue to earn substantially less than Anglo workers, and only a minority hold white-collar jobs.

In this era of greatly enlarged ethnic expression, the community constantly confronted the issue of identity, as Hispanic, Latino, Latin American, and Chicano labels were introduced both from within and from outside of the community. Old issues of immigration revived in the late 1970s served to remind Mexican Americans that when it came to nativistic sentiments, Americans had a long memory.

The turbulent sixties inaugurated an era of social and political activity for the Mexican American communities and included a protest movement with strong ethnic dimensions. Perhaps the best-known exponent of social protest in the Mexican American community during this time was a former migrant worker from Arizona. César Chávez, whose parents migrated to California during the terrible dust-bowl years, worked during the forties and fifties in the San Joaquin Valley picking crops. When Chávez began his famous grape boycott movement, the small family farm in California had all but disappeared as large corporations bought and operated increasingly vast sections of agricultural lands. These immense farms hired thousands of migrant workers at wages only slightly higher than the sixty cents an hour paid to the braceros of a decade earlier.[56] César Chávez's appeal to ethnic unity was apparent from his speeches, which he often gave in Spanish; also his dedication to the *Virgin de Guadalupe,* as well as his promotion of the famous *Teatro Campesino.*[57]

Chávez, who had learned about organizing from his particiapation in the Chicago urban-based Community Service Organization, left the barrios of San Jose, California, in 1962 to work among farmworkers in the Delano area. When his farmworkers' union joined Filipinos in a strike against grape growers, Chávez applied unique strategies to call attention to the efforts of the strikers. These included a nation-wide boycott of grapes, picketing of stores in urban areas, and a long, well-publicized protest march to the governor's mansion in Sacramento.[58]

The United Farm Workers Union (UFW) under the leadership of César Chávez and Dolores Huerta succeeded over the next ten years in its bid for collective bargaining, decent minimum wages, and workmen's compensation. The UFW's extended battle for these basic employee's rights captured the heart of the Mexican American community.[59] Out of the UFW struggle emerged a cultural organization as well, the Teatro Campesino under the direction of Luis Valdez. In time, other organizations and leaders employed tactics similar to those of the UFW.[60] The Chicano student movement in California and Texas, for example, called for boycott of classes and picketing of public schools. While their demands were different from those of the UFW, their desire to learn more Mexican American history and culture and their call for more Mexican American teachers and administrators nonetheless addressed both important grievances and ethnic issues.

In an earlier generation, Mexican Americans had fought in World War II and Korea with distinction. There was strong unity in the Spanish-speaking community for the war effort. Support for the Vietnam war, however, was no doubt affected by ethnic considerations. César Chávez protested that the Pentagon was engaged in "overbuying" of grapes to help offset losses for California growers resulting from the UFW boycott. Reports that the number of Mexican Americans killed in combat were greatly disproportionate to their population gave rise to a strong protest movement among Spanish-speaking youth in the West. One giant protest rally in Los Angeles, which drew more than twenty thousand participants, resulted in the death of Ruben Salazar, an outstanding spokesman for new ethnic issues among the Spanish-speaking population. Salazar had been the first American journalist to attempt to explain the new phenomena of Chicano power. Other journalists such as Tony Castro would write a full-length study on the topic. The theme of Chicanismo has engaged both scholars and community activists since that time. One consequence of this interest has been the creation of Chicano Studies programs in every western state. These programs, along with mainstream social science and humanities programs, enabled current scholars to assess the level of progress, the degree of change, and the social direction in Mexican American communities. With the exception of the biographies of César Chávez, however, there is still a dearth of published material on this epoch.

The publication of *Los Mojados: The Wetback Story* by Julian Samora of the University of Notre Dame, a study critical of unrestricted migration from Mexico, is an example of the new ethnic scholarship. Samora addressed for the first time the complex issues related to undocumented migration, arguing that illegal migrants displaced Mexican American workers, hindered wage increases, and stifled unionization as well.[61] That numerous Mexican American leaders voiced these concerns is further evidence that the Mexican-origin community in the West no longer viewed itself as an immigrant colony. At the heart of the debate was the question of whether immigrant labor was good or bad for the barrios of the West.[62] An essay in Samora's study by Mexican sociologist Jorge Bustamante calls attention to renewed academic interest by Mexican scholars on the subject of migration to the United States.

Bustamante and other scholars have compared today's undocumented migrants with the bracero workers of the past. Political leaders, economists, and labor spokesmen have also been vocal in blaming foreign workers for taking jobs from native workers and for depressing wages. But the economic situation has changed in the last quarter century. A recent study by the Rand Corporation found that only in the very low-skilled, menial jobs were foreign workers competitive with native workers.[63] Indeed, most Mexican immigrant workers claim less than an elementary school education and thus can hardly compete with the domestic workers whose median educational level is a high school diploma or beyond. In our society there are many menial jobs such as those of maids and busboys that native workers will not accept. Rand investigators also concluded that in an expanding economy, "by keeping costs low, slow wage growth enables the manufacturing sector to maintain a better competitive position vis-a-vis foreign producers."[64] Much more research is needed in this area to determine the economic and social impact—positive and negative—on local communities in the West.

Certainly, the new wave of Mexican immigration has little impact on how Americans view the Mexican American community. The terms "Hispanic" and "Latino" are gaining wide use in many areas. The federal bureaucracy in Washington, as well as Wall Street business and Madison Avenue marketing communities, has adopted the term Hispanic to refer to the U.S. Mexican population. While this term has historical significance in New Mexico and Colorado, it is not widely accepted among Mexican Americans in California and Texas where more than 50 percent of the ethnic group currently resides. On the other hand, the United States Census office, which in 1980 conducted its most comprehensive survey of the Latino population in its history, has been careful to draw distinctions

Mexican Americans in the New West

among the diverse cultural groups constituting the U.S. Hispanic population.[65]

The United States Census counted nearly 15 million people of Latino ethnicity in 1980. These figures confirmed that America accounted for the sixth largest Spanish-speaking population in the world. Latinos in the United States today number more than the combined populations of Nicaragua, Honduras, El Salvador, Costa Rica, and Panama. Los Angeles continues to lead in Latino population in America with two million, and California's four and a half million Latinos account for a population group larger than the national population of Paraguay, Uruguay, or Puerto Rico.[66] The new Latino population is obviously having a significant demographic impact on the urban communities of the West. How diverse Latino groups will interact with each other socially, as well as how they will behave politically is a question that scholars have only begun to research.

Growing ethnic diversification within the Latino community makes it increasingly difficult to classify and enumerate this population. The 1980 Census confirmed, for example, new migration and settlement patterns among U.S. Latinos. Houston, Texas, for example, which prior to the 1960s had a relatively small Mexican community, now has surpassed traditionally Latino cities such as Tucson and El Paso in its Spanish-speaking population. In numbers, California is still the West's largest receiver of new immigrants—based on data for foreign-born, although Florida has a larger percentage of Spanish-speaking foreign-born immigrants. Florida, the oldest Spanish settlement in the North American mainland, is a haven for new immigrants from Puerto Rico and Cuba as well as a center for Central American immigration.[67]

These new migration patterns suggest that the West still represents a major destination for foreign-born, Spanish-speaking migrants from Mexico and Central America (excluding the Caribbean region). In the 1970s Mexican migrants accounted for 40 percent of the new Latino immigration; however, 60 percent of the new Latino migration has been largely Cuban and Central American.[68] New York, with 1.5 million Latinos, now has the second largest concentration of Spanish-speaking people in America. Miami and Chicago, with half a million Latinos each, rank fourth and fifth respectively among the largest urban centers for Spanish speakers. Other Latino communites like those in New Jersey, Tampa, and Washington are also growing rapidly. Furthermore, these new settlement patterns for Latinos do not mean that the West will lose its traditional Mexican influences, but these changes do indicate that Washington politicians, New York media visionaries, and scholars will have to be more precise when they speak of a Hispanic population in the United States.

Conclusion

Mexican American communities of the West have been in a state of flux for well over a century. Eastern and southern migration set in motion by the gold strike and augmented by military activity and the construction of the railroad, converted old Mexican-origin pueblos into American cities. In Los Angeles, San Diego, Tucson, Santa Fe, El Paso, and San Antonio Spanish-speaking peoples quickly became a minority. By the turn of the century, Spanish-speaking communities of the West were thus inhabited by both descendants of a conquered population and participants in the recent migration. The incessant flow of migrants from Mexico into the borderland states contributed to the abilities of Spanish-speaking communities to preserve their Latino characteristics. The new migrants, however, entered the West in an era when barrios no longer remained immigrant colonies. Today's barrios are ethnic communities with growing political and economic power.

The consequences of this migration and the relationship between Mexico and the Mexican American community has attracted recent scholarly notice. Writing in *Daedalus: Journal of the American Academy of Arts and Sciences,* four Mexican American scholars conclude that only Mexico's new oil wealth will alter United States governmental policies that "deplete the resources of the Chicano community." These scholars argue that "a nation tends to treat descendants of foreign stock, even a militarily conquered population, with greater responsibility when it is obligated to negotiate with that foreign nation on an equal footing."[69] Since the expected Mexican economic revolution did not occur and United States officials speak instead of an imminent economic collapse, such a relationship could concern social scientists for another generation. Mexico's growing economic problems, many acknowledge, have already increased undocumented migration. That Mexican Americans could be affected by what happens in Mexico City is indeed a concern to many ethnic leaders. Nonetheless, immigration and economic development within Spanish-speaking communities are highly complex problems for which no simple answers exist. The economic and political problems will have to be worked out between Washington and the leaders of the western states. It is still too early to assess whether the political gains Mexican Americans have made since 1980 will lead to increased influence in foreign policy. One hopes that the solid foundation for a pluralistic society is well in place and that citizens are recognized on the basis of their contribution to American society rather than on ancestral issues.

Notes

*I would like to thank Richard W. Etulain, Gerald D. Nash, Rolando Hinojosa, Raymundo Paredes, Tomas Zigal, Dave Oliphant, and my wife Harriett Romo for their helpful suggestions in the preparation of this essay.

1. There are currently only two journals that publish exclusively in the field of Mexican American studies: *Aztlán: International Journal of the Social Sciences,* Chicano Studies Center at UCLA; and *The Revista Chicana-Riquena* [recently renamed *Journal of the Americas*], University of Houston.
2. See, for example, Frank Bean and Marta Tienda, *The Hispanic Population of the United States* (New York: Russell Sage Foundation, 1987).
3. Carey McWilliams, *North From Mexico: The Spanish-Speaking People of the United States* (New York: Greenwood Press, 1968) [first published in 1948], 207.
4. Ibid., 213.
5. Myron Weiner, "Transborder Peoples," in *Mexican Americans in Comparative Perspective* (Washington, D.C.: The Urban Institute Press, 1985), 130.
6. McWilliams, *North From Mexico,* 207.
7. Rodolfo Alvarez, "The Psycho-Historical and Socioeconomic Development of the Chicano Community in the United States," *Social Science Quarterly* 53 (March 1973): 927–28.
8. Rodolfo Acuña, *Occupied America: The Chicano's Struggle Toward Liberation* (San Francisco: Canfield Press, 1972), 4.
9. Rodolfo Acuña, *Occupied America: A History of Chicanos* 2nd ed. (New York: Harper and Row, 1981), vii.
10. Mario Barrera, *Race and Class in the Southwest: A Theory of Racial Inequality* (Notre Dame: University of Notre Dame, 1979), 218.
11. S. Dale McLemore and Ricardo Romo, "The Origin and Development of the Mexican American People," in Rodolfo O. de la Garza, et al., *The Mexican American Experience: An Interdisciplinary Anthology* (Austin: University of Texas Press, 1985), 3–32.
12. Arrell Morgan Gibson, *The West in the Life of the Nation* (Lexington, Mass.: D.C. Heath and Company, 1976), 574.
13. Edwin T. Bamford, "The Mexican Casual Problem in the Southwest," *Sociology and Social Research* 8 (July-August 1924): 363–71.
14. See, for example, Roger Daniels, *The Politics of Prejudice: The Anti-Japanese Movement in California* (Berkeley: University of California Press, 1962); Stuart Creighton Miller, *The Unwelcome Immigrant: The American Image of the Chinese, 1785–1882* (Berkeley: University of California Press, 1969); Paul R. Ehrlich, et al., *The Golden Door: International Migration, Mexico, and the United States* (New York: Ballantine Books, 1979), 62–65.
15. Victor S. Clark, "Mexican Labor in the United States," *Bureau of Labor Bulletin* No. 78 (Washington: Government Printing Office, 1908), 470.
16. Ibid., 470.
17. The discussion on Primo Tapia's experiences is compiled from Paul Fried-

rich, *Agrarian Revolt in a Mexican Village* (Chicago: University of Chicago Press, 1970), 64–77.

18. Robert Glass Cleland, *California in Our Time* (New York: Alfred A. Knopf, 1947), 82, 85.

19. For an examination of Flores Magon's formative years in the United States, see Ricardo Flores Magon, *Epistolaria revolucionario e intimo* (Mexico City: Ediciones Antorcha, 1978); John M. Hart, *Anarchism and the Mexican Working Class, 1860–1931* (Austin: University of Texas Press, 1978); and Juan Gómez-Quiñones, *Sembradores: Ricardo Flores Magon y el Partido Liberal Mexicano, a Eulogy and Critique* (Los Angeles: Chicano Studies Center, UCLA, 1973).

20. Thomas C. Langham, "An Unequal Struggle: The Case of Ricardo Flores Magon and the Mexican Liberals" (Master's thesis, San Diego State University, 1975), 80–90.

21. Friedrich, *Agrarian Revolt*, 67.

22. Robert V. Hine, *The American West: An Interpretive History* (Boston: Little, Brown and Company, 1984), 348.

23. John Blum, "Nativism, Anti-Radicalism, and the Foreign Scare, 1917–1920," *Midwest Journal* 3 (1950–1951): 47–53.

24. The distribution of Mexican workers in the West is examined in *Mexicans in California: Report of C. C. Young's Mexican Fact-Finding Committee* (Sacramento: California State Printing Office, 1930); Max S. Handman, "San Antonio: The Old Capital of Mexican Life and Influence," *Survey* 6 (May 1931): 163–66; "The Mexican Invaders of El Paso," *Survey* 36 (July 8, 1916): 380–82. Also consult James L. Slaydon, "Some Observations on Mexican Immigration," *Annals of the American Academy of Political and Social Sciences* 93 (January 1921): 121–26.

25. Clark, *Mexican Labor*, 475.

26. Mario T. García, *Desert Immigrants: The Mexicans of El Paso, 1880–1920* (New Haven: Yale University Press, 1981).

27. Carleton Beals, "Civil War in Mexico," *New Republic* 51 (July 6, 1927): 166. "Mexican Government Frees Imprisoned Catholics," *Current History* 26 (September 1927): 958–60.

28. Ricardo Romo, *East Los Angeles: History of a Barrio* (Austin: University of Texas Press, 1983), 61–65.

29. David Montejano, "Frustrated Apartheid: Race, Repression, and Capitalist Agriculture in South Texas, 1920–1930," in Walter Goldfrank, ed., *The World-System of Capitalism: Past and Present* (Beverly Hills: Sage, 1981), 131–68.

30. Earlier investigations of the work and distribution patterns of Mexican immigrants in the West include Manuel Gamio, *Mexican Immigration to the United States* (Chicago: University of Chicago Press, 1931); Emory S. Bogardus, *The Mexican in the United States* (Los Angeles: University of Southern California Press, 1934); John McDowell, *A Study of Social and Economic Factors Relating to Spanish-Speaking People in the United States* (Philadelphia: Home Missions Council, 1927); Ernesto Galarza, "Without Benefit of Lobby," *Survey* 66 (May 1, 1931): 181; Harold Fields, "Where Shall the Alien Work?" *Social Forces* 12 (December 1933): 213–14.

31. Albert Camarillo, *Chicanos in a Changing Society* (Cambridge: Harvard University Press, 1979), 207.

32. Harry E. Hull, "Protective Immigration," *American Labor Legislation Review* 20 (March 1930): 97–98; Kenneth L. Roberts, "Mexicans or Ruin," *Saturday Evening Post* 200 (February 18, 1928): 14–15.

33. Abraham Hoffman, *Unwanted Mexican Americans in the Great Depression: Repatriation Pressures, 1929–1939* (Tucson: University of Arizona Press, 1974), 43.

34. Ibid. See also Carey McWilliams, "Getting Rid of the Mexican," *American Mercury* 28 (March 1933): 323.

35. Francisco E. Balderrama, *In Defense of La Raza: The Los Angeles Mexican Consulate and the Mexican Community, 1929 to 1936* (Tucson: University of Arizona Press, 1982).

36. Reynolds R. McKay, "Texas-Mexican Repatriation During the Great Depression" (Ph.D. dissertation, University of Oklahoma, 1982), 560.

37. For a fuller discussion of strikes in San Antonio and in the Imperial Valley, see, for example, Julia K. Blackwelder, *Women of the Depression: Caste and Culture in San Antonio, 1929–1939* (College Station: Texas A & M University Press, 1984); Paul S. Taylor, *Mexican Labor in the United States: The Imperial Valley* (Berkeley: University of California Press, 1928).

38. Douglas O. Weeks, "The League of United Latin-American Citizens: A Texas-Mexican Civic Organization," *Southwestern Political and Social Science Quarterly* 10 (December 1928): 260.

39. Richard Polenberg, *One Nation Divisible* (New York: Penguin Press, 1980), 52.

40. Raul Morin, *Among the Valiant: Mexican Americans in WW II and Korea* (Alhambra, Calif.: Borden Publishing Co., 1966). See also Kay Briegel, "Alianza Hispano-Americana and Some Mexican-American Civil Rights Cases in the 1950s," in Manuel P. Servin, *An Awakened Minority: The Mexican-Americans* (Beverly Hills: Glencoe Press, 1974), 174–88.

41. Mauricio Mazon, *The Zoot-Suit Riots: The Psychology of Symbolic Annihilation* (Austin: University of Texas Press, 1984).

42. Carl Allsup, *The American G.I. Forum: Origins and Evolution* (Austin: Center for Mexican American Studies Monograph No. 6, 1982), 39–40.

43. A. Russell Buchanan, *The United States and World War II*, vol. I (New York: Harper and Row, 1964), 140–41. Entrance into the war is a vastly complex subject. Useful studies are William L. Langer and Everett Gleason, *The Challenge to Isolation: 1937–1940*, 2 vols. (New York: Harper & Brothers, 1952–53); Charles C. Tansill, *Back Door to War* (Chicago: Henry Regnery Company, 1952); Eric Goldman, *Rendezvous with Destiny* (New York: Alfred A. Knopf, 1952); and Frank Freidel, *Franklin D. Roosevelt*, 3 vols. (Boston: Little, Brown and Company, 1952).

44. Wilbert E. Moore, "America's Migration Treaties During World War II," *Annals of the American Academy of Political and Social Science* 262 (March 1949): 31–38.

45. "Summer Brings the Mexicans," *Commonweal* 48 (July 2, 1948): 275–78.

For an overall assessment of the labor contract program, see Richard B. Craig, *The Bracero Program* (Austin: University of Texas Press, 1971); Peter N. Kirstein, *Anglo Over Bracero* (San Francisco: R & E Associates, 1977).

46. *Newsweek* 32 (October 25, 1948): 80.

47. Ibid., 80. See also Thomas Gorman, "They Help Feed America: A Photo Story of the Braceros," *Today's Health* (October 1957): 24–27.

48. "Braceros," *Fortune* 43 (April 1951): 60–61.

49. American G.I. Forum and the Texas State Federation of Labor, *What Price Wetbacks?* (Austin: Texas Federation of Labor, 1953); Otey M. Scruggs, "The United States, Mexico, and the Wetback, 1942–1947," *Pacific Historical Review* 32 (February 1963): 153; and Scruggs, "Evolution of the Mexican Farm Labor Agreement of 1942," *Agricultural History* 34 (July 1960): 140–49.

50. Charles Wollenberg, "*Mendez v. Westminister:* Race, Nationality, and Segregation in California Schools," *California Historical Quarterly* 53 (Winter 1974): 317–33.

51. Ricardo Romo, "George I. Sanchez and the Civil Rights Movement: 1940–1960," *La Raza Law Journal* (University of California Berkeley), 1 (Fall 1986): 342–62.

52. *Hernandez v. Texas* 347 U.S. 482 (1954).

53. Ibid., 480.

54. Ibid., 482.

55. Ibid., 479–82.

56. George E. Coalson, "Mexican Contract Labor in American Agriculture," *Southwest Social Science Quarterly* 33 (December 1952): 228–38.

57. Chávez's early life is recounted in Peter Matthiessen, *Sal Si Puedes: Cesar Chavez and the New American Revolution* (New York: Random House, 1969).

58. Ronald B. Taylor, *Chavez and the Farm Workers* (Boston: Beacon, 1975), 129.

59. Ibid., 330–32.

60. Jorge Huerta, *Chicano Theater: Themes and Forms* (Ypsilanti, Mich.: Bilingual Press/Editorial Bilingue), 11–26; Luis Valdez, *Actos* (Fresno, Calif.: Cucaracha Press, 1971).

61. Julian Samora, *Los Mojados: The Wetback Story* (Notre Dame: University of Notre Dame Press, 1971). See also Jorge Bustamante, "Undocumented Migration from Mexico: Research Report," *International Migration Review* 11 (1977): 149–77.

62. "Illegal Immigrants are Backbone of Economy in States of Southwest," *Wall Street Journal* 89 (May 7, 1985).

63. Kevin F. McCarthy and R. Burciaga Valdez, *Current and Future Effects of Mexican Immigration in California* (Santa Monica, Calif.: The Rand Corporation, 1985), 24.

64. Ibid., 20. Related to this discussion is Gilberto Cardenas and Estevan T. Flores, *The Migration and Settlement of Undocumented Women* (Austin: CMAS Publications, University of Texas, 1986).

65. "The Hispanic Market A Growing Profile," *Caminos* (Special Issue: Hispanic Conventioneer, 1985): 15–16.

66. "Where the Hispanics Live" *Caminos* (Special Issue: Hispanic Conventioneer, 1985): 14. See also A. J. Jaffe, Ruth Cullen, and Thomas Boswell, *The Changing Demography of Spanish Americans* (New York: Academic Press, 1980).

67. "Where Hispanics Live," *Caminos* (Special Issue: Hispanic Conventioneer, 1985): 14.

68. Ibid., 14; Alejandro Portes and Robert L. Bach, *Latin Journey: Cuban and Mexican Immigrants in the United States* (Berkeley and Los Angeles: University of California Press, 1985).

69. Leobardo F. Estrada, F. Chris Garcia, Reynaldo Flores Macias, Lionel Maldonado, "Chicanos in the United States: A History of Exploitation and Resistance," *Daedalus* 110 (Spring 1981): 130; Marta Tienda and Vilma Ortiz, " 'Hispanicity' and the 1980 Census," *Social Science Quarterly* 67 (March 1986): 3–20.

5

Indians of the Modern West[1]

Donald L. Parman

Native Americans have been the West's oldest settlers, but only recently have historians begun to assess their experience in the twentieth century. If studies of American Indian life before 1890 abound, the historical literature about their experience in the years since 1890 is uneven and sparse. By the 1970s, however, a growing number of historians began to turn their attention to this significant period in the development of the first Americans. Among these scholars Donald Parman is preeminent. In this essay he surveys existing writings in the field and identifies major themes that can serve as guideposts for researchers seeking to know more about the subject.

Until recently, the general historiography on Indians of the West in this century has been slow to develop.[2] Except for Randolph C. Downes's article on pre–New Deal reforms,[3] historians largely ignored twentieth-century Indian topics until the 1960s, when graduate students first probed the subject. This early work focused on the 1920s and the New Deal because of the keen interest in John Collier's reforms. More recently, several young scholars have investigated the post–World War II policies of withdrawal, termination, and relocation. To date, few studies have been completed on the Progressive Era, 1900–1920. Except for polemical writings, little attention has been given to the "red power" period of the 1960s and 1970s. In short, the historiography of the field remains uneven and sketchy.

Perhaps the overriding theme for twentieth-century Indians of the West[4] has been the conflicts over their natural resources—land, water, oil and gas, various minerals, timber, and wild life—and whites' desire to develop the region. This conflict has involved white vested interests seeking to acquire or to utilize Indian natural resources, and the Indians' attempts to protect their wealth. Although economic competition between whites and Indians has been central, other elements have been involved. The federal government has played crucial roles in western reclamation, conservation, national parks and forests, and grazing on the public domain, and these programs frequently have involved Indian reservations. Because of the Indians' dependence on the Bureau of Indian Affairs (BIA), their fate has often been determined by that agency's relations with other federal agencies, particularly those within the Departments of Interior and Agriculture, which have been responsive to whites.

Other significant determinants include the federal government's Indian policies, public attitudes towards Indians, the legal status of Native Americans as expressed in court decisions, and cultural differences between the two races. These other topics, however, have usually been related to white attempts to secure Indian resources.

Another factor that must be kept in mind is that Indian affairs in the West have been influenced by the region's general development since 1900. At that time, three of the present sixteen states (Oklahoma, New Mexico, and Arizona) remained territories. Agriculture dominated the region, but even Kansas, Nebraska, and California, although settled first, lagged far behind the corn belt in value of crops raised. Annual farm production in Arizona, Idaho, Nevada, New Mexico, Utah, and Wyoming totaled less than twenty million dollars in 1899, compared to $365,411,528 for Iowa alone. Western manufacturing and urbanization similarly remained insignificant. Although major railroad lines existed in the West before 1900, the region's inadequate transportation hampered marketing in many localities.[5]

Despite the West's underdevelopment and economic subservience, the region in no way was stagnant or lacked optimism in 1900. The post–Civil War settlement boom continued, and western states and territories during the 1890s had experienced population increases of 50 to 90 percent. Western leaders, moreover, foresaw an almost unlimited potential for more settlement and economic growth. The one essential requirement, according to regional spokesmen, was to escape the domination of eastern financial interests. Confidence in the future, desire for regional development, and hostility against the East typified western attitudes in 1900, and they would affect how Indians and their resources would be treated.

Except that most western Indians lived on reservations supervised by the BIA, their conditions in 1900 were markedly diverse.[6] Tribal differences, geographic conditions, means of subsistence, wealth, and receptiveness to change were factors that created such diversity. Arizona, California, Oklahoma, New Mexico, and South Dakota clearly contained large Indian populations, while Colorado, Kansas, Nebraska, Oregon, Texas, Utah, and Wyoming held much smaller numbers.[7] Although the reservation and assimilation policies had been pursued since the 1850s, their impact varied greatly from tribe to tribe and even from individual to individual.

The passage of the General Allotment Act of 1887 also figured as an important factor in Indian lives.[8] This measure developed from a general belief that Indians possessed too much land, the resource that most attracted white interest, and their assimilation demanded the elimination of communal property and tribalism. Allotment or the assignment of tribal land to individuals was not a new concept. Earlier treaties, agreements, and legislation had repeatedly included allotment provisions, and some 11,000 allotments already existed by 1885. What made the General Allotment Act especially significant was that it authorized the president to order the allotment of nearly all reservations that he believed suited to either agriculture or grazing.[9]

The main provisions of the legislation were fairly simple. Heads of families received 160 acres, single individuals over eighteen and orphans received 80 acres, and unmarried tribesmen under eighteen received 40 acres. To protect against loss, the legislation placed the allotments under federal trust for twenty-five years, and this, in turn, meant that the lands could not be sold, encumbered, or taxed. The allottees automatically became citizens. Other provisions permitted Indians to gain citizenship if they left their reservation or if they took an allotment on the public domain.

The unassigned portions of reservations became "surplus land" that could voluntarily be sold to the federal government. In practice, however, few tribes successfully resisted official pressures to sell such land. Funds from these transactions were credited to the tribe in the federal treasury from which they were appropriated by Congress for education or "civilization." Once sold, the surplus lands became subject to entry on the same basis as regular public domain.

In addition to allotment by executive order, numerous reservations were opened after 1887 by special legislation. Invariably, the opening of reservations in this manner simply reflected western politicians' willingness to satisfy constituents' land hunger.

The leasing of allotments was first authorized in 1891, and it was originally intended to permit the very young, the elderly, and the physically handicapped to derive some income from undeveloped holdings. Despite restrictive criteria, leasing by 1900 became widespread among all categories of Indian allottees.

Scholars have lodged numerous complaints against allotment and other

BIA land policies. Individualized holdings on arid reservations subsequently impoverished residents; sales of surplus land seriously reduced the Indian land base and left insufficient resources for future population growth; and the government never provided adequate capital and practical training to develop Indian farming. Allotments later became so fractionalized by heirship that they could only be rented to whites. Leasing afforded little return to allottees and usually frustrated any chance that Indians would utilize their own land.[10]

The role of western leadership in the passage of the General Allotment Act has never been totally clear, but the prima facie evidence of a bargain between the West and eastern reformers appears unlikely.[11] Apparently, the pivotal legislation was entirely the handiwork of Indian reformers. If a western role existed, it dealt with the reformers' knowledge that allotment must make some concessions to salve whites' land hunger. Perhaps this underlies the reformers' numerous assertions that general allotment forestalled the abolition of all reservations.

Major policies and legislation of the early twentieth century usually supplemented the General Allotment Act. The Burke Act of 1906, for example, withheld citizenship at allotment but permitted allottees to apply for "competency certificates" that gave them both citizenship and fee simple land titles during the trust period. Other legislation of the time also complemented the 1887 enactment.[12] Allotment itself continued at a rapid pace and frequently included less desirable reservations ignored earlier.[13]

The relationship between Indian legislation and policies of the early twentieth century and broader national Progressive reforms remains unclear. Perhaps this is not surprising since scholars of general Progressivism increasingly seem to conclude that reforms and leaders often differed drastically in philosophy and approach. Moreover, relatively few studies of early twentieth-century Indian affairs have been completed, and perhaps the literature has not reached sufficient maturation to permit a full understanding of the ties between Indian affairs and the broader Progressive reforms. Certainly evidence exists for at least some tentative parallels. Herbert Welsh, head of the Indian Rights Association, and other Indian reformers frequently cited the evils of the spoils system within the Indian service as a means of achieving civil service reforms not only for the BIA but for government in general.[14] Progressivism likely helped inspire such BIA policies as scientific administration, Indian self-support, and administrative decentralization. One may also find other examples such as new legal protections, the creation of executive order reservations, and increased attention to education and health.

Several recent studies have focused attention on general Indian affairs of the early twentieth century. Frederick E. Hoxie in *A Final Promise*, for example, sees the "Indian question" transformed in the 1890s from the benevolent assimilation embodied in the Dawes Act to a malevolent assimilation because of President Theodore Roosevelt's reliance on a "cowboy cabinet" for advice, the increased political power of western congressmen, and by a growing white pessimism about the Indians' ability to assimilate and to survive without government supervision.[15] Assimilation, Hoxie argues, continued as a goal after 1900, but it was always secondary to regional development, usually at the expense of Indian land and resources.[16]

Brian W. Dippie's study of white attitudes and their impact on Indian policy agrees that a lessened faith in assimilation took place at the turn of the century, but he suggests that Progressive reformers such as Francis E. Leupp and Roosevelt, recognizing anthropologists' earlier warnings about overly rapid cultural change, concluded that the 1880s drive for rapid assimilation had failed and many Indians would need the reservations as a protective device in the foreseeable future.[17]

An interesting recent article by Henry E. Fritz suggests different conclusions. Although Fritz does not attempt to evaluate the impact of general Progressive reforms on Indian affairs, his revisionist study of the Board of Indian Commissioners argues against the standard interpretation that the board was virtually moribund after 1900. He maintains that new appointees after 1906 revitalized the advisory group and made it once again into an effective monitor over Indian affairs and legislation. While Fritz admits the board could not change established policy, its renewed activism forced the BIA to operate more humanely. More importantly, he concludes that board protests about health conditions, land policies, and other matters anticipated the reforms of the 1920s and 1930s.[18]

An article by Kenneth O'Reilly stresses the importance of Indian self-support throughout the Progressive Era. He identifies the start of the policy goal with Commissioner William Jones's (1895–1904) drastic cuts in rations. Leupp (1905–1909), Jones's successor and a central figure in Progressive reform, tried unsuccessfully to achieve self-support by attracting outside capital investment to reservations and by also aggressively recruiting Indians for outside employment. After Leupp's failure to secure outside capital, Commissioner Robert Valentine (1909–1912) sought to wring funds out of a reluctant Congress by securing reimbursable loans. Used to finance irrigation, livestock purchases, farm machinery, and other self-support projects, the reimbursable funds could be loaned to individuals or tribes. Since the loans were charged against tribal funds, groups without such wealth could not obtain this credit. The Cato Sells administration (1913–1921) enlarged the approach after an inaugural inspection of reservations in 1913. Sells' expansion of loans, however, brought mixed results. The amount of money was never adequate, and the loans were often used on unsuccessful projects, or they benefited whites more than Indians, especially on irrigation projects.[19]

Case studies of Indian reservations during the Progressive Era reveal serious BIA failures to protect Indian land and resources. Donald J. Berthrong's work on the Cheyenne-Arapaho reservation and William T. Hagan's book on the Kiowa-Comanche reservation, both in western Oklahoma, stress that the BIA failed badly to protect Indian land holdings from local whites.[20] In part, the failures may reflect the normal gap between national policy and agency implementation, but they largely reveal that Progressive Era officials were insensitive to the importance of Indians retaining a land base, both for future economic needs and preserving their tribal identities.

If there is any common agreement among existing scholarship on Progressive Era Indian affairs, it lies in the conclusion that Commissioner Sells' "forced patents" had disastrous results. Sells and Interior Secretary Franklin Lane saw in competency certificates and fee simple titles, permitted under the Burke Act, an opportunity to free the more capable Indians of government control. Instead of waiting for Indians to apply, Sells in 1915 and 1916 organized competency commissions that toured reservations, screened Indians, and issued certificates and fee simple titles to many. In April 1917, Sells' "Declaration of Policy" intensified such efforts by ordering that nearly all individuals with less than one-half Indian blood and adult graduates of government schools would receive fee patents. Sells also lessened restrictions over the sale of heirship lands and older Indians' trust holdings.

It was quickly evident that approximately 90 percent of Indians who gained full title to allotments quickly sold them, usually well under market value, and squandered the proceeds. Others lost their land because they neglected to pay local and state taxes. Despite these problems, Sells further "liberalized" fee patenting in 1919. Finally in 1920, a new secretary of interior, John Barton Payne, reinstituted the policy of processing only voluntary applications for competency. Some 34,000 fee patents had been issued during the previous decade with approximately half that number since the "Declaration of Policy."[21] The forced patents enriched white merchants and land owners, but they tragically left thousands of Indians landless and impoverished.

World War I had a varied but often decisive effect on western Indians. Both citizen and noncitizen Indians were required to register for selective service, but only the former would be drafted. According to the war department, 33,000 Indians were eligible for military duty, with 6,500 entering the army, 1,000 the navy, and 500 in other military positions. The government rejected an attempt to place Indians in separate units, and they were integrated with whites, evidently experiencing little dis-

Indians of the Modern West

crimination. Many Indian servicemen were accustomed to military life because of attending boarding schools. In at least one instance, the 36th Division, Choctaws frustrated German wiretaps by transmitting telephonic messages in their native language.[22]

Indians who remained at home were mainly affected by Sells' campaign to increase food production. The commissioner quickly ordered agency personnel to encourage Indians to place more land under cultivation. The acreage farmed increased by 31.6 percent in 1917 and about the same amount in the following year. The extra production, combined with higher farm prices, doubtlessly increased Indian income.[23] Unfortunately, not all of Sells' campaign worked to the advantage of Indians. On several reservations, superintendents pressured Indians to sell their cattle and to lease their land to white ranchers. Money from the cattle was quickly spent on automobiles and luxuries, and when prices plummeted after the war, white ranchers defaulted on lease payments. One author characterizes the wartime leasing policies as the worst disaster on the Pine Ridge reservation since the end of the buffalo.[24] Sells' wartime policies everywhere stressed the leasing of all types of land with a minimum of safeguards for the Indians.[25]

Some of the Indians' problems were simply by-products of wartime conditions. Increased inflation seriously reduced the real income of Indians and curtailed BIA services. Numerous resignations of field personnel also took place.

Another by-product of the war was passage of the Indian Citizenship Act of 1924. As early as 1918, individuals proposed such legislation because of the wartime contributions of Indians, and in 1919 Congress conveyed citizenship to all Indian veterans. General legislation, however, was delayed by fears that citizenship might jeopardize federal services and protections. This obstacle was overcome by the statement in the act that citizenship would not "in any manner impair or otherwise affect the right of any Indian to tribal or other property."[26] The legislation, however, did not guarantee voting rights, and several western states denied Indians the franchise until after World War II.[27]

During the 1920s, the government abandoned its aggressive self-support policies and displayed more interest in protecting Indian resources. Most studies see these changes as a reaction to the reform agitation of John Collier, a young native of Georgia.[28] Although Collier's philosophy is not easy to understand, he represented a major departure from earlier reformers. Repulsed by the industrial revolution, conservative social Darwinism, and rampant individualism, Collier saw a general need to return to the spiritual, social and moral virtues of pre-industrial communal life. For Indians, he rejected forced assimilation in favor of cultural pluralism or simply allowing tribesmen to accept voluntarily whatever aspects of white life they wanted while still retaining their own folkways. Although something of an idealist and a mystic, Collier became well versed in the complexities of Indian affairs, demonstrated extraordinary propaganda skills, and recognized the tragic results of allotment. In contrast to older reformers, Collier directly attacked the BIA rather than attributed its failures to corrupt or inept employees.[29]

After an initial contact with the Taos Indians in 1920, Collier took up Indian reform full time in 1922 because of the Bursum Bill. Introduced at the request of Interior Secretary Albert B. Fall, the measure attempted to resolve long-standing land disputes between Pueblo Indians and white settlers and to provide clear titles to owners. The Bursum Bill defined ownership but with a heavy bias by awarding whites clear title if they could prove continuous possession for ten years prior to 1912.[30]

Collier's campaign against the Bursum Bill foreshadowed his later agitation. He organized the Council of All Pueblos in November 1922, and shortly afterward a memorial from the group appeared in the *The New York Times*. Numerous protests and inquiries flooded the BIA. Later the same month, Senator William Borah of Idaho effectively killed the bill by asking for its recall. Collier continued his lobby activities in the subsequent struggle to obtain a more equitable law. A compromise measure finally passed in 1924.[31]

An issue with much greater potential harm to western Indians developed in the early 1920s with oil explorations on the Navajo reservation. All groups agreed that Indians were entitled to full revenues from oil on treaty reservations, but many western whites believed that tribes should not derive any money from leases on executive order reservations.[32] In 1922, Secretary Fall, claiming that executive order lands were legally still public domain and their surface was merely on loan to Indian residents, ordered that oil leases on executive order reservations fell under the General Leasing Act of 1920. Potentially, Fall's order would have denied the Navajos any revenues from the executive order portions of their reservation.[33] Fortunately, Fall's successor, Hubert Work, revoked the order, and in 1927 Congress approved an act guaranteeing Indians the revenues from all reservations, subject to some state taxes.[34]

Collier remained a constant critic of the BIA on numerous issues throughout the 1920s. He vigorously defended Indian religious freedom, attacked BIA education, fought against leasing a valuable power site on the Flathead reservation, criticized the expenditure of Navajo oil revenues, and demanded the cancellation of reimbursable loans. His major concern, however, always remained the ending of allotment.

By the mid–1920s, Collier's many protests prompted several major assessments of BIA administration. Secretary Work inaugurated these in December 1923 when he convened the Committee of One Hundred to evaluate Indian affairs. The group's mixed composition produced compromise resolutions that had little impact.[35]

In 1926 the Institute for Government Research, a private group, at Work's request, launched perhaps the most significant survey of Indian conditions ever made.[36] Lewis Meriam of the institute headed a panel of ten experts from such fields as law, economics, urban conditions, agriculture, health, family life, and education. Henry Roe Cloud, a Winnebago educator, served as "Indian advisor." After seven months of visiting reservations, schools, and medical facilities, the group returned to Washington and drafted a voluminous report, *The Problem of Indian Administration*.[37]

The report sharply criticized the quality of education and conditions at boarding schools, emphasized the intense poverty and health problems of reservations, and condemned allotment and forced assimilation, but it did not endorse radical solutions. Instead, the commission suggested making the BIA more efficient by adding a division of planning and administration, upgrading field personnel, and increasing appropriations.[38]

Collier, in the meantime, influenced Senator William T. King of Utah to begin a Senate investigation in 1928. Usually conducted in the field during recesses by a subcommittee of the Senate Indian Affairs Committee, the investigation lasted until 1943. The extensive hearings, "The Survey of Conditions of Indians in the United States," remain an unstructured but invaluable body of data about reservation conditions.[39]

That Collier secured the Senate investigation through Senator King points up his ability to avoid western politicians' traditional hostility toward Indian reformers. Collier probably also recognized that regional interests were more important than party affiliations, for he worked with both western Democrats and Republicans. Most western congressional figures agreed with Collier that the BIA ruled Indians dictatorially, but they failed to recognize, however, that his cultural pluralism differed sharply with their belief in rapid assimilation and abolishing the BIA.[40]

The wave of criticisms and investigations produced limited reforms during the Herbert Hoover administration. The policies of W. Carson Ryan, director of Indian education, were the most distinctive of these, but improved health facilities, some reorganization of the Washington office, and increased appropriations also occurred. However, the "benevolent assimilation" philosophy adopted by Commissioner Charles J. Rhoads and Assistant Commissioner J. Henry Scattergood and their weak support for ending allotment and the cancellation of reimbursable loans soon led Collier to renewed agitation.[41]

The onset of depression in 1929 doubtlessly created far more distress on reservations than any shortcomings of Rhoads and Scattergood. As a minority in a still underdeveloped region, Indians were especially vulnerable to economic woes. Normal income from ranching, farming, leasing, arts and crafts, and off-reservation jobs dropped sharply.

The appointment of Collier as commissioner in 1933 marked the first real departure from assimilation policies since the 1880s. It gave the longtime critic of the BIA an opportunity to effect the many changes he had advocated during the previous decade.[42]

Historians who have studied Collier's commissionership have raised serious questions about his effectiveness. Despite these reservations, Collier demonstrated remarkable ability to secure funds from numerous New Deal emergency programs. These included the Civilian Conservation Corps, Public Works Administration, Soil Conservation Service, and the Works Progress Administration. Collier's ties with Secretary of Agriculture Henry A. Wallace brought the BIA technical expertise impossible under its regular budgets. Emergency funds provided jobs and money for reservations, improved conservation, and built much-needed educational and medical facilities. Many older Indians still regard the New Deal not as a time of hardship but as a prosperous period.

Despite such successes, the keystone of Collier's administration was the Indian Reorganization Act (IRA) of 1934.[43] This important measure attempted to replace the General Allotment Act and the assimilation policy with cultural pluralism and other key Collier beliefs. Introduced in February 1934, the original bill of 48 pages was divided into four titles. The first title permitted tribes to establish themselves as federal municipalities, to charter tribal businesses, and to secure loans from a revolving fund. Title II endorsed the study of Indian arts, crafts, and traditions in BIA schools. The third title prohibited further allotment, returned surplus lands to tribes, and authorized one million dollars annually to acquire more land. The provisions also granted controversial powers to the secretary of the interior to consolidate restricted allotments and private reservation lands by either their purchase or exchange. Also title to restricted allotments could, at the death of the present owner, revert to the tribe rather than to heirs. Title IV called for a system of special Indian courts, using traditional Indian law, to exercise original jurisdiction over reservations.

After preliminary hearings, Collier staged ten Indian congresses in the West to explain the measure to tribal representatives in March and April. Few Indians fully understood the complex measure after the congresses, but most probably favored it. Some critics, however, saw cultural pluralism as retrogressive and forced land consolidation as confiscatory. Several extremists in Oklahoma denounced the bill as communistic and unAmerican.

A second round of congressional hearings drastically altered and shortened the bill. Amendments dropped the special Indian courts and made land consolidation voluntary and virtually inoperative. Collier, however, received increases in funds for revolving loans and scholarships. What remained virtually intact in the final bill, approved in June 1934, was a complicated process for creating local self-government and chartering of tribal businesses.

The formation of tribal councils, central to Collier's program after 1934, was rejected by 60 percent of the Indians in referendums on the IRA.[44] Where approved, mixed bloods often seized control of IRA councils, excluded the full bloods, and worsened existing factionalism. The new councils found decision making limited to internal tribal affairs, such as determining who would be allowed on rolls, not the control of budgets and personnel. Superintendents usually dominated the IRA councils by judiciously dispensing emergency program jobs.[45]

Collier as commissioner could no longer disguise his long-range goals from the Indian affairs committees. Representatives Theodore Werner of South Dakota and Isabella Greenway of Arizona, for example, opposed land consolidation during the 1934 hearings on the IRA because they saw it as prolonging the BIA. Committee members' proprietary attitudes about Indians also surfaced. After a heated exchange during the Senate hearings, Senator Elmer Thomas, claiming that the bill did not fit the conditions of Indians in his state, later amended the legislation to exclude Oklahoma.[46]

Despite two years of relative harmony with the Indian affairs committees after 1934, Collier experienced severe difficulties in 1936. Several factors explain the change. Major Indian opponents formed the American Indian Federation (AIF) in 1934. The AIF represented a diversity of views unified chiefly by members' opposition to Collier. Alice Lee Jimerson, the AIF's "brains" and Washington representative, repeatedly attacked Collier's administration before the Senate Indian Affairs Committee after 1934. The senators themselves strongly disagreed with his cultural pluralism or opposed him because of complaints of white constituents. Regardless of the motives of the senators, Collier's main concern after 1936 was to ward off numerous attempts to repeal or limit the application of the IRA. He survived as commissioner only by retaining the strong support of Interior Secretary Harold L. Ickes and the Roosevelt administration.

Despite the attention that the Collier administration has received, no strong interpretative consensus has yet emerged. Several writers suggest that Collier never really achieved greater Indian freedom from the BIA. What appeared as self-government was actually Collier's exercising administrative fiat to do what he thought best for the Indians. Reservations doubtlessly benefited from emergency programs, but some tribes experienced problems adjusting to a wage work and cash market economy. More importantly, the ability of these programs to bring about lasting prosperity and self-sufficiency was often negligible. Indeed, Richard

White's provocative study, *The Roots of Dependency*, concludes that livestock reductions on the Navajo reservation brought on tribal *dependency* and created mass trauma.[47] Several studies, however, see the Indian New Deal as economically beneficial, and they especially praise Collier's reversal of allotment and assimilation policies.[48] Given the evidence to date, perhaps the Indian New Deal can never be reduced to a simple formulation, but it must be evaluated almost reservation by reservation and program by program.[49]

In truth, Collier faced major obstacles in his attempts to upgrade the Indians' situation. Despite gaining money from emergency programs, he never received adequate funds to bring long-term prosperity to most reservations. Some, because of checkerboarded and fractionalized allotments, inadequate rainfall, and lack of natural resources, remained "basket cases" without the means to support their population except by constant infusions of federal aid. Finally, such Collier policies as canceling white leases, buying additional lands with IRA or emergency funds, and protecting Indian religious freedom contributed to his many difficulties with western congressional delegations.

The experience of western Indians during World War II paralleled those of World War I. Military service, greater employment opportunities, and diminished BIA services typified both conflicts. Because of the Citizenship Act of 1924, however, all Indians came under Selective Service legislation. More importantly, World War II had a much more intense and varied impact on Indians. One study of Zuni and Navajo veterans, indeed, suggests that the war created perhaps the most profound changes on the tribes since the arrival of the Spanish in the Southwest.[50] Most of the changes developed from important regional and national trends, particularly western economic development. Probably because Indian wartime experiences often lacked drama and are not readily studied by conventional research techniques, historians have yet to probe the topic adequately.[51]

Indian participation in the armed forces during the conflict was sizeable. Some 25,000 young men and women served, and as during World War I, they were integrated into white units without major difficulty. For most, military service greatly broadened their horizons and created the realization that better education was needed for Indians. Although much attention has centered on the Navajo "code talkers" and Ira Hayes's tragic postwar death from alcoholism, Indians served in all military branches in many capacities. Given their undereducation and the "sociology" of the military, probably a high percentage were assigned to combat units, which helps account for Indians' numerous decorations. The largest single group of Indians served in the 45th Division, a national guard unit from the Southwest, which fought extensively in Europe.

Indians of the Modern West

The broader impact of the war, however, involved the mass exodus of 40,000 Indians to off-reservation jobs. This relocation was particularly important because it established a continuing trend, and it signified that western economic development during the war gave Indians unprecedented job opportunities. Very strong ties also existed between New Deal emergency work programs and the 40,000 Indians who left their reservations between 1940 and 1945. Indians first became eligible for job training under the National Defense Vocational Training Act in early 1941, and Indian CCC officials arranged classes in welding, auto mechanics, sheet metal work, carpentry, and other subjects. Even without such training, thousands of Indians utilized skills learned in the CCC and other New Deal programs to win wartime jobs.[52]

The effects of off-reservation employment for Indian civilians varied much more than for military service. Many Indians found temporary and seasonal jobs that did not significantly alter their lives. Others who worked in west coast war plants and shipyards or interior cities such as Wichita, Minneapolis, or Denver apparently integrated into a white middle class lifestyle. The percentage who remained as permanent residents in the postwar period is unknown. Both categories benefited economically as Indians' average annual income rose from $400 in 1940 to $1,200 in 1945. In some instances, the war revived cultural traditions, particularly religious ceremonies asking for victory or blessing young servicemen as they left home. The postwar return of veterans sometimes created conflicts because their new ideas and behavior offended traditionalists.

The war produced severe dislocations in BIA services. Early in the conflict, the Washington office moved to Chicago, handicapping its day-to-day functions. The Indian CCC and other emergency programs quickly disbanded in early 1942. The BIA budget, with Collier and Ickes's consent, was pared. Perhaps the worst impact, however, was the numerous Indian Service workers who resigned for military service or better paying jobs. On the Navajo reservation, for example, half of the day schools closed, and the excellent medical staff and services developed after 1933 disintegrated quickly.[53]

The end of World War II left Indian affairs in disarray and drift. Veterans and former war workers returned to reservations still suffering from wartime dislocations. Collier resigned in January 1945, apparently frustrated by his ineffectiveness. His handpicked successor, William A. Brophy, promised during confirmation hearings that he would follow the policy dictates of Congress. Brophy spent his first months in office planning a decentralization of the BIA, and Congress in August 1945 authorized five district offices located throughout the West.[54] Illness, however, forced him to relinquish his duties to Assistant Commissioner William Zimmerman (a Collier holdover) most of the time after 1946. John R.

Nichols finally became commissioner in 1949 but spent most of his eleven month tenure inspecting reservations.

The most significant change in the postwar drift was passage of the Indian Claims Commission Act in 1946. Achievement of this long-advocated reform resulted from a peculiar alliance between liberals who saw it as redressing past wrongs and conservatives who wanted to get the government out of the "Indian business." The act itself permitted tribes to present evidence about government violations of treaties and other abuses of trust responsibilities. The quasi-judicial commission heard the cases presented by tribal and justice department attorneys, rendered a verdict (subject to judicial review), and determined damages. Although hailed as a major reform, the commission's work "was a mixture of positive results and substantial failure."[55] Particularly disappointing to Indians, the claims awards were based on land values at the time of treaty cessions, and they were further reduced by "offsets" or various past government expenditures for the tribes. The claim cases unquestionably have sensitized Indians to legal matters, and they also produced extensive research by historians, anthropologists, and other expert witnesses. After several revisions and extensions of the original legislation, Congress disbanded the commission in 1978 and assigned remaining cases to the court of claims.

The period of drift in Indian affairs ended with the appointment of Dillon S. Myer as commissioner in 1950. A professional administrator, Myer had headed several federal programs, including the War Relocation Authority. Despite inexperience with Indian affairs, Myer quickly sensed that western conservatives in Congress wanted a reversal of Collier policies. Without major new legislation, he launched a policy of "withdrawal" aimed at ending BIA services for Indians. He manipulated the new district offices to increase his own authority and to bypass Collier holdovers. He also initiated a relocation program that placed Indians in off-reservation jobs and began using revolving loans to upgrade tribes' economic conditions as a prelude to withdrawal.

Myer also moved toward the transfer of BIA services such as education and health to states or other federal agencies. In November 1951, the newly created division of programs in the BIA began a massive compilation of data on reservations aimed at creating a master plan for ending federal trust and service activities. After completion of the fact finding in mid-1952, Myer ordered BIA employees to draw up withdrawal programs for individual reservations. Although unable to implement any of the plans, Myer's studies greatly influenced the "termination" policy of the Eisenhower administration.[56]

Scholars who have studied the withdrawal and termination period have developed something of an interpretative consensus to explain the new trend. Nearly all trace the roots of withdrawal and termination to a 1943

Indians of the Modern West

report by the Senate Indian Affairs Committee that attacked Collier's policies as restrictive and advocated an abolition of the BIA. O. K. Armstrong repeated similar views in his widely read 1945 article, "Set the Indian Free," in *Reader's Digest*. Freeing the Indian also was reenforced by the conservative postwar public mood, the cold war, McCarthyism, and, somewhat ironically, the fledgling civil rights movement.[57]

BIA leadership tried to accommodate withdrawal-termination forces without much success. Acting Commissioner Zimmerman in February 1947 testified before the Senate Committee on Civil Service about how BIA personnel and expenditures might be reduced. Perhaps unwittingly, he provided a blueprint for terminationists by categorizing reservations according to their readiness for ending federal services, and he even presented a time table and model legislation to committee members. The influential Hoover Commission's Report on Indian affairs in 1948 strongly advocated a return to assimilation, the assumption of BIA services by other agencies, and the retention of tribal governments as only transitory devices.

During the postwar era the BIA also failed to maintain its trust responsibilities over Indian land and other resources. The granting of fee simple titles to restricted allotments had continued after 1933, but Collier approved such actions only in emergency cases or if owners sold holdings to their tribe or other Indians. In 1944, Secretary Ickes, surrendering to white and Indian pressures, relaxed Collier's rigid standards, and protections were eased even more after the war.[58]

A related problem was the loss of Indian land through the use of eminent domain by federal agencies. Examples of this can be found throughout the twentieth century, but the trend accelerated after World War II. In 1944 the Corps of Engineers and the Bureau of Reclamation negotiated the Pick-Sloan plan that led to a program of dam construction and water development on the upper Missouri river. The two agencies then secured land from five Sioux reservations (Standing Rock, Cheyenne River, Lower Brule, Crow Creek, and Yankton) and the Fort Berthold reservation. Included were the Indians' most valuable holdings for agriculture, grazing, hunting, timber, and gathering. The relocation of Indian population disrupted kinship ties, flooded religious shrines, and destroyed long-standing ties to land. In negotiating monetary settlements, the tribal leaders found themselves on the defensive because the Corps of Engineers presented the projects as *faits accomplis*. The relatively powerless BIA assisted tribal negotiators but usually advised compromises. The much-touted benefits of the Pick-Sloan projects (irrigation, flood control, production of hydroelectricity, navigation, tourism, etc.) have proven illusionary for the six reservations.[59]

True termination, the severing of legal ties between tribes and the federal government, developed quickly after the inauguration of President Dwight D. Eisenhower in 1953.[60] The new administration ignored its campaign promises to consult with Indians before major policy changes. House Concurrent Resolution 108 in August strongly endorsed termination and ordered the secretary of the interior to supply legislative recommendations for ending federal responsibilities over several tribes. Public Law 280, approved shortly afterward, authorized state control over civil and criminal laws for most reservations in California, Minnesota, Nebraska, Oregon, and Wisconsin. The act also permitted other states to extend law enforcement over Indian trust lands by unilateral legislative action. The two measures were inspired by Senator Arthur V. Watkins of Utah and fellow western terminationists in Congress.

Between 1954 and 1966, Congress passed legislation terminating twelve Indian groups. Ten of these involved western reservations: Klamath, Western Oregon (61 tribes and bands), Mixed Blood Ute, Southern Paiute, Wyandotte, Peoria, Ottawa, California Rancherias, Ponca, and Alabama-Coushatta.[61] The two remaining tribes, the Menominee and the Catawba, were eastern groups. Each termination act outlined basic provisions determining a final tribal roll, dividing tribal property, and the reassigning of trust responsibility.

Because the Klamath termination has been studied more than any of the other western groups, it seems legitimate to assess that group's experiences. The Klamaths had long been suggested as the ideal tribe for termination because of their relative prosperity and general acceptance of white life. Previous discussions had produced severe factionalism between those who wished to maintain the tribe's rich timber resources intact and those who demanded liquidation of the assets and per capita payments. The Klamath Termination Act tried (and failed) to satisfy both groups. It permitted an election to determine whether individuals wished to withdraw from the tribe and accept a per capita payment for a portion of the group's assets, or to remain tribal members with a share in the unsold part of the reservation. Outside trustees would then determine what percentage of the tribal holdings had to be sold to make the per capita payments and devise some sort of new trust arrangement for the unsold timber.

Bickering and confusion continued after passage of the termination measure. Conservationists expressed alarm about clear cutting the timber and the ecological effects on the Klamath marsh. Business interests became worried that all the Klamath lumber might be marketed at once. Other critics recognized that many Klamaths were totally unprepared for the shock of termination. These concerns led to two amendments. One extended the termination deadline, and the second further delayed the effective date and guaranteed sustained-yield harvesting of all timber sold, fair prices for the tracts, and protection of the Klamath marsh. At the election in 1958, 1,659 Klamaths (77 percent) opted to withdraw from the tribe and each eventually received $43,700. The remaining 474 stayed under tribal status. Although this was 23 percent, a total of 48.9 percent were deemed financially incompetent and placed under private trust. Another 13.6 percent, considered competent, chose to join the trust group. Klamath termination clearly "freed" a minority and mainly shifted trust responsibility from federal to private agencies.[62]

Although termination affected a small percentage of western tribes, it aroused intense fears and strident complaints among many Indians. These diverse reactions point up the truism that Indians may complain constantly about the BIA, but they will fight any attempt to reduce that agency's service and trust responsibilities. The National Congress of American Indians particularly lashed termination, charging that it was forced on tribes and played into the hands of white business interests. The organization's campaign fostered pan-Indianism and provided valuable experience at lobbying.

Another important side effect of termination was the emergence of a liberal Democratic faction of western congressional leaders who cooperated with the critics of termination. Richard Neuberger of Oregon and James E. Murray and Mike Mansfield of Montana headed the group in the Senate, while Representative Lee Metcalf of Montana acted as a counterpart in the House.[63] The faction's effectiveness increased in 1955 when the Democrats gained control of Congress, and Neuberger chaired the Senate Subcommittee on Indian Affairs. The group's presence may indicate that a sizable portion of western public opinion had become sympathetic to Indian needs. The old, harsh regional attitude that Indians must assimilate still survives, but it competes with a more tolerant acceptance of Indians.

By 1958, the terminationists' heady optimism that they could solve all Indian problems had faded. Secretary of Interior Fred A. Seaton virtually admitted this point in a radio address at Flagstaff, Arizona, in 1958 when he promised that termination henceforth would proceed slowly and only with Indian consent.

The relocation program served as a corollary to termination. Myer had initiated the program, but Commissioner Glenn L. Emmons, a banker from Gallup, New Mexico, formalized it and shifted the emphasis to a permanent transfer of Indians to urban jobs. In this later phase, the BIA actively recruited reservation residents, transported them to cities, supplied vocational training (after 1956), and offered placement services. Numerous problems plagued relocation, especially in its early years. The BIA did not adequately screen applicants, the low-paying jobs afforded little future opportunity, and no provision existed for individuals who failed or simply wanted to return to their homes. Certainly, many Indians found adjustment to urban life difficult. Some sank into alcoholism and destitution, while as high as half became demoralized and returned to their reservations.[64]

Since an estimated 40 to 50 percent of Indians today live in urban areas, the migration since World War II poses some important questions for future studies. The fact that 75 percent of urban Indians relocated on their own invites comparisons between these individuals and those relocated through federal assistance. Are there significant differences between the two in education, income, retention of native culture, and intermarriage with nonIndians? In some instances, divisions between urban Indians and those on reservations have appeared, particularly when per capita payments are to be made. The most important question that relocation raises, however, is how well urban Indians have retained their racial and tribal identities.

Commissioner Emmons pursued other programs that complemented termination and attempted to defuse criticism of his administration. Like Myer, he tried to move BIA services to other agencies. His most important transfer involved switching BIA health care to the Public Health Service (PHS) in 1954. Although this transfer sometimes led to initial problems, the PHS has improved medical services for Indians. Transfers of Indian youngsters to public schools also played a role in Emmons's educational programs, but his major effort centered on providing schooling for the Navajo reservation. Despite intensive efforts, Emmons's campaign to attract industry to the reservation enjoyed little success, and only four firms remained in operation when he left office.[65]

By liberalizing sales of restricted lands, Emmons sought to reduce heavy BIA expenses on leasing fractionalized allotments. In his early administration, he issued new regulations that encouraged sales of trust lands to whites. Grants of fee simple titles doubled in 1954, and Indians complained that sales of "key tracts," usually areas with water supplies, jeopardized range management. As one Blackfoot leader complained, the BIA insisted on more funds for relocation because reservations were overpopulated, but, at the same time, its land policies were destroying Indians' livelihoods. In 1958, Emmons, under fire from Indians and western liberal congressmen, retreated from his earlier regulations.[66]

Relatively few scholarly studies exist thus far on the red power period of the 1960s and early 1970s.[67] Certainly the topic offers fascinating drama with major policy revisions, increased Indian militancy, numerous marches and protests, seizure of Alcatraz, fish-ins, trashing of the BIA building, and Wounded Knee II. In addition, the Johnson and Nixon administrations proved remarkably innovative, often permitting a surprising degree of Indian participation in new federal services. These broke the BIA's traditional monopoly over cooperative programs. Indian affairs also took on an "urban orientation" during the 1960s with Indian centers in major cities becoming the focal points of protests against relocation, ghetto conditions, and refusals by local officials to offer social services to Indians. Western state governments have become more sensitive to Indian needs, and nearly all now possess some sort of agency or advisory commission which deals with Indian matters.

Almost hidden in the 1960s and 1970s militancy, Congress passed basic legislation affecting Indians. Included were the Indian Education Act (1972), the Indian Self-Determination and Educational Assistance Act (1975), the American Indian Policy Review Commission Act (1975), the Indian Health Care Improvement Act (1976), the American Indian Religious Freedom Act (1978), and the Indian Child Welfare Act (1978).[68] Underlying nearly all legislation were the dual but contradictory themes of government maintenance of trust responsibilities and of assumption of administrative functions by tribal governments. Even at this early stage, it is quite clear that federal trust roles and Indian self-determination have not been easily reconciled for either Indian leaders or white officials.

The events, legislation, and policies of the past two decades are too close to be understood fully. Clearly, more time must lapse to judge results, and diligent graduate students are needed for researching the voluminous documents and conducting interviews. Certainly, future scholars will find their research complicated by the many federal agencies involved in "war on poverty" programs for Indians and because tribes themselves administered many of these. The records, therefore, will be very diffuse.

Turning to the general field of twentieth-century Indian history, the need for additional research remains awesome. Even the 1920s and the New Deal, although studied the most, offer numerous unexplored topics. Although we are approaching the end of the century, tribal histories normally offer only a cursory treatment of the twentieth century. Future tribal histories will especially need to address recent social trends such as the impact of assimilation, intermarriage with whites, education, income sources and levels, health conditions, and care of the aged and handicapped. At the national level, the Progressive Era and period since World War II have scarcely been exploited. Very little has been done on reform organizations, Indian leaders and leadership techniques, and how Indian affairs fit into regional or national development. Even less attention has been given to the "urban orientation" of the postwar era despite the importance of the subject. As a scholarly field, twentieth-century Indian history in many ways resembles a forest that has been cruised and a few prime trees removed, but the bulk of timber remains untouched.

Federal policy has clearly dominated twentieth-century Indian scholarship, and very different approaches are needed. Recent works by Richard White, Loretta Fowler, and Garrick and Roberta Glenn Bailey demonstrate the exciting potential of ethnohistory and other methodologies.[69]

Although film critics and students of popular culture have suggested that postwar movies, especially *Broken Arrow* (1950) and *Little Big Man* (1970), and other media have revised the public image of Indians by depicting them, among other things, as innocent victims of white violence and as the original American ecologists, more serious investigations are needed to show the effects of these changes.[70] They may help explain, for example, the dramatic postwar changes in attitudes toward Indians by some western politicians and reform and missionary groups.

But problems facing twentieth-century Indian history are formidable. The field will never attract the readership that earlier periods have because of the absence of military topics. Perhaps because of Indian role models of success, few Native Americans have been attracted to scholarly history, and the field remains dominated by white scholars. Certainly new research techniques, interpretive approaches, and writing strategies will be needed for treating the complexities of post–World War II topics. In sum, twentieth-century Indian history offers real challenges but equally exciting opportunities.

Notes

1. A version of this chapter was read at a conference jointly sponsored by the D'Arcy McNickle Center for American Indian History and the Smithsonian Institution at Washington, D.C., on October 4, 1985. The author would like to thank Frederick E. Hoxie, director of the McNickle Center, for permission to use the earlier paper.

2. The only general study on twentieth-century Indian history is James S. Olson and Raymond Wilson, *Native Americans in the Twentieth Century* (Provo, Utah: Brigham Young University Press, 1984). Francis Paul Prucha, "American Indian Policy in the Twentieth Century," *Western Historical Quarterly* 15 (January 1984): 5–18, provides an overview, outlines major issues, and points out needed studies. Prucha's *The Great Father: The United States Government and the American Indians*, 2 vols. (Lincoln: University of Nebraska Press, 1984), offers a full discussion of federal policy and a bountiful bibliography. Peter Iverson, ed., *The Plains Indians of the Twentieth Century* (Norman: University of Oklahoma Press, 1985), presents several of the better existing writings on the topic. Vine Deloria, Jr., ed., *American Indian Policy in the Twentieth Century* (Norman: University of Oklahoma Press, 1985), is also a collective volume, but the essays are original and were drafted by specialists from several disciplines. Robert M. Kvasnicka and Herman J. Viola, eds., *The Commissioners of Indian Affairs, 1824–1977* (Lincoln: University of Nebraska Press, 1979), not only presents sketches of the commissioners but suggestions for sources. Margaret Szasz, *Education and the*

Indians of the Modern West

American Indian: The Road to Self-Determination, 1928–1973 (Albuquerque: University of New Mexico Press, 1974), is standard for Indian education, but no counterpart exists for the period before 1928. Basic to any research are Prucha's two bibliographies. See Francis Paul Prucha, ed., *A Biographical Guide to the History of Indian-White Relations* (Chicago: University of Chicago Press, 1977), along with his supplement, *Indian-White Relations in the United States: A Bibliography of Works Published 1975–1980* (Lincoln: University of Nebraska Press, 1982). The D'Arcy McNickle Center for the History of the American Indian has sponsored a series of bibliographies on specific tribes and topics that Indiana University Press has published.

3. Randolph C. Downes, "A Crusade for Indian Reform, 1922–1934," *Mississippi Valley Historical Review* 32 (December 1945): 331–54.

4. For this essay, I have defined the West as the area west of the eastern borders of the Great Plains states.

5. *Abstract of the Twelfth Census, 1900* (Washington: Government Printing Office, 1902), 32, 34, 36, 40, 230, 250, 296, 321–33.

6. Oklahoma particularly needs to be treated separately from other areas because of unusual legal conditions Indians faced. Except for the Osages' subsurface wealth, for example, no reservations remained after statehood in 1907. Unfortunately, these unique features cannot be discussed in a short paper.

7. *Abstract of Twelfth Census*, 40.

8. 24 *United States Statutes* 388–91.

9. The original legislation did not cover the Five Civilized Tribes and some other groups in present Oklahoma, Nebraska, and New York. A sizeable literature exists on the legislative history and implementation of allotment. For recent summaries, see Prucha, *The Great Father*, 2: 659–86 or Wilcomb E. Washburn, *The Assault on Indian Tribalism: The General Allotment Law (Dawes Act) of 1887* (Philadelphia: J. P. Lippincott Company, 1975). An interesting recent study by an economist, Leonard A. Carlson, *Indians, Bureaucrats, and Land: The Dawes Act and the Decline of Indian Farming* (Westport, Conn.: Greenwood Press, 1981), used developmental theory and quantitative techniques to contend that allotment actually harmed Indian farming attempts.

10. The impression is often created that Indian heirs only held a single share of a fractionalized allotment, but, as my colleague Donald J. Berthrong points out, tribal members usually owned parts of several such allotments.

11. One of the problems for understanding the legislative history of the act is that so little evidence exists on the subject. The first general allotment bill was introduced in 1879, but the only floor debate took place in the Senate in 1881. Ironically, a Westerner, Senator H. M. Teller of Colorado, vigorously warned that allotment after thirty or forty years would rob the Indians of their land.

12. 34 *United States Statutes* 182–83. Other major acts included the Indian Heirship Act of 1902 that permitted the sale of an allotment when the original holder died and a division of the proceeds among the heirs. A 1907 statute permitted the BIA to sell restricted lands of those considered incompetent. The Omnibus Act of 1910 considerably enlarged BIA authority over such matters as land, probation, forestry, and irrigation. See 32 *United States Statutes* 275; 34 *United States Statutes* 1018; and 36 *United States Statutes* 855–63.

13. Carlson, *Indians, Bureaucrats, and Land*, 64–65.

14. William T. Hagan, *The Indian Rights Association: The Herbert Welsh Years 1882–1904* (Tucson: University of Arizona Press, 1985), 162.

15. Frederick E. Hoxie, *A Final Promise: The Campaign to Assimilate the Indians, 1880–1920* (Lincoln: University of Nebraska Press, 1984), 151–68. Hagan, *The Indian Rights Association*, 234, also suggests the growing power of western leaders over Indian affairs.

16. Hoxie, *A Final Promise*, 171.

17. Brian W. Dippie, *The Vanishing American: White Attitudes and U.S. Indian Policy* (Middletown, Conn.: Wesleyan University Press, 1982), 179–85.

18. Henry E. Fritz, "The Last Hurrah of Christian Humanitarian Reform: The Board of Indian Commissioners, 1909–1918," *Western Historical Quarterly* 16 (April 1985): 146–62.

19. Probably no topic in twentieth-century Indian history has been more neglected than irrigation. Janet McDonald, "The Disintegration of the Indian Estate: Indian Land Policy, 1913–1929" (Ph.D. dissertation, Marquette University, 1980), provides information on the topic, especially see 250–55. Excellent treatments on Indian water rights can be found in Norris R. Hundley's two articles, "The Dark and Bloody Ground of Indian Water Rights: Confusion Elevated to Principle," *Western Historical Quarterly* 9 (October 1978): 455–82; and "The *Winters* Decision and Indian Water Rights: A Mystery Reexamined," *Western Historical Quarterly* 13 (January 1982): 17–42.

20. See Donald J. Berthrong, "Legacies of the Dawes Act: Bureaucrats and Land Thieves at the Cheyenne-Arapaho Agencies of Oklahoma" *Arizona and the West* 21 (Winter 1979): 335–54; and William T. Hagan, *United States-Comanche Relations: The Reservation Years* (New Haven: Yale University Press, 1976).

21. McDonald, "Disintegration of the Indian Estate," 167.

22. The recent article by Michael L. Tate, "From Scout to Doughboy: The National Debate over Integrating American Indians into the Military, 1891–1918," *Western Historical Quarterly* 17 (October 1986): 417–37, ably summarizes major issues involving Indian military participation. See also "Indians in World War I," Central Correspondence Files, National Archives, Record Group 120.

23. McDonald, "Disintegration of the Indian Estate," 171–202, discusses the wartime period.

24. Gordon McGregor, *Warriors without Weapons: A Study of the Society and Personality of the Pine Ridge Sioux* (Chicago: University of Chicago Press, 1946), 36–39. Ernest L. Schusky, *The Forgotten Sioux: An Ethnohistory of the Lower Brule* (Chicago: Nelson-Hall, 1975), 168, quotes a former chairman's statement that forced patents were issued to servicemen while on duty, and they returned to find that their allotments had been sold for taxes.

25. McDonald, "Disintegration of the Tribal Estate," 180–99.

26. 43 *United States Statutes* 253.

27. An interesting piece on this topic and recent Indian voting behavior is Daniel McCool, "Indian Voting," in Deloria, ed., *American Indian Policy*, 105–33.

28. Collier's career has been studied by Kenneth R. Philp, *John Collier's Crusade for Indian Reform, 1920–1954* (Tucson: University of Arizona Press, 1977), and

more recently by Lawrence C. Kelly, *The Assault on Assimilation: John Collier and the Origins of Indian Policy Reform* (Albuquerque: University of New Mexico Press, 1983), which carries up to 1927. Collier's autobiography, *From Every Zenith: A Memoir and Some Essays on Life and Thought* (Denver: Sage Books, 1963), and his other writings are partisan but helpful in understanding his philosophy.

29. In addition to the works cited above, Collier's philosophy has been treated in Stephen J. Kunitz, "The Social Philosophy of John Collier," *Ethnohistory* 18 (Summer 1971): 213–19.

30. Kelly, *Assault on Assimilation*, 213–54.

31. Ibid., 295–300.

32. Prior to a congressional ban in 1918, presidents had frequently set aside reservation lands from the public domain by proclamations. Key examples include the Hopi reservation in 1882, several extensions of the Navajo reservation after 1868, and the Papago reservation in 1916. The latter played a key role in the 1918 ban.

33. This matter is thoroughly discussed in Lawrence C. Kelly, *The Navajo Indians and Federal Indian Policy 1900–1935* (Tucson: University of Arizona Press, 1968), 37–101.

34. Ibid., 92–93, 99–103.

35. Prucha, *The Great Father*, 2: 807–8.

36. Donald T. Critchlow, "Lewis Meriam, Expertise, and Indian Reform," *Historian* 43 (May 1981): 325–44, discusses Meriam's approach and his efforts to implement reforms in the BIA afterward.

37. *The Problem of Indian Administration* (Baltimore: Johns Hopkins University Press, 1928). Copies of Meriam's field letters are often very revealing. See Donald L. Parman, ed., "Lewis Meriam's Letters during the Survey of Indian Affairs, 1926–1927 (Part I)," *Arizona and the West* 24 (Fall 1982): 253–80; "Part II" (Winter 1982): 341–70.

38. In addition to Critchlow's article, Frederick J. Stefon, "Significance of the Meriam Report of 1928," *The Indian Historian* 8 (Summer 1975): 2–7, discusses the commission's impact on subsequent educational reform.

39. See "Survey of Conditions of the Indian in the United States," *Hearings before a Subcommittee of the Committee on Indian Affairs*, United States Senate, 70th Congress to 78th Congress (1928–1943).

40. Despite excellent biographies on Collier, more attention needs to be given to his lobbying and propaganda techniques. These matters are treated somewhat in one of the first and best dissertations on Collier, John Leiper Freeman's, "The New Deal for Indians: A Study in Bureau-Committee Relations" (Ph.D. dissertation, Princeton University, 1952), but the study mainly examines Collier's relationships with the Indian affairs committees.

41. Collier gives his impressions of the "False Dawn" of the Rhoads-Scattergood administration in *From Every Zenith*, but this account should be balanced with Philp's biography and other writings.

42. In addition to previously cited works by Kelly, Philp, and Collier, several other books deal with the Indian New Deal. See Donald L. Parman, *The Navajos and the New Deal* (New Haven: Yale University Press, 1976); Graham D. Taylor,

The New Deal and American Indian Tribalism: The Administration of the Indian Reorganization Act, 1934–45 (Lincoln: University of Nebraska Press, 1980); Laurence M. Hauptman, *The Iroquois and the New Deal* (Syracuse: Syracuse University Press, 1981); and Robert F. Schrader, *The Indian Arts and Crafts Board: An Aspect of New Deal Indian Policy* (Albuquerque: University of New Mexico Press, 1983).

43. 48 *United State Statutes* 984–88. Prucha, *The Great Father*, 2: 954–63, summarizes the original bill, its legislative history, and provisions of the final measure.

44. Taylor, *The New Deal and American Indian Tribalism*, treats the formation and operation of tribal governments during the period. Lawrence C. Kelly, "The Indian Reorganization Act: The Dream and the Reality," *Pacific Historical Review* 44 (August 1975): 291–312, critically assesses the IRA, especially the number of Indians who came under its provisions.

45. One of the most typical criticisms of the IRA is that it followed white political forms rather than those of traditional Indian government. This objection, as Roy W. Meyer suggests, is questionable for it was never raised during the 1930s. See Meyer's *The Village Indians of the Upper Missouri: The Mandans, Hidatsas, and Arikaras* (Lincoln: University of Nebraska Press, 1977), 194.

46. Freeman, "New Deal for the Indians," 147–48, 215, 256. Thomas, however, in 1936 sponsored the Oklahoma Indian Welfare Act, a measure similar to the IRA. See Peter M. Wright, "John Collier and the Oklahoma Indian Welfare Act of 1936," *Chronicles of Oklahoma* 50 (Autumn 1972): 347–71.

47. Richard White, *The Roots of Dependency: Subsistence, Environment, and Social Change Among the Choctaws, Pawnees, and Navahos* (Lincoln: University of Nebraska, 1983).

48. Hauptman, *Iroquois and the New Deal*, places considerable stress on revitalization of culture and language.

49. Steven James Crum, "The Western Shoshone of Nevada and the Indian New Deal" (Ph.D. dissertation, University of Utah, 1983), and Roger Bromert, "The Sioux and the New Deal, 1933–1944" (Ph.D. dissertation, University of Toledo, 1980), are two recent reservation studies that appraise the Indian New Deal in a favorable manner.

50. John Adair, "The Navajo and Pueblo Veteran, A Force for Cultural Change," *The American Indian* 4 (1947): 5–11.

51. Three notable exceptions to this statement are Tom Holm, "Fighting a White Man's War: The Extent and Legacy of Indian Participation in World War II," *Journal of Ethnic Studies* 9 (Summer 1981): 69–81; Gerald D. Nash, *The American West Transformed: The Impact of the Second World War* (Bloomington: Indiana University Press, 1985), 128–47; and Alison Ricky Bernstein, "Walking in Two Worlds: American Indians and World War Two" (Ph.D. dissertation, Columbia University, 1986).

52. Donald Lee Parman, "The Indian Civilian Conservation Corps" (Ph.D. dissertation, University of Oklahoma, 1967), 222–27.

53. Hildegard Thompson, *The Navajos' Long Walk for Education: A History of Navajo Education* (Tsaile, Ariz.: Navajo Community College Press, 1975), 73–85; and Parman, *Navajos and the New Deal*, 285.

54. Implementation of the district offices was delayed by shortages of funds and additional legislation. Myer actually established a revised plan in 1950. See Larry J. Hasse, "Termination and Assimilation: Federal Indian Policy, 1943–1961" (Ph.D. dissertation, Washington State University, 1974), 100–103.

55. Prucha, *The Great Father*, 2: 1022.

56. Hasse, "Termination and Relocation," 108–64, provides a critical but thorough discussion of Myer's administration.

57. One exception to the consensus is Kenneth R. Philp's recent article. Philp discusses most of the trends mentioned above, but he argues that postwar policy changes can be attributed to the many failures of the Indian New Deal. See Philp, "Termination: A Legacy of the Indian New Deal," *Western Historical Quarterly* 14 (April 1983): 165–80.

58. Hasse, "Termination and Assimilation," 81, 142.

59. Michael L. Lawson, *Dammed Indians: The Pick-Sloan Plan and the Missouri River Sioux* (Norman: University of Oklahoma Press, 1982); and Meyer, *The Village Indians*, 211–34.

60. Three young scholars have dealt with termination. See Hasse, "Termination and Assimilation"; Larry W. Burt, *Tribalism in Crisis: Federal Indian Policy 1953–1961* (Albuquerque: University of New Mexico Press, 1982); and Donald L. Fixico, *Termination and Relocation: Federal Indian Policy, 1945–1960* (Albuquerque: University of New Mexico Press, 1986).

61. The Alabama-Choushatta group was unique. Although under the control of Texas, the joint tribe had received some federal services before its termination.

62. Theodore Stern, *The Klamath Tribe: A People and Their Reservation* (Seattle: University of Washington Press, 1966), 249–55; and Hasse, "Termination and Assimilation," 222–31, 283–96.

63. The group was somewhat larger than these individuals. Several others sometimes cooperated with the main leaders.

64. Fixico's study, *Termination and Relocation*, gives much attention to the human side of relocation. Kenneth R. Philp, "Stride toward Freedom: The Relocation of Indians to Cities, 1952–1960," *Western Historical Quarterly* 16 (April 1985): 175–90, is an able summary that offers a more favorable assessment.

65. Larry W. Burt, "Factories on Reservations: The Industrial Development of Commissioner Glenn Emmons, 1953–1960," *Arizona and the West* 19 (Winter 1977): 317–32.

66. See "Indian Land Transactions, Memorandum of the Chairman to the Committee on Interior and Insular Affairs, United States Senate," *An Analysis of the Problems and Effects of Our Diminishing Indian Land Base, 1948–57*, 85th Congress (1958), XVIII–XIX, 23, 50.

67. For a preliminary discussion that concentrates on the Nixon administration, see Donald L. Parman, "American Indians and the Bicentennial," *New Mexico Historical Review* 51 (July 1976): 233–49 and Jack D. Forbes, *Native Americans and Nixon: Presidential Politics and Minority Self-Determination* (Los Angeles: American Studies Center, University of California Los Angeles, 1981). The final chapters of Prucha, *The Great Father*, 2: 1085–1208, outline events and list the better sources.

68. Prucha, *The Great Father*, 2: 1139–70.

69. See White, *Roots of Dependency;* Loretta Fowler, *Arapahoe Politics, 1851–1978: Symbols in Crises of Authority* (Lincoln: University of Nebraska Press, 1982); and Garrick Bailey and Roberta Glenn Bailey, *A History of the Navajos: The Reservation Years* (Seattle: University of Washington Press for School of American Research Press, Sante Fe, N.M., 1986).

70. The standard work on the image of the Indian is Robert F. Berkhofer, Jr., *The White Man's Indian: Images of the American Indian from Columbus to the Present* (New York: Alfred Knopf, 1978). Raymond William Stedman, *Shadows of the Indian: Stereotypes in American Culture* (Norman: University of Oklahoma Press, 1982), is also a general treatment, and his final chapters discuss movie portrayal. A brief but useful introduction to the image of Indians in the movies is John E. O'Conner, *The Hollywood Indians: Stereotypes of Native Americans in Films* (Trenton: New Jersey Museum, 1980).

II

Economy of the Twentieth-Century West

Among the various aspects of western history after 1890, the region's economic development remains a field yet to be explored. Technical reports on particular issues concerning the economy may be plentiful, but historical assessments far less so. Histories of particular industries, of leading entrepreneurs, of unorganized as well as organized labor, of farms and ranches, of government policies on the local, state, and national level remain to be written. Nor has the history of economic ideas, attitudes, or theories been explored. Clearly, it would take volumes to do justice to the subject, but a brief essay can at least illustrate its potentials. Howard Lamar's piece provides a good example, as he compares American perceptions with those of Canadians during the Great Depression between 1929 and 1941. As Lamar indicates through his use of the comparative approach, it may be as important for historians to understand the attitudes and perceptions of Westerners as to detail the more practical aspects of their lives.

6

Comparing Depressions

THE GREAT PLAINS AND

CANADIAN PRAIRIE EXPERIENCES, 1929–1941

Howard R. Lamar

As Professor Lamar informs his readers, historians have for years compared the American frontier to that of other countries, including Australia, Canada, South America, and Siberia. But the comparison of a region like the West to similar areas elsewhere—for the years since 1890—has been less frequent. A major purpose of his essay is to compare three Dust Bowl areas—two in the United States and one in Canada—during the Great Depression. Such an analysis yields new insights, not only about the differing cultural reactions to economic crisis by Canadians and Americans. It also highlights the differing perceptions and assumptions with which Canadian and American scholars have approached the subject. In the effort to forge a clearer image of the twentieth-century West, comparative history has an important function, for it broadens an understanding of the Great Depression by placing it in multicultural context. Above all, it indicates which aspect of the western experience was unique, and which reflected similar conditions elsewhere.

At the mention of the word *comparative*, scholars in the field of frontier history almost automatically think of studies that compare the American frontier to those of Australia, Canada, and South America. Less frequently the American frontier has also been compared to those of Siberia and South Africa.[1] Comparing postfrontier or recent *Wests*, on the other hand, is still in its beginning stages. The purpose of this essay is to explore the promise of comparability by looking at three North American *dust bowl* regions during the traumatic drought and depression years of 1929–1941. The three regions are (1) the Southern Plains area that came to be known as the American *Dust Bowl*, and that, by general agreement embraced the Texas and Oklahoma Panhandles, northeastern New Mexico, southeastern Colorado, and western Kansas;[2] (2) a lesser known but equally severe *dust bowl* in the Northern Plains that included parts of North and South Dakota and eastern Montana;[3] and (3), the so-called Palliser's Triangle area of the Canadian Prairie Provinces.[4] This Canadian *dust bowl* was centered in southwestern Saskatchewan and southeastern Alberta.

Most historians are agreed that the combination of drought in a largely one-crop economy of wheat and grain production, low prices for what grain was produced, the drying up of the market due to national and international depression, and the lack of any alternative forms of employment made the "dirty thirties" the grimmest and most crucial decade in the history of the Great Plains and western Canada.[5] One would expect that almost identical problems in similar areas would provoke similar or even common responses. But each of the three regions named made different responses to drought and depression. It would seem logical that by comparing these responses one could gain further insight into the factors that produced distinctiveness and, perhaps equally important, ascertain which area suffered the most. The approach may supply a partial explanation as to why writers about the depression years in each of these regions took such different approaches and stressed such different themes. It is hoped that by a comparative approach we might even identify what has been missing or neglected in the history of one region as opposed to another.

There have been many studies of the Great Plains and Prairie Provinces in the 1930s. This essay frankly builds on their findings and makes no claim to originality except for its comparative approach. The first task is to identify the major themes and topics that need comparing. With that in mind, five questions seem worth pursuing: (1) how did people see themselves in relation to their environment before and during the depression years? (2) what were the major features and determinants of the regional economy? (3) what distinctive society or culture (if any) had developed in the regions under study? (4) how did the three populations view and participate in the systems of governance that could be found at the local, state and provincial, and national levels? and (5) what basic changes or reforms occurred in these regions, either social, economic, or political, as a result of the decade of drought and depression?

The Northern Plains

The area of the Northern Plains comprising present-day North and South Dakota and eastern Montana had been known to French explorers since the early 1830s when the fur trapper and trader, Sieur de la Vérendrye, and a party penetrated the region, explored the Red and Assiniboine Rivers and saw the Missouri.[6] A few years later French Canadian fur trappers had settled in the Red River Valley. Although agricultural settlement in the Red River Valley was attempted early in the nineteenth century by Thomas Douglas, the fifth earl of Selkirk, and produced conflict with the fur trappers, the larger issue of how these prairie lands would be used did not really arise until the 1850s.[7]

By the 1850s, however, Minnesota settlers were pressing west into the Red River Valley and along the Big Sioux River on the state's southwestern border, while speculators and settlers from the Midwest were pushing up the Missouri River.[8] Their coming, the optimistic propaganda of town site speculators, and the presence of official survey parties, opened the debate. Of the survey parties, two deserve mention: that of Isaac I. Stevens's Pacific Railroad Survey along the 47th parallel in 1853, and those of Gouverneur Kemble Warren from 1855 to 1859.[9] In his 1855 report, Warren said flatly that land west of the 97th meridian was not fit for agricultural settlement. "Agricultural settlements," he wrote, "have now nearly reached their western limits on our great plains; the tracts beyond must ever be occupied by a pastoral people, whether civilized or savage."[10] The Stevens and Warren surveys appear to have prompted both the British and the Canadian governments to make the first official survey of the prairie provinces.[11]

Warren's doubts were drowned out by the optimistic hawkings of speculators and the land hunger of settlers so that between the organization of Dakota Territory in 1861 and the achievement of statehood by North and South Dakota and Montana in 1889, the Northern Great Plains were settled and became one of the biggest wheat producing areas in the world.[12] Until the depression years of the 1890s, despite some drought and grasshopper plagued years in the 1870s and 1880s, the image of the land was very favorable and attracted a large number of Norwegian, Canadian, and German-Russian immigrants who believed the area somewhat replicated the climate and/or soils of their native land. Depression and drought severely troubled parts of the Northern Plains during the 1890s, but between 1900 and 1915 there was a new boom in settlers and wheat farming. In North Dakota, as D. Jerome Tweton has noted, "some 250,000 latterday pioneers entered the state from 1898 to 1915," and homesteading actually reached its peak there in 1906, so that by 1920 foreign-born men, women, and children made up 66.7 percent of the population, of which slightly more than 26 percent were from Scandinavia and 22 percent were of German origin.[13] (This essay will focus largely on North Dakota's experiences.)

Along with Minnesota and Kansas, North Dakota became the leading producer of wheat in the United States, and it was on that grain that the state's economy depended. With a one-crop economy, as is well known, came a price. The farmer depended on grain elevators and railroads to buy and ship his wheat, and he was subject to the strategems of grain merchants, bankers, and the national and international market. For North Dakotans their sense of being manipulated by all these agencies, by St. Paul-Minneapolis milling interests and control by Republican boss, Alexander McKenzie in particular, led them to seek remedies through political action between 1900 and 1915.[14]

Beginning with the election of John Burke, a Democrat, to the governorship in 1906, the state overthrew the McKenzie machine and engaged in a series of progressive reforms and the election of progressive senators to Congress.[15] Despite the prosperity of the war years, in 1919 wheat prices fell, and residents began to leave the state. During World War I, a group of radical agrarian leaders, headed by Arthur Charles Townley, William Lemke, and others, formed the Nonpartisan League, which by working within the Republican party had gained control of the state government by 1919.[16] Under Nonpartisan leadership the state legislature created a state-owned bank and flour mills and elevators so that North Dakota became known as the one American state that had gone over to "state socialism."[17]

D. Jerome Tweton has called the years from 1915 to 1945 in North Dakota a time of troubles, and indeed it was. As he has noted, the "value of North Dakota farm property fell by more than a half billion dollars in 1920–1925, and more than five hundred banks failed in the 1920s."[18] The continued exodus of population prevented normal growth and development. Thus when drought and depression hit the state in the 1930s, it was an unmitigated disaster. By then the North Dakotans had developed both a negative view of the environment they found themselves in and a paranoia about the causes of their difficulties. Having long learned to hate the absentee power brokers of St. Paul-Minneapolis and Wall Street, they applied this to the federal government and to many outsiders. Thus it was not surprising that North Dakota's public figures would take an isolationist stance when it came to foreign policy.[19] They also resented as much as any rural population the image of the farmer as a backward, uneducated hayseed whose problems were largely his own fault. While there is no way of measuring such a phenomenon, it seems that a profound general psychological depression existed alongside of the very real economic depression and the extremes in weather in North Dakota. This despairing attitude is captured in the diary of Ann Marie Low, the teenage daughter of an able farmer-rancher in central North Dakota in 1928. "Now times are hard, prices low, and this year we are hailed out. . . . Come to think of it, Dad never plays his violin anymore."[20] That was written a year before depression or drought struck the state.

Certainly the conditions that plagued North Dakota in the 1930s were grim enough to break the strongest spirit. Between 1929 and 1931 drought conditions were so bad in the northwestern section of the state that more than 50 percent of the farmers there needed relief.[21] The state escaped drought in 1932, but 1933 was "the fourth driest year ever recorded," and 1934 was "the driest year yet on record."[22] In May of that year a vast dust storm arose on the Northern Plains that scattered dust all the way to New York and Washington. Dust storms that came early in 1935 were alleviated by timely rain in the summer; but then came a plague of grasshoppers. However, in 1936 North Dakota experienced a combination of blizzards in winter and drought and 100° F. heat in the summer that was devastating. The rainfall for the next three years (1937, 1938, and 1939) was below normal, but happily the extreme conditions of 1934 and 1936 did not return.[23] Buttressing their accounts with tragic and telling statistics, historians of North Dakota's depression years note that the state produced only two normal wheat crops between 1929 and 1941 and that the per capita income for North Dakota was less than half that of the nation's during the 1930s.[24]

These conditions, juxtaposed with a general sense of alienation, negation, and despair, shaped North Dakota's response not only to drought and depression but to the relief programs designed to lessen their impact. Elwyn Robinson has noted that although North Dakotans had long had a liberal and progressive outlook and believed in cooperative farm efforts, they "resented the loss of freedom" implied by "aid and direction from the federal government." Rather than help, it seemed to "accentuate North Dakota's dependent status. . . ."[25] Thus the state remained Republican in its politics except to vote for Franklin D. Roosevelt in the national elections of 1932 and 1936; it had no major New Deal newspapers nor any "single leader in the State, Democrat or Republican," who "was a consistent supporter of the New Deal."[26] Moreover, North Dakota's best-known and most outspoken leader, Governor William Langer, while increasing his popularity by using his authority to place a moratorium on foreclosures and to force a rise in wheat prices by threatening a state-wide embargo on shipments, did not really address larger questions of reform in land use and agricultural production.[27] As did most state governments, North Dakota pursued a policy of retrenchment during the depression although it looks as if Langer kept a larger state bureaucracy in office— one source of his political power—than was perhaps the case in other Plains states.

At the outset of the Depression other state leaders, such as Congressman William Lemke, stressed a four point program that focused on money issues. Lemke wanted a Third Bank of the United States to issue money in place of the Federal Reserve, also refinancing of mortgages and debts, and bankruptcy legislation to protect the farmer as well as guaranteeing them the cost of production. Having been one of the first western figures to support Roosevelt, when his and Congressman Lynn Frazier's bankruptcy bill ran into trouble in Congress, he forced it out of committee only to have the Frazier-Lemke Bankruptcy Act of 1934 declared unconstitutional by the Supreme Court a short time later. Then a more moderate law was enacted. Lemke, feeling he had been betrayed by the New Dealers, broke with Roosevelt, and in 1936 ran for president against Roosevelt on the Union Party ticket.[28]

As sincere as these efforts were, none really addressed the more fundamental issues of the unwisdom of a one-crop economy, the need for land use reform, and provision of social services for the needy. Thus counties and private charities rather than the state were the first to furnish direct relief to those in dire need in 1931 and 1932. These resources were soon depleted, and a State Emergency Relief Committee undertook the task by borrowing funds from the Reconstruction Finance Corporation.[29]

Even so, its function was eventually superseded in late 1933 and 1934 when federal funds, handled by federal agencies after the passage of the Agricultural Adjustment Act of 1933 and the Civil Works Administration and, in 1934, the Federal Emergency Relief Administration (FERA), became mainstays for relief in North Dakota. The FERA, under the direction of Harry Hopkins, received an appropriation of a half billion dollars to assist the needy.[30] Together these federal agencies provided relief of three kinds to North Dakotans: (1) starving cattle were purchased from ranchers to be destroyed if diseased or unfit or shipped elsewhere for canning or to provide meat directly to families on relief; (2) cash payments were made to farmers in return for their restricting wheat production; and (3) direct relief funds went to suffering individuals and families.[31]

With the passage of the Social Security Act of 1935, a Public Welfare Board, operated by the state, assumed care for the aged and dependent and those unemployed but not on work relief. All in all, the federal government spent some $266,000,000 in North Dakota between 1934 and 1940 through an impressive number of programs, a large number of projects, and by providing a variety of services. Relief, writes Elwyn Robinson, "soon became the biggest business in the state."[32] As early as 1934 more than a fifth of the state's population were receiving relief; a year later it had jumped to 37 percent, and by 1936 more than 50 percent of the population were on relief; and even as late as 1939 some 37 percent were receiving some kind of relief.[33]

As many scholars have observed, even the federal government's actions did not really succeed in preserving land values, paying of debts and loans, mortgages, and delinquent taxes, and raising farm prices to parity levels. Nor did Washington find adequate jobs for the unemployed. Farmers continued to lose their farms, and people continued to leave the state. Moreover, so many agencies inevitably resulted in overlapping or confused jurisdictions. Indeed, Richard Lowitt has concluded that the New Deal efforts in all Great Plains states, as broad and humane as they were, remained fragmented with no overall direction.[34]

Beginning in 1935–36, however, Roosevelt and the New Deal officials did attempt to develop a long-range program that would, in effect, reform land use on the Great Plains by conserving land and water, by retiring submarginal lands to grass, by adjusting crops to the soil and climate, and by creating larger and more efficient farm units. All of these were articulated in a 1936 report entitled *The Future of the Great Plains*,[35] portions of which were to be implemented by two Great Plains Councils, one for the southern region and one for the northern region. The former was to have headquarters in Amarillo and the latter in Denver.[36]

Needless to say, North Dakota farmers and Plains residents generally were reluctant to engage in a change of attitude towards the agricultural economy they knew best. The government's own efforts flagged after 1939, and the coming of good weather and the prosperity of World War II prevented any really major actions except for the Department of Agriculture's efforts to conserve the soil and water resources and to urge the practice of more scientific approaches to farming.[37] At another level, the local political response to drought and depressions suggests that the vaunted western liberal progressivism of the first decades of the twentieth century and the so-called radicalism of the Nonpartisan League, the Farmers' Union, and the Farm Holiday Association, in retrospect, appear to have been neither radical nor reformist.[38] Indeed, even if all three groups believed in economic class warfare, they could not really ever achieve control over events that produced distress in the economy of the Great Plains. It is a paradox, and perhaps a tragic one, that the most positive lessons offered by the Nonpartisan League, the cooperative movements, and the ideology of state socialism—of nonpartisan political cooperation for the benefit of the people, of controlling both middlemen and prices by cooperation as practiced in Canada, and the use of the state to provide security for all citizens—were not really pursued at the state level at the time its citizens needed them most.

The Dust Bowl Region of the Southern Plains

Long before any of the central and southern Great Plains were organized as territories or states or were considered as a likely place for white settlers, Lieutenant Zebulon Pike in 1806 and 1807, and Major Stephen H. Long in 1820, described large portions of the region as a desert.[39]

Long and his expedition colleague, Edwin James, in fact named it "The Great American Desert" both on Long's map and in his report.

> We have little apprehension of giving too unfavorable an account of this portion of the country. Though the soil is in some places fertile, the want of timber, of navigable streams, and of water for the necessities of life, render it an unfit residence for any but a nomad population. The traveller who shall at any time have traversed its desolate sands, will, we think, join us in the wish that this region may forever remain the unmolested haunt of the native hunter, the bison and the jackall.[40]

That image was reinforced by the Santa Fe traders using the waterless sixty-mile Cimarron Cutoff, by the Mexican War soldiers, and by travellers until 1860.

After the Civil War, Southern Plains Indian tribes resisted surrender and acceptance of reservation life until the 1870s, by which time the Atchison, Topeka and Santa Fe had built its lines across Kansas and into eastern Colorado and northeastern New Mexico. That railroad's penetration allowed buffalo hunters to come and kill off the vast buffalo herds by 1879.[41] A similar phenomenon was taking place on the central plains, while the Northern Pacific became the conduit for buffalo robes taken from the slaughter of the herds on the northern plains.[42] Thus occurred what must be one of the most rapid and dramatic faunal transformations within a region in ecological history. Herds of native bison that had existed for thousands of years were exterminated in less than fifty years. With virtually no lag time, ranchers moved cattle into the Texas Panhandle, parts of Indian Territory (Oklahoma), western Kansas, and the eastern thirds of New Mexico and Colorado. Cattle also replaced the buffalo on the central and northern plains embraced by the territories or states of Nebraska, Wyoming, the Dakotas, and Montana.[43] As every school child knows, this vast open-range industry lasted only twenty years, for by 1890 it had been replaced by homesteads and farms and smaller ranches.

On what has been called the farmers' last frontier, men, families, and speculators were attracted to the region by the Homestead Act of 1862 and other generous land laws passed by Congress in the 1870s and 1880s.[44] They were further attracted by railroads anxious to sell their own land holdings and to create customers along their lines. State immigration bureaus and Atlantic steamship lines also poured out propaganda urging Europeans to migrate to America. All these attractions were enhanced by the discovery of new dry-farming techniques, the invention of machinery that allowed one to plow up the plains, and the introduction of hardy strains of grain.[45] Thus a third ecological revolution took place on the Great Plains between 1870 and 1900 in the form of a massive successful agricultural development. This revolution, too, had proceeded with such rapidity that in thirty years "more land was brought under cultivation . . . than in the entire previous history of the nation."[46]

Thus, as had been the case in the Northern Plains, an early negative view of the Southern Plains had been reversed. And despite the drought and depression-ridden years of the late 1880s and the 1890s, characterized by fierce populist protest in Kansas, Texas, and Colorado—and to a lesser degree in New Mexico—the positive image continued into this century. Even in the dry '90s, the opening of Indian and Oklahoma territories piece by piece, until statehood was achieved in 1907, kept the excitement of pioneering alive on the Southern Plains.

After World War I, Great Plains farmers suffered from depression from 1919 to 1923 and from poor agricultural prices for the rest of the twenties. This meant rising farm debts, increasing tenancy, and the fact that the lands, because of both poor farming practices and especially unwise soil plowing practices, were being eroded.[47] While it is dangerous to generalize about world views, it appears that residents of the future Southern Plains dust bowl area, due in part to their southern origins, were more passive and fatalistic about their environment, giving way not so much to despair in bad times but to fatalistic acceptance that things were bad. This attitude was reinforced by what Donald Worster has called a "next year" philosophy—whereby people in the Plains explained away present difficulties by saying it will be better next year. "It is," he writes, "an optimism at heart fatalistic," a belief in an upwardly mobile society, that asserted "Providence and not Washington would see them come out all right."[48] It also appears likely that persons with farms that were really too small to sustain a family in bad times were more numerous than in North Dakota.

As to the major features and determinants of the Southern Plains economy, this was also an area that saw itself controlled by outside forces like Wall Street, big business, and eastern capital. There had always been a problem of absentee-owned ranch and farm lands on the Southern Plains, similar perhaps to the Minnesota and eastern-owned bonanza farms in North Dakota. But by the 1920s those in the Southern Plains had been increasingly replaced by a new group, the "suitcase farmers," persons living in cities or in other areas who bought farms in good years, paid tenants or workers to farm them, and benefitted from the profits made. In most cases suitcase farmers already had an income to which was added farm income.[49] At the same time, cattle ranching continued to be a part of the local economy.[50]

As Arrell Gibson has noted, there were other determinants of the Southern Plains economy as well. "New oil field discoveries in Texas, Oklahoma, Kansas and California produced pockets of boom-type developments and assuaged some of the economic suffering by employing large numbers of workers."[51] In a kind of reverse of the suitcase farmer operation, in off seasons, small farmers, even in good years, took employment in the oil fields. Paul Bonnifield argues that oil and natural gas discoveries on the eve of and during the drought and depression years allowed farmers to seek seasonal employment in the oil industry. Ironically, Dalhart, Texas, often described as the "capital"[52] of the dust bowl, was one of the urban centers benefitting from a local oil boom. Certainly the prospect of alternative employment created a different mindset and even a different economy in the depression years. At the same time it should be remembered that the oil industry itself was suffering from low prices because of overproduction and the national depression. Indeed, conditions were so bad that the governors of Oklahoma, Texas, and Kansas engaged in state-imposed control on production and created a regional conservation and production control organization called the Interstate Oil Compact Commission.[53]

If a sizable portion of North Dakota's population was foreign-born in the 1930s, that of the Southern Plains was less so although Spanish Americans were to be found in Texas, New Mexico, and Colorado and a number of European immigrants could be found in all the states with dust bowl counties.[54] On the other hand, they do not appear to have been as much of a force in politics as were the Scandinavians and the German Russians in North Dakota. It was also a fact that these areas constituted the fringe regions of five states and could not speak with a single political voice or through a single leader. Texas and Oklahoma were Democratic and Kansas was Republican. And certainly there was no great cooperation between such individualistic leaders as Ma and Pa Ferguson in Texas, Alfalfa Bill Murray in Oklahoma, and Alf Landon in Kansas.[55]

All these factors suggest that for reasons quite different from those in North Dakota, the Southern Plains people turned more willingly to the federal government for relief, and they did so knowing they had *three* major products—cattle, grain, and oil—all of which needed relief, control, and subsidy.

In the Southern Plains the drought roamed around, and given the fact that 1934 was a grim year for the entire Great Plains, dust storms came at different times than in other areas.[56] One of the peak years was 1938 when up to 10 million acres lost the upper five inches of top soil, and another 13.5 million lost two and one-half inches.[57] As Donald Worster has pointed out, there are seeming contradictions as well. For example, in the dust bowl center farm population decreased less than 3 percent between 1930 and 1935, but between 1935 and 1937 more than 34 percent of the population left.[58]

The image of Okie, Arkie, and Plainsman trekking to California over

Route 66 or to the Pacific Northwest also needs correction in that many dust bowlers simply went into town or to the next county. Of the 309,000 residents of Oklahoma who left between 1935 and 1940, 142,000 went to contiguous states such as Texas, and 167,000 went to noncontiguous states.[59]

Residents of the Southern Plains region, while accepting and benefitting enormously from the New Deal programs, were as resistant to change as the North Dakotans were. Elaborating on this theme, Donald Worster argues that despite the plans for a fresh long-range approach to Great Plains land use, in the end the government itself never faced the fact that it was our capitalistic culture that prevented us from thinking in new ways. The Dust Bowl, he wrote, was "the inevitable outcome of a culture that deliberately, self-consciously, set itself the task of dominating and exploiting the land for all it was worth."[60]

> This failure of adaptation may be the region's most important value—as a model from which we can learn much about the ecological insensitivity of our culture. Out on the high tableland of the plains occurred one of the most tragic, revealing and paradigmatic chapters in our environmental history— one with increasing relevance to mankind's future.[61]

For the historian of the West the images of the Great Plains as revealed in its historiography have undergone a fascinating evolution and are full of remarkable contradictions. As we have already noted, the first American explorers and scientific surveyors were generally negative. After the Civil War, John Wesley Powell revived the negative image but with a highly intelligent plan for coming to terms with nature beyond the 100th meridian.[62] Curiously, while Powell's warnings about changing the water laws, size of ranches and farms, and the necessity for irrigation were partially accepted, the larger message that this was a land that could do only limited things was not. It was a further irony that during the antebellum years when Americans were talking about a Great American Desert, Indian tribes, assisted by horse and gun, moved into this desert and achieved such a successful new economy and lifestyle that they became more powerful than they had ever been before. In the case of the Sioux, they actually expanded their territory as well as their power.[63] Both the Powell and the Indian messages of successful adaptation were generally lost on the American government and on the settler. Yet, as has also been observed earlier, the two American adaptations—open-range cattle raising and dry farming—seemed for our society as masterful and successful as any in American history. The challenge of a decade of drought and depression in the 1890s, poor farm prices, and population exodus did not really result in any fundamental changes.

Throughout the telling of the story there has been an intriguing shift of villains and heroes. In the 1880s and 1890s the villains were the railroads, the middleman, Wall Street, the tariff, and tight money. In this century they have continued to be the heavies plus depression, drought, and, at the local level, continued belief in a conspiracy theory that "others" on the outside are scheming to hold the Great Plains in colonial bondage.[64]

During and after the 1930s, however, the federal government attempted to write its own historical scenario. Indeed, the amount written to explain both general American and agricultural history is simply staggering, and the way it was disseminated by radio, the press, speeches, studies, and reports represents one of the greatest propaganda efforts in American history.[65] In the government's view the real villains, though always subtly portrayed, were over-aggressive pioneers who raped the land and ignorant farmers who brought humid concepts of farming to the Great Plains and failed to adjust them. Further, in their greed, the farmers unwisely plowed them up when they should have been left for grass and cattle ranching.[66] In this history the government, with its brains trusters, its thousands of studies, its flood of monies for relief, rehabilitation, and reform, became the hero and remained safely so until the 1970s.

Then came the next switch in heroes and villains. Inspired at first by Westerners rebelling against government control of so many western resources, for it had, in fact, replaced the private eastern investor as the controller of the "colonial" West, the government was blamed for stifling the West's economy and limiting the right of the individual.[67] Whether it took the form of resistance to Washington, support for Barry Goldwater and conservative political candidates, or the assertion of independence by virtue of their own postwar prosperity, the rebellion actually implied that the West had a new confidence.[68] This new entrepreneurial spirit was backed by a new economic and demographic clout as the Sun Belt and especially states like Texas and California came into prominence in terms of industry, wealth, and population.[69]

With the publication of his *Dust Bowl: The Southern Plains in the 1930s* in 1979, Donald Worster moved the blame on to fresh villains. Arguing that while the New Deal planners and reformers had been sincere in their efforts to remake the Great Plains, he thought that they did not, or could not, challenge the capitalistic ethic that said the Great Plains must be used in a practical way. Nor did Great Plains residents try to think in new ways. In short, it was the blinders of our capitalistic culture that had kept us from developing an intelligent response to the realities of the Great Plains environment.[70] Worster has been joined in his plea to take an informed ecological approach to the Great Plains and to the whole of America by an entire new generation of scientists, social scientists, historians, and popular writers.[71]

However, the new environmentalists have not yet swept all before them. Paul Bonnifield, in his *Dust Bowl: Men, Dirt and Depression*, which also appeared in 1979, finds a villain of sorts in nature itself in that dust storms existed long before farmers plowed up the plains.[72] Further, he argues that dust storms are caused by wind erosion and that neither the scientist nor the government addressed this problem before 1929 or during the early thirties. In short, the farmer, the experts, and the government were all going after the wrong thing in their initial efforts to save the Great Plains.[73] Bonnifield also suggests that farmers and the public simply did not understand the implications of improved mechanized farming for the Great Plains. That is to say, it was the capacity of machinery to farm more land that enabled farmers to use more land and expand their operations and thus produce more grain. It was also specializing machines such as disc plows and harrows that broke the soil in such a way that it could blow.[74]

At the same time Bonnifield is anxious to correct the government's and the public's image of the Southern Plains as being completely poverty struck and subject to a massive exodus of peoples. It is he who argues that deep depression did not hit there until 1932 and that total crop failure occurred only in 1933.[75] Some farmers continued to live on oil lease royalty checks; bank failures were not epidemic; and sales of such durable goods as automobiles in the larger towns did not go below a point of no return.[76]

Perhaps most important, Bonnifield argues that while the farmers were unprepared to meet the dust bowl crisis in 1932, they were beginning to come to grips with it by 1934, both in terms of better conditions and a realization that they had been engaged in wrong agricultural practices. Nor does he downplay the crucial role of federal help. But in the end Bonnifield believes that the people of the dust bowl region saved themselves. It was government land policy and long-range planning that bungled things and drove people from the land with talk of relocation and the switch from wheat to grazing. Thus the tragic hero of the government scenario, land reform, becomes the villain.[77]

R. Douglas Hurt, in his *The Dust Bowl: An Agricultural and Social History*, which appeared in 1981, agrees with Bonnifield that the dust bowlers were a tough courageous people who, while naive at the beginning, did accept professional advice about soil conservation and that farmers working through the soil conservation districts made considerable progress. Here the Soil Conservation Service retains its status as a hero.[78] Unlike Bonnifield, Hurt believes that the government helped considerably and that the behavior of the dust bowl farmers in the drought of the 1950s suggests how much they had learned.[79] If one adds Richard Lowitt's assessment that while New Deal programs really benefitted the

Great Plains, they were not designed to bring about basic economic change, and this meant "that the conditions and practices fostering erosion and drought would not disappear," it is clear that it is now open season in Great Plains historiography.[80] As new studies are undertaken, one hopes that scholars will remember that government programs that were unique and controversial from the beginning and that never achieved their ultimate goals, should not be judged with hindsight but in the context in which they operated and with the knowledge of what limitations constrained them.[81]

In the perspective of time, and on the basis of the new studies cited above, it looks as if conditions in the most publicized dust bowl—that in the Southern Plains—were probably not as severe as those in North and South Dakota or perhaps even those in Wyoming and eastern Montana. It also appears that local and state political leaders, despite their vigor and their proposals for helping the farmer in a business sense, had very limited ideas about how to cope with either drought or the larger social consequences of the depression. It was the national government using floods of money distributed by a bewildering variety of agencies that stepped into the void and temporarily saved the day. If the verdict is not yet in on how much the New Deal achieved in the way of conservation and improved land use, it seems clear that there was a general improvement in peoples' lives if only as a result of such programs as Rural Electrification and Social Security.[82]

One should also remember that there was no real social or economic revolution in the 1930s on the Great Plains. Local writers have praised Great Plains farmers and residents for showing their pioneer spirit in the 1930s.[83] While it was certainly there, so too was a strain of thought that must be called conservative rather than liberal, cautious rather than daring, and traditional rather than reformist. Until we can get past elections, circus politics, and journalistic reports to know, without prejudice aforethought, about the thoughts and makeup of the people of the Great Plains themselves, the history of the southern and northern Great Plains will remain unwritten.[84]

One of the problems in coming to grips with that task is the concept of regionalism that has been so popular in Great Plains historiography for so long. Although John Wesley Powell was a founder of the concept, its popularity dates from Walter Prescott Webb's seminal book, *The Great Plains* (1931), which gave a set of vast and varying regions a single regional image, a coherent past, a distinct culture, and a sense of being different in a way that no other book before or since has done.[85] The sense that region was the ultimate reality was central to the thinking of both New Deal programs and New Deal long-range planners. The dust bowl was, in fact, called Region VI in official reports. These are all concepts imposed from above by scientists, scholars, and bureaus. Within the Great Plains, local initiation of such things as tri-state oil compacts or interstate conferences on grasshopper control, for example, seem more rare than common.[86] These facts would suggest that the historian in tackling the immensely complex but fundamentally important history of the Great Plains environment must not forget that people think in terms of state and local economic and political units rather than regions in their everyday lives. Indeed, one of the most valuable contributions environmental and ecological historians might make is to highlight the contrast between local traditional spatial and environmental conceptualizations and those that scholars and experts believe better explain the actual environment.

The Prairie Provinces

In 1847 a British sportsman appeared in the upper Missouri and Yellowstone River areas to hunt buffalo and grizzly bears. His name was John Palliser. Born into a family of wealthy landowners in Ireland, Palliser spent much of his time traveling and big game hunting in all parts of the world. Although he attended Trinity College, Dublin, he did not graduate. Nevertheless he was a well-educated person, highly intelligent, and very observant. Fluent in French, German, and Italian, he enjoyed the company of scholars and scientists. Often sojourning in London he had close friends who were on the staff of the British Museum.[87]

Ten years after he had been on the upper Missouri, Palliser found himself heading a scientific expedition sponsored by the Royal Geographic Society and Parliament with orders to survey the prairie provinces of Canada. Because the findings of that 1857 expedition, particularly with regard to soil and climate, shaped British and Canadian policy for Canadian prairie settlement for the next thirty years and continue to be part of a debate about the region down to the present, Palliser's report deserves some attention in this essay.[88]

How had Palliser become interested in Canada and why was he, who was neither a professional scientist nor an engineer, nor an experienced army man, chosen for this task? Irene M. Spry, editor of the Palliser Papers, believes that Palliser became personally interested in the idea of exploration after meeting Commander Cadwalader Ringgold who had been with the Charles Wilkes Expedition from 1838 to 1842.[89] In 1856 Palliser was elected to the Royal Geographic Society, having been sponsored by Francis Galton and seconded by John Arrowsmith, the great cartographer.[90] By the time Palliser joined the Royal Geographic Society, it appears that the Society had already become interested in exploring the Canadian plains and prairies above the 49th parallel. Although the evidence is somewhat circumstantial, the society was interested in Governor Isaac I. Stevens' Railroad Survey along the 47th parallel that took place in 1853. They followed Lieutenant Gouverneur Kemble Warren's topographical forays into the Northern Plains (embraced by the future states of North and South Dakota) between 1855 and 1857. It does not seem mere coincidence that Arrowsmith produced a fine map of Western Canada in 1854 and Warren completed the first general map of the American West in 1857.[91]

After receiving the added support of the Royal Society, and aided by the support of John Bell, a friend of Palliser's who was under-secretary of state at the time, Parliament approved the funding. The expedition was to explore the country from "the headwaters of the Assiniboine River to the foot of the Rocky Mountains, and from the northern branch of the Saskatchewan to the 49th parallel of Latitude."[92] Although this region was well known to the fur trappers of the Hudson's Bay and Northwest Company, it had never been officially explored.

The scientific members of the expedition included a distinguished French Botanist, Eugene Bourgeau, a "magnetical observer," Lieutenant Thomas Wright Blakiston, a naturalist-geologist, James D. Hector, who was also a medical doctor, and John W. Sullivan, an astronomer who also served as the party's secretary.[93]

Palliser's expedition was designed to answer a number of questions: (1) Were the western plains of Canada suitable or unsuitable for agriculture and settlement? (2) Was there a logical access route through British territory to the prairie region and from there westward to the Pacific? It was not lost on Palliser or the Royal Geographic Society that he and the scientists had to come via New York and thence to Sault Ste. Marie in order to reach the prairies. A trans-Canada route was even more important, for if the prairies could be farmed, the British were anxious to settle them "before the swelling tide of American expansion flooded the British West." (3) Should the Hudson's Bay Company be left in control of the area, or superseded by a regular government organization?[94]

Palliser and his scientists did their work well, staying for nearly three years (1857–1860). Their careful report on the topography, soil, rainfall, and climate left one with the image of clearly defined belts of vegetation, some of which were fine for agriculture. They also pointed out routes by which to communicate with Ontario and with the Pacific and thus, by implication, laid the basis for a trans-Canada railroad just as Americans had been laying out routes for American transcontinental lines.[95] Moreover their own survey was supplemented and sometimes paralleled by a Canadian government expedition taking place at the same time headed by S. J. Dawson and H. Y. Hind. Together they provided a very comprehensive report on the Canadian prairie provinces.[96]

As part of his report Palliser described a semiarid and arid zone, roughly triangular shaped with the 49th parallel for its base from longitude 100° west to longitude 114° with the apex at the 52nd parallel of latitude. Palliser saw it as an extension of the "Great American Desert" south of the border. Impressed by the bunch grass, sagebrush, cactus, and grasshoppers he found in the triangle, Palliser said it would "forever be comparatively useless."[97] Both the government and settlers of the prairie provinces of Canada have roundly condemned Palliser for his negative image of the region that now forms the southwestern part of Saskatchewan and the southern portion of Alberta. But it is an area that borders on the dust bowl area of western North Dakota and the eastern half of Montana.

The first new province in the Dominion of Canada was Manitoba. Created in 1870 it was then, as Gerald Friesen has noted, largely a *métis* settlement, but only a decade later it could be described as a British-Ontarian community, and by 1900 "a stable, comfortable civilization had been set in place" there. The *métis* had moved west and north, and the French-speaking population had lost all power in the intervening years.[98]

Although Manitoba was destined to be a rural agricultural province, whose settlements were determined by the route of the Canadian Pacific railroad, it was less rural than North Dakota or the Southern Plains because it had its own "metropolis" of Winnipeg, a city that boasted 40,000 inhabitants by 1900. Moreover, Winnipeg had a high opinion of itself as a future Canadian equivalent of St. Louis or Chicago. Dominated by merchants, it challenged Toronto's control of the grain trade and established its own exchange.[99] Somewhat like the Northern Plains area of the United States, Manitoba boomed in the 1880s with a large influx of immigrants and good crops. Similarly, between 1887 and 1897 the province experienced drought, fewer settlers, trouble with new ways of farming, and new strains of wheat, and its municipalities bore a heavy burden of debt. There were agrarian protests that resembled and even paralleled those of the Farmers' Alliance and the Populists in the United States, though it should be pointed out that some of the most outspoken "American" populist leaders, such as Henry Loucks, had been Canadian citizens.[100]

On Manitoba's western border lay the North-West Territories (embracing the future provinces of Saskatchewan and Alberta). Still occupied by a *métis* population, faced with uncertainty about its future economy in the Dry Belt (Palliser's Triangle), and hampered by the lack of farm-to-market branch railroad lines, there was no real agricultural takeoff until 1896 and thereafter. On the other hand, the southwestern district of the North-West Territories flourished as open-range cattle country from 1874 onward. Indeed, writes Gerald Friesen, Ottawa authorities treated the semiarid southwestern land of the Territories as a country apart, a unique cattle-kingdom with a British and equestrian tradition, "where hot autumn weather cured the short grass and warm winter winds melted the snow" frequently enough for there to be year-round grazing.[101] Attracted by the Ottawa government's policy of generous land leases, a good market for beef in Great Britain, and the presence of the railroad and the refrigerator car, a golden era of Canadian ranching occurred.[102]

It was not really until Alberta and Saskatchewan were made provinces in 1905 and the government began to break up the big ranches and promote agricultural settlement that the ranchers began to lose their power.[103] It was in this period that the more arid regions of those two provinces were settled by farmers.

Of the two new provinces, Saskatchewan grew more rapidly. Devoted largely to wheat raising, it developed a real identity whereas Alberta, with a mixed population and a mixed economy of ranching, mining, and agriculture, had a less clear self-image. At the same time the settlers of Saskatchewan were of mixed origins. Because the Canadian government had recruited settlers from central and eastern Europe, by 1914 almost half the prairie residents had been born in another country. Moreover, in contrast to the United States after World War I, Canada continued to sponsor immigration right up to 1929, so that in 1931 one-third of the population could still be described as foreign-born.[104] Many of the European immigrants, among them Mennonite sects and the Doukabours, came only because the government had promised them that their religion and native culture would not be suppressed. Thus "the map of the southern half of the western interior was a great checkerboard of culturally and linguistically distinctive settlements."[105]

In the space of one essay it would be impossible to identify similarities and contrasts between Canadian and American plains settlement and evolving institutions. One thing that does stand out, however, is different styles of governance. Not only did the Canadian government accept the British class system; the government of the North-West Territories, writes Friesen, resembled that of a crown colony in the British empire where "local inhabitants would learn the ropes by observing government rather than by governing themselves."[106] This meant that a tradition of government decision making concerning land use, agricultural development, immigration, transportation, and marketing was there from the start. The history of the prairie provinces is filled with instances of Ottawa ministers determining the fate of the area and of pursuing policies that Americans would think belonged in the private sector. Even so, there was the countervailing factor that the powers of the Ottawa federal government were limited so that provincial premiers and representatives to the Canadian parliament actually had and still have more clout than American governors and congressmen.

Comparing Depressions

And finally in the category of similarities and differences, it is important to realize that although both American and Canadian agriculture experienced an acute price depression between 1919 and 1923–24, the Canadian prairie farmers made a comeback whereas American farmers continued to be depressed. On the other hand, prairie towns and cities in Canada had a major problem with unemployment throughout the 1920s.[107]

When the depression did hit the prairie provinces it proved to be "as important in the development of a regional society as the era of the pioneer."[108] R. D. Francis and H. Ganzevoort called the depression decade

> possibly the most significant and memorable decade in prairie history. The very phrase conjures up awesome pictures of defeat, despair, long lines of unemployed, boxcars covered by men 'riding the rods'; the boredom of relief camps; windfall apples and surplus cod; whirling plagues of dust and grasshoppers; the interminable bitter heat of prairie sun.[109]

Having focussed their livelihood on a single export crop that represented 60 percent of their cash income, prairie grain, farmers were not hit just by drought and the fall of agricultural prices, but by the failure of foreign markets that purchased 70 percent of Canada's wheat.[110] In some parts the drought came in 1929 followed by dust storms in 1931. Then after two poor but not devastating crop years, the dust storms came in 1934 with renewed fury, but there was a respite again in 1935. Both 1936 and 1937 were also disasters in which residents experienced blizzards in winter and heat and drought in the summer, along with dust storms. The crops were so poor that year there was not enough grain for seed. Then in 1938 grasshoppers and stem rust came to plague the farmers.[111]

As had been the case in North Dakota and on the Southern Plains, there was an exodus. Between 1931 and 1941, 250,000 people left the prairies. Some went to cities and particularly to Vancouver; others rode the rails and spread all over Canada, and an additional 50,000 moved to the parklands to the north and started all over again.[112]

Because Saskatchewan was the hardest hit by the depression and the scene of the most acute drought, it seems logical to compare its experiences with those of North Dakota and the Southern Plains dust bowl. As P. A. Russell has noted, the average per capita income in Saskatchewan fell by 72 percent between 1928 and 1933, the largest drop for any province. That meant a decrease in the farmers' purchasing power of 63.8 percent. While drought conditions were spotty between 1929 and 1931, they became general for the province between 1931 and 1933 with extreme conditions continuing in many parts right down to World War II.[113]

How did the government respond to the crisis? By provincial law Canadian municipalities were responsible for local relief, and throughout the thirties the laws never really changed. The provincial government was expected to provide "aid to junior governments only in dire distress," and the government at Ottawa said "relief" was strictly a provincial affair. Since no one believed the depression would last long, relief was never organized on a long-range basis. Alma Lawton has concluded that it became "a veritable patchwork quilt of yearly arrangements."[114] A government commission appointed to inquire into relief systems reported in 1938: "It is clear there was no coordinated or carefully planned relief policy in Canada in the Depression." Lawton finds that "Posterity has almost universally condemned the way in which the problem of relief was tackled."[115]

The Saskatchewan municipalities identified four types of relief recipient: "residents, transients, physically fit single, homeless men, and physically unfit single homeless unemployed." Since the cities were legally responsible for the welfare of bonafide residents only, the federal and provincial governments tried to handle all the rest.[116] Most Saskatchewan municipalities of any size had a Relief Board, and, depending on its head and the policies it adopted it could be very unpopular. In Saskatoon, for example, the relief recipients were so discontented and especially at being given clothing, food, and goods handouts in lieu of cash that they organized into unions or protest groups.[117]

The relief camp for single homeless men located on the Saskatoon fairgrounds proved to be such a "hotbed of discontent and radicalism" that the camp was closed and its inmates sent to a Federal Relief Camp. Alma Lawton estimates that between 10 and 25 percent of the urban population of Saskatoon was on relief in the 1930s, and that in contrast to the experience of the Great Plains, the problem became worse in the second half of the decade.[118]

Meanwhile the provincial and federal governments had their hands full in dealing with the estimated 70,000 single, homeless unemployed. Between 1932 and 1936 a number of camps were established for this group of which Dundurn was the major one in the province. According to Lorne Brown, the primary purpose of the camps was to keep young men out of the cities, but by 1936 the government saw them as seed beds for communism. The evidence suggests that Dundurn was run in military fashion but by a corrupt and inefficient staff that denied men their rights and gave them a sense that they were wasting their lives. Used to repair highways and build airports, their response to their work contrasted with the attitudes found in the American Civilian Conservation Corps or other public works programs.[119] The dissatisfaction was so great, in fact, that when a British Columbia group of unemployed mounted a march to Ottawa—the

Ottawa Trek—200 Dundurn inmates joined their ranks. Meanwhile others started a Relief Camp Workers' Union.[120] While the Dundurn experiences may not be typical, they do contrast with the sense of esprit and purpose that most of the American CCC camps seemed to have.

The Canadian federal government at the beginning of the depression was controlled by the Conservative Party with R. B. Bennett as Prime Minister. It followed a conservative course and did not really engage in New Deal style programs although Bennett was tempted to do so, in part to remain in power.[121] Yet when the Liberals and MacKenzie King took over in 1935, they also pursued a very cautious course of action. This meant that there was a constant pummelling of the federal government by the provincial authorities, and there were some dramatic showdowns when the King government actually tried to abolish government support of the Wheat Board and the long-established tradition of wheat pools.[122] What happened at the provincial level of government, then, was extremely important.

In Manitoba the government was run by a coalition of United Farm Workers and Progressives under the remarkable leadership of Premier John Bracken who remained in power throughout the depression years. In effect, it was a nonpartisan government whose password was that "times of crisis required a united front."[123] Under his leadership Manitoba suffered less than the other two prairie provinces.

In Saskatchewan the Liberal Party that had dominated the province in the twenties had unfortunately come under the leadership of James G. Gardiner whose narrow partisanship and pro-Catholic and pro-European stance led to a nativist anti-Catholic and anti-Central European backlash and the Liberal downfall in 1929. In 1930 the Conservatives took over the government. But even they consisted of a coalition of Conservatives, Progressives, and Independents and called themselves "the Co-operative Government." Headed by Premier J. T. M. Anderson, it first pursued "the traditional response of relief and retrenchment before turning to tax consolidation and debt adjustment." Promising that "No one will starve," the Cooperative Government gave municipalities special relief grants in 1930–31, but by the latter year it had set up a "single provincial agency responsible for supervising all rural relief and administering provincial relief programs."[124] Known as the Saskatchewan Relief Committee (SRC), it supplied, writes P. A. Russell, "food, clothing, heating fuel, feed, fodder, seed grain, medical and dental aid, fuel for schools, relief payments to allow teachers to continue teaching and money for machinery repairs." On the whole the SRC managed its limited resources "ably."[125] Relatively speaking, the relief burden in Saskatchewan was five times that of Ontario and the Maritimes.

During its four years in power the Co-operative Government passed measures deferring all delinquent tax sales, promoted public works to absorb the unemployed, passed a provincial income tax as well as an act to adjust agricultural debts, measures that in some form or another were also adopted by the Great Plains state governments.[126]

By 1934, however, the Conservative government had failed, miserably in the eyes of many, and the Liberals took over again and held power until a new party, the Co-operative Commonwealth Federation (CCF), won in 1944. The CCF began as a Farmer-Labour coalition in the thirties and then began to embrace both Catholic and east European groups, British immigrants believing in the Labour Party heritage, and socialist ideas.[127] As Gerald Friesen has written:

> The CCF was prairie Canada's version of socialism; it was an alliance of farmers, labourers, and professionals who shared a deep faith in British parliamentary institutions and an abiding distrust of the competitive market economy; it was quite willing to mix private enterprise with state ownership, but it would not, given the opportunity, permit the market to dictate the availability of health and education services, to bankrupt thousands of family farms, or to develop provincial resources in such a manner that the people did not benefit. It was an indigenous response to long-term urban and class issues as well as to the immediate crisis of the agricultural depression. The CCF was a movement, at times radical, at times moderate in outlook, seeking economic security and the amelioration of social injustice.[128]

Put another way, the trauma of the depression did in the Conservatives and spawned a new party that tried to address the more fundamental social as well as economic issues plaguing the prairie provinces.

In neighboring Alberta, the United Farmers were in power until 1935, and though they claimed to speak for the farmers they proved unable to cope with the problems brought on by drought and depression. By 1935, William Aberhart, a fundamentalist Baptist who, in addition to being a high school principal, ran a Bible Institute and had a popular Sunday radio broadcast that is said to have had 350,000 listeners, succeeded as the first premier representing a new group called the Social Credit Party.[129]

Social Credit took its ideas and name from the economic doctrines of C. H. Douglas, an English engineer. At the risk of excessive over-simplification, Douglas and Aberhart's Social Credit philosophy argued that modern technology has produced an era of great plenty and leisure and both the riches and the free time should be distributed throughout the economy as unearned income.[130] In some sense it resembled the Townsend Plan in California that argued that all senior citizens deserved a certain amount to spend each month.[131] Social Credit should probably even acknowledge a certain indebtedness to Henry George's concept of the unearned increment. (George's ideas had been popular with a previous generation in Canada.) The Social Credit Party, however, argued that banks and credit must be controlled so that the unused income could be shared by the general public. Social Credit did not object to the way businesses were run or to private enterprise. In actual fact the "funny money" people, as their opponents dubbed them, did little more than practice, in the words of Gerald Friesen, "reform capitalism and Christian fundamentalism."[132]

While it is probably premature to draw firm conclusions, it does appear that social and political reforms prompted by the depression took place at the provincial level rather than in Ottawa. Further, at first appearance the Co-operative Commonwealth Federation and the Social Credit party may have seemed radical, but once in power each party pursued a moderate course.[133]

It also appears that an impressive amount of cooperation took place between farmers, government experiment stations, and the farmers themselves in a search for better farming practices, soil conservation, and other land-use problems.[134] Farmers attended institutes for retraining and often came up with ideas that the experts then adopted. Paul Bonnifield has suggested that the Southern Plains farmers who stayed responded in somewhat the same way by cooperating with others to solve their problems, but the Canadian example seems far more positive and elaborate.[135]

It may seem a paradox, but the long tradition of government activism at the provincial level led people to expect government to do many things to respond to the depression, while in the Great Plains less was expected from the state governments. The antics of William Langer, Alfalfa Bill Murray, and Ma and Pa Ferguson and the sometimes rapid turnover in officials (North Dakota had four governors in seven months) contrasts with the long tenure of William Aberhart of Alberta, Paul Bracken of Manitoba, and the Liberals in Saskatchewan.[136] And yet, as Seymour Lipset observed many years ago, the antibank stand of the Social Credit party and the CCF critique of capitalism bear some extraordinary similarities to American populist ideas and the policies of the Nonpartisan League.[137] New comparative studies of these political responses are needed.

The main point is that Saskatchewan and Alberta emerged from the Great Depression with a more sober realistic view of the farming economy, a willingness to use the state to underwrite that economy and, a concept, not really put into law until after World War II, that "Social and economic security were recognized as the fundamental right of every human being."[138]

Many Canadian writers about the depression in the prairie provinces have concluded that the experience created a grassroots sense of regional unity that had never been there before, along with a recognition that problems must be approached regionally. As B. Y. Card, a sociologist writing about prairie society and culture in 1960, noted:

> the regional point of view is vital in understanding social change and in attempting to create a valid theory of human behavior and society.
>
> A second assumption is that the Prairie Provinces constitute a region, that they are a well-delineated natural area whose population faces an assortment of social and economic problems related more or less directly to the area's geography and unique historical-cultural experiences.[139]

Perhaps most important, Card and others believe that the Canadians came out of the depression with an increased sense of community and a renewed spirit that, far from being broken, had been enhanced by adversity.[140]

The emphasis of Canadian writers on a sense of regional awareness and unity suggests that they have approached the story of the depression in sociological and systemic ways that American writers about the plains have not fully explored. And though the pioneer period is as important in prairie history as it is in Great Plains history, unlike the Great Plains, it does not seem to have been a factor in the prairie region's response to drought and depression.[141] Thus it would seem worthwhile to study themes stressed by American historians of the Great Plains depression as opposed to those stressed by Canadian historians. But there is a more subtle semantic problem as well. What, for example, does the word *region* mean to Canadians and Americans and to their respective historians? What does the word *relief* mean, and were the Canadian and American responses to this word similar or different? The same question can be asked about other key words such as *rural, party,* and *unions*.

Questions could also be raised about images of a policy, an institution, or even about the origin of a proposed reform. It has been suggested earlier that relief camps were an abomination to the young unemployed men in Canada. In contrast, government camps for transient labor as portrayed in John Steinbeck's *Grapes of Wrath* seem like bright oases in a barren landscape, and the praise of the CCC camps and their accomplishments has been nearly universal. What factors determined the different responses?

Laws and government policies could also be compared. While farmers in both the Great Plains and Canada responded positively to soil conservation practices, it appears that in the United States the impetus came from the federal government; whereas in Canada it appears that provincial representatives pressured Ottawa to pass legislation for soil conservation.[142] How much did farmers' views about conservation change over time?

Nor should one ignore how political ideas, economic systems, and people themselves move back and forth across borders. For many years it was assumed that the nineteenth-century cattle frontier in Canada was simply an extension of an America one that moved north. Recent scholarship suggests that a distinct British Canadian cattle frontier existed first, and only later did American practices and American cattlemen come to dominate some areas of Canada.[143] By using a comparative approach to the cattle industry of the two countries we might be able to be more precise in saying what features are unique to one, what is common to the two, and what is, indeed, universal in the age-old occupation of cattle raising.

And finally there are questions of periodization, continuity, and discontinuity, and of the need for more synthesis as opposed to monographic studies. Curiously, in spite of all the fame of Walter Prescott Webb's classic, *The Great Plains,* and Steinbeck's dramatization of a depressed rural population leaving for California, there has been no body of American historians dealing with recent Plains history. Canada, on the other hand, has its prairie historians, of whom W. L. Morton and Gerald Friesen are outstanding examples.[144] Nor have plains writers quite equaled Wallace Stegner's *Wolf Willow: A Story and a Memory of the Last Plains Frontier* or James H. Gray's *The Winter Years: The Depression on the Prairies.* The fictional works of Sinclair Ross, *As for Me and My House,* Margaret Laurence's *The Stone Angel,* and W. O. Mitchell's *Who Has Seen the Wind* create a rich image of prairie life even in vicissitude that has no equivalent in fiction about the Great Plains in the 1930s,[145] although the works of Willa Cather, Ole Rölvaag, and Ruth Suckow touch on the 1930s.

On the other hand the burgeoning Center for Great Plains Studies at the University of Nebraska, along with other regional centers in the Northern Plains and Canada pursue a broad interdisciplinary approach that, along with such recent works as Donald Worster's *Dust Bowl* and Richard Lowitt's *The New Deal and the West,* promise a long-delayed renaissance in Great Plains history.[146] In that reawakening one would hope that recent history and the comparative approach will not be neglected.

Notes

1. Paul F. Sharp, "Three Frontiers: Some Comparative Studies of Canadian, American and Australian Settlements," *Pacific Historical Review* 24 (November 1955); Fred Alexander, *Moving Frontiers: An American Theme and its Applica-*

tion to Australian History (Victoria: Melbourne University Press, 1947); H. C. Allen, *Bush and Backwoods: A Comparison of the Frontier in Australia and the United States* (East Lansing: Michigan State University Press, 1959); and William Turrentine Jackson, "A Brief Message for the Young and/or Ambitious: Comparative Frontiers as a Field for Investigation," *Western Historical Quarterly* 9 (January 1978), are but a sampling of works comparing the American-Australian frontiers.

Canadian-American comparisons abound, but see Michael S. Cross, ed., *The Frontier Thesis and the Canadas* (Toronto: Copp Clark Publishing Co., 1970); Paul F. Sharp, *Whoop-Up Country: The Canadian American West, 1865–1885* (Minneapolis: University of Minnesota Press, 1955); William J. Eccles, *The Canadian Frontier, 1534–1760* (New York: Holt, Rinehart and Winston, 1969); Robin W. Winks, *The Myth of the American Frontier: Its Relevance to America, Canada and Australia* (Leicester, England: Leicester University Press, 1971); and a forthcoming study by Roger Nichols that compares Canadian and American policies towards Indians.

For Latin America, see Alastair Hennessey, *The Frontier in Latin America* (Albuquerque: University of New Mexico Press, 1978); and David J. Weber, *The Mexican Frontier, 1821–1846: The American Southwest under Mexico* (Albuquerque: University of New Mexico Press, 1982).

Walker D. Wyman and Clifton B. Kroeber, eds., *The Frontier in Perspective* (Madison: University of Wisconsin Press, 1957), contains an essay on the Siberian frontier. The South African experience is treated in Howard R. Lamar and Leonard M. Thompson, eds., *The Frontier in History: North America and Southern Africa Compared* (New Haven: Yale University Press, 1981).

2. Donald Worster, *Dust Bowl: The Southern Plains in the 1930s* (New York: Oxford University Press, 1979), 29.

3. Elwyn B. Robinson, *History of North Dakota* (Lincoln: University of Nebraska Press, 1966), 396–419; Richard Lowitt, *The New Deal and the West* (Bloomington: Indiana University Press, 1984), 9–13, 33–46 passim., 53–63; Robert P. Wilkins and Wynona Huchette Wilkins, *North Dakota: A Bicentennial History* (New York: W. W. Norton, 1977); Herbert S. Schell, *History of South Dakota* (Lincoln: University of Nebraska Press, 1969), 288–95.

4. Gerald Friesen, *The Canadian Prairies: A History* (Toronto and London: University of Toronto Press, 1984), 382–400; W. L. Morton, "A Century of Plains and Parkland," in Richard Allen, ed., *A Region of the Mind: Interpreting the Western Canada Plains* (Regina: Canadian Studies Centre, University of Saskatchewan, 1973), 165–99 passim.; B. Y. Card, *The Canadian Prairie Provinces from 1870 to 1950: A Sociological Interpretation* (Toronto: J. M. Dent and Sons, 1960), 1–7, 18–21, and bibliography, 43–46.

5. R. D. Francis and H. Ganzevoort, eds., *The Dirty Thirties in Prairie Canada* (Vancouver: Tantalus Research, Ltd., 1973), 5; Wilkins and Wilkins, *North Dakota*, 102; Lowitt, *The New Deal and the West*, 10–13.

6. Robinson, *North Dakota*, 28–32; Schell, *South Dakota*, 27–30.

7. "Red River Valley of the North," in Howard R. Lamar, ed., *Reader's Encyclopedia of the American West* (New York: Harper and Row, 1986), 1005–6 (hereafter cited as *REAW*); Robinson, *North Dakota*, 62–67, 128–31.

8. Howard R. Lamar, *Dakota Territory, 1861–1889: A Study of Frontier Politics* (New Haven: Yale University Press, 1966), 34–66; Robinson, *North Dakota*, 109–32.

9. Isaac I. Stevens, *Narrative and Final Report of Explorations for a Route for a Pacific Railroad near the Forty-Seventh and Forty-Ninth Parallels of North Latitude from St. Paul to Puget Sound*, in *Reports of Exploration and Surveys to Ascertain the Most Practical and Economical Route for a Railroad from the Mississippi River to the Pacific Ocean, 1851–1858* (Washington, 1860), XII.

10. Lieutenant G. K. Warren, *Exploration in the Dacota Country in the Year 1855*, Senate Executive Document No. 76, 34th Cong., 1st sess. (1856), 21–22.

11. *The Papers of the Palliser Expedition, 1857–1860* (Toronto: The Champlain Society, 1968). Edited with an Introduction by Irene M. Spry. See also H. Y. Hind, *North-West Territory Reports of Progress: Together with a Preliminary and General Report of the Assiniboine and Saskatchewan Exploring Expedition* (Toronto: John Lovell, 1859).

12. The boom years are fully treated in Robinson, *North Dakota*, 133–55 and in Schell, *South Dakota*, 158–74.

13. D. Jerome Tweton, "North Dakota," in *REAW*, 848.

14. Robinson, *North Dakota*, 219, 230–31, 257–58.

15. Robinson, *Ibid.*, 260, 263–64, 266–67.

16. Robinson, *Ibid.*, 330–45; Wilkins and Wilkins, *North Dakota*, 137–52.

17. Robinson, *North Dakota*, 327–51; Wilkins and Wilkins, *North Dakota*, 137–52.

18. Tweton, "North Dakota," *REAW*, 848.

19. Robinson, *North Dakota*, 354–57, 421–24.

20. Ann Marie Low, *Dust Bowl Diary* (Lincoln: University of Nebraska Press, 1984), 13.

21. Robinson, *North Dakota*, 398.

22. Robinson, *Ibid.*, 398.

23. Robinson, *Ibid.*, 399.

24. Robinson, *Ibid.*, 399–400; Wilkins and Wilkins, *North Dakota*, 102.

25. Robinson, *North Dakota*, 397.

26. Robinson, *Ibid.*, 397.

27. Wilkins and Wilkins, *North Dakota*, 114–19.

28. Wilkins and Wilkins, *Ibid.*, 126–31.

29. Robinson, *North Dakota*, 406–9.

30. Robinson, *Ibid.*, 406–7.

31. A full coverage of New Deal programs operating in a given state is difficult to find, but see Robinson, *Ibid.*, 406–9; Lowitt, *The New Deal*, 33–80 passim.; Schell, *South Dakota*, 288–95.

32. Robinson, *North Dakota*, 407–8.

33. Robinson, *Ibid.*, 408.

34. Lowitt, *The New Deal*, 53–63.

35. Lowitt, *Ibid.*, 40–45.

36. Worster, *Dust Bowl*, 192–97.

37. Lowitt, *The New Deal*, 62–63; Robinson, *North Dakota*, 196–419.

38. Robinson, *North Dakota*, 402–6.

39. Zebulon M. Pike, *Explorations and Travels Through the Western Territories of North America* (Philadelphia: C. & A. Conrad & Co., 1810).

40. Edwin James, *Account of an Expedition from Pittsburgh to the Rocky Mountains, 1819–1820*, in *Early Western Travels, 1748–1865*, ed. by Reuben G. Thwaites (Cleveland: Arthur H. Clark Co., 1905–7), 174.

41. Wayne Gard, *The Great Buffalo Hunt* (New York: Knopf, 1959); C. C. Rister, *The Southwest Frontier* (Cleveland: 1928); Robinson, *North Dakota*, 71–72, 77–78, 185–86; Arrell M. Gibson, *The West in the Life of the Nation* (Lexington, MA: D. C. Heath and Co., 1976), 474–76.

42. Robinson, *North Dakota*, 71–72, 77–78, 185–86.

43. Gibson, *The West in the Life of the Nation*, 476–77; Edward E. Dale, *The Range Cattle Industry* (Norman: University of Oklahoma Press, 1929); Lewis Atherton, *The Cattle Kings* (Bloomington: Indiana University Press, 1961); Ernest S. Osgood, *The Day of the Cattleman* (Minneapolis: University of Minnesota Press, 1929); Maurice Frink, W. T. Jackson, and A. W. Spring, *When Grass Was King* (Boulder: University of Colorado Press, 1956); Louis Pelzer, *The Cattlemen's Frontier* (Glendale, CA: Arthur H. Clark Co., 1936).

44. A convenient survey is in Chapters 34 and 35 of Ray Allen Billington, *Westward Expansion* (New York: Macmillan Company, 1960); for fuller coverage see Paul W. Gates, *History of Public Land Law Development* (Washington: U.S. Government Printing Office, 1968).

45. Walter Prescott Webb, *The Great Plains* (Boston: Ginn and Company, 1931); Gilbert C. Fite, *The Farmers' Frontier, 1865–1900* (New York: Holt, Rinehart and Winston, 1966).

46. John P. Stover, *American Railroads* (Chicago: University of Chicago Press, 1961), 98.

47. Gerald D. Nash, *The American West in the Twentieth Century: A Short History of an Urban Oasis* (Englewood Cliffs, N.J.: Prentice-Hall, 1973), 98; Worster, *Dust Bowl*, 90–97; R. Douglas Hurt, "Agricultural Technology in the Dust Bowl, 1932–40," in Brian Blouet and Frederick C. Luebke, *The Great Plains: Environment and Culture* (Lincoln: University of Nebraska Press, 1979), 139 ff.

48. Worster, *Dust Bowl*, 28.

49. Lewlie Hewes, *The Suitcase Farming Frontier* (Lincoln: University of Nebraska Press, 1973).

50. Paul Bonnifield, *Dust Bowl: Men, Dirt and Depression* (Albuquerque: University of New Mexico Press, 1979), 28, 47, 95.

51. Gibson, *The West in the Life of the Nation*, 579.

52. Bonnifield, *Dust Bowl*, 37–38, 98; Lowitt, *The New Deal*, 59.

53. Gibson, *The West in the Life of the Nation*, 579.

54. Nash, *American West*, 80, notes that "one-fourth of all Texans were of Mexican or Chicano descent." This suggests yet another difference between the dust bowls. Immigrant groups were active in North Dakota politics and in the Prairie Provinces of Canada. By contrast, during the 1930s, Mexicans and Chicanos had very little role as active participants in Texas politics or the dust bowl region.

55. Lewis L. Gould, "James Edward Ferguson," in *REAW*, 362–63; Seth S. McKay, *Texas Politics, 1906–1944* (Lubbock: Texas Tech Press, 1952).

56. This theme is pursued in Bonnifield, *Dust Bowl*, 61–86, and in Worster, *Dust Bowl*, 29 ff.

57. Worster, *Dust Bowl*, 29.

58. Worster, *Ibid.*, 49.

59. Worster, *Dust Bowl*, 49.

60. Worster, *Ibid.*, 4.

61. Worster, *Ibid.*, 4.

62. Lawrence B. Lee, "John Wesley Powell," in *REAW*, 597–99; John Wesley Powell, *Report on the Lands of the Arid Region of the United States* (Washington: Government Printing Office, 1878).

63. Richard White, "The Winning of the West: The Expansion of the Western Sioux in the Eighteenth and Nineteenth Centuries," *Journal of American History* 65 (September 1978): 319–43.

64. This theme is sensitively treated in Robinson, *North Dakota*, 397, 550–52, and in Wilkins and Wilkins, *North Dakota*, 122–25.

65. Elise L. Broach, "The Unsettling Frontier: New Deal Resettlement and the Turnerian Legacy" (Research Paper, Yale University, May 1987). I am grateful to Ms. Broach for allowing me to cite her paper, which traces the speeches and broadcasts of Rexford G. Tugwell and other New Deal officials concerned with agricultural reform and resettlement.

66. Broach, *Ibid.*, and Lowitt, *The New Deal*, 58–62.

67. Barry Goldwater, *Where I Stand* (New York: McGraw-Hill, Inc., 1964).

68. See Peter Wiley and Robert Gottlieb, *Empires in the Sun: The Rise of the New American West* (New York: G. P. Putnam's Sons, 1982), and Gerald D. Nash, *The American West Transformed: The Impact of the Second World War* (Bloomington: Indiana University Press, 1985); Robinson, *North Dakota*, 442–66.

69. Walton Bean and James J. Rawls, *California, An Interpretive History* (New York: McGraw-Hill, 1983), 429–44.

70. Worster, *Dust Bowl*, 198, 229.

71. Richard White, *Land Use, Environment, and Social Change: The Shaping of Island County Washington* (Seattle: University of Washington Press, 1980); and Marc Reisner, *Cadillac Desert: The American West and its Disappearing Water* (New York: Viking Press, 1986); and Brian W. Blouet and Frederick C. Luebke, *The Great Plains: Environment and Culture*.

72. Bonnifield, *Dust Bowl*, 1–19, but especially 10.

73. Bonnifield, *Ibid.*, 40–42, 44–45.

74. Bonnifield, *Ibid.*, 49 ff.

75. Bonnifield, *Ibid.*, 105, even asserts that the world of the local depression may have been over "by the time the nation discovered the dust bowl."

76. Bonnifield, *Ibid.*, 89–98.

77. Bonnifield, *Ibid.*, 170, 188.

78. Hurt's argument is well summarized in his essay, "Agricultural Technology in the Dust Bowl, 1932–40," in Blouet and Luebke, *The Great Plains*, 139–56.

79. Hurt, *Ibid.*, 145–51.

80. Lowitt, *The New Deal*, 62.

81. The extraordinary prosperity of the postwar years, advances in technology, the complexity and range of current government services, and a new range of critical thought about capitalism make it almost impossible to see the depression in proper context.

82. Lowitt, *The New Deal*, 33. Curiously, there are no index references to the Social Security Act of 1935 in Lowitt, Bonnifield, and Robinson, and only passing reference in Worster. However, beginning in the late 1970s both *South Dakota History*, vols. 7 ff., and *North Dakota History*, vols. 47 ff., have explored the social aspects of the New Deal in those states. See for example, Kenneth E. Hendricksen, "The National Youth and the New Deal, 1935–1943," *South Dakota History* 9 (Spring 1979): 131–51; also his "The Civilian Conservation Corps in South Dakota," *Ibid* 11 (Winter 1980): 1–20; and Harry C. McDean, "Federal Farm Policy and the Dust Bowl: The Half-Right Solution," *North Dakota History* 47 (Winter 1980): 21–31.

83. Bonnifield, *Dust Bowl*, 185–86.

84. Elwyn B. Robinson's chapter, "The Character of a People," in his *North Dakota*, 547–65 is a good model to emulate.

85. Walter Prescott Webb, *The Great Plains* (Boston: Ginn and Company, 1931).

86. Robinson, *North Dakota*, 399, and Gibson, *The West in the Life of the Nation*, 579.

87. Spry, *The Palliser Papers*, xv–xxii.

88. Irene M. Spry, *The Palliser Expedition: An Account of John Palliser's British North American Expedition, 1857–1860* (Toronto: Macmillan Company, 1965), is a useful summary.

89. Spry, *Palliser Papers*, xxi.

90. Spry, *Ibid.*, xxii–xxiii.

91. William H. Goetzmann, *Exploration and Empire: The Explorer and the Scientist in the Winning of the American West* (New York: Knopf, 1966), 314–16.

92. Spry, *Palliser Papers*, xxiv.

93. Spry, *Ibid.*, xxvi–xxxviii passim.

94. Spry, *Ibid.*, xli–xliii.

95. Spry, *The Palliser Expedition*, 278–87.

96. H. Y. Hind, *North-West Territory, Reports of Progress.* . . . See also John Warkinton, *The Western Interior of Canada: A Record of Geographical Discovery, 1612–1917* (Toronto: 1964), 144–230.

97. Spry, *Palliser Papers*, cix–cxii.

98. Friesen, *Canadian Prairies*, 195.

99. Friesen, *Ibid.*, 204–10, 218.

100. "Henry L. Loucks," in *Dictionary of American Biography*, vol. 11 (New York: Charles Scribner's Sons, 1933), 426–27.

101. Friesen, *Canadian Prairies*, 221.

102. David H. Breen, *The Canadian Prairie West and the Ranching Frontier, 1874–1924* (Toronto: University of Toronto Press, 1983), I, 3–98.

103. Breen, *Ibid.*, 136–61.

104. Friesen, *Canadian Prairies*, 242.
105. Friesen, *Ibid.*, 244.
106. Friesen, *Ibid.*, 223.
107. Friesen, *Ibid.*, 396.
108. Friesen, *Ibid.*, 382.
109. Francis and Ganzevoort, *Dirty Thirties*, 5.
110. Friesen, *Canadian Prairies*, 384.
111. Friesen, *Ibid.*, 386.
112. Friesen, *Ibid.*, 388.
113. P. A. Russell, "The Co-operative Government's Response to the Depression, 1930–1934," *Saskatchewan History* 24 (Autumn 1971): 81.
114. Alma Lawton, "Relief Administration in Saskatoon During the Depression," *Saskatchewan History* 22 (Spring 1969): 42.
115. Lawton, *Ibid.*, 42.
116. Lawton, *Ibid.*, 42–43.
117. Lawton, *Ibid.*, 44–45, passim.
118. Lawton, *Ibid.*, 45, 58.
119. Lorne A. Brown, "Unemployment Relief Camps in Saskatchewan, 1933–1936," *Saskatchewan History* 23 (Autumn 1970): 81–83.
120. Brown, *Ibid.*, 90–98.
121. Donald Foster and Colin Read, "The Politics of Opportunism: The New Deal Broadcasts," *Canadian Historical Review* 60 (Fall 1979): 324–49, but especially 324–31.
122. Compared to the number of times Franklin D. Roosevelt and federal New Deal officials are mentioned in all texts on the Great Plains, Prime Minister Bennett and his successor Mackenzie King are mentioned only in passing in Friesen's *Canadian Prairies;* Bennett four times and King only three. The Bennett government reluctantly agreed to a Canadian Wheat Board in 1935 that in effect guaranteed the wheat farmer a fair price. When King tried to abolish the Wheat Board in 1939, prairie anger was so great he had to keep it, give the small farmer added protection, and establish a system of crop insurance as well. The federal government created the Prairie Farm Rehabilitation Administration in 1935 that established additional experiment stations to teach farmers how to deal with soil and water conservation and to adjust crops to the soils, especially in the Palliser's Triangle area. However, if the federal government seems overly unsympathetic to the farmer, it should be noted that it passed an Unemployment Relief Act in 1930 and a series of farm and unemployment relief acts in subsequent years as well as other legislation (Friesen, *Canadian Prairies*, 391–92, 395).
123. Friesen, *Ibid.*, 401.
124. Friesen, *Ibid.*, 403–7; Russell, "Co-operative Government's Response," 81–84.
125. Russell, *Ibid.*, 82.
126. Russell, *Ibid.*, 86–100.
127. Friesen, *Canadian Prairies*, 408–9. The early history of the CCF is traced in Michael Horn, "Frank Underhill's Early Drafts of the Regina Manifesto 1933," *Canadian Historical Review* 54 (December 1973): 393–418, and in Peter R.

Sinclair, "The Saskatchewan CCF: Ascent to Power and the Decline of Socialism," *Ibid.*, 419–33.

128. Friesen, *Ibid.*, 409.

129. Friesen, *Ibid.*, 410 ff.; see also John A. Irving, *The Social Credit Movement in Alberta* (Toronto: University of Toronto Press, 1959); Seymour M. Lipset, *Agrarian Socialism* (Berkeley: University of California Press, 1959); C. B. MacPherson, *Democracy in Alberta: Social Credit and the Party System* (Toronto: University of Toronto Press, 1962), and David Elliot, "William Aberhart: Right or Left?" in Francis and Ganzevoort, *Dirty Thirties*, 11–32.

130. Friesen, *Canadian Praries*, 412–15.

131. Lowitt, *The New Deal*, 172; Robert S. McElvane, *The Great Depression: America, 1921–1941* (New York: Times Books, 1984), 236, 241, 243.

132. Friesen, *Canadian Prairies*, 416.

133. This is a major theme in Friesen's analyses of Social Credit and the CCF, *Ibid.*, 410–17.

134. Friesen, *Ibid.*, 391.

135. Bonnifield, *Dust Bowl*, 155; Hurt, "Agricultural Technology," 139–56.

136. Robinson, *North Dakota*, 411.

137. Lipset's findings in his *Agrarian Socialism* are strongly challenged in J. F. Conway, "The Prairie Populist Resistance to the National Policy: Some Reconsiderations," *Journal of Canadian Studies* 14 (Autumn 1979): 77–91.

138. Lawton, "Relief Administration," 58.

139. Card, *The Canadian Prairie Provinces*, ix.

140. This is a major theme in Friesen, *Canadian Prairies*, 382–417, and in A. W. Rasporich, *Western Canada: Past and Present* (Calgary: McClelland and Steward West, 1975), 9–10, who argues that the sense of community was there from the start in "the complex network of collective social systems and formal organizations which permeate the farm community."

141. John W. Bennett and Seena B. Kohl writing in Raspovich, *Ibid.*, 9, 15 and 17, assert that the stress on individualism comes from academics not from the residents themselves.

142. Friesen, *Canadian Prairies*, 391–95.

143. Breen, *The Canadian Prairie West*, discusses the American presence, 162–79.

144. Friesen's *Canadian Prairies* is an outstanding study. See also W. L. Morton, *The Critical Years: The Union of British North America, 1857–1872* (Toronto: University of Toronto Press, 1964) and his *Manitoba: A History* (Toronto: University of Toronto Press, 1967).

145. Of these, historians agree that Gray's *The Winter Years* is extraordinary for its understanding and sensitivity.

146. There are several fine centers and programs for regional study in the Great Plains and Canada, but the Nebraska Center is engaged in interdisciplinary approaches, reflected in its conferences and the *Great Plains Quarterly*. In addition to ecological, environmental, and political and economic topics, the center has stressed literature and culture and the comparative approach. Both in conferences and in publications the history of the Canadian Prairie Provinces have been treated.

III

Environment of the Twentieth-Century West

Although the impact of environmental influences on the American West after 1890 was less significant than in the earlier frontier stages, nevertheless it continued to be significant. Climate, topography, open spaces, and natural resources clearly contributed to shaping the contours of the twentieth-century West and are essential elements of its image. Indeed, some of the most distinctive characteristics of the West originated in environmental conditions. As John Opie indicates in his essay, the extraordinary range of environmental influences on the West provides a particularly revealing case study of the impact that European civilization had on what not very long ago was a virgin continent. That experience must clearly be an essential part of any image of the twentieth-century West that will be developed in the future. But the extent of the influence of environmental conditions can best be understood with reference to particular factors. William Robbins provides such a perspective by subjecting the western lumber industry to close analysis. As he indicates, the story of the exploitation of western lumber is largely a twentieth-century phenomenon. It reveals much about the society that it also helped to shape. That theme could be applied as readily to the influence of water in the development of the twentieth-century West. Donald Pisani explores one aspect of this extensive subject by analyzing irrigation districts and their relation to federal authorities. Water did much to shape the semiarid regions of the West and the society that developed there, as much as eastern institutions that settlers brought with them to the area. But whatever institutions twentieth-century settlers brought were clearly modified and adapted by them to the new western environment that they encountered.

7

Environmental History in the West

John Opie

Environmental influences, John Opie reminds us, are not necessarily fixed and immutable. They depend on the cultural perceptions of individuals and civilizations that view them from differing perspectives. Utilizing this approach, Opie raises questions about the environmental changes introduced by newcomers to the twentieth-century West. He wonders whether they were desirable or whether they were amenable to effective management, particularly under the pressures of an increased population. Opie suggests various frameworks for the study of the western environment and also indicates how these can illuminate the values—and the image—of the society of which the landscape is a part.

The American Indians possessed, but benefited little from, the fertile soil that formed an unprecedented source of wealth for the colonists: the colonists gained little more than the grinding of their grain from the water power which made magnates of the early industrialists; the early industrialists set little store by the deposits of petroleum and ore which served as a basis for the fortunes of the post–Civil War period; the industrial captains of the late nineteenth century had no conception of the values that lay latent in water power as a force for generating electricity, which would be developed by the enterprisers of the twentieth century; and these early twentieth-century enterprisers were as little able to capitalize the values of uranium as the Indians had been five centuries earlier. The social value of natural resources depends entirely upon the aptitude of society for using them.
—David Potter (1950)[1]

To the Arid Region of the west thousands of persons are annually repairing . . . a region where the climate is so arid that agriculture is not successful

> without irrigation. . . . [For example,] Utah has an area of 80,000 square miles, of which 2,262 square miles are irrigable. That is, 2.8 percent of the lands. . . . It is probable that the percentage in the entire [western] region is [only] somewhat greater than in the [Utah] territory which we have considered.
> —*John Wesley Powell (1878)*[2]

> Growth for the sake of growth is the ideology of the cancer cell.
> —*Edward Abbey*[3]

As David Potter noted almost four decades ago, natural resources in today's West are like a moving point on a moving line. One man's dross is another man's gold. It is particularly inappropriate in today's West simply to accept its diverse geographies, from the Rocky Mountains to the Pacific Coast, as a fixed and immutable foundation for the historian to ignore as he gets on to more important matters. Nor is the American West hell-bent toward some ecological collapse (forbidding earthquakes and erupting volcanoes). But it is far less clear whether the inevitable environmental changes introduced by European exploitive settlement are invariably desireable or always open to effective management. Today, for example, California and Arizona each struggle internally to allocate scarce water for expanding urban populations and strategic agriculture. They also fight water wars with each other over access to Colorado River supply. No one, not even the redoubtable John Wesley Powell, anticipated the scale of the civilizational pressures placed upon limited essential resources, such as water, in the West.

The modern West is a region that is particularly appropriate for environmental analysis. Its modern appeal is tied more directly to natural resources than is the East. This ranges from the profitability of Santa Barbara's oil to the aesthetic appeal of the Oregon coast. In addition, the West's settlement and modernization are more recent, more fluid, and more clearly associated with local environmental resources, such as the mix of climate, soil, and groundwater in the San Joaquin Valley. Environmental history has the opportunity to introduce and adapt an *Annales*, Braudellian, or New Social History approach for western history.[4] This "history from the ground up" is a multipath approach that integrates natural resources, exploitive technologies, and resulting societal structures. Such analysis is particularly appropriate to the American West where environmental change is more recent, visible, and ongoing than elsewhere in the nation. Such an approach also emphasizes that environmental history cannot be separated from economic, political, and social history, nor from other disciplines such as agricultural economics, cultural anthropology, or historical geography.

Environmental History in the West

Only with a broad multipath approach can environmental impacts, for example, be traced to their origins. For example, groundwater supplies are all-important for agriculture in many western regions, but groundwater was inaccessible before mid-century, until water pumping technologies, cheap fuels, farmers' cash resources, mechanization, and new markets together improved irrigation opportunities. Only a broad multipath approach could conceivably assess the extraordinary environmental effects of the 1973 Oil Crisis, as the nation rushed, sometimes heedlessly, to lower its dependence upon foreign supplies, explore alternatives like nuclear, solar, and wind, and change American energy consumption habits.

Since environmental history does not exist in a vacuum, its historians should open their studies of the contemporary West by first looking at the viewpoints established by nonenvironmental historians. Attention should be paid to Earl Pomeroy's non-Turnerian 1965 regional history, Gerald D. Nash's successful integrative 1973 survey, Donald W. Meinig's fresh views of the Pacific Northwest in 1968 and the changing fortunes of Hispanic Arizona and New Mexico in 1971, W. Eugene Hollon's 1961 southwestern review, Neil Morgan's 1961 contemporary analysis, and Charles Gates and Dorothy O. Johansen's 1967 analysis of the Pacific Northwest.[5] Nash, for example, makes important connections between a post–World War Two "Eco-Technostructure" in the West, large infusions of federal funds, a booming consumption-oriented lifestyle, and rapid environmental degradation. A 1984 article by Paul W. Gates and Lillian F. Gates, goes far beyond the scope of its title, "Canadian and American Land Policy Decisions," to look into key issues on federal policies, environmental protection, and the Sagebrush Rebellion, as well as the internationalization of environmental debate.[6] Nor can the historian look into western environmental issues without taking into account the viewpoints over two decades of the small but growing legion of environmental historians, particularly Joseph Petulla, Donald Worster, and Roderick Nash.

The American West is hardly environmentally homogeneous, ranging from southwestern deserts to northwestern rainforests, from uninhabitable mountains and deserts to sybaritic coastlines. Nor are all parts of the West equally under environmental or human stress. Hence the following observations will target specific issues or regions experiencing high risk that demand the historian's perspective more than others. In this sense the environmental historian very often finds himself in an activist mode. He offers long-term viewpoints to inform heated public debates. The environmental historian rarely wonders whether he is relevant. But he does concern himself about the question of taking sides and advocacy. No doubt the linkage between environmental history and environmental ethics will be debated forever.

Major Environmental Issues*

AGRICULTURE

The oldest environmental use pattern in the West is agriculture. It is also the most continuous. It also provides the greatest wealth and is the single largest employer. After World War II, California became the nation's leading farm state, with fruits, vegetables, and other table foods. In his 1969 history, William H. Hutchinson spoke for much of the West when he wrote, "California's remarkable ability to sustain an ever accelerating growth since 1849 has been made possible through technological utilization of a most bounteous natural resource base."[7] Yet western agriculture remains the stepchild of historical analysis. Of all environmental impacts in the West it is the most pervasive and least understood. Regions like the San Joaquin and Imperial valleys have national roles; the interaction between mechanization, water, markets, migrant workers, federal incentives and regulations, and direct environmental impacts of soil erosion and chemical pollution deserve attention. The impacts of continued and expanding federal support, growth in the size of holdings, increasing irrigation, regional specialization, corporate farming, the decline in numbers of farmers, and vertical integration "from seedling to supermarket" need attention.[8]

The impact of the transfer of the public domain into private property by means of the land survey and land sale offices has not been adequately chronicled for the West, despite Paul Gates's monumental history. The "eastern" gridiron often did not serve western agriculture well, as Powell argued in his 1878 report. Even 640-acre square tracts were not large enough in arid regions. Farmer-settlers found themselves "in harm's way" well into the twentieth century. Rescuing stranded farmers was too immense a problem for the states or private interests. Federal rescue operations, notably the 1902 Reclamation Act, New Deal farm programs, and post–World War Two subsidies, would soon be taken for granted, and eventually become problems as well.

Not the least, California and other Mexican-Spanish oriented southwestern states carry into the twentieth century large-scale private ranch and farm ownership of the best agricultural lands.[9] The historic survey-sale method butted into these private fiefdoms and failed. The fabled American independent family farmer also failed to take hold as effectively in the Southwest as he did in the upper Midwest. The West's extraor-

---

*The list of individual agendas here is weighted to emphasize areas that have been little developed or promise to be major environmental issues well into the future. No doubt some deserving specialties will be slighted and others treated idiosyncratically. But it is hoped that the subjects selected will at least provoke interest in new and important directions to improve an environmental perception of the modern American West.

dinarily productive farmland was largely captured by railroad interests, wealthy speculators, and other prototypes of today's agribusiness.

The result has been to make the Southwest an unusual agricultural region that prospers at the price of environmental "mining" of land and water. The region is not self-sufficient or self-supporting agriculturally, but demands heavy external inputs of chemicals, technologies, capital, favorable government agricultural policies, and low-cost labor, in order to guarantee the year-round, high-yield food production expected by the rest of the nation.

Farmland has been historically a low-cost resource, but not as renewable as once believed. The pressure to preserve farmland is not high because agriculture's extraordinary productivity demands only half of today's cultivated acreage. But a scare arose concerning the limits of American farmland in the early 1970s when "fencerow to fencerow" high-yield farming did not appear sufficient, for the first time in American history, to feed the nation and the world. In addition, approximately 5 percent of America's farmland has already been lost to urbanization and erosion, and the pace is quickening. A determined and cliometrically minded historian would find a wealth of largely untapped information in the annual USDA statistical reports. In addition, the controversial USDA National Agricultural Lands Study of 1980 has not been adequately placed in historical context. It emphasizes various programs of farmland protection and preservation through zoning, districting, easements, tax relief, and other legal controls in California, Oregon, Washington, and Hawaii.[10]

WATER

Of the 612 million acres suitable for continuous cultivation in the U.S., more than 10 percent is irrigated land, producing a third of the total crop value, mostly in the West. Eight million acres are under irrigation projects of the federal Bureau of Reclamation. This amount compares to only 4 million total acres under irrigation in 1900.

The search for large quantities of fresh water has dominated the history and development of the American West for at least the last 100 years. In 1900, when the population of Los Angeles reached 100,000, it reached the maximum that local water sources could support. The city's legal rights to water from the agricultural Owens Valley, hundreds of miles to the north, its demands upon the Colorado River, and the Peripheral Canal battle, have been well chronicled. California water consumption, whether irrigation or urban, has received the lion's share of attention in the West, with important interpretations by Donald J. Pisani, Donald Worster, Abraham Hoffman, William L. Kahrl, and others.[11] Arizona's controversial Central Water Project, with new demands of Colorado River water for growing metropolitan Tucson and Phoenix, and the resulting denial of agricultural needs, requires reinterpretation.[12]

The wider complexities and priority struggles over scarce water are analyzed well by Robert G. Dunbar's 1983 *Forging New Rights in Western Waters*.[13] Urban water demands are far surpassed by agriculture's needs. Over 80 percent of the West's limited water resources historically go to farming. John Wesley Powell's 1878 *Report on the Arid Region of the United States*, despite its dated vision, offered to a disbelieving "humid East" public a realistic picture of the absolute limits water shortages placed on agriculture. Only after many settler failures, and the inability of private enterprise and individual states to improve farming opportunities, was federal intervention invited with the Reclamation Act of 1902. But reclamation did not always fulfill its promise. Lawrence Lee opened up the subject of western waters in his exemplary bibliographical essays. Western reclamation has received attention in Donald Worster's magisterial 1986 *Rivers of Empire* and Charles Coate's unpublished 1977 Western History Association paper. Conflicting views in these studies suggest that major historical and policy issues have hardly been set to rest.[14]

The Colorado River Compact of 1922, a litigation historian's dream, continues to control access to water by farmers and cities from the major surface water source in the arid southwest (the Rio Grande and Pecos rivers also deserve attention).[15] The compact is admirable as an early intrastate agreement for scarce water allocation, but it was flawed from the beginning because water was measured on the historically highest flow of the Colorado that has rarely if ever been matched since. The compact in recent years is the arena for "water wars" involving competing claims and excess use between states, especially California and Arizona, and between the United States and Mexico, as the river became a saline trickle by the time it reached the border. As an interstate and international water-transfer agreement, the compact deserves attention as a precedent for massive water management proposals, several of which, including the 1964 North American Water and Power Alliance (NAWAPA) and the 1968 Lewis G. Smith water import plan, would unite the entire West, American and Canadian, under one water development system.[16] The environmental impacts of these plans, as they would flow water down in massive sheets from Canada between ranges of the Rockies, and reverse the flow of major rivers, would be staggering.

URBAN SPRAWL: THE BOOMTOWN MENTALITY

It is no news that the American Southwest has been the fastest-growing part of the United States for most of the twentieth century. Attention has also been paid in the 1970s and 1980s to the uncontrolled rise of "boomtowns" connected to petroleum and coal exploitation in the American and Canadian West.[17] Gilette and Rock Springs, Wyoming, are notorious examples of chaotic human communities and degraded natural environments.

The history of boomtowns is invariably an environmental history, although it was first examined in terms of the mining frontier. Natural resources, whether gold, silver or copper, lumber, oil or coal, a pass through the mountains or a good harbor, create momentum for rapid localized development. This almost invariably means the invasion of a human population far beyond local capacity to support. The results are not only the spoilation of the land, but also community pollution, waste, crowding, violence, and other human hardships. These developments are often justified as an extension of historic American individualism, freedom of opportunity, the entrepreneurial spirit, and acquisition of wealth.

But the haste and instant riches of boomtowns are not a new phenomenon in the American experience. As John W. Reps has demonstrated, most of American frontier and western history is a boomtown history, including mining, settlement, and railroad frontiers.[18] In a longer-term perspective, urban centers such as Los Angeles, Las Vegas, Phoenix, and Tucson were conceived (if *any* planning took place) and went through their early years as classic American boomtowns.[19] It may be useful to consider several historic boomtown phases that may offer a recognizeable pattern: (1) initial, primitive, unexpected, and unplanned growth "from nothing," (2) a chamber-of-commerce structured boosterism, (3) the rapid push of wealth to the suburbs (tract housing and shopping malls) with parallel city-center decay.

ENERGY

Together with available water, the West's prosperity turns on an abundance of energy. Across the United States, energy consumption doubled almost every decade since 1850. The West far surpassed this pace. But energy growth created environmental problems that often overshadowed its benefits.[20]

The changing viewpoint is astounding. In 1940, Woody Guthrie, already famous for his protest folk songs about Sacco and Vanzetti and the Dust Bowl, travelled along the Columbia River in the Pacific Northwest and wrote 41 songs in 33 days. Some of these songs, "Pastures of Plenty" and "Roll on, Columbia," made the hit parade. Unlike a later day, the songs uncritically praised the dams and power plants of the Bonneville Power Administration as, in one of the songs, "the greatest thing man has ever done." The hydroelectric projects were judged benevolent technological achievements to enhance the well-being of America's common man. Guthrie's protest was against underdevelopment and its resulting human hardship. Together with the demand for water, boomer growth so characteristic of the twentieth-century West depends upon massive supplies of on-demand electric power. It is not surprising that many federal reclamation projects paid their bills more from selling electricity than water.

By the 1970s and 1980s, Woody Guthrie's lyrics would have run into a thicket of environmental contradictions. Even apparently benign hydroelectric development—Flaming Gorge and Glen Canyon are prime examples—was damned for stopping free-flowing rivers, flooding spectacular scenery, terminating rare species, and creating unneeded excess electricity. The famous 1969 Sierra Club newspaper advertisement, which compared a proposed dam in the Grand Canyon to a flooded Sistine Chapel, set a powerful antidevelopment preservationist tone.

Nowhere has the adversary confrontation between growth and conservation been more visible than over energy projects, and nowhere more than in the American West. Nowhere have there been more contradictions. Western environmental organizations, far better organized than in the East, have often succeeded in stemming federal pork-barrel growth-for-growth's-sake projects, including dramatic cutbacks on extensive reclamation projects at Hell's Canyon on the Snake River and the Garrison Diversion Project on the Missouri River in North Dakota. On the other hand, the so-called Sagebrush Rebellion fights federal intervention, such as environmental protection, for the sake of local development, as in the Four Corners coal-fired power project.

The debate over energy has become the primary surrogate arena where the issues of growth versus no-growth are fought, and where the historic environmental contrasts between development, conservation, and preservation of natural resources come to the surface.

RENEWABLE AND NONRENEWABLE RESOURCES

One of the early agendas of environmental history was the assessment of western extractive industries: copper, iron ore, lead, zinc, silver, and gold. Exotic but strategic minerals were tungsten, manganese, molybdenum, antimony, beryllium, lithium, and uranium. In many ways this is another extension (like boomtowns) of the historic mining frontier, but with a critical eye toward waste, damage, and loss rather than the positive emphasis that mining did much to populate and develop the West. A representative dispute that shows the complexity of the issues is the ongoing brouhaha at Crested Butte in western Colorado between major mining interests, a national historic district (tourism), protection of scenic wilderness, and local booster development. Highly visible debates concern coal and offshore oil, with national rules for debate set by the Santa Barbara oil spill and the large scale of the Prudhoe Bay 800 mile pipeline project.

Renewable resources include fishing and lumbering. Forest history, well-served for years by the journal and society of the same name, has acquired a new sophistication and comprehensiveness beginning with the work of Harold K. Steen, Ronald J. Fahl, Tom Cox, and William G. Robbins.[21]

American demands upon natural resources remain as changeable as David Potter claimed almost forty years ago. The environmental historian working with mineral resources needs to take into account technological change, including new, more efficient modes of exploration, including satellites, new modes of extraction, particularly of coal and oil, and new modes of processing and delivery, such as coal slurry. But technological "fixes" create as many problems as they solve.

TOURISM

The West is America's playground. The cash value of tourism in the West compares in scale to vast federal expenditures for the region. Seasonally, important and fragile regions of the American West are invaded by temporary visitors, who swell local populations by multiples of two, three, four or more. Environmentally vulnerable seashores, mountains, and deserts become, one might say, seasonal boomtowns. The historic western example is the extreme population pressure placed upon Yosemite Valley. But urbanized zones like Disneyland also risk overuse and collapse.

In 1968 the futurist Herman Kahn did show prescience when he argued that "excessive tourism" would rank among the ten major factors, together with radioactive debris, overcrowding, and pollution, bringing large-scale environmental contamination and degradation before the end of the century.[22]

But Americans take freedom of movement as a national birthright, and rightly so. Beginning with the New York-New England "Grand Tour" taken by Manhattanites in the 1830s, and the traditional middle class "summer vacation" first by train and later by automobile, tourism became an intrinsic feature of American life. Soon it became more than the young gentleman's adventure, and more a family expedition. John Muir's Sierra Club and Theodore Roosevelt's "strenuous life" encouraged wilderness communion with nature that by the 1970s involved tens of thousands of campers and backpackers. Even during the 1930s Depression, Americans took to the vacation road. After World War II new records for tourism were set every season in the 1950s, 1960s, 1970s, and 1980s. Tourism is taken for escape, education, health, renewal, refreshment, adventure, and innumerable other reasons. It was seen as wholesome recreation for a democratic society.

John A. Jakle, a historical geographer and leading interpreter of twentieth-century tourism, argues persuasively that "tourism is a nearly universal behavior in advanced, industrialized societies. Through firsthand observation in pleasurable circumstances, tourists explore the complexities of the world beyond everyday existence. Thus tourism is a significant means by which modern people assess their world, defining their own sense of identity in the process."[23] Jakle argues that tourism is not a superficial activity, but reflects (and creates) important cultural attitudes toward landscape. The academic's bias, says Jakle, is the prejudice against leisure inherent in the work ethic and the sometime-justified complaint of shallowness. But he also notes that tourism is a powerful test of the visitor's self-identity. Psychologists speak of the essential process of "cognitive mapping" that involves personal self-orientation.[24] In contrast to the passivity of television and even the classroom and library, Jakle says, "In tourism we are freer to explore the unexpected, to face experiences directly and immediately through our senses, unedited by other minds."[25] It is usually strongly aesthetic (another neglected environmental field) and an outsider's view that focuses on the unique qualities of place often little appreciated by local inhabitants.

Above all, tourism, and its environmental impact, is one of the most rapidly expanding features of contemporary society, and has been little served by the historian. Jakle for example notes that "Tourism created a favorable political environment for an expanded highway system and was a significant force behind North America's highway reorientation, the most significant environmental change to occur in the United States and Canada in this century."[26] The Federal Highway Acts of 1956 and 1958 projected 40,000 miles of roads with $40 billion spent by 1970, and spawning over 130 million autos by 1985.

But as the nation's population, leisure time, surplus money, and mobility expand, pressure upon fragile environments has become unbearable in some of the most desireable tourism targets. As a result, for example, the National Park Service and other federal and state agencies find themselves caught in the paradox between service to the nation's *recreation* expectations and their historic mandate for environmental *preservation*.

This contradictory yoking of tourist recreation and nature preservation has dominated the historic move toward national parks since the creation of Yellowstone in 1872, the formation of the Sierra Club in 1893, the National Park Service in 1916, and the Wilderness Act of 1964. Great resort places, such as California's Monterey, Colorado's Estes Park, Canada's Banff Springs, Yellowstone's Old Faithful, and the Grand Canyon's South Rim, would in time point the way to extremely contrived attractions such as Disneyland, controversial ski resorts like Sun Valley, and the phenomenon called Las Vegas. These are all far too powerful western institutions to be ignored by the historian. The West continuously draws more tourists than any other part of the country. The reasons for and meaning behind the West's attractiveness to the rest of the United States deserve attention.

Environmental Issues Unique to the West
EXTRAORDINARY ROLE OF THE FEDERAL GOVERNMENT

West of the Rocky Mountains the federal government never relinquished control of the land as it had in the eastern 60 percent of the nation: half of all western lands, up to 65 percent in Utah and 87 percent in Nevada. The Bureau of Land Management, Forest Service, the military, and to a lesser extent the National Park Service hold in perpetuity vast tracts across the West. Public land sales ended in the mid-1930s. Instead, it is possible that public lands have actually increased through the eminent domain acquisitions for the interstate highway system and rationalization of private land enclosed by national parks, forests, and monuments. Serious questions of land management, taxation, and jurisdiction remain moot in the West.

The historic plan for national expansion since before the Constitution, exemplified by the Land Survey Ordinance of 1785 and the Northwest Ordinance of 1787, was to turn public lands over to private hands—farmers, speculators, railroads—as speedily and reasonably as possible. The constitutional word was "disposal." The unexamined western complaint is that this tradition, bound up with the free individual and manifest destiny, was not fulfilled in the West, to the extent that it has a different and "unAmerican" history. The complaint is exaggerated, but the federal lands are resented. They are said to impede private growth and development.

Contrarily, the West benefited most from federal assistance. Railroad land grants between 1850 and 1870 provided far easier access for immigrants and movement of goods eastward. Post–Civil War settlers acquired federal lands at little or no cost. Military protection and Indian removal offered safe access. By the twentieth century, the 1902 Reclamation Act set a historic precedent by promising farmer's paradises where only uninhabitable desert had existed. The seemingly endless debates over western water rights are classic cases of the historic American tension between private property and public interest, as examined in two articles by Clayton R. Koppes and Donald J. Pisani.[27]

Since World War II, the lion's share of federal funds for military procurement, highway development, wilderness preservation, and energy production has been siphoned into the West. The Bureau of Reclamation and Department of Defense are major actors. Between 1945 and 1960 alone, more than $150 billion was poured into the West, and the funds have not diminished since. In addition, despite Sagebrush Rebellion complaints, the rush of environmental protection laws, beginning with the 1967 Air Quality Act and reaching a climax with NEPA in 1969–1970, controlling air, water, wilderness, and pollution, did much to preserve the West's vaunted quality of life and prevent undesireable degradation. John D. Leshy's calm 1980 analysis of the Sagebrush Rebellion is still the clearest presentation of the issues.[28]

The scale of federal holdings and the resulting federal presence in the West is like a burr under the saddle for many Westerners. The absolute autonomy of private property—the Lockean rights of the owner to do what he pleases—is a historic tenet of American society. It is protected by the Constitution and the Fifth and Fourteenth Amendments. But the conservationist commitment to public lands—a national commons—has been well-entrenched since the establishment of the first national parks and national forests. The study of zoning, easements, eminent domain, and other so-called public "takings" belongs to the historian as well as the attorney.[29]

THE INTERNATIONAL DIMENSION OF ENVIRONMENTAL ISSUES

The American West does not stop at the Pacific Ocean or the Mexican or Canadian Borders. In his stimulating 1981 *Nine Nations of North America*,[30] journalist Joel Garreau crossed international borders when he used environmental logic to divide the West into three nations: MexAmerica, Ecotopia, and The Empty Quarter. His popular approach should not negate his insights. MexAmerica covers southern California, lower Arizona, and New Mexico together with Old Mexico. Ecotopia claims an environmentally responsible culture covering a narrow California coastal strip from Santa Barbara north into the Pacific Northwest, and from Vancouver into Alaska. The Empty Zone emcompasses the low-populated desert and mountain regions of the rest of the West. Garreau displayed considerable insight when he justified the "nations" because they reflected radically different social, economic, political, and environmental conditions.

Just as acid rain provoked conflict between Canada and the United States in the East, so water, specifically lack of good Colorado River water, raised costly tensions between Mexico and the United States.[31] The result has been hundreds of millions of dollars spent on controversial desalination operations near Yuma, Arizona, to bring water quality up to treaty levels when the Colorado River reaches the Mexican border.

Equally controversial has been the inability of the United States to provide the quantity of water guaranteed by treaty to Mexico after the thirsty cities and farms of the Southwest take their shares. Nor has the major environmental impact of population pressures from Mexican immigration into the southwestern states been adequately examined. The environmental pressures upon both the United States and Canada in the Pacific Northwest are not as demanding, but conflicting (and similar) policies toward forestry, land use, industrial development, and pollution can create serious distortions in the future. Environmental risks do not stop at borderlines drawn by politicians and soldiers. If the West had been mapped according to watersheds, ecosystems, habitats, or human liveability, the political map would have looked very different. International boundaries often act to inhibit environmental conservation and preservation, and complicate debates over massive water transfers (see NAWAPA above), the Glacier-Waterton National Park, and diverse problems along the Mexican border.

Not the least, the coastline West is increasingly lured into the rapidly growing Pacific Rim economy. The future of Vancouver, Seattle and Portland—including timber, tourism, coal, oil, fishing—may be tied more to the interests of Japan and China than to a distant Atlantic Community. Hawaii and Alaska are already divided between conflicting Pacific and national ties. The Pacific Ocean has become less a barrier than a trade link, just as the Atlantic Ocean was for early American history. A new western history is in the offing.

WILDERNESS PRESERVATION AND AESTHETICS WITHOUT ELITISM

Environmental history is primarily recognized, rightly or wrongly, for its aggressive promotion of wilderness preservation. Roderick Nash's *Wilderness and the American Mind*, Joseph Petulla's *American Environmental History*, and Alfred Runte's *National Parks: The American Experience*, all praise national park expansion, indict commercialization of the parks, and advocate wilderness preservation while decrying the use of the parks for public amusement. In turn, they are attacked for effete elitism. The value attached to national parks and monuments seems to change with presidential administrations. But for at least fifty years, until the Reagan administration, public appreciation and the creation of a highly professionalized National Park Service, made wilderness advocacy as American as apple pie. And there are roots, of course, going back at least to the Progressive movement. Reassessment of this wilderness advocacy, however, may place it in a specific societal context rather than as an intrinsic feature of the American character. Nash, Joseph Sax, and those who debate with Runte, have already pointed in this direction.[32]

National Park writing has more depth and maturity than most environmental history. Specific parks have been well-served by Richard Bartlett and Aubrey Haines on Yellowstone, Robert Righter on Grand Teton National Park, C. W. Buchholtz on Rocky Mountain National Park, and by Susan Schrepfer's insightful work on the Redwoods, although Yosemite remains neglected until Runte's research is published.[33]

One aspect of wilderness preservation inside and outside the national parks is surprisingly neglected: the human experience of wilderness, by tourist or professional, centers largely on a visual aesthetic. The linkage between environmental history, aesthetic theory, art history, and the psychology of visual thinking has not been elaborated. The work of Richard Smardon, R. Burton Litton, and Barbara Novak opens doors for a highly suggestive viewpoint on the American wilderness experience.[34] Attention should also be given to landscape historians and planners.

Skeletons in the Environmental Historian's Closet

Like most new approaches to history, environmental history undergoes criticism through "guilt by association," doubts about its professional standards, and the worth of its subject matter. Several important essays by Joseph Petulla, Richard White, and Donald Worster explore environmental history as a new historical field, and related pitfalls and opportunities.[35] One hopes that the field can soon move beyond the following problems.

THE GHOST OF FREDERICK JACKSON TURNER

The once-powerful "frontier thesis" of American history is in eclipse today, but hangs on the environmental historian's neck like the proverbial albatross. In his provocative 1984 article, Gene M. Gressley wrote of the Turnerian burden for all western historians: "In spite of a half century of diligent searching, we simply have not found a monolithic, overarching thesis to replace Turner's, nor are we, it would appear, likely to do so. But why should this realization fill us with anxiety?"[36] For environmental historians, the troublesome linkage is twofold. Does the environmental historian, as Turner once did, promote a latter-day version of geographical determinism? In addition, is the environmental historian prone to a single-cause historical explanation? When so much western history is tied to resources, geography, climate and region, and the ability or inability to consume and shape the environment, the neo-Turnerian trend of some environmental historians' conclusions must be taken seriously. Western historiography, beginning with Earl Pomeroy's 1955 statement, downplays the determining power of geography and emphasizes "man-directed movements."[37] Second only to Turner as a problem for the environmental historian are the writings of Walter Prescott Webb, notably his 1931 classic, *The Great Plains,* which is yet to be replaced.[38] In an interesting turn of events, Ralph Mann suggested in 1984 that one major agenda for the New Social History (see Braudel above) in the West is to test Turner's folk belief that the frontier not only symbolized but realized personal success for settlers.[39] This topic may be the environmental historian's liberation from Turner, who believed the abundant untouched resources of the frontier provided unlimited opportunity for the acquisition of wealth, rather than a frontier of limited resources that deserved to be carefully managed.

GEOGRAPHERS AS ENVIRONMENTAL HISTORIANS

If they have read Carl Sauer, Clarence Glacken, Yi-Fu Tuan, David Lowenthal, Donald Meinig, Pierce Lewis, and others, environmental historians must feel that historical geographers are looking over their shoulders at long-familiar subjects. But environmental historians ought also to be looking forward at the geographer's dust far ahead of them.

Between the 1920s and 1960s the geographer Carl Ortwin Sauer applied innovative environmental principles to history that transformed geographers' views of the historic American West. Beginning with a 1929 paper, "Historical Geography and the Western Frontier,"[40] Sauer argued for a methodology that would begin by establishing the physical character (climate, soil, vegetation) of a region before human intrusion. Only then could adequate analysis of settlement patterns be made, in response to this known environment. Sauer attempted to reduce western expansion to a small number of essential material and technological factors to determine more clearly (1) historic human modification of plant and animal life, (2) criteria set by settlers for a successful frontier society, and (3) the man-nature interactions leading to permanence or change. In the same 1929 paper, Sauer wrote, "The kind of frontier that develops is determined by the kind of group that is found on it. The external pluralism of history asserts itself on the American frontier: there was no single type of frontier, nor was there a uniform series of stages." Instead, frontier societies are essentially a series of "secondary cultural hearths," depending for their original identity and resources upon settled eastern societal centers.

In Carl Sauer's environmental perspective, America's western history is the story of three centuries of progressive suicide. By mid-twentieth century, "the saving of worn land requires more labor, more skill, and more capital than the farming of good land, and then is of uncertain results. . . . We have not yet learned the difference between yield and loot." Sauer also argued that the answer was not the touted shift from a temporary "frontier of nature" to an enduring "frontier of technology," since resource exploitation remains the prevailing mode. Sauer developed his environmentalist approach in classic methodological and definitional essays: "The Morphology of Landscape" (1925) and "Foreword to Historical Geography" (1941), and "The Agency of Man on the Earth" (1955).[41]

Ralph H. Brown's masterly but seriously outdated 1948 *Historical Geography of the United States* will soon be supplanted by Donald Meinig's long-awaited multivolume history and interpretation, *The Shaping of America . . . A Geographical Perspective on 500 Years of History,* of which the first volume, *Atlantic America, 1492–1800,* was published in 1986 by the Yale University Press. See Meinig's rationale in his 1978 article, "The Continuous Shaping of America: A Prospectus for Geographers and Historians."[42] Meinig revolutionized geographers' perceptions of the American West with his emphases upon cores, domains, and "culture regions" as total man-nature entities, using as a key model Mormon culture and communities. See his widely reprinted 1972 essay, "American Wests: Preface to a Geographical Interpretation."[43]

By the 1960s and 1970s, historical geographers took another quantum step as they sought to reconstruct the *behavioral environment* of the American West. The new agenda for historical geography, said John K. Wright in his pioneering 1947 article, "Terrae Incognitae: The Place of Imagination in Geography,"[44] was to recover the environmental setting, but as anticipated, observed, and remembered in settlers' minds, as well as the real-world place. These perceptions play a powerful role in human behavior, and do much to create the values and potential attached to a region. Important essays are conveniently collected by David Lowenthal and Martyn J. Bowden, *Geographies of the Mind,* Donald W. Meinig's *The Interpretation of Ordinary Landscapes,* and David Ward, *Geographic Perspectives on America's Past.*[45] A philosophical base for environmental perception, using resources from cultural anthropology, has been attempted in Yi-Fu Tuan's 1974 *Topophilia: A Study of Environmental Perception, Attitudes, and Values* in 1974 and his 1977 *Space and Place: The Perspective of Experience.*[46] For methodology, see Peter Gould and Rodney White in their 1974 *Mental Maps,* and Roger M. Downs and David Stea in their 1977 *Maps in Minds: Reflections on Cognitive Mapping.*[47]

NATIVE AMERICANS

Treatment of native Americans by environmental historians tends toward two biases. As heroic "original" inhabitants, native Americans have legal treaty rights and claims that have been shamefully ignored. Or as

Environmental History in the West

"keepers" of the American land, their lifestyle in harmony with nature is admirable and probably superior to industrialized society. As a result, histories of native Americans tend to promote land renewal and preservation in the Indian way in sharp contrast to development or exploitation.[48] Yet, as Philip Reno notes, tribes like the Navaho seek to have modern economic benefits through industrial development of their lands.[49] We need a William Cronon for the West.[50]

NEGATIVE IMPACTS OF ENVIRONMENTAL PROTECTION

Little has been written about the sometime severe restrictions that environmental controls have placed upon parts of society. Environmental issues continue to be treated as a counterpoint to capitalism, technological innovation, and economic growth. The independent family farmer, so publicly praised and privately ignored, finds environmental restrictions upon cheap pesticides and fertilizers contribute to his bankruptcy. Complaints about loss of employment because of new environmental restrictions in traditional heavy industries, such as steel or rubber, need verification. EPA rulings are damned as unnecessary federal interventions in private business. Entire regions, such as the southwestern Four Corners, are convinced that their growth is delayed and diminished, or prohibited, because of environmental regulations or outside interventions by activist groups. While most environmental historians successfully keep their personal pro-environment viewpoints out of their academic research, a prejudice against the negative impacts has delayed important research. Pro-business and pro-development historiography does not fill the gap well and the subject deserves attention.

Mary Douglas and Aaron Wildavsky, in their pathbreaking 1983 *Risk and Culture*, urge environmental historians to balance their tendency to protest environmental exploitation and acknowledge the benefits of a technological resource-based society.[51] Americans historically have been horsetraders between levels and types of risk; risk-taking has been part of a powerful entrepreneurial tradition. Douglas and Wildavsky imply that "environmental sectarians" dedicated to safety contradict the historic aggressive "full speed ahead" tradition of western expansion. But they argue that choices of risk reflect the priorities of society. Major environmental issues, such as the contradictions in nuclear power and coal-fired power, need to be examined in light of risk-benefit assessment.

ACTIVISM, MORAL SUPERIORITY, AND SEARCH FOR AN ETHIC

Many environmental historians, including this one, have been accused of "strident" writing. Environmental history still remains suspect for two bad habits. One is a reformist tone that sharply, simplistically, inaccurately, and piously divides issues into pro-environment and anti-environment.[52] Most environmental historians have important convictions about environmental development and protection, but good historical writing is unlikely to be good lobbying fodder, and vice versa. A second debateable trend is nostalgia for a simpler life that repudiates technological innovation and industrial growth.[53] In some cases this viewpoint becomes virulently anticapitalist without being Marxist. A simpler life may be desireable for many reasons, but few of us would enjoy the hard labor and physical hardship of "back to nature" farming, or even mechanical typewriters instead of word processors.

Conclusion

The above agendas for environmental history in the American West are hardly comprehensive. No doubt the following items should also receive attention: (1) comparative environmental history (eastern U.S., international); (2) scientific (ecological) foundations for environmental research; (3) the West as a maturing region, with environmental stabilization; (4) environmental foundations of widely appealing western life-styles, including the contrasts between California consumerism and "small is beautiful" in Ecotopia; (5) potential of environmental modelling for historians, together with a history of the environmental implications of the "limits to growth" paradigm.

In 1978 Wilbur Jacobs wrote, "Environmental history can be a window to a clearer image of the past and can offer us unique perspectives on generally accepted historical concepts of unlimited growth, frontier expansionism, and the rapid use of nonrenewable natural resources."[54] This quote sums up the contribution toward clarification of the American West that environmental history can provide. The civilizational process, after all, is the history of the modification of the earth for human benefit; environmental history seeks to evaluate the beneficial use of the earth in terms not only of humanity, but to include all other earthly entities, organic and inorganic, on the premise that loss or degradation anywhere has universal impact.

Notes

N.B. The bibliographical references in this essay are intended to identify significant starting points or provocative interpretations for continued research in western environmental history. They are not comprehensive.

1. David M. Potter, *People of Plenty: Economic Abundance and the American Character* (Chicago: University of Chicago Press, 1950), 85.
2. John Wesley Powell, *Lands of the Arid Region of the United States,* 2nd ed. (Washington: USGPO, 1879; Harvard Common Press reprint, 1983), viii, 1, 9.
3. Quoted in Joel Garreau, *The Nine Nations of North America* (Boston: Houghton Mifflin, 1981), 266.
4. See particularly the approach used in Fernand Braudel, *Civilization and Capitalism: 15th–18th Century,* 3 vols., Sian Reynolds, trans. (New York: Harper and Row, 1971–1984). There is no comparable work in American history, but the Braudel Institute, SUNY, Binghamton, has a publishing program, and the "new social history" has *Annales* roots. See also Richard Griswold del Castillo, "Quantitative History in the American Southwest: A Survey and Critique," *Western Historical Quarterly* 15 (October 1984): 407–26, and Ralph Mann, "Frontier Opportunity and the New Social History," *Pacific Historical Review* 53 (November 1984): 463–91.
5. Earl Pomeroy, *The Pacific Slope: A History of California, Oregon, Washington, Idaho, Utah, and Nevada* (New York: Alfred A. Knopf, 1965), Gerald D. Nash, *The American West in the Twentieth Century: A Short History of an Urban Oasis* (Englewood Cliffs, N.J.: Prentice-Hall, 1973; Albuquerque: University of New Mexico Press, 1977); Donald W. Meinig, *The Great Columbia Plain: A Historical Geography, 1805–1910* (Seattle: University of Washington Press, 1968), and *Southwest: Three Peoples in Geographical Change, 1600–1970* (New York: Oxford University Press, 1971); W. Eugene Hollon, *The Southwest: Old and New* (New York: Alfred A. Knopf, 1961); Neil Morgan, *Westward Tilt: The American West Today* (New York: Random House, 1963); Dorothy O. Johansen and Charles M. Gates, *Empire on the Columbia: A History of the Pacific Northwest,* 2nd ed. (New York: Harper and Row, 1967); see also Peter Wiley and Robert Gottlieb, *Empires in the Sun: The Rise of the New American West* (New York: G. P. Putnam's Sons, 1982), and Michael Malone, ed., *Historians and the American West* (Lincoln: University of Nebraska Press, 1983). A special issue of the *Pacific Historical Review,* 50 (November 1981), on western state histories, also deserves attention.
6. Paul W. Gates and Lillian F. Gates, "Canadian and American Land Policy Decisions, 1930," *Western Historical Quarterly* 15 (October 1984): 389–405.
7. *California: Two Centuries of Man, Land, and Growth* (Palo Alto: American West Publishing Company, 1969), 13.
8. Selected reading should include Paul W. Gates, *History of Public Land Law Development* (Washington: USGPO, 1968), 115 ff, 301 ff; W. W. Robinson, *Land in California* (Berkeley: University of California Press, 1948), and Lawrence J. Jelinek, *Harvest Empire: A History of California Agriculture* (San Francisco: Boyd and Fraser, 1979), together with a rash of articles in *Agricultural History, Pacific Historical Review,* and *Western Historical Quarterly* on agribusiness. See also references below to irrigation.
9. Ellen Liebman, *California Farmland: A History of Large Agricultural Landholdings* (Totowa, N.J.: Rowman and Allanheld, 1983).
10. See the preliminary assessment in John Opie, *The Law of the Land: 200*

Years of American Farmland Policy (Lincoln: University of Nebraska Press, 1987), chapter 11.

11. See Donald J. Pisani, *From the Family Farm to Agribusiness: The Irrigation Crusade in California and the West, 1850–1931* (Berkeley: University of California Press, 1984); Abraham Hoffman, *Vision or Villainy: Origins of the Owens Valley-Los Angeles Water Controversy* (College Station: Texas A & M University Press, 1981); William L. Kahrl, *Water and Power: The Conflict Over Los Angeles' Water Supply in the Owens Valley* (Berkeley: University of California Press, 1982). Donald Worster breaks new ground in "Hydraulic Society in California: An Ecological Interpretation," *Agricultural History* 56 (July 1982): 508–20, which anticipated his critique of western water institutions in *Rivers of Empire: Water, Aridity, and the Growth of the American West* (New York: Pantheon Books, 1986).

12. Dean E. Mann, *The Politics of Water in Arizona* (Tucson: University of Arizona Press, 1963).

13. (Lincoln: University of Nebraska Press, 1983).

14. See endnote 11 and the brief study by Michael G. Robinson, *Water for the West: The Bureau of Reclamation, 1902–1977* (Chicago: Public Works Historical Society, 1979). Research must begin with Lawrence B. Lee's *Reclaiming the American West: An Historiography and Guide* (Santa Barbara: ABC-Clio Press, 1980); see also Lee's "Environmental Implications of Governmental Reclamation in California," *Agricultural History* 49 (Fall 1975): 223–30. And see Paul W. Gates, et al., *Four Persistent Issues: Essays on California's Land Ownership Concentration, Water Deficits, Sub-State Regionality, and Congressional Leadership* (Berkeley: Institute for Government Studies, 1978).

15. Researchers must begin with Norris Hundley, jr., *Water and the West: The Colorado River Compact and the Politics of Water in the American West* (Berkeley: University of California Press, 1975); see also Philip L. Fredkin, *A River No More: The Colorado River and the West* (New York: Alfred A. Knopf, 1981).

16. See the useful summary of these and other plans in Morton W. Bittinger and Elizabeth B. Green, *You Never Miss the Water Till . . . (The Ogallala Story)* (Littleton, CO: Water Resources Publications, 1980), 94–111.

17. One of the best collections of modern boomtown studies is available in *Abstracts of Papers, Proceedings of The Human Side of Energy: 2nd International Forum, August 16–19, 1981* (Alberta: University of Alberta, 1982).

18. John W. Reps, *Cities of the American West: A History of Frontier Urban Planning* (Princeton: Princeton University Press, 1979), and *The Forgotten Frontier: Urban Planning in the American West before 1890* (Columbia: University of Missouri Press, 1981).

19. See, for example, Carl Abbott, *The New Urban America: Growth and Politics in Sunbelt Cities* (Chapel Hill: University of North Carolina Press, 1981), and Bradford Luckingham, "The American Southwest: An Urban View," *Western Historical Quarterly* 15 (July 1984): 261–79.

20. The energy debate has produced a very large literature. See the historical perspective and contemporary analysis in Ian Barbour, Harvey Brooks, Sanford Lakoff, and John Opie, *Energy and American Values* (New York: Praeger Special Studies, 1982).

21. Thomas R. Cox writes widely for *Forest History, Agricultural History, Environmental Review*, and other journals. See Cox, et al., *This Well-Wooded Land: Americans and Their Forests from Colonial Times to the Present* (Lincoln: University of Nebraska Press, 1985), as well as Harold K. Steen, *The U.S. Forest Service: A History* (Seattle: University of Washington Press, 1976), Ronald J. Fahl, *North American Forest and Conservation History: A Bibliography* (Santa Barbara: ABC-Clio Press, 1976), William G. Robbins, *Lumberjacks and Legislators: Political Economy of the U.S. Lumber Industry, 1890–1941* (College Station: Texas A & M University Press, 1982), and Richard C. Davis, ed., *Encyclopedia of American Forest and Conservation History*, 2 vols. (New York: Macmillan Publishing Company, 1983).

22. Herman Kahn and Anthony J. Wiener, "Faustian Powers and Human Choices: Some Twenty-First Century Technological and Economic Issues," in *Environment and Change: The Next Fifty Years* (Bloomington: University of Indiana Press, 1968).

23. John A. Jakle, *The Tourist: Travel in Twentieth-Century North America* (Lincoln: University of Nebraska Press, 1985), xi; and see the pathbreaking and still unexcelled study by Earl Pomeroy, *In Search of the Golden West: The Tourist in Western America* (New York: Alfred A. Knopf, 1957).

24. See John Opie, "Shaping the Visual Experience: Historic Origins of Wilderness and Desert Aesthetic," in Robert D. Rowe and L. G. Chestnut, eds., *Managing Air Quality and Scenic Resources at National Parks and Wilderness Areas* (Boulder, CO: Westview Press, 1983), 13–20; and "Seeing Desert as Wilderness and as Landscape," in Richard Smardon, ed., *Proceedings: National Conference on the Visual Resource* (Berkeley: U.S. Forest Service, 1979), 101–8.

25. Jakle, *The Tourist*, 2.

26. Jakle, *The Tourist*, xii.

27. Clayton R. Koppes, "Public Waters, Private Land: Origins of the Acreage Limitation Controversy, 1938–1953," *Pacific Historical Review* 47 (November 1978): 607–38, and Donald J. Pisani, "State vs Nation: Federal Reclamation and Water Rights in the Progressive Era," *Pacific Historical Review* 51 (August 1982): 265–82.

28. John D. Leshy, "Unravelling the Sagebrush Rebellion: Law, Politics and Federal Lands," *University of California (Davis) Law Review* 14 (1980): 317–55; and Gene Gressley, "Whither Western American History? Speculations on a Direction," *Pacific Historical Review* 53 (November 1984): 496–97, argued that issues of bureaucracy and federalism have come to dominate western history.

29. See John Opie, *The Law of the Land: 200 Years of American Farmland Policy*, chapter 11.

30. (Boston: Houghton Mifflin, 1981).

31. See Norris Hundley, jr., *Dividing the Waters: A Century of Controversy Between the United States and Mexico* (Berkeley: University of California Press, 1966).

32. Required reading includes Gregory Thompson, *Parks in the West and American Culture* (Sun Valley, ID: Institute of the American West, 1984); John Ise, *Our National Park Policy: A Critical History* (Baltimore: Johns Hopkins University Press, 1961), Alfred Runte, *National Parks: The American Experience* (Lin-

coln: University of Nebraska Press, 1979), and Joseph L. Sax, *Mountains Without Handrails: Reflections on the National Parks* (Ann Arbor: University of Michigan Press, 1980).

33. Richard A. Bartlett, *Nature's Yellowstone* (Albuquerque: University of New Mexico Press, 1974), Aubrey L. Haines, *The Yellowstone Story: A History of Our First National Park*, 2 vols. (West Yellowstone: Yellowstone Library and Museum Association, 1977), Robert Righter, *Crucible for Conservation: The Creation of Grand Teton National Park* (Boulder: Colorado Associated University Press, 1982); and C. W. Buchholtz, *Rocky Mountain National Park* (Boulder: Colorado Associated University Press, 1983), and Susan R. Schrepfer, *The Fight to Save the Redwoods: A History of Environmental Reform, 1917–1978* (Madison: University of Wisconsin Press, 1983).

34. Richard C. Smardon, *Prototype Visual Impact Assessment Manual* (Berkeley: U.S. Forest Service, 1979). Smardon also edited *Our National Landscape . . . Applied Techniques for Analysis and Management of the Visual Resource* (Berkeley: U.S. Forest Service, 1979). See also R. Burton Litton, et al., *Water and Landscape: An aesthetic overview of the role of water in the landscape* (Port Washington, NY: Water Information Center, 1974), Barbara Novak, *Nature and Culture: American Landscape and Painting, 1825–1875* (New York: Oxford University Press, 1980), and John Opie, "Shaping the Visual Experience: Historic Origins of Wilderness and Desert Aesthetic," and "Seeing Desert as Wilderness and as Landscape."

35. See particularly Joseph M. Petulla, *American Environmentalism: Values, Tactics, Priorities* (College Station: Texas A & M University Press, 1980); Richard White, "American Environmental History: The Development of a New Historical Field," *Pacific Historical Review* 54 (August 1985): 297–335; Donald Worster, "History as Natural History: An Essay on Theory and Method," *Pacific Historical Review* 53 (February 1984): 1–19; and see also John Opie, "Environmental History: Pitfalls and Opportunities," *Environmental Review* 7 (Winter 1983): 8–16.

36. Gene M. Gressley, "Whither Western American History?" 493–501.

37. See Earl Pomeroy, "Toward a Reorientation of Western History: Continuity and Environment," *Mississippi Valley Historical Review* 41 (December 1955): 579–600; to be contrasted with Wilbur J. Jacobs, "The Great Despoliation: Environmental Themes in American Frontier History," *Pacific Historical Review* 47 (February 1978): 1–26, and Richard White's brief observations in the same issue, "American Environmental History," 297–98, 319–20, as White joins other environmental historians in appropriating James Malin's critique of Turner. Also see Robert P. Swierenga's introduction in the new Malin collection, *James C. Malin, History and Ecology: Studies of the Grassland* (Lincoln: University of Nebraska Press, 1984).

38. (Boston: Ginn and Company, 1931).

39. "Frontier Opportunity and the New Social History."

40. Many of Sauer's significant papers are conveniently collected in John Leighly, ed., *Land and Life. A Selection from the Writings of Carl Ortwin Sauer* (Berkeley: University of California Press, 1967).

41. The 1925 and 1941 essays are in Leighly, *Land and Life*, 313–79; the 1955

essay appeared in William L. Thomas, Jr., ed., *Man's Role in Changing the Face of the Earth* (Chicago; University of Chicago Press, 1956), I: 49–69.

42. Donald W. Meinig, "The Continous Shaping of America: A Prospectus for Geographers and Historians," *American Historical Review* 83 (December 1978): 1186–1205, and commentary on 1206–17. See also Ralph H. Brown, *Historical Geography of the United States* (New York: Harcourt, Brace and World, 1948), and Donald W. Meinig, *The Shaping of America: A Geographical Perspective on 500 Years of History: Atlantic America, 1492–1800*, vol. 1 (New Haven: Yale University Press, 1986).

43. Meinig, "American Wests: Preface to a Geographical Interpretation," *Annals of the Association of American Geographers* 62 (June 1972): 159–84.

44. John K. Wright, "Terrae Incognitae: The Place of Imagination in Geography," *Annals of the Association of American Geographers* 37 (March 1947): 1–15.

45. David Lowenthal and Martyn J. Bowden, eds., *Geographies of the Mind: Essays in Historical Geosophy in Honor of John Kirkland Wright*. (New York: Oxford University Press, 1976); Meinig, ed., *The Interpretation of Ordinary Landscapes: Geographical Essays* (New York: Oxford University Press, 1979); David Ward, ed., *Geographic Perspectives on America's Past* (New York: Oxford University Press, 1979).

46. Yi-Fu Tuan, *Topophilia: A Study of Environmental Perception, Attitudes, and Values* (Englewood Cliffs, N.J.: Prentice-Hall, 1974) and *Space and Place: The Perspective of Experience*, (Minneapolis: University of Minnesota Press, 1977).

47. Peter Gould and Rodney White, *Mental Maps* (New York: Penquin Books, 1974), and Roger M. Downs and David Stea, *Maps in Minds: Reflections on Cognitive Mapping* (New York: Harper and Row, 1977).

48. See Richard White, "Native Americans and the Environment," in W. R. Swagerty, ed., *Scholars and the Indian Experience* (Bloomington: Indiana University Press, 1984), 179–204; Christopher Vecsey and Robert W. Venables, eds., *American Indian Environments: Ecological Issues in Native American History* (Syracuse: Syracuse University Press, 1980); J. Donald Hughes, *American Indian Ecology* (El Paso: Texas Western Press, 1983), Calvin Martin, *Keepers of the Game: Indian Animal Relationships in the Fur Trade* (Berkeley: University of California Press, 1978).

49. Philip Reno, *Mother Earth, Father Sky, and Economic Development: Navaho Resources and Their Use* (Albuquerque: University of New Mexico Press, 1981).

50. *Changes in the Land: Indians, Colonists, and the Ecology of New England* (New York: Hill and Wang, 1983).

51. Mary Douglas and Aaron Wildavsky, *Risk and Culture: An Essay on the Selection of Technological and Environmental Dangers* (Berkeley: University of California Press, 1983); an entire literature on risk assessment deserves attention from environmental historians.

52. This is an issue, considered directly or indirectly, in several intellectual history classics: Roderick Nash, *Wilderness and the American Mind*, 3rd ed. (New

Haven: Yale University Press, 1982), Hans Huth, *Nature and the American: Three Centuries of Changing Attitudes* (Lincoln: University of Nebraska Press, 1957), Arthur A. Ekirch, *Man and Nature in America* (New York: Columbia University Press, 1963), Peter J. Schmitt, *Back to Nature: The Arcadian Myth in Urban America* (New York: Oxford University Press, 1969).

53. Examples of pro-environment bias include Michael P. Cohen, *The Pathless Way: John Muir and the American Wilderness* (Madison: University of Wisconsin Press, 1984), and Frederick Turner's disappointing *Beyond Geography: The Western Spirit Against the Wilderness* (New York: The Viking Press, 1980). This is not the place to look into the feminist writings of Annette Kolodny, the controversial "deep ecology" of William Duvall and others, or the debate over the "Gaia Principle" as a guide for the environmental historian as activist.

54. "The Great Despoliation," 1.

8

The Western Lumber Industry

A TWENTIETH-CENTURY PERSPECTIVE

William G. Robbins

From the beginnings of European settlement in America, forests played a major role. That role was in no way diminished in the twentieth century when the industrial complex that arose further embellished the importance of timber. But the passage of time after 1890 dimmed the romantic aura that had once surrounded lumbermen and companies and their prodigious production records of earlier years. Robbins emphasizes instead the impact of corporate capitalism in shaping the forest environment of the twentieth-century West and the communities dependent on it. Like other scholars in the field, Robbins explores the reciprocal impact of American culture and its values and the western environment. That interplay provides a context for an emerging image of the West in the twentieth century.

The North American continent is blessed with one of the most extensive and productive forest environments in the world. That wooded wealth attracted commercial interests from Europe as early as the sixteenth century as French, British, Dutch, and Spanish ships explored the coastal shores and major river systems of the eastern seaboard. In an age when sea power meant dominion over the far places of the globe, the timbered regions of the New World were important to mercantilist-minded empire builders.[1] The significance of North American forests to the expansion of early modern capitalism, therefore, was established at the onset of the seventeenth century. And, until the development of alternative sources of fuel and construction materials in the late-nineteenth and early-twentieth centuries, wood products remained the most critical and essential natural resource to economic expansion.[2]

According to Raphael Zon, a disciple of Gifford Pinchot and one of the central figures in American forestry during the first half of the twentieth century, "no other geographical factor has so profoundly affected the development of this country as the forest." From the New Brunswick and Maine woods south to Spanish Florida, soft and hardwood species provided subsistence materials for European newcomers in the form of shelter, crude furniture, fencing, and cooking and heating. Those early uses only mirrored the native Indians who had skillfully adapted to the eastern woodlands for centuries. But the immigrants who came from England and western Europe, steeped in the acquisitive values of an expanding market system, quickly began to exploit the forest for commercial purposes.[3]

The use of forest products in the shipbuilding industry in the seventeenth and eighteenth centuries, the burning of wood for fuel and the production of charcoal, and the clearing of "brush" for agriculture slowly began to take its toll on the forest. When the westward press of large-scale urban settlements reached the Mississippi River Valley, the commercial exploitation of the eastern woodlands, especially in the Great Lakes pineries, was in full swing. By the time the transcontinental rail lines pushed onto the arid and largely treeless Great Plains, the end of the pine forests in Michigan, Wisconsin, and Minnesota was in sight. Although the South dominated production in the early twentieth century, the Pacific Northwest was rapidly developing as the lumbering center of the country.[4]

The expansion of the industry in the West, therefore, is largely a story for the twentieth century. As with the eastern half of North America, the commercial exploitation of the western forests dates from the initial Euro-American settlements—the establishment of the Spanish missions in California, the coming of the Hudson's Bay Company and the Russian fur trading posts to the northern coast, and finally, the burgeoning number of immigrants who swarmed to the Pacific slope in the mid-nineteenth century. But, with the exception of a fledgling business with the Hawaiian Islands and the Far East, most of the nineteenth-century lumber trade was a coastal affair. Waterways provided the vital means to transport the huge logs to mills and the finished lumber to market. The exceptions were the mining districts along the Rocky Mountain cordillera where piñon, juniper, ponderosa, and other pines were harvested for fuel and tunnel construction.[5] At the onset of the twentieth century, however, the center of the lumber entrepreneur's attention was shifting to the great stands of virgin forest extending from Humboldt Bay north to the Alaskan panhandle.

Unlike the eastern woodlands, broad alluvial valleys, wide stretches of grazing land, and parched and arid deserts separate the forested regions of the West. From an area standpoint the most prominent western tree is the

The Western Lumber Industry

ponderosa pine, a species that grows at higher elevations from Montana, Idaho, and Washington south to New Mexico and Arizona. Its rate of growth and density is directly related to precipitation. The primary center for most lumber production in the twentieth century, however, has been the redwood, cedar, spruce, and Douglas fir country that stretches from northern California to British Columbia. And, in terms of manufacturing volume, Douglas fir is by far the dominant species.[6]

Other differences exist between the eastern forests and those in the West. In the Rocky Mountain and Pacific states where most of the national forests are located, two-thirds of all timberland is in public ownership. But in some western states, especially California, Oregon, and Washington, the forest industry owns a large percentage of the most productive land. The ownership pattern has meant that powerful and well-organized groups in the lumber industry have been able to exert great leverage in legislative policy at the state and federal level.[7] In Oregon and Washington, where timber dominates industrial activity, that influence is most obvious.

The north Pacific slope, which has far outstripped other western states in forest products manufacturing in the twentieth century, was, in a sense, the last "frontier" for a migrating industry that could trace its roots to colonial New England. Several important factors limited the extensive exploitation of the far-western forests until the beginning of the twentieth century—a small population, distance from markets, a limited technology, and the ruggedness of the landscape. But, the extension of two transcontinental railroads to the Pacific Northwest in the 1880s and 1890s spurred population growth, invited capital investment in timber and mining ventures, and provided better access to markets.[8] The development of the steam donkey and the dramatic expansion of logging railroads in the Humboldt Bay region, around Puget Sound, and in the Willamette Valley aided the logger's ability to haul timber to mill sites.

But the transcontinental lines, more than any other development, boosted the far-western economy. According to Thomas R. Cox, the railroads that penetrated the Rocky Mountain West encouraged investment in the region and ushered in "a new economic order in which the Pacific Coast's lumber industry was to grow apace." Although markets beyond the West continued to expand and talk of a canal across the isthmus of Panama promised even more, the burgeoning population of California, Oregon, and Washington provided the greatest boon to increased lumber production. In the first decade of the twentieth century, Washington grew by 120 percent, Oregon by 62 percent, and California by more than 60 percent.[9] A continually expanding regional market provided the most important single sustaining force in the western lumber industry through the 1970s.

235

In the state of Washington, Seattle and Tacoma emerged as important metropolitan communities within two decades. And around Alberni Inlet in British Columbia, the city of Vancouver quickly established itself as an important lumber port and terminus for the Canadian-Pacific railroad. Other centers of forest products activity also expanded during the first decade of the twentieth century—Grays Harbor and Willapa Bay on the Washington coast, several smaller sites on the lower Columbia River, the Coos Bay region on the southern Oregon coast, and the great redwood manufacturing district around Humboldt Bay in northern California. At the same time, the numerous rail lines that crisscrossed the interior opened the ponderosa pine region to axe and saw. Fledgling post office stopovers like Bend, Oregon, and other former stagecoach rest areas in California's northern interior mushroomed into sizable lumbering centers overnight.[10]

In the first decade of the twentieth century the north Pacific slope had taken on the aura of an investor's frontier as timber locators prowled the slopes of the Douglas fir and ponderosa country in their efforts to "block-up" large acreages of forest land. Presidential withdrawals of the forest reserves and rumors of an impending timber famine probably quickened speculation in the region. In the process, company land agents played fast and loose with state and federal land laws, shenanigans that landed some of the perpetrators in prison.[11] But, with the deed accomplished, the lumber capitalists proceeded to process and market their newly acquired timber purchases to help pay the costs of the investment.

The speculative mania in western timberlands and the new mills that came on line after 1900 contributed to a great increase in production. In the process, lumbermen had constructed manufacturing plants with a productive capacity that far exceeded market demand. Shortly after output reached its all-time high in 1906, lumber prices began to fall and the market entered a period of protracted instability that persisted until the outbreak of the First World War. Fluctuating and often depressed prices wreaked havoc on the financial world of timberland owners in the Pacific Northwest; in truth, many were overextended. Because they had borrowed capital for their land purchases and then bonded those forest stands to finance sawmill construction and the building of transportation arterials, many lumbermen were forced to liquidate their timber rapidly to avoid bankruptcy. The result was a perpetually depressed market and even greater instability in an industry plagued with problems.[12]

There were, of course, social costs for the timber-dependent communities, especially when the lumber capitalist curtailed or suspended operations. That risky financial world, as Norman Clark has stated so well in his study of Everett, Washington, provided little security for working people; it "was not and could not be a humane system." Moreover, the vagaries of the forest products trade have always struck hardest at loggers

The Western Lumber Industry

and millworkers; for it was they, not the owners, who suffered the brunt of the industry's mercurial financial world. In addition to market-induced lay-offs, weather conditions regularly closed the woods and mill operations and coastwide maritime strikes also brought production to a standstill.[13] Those boom-and-bust cycles plagued the industry throughout the twentieth century.

Lumbermen responded to their economic problems in several ways. To cut expenses, they lowered wages, reduced the labor force, and in some cases closed their operations altogether to ride out market slumps. In a state like Washington, where—according to William Greeley—the people relied on "the lumber business in the same way that the citizens of Iowa are dependent upon corn," there were few alternative forms of income. The social and economic misery inherent to those conditions helped bring into being the Industrial Workers of the World, a radical union whose popularity was widespread among other resource industries in the American West.[14]

Lumbermen countered problematic market conditions—and to a lesser extent "labor troubles"—by forming trade associations, organizations committed to bringing order to the conduct of market activity. Although the early associations in the western lumber trade were limited and relatively ineffective, they gradually evolved as a powerful voice for the industry. The West Coast Lumbermen's Association, the Western Pine Manufacturer's Association, and the California Redwood Association emerged as the most important of the early twentieth-century trade groups on the Pacific slope.[15]

The most powerful of the western trade organizations for the first half of the twentieth century was the West Coast Lumberman's Association. Organized in 1911 and concerned with prices, standardizing grades of lumber, and equitable railroad rates, the trade group represented the tremendously productive Douglas fir region of western Oregon and Washington and southern British Columbia. In addition to its efforts to stabilize market conditions—primarily through price fixing—the association worked for lower timberland taxes in state legislatures, lobbied at the federal level for a duty on forest products imports, and engaged in a variety of market expansion programs. Although not as large or influential, the Western Pine Manufacturer's Association (Western Pine Association after 1931) ranked third in order of production, surpassed in output only by the Southern Pine Association and the West Coast Lumbermen's Association before the Great Depression. The highly specialized California Redwood Association, founded in 1916, represented a few large mills with a large volume of production.[16]

Allied with the associations in terms of ideology and political commitment and devoted to a wide variety of business and professional activities were several lumber trade journals. Those weekly and monthly magazines served as advertising media for mill and logging equipment and took an active part in shaping forest policy and informing lumbermen on matters of national importance. Two journals—*The Timberman* and the *West Coast Lumberman*—enjoyed the widest circulation in the lumber-producing areas of the West. *The Timberman*, established in Portland in 1890, focused on the region west of the Rocky Mountains but enjoyed a much wider circulation. Under publisher and editor George Cornwall, it promoted fire protection, reforestation, lower timberland taxes, standardized and equitable long-haul railroad rates, and a myriad of other causes important to lumbermen.[17]

Another organization, the Western Forestry and Conservation Association (WFCA), was not a trade group in the strict sense of the word. But from the time it was established in 1909 to the present day, it has served as an umbrella organization to represent large timber holders in matters of fire protection, the taxation of forest land, and other issues of importance. The WFCA quickly extended its membership to include forest protection associations in Washington, Oregon, Idaho, Montana, northern California, and British Columbia.[18] For the first half of the twentieth century no other organization had a greater influence on forestry policy.

The association attracted some of the ablest of the early forestry experts in the West such as two young Forest Service officials, Edward Tyson Allen and William B. Greeley, who attended its organizational meeting. Within the year Allen had resigned from the service to accept an appointment with the WFCA, a position he held until 1942. As for Greeley, he was soon transferred to the central offices of the Forest Service in Washington, DC, where he exercised an influence over national forest policy second only to that of Gifford Pinchot. After an eight-year stint as chief forester (1920–1928), Greeley resigned and returned to the Northwest to serve as executive manager of the West Coast Lumbermen's Association.[19] Like the organization they helped establish early in the century, Allen and Greeley were persuasive spokesmen for the lumber industry.

Although lumber output in the Douglas fir and redwood districts has been the focus of attention for most scholars in the twentieth century, there were small but significant centers of production scattered throughout the extensive ponderosa pine regions of the West. There also was an important feature to the high pine country of Arizona, New Mexico, Colorado, Wyoming, and Utah—virtually all of the timbered area in those states had been set aside as national forests. Moreover, those scattered forests could be exploited effectively only with the use of logging railroads. Even then, the limited resource and distance from major population centers meant that the finished product usually was sold locally, or in some instances, in specialty markets. As Stephen Pyne has pointed out, in states like Arizona logging was "tied to local and regional markets, not national ones."[20]

The most productive of the southwestern interior forests are the ponderosa pine stands that grow along the broad mountain belt that extends north along the Arizona and New Mexico border to the Colorado Plateau and then northwesterly through central Arizona. Commercial lumbermen operating on the fringe of the plateau—the Mogollon Rim—date from the mid-1920s and the arrival of capitalists from the Great Lakes states and a large lumber operation from Louisiana. James G. McNary, a New Mexico banker with a large investment in the Gulf coast company of W. M. Cady, led the move to tap the pine stands in Arizona. For twenty-five years (1925–1950), he directed Southwest Lumber Mills, one of the largest ponderosa pine operations in the country. The firm had plants in McNary (the company town) and Flagstaff, and distributing yards throughout the region.[21]

Another firm, the New Mexico Lumber Company with offices in Denver, shipped lumber from Arizona's pine country northeast by rail to its home city. Like other producers in the region the McNary and New Mexico operators relied on national forest timber to supply their mills with logs. With the growth of the Sunbelt cities of Phoenix, Tuscon, and Albuquerque, especially after the Second World War, the ponderosa manufacturers had a booming market for their products (albeit for special uses). By that time, however, recreational and preservationist demands had limited the extent of the forest available for harvest. In the interim, the Forest Service had established sustained yield units on its federal lands with the intention of stabilizing nearby communities dependent on logging and sawmilling. That effort has achieved little success because technological improvements and limits on harvests from the national forests have diminished the size of the workforce.[22]

California's northern interior also has been the center of a thriving pine industry. As it did elsewhere, the large-scale exploitation of those forests awaited the completion of the Oregon and California Railroad northward to Redding in 1872. Until that time, coastal sawmills in the redwood country and Puget Sound produced most of the lumber shipped to Sacramento. By the turn of the century, however, pine from California's northeastern counties enjoyed a thriving market in the mining centers of Arizona and New Mexico territories. Using a system of chutes and flumes to transport logs and lumber out of the northern Sierras to towns like Chico, Red Bluff, and Redding, the interior pine industry became an important contributor to western lumber production.[23]

But the most significant center of lumber manufacturing in California was the redwood coast, an area extending from Monterey Bay north to the Oregon border. Although the gold rush spurred the exploitation of the redwood forests in Mendocino, Humboldt, and Santa Cruz counties, the state continued to import large quantities of lumber from Oregon and Washington. Redwood, like ponderosa pine, had specialized uses. California's northern coastal towns shipped their products by sea until 1915 when a railroad was built between San Francisco Bay and Eureka in the heart of timber country. Long before the rail connection to the south, however, logging railroads had crisscrossed the Humboldt region.[24]

At the onset of the twentieth century, some of the choicest redwood stands adjacent to the river systems entering Humboldt Bay already had been logged off. Further south in Mendocino County, where rivers provided the means to transport logs to mills located on tidewater, timber also was becoming less accessible. Two pioneering Eureka area redwood capitalists, John Dolbeer and William Carson, passed from the scene after the turn of the century—Dolbeer in 1902 and Carson in 1912. But the great stands of redwood away from water's edge continued to invite capital. Those attractions appealed to a Montana lumberman, Andrew B. Hammond, who purchased timberland and mills in the area in 1900. In the following years the Hammond Lumber Company added to its holdings until it held some of the most valuable stands of redwood on the coast. The firm was the largest producer in northern California until it sold out to the expanding Georgia-Pacific Company in the midst of the postwar housing boom.[25]

Despite the heavy cutting in the redwood forests through the years of the Great Depression, the heyday of lumbering in northern California lay in the future. Because most of the old growth forests in western Washington had been cut over by the end of the Second World War, many lumber capitalists (like the Simpson Company) headed south to the still largely untapped Douglas fir stands on the California coast. Billed as the "lumber center of the world" by local boosters, the Humboldt Bay area vied with counties in southwestern Oregon who claimed the same honor in the postwar era.[26] And, through all those years of hectic activity, the market reigned supreme. The availability of accessible and cheaper privately owned timber retarded the logging of public land. It was not until after the Second World War that the forest products industry brought political pressure to increase the annual cut on those ownerships.

Western Montana and much of northern Idaho, with mixed stands of conifers, western hemlock, and Douglas fir, has been the center of both a thriving mining and lumber industry. In each case, commercial investment in those endeavors followed the rails of the first transcontinental line to penetrate the area, the Northern Pacific Railroad in 1881. By the second decade of the twentieth century sawmills operated from Bonners Ferry in

The Western Lumber Industry

northern Idaho to Boise at the southern edge of the pine country, many of them (i.e. Potlatch) linked directly or indirectly to the sprawling Weyerhaeuser interests. Across the border in western Montana the lumber industry served the state's mining districts in the early years. Until the Second World War the Montana lumber trade was small and dominated by a few large producers like Anaconda that owned more than one million acres of timberland. But those mills also shipped some finished material to midwest and eastern markets.[27]

Because it is part of the same extensive forest environment and because it often competes for the same markets, the Canadian province of British Columbia has been a vital segment of the western North America lumber scene. Like its industrial competitors to the south, the forest products industry in Canada evolved westward from the eastern provinces. Even the ownership patterns—with private holdings dominating in the East and public in the West—are similar to those in the United States.

Except for a small quantity of the most marketable timber in the coastal region, the provincial government owns virtually all of the forest land in British Columbia. Those circumstances have made the government a major influence in harvesting policies and in determining the basic structure of the lumber industry. Although the province became part of the world market economy because of its fur resource base, mining, agriculture, and lumbering had surpassed the fur trade in importance by 1900. When J. H. Bloedel moved to British Columbia from Washington state in 1911, forest products was the third largest industry in the province, ranking behind agriculture and mining. By the time his future partner, H. R. MacMillan, had established his lumber export business in 1919, wood products had clearly emerged as the mainstay of the provincial economy.[28] And through depression and boom times, it has remained so to the present day.

Even more than their industrial competitors south of the border, the lumber industry in British Columbia has been a function of the twentieth century. And for much of that period, large capital operations—Bloedel, H. R. MacMillan, and the Powell River Company Limited—have dominated production. The greatest market for the province's lumber for the first half of the twentieth century was Great Britain, and by the 1930s H. R. MacMillan Export was handling 50 percent of that trade. By the time Bloedel and Powell River merged with MacMillan (1951 and 1962 respectively), the organization was a fully integrated forest products firm and the largest corporation in British Columbia.[29]

From the time of the earliest forestry legislation (1912) in British Columbia, provincial timber has been harvested under various licenses granted to private companies. That these licenses have progressively favored the larger companies, as Patricia Marchak and others have shown, is also an established fact. Although the British Columbia lumber industry included hundreds of competitors in the early years, after the First World War the larger firms began to control a greater share of the market. The timber sale license system contributed to that shift. But, it was not until after the Second World War that the forest products industry in the province experienced its greatest boom.[30] And part of that expansion involved the domination of production in the interior of British Columbia by United States-based firms.

Only periodically glutted markets and the dislocations of two major wars curbed the great harvests of forest resources on the private timberlands of the north Pacific slope. Indeed, one economist argues that the privately owned old growth Douglas fir would have been cut over much earlier had it not been for the demoralized market conditions of the 1930s. Even at that, there were warnings that the old pattern of a rapidly depleted timber inventory was being repeated in parts of Oregon and Washington. Oregon's state forester warned in 1912 that the experiences of earlier frontiers "proves the fallacy" that forests are inexhaustible. A decade later Henry Graves, dean of the forestry school at Yale University and former head of the Forest Service, cautioned against "a feverish haste to cut the choicest" of the remaining timber in the Northwest.[31]

Despite rumblings of concern in the forestry profession and in Congress, neither state nor federal governments took action to restrain private harvesting practices. At the same time, reports about diminished private timber supplies—many of them from the Far West—continued to multiply. The Pacific Northwest Forest and Range Experiment Station reported in 1927 that almost half of the privately owned forests of the Douglas fir region was not being adequately reforested. When the Great Depression struck the area in the early 1930s, several western Washington communities already were suffering the consequences of the rapid liquidation of the timber resource. Although lumber production in Washington peaked in 1929 and the state continued to lead the nation in timber manufacturing until about 1940, the center of the forest products trade was shifting south to the virgin stands in Oregon.[32]

A case example—in the year that Washington lumber production reached its greatest output, Grays Harbor County produced more board feet of lumber than any other county in the United States. Yet, just before the outbreak of the Second World War the Forest Service Region 6 forester described the area as "vast expanses of cutover land largely barren of conifer growth." I. J. Mason of the Forest Service conducted a study of the area in 1935; his findings showed that the market reigned supreme, conditions that had characterized the industry's practices in earlier centers of lumbering activity. In the Grays Harbor vicinity, Mason pointed out, "the huge . . . original timber supply and the restrictions on production imposed by general market conditions" were the sole factors restraining the rate of the harvests.[33]

Planning commissions in Oregon and Washington—by far the leading timber producing states in the country—took up the cause of their impoverished communities in the late 1930s. The Oregon State Planning Board cautioned against the "present 'cut-out and get-out' policy" of forest harvests that would "result in a brief period of industrial activity, followed by inevitable economic and social disaster." Because of Oregon's still extensive virgin stands, the authors of the planning board report pointed out that the state could implement a sustained-yield program without curtailing production. The Northwest Regional Planning Council added its support for similar programs in 1940. Unless "sustained-yield management" was adopted, the council warned, "serious economic and social dislocation is inevitable."[34] The idea of sustained-yield management, however, did not originate with Northwest planning commissions.

In an effort to rationalize the process of liquidation and reforestation in the fast-growing forest environment of the Pacific Northwest, David Mason, a consulting forester in Portland, and a few others had been promoting sustained-yield management since the 1920s. They argued that cooperatively managed units of public and private timberland (one form of implementing sustained-yield practices), would regularize the rate of harvests and contribute to community stability. It also should be noted that the foremost proponents of sustained yield were people like Mason who had ideological ties to the largest producers; they were anxious to control the availability of timber and to manage it in the interests of those who dominated the industry. Regulate the supply, they believed, and prices would stabilize and lesser competitors would be without timber.[35] It was a grand scheme and received a great deal of attention from foresters and legislators for more than five decades.

Until at least the Second World War, industry leaders as well as the Forest Service gave broad support to sustained-yield proposals. That the most ardent proponents of the idea came from the Pacific Northwest should come as no surprise; for it was on the north Pacific slope—the center of lumbering activity during those years— that the greatest harvests were taking place. Thus, the region figured in the only two pieces of legislation ever passed by Congress that authorized cooperative sustained-yield units: the Oregon and California (O & C) Revested Lands Act of 1937 and the Sustained-Yield Forest Management Act of 1944.[36] Because they were designed to provide an even harvest of timber in well-defined areas and to stabilize communities that relied on forest resources, progressive industry leaders and foresters alike singled out those measures as the way to conserve resources and to provide a continual supply of timber.

Enacted at the end of a prolonged period of depressed prices, neither piece of legislation achieved significant and long-range success. Market forces, especially the construction boom after 1945 and the heavy demands placed on the remaining private timber reserves in the Northwest, made the *real* goals of the legislation—a mechanism to control production—a moot point to its industrial supporters. The Bureau of Land Management dropped its "marketing area" requirement (that timber be processed within a certain distance of its harvest) in 1957; that change removed one of the fundamental assumptions of the original O & C law. As for Public Law 273, the Sustained-Yield Forest Management Act, only one cooperative agreement was signed under the much-ballyhooed measure. The Simpson Logging Company of Shelton, Washington, signatories with the Forest Service in 1946 to manage cooperatively more than 200,000 acres of timberland for the next century, began to have reservations about that arrangement in the 1980s.[37]

The Second World War had a profound and disrupting influence on most American communities. It brought an abrupt end to years of unemployment and deprivation; it drew thousands of women into wage-earning jobs for the first time; and it sent people to far away places—to the armed forces or to defense industry jobs. Those who had experienced long periods without work during the Great Depression suddenly realized they were sellers in a buyer's market. The wars in Europe and in Asia also had far-reaching effects upon the forest products trade and communities dependent on logging and lumbering.[38] After decades of seasonal and market-induced unemployment, the timbered regions of the West—especially those with large virgin forests—entered a period of economic expansion that brought full employment, regular paydays, and, for laborers, greater control over the conditions of work.

The war and the rekindling of patriotism removed all restraints on harvesting practices as industry leaders moved to fill wartime production objectives. A forester with the National Lumber Manufacturer's Association, George Harris Collingwood, told the head of the Forest Service that trees were less important than human lives and that the United States would "have to sacrifice future needs for immediate demands." Appeals to good forestry practices and community welfare, therefore, had to give way to greater production.[39] The war precipitated a prolonged boom in the lumber trade that lasted—with a few interruptions—for nearly thirty years. And the timbered areas of the West where private stands were still extensive—the northern California coast, southwestern Oregon, and British Columbia—enjoyed the distinction of being the center of the forest products trade.

For its part, the industry had problems of another kind during the war—a shortage of labor. When people began to leave in large numbers for the armed forces or to defense plants in Portland, Seattle, and southern California, logging operators and mill owners pressured the government to protect against further job raids. An inadequate labor force and drastically altered marketing arrangements affected production. By the spring of 1942, according to Vernon Jensen, "the lumber problem [was] one of the most critical in the nation." Eventually, the War Manpower Commission issued an order "freezing" workers in "certain essential occupations," including logging and lumbering.[40] The purpose of the plan was to halt the pirating of workers to other industries through the offer of better wages or working conditions. The order had limited effectiveness, however, and job mobility remained high during the war.

But the West coast logging industry experienced great changes during the 1940s. Because of the shortage of manpower, employers devised new schemes to speed production, placed a premium on labor-saving devices like the chain saw, accelerated the introduction of other technological innovations, attracted workers from other sections of the country, and brought women into the workforce in large numbers. Although the shortage of help meant longer hours and faster work, loggers and millworkers were in a better position to exact a "pound of flesh" in exchange for their labor. Nevertheless, for employers the "production problem" persisted—in the Puget Sound and Grays Harbor area the lack of logs caused mills to close periodically, and elsewhere on the coast workers experienced shortened weeks for the same reason.[41]

The ending of the war, of course, did not lessen the heavy demands on labor and the timber resource. The booming lumber market seemed to mock an earlier Forest Service report that "concentrated and unnecessarily destructive cutting" was taking place in the Pacific Northwest. Gasoline-driven chain saws and the use of diesel-powered donkeys to yard logs vastly increased the speed of production in the woods; at the same time, those devices meant that operators required fewer workers to deliver logs to the mills. Wartime savings also meant large accumulations of capital seeking investment prospects. British Columbia's large timber reserves and relatively undeveloped forest industry was one of many attractive possibilities.[42]

Even before hostilities in Asia had ended and well before the domestic demand for building materials rose sharply, lumber orders for rebuilding ravaged European cities began flooding mills on the north Pacific slope. In the ensuing years, producers sold a large volume of lumber on the foreign market, but the bread and butter for the trade was the burgeoning domestic home building industry, especially in the fast-growing metropolitan centers of southern California.

The combination of an expansive postwar economy and an increasingly efficient technology vastly stepped up timber harvests everywhere. Lumber manufacturing figures for the leading producers (table 8.1) reveal sharp increases in every state except Washington, where the heaviest cutting had taken place before the war. Oregon surpassed Washington in 1940 and has remained the leading forest products manufacturing state, and California, ranked second since 1948, has held onto that position. Washington's output, more than 7 billion board feet in 1925 and 4.5 billion in 1940, has remained fairly constant at about 3.5 billion board feet. The leading producer, Oregon, increased from 4.2 billion feet in 1925 to 5.2 billion feet in 1940 and a postwar high of 9.1 billion board feet in 1955. California's output increased steadily after the war and reached a peak of just over 5 billion board feet in 1959.[43]

In the midst of the postwar production boom, Michael Bigley, a consulting forester from Eugene, reminded readers of *The Timberman* that little had changed in the long migratory habit of the lumber industry. "With the exhaustion of the open market timber supply in Washington and northern Oregon," he pointed out, "the past several years have witnessed a shift of mills to southern Oregon and northern California with a consequent disturbance of local communities." Bigley was not optimistic that anything could be done about the migration of the business: "it is the tailend of the movement which started in the Northeast many years ago, moved to the Lake States, the South and then shifted West." In the Pacific Northwest, however, he thought the work of foresters had "lessened the ... impact of this cut and get out philosophy."[44] The work of professional foresters, however, was not the factor determining the rate of harvesting on private timberlands.

Although large firms like Weyerhaeuser, Simpson, Georgia-Pacific, and MacMillan-Bloedel in British Columbia set the pace for that tremendous output, those were also the years of the famed gyppo logging and sawmill units—operators who did business on marginal capital and through subcontracts and whose machinery often was pieced together with baling wire. The big companies controlled the marketing outlets, but the hundreds of small operators who logged second-growth stands or in less desirable old-growth timber, provided a valuable source of employment and contributed to the great production records.[45]

The Western Lumber Industry

Table 8.1
Western Lumber Production, 1940–1979 (in million board feet)

	1940	1945	1950	1955	1960	1965	1970	1975	1979
Oregon	5,202	5,003	5,239	9,181	7,401	8,206	6,680	6,342	7,312
Washington	4,541	3,257	3,606	3,118	3,377	3,958	3,189	3,104	3,841
California	1,954	2,260	4,262	5,319	5,160	5,032	4,979*	4,153*	4,639*
Idaho	773	780	1,126	1,413	1,654	1,750	1,631	1,631	1,893
Montana	325	341	480	785	1,035	1,311	1,281	1,038	1,257
Arizona	128	157	842	887	330	398	319	316	337
Colorado	79	88	—	—	181	245	230	181	170
Wyoming	57	54	—	—	228	—	—	162	198
New Mexico	112	99	—	—	224	256	297	210	227
Utah	15	28	—	—	179	—	—	—	—

*Includes Nevada.

There were a few gyppos in the southwestern pine country, many more in the interior of the Northwest, but most of them logged and milled in the Douglas fir region from Humboldt Bay north to British Columbia. The number of gyppo operators dropped sharply in northern California, Oregon, and Washington in the late 1950s when easily accessible timber was no longer available. And in British Columbia a system of granting cutting rights that favored large integrated firms thinned the ranks of independent loggers and sawmill operators, according to one authority, "almost to extinction."[46]

The story of the modern lumber industry is also a tale of merger, consolidation, corporate takeovers, and the increasing concentration of land ownership among the largest units. For their part, the corporate directors and executives who spoke the loudest on behalf of free enterprise began to pursue business policies that worked to undermine a competitive economy. Although not all of the financial consolidations that have taken place since 1945 are significant, some—like the emergence of Georgia-Pacific from a small financial base in Georgia to an industrial giant—truly have been striking. Between 1956 and 1959 the firm made its most significant purchases along the rich timber belt in northern California and Oregon—the Coos Bay Lumber Company in southwestern Oregon and 120,000 acres for $70,000,000; the Hammond Lumber Company on the redwood coast and 127,000 acres for $80,000,000; and the lush 200,000 acres, manufacturing plants, and logging railroads of the Booth-Kelly Lumber Company in Springfield, Oregon, for $93,000,000.[47]

Georgia-Pacific's huge purchases, its sharply increased harvests, and its subsequent timber sales to create a "cash flow" to help pay for the acquisitions, revolutionized the West coast lumber industry. From its

Douglas fir stands on the old Hammond Lumber Company lands north to the Coos Bay, Booth-Kelly, and the C. D. Johnson forests (the latter near Toledo, Oregon), Georgia-Pacific's sales of old-growth trees sustained for a decade firms that otherwise had access to very little timber. A strong lumber market and rising prices were the sole factors determining the harvesting rate on most private timberlands during the period. Although the tremendous volume of the harvests created a multitude of jobs at the outset, the long-range consequences for many communities were fraught with danger.[48]

The Georgia firm's sudden emergence as a giant in the forest products trade attracted the attention of the Federal Trade Commission in the early 1970s; in order to preserve its right to make more purchases, Georgia-Pacific reached an agreement with the commission, and the Louisiana-Pacific Corporation was created to pare down the size of the parent firm. Today, Louisiana-Pacific is one of the largest companies operating in the United States with manufacturing plants and timberland in the Northwest, the Southeast, the Great Lakes states, and in New England. Under the leadership of Harry Merlo, the new firm has earned a reputation for aggressive business practices; Louisiana-Pacific also has led the charge during the recession of the early 1980s to decertify labor unions.[49]

Through all of the production records established during the postwar years, the huge Weyerhaeuser empire remained in the lead in virtually every sales category. The firm built new manufacturing facilities near its extensive holdings (Cottage Grove and Coos Bay, Oregon, are two examples). The company also increased the volume of its harvests in the 1960s in some areas—selling timber to other firms and initiating a major log export program, primarily to Japan. On one of its large holdings in southwestern Oregon, a forester notes that local residents were aware that Weyerhaeuser was "cutting a great deal faster than they could sustain."[50] But the same could be said for the rate of harvesting from Eureka north to British Columbia.

In the two decades following the Second World War, the availability of timber and the seemingly unlimited marketing opportunities created an aura of optimism, a widespread belief that the good times would last forever. Even in the Intermountain region where limited national forest harvests provided most of the timber, work was steady and markets were good. In southwestern Oregon and northern California, newspapers headlined the monthly and annual production records, and there were frequent references to the permanence of the industry. The concern of many producers during those years, however, was in the scramble for access to more timber.

But, amidst the great boom in production, there were indications that the tide was beginning to run out. There were voices of caution, some of them coming from the areas of greatest output. A Forest Service study of the Douglas fir region warned of a rapid "inventory depletion," inadequate reforestation, and that the "high rates of log production . . . have a limited future." The extraordinary harvests and the increasing mechanization of the woods and mill operations contributed to a reduction in the industry's workforce as early as the 1960s. And there were occasional mill closures in the region—the companies usually citing the lack of timber and a soft market as the reasons for their decision.[51]

Not until the early 1970s (and in British Columbia, more recently) did public officials begin to examine in greater detail the consequences of the tremendous volume of the harvests on private timberlands. And even in those instances, concern at the grass roots level—from loggers, union leaders, and local communities—finally spurred legislative action. A study conducted by Oregon State University in the mid-1970s predicted declining timber harvests in the western part of the state for the rest of the century. In British Columbia, where forestry is to the province as oil is to Saudi Arabia, studies indicated timber shortages as great as 30 percent by 1995. Les Reed, a respected forester and former deputy minister in the Canadian Forest Service, predicts that "more than half the people now employed in mill towns will have to move to find other work."[52] Reed's comments were made in the midst of booming Canadian sales in the United States market.

And then the whirlwind—a rash of mill closures beginning in 1979 and continuing into the early 1980s. That social and economic disaster struck especially hard in the lumber producing regions of northern California, Oregon, Washington, Idaho, and western Montana. A severe recession in the United States in the early 1980s and an expanding southeastern wood products trade have compounded the problems for the north Pacific slope (with the exception of British Columbia where production is still high). The federal government's borrowing and runaway federal deficits have kept interest rates high; the strong American dollar, another reflection of costly interest rates, has driven up the price of lumber for foreign buyers; and that has made it possible for Canadian lumbermen to undersell domestic producers in the United States market. Imports from Canada represented 18.7 percent of the lumber products consumed in the United States in 1975 and 32.6 percent in 1985.[53]

That state of affairs has meant protracted depression for timber-dependent regions of the American West. And the outlook for the immediate future is not bright. The great harvests on private timberlands since the Second World War, the expanding production in the Southeast, and large Canadian sales to its southern neighbor indicate that the present troubles will persist. Under these circumstances, it is the sawmill towns and lumber communities that bear the brunt of the suffering. The corporate giants cut back on production, extra shifts and speciality production units are laid off, and some of the smaller operators are forced to close permanently. As for the plant owners and managers, their investment capital is diversified to the point that they are able to ride out the slump in the market. A forest products executive put that in classic form in an address to the Oregon Logging Conference in March 1985: "We are engulfed in a tidal wave of overcapacity and overproduction. But tidal waves subside and there will be survivors."[54]

The history of the twentieth-century forest products trade—like the automobile, steel, and farming industries—is instructive to an understanding of the pervasive influence of modern capitalism and its ability to move on the national and international stage. Always multinational in character because of its marketing network, the industry usually has been subject to influences far from the location of its forests.[55] Because of the limitations of indigenous capital, investments from earlier lumbering frontiers made possible the "opening up" of much of the forested region of the American West to saw and axe. For their part, historians have written extensively about the migration of the industry from one center of logging and lumbering activity to the next. But with only a few exceptions, they have ignored the broader significance of the role and movement of capital, the social and human costs inherent to a system of unbalanced production, and the industry's powerful influence in shaping regional economies to meet its competitive requirements.

Until recently, the rich tradition of folklore, the stories that glorified hardship and dangerous work, and an emphasis on biography and company history have dominated much of the published work on the lumber industry. In short, we have been treated to romantic and nostalgic stories about workers, commissioned histories of corporations and their chief executive officers, and celebrations of the contributions of the forest products trade to the national welfare. As one writer remarked, the industry "has an enormous capacity to believe its own myths."[56] And, it should be added, to pass that version on to others.

Less conspicuous in the published literature of this vital industry are studies that examine how these emerging multinationals fit within the framework of modern capitalism and how the market relationship has shaped both the forest environment and the communities dependent on the timber resource. The segment of society that has reaped a large share of the benefits of the industry's activity in the twentieth century has also heavily influenced the historical pageant as well.

The Western Lumber Industry

Future scholarship needs to assess the history of the western lumber industry in the context of its position in a world-wide network of market relations and how those connections have affected conditions in forest communities. The economic health of those areas always has been dependent on the extent of the resource in other regions of the United States and Canada. We need to understand better the long-range consequences of those interrelationships, their broader meaning for the United States economy, and their implications for the future. Is the industry prone to periodic geographic shifts to new centers of production as the stands in one section of the continent are cut over? With reforestation lagging badly in both the southeastern United States and in British Columbia, there are indications that the old cyclical pattern may repeat itself in the future.

Except for one or two conspicuous exceptions,[57] scholars also have neglected the study of the interplay between the industry and the forest environment. The timbered regions of the West have undergone dramatic ecological change in the transformation of the old-growth forests of the turn of the century to the tree-farm landscape of the present. While historians like Donald Worster have written excellent accounts of ecological and economic disasters like the Dust Bowl, there are no comparable studies of the forested West. The interplay between "economic culture"[58] and environment deserves much greater detail.

Finally, historians should pay more attention to the influence of federal and state policy and its relation to the lumber industry. The failure to reforest public and private lands, for instance, has dire implications for the future economic health of timber-dependent areas. In the same way, national and international development—depression, trade volume, and war—have exercised a critical influence in shaping policy toward resources. What has this meant to heavily forested states like Washington and Oregon or the province of British Columbia? These and other questions are the task of future scholarship. It is time that historians move beyond the celebration of production records and corporate successes and address the more fundamental issues associated with this vital industry.

Notes

1. Curtis P. Nettels, *The Roots of American Civilization: A History of American Colonial Life*, 2nd ed. (New York: Appleton-Century-Crofts, 1963), 146–47, 244–45. For works that treat extensively the early timber trade, see R. G. Albion, *Forests and Sea Power; The Timber Problem of the Royal Navy, 1652–1862*, Harvard Economic Studies, 29 (Cambridge, Mass.: Harvard University Press, 1926); A. R. M. Lower, *'Great Britain's Woodyard': British America and the Timber Trade, 1763–1867* (Montreal: McGill-Queen's University Press, 1973);

and Graeme Wynne, *Timber Colony: A Historical Geography of Nineteenth Century New Brunswick* (Toronto: University of Toronto Press, 1981); Thomas R. Cox, et al., *This Well-Wooded Land: Americans and Their Forests from Colonial Times to the Present* (Lincoln: University of Nebraska Press, 1985), 11, 17.

2. For general studies that underscore the importance of resources from the forest, see John Ise, *The United States Forest Policy* (New Haven: Yale University Press, 1920; reprint ed., New York: Arno Press, 1972); Nelson C. Brown, *The American Lumber Industry: Embracing the Principal Features of the Resource, Production, Distribution, and Utilization of Lumber in The United States* (New York: John Wiley and Sons, 1923); Samuel Trask Dana, *Forest and Range Policy: Its Development in the United States* (New York: McGraw-Hill, 1956); William G. Robbins, *Lumberjacks and Legislators: Political Economy of the U.S. Lumber Industry, 1890–1941* (College Station: Texas A & M University Press, 1982); and Cox, *This Well-Wooded Land*.

3. Raphael Zon, "The Vanishing Heritage," unpublished manuscript in Research Compilation File, Records of the Forest Service, Record Group 95, National Archives and Record Service (NA/RG95). For Indian uses of forest resources, see Richard White, *Land Use, Environment, and Social Change: The Shaping of Island County, Washington* (Seattle: University of Washington Press, 1980), 23–25; and William Cronon, *Changes in The Land: Indians, Colonists, and the Ecology of New England* (New York: Hill and Wang, 1983), 38, 45, 62.

4. For sources that focus, in part, on the southerly and westward shift of the lumber industry, see Brown, *The American Lumber Industry;* Ralph Clement Bryant, *Lumber: Its Manufacture and Distribution* (New York: John Wiley and Sons, 1922); Charlotte Todes, *Labor and Lumber* (New York: International Publishers, 1931); Stewart Holbrook, *Holy Old Mackinaw: A Natural History of The American Lumberjack* (New York: Macmillan, 1938; Comstock Books, 1971); Vernon Jensen, *Lumber and Labor* (New York: Farrar and Rinehart, 1945); William Buckhout Greeley, *Forests and Men* (New York: Doubleday, 1951); Ralph W. Hidy, Frank Ernest Hill, and Allan Nevins, *Timber and Men: The Weyerhaeuser Story* (New York: Macmillan, 1963); Thomas R. Cox, *Mills and Markets: A History of the Pacific Coast Lumber Industry to 1900* (Seattle: University of Washington Press, 1974); Robbins, *Lumberjacks and Legislators;* Jamie Swift, *Cut and Run: The Assault on Canada's Forests* (Toronto: Between The Lines, 1983); and Cox, *This Well-Wooded Land*.

5. Thomas R. Cox, "Trade, Development, and Environmental Change: The Utilization of North America's Pacific Coast Forests to 1914 and Its Consequences," in Richard P. Tucker and John F. Richards, eds., *Global Deforestation and the Nineteenth Century World Economy,* (Durham, N.C.: Duke University Press, 1983), 14–25. For sources on the early exploitation of forests in the arid West, see James A. Young and Jerry D. Budy, "Historical Use of Nevada's Pinyon-Juniper Woodlands," *Journal of Forest History* 23 (July 1979): 112–21; and Conrad J. Bahre and Charles F. Hutchinson, "The Impact of Historic Fuelwood Cutting on the Semidesert Woodlands of Southeastern Arizona," *Journal of Forest History* 29 (October 1985): 175–86. The best general discussion of the nineteenth-century lumber trade on the Pacific coast is Cox, *Mills and Markets*.

6. U.S. Department of Agriculture, Forest Service, *Timber Resources for Amer-*

ica's Future, Forest Resource Report No. 14, 1958, 114–16. This massive collection of data had been ready for printing since 1954, but the Forest Service withheld it from publication because of opposition from powerful lumber trade organizations. See William G. Robbins, *American Forestry: A History of National, State, and Private Cooperation* (Lincoln: University of Nebraska Press, 1985), 189.

7. *Timber Resources for America's Future*, 119–21; William G. Robbins, "Land: Its Use And Abuse," Series no. 6, *Man and His Activities as Related to Environmental Quality* (Oregon State University: Corvallis, 1974), 32; and Thomas P. Clephane, "Ownership of Timber: A Critical Component in Industrial Success," *Forest Industries* 105 (August 1978): 30–33.

8. Cox, "Trade, Development, and Environmental Change," 17–18; Norman Clark, *Mill Town: A Social History of Everett, Washington* (Seattle: University of Washington Press, 1970), 19–42, 58–76; and Murray Morgan, *The Mill on the Boot: The Story of the St. Paul and Tacoma Lumber Company* (Seattle: University of Washington Press, 1982), 48–54. For an elaboration of the Northwest as the last forest frontier, see William G. Robbins, "The Social Context of Forestry: The Pacific Northwest in the Twentieth Century," *Western Historical Quarterly* 26 (October 1985): 413–27.

9. Cox, "Trade, Development, and Environmental Change," 18.

10. Holbrook, *Holy Old Mackinaw*, 160–62; Donald MacKay, *Empire of Wood: The Macmillan Bloedel Story* (Toronto: Douglas & McIntyre, 1982), 15–20; Robert E. Ficken, *Lumber and Politics: The Career of Mark E. Reed* (Seattle: University of Washington Press, 1978), 9–21; Ficken, "Weyerhaeuser and the Pacific Northwest Timber Industry, 1899–1903," *Pacific Northwest Quarterly* 70 (October 1979): 146–54; William G. Robbins, "Timber Empire: Market Economics in Coos Bay, Oregon, 1850 to the Present," *Pacific Northwest Quarterly* 75 (October 1984): 148–49; and Patricia Marchak, *Green Gold: The Forest Industry in British Columbia* (Vancouver: University of British Columbia Press, 1983), 35–36.

11. Ficken, "Weyerhaeuser and the Pacific Northwest Timber Industry," 146–54; Kenneth A. Erickson, "Morphology of Lumber Settlements in Western Oregon and Washington" (Ph.D. diss., University of California, Berkeley, 1965), 16–20; John M. Cox, "Trade Associations in the Lumber Industry of the Pacific Northwest," *Pacific Northwest Quarterly* 41 (October 1950): 285–87; Clark, *Mill Town*, 58–76; Swift, *Cut And Run*, 44–45; MacKay, *Empire of Wood*, 6–19; and R. N. Bryon, "Community Stability and Forest Policy in British Columbia," *Canadian Journal of Forest Research* 8 (March 1978): 62.

12. Greeley, *Forests and Men*, 13; Greeley, *Some Public and Economic Aspects of the Lumber Industry*, USDA, Report No. 114 (Washington, D.C.: GPO, 1917), 4, 61; Edmund Meany, "The History of the Lumber Industry in the Pacific Northwest to 1917" (Ph.D. diss., Harvard University, 1935), 234–36; and Jensen, *Lumber and Labor*, 26–29.

13. Clark, *Mill Town*, 234; Robbins, "Timber Town," 149, 154–55; and Robbins, "Labor in the Pacific Slope Lumber Industry: A Twentieth-Century Perspective," *Journal of the West* 25 (April 1986): 8–13.

14. The best history of the Industrial Workers of the World (IWW) is Melvyn Dubofsky, *We Shall Be All: A History of the Industrial Workers of the World*

(Chicago: Quadrangle Books, 1969). For an account of the IWW in the lumber industry of the Pacific Northwest, see Robert W. Tyler, *Rebels of the Woods: The I. W. W. In The Pacific Northwest* (Eugene: University of Oregon Books, 1967).

15. Cox, "Trade Associations in the Lumber Industry," 285–311; and Brown, *American Lumber Industry*, 240, 243, 247. For a brief history of lumber trade associations, see William G. Robbins, "Trade and Promotional Associations," in Richard C. Davis, ed., *Encyclopedia of American Forest and Conversation History*, vol. 2 (New York: Macmillan, 1983), 651–54.

16. Cox, "Trade Associations in the Lumber Industry," 291, 307; and Brown, *American Lumber Industry*, 243, 247.

17. Robbins, *Lumberjacks and Legislators*, 46; and Brown, *American Lumber Industry*, 255–56, 259.

18. George T. Morgan, Jr., "The Fight Against Fire: Development of Cooperative Forestry in the Pacific Northwest, 1900–1950" (Ph.D. diss., University of Oregon, 1964), 58–59; Morgan, "Conflagration as Catalyst: Western Lumbermen and American Forest Policy," *Pacific Historical Review* 47 (May 1978): 179–81; and *Forty Years of Western Forestry: A History of the Movement to Conserve Forest Resources by Cooperative Effort* (Portland: Western Forestry and Conservation Association, 1949), 8–10.

19. Ralph R. Widner, ed., *Forests And Forestry in the American States: A Reference Anthology* (Washington, D.C.: Association of State Foresters, 1968), 168–69; and Robbins, *American Forestry*, 266–68.

20. Edwin A. Tucker and George Fitzpatrick, *Men Who Matched The Mountains* (Washington, D.C.: GPO, 1972), 125–32; and Stephen Pyne, *Fire in America: A Cultural History of Wildland and Rural Fire* (Princeton, N.J.: Princeton University Press, 1982), 521.

21. Pyne, *Fire In America*, 516; James G. McNary, *Briefly: The Story of a Life* (New York: Newcomen Society, 1957), 10–17; and D. W. Meinig, *Southwest: Three Peoples in Geographical Change, 1600–1970* (New York: Oxford University Press, 1971), 42.

22. Tucker and Fitzpatrick, *Men Who Matched the Mountains*, 130–31, 190; and Harold K. Steen, *The U.S. Forest Service: A History* (Seattle: University of Washington Press, 1976), 252.

23. W. H. Hutchinson, *California Heritage: A History of Northern California Lumbering*, rev. ed. (Santa Cruz, Calif.: Forest History Society, 1974), n.p.; Walton Bean, *California: An Interpretive History*, 2nd ed. (New York: McGraw-Hill, 1973), 205; and Cox, "Trade, Development, and Environmental Change," 15.

24. Bean, *California*, 205; Hutchinson, *California*, 165; and Lynwood Carranco, *Redwood Lumber Industry* (San Marino, Calif.: Golden West Books, 1982), 117–39.

25. Carranco, *Redwood Lumber Industry*, 143, 149, 152, 155, 159, 169.

26. Ibid., 162–63; and Robbins, "The Social Context of Forestry," 421.

27. Charles E. Twining, *Phil Weyerhaeuser: Lumberman* (Seattle: University of Washington Press, 1985), 36–92; Hidy, Hill, and Nevins, *Timber and Men*, 248–68; and Michael P. Malone and Richard B. Roeder, *Montana: A History of Two Centuries* (Seattle: University of Washington Press, 1976), 253–54.

28. Marchak, *Green Gold*, 29, 31–32; MacKay, *Empire of Wood*, 66–67; and Martin Robin, *The Rush for Spoils: The Company Province, 1871–1933* (Toronto: McClelland and Stuart, 1972), 12–18. For an excellent, albeit fictional, account of turn-of-the-century logging in British Columbia, see M. Allerdale Grairger, *Woodsmen of the West* (Toronto: McClelland and Stuart, 1964).

29. MacKay, *Empire of Wood*, 92–93, 118, 244.

30. Marchak, *Green Gold*, 30–36; and Keith Reid and Don Weaver, "Aspects of the Political Economy of the British Columbia Forest Industry," in Paul Knox and Philip Resnick, eds., *Essays in British Columbia Political Economy*, (Vancouver: New Star, 1974), 13–24. The British Columbia government holds approximately 94 percent of the forests in the province. See Ken Drushka, *Stumped: The Forest Industry in Transition* (Toronto: Douglas & McIntyre, 1985), 15.

31. Conversation with Con Schallau, Oregon State University, February 20, 1985; Oregon, *Report of the State Forester* (Salem, 1912), 19–21; and Henry S. Graves, "Federal and State Responsibilities in Forestry," *American Forests and Forest Life* 31 (November 1925): 677.

32. Thorton Munger, *Timber Growing Practices in the Douglas Fir Region*, USDA Bulletin no. 1493 (Portland, Ore., June 1927), 14; Brian Wall, *Log Production in Washington and Oregon, An Historical Perspective*, U.S. Forest Service, Resource Bulletin PNW-42, Pacific Northwest Forest and Range Experiment Station (Portland, 1972), 5–6; and F. L. Moravets, *Production of Logs in Oregon and Washington, 1925–1948*, USDA, Forest Service, Forest Survey Report no. 101, Pacific Northwest Forest and Range Experiment Station (Portland, 1950), 7.

33. Andrews is quoted in Wall, *Log Production In Washington and Oregon*, 6; I. J. Mason, "Grays Harbor Study," April 4, 1935, in S Plans, Timber Management, Olympic, 1927–1935, box 54139, Federal Records Center, Seattle, Wash.

34. Oregon State Planning Board, *Oregon's Forest Problems* (Portland, 1936), 1–2, 4; and Northwest Regional Council, *Forest Depletion in Outline* (Portland, 1940), iii–iv.

35. For details about Mason's proposal, see Timber Conservation Board, Report of the Subcommittee on Publicly Owned Timber, November 14, 1931, box 71, National Forest Products Association (NFPA) Records, in Forest History Society Archives, Durham, N.C.; and Robert Y. Stuart to Timber Conservation Board, October 31, 1931, "Agriculture—Forest Service, Forest Management," Presidential Papers, Hoover Papers (PPHP) in Herbert Hoover Presidential Library, West Branch, Iowa. For an account of Mason's ideas, see Elmo Richardson, *David T. Mason: Forestry Advocate* (Santa Cruz, Calif.: Forest History Society, 1983).

36. Richardson, *David T. Mason*, 76–79, 84–87; and Roy O. Hoover, "Public Law 273 Comes to Shelton: Implementing the Sustained-Yield Forestry Management Act of 1944," *Journal of Forest History* 22 (April 1978): 86–87.

37. Elmo Richardson, *BLM'S Billion-Dollar Checkerboard: Managing the O & C Lands* (Santa Cruz, Calif.: Forest History Society, 1980), 147; and Hoover, "Public Law 273 Comes to Shelton," 101.

38. Although badly dated, Vernon Jensen's *Lumber and Labor* is still the standard account of the industry during the Second World War.

39. G. H. Collingwood to Earle Clapp, March 19, 1942, box 54, NFPA Records.

40. Jensen, *Lumber and Labor*, 276; and *Coos Bay* (Oregon) *Times*, September 11, 19, 1942.

41. Author's interview with Wylie Smith, Coos Bay, Oregon, April 16, 1984.

42. Drushka, *Stumped*, 70.

43. The figures in Table 1 are gleaned from the following sources: *Statistical Yearbook, 1952* (Portland: West Coast Lumbermen's Association, 1953), 7; *Statistical Yearbook, 1962* (Portland: West Coast Lumbermen's Association, 1964), 7; *Statistical Supplement to Facts, 1968* (Portland: Western Wood Products Association, 1969), 23; *Statistical Yearbook, 1972* (Portland: Western Wood Products Association, 1973), 25; and *Statistical Yearbook of the Western Lumber Industry* (Portland: Western Wood Products Association, 1981), 27.

44. *The Timberman* (February 1949), 56.

45. *Coos Bay Times*, November 2, 1944, August 14, 1945, April 5, 8, 1946, April 3, 1947, and May 1, 1951; and *Portland Oregonian*, December 15, 1946.

46. Drushka, *Stumped*, 81.

47. Ibid., 210; Dennis C. LeMaster, *Mergers Among the Largest Forest Products Firms, 1950–1970*, Washington State University, College of Agriculture Research Center, Bulletin 854 (Pullman, 1977), 1; and Carranco, *Redwood Lumber Industry*, 163.

48. *Portland Oregonian*, August 29, 1958, and *Coos Bay Times*, April 8, 1959.

49. Carranco, *Redwood Lumber Industry*, 166–67.

50. Nathan Douthit, *The Coos Bay Region, 1890–1944* (Coos Bay, Oregon: River West Books, 1981), 117–23; and author's interview with Jerry Phillips, April 6, 1984.

51. Wall, *Log Production in Washington and Oregon*, 7–8, 29. Also see Alan H. Muir and Richard A. Searle, *A Study of Industrial Development Possibilities for the Coos Bay District* (Menlo Park, Calif.: Stanford Research Institute, 1956), 17–20; and John A. Young and Jan M. Newton, *Capitalism and Human Obsolescence: Corporate Control Versus Individual Survival in Rural America* (Montclair, N.J.: Allenheld, Osmun, 1980), 34–38. For an account of an early mill closure, see Portland *Oregonian*, January 17, 1959.

52. John F. Beuter, K. Norman Johnson, and H. Lynn Scheurmann, *Timber For Oregon's Tomorrow*, Research Bulletin 19, Forest Research Laboratory, School of Forestry, Oregon State University (Corvallis, 1976), 1, 18, 43; Russel Sadler, "John Beuter Reckons With Timber," *Willamette Week*, December 26, 1977; and Jane O'Hara, "Canada's Vanishing Forests," *Macleans*, January 14, 1985, n.p.

53. Portland *Oregonian*, November 27, 1985.

54. Ibid., March 10, 1985.

55. Drushka, *Stumped*, 202.

56. Ibid., 223.

57. White, *Land Use, Environment, and Social Change*.

58. Donald Worster, *Dust Bowl: The Southern Plains in the 1930s* (New York: Oxford University Press, 1979).

9

The Irrigation District and the Federal Relationship

NEGLECTED ASPECTS OF WATER HISTORY

IN THE TWENTIETH CENTURY

Donald J. Pisani

As no other natural resource, water provides the key to the development of the semiarid regions of the West. Even in the midst of sophisticated technology of the twentieth century, availability of water is often the essential resource that determines patterns of population growth and the expansion or decline of cities. The legal and institutional framework governing the distribution of water was thus of crucial importance to the West. In his essay Donald Pisani discusses two variations related to this major theme. He evaluates the development of the irrigation district in the West and also the changing relationship between the states and the federal government regarding water rights. In both instances environmental conditions and legal institutions interacted to produce new and distinctive conceptions about the role of water in the West.

In the last decade, the history of water in the American West has come of age. Historians have long recognized that the region's past and future have much to do with the intricate network of dams and canals that move water great distances from moisture-rich mountains to arid valleys and plains. Now they are beginning to see that the way Westerners have tackled the "water problem" says much about values and aspirations. In other words, the West's water systems have not simply permitted the adaptation of familiar eastern institutions to a new environment; they have, at least to some extent, redefined those institutions and the society itself. Readers who want an overview of the literature should consult Lawrence B. Lee's excellent bibliography.[1] In the pages that follow, I shall appraise some of the most significant work, especially that published during the last decade, in effect picking up where Professor Lee left off in the late 1970s. That done, I shall examine two major topics in the relationship between law and economic growth, the irrigation district and the persistent struggle between the federal government and states over water rights.

The history of water resource development in the trans-Mississippi West has always been intwined with the basic themes in American history, including parochialism, sectionalism, and "colonialism." Not surprisingly, the first popular works dealing with arid land reclamation followed hard upon the closing of the frontier.[2] With the best farmland in the humid half of the nation taken up, the American deserts offered the last free or cheap land, but they could not be conquered without water. Moreover, reclamation fitted the spirit of a new age that emphasized cooperation over individualism, central planning over haphazard economic growth, and the expert over the generalist. After World War II, led by the enormously productive and perceptive Paul Wallace Gates, American historians produced many fine studies of American land policy. But until the 1960s and 1970s, few books and articles were devoted exclusively to the history of water. To be sure, its importance had long won recognition from historians interested in such broader themes as the winning of the West[3] and the emergence of the conservation movement.[4] They built on the earlier work of such engineers as William Hammond Hall, Frederick Haynes Newell, Elwood Mead, Arthur P. Davis, and Ray Palmer Teele whose writings often emphasized the theme of modern technology pitted against raw, untamed nature.[5]

If any book can be said to mark the emergence of water history as a separate field it was Samuel P. Hays's justly celebrated *Conservation and the Gospel of Efficiency* (1959).[6] Not only did Hays trace the evolution of "multiple-purpose" water planning in the United States; his pathbreaking survey brought the West into a national focus. Hays analyzed natural resource policies as they reflected the increasing influence of specialists in government, the growth of bureaucracy, and the quest for efficiency. In short, water policy and conservation became a mirror to understand broader political and economic changes.

Oddly enough, while several historians produced excellent histories of conservation that complemented or built on Hays, only Donald C. Swain and Elmo Richardson surveyed water resource development after the Progressive period.[7] In the 1960s and 1970s, much of the best work on reclamation focussed on individual leaders.[8] Other excellent studies explored interstate conflicts over water, the 160-acre limitation, and the origins of the Reclamation Act of 1902.[9]

Only since the late 1970s—in a decade of synthesis—have historians tried to fit reclamation history into a broader framework. The decade began with the publication of a sophisticated, suggestive comparative study by political scientist Arthur Maass and economist Raymond Anderson that deserved more attention from historians.[10] Many nineteenth-century American scientists and engineers were close students of dam and canal construction, irrigation techniques, and water laws outside the United States; but Maass and Anderson were the first to address the question George Perkins Marsh posed in the 1870s, and Karl Wittfogel reiterated in this century: what effect did irrigation have on the structure and processes of government, and was it fair to talk about "hydraulic societies"?[11] The two authors examined irrigation institutions and policies in three parts of Spain and compared them to conditions in three parts of western America—the Kings River Basin of California's San Joaquin Valley, the South Platte Basin in northeastern Colorado, and the Utah Valley south of the Salt Lake City, served mainly by the Provo, Spanish Fork, and American Fork rivers. They found that institutions and policies devoted to water allocation in each of these areas had comparable goals, including "orderly conflict resolution, popular participation, local control, increased income, justice in income distribution and equity."[12] The two authors directly challenged Wittfogel's contention that irrigation agriculture contributed to centralization of power and, inevitably, despotism. Quite to the contrary, the farmers controlled their destinies to a remarkable degree. Maass and Anderson's conclusions are worth quoting at length:

> The most powerful conclusion that emerges from the case studies is the extent to which water users have controlled their own destinies as farmers, the extent to which the farmers of each community, acting collectively, have determined both the procedures for distributing a limited water supply and the resolution of conflicts with other groups over the development of additional supplies. With important variations to be sure, local control has been the dominant characteristic of irrigation in these regions, regardless of the nationality or religion of the farmers, the epoch, whether formal control is vested in an irrigation community or in higher levels of government, the forms of government at the higher levels, and perhaps even the legal nature of water rights. In this realm of public activity—and one wonders in how many others—formal centralization of authority, where it has occurred, has not meant substantial loss of local control *de facto*.[13]

In fact, the institutions developed were an antidote to centralized, despotic political power. "Systems that were in existence before the central government invested money and technical expertise," Maass and Anderson conclude, "have to a remarkable extent protected their autonomy and even defied national policies that are supposed to accompany national money if these policies have been a serious threat to local custom." In the western United States, state water laws have been a powerful counter to federal policies, as has the federal system generally. Thus, in California the national policy of restricting water to small farms has been thwarted by large, powerful interests at the local level.[14]

No historian has responded to the challenge of Maass and Anderson to study comparatively irrigation institutions. But a few have helped break down the assumption that agriculture has been the only determinant of water policy in the West. As the largest city in the West, Los Angeles' search for water has attracted plenty of attention. In 1900, the city's population stood at 100,000, but that number doubled by 1905 and reached 576,000 in 1920. In 1899, local voters approved a $2,000,000 bond issue that allowed the city to buy out the Los Angeles City Water Company and establish a publicly owned water system. Subsequently, a persistent drought at the beginning of the twentieth century, and the need for a water supply to encourage future economic growth, prompted city officials to look for water outside the arid Los Angeles Basin.

Abraham Hoffman and William Kahrl have told the story of Los Angeles' attempt to tap the water supply of the Owens Valley in quite different ways. Hoffman sees the story as an odd set of circumstances inspired more by "vision" than "villainy." Kahrl, however, largely accepts the notion that a "conspiracy" robbed the valley of its water. He argues that a handful of civic leaders, led by the aqueduct's chief architect, William Mulholland, repeatedly and consciously exaggerated the city's existing and anticipated water needs. The invention of "paper droughts" as well as the clever manipulation of population and industrial growth statistics persuaded the city's gullible voters to approve bond issue after bond issue by overwhelming majorities.[15]

While Hoffman sticks closer to the evidence, Kahrl does more to place his story in a broad historical perspective. The Owens Valley Aqueduct marked a sharp break with nineteenth-century traditions of corporate water development, and Kahrl properly recognizes that the spirit behind the great canal was but one facet of the booster mentality that built San Pedro Harbor and fueled southern California's frequent real estate booms. The book also demonstrates the persistent rivalry between rural and urban water users as well as between Los Angeles and San Francisco. Los Angeles clearly "created itself" using cheap water as an enticement for adjoining communities to merge with the city. Unfortunately, Kahrl's evidence does not support the author's contention that the construction of the Los Angeles Aqueduct directly influenced either the planning or construction of California's twentieth-century water transfer systems, such as the Central Valley Project. The influence of urban water use on comprehensive water plans—including the demands of cities for cheap hydroelectric power—begs for much more attention from historians of water. In particular, we need comparative studies of the part water politics played in urban growth in different parts of the arid West.

The Irrigation District and the Federal Relationship

In the year after Kahrl's book appeared, Robert Dunbar published the first survey of water law in the West, *Forging New Rights in Western Waters*.[16] No subject in water history has received more attention in the last decade.[17] Dunbar's concise book was the culmination of decades of careful, thoughtful work in irrigation agriculture and western water law.[18] He went well beyond the existing historical literature by treating twentieth- as well as nineteenth-century water law, and groundwater rights—which have become increasingly important in recent years—as well as surface water. Understandably, a book that tried to do so much also contained basic weaknesses. For one thing, it largely ignored the relationship of water law to the law as a whole, despite the suggestive work of such leading legal historians as Willard Hurst, Harry Scheiber, and Morton Horwitz. Dunbar's water law appears to have been made out of whole cloth. Yet the doctrine of prior appropriation was not a western innovation. Rather it was a response to the first phase of industrialization in New England. I have built on Hurst, Scheiber, and Horwitz by arguing that aridity had less influence on the evolution of water law than immediate economic needs.[19] Finally, Dunbar pays too much attention to water rights applied to irrigation, not enough to changes in the laws pertaining to municipal water uses of water or rights to water to generate hydroelectric power.

The same criticism can be levied against my own *From the Family Farm to Agribusiness* (1984),[20] where I tried to provide a case study of the development of water law—statutory, administrative, and court-made—in the leading irrigation state. I was interested in the relationship of law to basic social and economic values, particularly the ideal of the family farm. California told a poignant story of how legislation such as the irrigation district laws—designed in the 1870s and 1880s to promote small scale, diversified agriculture and democratic values—had by the 1920s and 1930s been perverted to serve as the foundation for agribusiness. Along the way, I also tried to show how ineffective water resource planning had been in California, whether it was undertaken by the federal government, state, local water districts, or private enterprise. Because California was a model for the rest of the arid West, much of what I found had significance far beyond that state.

My book reflected a disillusionment with western water policies that has now reached full flood. No longer is the Bureau of Reclamation celebrated as the liberator of the West; public respect for dams and canals and dam-builders has been seriously tarnished.

Donald Worster's *Rivers of Empire,* like all his books, is written with a passionate dedication to saving the land.[21] In many ways it does for the Far West what his prize-winning *Dust Bowl* did for the Great Plains states.[22] Worster is not one to temporize or equivocate, and he has the great gift of being able to write history for a broad audience. There is lyric beauty to his prose; his vision is breathtaking; his ability to generalize is deft; his eye for detail almost uncanny. All in all, he is a spellbinder. And yet his history is also deeply flawed—arrogant, distorted, and moralistic.

The book is built on the assumption that the West is "a land of authority and restraint, of class and exploitation, and ultimately of imperial power" and that it exhibits those characteristics more sharply and in greater measure than any other part of the nation. Worst of all, according to Worster, it might have been different. The West is a land of missed opportunities and dreams, a place where American democratic values might have reached their full potential. This romantic quality to Worster's work, evident also in *Dust Bowl,* gives his book an intensity rare in historical writing.[23]

The key to Worster's argument is Wittfogel's thesis. Worster assumes that the principles of "hydraulic empire" transcend time and place, that the lessons Wittfogel drew from ancient China can be applied to a technological twentieth-century society with very different values and culture. He traces three stages of irrigation development, a localized, autonomous irrigation society that began with the first Mormon settlement and lasted into the 1890s ("incipience," to use his word); a more centralized phase after 1902 when the "federal government took firm charge of the western rivers, furnishing the capital and engineering expertise to lift the region to a higher plateau of development" ("florescence"), and a third phase beginning in the 1940s ("empire") when "the two forces of government and private wealth achieved a powerful alliance, bringing every major western river under their unified control and perfecting a hydraulic society without peer in history."[24] All of this is buttressed with many sound observations about the dangers reclamation posed to the future of the West.

Yet for all its insights, little in *Rivers of Empire* is new. While we have needed a good synthesis for a long time, it pretends to be something more than that, for Worster promises to "brush away the obscuring mythologies and the old lofty ideals and to concentrate on that achieved reality."[25] There is no substantive research in archival or manuscript sources, and a good deal presented as fresh material was articulated or anticipated long ago, particularly by the Ralph Nader Study Group's report on the Bureau of Reclamation published in 1973.[26]

More important, Worster knows full well that the eastern half of the nation, as well as the West, was built by man's exploitation and will to dominate nature. The ruthless values of capitalism—what Worster is really talking about—know no regional boundaries. Forests were stripped away, millions of acres of swamps drained, soil eroded, and species after species of wildlife destroyed as Americans subdued the humid half of the continent. In fact, as Marc Reisner has pointed out, flood control structures of the Corps of Engineers *in the East* have reclaimed more land for agriculture than the storage reservoirs the Bureau of Reclamation built in the West. Admittedly, there is a difference, but the assumption that man's impact on the land is substantially greater in a region heavily dependent on irrigation remains unproven.[27]

All large states, hydraulic societies or not, have been ruled by elites given over to pride and arrogance, often blindly optimistic about the future. Unfortunately, Worster never tells us how the structure of a hydraulic empire differed from a nonhydraulic empire, or how politics and institutions in the western United States differ from those in the eastern half of the nation, or how government and the economy in the West differ from other countries that practice irrigation extensively, such as Egypt or India. Moreover, by regarding the West as a "hydraulic empire"—though most of the evidence provided comes from the California experience—we miss the fact that there are many variations within the West; it is not a monolithic entity.

Worster cannot decide whether the will to dominate nature is endemic to western man, a sort of original sin, or the creation of a greedy, manipulative elite—in this case the "water hustlers." Given the acquisitive spirit of all Americans, he is hard put to demonstrate that Westerners are unique. Unfortunately, Worster's world is one of "either-or" choices. "Was it a society in which power and profit were broadly diffused—was it, after all, a people's Eden?" Worster asks plaintively of his failed dream, "Or was it instead, more or less as the earlier hydraulic societies had been, a hierarchical system of power, of unequal life-chances, of some humans dominating others?" Such a question, like Worster's naive suggestion that the answer to the West's problems is a return to something akin to the simple river basin communities John Wesley Powell called for a century ago, demonstrate that a book written as an extended jeremiad cannot fairly evaluate the complexity of human decision making.[28]

The charm of Worster's book is in the marvelous prose, in his Cassandralike moralizing, and in the haunting thought that no society has managed to defy forever those natural forces that have helped undermine so many earlier empires—siltation, erosion, soils choked with salt residues, collapsing dams. His warning is remarkably similar to Marc Reisner's message in *Cadillac Desert*.

Reisner's book is written with the same passion as Worster's, the same set of manipulative, conspiratorial elites, the same sense of foreboding and the impermanence of the West's "oasis civilization."[29] That Reisner is a journalist, not a professional historian, is obvious throughout. The book lacks footnotes and often overlooks basic historical sources—for example, Norris Hundley's books on the Colorado River and Paul Gates's *History of Public Land Law Development* are left out of the bibliography.

Moreover, the author crams his book full of stories (Powell's running of the Colorado, the Owens Valley controversy, and the construction of Boulder Dam, to name a few) that have already been very well told and have little bearing on his major concern, federal water policies in the West. Yet for all its flaws, the book is well-written and much more original than Worster's. No one has done a better job of exploring decision making within the Bureau of Reclamation, the complicated relations among federal bureaus, and the Congressional appropriations gauntlet.

Until quite recently, Reisner maintains, water projects were "the grease gun that lubricates the nation's legislative machinery."[30] The dam-building binge following World War II resulted in an intense and incredibly wasteful rivalry between the Bureau of Reclamation and Corps of Engineers, each of which saw survival in terms of responding to, or creating, local support for water projects. "Across the entire West, the Corps, as opportunistic and ruthless an agency as American government has ever seen," according to Reisner, "was trying to seduce away the Bureau's irrigation constituency; it was toadying up to big corporate farmers who wanted to monopolize whole rivers for themselves.... As a result, the business of water development was to become a game of chess between two ferociously competitive bureaucracies."[31]

Reisner tells many incredible stories, none more incredible than the tale of the Bowman-Haley Project, a dam on the Grand River in North Dakota. In May 1962, according to Reisner, the bureau's regional director in Billings warned Commissioner of Reclamation Floyd Dominy that the Corps of Engineers intended to build the structure. The bureau had surveyed the feasibility of such a dam for thirty years but always concluded that the dam would not store sufficient water to provide for either irrigation or flood control. Municipal water use was the only conceivable justification, but the town of Haley was a dot on the map, and Bowman had only about 1,300 people. In the end the corps built a gigantic dam more than a mile across and 79 feet high to impound just 19,780 acre-feet of water (by comparison, the dam was about half the size of the smallest dam on the Missouri River, but held only about 1/90th the volume of water). The significance of the story is obvious. After the corps moved into California during World War II, it "kept a full-court press on the Bureau." In their competition for appropriations, the two agencies built many financially infeasible projects, and, as the most stable sites for dams were taken, they built more and more dams that posed safety risks. The Teton Dam disaster of 1976—which occurred despite warnings from the U.S.G.S. concerning safety hazards—symbolized the destructive effects of such crazed rivalries. On one occasion, according to Reisner, Commissioner Michael Straus lectured the Billings Division of the Reclamation

The Irrigation District and the Federal Relationship

Bureau. "I don't give a damn whether a project is feasible or not. I'm getting the money out of Congress and you'd damn well better spend it."[32]

Reisner differs from Worster in several important respects. First, while both agree that the federal government's water resource policies have been enormously wasteful and destructive, Reisner emphasizes that the weaknesses of policy derived as much from federal agencies trying to cater to local interests as to dictatorial policies handed down by a remote, aloof bureaucracy. In this sense, his analysis is closer to Maass and Anderson than Worster. Second, and perhaps even more important, individual actors matter to Reisner. The book's greatest virtue is that it is written using the knowledge of "insiders," a knowledge derived from hundreds of interviews, some lengthy, of such public figures as James Watt, Stewart Udall, David Brower, Floyd Dominy, George Ballis, and Ben Yellen. There are also interviews with many of those responsible for the day-to-day operations of the Bureau of Reclamation, Corps of Engineers, and other federal agencies. Reisner does not pull punches. His chapter on Dominy notes:

> It wasn't his blindness, his stubborness, his manipulation of Congress, his talent for insubordination, his contempt for wild nature, his tolerance of big growers muscling into the Reclamation program—in the end, it wasn't any of this that did Dominy in. It was his innate self-destructiveness, which manifested itself most blatantly in an undisguised preoccupation with lust. His sexual exploits were legendary. They were also true. Whenever and wherever he traveled, he wanted a woman for the night. He had no shame about propositioning anyone. He would tell a Bureau employee with a bad marriage that his wife was a hell of a good lay, and the employee wouldn't know whether he was joking or not. He preferred someone available, but his associates say he wasn't above paying cash. . . . As he bullied weak men, Dominy preyed on women whom he considered easy marks.[33]

Unfortunately, Reisner too often portrays federal bureaucrats and politicians as comic-book caricatures, their motivation reduced to greed, lust, and elemental drives to dominate. There are plenty of "bad guys" here, fewer "good guys," and still fewer believable human beings. Nevertheless, the quoted dialogue is fascinating and revealing.

In his survey of water politics since 1945, Reisner's book is invaluable; it offers a thousand tantalizing leads for historians to pursue. For example, in assessing Jimmy Carter's "hit list" he notes that many advisers close to the president recognized that the list contained far too many projects in too many parts of the country. Had the president begun by attacking the most vulnerable western projects—such as the Auburn Dam in California—he might have made headway. Instead, he stubbornly, though for all the right reasons, insisted on trying to kill 19 or 32 projects—the size of the list varied. His short-sighted strategy insured that the traditional porkbarrel coalitions in Congress would manage to hang onto the spoils. Moreover, Carter spent too much time talking about the threat the projects posed to the environment, not enough on their contribution to the deficit. The American public might respond to appeals to balance the budget, but they were less sympathetic to protecting nature.[34]

In the end, the laudable attempt of Worster and Reisner to take the broadest possible view of their subject is also a weakness. As Maass and Anderson show, we can learn as much studying institutions from the ground up as from the top down. The development of water resources followed a pattern in many parts of the West. Almost everywhere, the first farmers individually or in small groups dug simple, inexpensive, and inefficient diversion ditches. At this time, roughly from the 1850s through the 1870s, mining and stock raising dominated the western economy. But toward the end of the 1870s the Desert Land Act (1877) and a protracted drought touched off a corporate irrigation boom that lasted into the 1890s. Few of these companies made money. Farmers resented depending on a private monopoly, and most ventures could not control a sufficient body of land to make their scheme pay as speculation. To compound the problems of private enterprise, states like Colorado and Wyoming prohibited the sale of water rights by private companies on grounds that surplus water belonged to the people; so title could be acquired only through use, not through delivery. (That limitation could be evaded, however. Where possible, companies first bought the land to be watered, then sold farms for a price that included the cost of a water right.) The government owned most of the West, but by the 1880s the best agricultural land was already in private hands, and the mere whisper of a canal survey sent land sharpers scurrying to buy up all the property they could to resell. So while private companies built many works later absorbed into thriving irrigation projects, and contributed mightily to western economic development, they rarely profited from their investment.[35]

The mutual water company proved much more acceptable to farmers. These cooperative organizations usually took over irrigation works that private companies constructed. After estimating their dependable water supply, farmers apportioned it by selling stock (though farmers often contributed labor rather than money to the venture). Although the stock did not pay dividends, each share entitled the bearer to a certain quantity of water, usually enough to irrigate an acre of land, but sometimes a fraction of streamflow. The mutual company had many advantages. It was administered by the farmers it served, and the largest water users had the greatest say in how it was run. Moreover, since the water was not attached to the land, rights could be transferred easily from one parcel of land to another, and the cost of maintaining the ditches was easily apportioned. If an individual failed to pay an assessment, or to contribute labor, he forfeited his stock. Some mutual water companies became very large. For example, the Peoples Ditch and Last Chance Ditch companies on California's Kings River had 60 and 30 miles of main canals respectively in 1918. In the twentieth century the mutual water company lost in popularity as water projects dramatically increased in size and complexity, but as late as 1969 such institutions served more than 20,000,000 acres in 17 states, about 45 percent of all the West's irrigated land. Utah, where the Mormon Church encouraged farmers to build cooperative enterprises, led with 87 percent of its irrigated land served by mutual companies.[36]

Mutual water companies had great advantages. Since they delivered water to consumers at cost, they were exempt from state regulation. That meant they were easier to form. Moreover, unlike irrigation districts, such companies were controlled by stockholders, not the residents of the service area at large. Consequently, a direct relationship existed between costs and benefits because the largest investors were also the largest landowners. But such companies also had one major weakness: the amount of money they could raise for construction was small because their financial liability was limited. Although individual water users forfeited part of their stock if they refused to comply with company policies, their land and property could not be attached; hence the company could not use land values as security to borrow money. California was the first to find a way to combine the home-rule the mutual company offered with an institutional mechanism to raise money to build large irrigation works. This achievement became increasingly important at the end of the nineteenth century because most of the West's streamflow had already been claimed, and future economic development depended on storing floodwater that ran to waste each spring when the snow melted.

Nineteenth-century Westerners had a healthy fear of monopoly in all forms, including public monopolies. If American virtue was reborn on the frontier, and if the West was the safeguard of republican values, politics west of the Mississippi were not notably cleaner than in other parts of the nation during the last decades of the nineteenth century. For example, in 1872 at the adjournment of the California Legislature, the *Stockton Daily Independent* lamented: "When the Legislature convenes it is usually pronounced a superior body of men, and when it adjourns it is most generally denounced as excelling all of its predecessors in incompetency and corruption. It is to be presumed that the Legislature just adjourned will not be an exception."[37] In short, lawmakers could not be trusted to spend money fairly or efficiently. Moreover, with the possible exception of California, the financial resources of western states were too limited to pay for massive public works projects. In the 1890s, especially during the dark months and years following the economic collapse of 1893, when private capital dried up in the West, many boosters argued that the nation should do what the states could not. But a massive federal reclamation program posed many potential problems. Other Westerners warned that the arid and semiarid states and territories were little more than economic fiefdoms or provinces of an overweening, dictatorial central government. Ironically, while federal reclamation promised to spur western economic development, and perhaps lay the foundation for later financial independence, it would do so only at the cost of weakening the role of the states in the federal relationship. Government aid was fine, but could Washington be expected to provide *unconditional* assistance? Few western leaders could escape the fear that any federal program would undermine existing water rights and lead to efforts by federal agencies to monopolize the region's surplus water.[38]

The irrigation district became one answer to this dilemma. Utah passed a district law as early as 1865, but while farmers there formed many districts, that law did not provide an effective method to raise money to build or purchase irrigation works. California experimented with legislation throughout the 1870s and 1880s but did not adopt an effective law until 1887.[39] The California irrigation district had certain distinct features. It was a quasi governmental institution, much like a school district, in which all eligible voters—not just landowners—had a voice in policies. In effect, the needs of the community were placed above individual property rights. A majority of voters—in some elections a simple majority, in others a two-thirds plurality—could, in theory, decide to irrigate even if large landowners remained committed to preserving their land for stock grazing or dryland farming. The greatest strength of the district was that it could force an economically powerful and vocal minority to accept the will of the majority. Districts had the power to tax all property within their boundaries, including town lots and buildings, not just agricultural land. Moreover, taxes were levied uniformly, not according to specific benefits conferred on individual parcels of land. Districts also had the power to issue bonds. Particularly where districts included a great deal of virgin land, direct taxes were inadequate because unimproved land provided a small tax base. However, since the mere promise of irrigation usually drove up land values—particularly in places where part of a proposed district had already been successfully cultivated—bonding allowed irrigation promoters to take advantage of the cycle of speculation that inevitably followed the designation of a district.[40]

Several states were quick to follow California's lead. Washington adopted a district law in 1890, Kansas and Nevada followed in 1891, and

Oregon, Idaho, and Nebraska in 1895.[41] But this first phase of institutional experimentation ended in failure. In California, land speculators thoroughly discredited the district concept by including too much undeveloped, unirrigable land within districts. They concocted bizarre schemes matched only by the greed and gullibility of their victims. For example, the land sharks who organized the Manzana District in Los Angeles County in December 1891 knew the proposed district did not have access to an adequate water supply. Not many months earlier, no more than a dozen people lived in the district. Since this number was far below the fifty residents required to petition for the formation of a district, the company gave away part of its worthless land—some of which actually belonged to the Southern Pacific Railroad—to increase the district's population. Once the district was formed, the promoters exchanged property worth at most $5 an acre for $200 an acre in bonds, hoping that as settlers flooded in the paper could be unloaded on bona-fide investors. Such schemes, and the opposition of many large landowners to taxing their land for improvement they did not want, clogged the state's courts with suits. An emasculated version of the 1887 law survived, but of 51 districts formed in California before 1912—covering nearly 3 percent of the state's land area—only a handful flourished. As of 1909, only about 4 percent of the West's irrigated land was within districts. This amount was more than the acreage then irrigated in the fledgling federal projects, but only about 11 percent of the land irrigated by cooperative enterprises such as mutual water companies.[42]

The new Reclamation Service, established in 1902, quickly recognized the potential value of districts to its own efforts. In November 1904, one of the patron saints of western reclamation, William Ellsworth Smythe, proposed a plan to revive the moribund district idea at the request of California governor George Pardee, who recognized that the absence of public land in the Golden State limited the field for federal reclamation there. "The California District Law failed," Smythe explained, "largely because of lack of expert supervision. . . . Under the new plan, districts would be formed only after investigation by the Reclamation Service." The secretary of the interior would locate likely districts and supervise the sale of bonds. The Reclamation Service would construct the irrigation system. When the works had been finished, they would be turned over to local management. The scheme attracted the Reclamation Service as a way to inflate the reclamation fund, but it won little support in the states. Federal supervision promised to breathe new life into the irrigation district, and it would have insured the construction of high-quality hydraulic works. Nevertheless, most farmers must have wondered why they should vote for interest-bearing bonds when the federal government advanced construction costs interest free.[43]

The great turnaround in irrigation district fortunes came with state supervision. For a variety of reasons, particularly the fear that the state would have to assume financial liability for district debts, none of the district laws passed between 1887 and 1895 gave the state any direct control over either the process of organization or the issuance of bonds. In 1911, the desire to create safe markets for bonds prompted California to create a state commission, headed by the state controller, to certify that no bond issue exceeded 60 percent of the value of the land, water rights, and other assets within a proposed or existing district. No districts had been formed in California since 1895, but Imperial Valley farmers were eager to create the largest district ever established in California, one that contained more than 600,000 acres. Then, in 1913, the legislature required the state engineer to report on the feasibility of all plans for new districts. If he issued an adverse report, the district could still be created, but only with the approval of three-fourths of district residents.[44]

By 1920, every state with a district law except Kansas had instituted some form of state review, though the form varied from place to place. And at least five states—Utah, California, Nebraska, Washington, and Oregon—used state funds to purchase district bonds to bolster public confidence in this new institution and because such bonds paid a good return.[45]

The demand for food during World War I provided a tremendous stimulus to the formation of districts. By the beginning of the war, the opportunity to construct small-scale irrigation systems had disappeared in the West as farmers relied more and more on stored water. (Only the use of underground water on parts of the Great Plains, southern California, and the Southwest, offered much opportunity for individual enterprise.) Consolidation hit irrigation just as it had industry, and many districts formed during the war involved storage projects that unified smaller systems. In the two years of 1919 and 1920, 156 districts were created, more than 25 percent of those established since 1887. By 1922, 598 districts had been formed in the seventeen western states covering about 16,000,000 acres, though only 3,000,000 acres were irrigated. The organization of districts passed through distinct phases in different parts of the West depending on a variety of economic factors ranging from drought, railroad construction, the technology of dam building, mining and lumber booms, and the price of beef. For example, most of western Nebraska's districts were formed during the 1890s, while Colorado's district boom came in the first decade of the twentieth century—especially in 1908 and 1909—and the greatest activity occurred in Montana and Oregon during World War I.[46]

The boom was not uniform. Eighty-eight percent of the districts formed before 1922 were in the seven states of California, Washington, Oregon, Idaho, Nebraska, Colorado, and Montana. Great Plains farmers relied

The Irrigation District and the Federal Relationship

too heavily on dry farming, and their land offered few potential reservoir sites. Nevada, Arizona, and New Mexico were too sparsely settled and dry. The climate and elevation of most parts of Wyoming provided too short a growing season to take full advantage of irrigation. And in most parts of Utah, the cohesive force of the Mormon Church made mutual companies adequate substitutes for districts. Nevertheless, at the end of World War I irrigation districts watered 50 percent more land than federal projects (though together they served only 3,000,000 acres, about 20 percent of all the West's irrigated land). Still, this increase accounted for much of the growth in acreage from 1900 to 1920.[47]

Of course, the two forms of enterprise were not mutually exclusive. The Reclamation Service encouraged the formation of irrigation districts, particularly after it began to relinquish control over its projects to the farmers after the middle 1920s. Districts had distinct advantages over the more informal water user's associations, upon which the Reclamation Service had relied during the early years of federal reclamation. The latter organizations were simply collections of individual farmers, so each landowner had a separate contract and account with the government. Not only did this increase accounting costs, but it meant that in case of nonpayment, the government was forced to file individual suits. Moreover, such an arrangement provided no way to force landowners who had not filed for a government water right to pay for operation and maintenance charges, and it also prevented individual farmers from obtaining federal farm loans. By relying on districts, the government substituted one contract for many and depended on district taxes to repay construction costs. This change relieved the Reclamation Bureau of its most onerous burden. Ironically, while the nineteenth-century irrigation district had been created to encourage and protect home rule over water—as an alternative to federal reclamation—in the twentieth century it became a tool of centralization.[48]

Much work needs to be done on irrigation districts and the many other institutional forms they spawned to stimulate economic development. As with almost all irrigation innovations, California led the West. There, large landowners sponsored water storage and conservation districts during the 1920s as alternatives to the "one man, one vote" philosophy upon which the irrigation district rested. The irrigation district was much more than a way to irrigate land. It also influenced the size of estates, patterns of farming, and political leadership within rural communities. The storage district was an attempt by agribusiness interests to maintain the status quo in the San Joaquin Valley. Votes within these districts were apportioned according to property, one for each $100 in assessed value, and landowners did not have to reside in the district, let alone live on the land. The political implications of such districts were enormous. For example, the famous Kern County Land Company petitioned for the formation of a storage district in 1922. An election was held in November 1923, and the district approved the measure by 68,465 to 21,929. However, the land company held about half the votes. Without its support, the district proposal would have lost by more than two to one. By 1970 there were twenty different kinds of water districts in California, ranging from county districts to the unique, gigantic Metropolitan Water District, which provided Los Angeles, San Diego, and many other southern California cities with water. Most of these districts were formed after World War II as a result of the state's dramatic industrial and population growth, and many were created in conjunction with the Central Valley Project and State Water Plan. But all owed much of their success to the irrigation district.[49]

The irrigation district was a legal experiment state legislatures conducted, but the courts also had plenty to say about the shape of water law. Fortunately, there has been much good work done in recent years to complement Robert Dunbar's lucid, concise overview.[50] However, one very significant story, the persistent struggle between the federal government and arid states for sovereignty over water, largely has been ignored.

The roots of that story stretch well back into the nineteenth century. Most of the West's largest streams are interstate, and the drought of the late 1880s and 1890s touched off conflicts on many of those rivers. For example, residents of New Mexico bitterly complained that diversions upstream to water 400,000 acres in Colorado's San Luis Valley had dried up the river, destroying farms downstream.[51] Many different solutions were proposed including a federal code to regulate water use on interstate streams, the extension of prior appropriation across state borders, the creation of special tribunals to adjudicate interstate disputes, and even the adjustment of state boundaries to conform to natural drainage basins. However, partly because of the complexity of the problem, partly because the western states could not agree on a unified course of action, and partly because Congress showed scant interest in "western problems," little was done.[52]

The jurisdictional problem became even more acute in 1902, following passage of the reclamation act. Section 8 of that law promised that "nothing in this act shall be construed as affecting or intended to affect or in any way interfere with the laws of any State or Territory relating to the control, appropriation, use, or distribution of water used in irrigation, but State and Territorial laws shall govern and control . . . the waters rendered available by the works constructed under the provisions of this act."[53] What authority the nation had to store the waters of interstate streams remained an open question, especially after the U.S. Supreme Court refused to define the nature or the extent of federal water rights in its 1907 decision pertaining to the conflict between Kansas and Colorado over the Arkansas River.[54] In that decision the court implied that the states owned the water of *all* streams, even those that were shared by two or more states. But it did not say so directly. As in so many of its cases, the court stuck to the facts at issue in the case at hand and refused to make a broad declaration about the nature of water rights.

Since the court did not close the door on federal rights, legal officials in the Reclamation Service clung to a theory of national ownership of the West's surplus or unappropriated water that they had been polishing since at least 1904. Their theory built on the assumption that the federal government, as original owner of the public domain, also owned all the resources on or in the land. Although Congress had passed many laws granting public lands to states, private companies, and individuals, and others permitting settlers on public lands to appropriate water, it never formally gave up ownership. That Congress had permitted the arid states to pass laws regulating the allocation of water did not modify the federal-state relationship. Congress could deed away what belonged to the nation *only by explicit grant*. The states had been allowed to record rights and determine priorities because they could do that job more efficiently under nineteenth-century frontier conditions. But when they had granted water, title passed from the nation to individual claimants, not through the states. This theory not only maintained government ownership of the West's unused water, it also suggested that the federal government could at any time abrogate state administrative control. In 1904, Frederick H. Newell, first director of the Reclamation Service, warned: "The States are recognized by the Federal Government as in control of the regulation of the use of water merely because the Federal Government has not undertaken to regulate such matters."[55]

The Reclamation Service's need to maintain political support in Congress discouraged the use of this weapon. In practice, the government filed for water like other claimants in the arid states, though it used a variety of tactics to guarantee an adequate supply for its projects. It made "blanket claims" to water, often demanding a large enough supply to meet ultimate rather than immediate needs. Here it held a trump card. It could threaten states that did not grant the government special consideration with the loss of a government project or a delay in construction. The Reclamation Service also reserved vast areas of public land and potential reservoir sites to prevent their use by competing private water companies, and it used friendly federal courts to define and adjudicate project and nonproject rights. The federal attorney responsible for these adjudication suits privately observed in 1918: "In practice we only use the theory of Federal ownership as an anchor to the leeward. We strive strenuously to show that we have complied with every State law and therefore [that] our rights are good upon that theory; but we say that even if we have failed in some particular, they would be good anyway because the Government does not have to comply with State statutes."[56]

In 1922, the Reclamation Service tried again to get the Supreme Court to define reserved rights in an interstate conflict between Wyoming and Colorado, but once again the court dodged the issue.[57] Meanwhile, the technological potential to transmit electrical power long distances made gigantic projects like Boulder Dam possible, and the Reclamation Service quickly took advantage of the subsidy cheap power offered to irrigation. As usual, the service followed an erratic, and sometimes inconsistent, course. On the one hand, it encouraged states to resolve their differences by negotiating compacts to divide up interstate streams. These agreements, almost treaties, became very attractive as a way to reserve water for future needs. On the other hand, the service continued to insist that the government held paramount rights and did not have to consult the states.

The issue came to a head in the debate over the Boulder Dam legislation. Nevada's U.S. Senator Key Pittman recognized that a new chapter had opened in the legal conflict between states and nation. The government had argued that it did not have to comply with state water laws because the Colorado River was navigable. Pittman and other proponents of state's rights accepted the federal government's power over commerce, but questioned whether that power could be used to justify the construction of federal dams for hydroelectric power, flood control, and irrigation without regard to state water laws. Neither Secretary of the Interior Hubert Work nor Secretary of Commerce Herbert Hoover had any sympathy for the water rights of the states, Pittman declared. "Are we to remain silent," he asked, "while the United States Government through its delegated authority to regulate navigation assumes authority of the streams for all other purposes, although such additional authority has never been delegated by the States to the Federal Government?" Pittman embraced the classic states' rights thesis of enumerated powers: The states antedated the Union and had joined together for reasons specified in the Constitution. All rights not specifically granted to the federal government remained with the states. Since the colonies had control over all but coastal waters, that sovereignty was inherited by the states, save for a *limited* power over navigation.[58]

By the 1930s, federal water rights still had not been well defined. The theories used to explain them were profoundly ambiguous. Did federal water rights issue from the treaty rights by which the United States acquired property from France or Mexico, or from the formal withdrawal of lands from the public domain and their reservation for federal purposes, such as parks, forests, and game preserves? At times federal officials

The Irrigation District and the Federal Relationship

argued that the nation owned *all* unclaimed water on the public domain as a legacy of its original land ownership. At others, they argued that the nation owned sufficient water to improve federal lands, following the lead established by Supreme Court cases decided at the turn of the century. But there was a third alternative: that the federal government enjoyed jurisdiction over the water of all interstate streams because they were beyond the control of the individual states.[59] During the 1930s and 1940s, a much more sympathetic Supreme Court stretched the "navigation servitude," as lawyers called it, to fit a variety of new circumstances. Navigation was defined to include not just streams actually used for navigation, but those capable of being *rendered* navigable.[60] Since most of the water projects of the 1930s and 1940s were multiple purpose, and since most large western streams were navigable for at least part of their course, this new claim implied a dramatic expansion of federal power over water. However, despite the expansion of federal authority after the Boulder Dam Act, western dependence on federal aid diluted states' rights protests. Not until the post–World War II period, after the Central Valley Project, Big Thompson Project, Grand Coulee Project, and others had been built, did the pitch of dissent return to the shrill level of the 1920s.

After World War II, the political power of the Reclamation Bureau in the West continued to increase.[61] During the 1930s, the bureau added urban water needs to its list of multiple-purpose benefits, and by 1976 it provided more than sixteen million Westerners, from San Diego to Rapid City, with all or part of their municipal and industrial supply. It also generated cheap electrical power to help build cities like Portland and Los Angeles. In 1940 federal water projects served about five million people, more than five times the number benefitted in 1933.[62] But even these numbers pale in comparison to the post–World War II period, when irrigated acreage in the West doubled largely because of Bureau of Reclamation and Corps of Engineers projects. Before the 1930s, Supreme Court decisions limited the power of federal agencies over western waters, but during the New Deal the court acknowledged and justified the increasing federal presence in the region. Soaring demands for water after the war raised the spectre of unified federal control over river basins for the sake of efficiency, if nothing else.[63]

Even during the war, Westerners could see that the postwar period would produce a cornucopia of federal benefits. In 1943, the Corps of Engineers drafted a master plan for river development within the Missouri Basin that became known as the Pick Plan. It involved an expenditure of $658,000,000. Not to be outdone, the Bureau of Reclamation, after its own study, proposed the Sloan Plan, which called for spending $1,258,000,000 on reservoirs designed to accomplish the same objectives in different locations. Congress deadlocked over which plan to accept, so, in the grand tradition of logrolling, included both in the Flood Control act of 1944.[64]

In the decades after the war, Westerners came especially to fear the commerce and general welfare clauses of the U.S. Constitution. In the case of navigation, California's deputy attorney general observed: "So long as Congress uses the word in a statute and the case relates to something moist, the Court takes at face value the declaration that the legislation is in furtherance of navigation. . . . [T]he test of what constitutes a navigable stream," he continued, "has been stretched to embrace most of the waters in the United States. It has been suggested that the contemporary test may be whether a stream is navigable enough to float a Supreme Court opinion. . . ."[65] The court, of course, had not relied entirely on the commerce clause. In 1950 it affirmed what had become obvious since the 1930s, that the general welfare clause was not limited in the way enumerated powers were. "[T]he power of Congress to promote the general welfare through large-scale projects for reclamation, irrigation, or other internal improvement," the court concluded, "is now as clear and ample as its power to accomplish the same results indirectly through resort to strained interpretation of the power over navigation."[66]

Hard upon this decision, which had little immediate impact in the West, came a much more dramatic confrontation between the nation and states. It occurred at a time of mounting public concern over "big government," centralization, and the "Soviet menace," a time when many Americans were having a hard time adjusting to the new "welfare-warfare state" that had been created over the previous two decades. The suit was tailor-made for the times, filled with symbolic overtones: David versus Goliath; the hinterland versus the metropolis; common sense versus abstruse points of law, and the people versus remote, isolated, unresponsive bureaucrats.

The scene for the suit was Fallbrook, California, a small town on the Santa Margarita River about forty miles north of San Diego and ten or twelve miles inland from Camp Pendleton, a Marine Corps training base. The camp had been carved out of the 135,000-acre Santa Rita Ranch at the beginning of World War II; in 1951 it was home to 28,000 soldiers, most destined for service in Korea. The post's growth had created a serious water shortage.

Nevertheless, Fallbrook farmers continued to divert water from the Santa Margarita to water avocado and lemon orchards, as they had for years before the post was created. They were small farmers; more than 80 percent owned ten acres or less. In 1949, the problem had seemed near solution when local marine authorities worked out a deal with the farmers and townspeople to construct a storage reservoir. They promised 37 percent of the impounded water to the farmers, who, in turn, agreed to

The Irrigation District and the Federal Relationship

help pay for the structure. A second promising alternative also presented itself. The farmers and Marine base might tap into a canal planned to connect San Diego and the Metropolitan Water District of Los Angeles's canal from the Colorado River.

These alternatives were abandoned in early 1951. William Veeder, a Department of Justice lawyer in Washington—destined in the 1960s to become a leading champion of "reserved" Indian water rights—heard of the Fallbrook water shortage and decided to turn it into a test case. Justice Department officials supported him, and soon federal marshals delivered court summons to everyone from the pastor of the town's Methodist Church to ninety-year-old Mary Hubbard, whose well had run dry and who had subsisted on two buckets of water each day that sympathetic neighbors provided. Veeder contended that the federal government had the right to *all* the river's flow because of its paramount rights to sufficient water to develop reserved lands. The *Los Angeles Times* branded the suit as "the boldest attempt yet made on the part of the 'centralization bureaucrats' in Washington to tear down the last vestige of states' rights and confiscate private property in defiance of the injunction in the Fifth Amendment. . . ." If the government could seize water at will, it might soon confiscate private coal mines in Pennsylvania, iron mines in Michigan, or oil wells in Texas. Congressman Clair Engle of California, head of a special House Interior and Insular Affairs subcommittee chosen to investigate the Fallbrook case in the summer of 1951, called the government attorneys "legal sadists" and branded the suit "unreasonable and incomprehensible." The case became such a *cause celebre* that it won coverage even in such popular journals as the *Saturday Evening Post* and *Reader's Digest*.[67]

It also won attention in Congress. In 1952, Senator Pat McCarran of Nevada pushed through legislation to force the federal government to waive its immunity and participate in all suits to adjudicate or administer water rights on any stream to which the government held claims. The new law provided that when drawn into such contests, the government would "be deemed to have waived any right to plead that the State laws are inapplicable or that the United States is not amenable thereto because of its sovereignty" and would be required to obey state court decisions "in the same manner and to the same extent as a private individual under like circumstances." Many lawmakers assumed that this decision had put the genii back in the bottle once and for all.[68]

They had not considered the persistence of federal bureaucrats or the logic of the United States Supreme Court. If Congress was in a mood to protect states' rights in the 1950s, as it had not been in the previous two decades, the court continued to interpret federal power broadly. In 1955, it rendered its most controversial postwar water decision. The Federal

Power Commission had authorized a private company to build a dam on the Deschutes River in Oregon, entirely on federal land, to generate hydroelectric power. Since the FPC did not consult state authorities, Oregon sued. It resurrected perhaps the oldest defense of states' rights—that when Congress authorized the appropriation of water on the public domain in 1866, 1870, and 1877, the exclusive right to regulate and distribute western waters had been delegated or conveyed to the states. These laws, the argument ran, took precedence over any powers conferred on the Federal Power Commission by the Water Power Act of 1920. But the court dismissed this reasoning. The nineteenth-century legislation, it ruled, applied to the "public lands" but not federal reserved land, such as that set aside for power sites. "Accordingly, it is enough, for the instant case," the court warned, "to recognize that these Acts do not apply to this license, which relates only to the use of waters on reservations of the United States."[69]

That the justices were well aware of the implications of their decision can be seen in the eloquent dissent of Justice William O. Douglas, a friend of the West who on many occasions had defended national power. He warned that the law of 1910 that justified the creation of most reserved lands was open-ended and could apply as easily to irrigation and "other public purposes" as to power. "In the West," he observed, "the United States owns a vast amount of land—in some States over 50 percent of all the land. If by mere Executive action the federal lands may be reserved and all the water rights appurtenant to them returned to the United States, vast dislocations in the economies of the Western States may follow." About 700,000,000 acres in the West remained part of the public domain, and most of the region's water originated on reserved lands, mainly forests and parks.[70]

The Pelton Dam case, as it came to be called, had profound significance. Before the 1930s, most water and power projects grew out of the tug and pull of local pressure groups (which helps explain why so many federal reclamation projects established under the Reclamation Act of 1902 failed). Government engineers may have worshipped the ethic of efficiency, but there were other gods to propitiate. Farmers on government reclamation projects received a substantial subsidy in the form of interest-free loans, but they still had to pay the full cost of construction. Multiple-purpose water projects generated massive sums of money through sales of hydroelectric power and water to municipalities. This new source of income freed the bureau from the burden of requiring reclamation to pay for itself. As a result, more and more projects were conceived in Washington. The Pelton case contributed to this centralization of planning.[71]

Few Westerners schooled in the law granted the existence of federal reserved water rights, and most of those who did argued that such rights applied only to Indian lands.[72] As always, the Supreme Court's decision raised a bewildering, challenging array of questions. For example, if reservation of the dam site guaranteed a sufficient quantity of water to turn generators, then would water rights date to the reservation of the site in 1909 or to 1951, when the FPC approved the power company's permit to build? Moreover, how would future appropriations for irrigation or domestic use rank against rights that the federal government granted to the power company? Even more ominous, could the federal government claim reserved rights to land acquired by purchase or condemnation? And could the federal government claim water to develop oil, oil shale, gas, or mineral lands? The two greatest fears among western politicians were that water rights established under state laws might be seized without compensation, and that future state water planning was hopeless and futile because of the unknown dimensions of reserved rights. Not surprisingly, though federal agencies had joined in state court adjudications following the McCarran Amendment in 1952, the Pelton decision ended such cooperation.[73]

Congress considered more than fifty different bills to define or limit federal reserved rights during the second half of the 1950s and 1960s. The best-known, the Barrett Bill—which Senator Frank Barrett of Wyoming introduced on behalf of himself and seven other western senators—provided that unappropriated water could be claimed only under state laws. It denied the existence of any special federal rights. Other bills proposed recognizing such rights, but not until federal agencies defined specific needs and promised to honor earlier claims vested under state law.[74]

The fears of the West were not groundless, though the suspicion that bureaucrats in Washington wanted to replace existing water rights with a federalized system had no basis in fact. Nevertheless, the federal government had dramatically expanded its interest in water resource management. To the four major water resource responsibilities the nation assumed before World War II—irrigation, navigation improvement, power generation, and flood control—many others were added from 1955 to 1965. For example, the Water Supply Act of 1958 required that federal multiple-purpose water projects grant domestic and industrial water uses top priority. The Fish and Wildlife Act of the same year added the responsibility to maintain stream flows to protect aquatic life. The Water Pollution Control Act of 1960 added the protection of water quality, mainly through augmentation of streamflow to aid the efforts of waste treatment plants. Then, in 1962, new flood control legislation finally defined recreation as a primary, rather than incidental, purpose of Corps of Engineers's projects. Three years later, the Reclamation Bureau accepted this new responsibility.[75]

Despite the furor over the Pelton Dam opinion, the worst was yet to come. The states were dedicated to protecting the doctrine of prior appropriation and vested rights inherited from a pastoral, agricultural past, while, by the 1960s, the West was becoming increasingly urbanized and industrialized. The bedrock assumption upon which federal water rights rested was that only Washington could provided unified, centralized economic planning. The two positions were irreconcilable.

Much of the uncertainty of the Pelton decision arose because it never dealt *directly* with federal water rights. *Arizona v. California,* decided in 1963, was the first explicit discussion of reserved rights since the Winters decision in 1908. It was also the first explicitly to extend federal rights to uses outside Indian lands, and the first to divide up water claimed under reserved rights. The basic question before the court was how much water California and Arizona deserved from the Colorado River. It reaffirmed the Winters Doctrine and argued that the creation of reservations not only set aside sufficient water for uses at the time but for *future* (for example, "practicable irrigable acreage") uses as well. The decision granted the federal government specific allocations to serve the Lake Mead Recreation Area, Havasu Lake National Wildlife Refuge, Imperial National Wildlife Refuge, and the Gila National Forest. In effect, the court concluded that the Commerce and Property clauses granted Congress not just the power to dam and store water from navigable streams, but also to distribute that water to the states and even to individual water users without regard to state laws.[76]

The water allocated amounted to less than 1 percent of existing diversions, but the principles established and reaffirmed in the decision elicited another angry dissent from Justice Douglas. "It will, I think, be marked as the boldest attempt by judges in modern times to spin their own philosophy into the fabric of the law, in derogation of the will of the legislature," he declared. "The present decision ... grants the federal bureaucracy a power and command over water rights in the 17 Western States that it never has had, that it always wanted, that it could never persuade Congress to grant, and that this Court up to now has consistently refused to recognize."[77] Many students of water law agreed. One remarked that "the national powers granted by the property clause, the commerce clause, and the general welfare clause are so blended that the national government, were it so disposed, could proceed to develop natural resources without regard to the desires of the states."[78] Another noted that the federal government could also use the war power, treaty power, and property power

> to plan, develop, and allocate western water resources in disregard of state rights and state laws.... Provided it acts in exercise of the navigation power, moreover, it could dislocate and destroy vast private investments

without compensation.... In the case of nonnavigable waters in the public land states the United States has proprietary [riparian] rights, based on its original ownership of the lands, to all waters of which it has not been divested by valid appropriations under state laws. One way of immunizing itself against further divestment is to withdraw the public lands from entry.[79]

In 1963, few lawyers or government officials could anticipate that the high tide of reserved rights had been reached and would recede by the end of the decade. This fact was partly obscured by the increasing attention paid to reserved Indian water rights during the 1960s and 1970s.[80] Federal officials continued to argue that without reserved rights, weaknesses and variations in state water laws would forestall a uniform or comprehensive public lands policy. Not only did reserved rights insure sufficient water to improve designated federal lands, but many recreation and conservation uses—especially minimum flows for the protection of fish or for pollution control—were not recognized as beneficial uses in some states. Ironically, given the strong opposition of conservation groups to federal water storage projects in the 1970s and 1980s, federal agencies could not have maintained the need for reserved rights without their pragmatic alliance with conservation groups (which were convinced that state laws provided little protection to the environment).[81]

In the 1970s, the Supreme Court backed away from its earlier decisions without rejecting them entirely. In two cases, it ruled that state courts in Colorado could, under the McCarran Amendment, adjudicate federal reserved water rights. However, it did not limit the government to the amount of water reasonably needed to improve a reservation, nor did it require compensation for confiscated private rights perfected under state law prior to federal declaration of reserved rights, nor were Indian water rights included. Following these decisions, the United States filed claims for reserved rights in northwestern Colorado covering seven national forests, one national park, three national monuments, fifteen hundred springs and waterholes, two hot springs, and two oil shale reserves.[82] Then, in 1976, the court *implied* that the federal government held reserved rights to groundwater, as well as streamflow, to serve government preserves. Since groundwater had become an increasingly important source of irrigation and domestic water in the West since the mid-1950s, this decision represented an important extension of federal authority.[83]

The court's decisions on reserved rights did not extend to all federal water projects. For example, in 1978 it rejected a Bureau of Reclamation argument that the government could store unappropriated water for reclamation without observing state laws. This decision reversed a tendency since the 1930s for the court to give the bureau, rather than states, control over water impounded by federal projects. The justices, speaking through William Rehnquist, a Nixon appointee, delved into the history of the Reclamation Act of 1902 and concluded that the courts had never abrogated or limited Section 8, long recognized as the foundation block of states' rights in the arid West. But, as always, the decision left doubt as to whether the court had changed course. The Stanislaus River was not navigable, nor was a federal reservation involved.[84]

From the 1930s through the 1960s, the Supreme Court strengthened federal water rights on almost all fronts, but it equivocated in the 1970s. In a case involving the Rio Mimbres in New Mexico, the court acknowledged that Congress had tacitly reserved an unspecified amount of water when it created the Gila National Forest in 1899. The court refused, however, to acknowledge claims to preserve fish and wildlife, or for aesthetic, environmental, or recreation purposes. It suggested that at least nonIndian reserved rights were restricted to those water uses recognized as beneficial *at the time of reservation*. Consequently, it sustained federal claims only for timber and watershed protection. Reserved rights, the opinion stated, would be confirmed only in the amount necessary to fulfill the purpose of the reservation, and only for "direct" as opposed to "secondary" or "supplemental" purposes. The prime test was whether "the purposes of the reservation would be entirely defeated" without the water.[85] On the other hand, the court flatly rejected exclusive state claims to the ownership of western waters as legal "fiction."[86]

"If every speaker who has talked in the last twenty years or so about federal-state relations in water law were laid end to end," a professor of law at the University of Washington commented in 1971, "it would be a good and merciful thing."[87] Certainly, since the early 1950s there has been endless legal speculation concerning the meaning of various Supreme Court decisions, the nature of the federal-state relationship, and the future of water use in the arid West. But for all the national government's theoretical powers, federal agencies have been careful not to undermine or supersede existing rights. Reserved rights were like the sword of Damocles, always ready to fall. Nevertheless, few if any established rights were disrupted. What changed most in Washington was the conception of the purpose of the public lands. In 1902 their disposal had been a tool to encourage western settlement and economic development. By the postwar period, disposal had given way to reservation and management. That trend explains why reserved rights became so important. The acreage involved was vast indeed—more than 52 million acres in Indian lands and nearly 139 million in national forests alone.

Many questions about reserved rights remain unanswered. Can anyone maintain a secure title to water that originates on public land when federal agencies claim they can use the water to make virtually any improvements

The Irrigation District and the Federal Relationship

to government property? Does reserved water have to be used on the reservation where the water originates, or can it be carried to contiguous government lands, or lands far removed from the source? Although the Supreme Court has restricted reserved rights in certain ways, many lawyers still regard them as an indeterminate mortgage on the West's water supply. Ironically, so far their indefinite nature has prevented opponents from being able to point to concrete damage. This, and the fact that some water users *within* each state look to the national government to protect their interests against opposing forces dominant in the state legislature, has prevented effective opposition to reserved rights. Most of the legislation proposed to limit reserved rights has been infeasible, if not unconstitutional. While one can confidently say that federal control will not be abandoned, one cannot predict what the future will bring.

In conclusion, these two subjects—the expansion of irrigation districts and the federal-state legal relationship—suggest the rich potential for analyzing western economic development through the law and public policy. The surface of potential subjects has only been scratched. American historians need a survey of water resource development in the West that looks as hard at state and private reclamation projects—and not just in California—as at federal activities. We need to understand the variety of economic conditions in the West and how they affected local water policies. We must consider such intriguing questions as why, given the massive projects launched in the wake of the Boulder Canyon Act of 1928, the TVA idea did not win wider acceptance in the region. A survey of the evolution of urban water systems is also needed, focussed particularly on the question of how politicians reformed western water law to allow rapidly growing cities to reserve gigantic supplies of water to meet future domestic and industrial needs.[88] Lacking as well is an overview of the hydroelectric power industry in the West that considers how cheap energy stimulated western industrial development. Without cheap water power, the impact of the New Deal and World War II on the West would have been very limited. These research opportunities, and many others, suggest that historians of natural resources will play a vital role in writing the "new history" of the American West.

Notes

1. Lawrence B. Lee, *Reclaiming the American West: An Historiography and Guide* (Santa Barbara: ABC—Clio Press, 1980).
2. See, for example, William Ellsworth Smythe, *The Conquest of Arid America*

(New York: Harper & Bros., 1900), and Elwood Mead, *Irrigation Institutions* (New York: Macmillan Co., 1903).

3. For example, see Walter Prescott Webb, *The Great Plains* (New York: Ginn and Company, 1931); Robert Sterling Yard, *Our Federal Lands: A Romance of American Development* (New York: C. Scribner's Sons, 1928); George Wharton James, *Reclaiming the Arid West* (New York: Dodd, Mead, 1917); and Wallace Stegner, *Beyond the Hundredth Meridian* (Boston: Houghton Mifflin Co., 1954).

4. Charles R. Van Hise, *The Conservation of Natural Resources in the United States* (New York: Macmillan Co., 1910); Gifford Pinchot, *The Fight for Conservation* (New York: Doubleday, Page & Co., 1910); Stuart Chase, *Rich Land, Poor Land* (New York: McGraw-Hill, 1936); Roy Robbins, *Our Landed Heritage* (Princeton: Princeton University Press, 1942).

5. William Hammond Hall, *Irrigation in Southern California* (Sacramento: State Printing Office, 1888); Arthur Powell Davis, *Irrigation Works Constructed by the United States Government* (New York: John Wiley and Sons, 1917); Frederick H. Newell, *Irrigation in the United States* (New York: T. Y. Crowell & Co., 1902); Ray P. Teele, *Irrigation in the United States* (New York: D. Appleton & Co., 1915); Mead, *Irrigation Institutions*.

6. Samuel P. Hays, *Conservation and the Gospel of Efficiency: The Progressive Conservation Movement, 1890–1920* (Cambridge, Mass.: Harvard University Press, 1959).

7. Elmo Richardson, *Dams, Parks and Politics* (Lexington: University of Kentucky Press, 1973); Donald C. Swain, *Federal Conservation Policy, 1921–1933* (Berkeley: University of California Press, 1963).

8. Gene M. Gressley, "Arthur Powell Davis, Reclamation, and the West," *Agricultural History* 42 (July 1968): 241–57; Paul Conkin, "The Vision of Elwood Mead," *Agricultural History* 34 (April 1960): 88–97; James R. Kluger, "Elwood Mead: Irrigation Engineer and Social Pioneer" (Ph. D. dissertation, University of Arizona, 1970); Lawrence B. Lee, "William Ellsworth Smythe and the Irrigation Movement: A Reconsideration," *Pacific Historical Review* 41 (August 1972): 289–311; Andrew Hudanick, Jr., "George Hebard Maxwell: Reclamation's Militant Evangelist," *Journal of the West* 14 (July 1975): 108–21; Charles P. Korr, "William Hammond Hall: the Failure of Attempts at State Water Planning in California, 1878–1888," *Southern California Quarterly* 45 (December 1963): 305–22; Harwood P. Hinton, "Richard J. Hinton and the American Southwest," in Donald C. Dickinson, et al., eds., *Voices from the Southwest: A Gathering in Honor of Lawrence Clark Powell* (Flagstaff, Ariz.: Northland Press, 1976), 82–91.

9. Norris Hundley's superb *Water and the West: The Colorado River Compact and the Politics of Water in the American West* (Berkeley: University of California Press, 1975), told the story of the most important interstate conflict. Paul S. Taylor, an agricultural economist at the University of California, Berkeley, was a leader in the fight to enforce the 160-acre provision and the ideal of the family farm. See his "Central Valley Project: Water and Land," *Western Political Quarterly* 2 (June 1949): 229–54; and "Mexican Migrants and the 160 Acre Water Limitation," *California Law Review* 63 (May 1975): 732–50, as well as his oral history transcript of 1975 at the Bancroft Library. The best overview of the 160-acre

controversy is Clayton R. Koppes, "Public Water, Private Land: Origins of the Acreage Limitation Controversy, 1933–1953," *Pacific Historical Review* 47 (November 1978): 607–36. For a provocative study of the origins of the reclamation act, see William Lilley II and Lewis L. Gould, "The Western Irrigation Movement, 1878–1902: A Reappraisal," in Gene Gressley, ed., *The American West: A Reorientation* (Laramie: University of Wyoming Press, 1966), 57–74.

10. Arthur Maass and Raymond L. Anderson, *. . . and the Desert Shall Rejoice: Conflict, Growth, and Justice in Arid Environments* (Cambridge, Mass.: MIT Press, 1978).

11. George Perkins Marsh, *Irrigation: Its Evils, the Remedies, and the Compensations*, S. Misc. Doc. 55, 43 Cong., I sess., serial 1584 (Washington, D.C.: GPO, 1874); Karl Wittfogel, *Oriental Despotism: A Comparative Study of Total Power* (New Haven: Yale University Press, 1957).

12. Maass and Anderson, *. . . and the Desert Shall Rejoice*, 1.

13. Mass and Anderson, *. . . and the Desert Shall Rejoice*, 366. Wittfogel's work is discussed on 4–5, 366–68.

14. Maass and Anderson, *. . . and the Desert Shall Rejoice*, 4.

15. Abraham Hoffman, *Vision or Villainy: Origins of the Owens Valley-Los Angeles Water Controversy* (College Station: Texas A & M University Press, 1981); William Kahrl, *Water and Power: The Conflict Over Los Angeles' Water Supply in the Owens Valley* (Berkeley: University of California Press, 1982).

16. Robert G. Dunbar, *Forging New Rights in Western Waters* (Lincoln: University of Nebraska Press, 1983).

17. Although Michael C. Meyer's *Water in the Hispanic Southwest: A Social and Legal History, 1550–1850* (Tucson: University of Arizona Press, 1984) does not discuss law in the American Southwest either before or after 1850, its thorough analysis of the nature of Spanish water law makes it required reading. Also see Gordon R. Miller, "Shaping California Water Law, 1781–1928," *Southern California Quarterly* 55 (Spring 1973): 9–42; Douglas R. Littlefield, "Water Rights during the California Gold Rush: Conflicts over Economic Points of View," *Western Historical Quarterly* 14 (October 1983): 415–34; M. Catherine Miller, "Riparian Rights and the Control of Water in California, 1879–1928: The Relationship Between an Agricultural Enterprise and Legal Change," *Agricultural History* 59 (January 1985): 1–24; Norris Hundley, Jr., "The Dark and Bloody Ground of Indian Water Rights: Confusion Elevated to Principle," *Western Historical Quarterly* 9 (October 1978): 455–82, and "The 'Winters' Decision and Indian Water Rights: A Mystery Reexamined," *Western Historical Quarterly* 13 (January 1982): 17–42; and Donald J. Pisani, "Irrigation, Water Rights, and the Betrayal of Indian Allotment," *Environmental Review* 10 (Fall 1986): 157–76, "Water Law Reform in California, 1900–1913," *Agricultural History* 54 (April 1980): 295–317, and "Federal Reclamation and Water Rights in Nevada," *Agricultural History* 51 (July 1977): 540–58.

18. For a summary of Dunbar's major ideas, see his "The Adaptability of Water Law to the Aridity of the West," *Journal of the West* 24 (January 1985): 57–65.

19. Pisani, "Enterprise and Equity: A Critique of Western Water Law in the 19th Century," *Western Historical Quarterly* 18 (January 1987): 15–37.

20. Pisani, *From the Family Farm to Agribusiness: The Irrigation Crusade in*

California and the West, 1850–1931 (Berkeley: University of California Press, 1984).

21. Donald Worster, *Rivers of Empire: Water, Aridity, and the Growth of the American West* (New York: Pantheon Books, 1985).

22. Worster, *Dust Bowl: The Southern Plains in the 1930s* (New York: Oxford University Press, 1979).

23. Worster, *Rivers of Empire*, 4.

24. Worster, *Rivers of Empire*, 64.

25. Worster, *Rivers of Empire*, 4.

26. Richard L. Berkman and W. Kip Viscusi, *Damming the West* (New York: Grossman Publishers, 1973).

27. Marc Reisner, *Cadillac Desert: The American West and Its Disappearing Water* (New York: Viking Penguin, Inc., 1986), 504.

28. Worster, *Rivers of Empire*, 279.

29. For example, Reisner observes that "Westerners call what they have established out here a civilization, but it would be more accurate to call it a beachhead. And if history is any guide, the odds that we can sustain it would have to be regarded as low" (*Cadillac Desert*, 3. Also see pp. 5, 306, 499, 505).

30. Reisner, *Cadillac Desert*, 319.

31. Reisner, *Cadillac Desert*, 178.

32. Reisner, *Cadillac Desert*, 154. One other casualty of this interagency rivalry was the 160-acre limitation. It had been difficult to enforce in the first place, and many exceptions had been made, as in the Imperial Valley of California. But the fact that the corps, under the guise of flood control and navigation, could provide subsidized water with no strings attached made the bureau even more reluctant to enforce the provisions of the Reclamation Act of 1902. In 1982, Congress expanded the acreage limitation from 160 to 960 acres.

33. Reisner, *Cadillac Desert*, 259.

34. Reisner, *Cadillac Desert*, "The Peanut Farmer and the Pork Barrel," 317–43, especially 342.

35. By 1915, water companies not owned by water users irrigated only about 10 percent of the land in the West (Teele, *Irrigation in the United States*, 203–4, 206–7).

36. Teele, *Irrigation in the United States*, 185–87; Dunbar, *Forging New Rights in Western Waters*, 23–33; Maass and Anderson, . . . *and the Desert Shall Rejoice*, 188–96; C. S. Kinney, *A Treatise on the Law of Irrigation and Water Rights and the Arid Region Doctrine of Appropriation of Waters*, v. 3 (San Francisco: Bender-Moss Co., 1912), 2659–78; J. A. Alexander, *The Life of George Chaffey* (Melbourne, Australia: Macmillan and Co., Ltd., 1928), 51–52; Luther A. Ingersoll, *Ingersoll's Century Annals of San Bernardino County* (Los Angeles: L. A. Ingersoll Publishing Co., 1904), 227–28. Southern California spawned a variant of the mutual company, called by Robert Dunbar in *Forging New Rights in Western Waters* the "development corporation." It helped build San Bernardino, Pomona, Pasadena, and Redlands, among other communities. Promoters formed a land company and mutual water company simultaneously, then constructed a water system. They expected to profit from selling the land, not water. The land com-

pany granted shares in the water company without further charge, one share per acre. When all the land was sold, the settlers owned the water company (pp. 31–32).

37. Stockton (California) *Daily Independent*, April 2, 1872.

38. For a discussion of the origins of the federal-state conflict, see Pisani, "State vs. Nation: Federal Reclamation and Water Rights in the Progressive Era," *Pacific Historical Review* 51 (August 1982): 267–69.

39. Pisani, *From the Family Farm to Agribusiness*, 129–53.

40. Pisani, *From the Family Farm to Agribusiness*, 250–82.

41. Roy E. Huffman, *Irrigation Development and Public Water Policy* (New York: The Ronald Press, 1953), 75.

42. Pisani, *From the Family Farm to Agribusiness*, 266–67; Teele, *Irrigation in the United States*, 218.

43. William Ellsworth Smythe, "A Success of Two Centuries," *Out West* 22 (January 1905): 75; "The Reclamation Service," *Forestry and Irrigation* 11 (June 1905): 280; Francis G. Newlands to Secretary of the Interior, January 26, 1905, and Charles Walcott (letter prepared by A. P. Davis) to the Secretary of the Interior, June 3, 1905, Record Group 48, Records of the Department of Interior, "(1420–1904) Miscellaneous Projects: State Irrigation Under National Control, F. G. Newlands," National Archives, Washington, D.C.

44. Frank Adams Oral History Transcript, Bancroft Library, University of California, Berkeley, 232–39; *Sixth Biennial Report of the Department of Engineering of the State of California, December 1, 1916 to November 30, 1918* (Sacramento: California State Printing Office, 1919), 74.

45. Wells A. Hutchins, "Irrigation District Operation and Finance," U.S. Department of Agriculture, *Bulletin No. 1177* (Washington: G.P.O., 1923), 31–32; Teele, "Land Reclamation Policies in the United States," U.S. Department of Argiculture, *Bulletin No. 1257* (Washington: G.P.O., 1924), 16–17. The arid states had many ways to encourage irrigation. For example, the state constitutions of Colorado and Utah prohibited the taxation of irrigation works owned by individual farmers or groups of farmers; only ditches, canals, and flumes that carried water for hire were taxed. Arizona exempted ditches from taxation by statute.

46. Hutchins, "Irrigation District Operation and Finance," 4, 5, 54.

47. *Ibid.*, chart on p. 4; Teele, "Land Reclamation Policies in the United States," 27.

48. Frank Adams, "Irrigation Development through Irrigation Districts," *Transactions of the American Society of Civil Engineers* 90 (June 1927): 773–90.

49. Pisani, *From the Family Farm to Agribusiness*, 390–92; *California Water Atlas*, 63 (chart).

50. For example, see Miller, "Shaping California Water Law, 1781–1928"; Norris Hundley, Jr., "Clio Nods: *Arizona v. California* and the Boulder Canyon Act: A Reassessment," *Western Historical Quarterly* 3 (January 1972): 17–51, "The Dark and Bloody Ground of Indian Water Rights: Confusion Elevated to Principle," and "The 'Winters' Decision and Indian Water Rights: A Mystery Reexamined"; Littlefield, "Water Rights during the California Gold Rush: Con-

flicts over Economic Points of View"; M. Catherine Miller, "Riparian Rights and the Control of Water in California, 1879–1928: The Relationship Between an Agricultural Enterprise and Legal Change"; Dunbar, "Pioneering Groundwater Legislation in the United States: Mortgages, Land Banks, and Institution-Building in New Mexico," *Pacific Historical Review* 37 (November 1978): 565–84, and "The Adaptability of Water Law to the Aridity of the West," *Journal of the West* 14 (January 1985): 57–65; Pisani, "Federal Reclamation and Water Rights in Nevada," "The Strange Death of the California-Nevada Compact: A Study in Interstate Water Negotiations," *Pacific Historical Review* 37 (November 1978): 637–58, and "Water Law Reform in California, 1900–1913," *Agricultural History* 54 (April 1980): 295–327.

51. "Report of the Governor of New Mexico," in *Report of the Secretary of the Interior for the Fiscal Year Ending June 30, 1889* (Washington: G.P.O., 1890), 457; *Report of the Special Committee of the United States Senate on the Irrigation and Reclamation of Arid Lands*, v. 3, pt. 4 (Washington: G.P.O., 1890), 89.

52. Elwood Mead, "An Unsolved Western Problem: The Division of the Waters of Interstate Streams," *Irrigation Age* 7 (July 1894): 12–15, and "Influence of State Boundaries on Water-Right Controversies," *Independent* 57 (December 8, 1904): 1300–1303; J. M. Wilson, "State and National Control of Water," *Irrigation Age* 14 (November 1899): 45–46; "Our Rapidly Growing Irrigation Areas," *Scientific American* 82 (March 3, 1900): 131.

53. U.S., *Statutes at Large* 32 (1902), 388.

54. *Kansas v. Colorado*, 206 U.S. 46 (1907).

55. F. H. Newell to T. A. Noble, April 13, 1904, file 110–E16, "Legislation: Irrigation Law; Water Codes, etc., Washington thru 1910," Records of the Bureau of Reclamation, RG 115, National Archives, Washington, D.C. The architect of the theory of "reserved" federal water rights was Morris Bien, chief legal officer of the Reclamation Service. See his February 6, 1904 "Memorandum Concerning the Origins of the Right of Appropriation of the Waters of the Public Domain," and "Informal Statement Concerning the Right of Appropriation of Water and Riparian Rights in the Arid Region" (1906) in file 762, "Legal Discussions—General," RG 115, National Archives; "Relation of Federal and State Laws to Irrigation," in *Official Proceedings of the Eleventh International Irrigation Congress, 1903* (Ogden, Utah: 1904), 397–402; and his paper bearing the same title in U.S. Geological Survey, *Water Supply and Irrigation Paper #93* (Washington, D.C.: G.P.O., 1904), 232–37.

56. John F. Truesdell to J. F. Richardson, May 15, 29, 1918, "Truckee River Water-Right Adjudication, 1918," Truckee-Carson Irrigation District Archives, Fallon, Nevada.

57. *Wyoming v. Colorado*, 259 U.S. 419 (1922).

58. Key Pittman speech at the Colorado River Conference of the Seven Colorado River Basin States held at Denver, Colorado, August 22 to September 2, 1927, Key Pittman Collection, Container 129, file "Boulder Dam, 1919–1926," Library of Congress, Washington, D.C.

59. In *United States v. Rio Grande Dam and Irrigation Company*, 174 U.S. 690 (1899), the court ruled that "in the absence of specific authority from Congress a

The Irrigation District and the Federal Relationship

State cannot by its legislation destroy the right of the United States, as the owner of lands bordering on a stream, to the continued flow of its waters; so far at least as may be necessary for the beneficial uses of the government property." In *Winters* v. *United States*, 207 U.S. 564 (1908), the court maintained that on Montana's Fort Belknap Indian reservation water had been reserved for the use of Indians apart from state laws. Both cases posed a dilemma for the Reclamation Service. The Rio Grande case clearly suggested that the federal government held some species of riparian rights to the waters of the public domain. This theory clashed with the idea that the federal government could dispose of water and land separately and that it had reserved the ownership of water even as title to the land passed to private parties. Many western states had followed California's lead and accepted both riparian and appropriative rights. Since the Reclamation Service opposed the assertion of riparian rights by the states, it could not easily use this argument on its own behalf. For statements of the Reclamation Service's view of water rights in the 1920s, see Ottamar Hamele, Chief Counsel for the Reclamation Bureau, "Federal Water Rights in the Colorado River," American Academy of Political and Social Science, *Annals* 135 (January 1928): 143–49, and his testimony before the House Committee on Irrigation and Reclamation re H. R. 2903, March 25, 1924, 68 Cong., 1 sess., 881–900; and Ethelbert Ward, special assistant to the U.S. Attorney General, "Memorandum: Federal Irrigation Water Rights," January 22, 1930, in the Wells Hutchins Collection, item #588, California Water Resources Archives, University of California, Berkeley.

60. *Oklahoma* v. *Atkinson*, 313 U.S. 508 (1941); *First Iowa Hydro-Electric Cooperative* v. *Federal Power Commission*, 328 U.S. 152 (1946).

61. Although Reclamation Bureau projects were most responsible for conflicts between the national government and states, many other federal agencies became involved, including the Geological Survey, Forest Service, and Park Service. The western states had no power to approve permits to use water on government lands, such as within national forests. Moreover, even in cases where state officials could issue permits, they could not guarantee the right to use water. Since federal agencies had withdrawn most of the likely storage and hydroelectric power sites in the West, water users often secured permits to irrigate only to find their "right" useless without control over the sites. This, added to the uncertainty of Indian water rights, the cloudy issue of who controlled interstate streams, and federal control over navigation, provided countless opportunities for friction.

62. Richard Lowitt, *The New Deal and the West* (Bloomington: Indiana University Press, 1984), 224.

63. The U.S. Senate's Select Committee on National Water Resources, in its "National Water Resources," S. Rep. 29, 87 Cong., 1 sess., 1961, p. 4, predicted that the West's use of water would double by 1980 and triple by 2000. Such statistics provided a powerful justification for unified federal control. Of course, national control was not necessarily "unified control." In 1955 there were twelve federal agencies responsible for flood control, nine for irrigation, seven for navigation improvements, nine for pollution control, ten for watershed improvement, fifteen for power generation, and thirteen for water supply (Clyde O. Martz, "The Role of the Federal Government in State Water Law," *Kansas Law Review* 5 [1957]: 628).

64. H. Doc. 475, 78 Cong., 2 sess., 1943; S. Doc. 191, 78 Cong., 2 sess., 1944; U.S., *Statutes at Large*, 68 (1944), 887.

65. Charles E. Corker, "Water Rights and Federalism—The Western Water Rights Settlement Bill of 1957," *California Law Review* 451 (1957): 616–17.

66. *United States v. Gerlach Live Stock Co.*, 339 U.S. 725 (1950). Also see *Ivanhoe Irrigation District v. McCracken*, 357 U.S. 275 (1958).

67. Stanley High, "Washington Tyranny: Another Case Study," *Reader's Digest* 59 (December 1951): 65–69; Ed Ainsworth and Cameron Shipp, "The Government's Big Grab," *Saturday Evening Post* 224 (January 5, 1952): 26–27, 55–56; Carl G. Mueller, Jr., "Federal Ownership of Inland Waters: The Fallbrook Case," *Texas Law Review* 31 (April 1953): 404–17.

68. U.S., *Statutes at Large*, 66 (1952), 560; W. Michael Kleppinger, "Determination of Federal Water Rights Pursuant to the McCarran Amendment: General Adjudications in Wyoming," *Land and Water Law Review* 12 (1977): 457–84.

69. *Federal Power Commission v. Oregon*, 349 U.S. 435, 447–48 (1955).

70. *Federal Power Commission v. Oregon*, 349 U.S. 435, 457 (1955).

71. The Supreme Court's water decisions had passed through several distinct phases. In the 1930s and 1940s, it had justified multiple-purpose projects largely through the commerce clause. Then, in the 1950 *Gerlach* case it argued that such projects could be justified under the general welfare clause as well. The Pelton case carried the process one step forward. The court had not discussed water rights per se, but, rather, implied that under the property clause the government had the power to do whatever it needed to maintain and improve government lands. Thus the court added much to the legal arsenal of federal agencies (Richard A. Hillhouse, "The Federal Reserved Water Doctrine—Application to the Problem of Water for Oil Shale Development," *Land and Water Law Review* 3 [1968]: 83).

72. Frank J. Trelease, "Federal Reserved Water Rights Since PLLRC [Public Land Law Review Commission]," *Denver Law Journal* 54 (1977): 475; Catherine L. Dirck, "Federal Reserved Rights and the Interstate Allocation of Water," *Land and Water Law Review* 13 (1978): 815.

73. Corker, "Water Rights and Federalism," 609–12; Frank J. Trelease, "Water Resources in the Public Lands PLLRC's Solution to the Reservation Doctrine," *Land and Water Law Review* 6 (1970): 89–107; Kleppinger, "Determination of Federal Water Rights Pursuant to the McCarran Amendment," 463; William H. Veeder, "The Pelton Decision," *Montana Law Review* 27 (Fall 1965): 40; James Munro, "The Pelton Decision: A New Riparianism?", *Oregon Law Review* 36 (April 1957): 222.

74. Corker, "Water Rights and Federalism," 606, 635–37; Sho Sato, "Water Resources—Comments Upon the Federal-State Relationship," *California Law Review* 48 (March 1960): 54–56; David R. Warner, "Federal Reserved Water Rights and Their Relationship to Appropriative Rights in the Western States," 11 Rocky Mountain Mineral Law Institute, *Proceedings, 1969* (New York: Matthew Bender, 1970), 415–16; B. Abbott Goldberg, "Interposition—Wild West Water Style," *Stanford Law Review* 17 (1964): 6–7.

75. U.S., *Statutes at Large*, 72 (1958), 297; 72 (1958), 563; 75 (1961), 204; 76 (1962), 1173; 79 (1965), 213.

76. *Arizona* v. *California*, 373 U.S. 546 (1963); Raphael J. Moses, "The Federal Reserved Rights Doctrine—From 1866 Through Eagle County," *Natural Resources Lawyer* 8 (1975): 221–35; Gary King, "Federal Non-Reserved Water Rights: Fact or Fiction," *Natural Resources Journal* 22 (1982): 424–25; Eva Hanna Hanks, "Peace West of the 98th Meridian—A Solution to Federal-State Conflicts Over Western Waters," *Rutgers Law Review* 23 (1968): 36; William H. Veeder, "Winters Doctrine Rights: Keystone of National Programs for Western Land and Water Conservation and Utilization," *Montana Law Review* 26 (1965): 152; Norris Hundley, "Clio Nods: *Arizona* v. *California* and the Boulder Canyon Act: A Reassessment," *Western Historical Quarterly* 3 (January 1972): 17–51.

77. *Arizona* v. *California*, 373 U.S. 546, 628 (1963).

78. Goldberg, "Interposition—Wild West Water Style," 35.

79. Eva Hanna Morreale, "Federal-State Conflicts over Western Waters—A Decade of Attempted 'Clarifying Legislation,'" *Rutgers Law Review* 20 (1966): 445.

80. For a good bibliography of recent writings on Indian water rights, see Hundley, "The 'Winters' Decision and Indian Water Rights: A Mystery Reexamined," and Francis Paul Prucha, *Indian-White Relations in the United States: A Bibliography of Works Published, 1975–1980* (Lincoln: University of Nebraska Press, 1982), 66–68.

81. David R. Warner, "Federal Reserved Water Rights and Their Relationship to Appropriative Rights in the Western States," 410–12.

82. *United States* v. *District Court for Eagle County*, 401 U.S. 520 (1971); *United States* v. *District Court for Water District No. 5*, 401 U.S. 527 (1971); Laurie B. Craig, "Limiting Federal Reserved Rights Through the State Courts," *Utah Law Review* 48 (1972): 48–59; Harold A. Ranquist, "The *Winters* Doctrine and How It Grew: Federal Reservation of Right to the Use of Water," *Brigham Young University Law Review* (1975): 697; John C. Guadnola, "Adjudication of Federal Reserved Water Rights," *University of Colorado Law Review* 42 (1970): 161–72; Frank J. Trelease, "Federal Reserved Water Rights Since PLLRC," *Denver Law Journal* 54 (1977): 487. The U.S. Supreme Court authorized state courts to adjudicate Indian reserved rights, continuing the policy established in the Eagle County case, in *Colorado River Water Conservation District* v. *United States*, 424 U.S. 800 (1976).

83. *Cappaert* v. *United States*, 426 U.S. 128 (1976); Walter Kiechel, Jr., and Martin Green, "Riparian Rights Revisited: Legal Basis for Federal Instream Flow Rights," *Natural Resources Journal* 16 (1976): 969–74; James Spitzenberger, "Expansion of the Reservation of Water Rights Doctrine," *Nebraska Law Review* 56 (1977): 410–21; John E. Masters, "Water and Water Courses—Limiting the Reservation Doctrine," *Land and Water Law Review* 13 (1978): 501–11; Ned Lawrence Bork, "The Application of Federal Reserved Rights to Groundwater in the Western States," *Creighton Law Review* 16 (1982–1983): 781–813.

84. *California* v. *United States*, 438 U.S. 645 (1978); Roderick Walston, "Reborn Federalism in Western Water Law: The New Melones Dam Decision," *Hastings Law Journal* 30 (1979): 1645–82; Bork, "The Application of Federal Reserved Water Rights to Groundwater in the Western States," 791.

85. *United States* v. *New Mexico*, 438 U.S. 696 (1978); Frank J. Trelease, "Uneasy Federalism—State Water Laws and National Water Uses," *Washington Law Review* 55 (1980): 758–59.

86. *Hughes* v. *Oklahoma*, 441 U.S. 322, 334 (1979); *Sporhase* v. *Nebraska*, 458 U.S. 941, 951 (1982).

87. Charles E. Corker, "Federal-State Relations in Water Rights Adjudication and Administration," Rocky Mountain Mineral Law Institute, *Proceedings, 1971* (New York: Matthew Bender, 1972), 579.

88. The doctrine of due diligence, which grew out of the mining and agricultural economy of the nineteenth century, required evidence of steady progress toward completion of water projects to retain and perfect titles. Private water users could not claim water for ultimate needs unless their dams, canals, and ditches could be completed within a few years. The rapid growth of such cities as Denver and Los Angeles was possible only after urban water needs were given primacy over rural needs, and after cities were allowed to "cold storage" water.

IV
Politics of the Twentieth-Century West

Invariably many of the issues concerning changes in population, the economy, or the environment entered into the political arena. Surprisingly, however, the history of politics in the twentieth-century West is still largely unwritten. The development of political parties in localities and the states, the political alignments of western representatives in Congress, or even needed biographies of political figures in the West after 1890 still await adequate treatment. Nor have western voting patterns been analyzed in depth, or the political motivation of voters in the region. In his pioneering essay Paul Kleppner addresses this latter issue to determine what is distinctive about voters in the West within the context of national political patterns. Focussing on another aspect of the political scene, William D. Rowley discusses what he considers as the distinctive tradition of political reform in the West that has differentiated the region's political style from those in other areas in the nation. Both of these essays contribute to fashioning a clearer image of political life in the twentieth-century West by emphasizing the fluid and transitory nature of its political institutions, in contrast to greater rigidity elsewhere.

10

Politics without Parties

THE WESTERN STATES, 1900–1984

Paul Kleppner

How did the political complexion of the West change in the twentieth century—in comparison to that of earlier periods? Historian Paul Kleppner addresses this central question in this suggestive essay based on an extensive investigation of electoral statistics, with the aid of computer analysis. Perhaps the most fundamental transformation, he suggests, was the increasingly conservative political posture of the region. This contrasts with the later nineteenth century when the West was more readily identified with radical politics, particularly Populism. Waves of new migrants to the West after 1890 and a changing economic structure altered the political outlook of the region, however, and led to the weakening of party loyalties. In comparison with older and more settled parts of the United States this came to be a distinguishing characteristic of western politics and became part of its image.

It might seem that any effort to probe the grassroots patterns of electoral behavior in the Mountain and Pacific states during the twentieth century should appropriately be titled "The Radical West Becomes Conservative." The West at the turn of the century was associated with unorthodox economic nostrums, Populist insurgency, and "radical" political ideas—like giving women the right to vote and allowing the electorate to legislate directly. But the West of the 1980s is popularly identified with conservative Republicanism, entrepreneurial capitalism, and "traditional" values. Thus, the radical-to-conservative theme might seem to capture the overarching change that has occurred in the region's electoral politics and political culture.

Political patterns are rarely as easy to fathom as they appear at first glance, however. And the behavior and values of western voters, no less than those of their counterparts elsewhere in the country, defy simple ideological categorization. Westerners have espoused some political innovations, but they have resisted others. They have denounced "big government" while simultaneously calling for massive federal involvement in their region's reclamation and power projects. Actions such as these, which most westerners would not see as being at all contradictory, do not fit neatly into ideological boxes. And explanations that focus mainly on ideological change will miss much of the variety and volatility that have always been a feature of the region's voting behavior. As a result, such explanations will overlook the very characteristics that are most revealing of the area's political culture.

This is not to say that the radical-to-conservative theme is wholly inaccurate or without merit. But the truth it reveals is only one part of a more complicated picture. My aim here is to put this truth into a more useful analytic context by bringing into focus the underlying dimensions of that larger and richer reality.

Patterns of Party Strength

Despite its popular association with insurgency and radical movements, the West has been rather reliably Republican for most of this century. The Republicans held the lead in 26, or 61.9 percent, of the 42 presidential and off-year congressional elections between 1900 and 1984.[1] With the exception of the three-way presidential contest in 1912, they enjoyed an unbroken string of successes between 1900 and 1916, when Woodrow Wilson carried all the western states except Oregon. But though 50.6 percent of the West's voters cast their ballots for Wilson, only 34.4 percent of them voted for Democratic congressional candidates. And after 1916, the Republicans reasserted their political dominance, carrying the region in every biennial contest between 1918 and 1930.

The Great Depression had the same sort of political impact in the West as it did in other parts of the country. The area swung sharply toward the Democrats, as Franklin Roosevelt carried all eleven western states in 1932 and 1936, ten in 1940, and nine in 1944. But the Democrats were not equally successful in elections for other offices, although they did win 73 percent of both the gubernatorial and U.S. Senate elections between 1932 and 1944, as well as 65.7 percent of the seats in the U.S. House of Representatives and 63.6 percent of the seats in the lower house of the legislatures of the western states.[2] But despite this impressive list of Democratic victories, the Republicans remained a viable competitive factor in

Politics without Parties

Table 10.1
Patterns of Partisan Strength, 1900–1984

	Democratic Percent of Vote				Partisan Lead[1]			
	West	Mntn	Pacific	North	West	Mntn	Pacific	North
1900–1916	36.9	42.5	32.7	36.5	−11.4	−3.7	−17.4	−14.2
1918–1930	22.6	40.1	17.7	36.7	−23.0	−13.3	−29.2	−17.7
1932–1944	52.0	57.3	49.6	50.9	15.6	15.9	15.3	4.0
1946–1966	46.2	48.8	45.2	49.7	−1.6	−1.9	−1.6	.7
1968–1984[2]	40.3	34.6	42.3	45.2	−13.8	−25.1	−9.8	−4.5
1970–1982[3]	52.3	48.8	53.5	54.4	6.5	−.6	9.0	13.1

[1] Democrat minus Republican percent of vote, so negative signs indicate Republican lead.
[2] Presidential contests only.
[3] Off-year congressional contests only.

most states, and a surprisingly successful one in California, Colorado, Oregon, and even Idaho.

After 1944 the partisan tide turned once more. The Republicans led in seven of the eleven biennial elections between 1946 and 1966, although neither party ran ahead for more than four successive contests. And after 1966 the presidential and off-year results diverged significantly, with the Republicans winning in presidential years and the Democrats in off years.

Summarized in table 10.1 are these patterns of partisan strength for the West as a whole and for its two major subparts, and it allows for comparisons by including similar data for the North—that is, the Midatlantic and New England states.[3] The data add point to the earlier description. Through the first three decades of this century, the Democrats were a weak minority in the West and in both of its geographic components, although they ran more competitive races in the Mountain states than in those bordering the Pacific. During the 1930s and early 1940s, they reached the majority level in the area as a whole, fell barely below that mark in the Pacific states, and throughout the region enjoyed a reasonably wide lead over the Republicans. But with the end of World War II, Democratic support declined and the Republicans rebounded, although neither party regularly commanded a comfortable lead. The same patterns of movement marked the region's presidential elections after 1966, while support for the Democrats in off years approximated the party's New Deal peak. Significantly, however, the Democrats owed their continuing success in off-year contests to growing strength in the Pacific states, the area in which they had been especially weak prior to the 1930s.

Sometimes data aggregated to the regional level mask significant varia-

Table 10.2
Partisan Leads at the State Level, 1900–1984[1]

	1900–16	1918–30	1932–44	1946–66	1968–84[2]	1970–82[3]
Arizona	22.2	23.1	38.0	1.3	−26.7	−3.9
Colorado	3.2	−17.0	7.7	−1.7	−20.2	−.7
Idaho	−15.2	−30.2	12.8	−5.1	−34.8	−15.3
Montana	−2.3	−9.3	20.4	1.6	−16.6	16.0
Nevada	−5.7	−2.0	28.0	6.8	−21.7	32.7
New Mexico	−7.0	−1.3	15.6	7.7	−15.5	3.8
Utah	−16.7	−13.9	22.4	−7.4	−38.2	−7.6
Wyoming	−18.8	−26.4	7.4	−9.7	−31.0	−12.3
California	−17.7	−27.7	15.3	−1.1	−10.2	6.3
Oregon	−20.0	−27.1	4.5	−4.7	−7.6	20.8
Washington	−24.5	−36.2	21.9	−1.8	−9.1	12.4

[1] Democrat minus Republican percent of vote, so negative signs indicate Republican lead.
[2] Presidential contests only.
[3] Off-year congressional contests only.

Politics without Parties

tions among states. To explore this possibility, table 10.2 presents summaries of the patterns of partisan strength at the state level for each of the eleven western states. These data indicate that the behavior of most western states followed the same general contours as the region. Prior to the 1930s, the Democrats were dominant only in Arizona, especially weak in the three Pacific states, and competitive in Nevada, New Mexico, and Montana. The political change that occurred during the 1930s revived Democratic fortunes, with the party soaring to double-digit leads in all but Colorado, Oregon, and Wyoming, and it remained competitive everywhere through the mid-1960s. Thereafter, wide differences between presidential and off-year leads occurred in all of the states, and in every case the Democrats ran better in off-year contests.

With minor exceptions, the West's levels of party support and patterns of partisan change parallel those in the North. Northern Republicans did not so greatly increase their lead during the 1920s, and their 1968–84 presidential margin was only about one-third the size of the western lead. But otherwise the data indicate that electoral politics in both areas reflected trends that were not regionally distinctive.

These comparative data do suggest a regional difference of considerable importance, however. While the patterns of party support in both the West and the North tended to move pretty much in tandem, the size of the swings in the West was generally larger than in the North. This difference was most noticeable under the politically convulsive conditions that marked the 1930s. Between 1928 and 1936, the North switched from a 13.3 percentage-point Republican lead to a 15.9 percentage-point Democratic margin, a total swing of 29.2 points. Yet as large and dramatic as this change was, it paled beside the West's 62.4 percentage-point swing over the same eight-year period. Even under more normal conditions, the West for most of the past century has displayed much greater volatility from one election to the next. From 1900 through 1956, for example, the change in partisan lead between successive presidential elections averaged 17 percentage points in the West, but it was only 10 percentage points in the North.[4] Occurring under politically placid conditions for the most part, swings of this size suggest that the responses of western voters were more susceptible to short-term influences than those of the northern electorate.

Partisan Instability

Large swings from one election to the next provide evidence of an electorate whose collective response is not securely anchored in ongoing partisan attachments. When partisan norms are widely accepted, voters do not usually switch their party choices between elections, and the collective results do not fluctuate a great deal. Under these conditions, there is little opportunity for the short-term factors associated with each election to influence the outcome, and past voting returns serve as good predictors of current election results. On the other hand, when the electorate is composed mainly of weak partisans and independents, the short-term factors have larger impact, and the voting results fluctuate greatly from one contest to the next.

For the larger part of the U.S. electoral past, we cannot directly measure the strength of individual partisan identifications. But since strong partisans are likely to support their party's nominees in successive elections, consistency in partisan choice serves as a good indicator of whether party norms guided individual behavior. And we can derive estimates of party-vote consistency from one election to the next by applying multiple regression procedures to county-level election data, with all the vote variables calculated as percentages of the eligible electorate at the second contest. The regression equations allow us to develop estimates representing the proportions of each party's supporters at the first election who voted for the same party at the second election, who switched their choice to another party, and who simply did not vote at the later contest. We can use this approach to measure party-vote consistency between successive presidential or biennial elections, and we can express the estimates as percentages of the total electorate simply by multiplying each by the appropriate party's proportionate turnout at the first election.[5] Table 10.3 summarizes the results of applying these procedures for successive pairs of presidential and biennial elections between 1876 and 1984.

The regional contrast is sharp for most of the periods displayed. Regardless of which series we examine, through the 1960/1964 pair of presidential elections (or the 1962/1964 pair of biennial elections), western voters were considerably less likely than northerners to cast ballots for the same party's candidates at successive contests. The difference was largest on each series prior to 1900, and it narrowed after the turn of the century as partisanship among northerners began to weaken. During the 1930s through the mid-1960s, partisan behavior became more widespread in both areas, although the increases in the West were larger. As a result, the regional difference, while still evident, continued to narrow. This tendency toward regional convergence finally culminated during the 1960-to-1984 period. And when it did, it was northern behavior that had shown the greater change over time, as westerners were only slightly more likely than they had been in the late-nineteenth century to vote for the same party's candidates in two consecutive elections.

Party-vote consistency over a pair of elections may be thought of as only a minimal test of the diffusion and operation of party norms. What of the

Table 10.3
Estimates of Party-Vote Consistency[1]

	President to President		President to Off Year	
	West	North	West	North
1876–1900	40.8	69.3	37.0	58.3
1900–1932	37.3	55.9	29.8	42.3
1932–1944	55.3	61.9	34.5	47.6
1944–1964	55.2	59.5	40.5	50.5
1964–1984	47.6	46.9	37.0	36.0

[1] Entries are mean percentages of the electorate repeating the same partisan choice at successive elections.

longer term? Were voters who supported the same party in two contests likely to repeat that performance over a longer series of elections? While we cannot answer this question directly with aggregate data, we can use a measure of the extent to which earlier voting patterns explain current outcomes as a reasonable proxy. For this purpose, we need to construct an indicator of each party's baseline support, its normal vote, by calculating the mean of its percentage of the total vote in each county for the four biennial elections immediately preceding the current one. This measure of a party's normal vote covers a six-year period, it includes an equal number of presidential and off-year elections, and it cycles forward with each succeeding contest. If underlying party attachments shape vote choices, we would expect each party's normal vote to offer a good approximation of its current vote. The stronger the fit between these two, the more the current results can be said to be a product of long-term partisan behavior. We can measure the fit by calculating the simple correlation coefficient, with the square of that coefficient (r^2) indicating the percentage of the variance of the current distribution that can be accounted for by its normal vote—the measure of long-term partisan forces. The variance unexplained by the normal vote estimator ($1-r^2$) measures the impact of the short-term factors that operated at each election.[6] Table 10.4 presents the results of this normal vote analysis for the Democrats and Republicans in the North and the West for the relevant time periods, and it also includes the same measures for the late-nineteenth century to provide another point for comparison.

Once again, the contrasts between the two areas are sharp. Within each period and for both parties, the normal vote estimator explains a lower proportion of the variance of the current vote in the West than in the

Table 10.4
Normal Vote Analysis Means of (r^2) *and* $(1 - r^2)$

	Democrats				Republicans			
	West		North		West		North	
	r^2	$1 - r^2$	r^2	$1 - r^2$	r^2	$1 - r^2$	r^2	$1 - r^2$
1876–1900	.337	.663	.647	.353	.490	.510	.689	.311
1900–1930	.343	.657	.501	.499	.351	.649	.564	.436
1932–1944	.300	.700	.561	.439	.439	.561	.591	.409
1946–1966	.435	.565	.742	.258	.461	.539	.756	.244
1968–1984	.341	.659	.424	.576	.331	.669	.431	.569

North. Indeed, until the most recent period, the normal vote in the North routinely explained over half, and often over three-fifths, of the variance of the current returns. But the estimator did not account for that much during any period in the West, and it often left over three-fifths of the variance unexplained. Western election results, in other words, were clearly and consistently more susceptible to the operation of short-term forces than northern outcomes were. This finding offers strong inferential evidence that for most of this century the western electorate has contained much larger proportions of weak partisans and independents than its counterpart in the northern states.

It is also important to notice that the patterns for the two regions are quite similar during the most recent period. The normal vote estimator now routinely leaves about two-thirds of the variance of the Democratic vote and over half of the variance of the Republican vote unexplained in both areas. Notice, too, that this convergence has occurred because the northern electorate has changed: short-term factors now play larger roles in shaping its election outcomes than standing partisan identifications. In this respect, the current behavior of the northern electorate closely resembles the historical norm among westerners.

Strong partisans also tend to participate regularly, so that an electorate with a high proportion of committed party behavers tends to be a highly participant electorate. On the other hand, when party norms are weak and narrowly diffused, and when short-term forces play large roles in shaping the results, the electorate is likely to exhibit relatively low and erratic levels of mobilization.

Differences in the levels of mobilization reveal a great deal about citizens' orientations toward electoral politics, especially about their collective degree of psychological involvement. Generally, the stronger an individual's psychological commitment to electoral politics, the greater the

Politics without Parties

likelihood of participation. Using this relationship allows us to distinguish three types of voters. *Core* voters are those whose levels of involvement and interest do not change much in response to short-term forces and who can therefore be expected to vote in most elections. *Marginal* voters have lower levels of involvement, and the likelihood of their participating depends on the stimulus associated with current political events or candidates. Finally, the levels of psychological involvement are uniformly low among persistent *abstainers,* and they do not go to the polls even in high stimulus contests.[7]

Regression procedures applied to county-level voting data allow us to estimate the sizes of these components of the electorate. By regressing proportionate turnout (across the counties within each region) from one election on the same measure for an earlier election, we can derive estimates of the percentages of voters who case ballots at both, one, or neither of the two contests. And we can express these estimates as percentages of the eligible electorate by multiplying them by the known turnout at the first election.[8] We can develop these estimates by comparing successive presidential or biennial elections. In either case, core voters turned out at both elections being compared and abstainers sat out both. How marginal voters are defined operationally depends on which elections are compared. They participated at the first but not the second election if the comparison is between a presidential and an off-year contest, but participation at either of the pair is adequate if the comparison involves two consecutive presidential elections. Table 10.5 presents the results derived from applying these procedures and definitions to both types of election pairs.

In the late-nineteenth century and through the first third of the twentieth, the North's core electorate was larger than the West's. The difference was somewhat smaller after 1900, however, primarily due to an increase in the proportion of abstainers in the North. During the New Deal era, western states apparently experienced a reinvigoration of both partisanship and participation, as the region's core electorate increased in size, mainly at the expense of its marginal elements, and reached rough parity with its northern counterpart. Thereafter, the difference between the two areas has been relatively small. More significantly, during the post-1964 period, in both areas the size of the core electorate has declined and abstention has increased, producing a tendency toward a distinctly bimodal distribution in each region.

Taken together, the data in tables 10.3, 10.4, and 10.5 support two general observations. First, there is evidence of stronger partisan constraint in the North, especially prior to the 1930s. Second, on each of these series, the two areas tend to converge when viewed longitudinally, and it is a convergence that occurs on western terms, that is at the lower levels of

Table 10.5
Components of the Electorate[1]

	West			North		
	Core	Marginal	Abstain	Core	Marginal	Abstain
President to President						
1876–1900	55.3	22.3	22.2	78.6	4.1	17.1
1900–1932	50.6	21.5	27.6	62.5	8.0	29.1
1932–1944	61.6	9.6	27.0	62.4	11.8	25.7
1944–1964	63.4	6.2	30.1	65.2	6.1	28.5
1964–1984	56.1	7.4	36.3	55.7	6.1	38.2
President to Off Year						
1876–1898	52.9	21.0	24.4	66.9	15.5	17.4
1900–1930	46.8	18.0	34.9	51.6	18.1	28.8
1932–1942	57.8	10.8	31.1	53.4	17.9	28.5
1944–1962	58.4	7.1	34.2	54.3	14.1	31.4
1964–1982	52.9	6.0	41.0	48.1	11.0	40.7

[1] Entries are mean percentages of the electorate. For each region and sequence, rows sum to 100 percent except for rounding error.

partisanship and participation. In other words, over time, and especially since the mid-1960s, northern voters have begun to behave in the same ways that western citizens have for most of the past century.

Voting Support, 1900 to 1930

When partisanship is weak and short-term factors play important roles in determining voters' choices, we should not expect the coalitions of the major parties to exhibit a great deal of stability. Indeed, under these conditions, it becomes nearly a misnomer to refer to "standing" partisan coalitions, since so much voter movement occurs between elections. A group that displays a bias for one party's candidates at the first contest may switch its collective preference within two or four years, perhaps even showing a bias for the other major party at the second election. Movement of this sort can always be accounted for; however, the explanations must focus on factors unique to each election and each set of competing candidates. They must draw attention to what distinguished each contest from the others rather than to what was common to all of them.

For the most part, this summary aptly describes western political conditions during the first three decades of this century. Where less than half of an area's voters repeated their party-vote choices at two consecutive elections (see table 10.3), and where past voting patterns normally explained barely a third of the variance of the current results (see table 10.4), few social groups could have displayed any consistent partisan bias. Instead, significantly sized segments of most groups seem to have shifted their preferences in response to the particular stimuli associated with each election.

Multiple regression techniques allow us to describe the behavior of demographic groupings and indicators at each election. In this case, I executed three separate equations for each election: one using the Democratic proportion of the electorate as the dependent variable, a second using the corresponding Republican measure, and a third using the percentage of abstainers. The independent variables included nineteen economic, ethnic, and religious predictors, and additional control variables were included for urbanism, the decade's proportionate population change, and the prevailing voter registration requirements.[9] Total turnout at each election was also entered as a control variable except in those equations using abstention as a dependent variable. Each equation was weighted by the square root of the size of the voting age population at each election, and each set of three equations for each election was executed for counties within the West as a whole, for the Mountain and Pacific counties separately, and finally for the counties within each state individually.[10]

These operations produced a very large number of regression coefficients, and the search for patterns required developing and applying clear guidelines.[11] First, a demographic grouping was judged to have a partisan bias at an election when it showed a positive and statistically significant association with one major party, a statistically significant negative association with the other, and an indeterminate or statistically significant negative association with abstention. Only this pattern of coefficients warrants the inference that the group behaved cohesively in responding to its political environment. And this type of cohesive behavior is a minimal requirement for any argument that norms deriving from the group's shared culture and experiences shaped its collective choice.[12]

Second, for how many elections must a group display the same partisan bias to support the conclusion that a consistent pattern of partisanship existed? There is no simple and unassailable answer to this question. But it does not seem unreasonable to expect a group to show the same bias in five consecutive biennial contests, or at least in five of six such elections. These sequences span only ten or twelve years, roughly a third of the longer period under examination, and thus might be seen as a reasonable but minimal criterion.

Fortunately, the operational definition of "consistent pattern" turns out not to be of much practical importance. Whether examined within regional or state contexts, no group displayed the same partisan bias for more than four consecutive biennial elections, and most failed to do so across as many as three contests. The data in table 10.6 *illustrate* how unstable the regression coefficients were.[13]

William Jennings Bryan was the Democratic candidate for president in both 1900 and 1908; and, given his earlier association with Populism and his electoral success in the region in 1896, one might have expected most groups of westerners to have responded cohesively and positively to his later candidacies. Or, if the circumstances surrounding the 1896 election were unique, one might at least have expected most western voters to have responded to Bryan in 1908 as they had in 1900.[14] The data do not support either expectation, but instead point to great instability in the social group bases of voting support.

Only the Irish escape that generalization, showing a pro-Democratic bias in both years.[15] The Episcopalians are at the other extreme, displaying a strong Republican bias in 1900 and a Democratic tilt eight years later. However, the other four ethnic and religious categories simply did not react as groups in either 1900 or 1908. But while each shows no partisan bias at either election, the size and even the direction of their coefficients changed considerably over the eight-year interval.

Finally, notice the behavior of the two measures of economic prosperity or wealth. These are not proxies for groups, but indicators of the relative standing of counties on two statistically independent economic scales.[16] As a result, to interpret these coefficients we cannot simply search for a pattern that gives evidence of group cohesiveness or partisan bias. Instead, we must examine each separately, remembering that a negative association between these measures and any of the dependent variables indicates that the percentage of the latter increased as economic status (or farm wealth) decreased.

With the exception of the unexpectedly positive association between Democratic voting and economic status in 1900, the coefficients generally sustain the observation that Democratic support was higher in counties with lower levels of economic status and farm wealth. But abstention was also higher in the same places; and, as the economic measures decreased, the rate of increase in nonvoting outpaced the growth in Democratic support. In other words, the coefficients for these elections, as well as those from the much longer time series, suggest that while Democrats had noticeable appeal in the poorer counties, they were not very successful in mobilizing this constituency.

It is not especially surprising that Democratic candidates continued to have some appeal in economically weaker areas. The party's aura was still strongly colored by its fusion with the Populists during the turbulent 1890s, and an identification with anticorporate, redistributive policies

Table 10.6
The Social Instability of Partisan Choice: The West, 1900 and 1908[1]

	1900			1908		
	Democrat	Republican	Abstain	Democrat	Republican	Abstain
Catholic	.17	−.03	.13	.00	−.05	.25
Episcopal	−.19	.88	−.43	.42	−.20	−1.31
Methodist	.29	.15	−.36	−.62	−.15	.53
German	−1.53	.79	1.26	.26	.29	1.14
Irish	.25	−.45	−.59	.40	−.84	−1.99
Native stock	−.27	.07	.29	−.01	.16	.25
Economic status	1.09	−.44	−2.24	−.51	−.06	−1.57
Farm wealth	−1.03	.99	−1.37	−.71	−.05	−2.62

[1] Entries are unstandardized partial regression coefficients controlled for the effects of the other variables and the following: Baptist, Congregationalist, Lutheran, Presbyterian, Unaffiliated, Black, Norwegian, Swedish, population change, percent urban, registration requirements, and total turnout. Coefficients *not significant* at .001 are italicized.

was one lingering consequence of that association. But the Democrats were unable to transform this latent appeal into active and consistent voting support among lower income voters. In part, this failure resulted from ongoing factional struggles that prevented the party from developing a clear image and coherent program capable of tapping this source of discontent and translating it into an active and partisan commitment. These factional battles, in turn, often reflected differences in outlooks and values between the old-line and economically conservative Democratic leaders and the newly recruited "Popocrats" who sought to reshape the party's image and reorient its programs.[17]

Unable to resolve their internal conflicts and to develop and solidify an economically distinctive voting coalition, Democrats in most of the western states lapsed into the condition of a forlorn minority. As a result, the interests of lower-income voters remained for the most part unarticulated, unmobilized, and consequently unrepresented in the political systems of the states within the region. What emerged in most of these states was a dominant one-party system, in which the hegemonic Republicans depended for their success on a combination of high turnout in the economically better-off counties and high abstention in those areas at the other end of the economic scales.[18]

When this combination broke down, as it did in 1912 and again in 1916, the electoral success of the Republicans was jeopardized. Since these two elections, along with 1924, show that an economically based coalition was potentially mobilizeable, they merit a closer look.

The circumstances surrounding the 1912 election were certainly unusual. Conflict among the Republican party's national leaders led eventually to the formation of a separate party and the nomination of a former Republican president, Theodore Roosevelt, as its candidate for the presidency. In the ensuing three-way contest, Roosevelt's past Republican credentials were as important in garnering votes as his Progressive campaign rhetoric. The bulk of his voting support, in most states, came from the ranks of those who had cast Republican ballots in 1908. This sharp split in the Republican support base opened the way for a Democratic victory, even though Wilson polled a lower percentage of the national vote (and of the electorate) than Bryan had in any of his three unsuccessful efforts.[19]

What happened in the West represented only a minor variation on this national theme (table 10.7).

Roosevelt's popular appeal was uneven, cutting more sharply into the Republican base in the Pacific states and into the Democratic coalition in the Mountain states. However, in both areas, he outpolled Wilson and William Howard Taft among those who had abstained in 1908 and among those who only became eligible to vote between then and 1912.[20]

Table 10.7
*Political Origins and Destinations
of 1912 and 1924 Progressive Voters*[1]

	Democrat	Republican	Abstain	New Voter
1908 to 1912 Progressive[2]				
Mountain	20	15	6	25
Pacific	13	18	5	25
1912 Progressive to 1916[3]				
Mountain	38	53	9	NA
Pacific	12	60	28	NA
1920 to 1924 Progressive[2]				
Mountain	29	9	10	14
Pacific	41	2	11	10
1924 Progressive to 1928[3]				
Mountain	47	28	22	NA
Pacific	39	19	14	NA

[1] All entries are weighted means of regression estimates calculated for each state.
[2] Entries are percentages of the itemized category voting Progressive in 1912 or 1924.
[3] Entries are percentages of the Progressive voters selecting each itemized option in 1916 or 1920.

But even these levels of voter recruitment were not enough to give the former president a regional victory. While Roosevelt polled a third of the region's total vote, running 4 percentage points behind Wilson, he carried only two western states, California (with 42.1 percent) and Washington (with 35.2 percent). Wilson, without receiving a majority anywhere, carried eight western states, including Oregon and all the Mountain states except Utah, in which he ran second behind the victorious Taft. This successful effort by the Democratic nominee derived from holding the support of nearly two-thirds of those who had voted for Bryan in 1908, while attracting 8 percent of the abstainers and 18 percent of the newly eligible voters.[21]

Four years later in 1916, Wilson polled a majority in nine of the western states, scored a plurality victory in California (with 46.6 percent), and lost only Oregon (with 45.9 percent). In both major subparts of the West, he constructed his reelection victory by retaining the loyalty of about 80 percent of his 1912 voters, while attracting over a quarter of Taft's supporters and of the newly eligible voters. Most Progressive party voters cast Republican ballots in 1916, but Wilson attracted support from a reasonable proportion, especially in the Mountain states where over a third of Roosevelt's supporters voted to reelect a Democratic president. And while he polled a considerably smaller share in the Pacific states, Wilson could not have carried California without the 16 percent support he received from citizens who had cast ballots for Roosevelt four years earlier.

These patterns of voter movement are important in themselves, but the economic dimension underlying them is even more significant. It is plausible that Theodore Roosevelt's candidacy worked to mobilize lower income voters. This inference follows from the fact that his proportionate voting strength increased as indicators of economic status and farm wealth decreased (table 10.8), while abstention in 1912 (unlike 1908) showed only a statistically indeterminate association with the same measures. By 1916 recruitment from the Progressive ranks combined with new mobilization to give the Democratic voting base a distinct economic tilt. In that year abstention again failed to show a steep negative association with these economic indices, and the Democrats' share of the electorate looked economically more like Roosevelt's support in 1912 than like Wilson's in that year or even like Bryan's in 1908.

But Wilson's was a personal, not a party, coalition, and the Democrats were unable to sustain it beyond 1916. Indeed, it was during the 1920s that the Democrats hit their low point in most of the western states. Their voting clientele contracted even further, and the party's leaders devoted as much, or more, energy to fighting each other as they did to battling the Republicans. However, Democratic prospects in the West, and elsewhere, seemed to brighten in 1924, when the Republicans had to contend with yet another open schism.

But Senator Robert M. LaFollette, who headed the Progressive party's ticket in 1924, was not the energetic, charismatic Theodore Roosevelt. Besides, by 1924 the Republican lead was so wide in many states that the party could have won even if a large slice of its support base had defected to the new party of protest. In reality, however, that did not occur in the western states. There LaFollette's candidacy attracted a higher percentage of 1920 Democratic than Republican voters. And with LaFollette's fracturing the already small Democratic coalition, Calvin Coolidge not only carried all eleven western states, but John W. Davis ran second in only four of them—Arizona, Colorado, New Mexico, and Utah.[22]

In one important respect, however, Roosevelt's and LaFollette's efforts had similar results. Each ran best in counties of low economic status and farm wealth, and when they did the usually steep negative association between these measures and abstention dropped to an indeterminate one (table 10.8). In other words, both Progressive candidacies seem to have tapped and activated support among comparatively poorer groups. In 1916 Wilson was able to recruit enough of this already mobilized support base to enable him to carry the region and, not coincidentally, to be reelected. The Democratic standard bearer in 1928, Alfred E. Smith,

Table 10.8
Mobilizing an Economic Coalition in the West[1]

	Democrat		Progressive	Abstain	
	1912	1916	1912	1912	1916
Economic status	.42	−.70	−.77	−.18	−.07
Farm wealth	.16	−1.29	−.80	−.37	−.18
	1924	1928	1924	1924	1928
Economic status	.50	.53	−.52	−.13	−1.06
Farm wealth	*−.31*	*.10*	−.68	*.28*	−.81

[1] Entries are unstandardized partial regression coefficients, and see Table 10.6 for the list of control variables. Coefficients *not significant* at .001 are italicized.

apparently lacked Wilson's appeal: the economic character of the Democratic voting support did not change much between 1924 and 1928, and in the latter year abstention reverted to its customarily inverse relationship with the economic indicators. Obviously, the Smith-Hoover contest in the West, as elsewhere, pivoted on issues and identifications other than economic ones.

This view of the 1912, 1916, and 1924 elections in the West does complement the earlier generalization. While voters in lower status areas of the West were comparatively unmobilized and consequently unrepresented, these elections show that they were mobilizeable. Their turnout increased when candidates like Roosevelt, LaFollette, and even Wilson in 1916, articulated themes that appealed to their interests. But what resulted from these efforts were personal coalitions, ones that did not even extend to other offices at the same election, and neither major party was able, or perhaps even willing, to build an electoral base through sustained appeals to these economic groups.

Finally, it is important to emphasize that weak partisanship was the basic reason why the voting choices of social groups in the West fluctuated so much from one election to the next. The failure to sustain an economic cleavage at the electoral level, despite the fact that it appears to have been mobilizeable, can be attributed to the same factor.

In turn, partisan norms were weak in most western states because political parties there were underdeveloped. In some cases, the experiences of lengthy territorial periods worked to retard party development while encouraging the spread of antipartisan sentiments. And the political tumult of the 1890s further undermined partisanship, encouraging cross-party movement among leaders as well as among the mass electorate. As a result, most western states faced the new century with incompletely institutionalized political parties, entities incapable of performing the functions usually attributed to mature political organizations. That is, most western states lacked effective institutions that enjoyed wide and habitual support and were capable of uniting activists, officeholders, and voters for common purposes through shared symbols and tangible programs. They lacked durable mechanisms to penetrate to the grassroots, aggregate mass interests, and then convert them into public policy.[23]

Parties that were themselves not fully developed proved incapable of accommodating to the rapidly changing conditions of western life. As new differences arose among groups over land-use and water-rights issues, for example, leaders of existing party formations were not able to manage this conflict—to bargain, compromise, and develop "a 'joint preference ordering' of organizational objectives." They could not channel new conflict in this way, and thus avoid rupturing the party's electoral base, because the involved groups simply did not value the party's goals highly enough to subordinate their competing demands for the sake of its electoral success. Since party leaders could neither avoid local conflict nor subordinate it to organizational goals, they were unable to design their acts, speeches, and postures to "take the roles of the publics whose support they need[ed]." Consequently, their behaviors and pronouncements failed to evoke common meaning among their party's potential supporters and, hence, failed to contribute to cementing the strong and durable bonds of psychological rapport among activists, officeholders, and voters that typically mark fully developed parties.[24]

The West's weakly institutionalized parties were also incapable of adjusting to the large-scale population migration that the region experienced after 1900, especially the influx of midwesterners during the 1910s and 1920s.[25] The arrival of these newcomers altered the population mixture, created new demands for action and services from government, and generated new economic and cultural tensions with other groups. However difficult the task, strongly entrenched parties would have weathered these demographic shocks. But political parties in most western states were simply too feeble, their hold on the electorate too shallow and shaky to allow them to integrate these new groups into their voting clienteles while also placating earlier supporters.

Thus, after the turn of the century, when reform groups stepped up their rhetorical assaults on the baleful influences of parties and partisanship, for the most part they were attacking infirm institutions. Far from being the all-controlling factors that the reformers depicted, the region's party organizations—even the Republicans in California—were porous and without diffuse support among the mass electorate. Strong parties could have repulsed the reformers' attacks, as they did in northern and midwestern states. But the outcome was different in the West, as reformers institutionalized their antiparty measures. The initiative and referendum, open primaries, and ballots that eliminated straight-ticket voting were parts of their arsenal. In California, antiparty reformers went even further: they eliminated party labels in county and local elections and allowed candidates for other offices to run in the primaries of more than one party. Each of these measures operated differently; but, in one way or another, all of them worked as they were intended—to weaken parties and partisanship even further.

Voting Support, 1932 to 1984

The Great Depression of the 1930s ended Republican hegemony in the West. From 1932 through 1944, the Democrats enjoyed a lead in the region as a whole and in every one of its states (tables 10.1 and 10.2). Democratic candidates also carried just under three quarters of the region's gubernatorial and Senate elections, and the party won a majority in the lower houses of the state legislatures in every year except 1942.

But this was hardly a case of the Democrats quickly becoming the area's new hegemonic party. In fact, it was not even a case of a *party* triumph. In presidential years, Franklin Roosevelt ran considerably ahead of Democratic congressional and state candidates. His lead in the region averaged 20.1 percentage points in his four races, while in the same years the Democratic congressional vote was only 9 points greater than Republican support. And in the intervening off-year elections, Democratic candidates collectively led their Republican opponents by only 5 percentage points. By 1946 the Democratic lead in the region had evaporated, as Republican candidates outpolled their major opposition by 8.5 percentage points. Two years later, the Republicans again won the congressional vote (by 2.3 percentage points), while Harry Truman captured the region's presidential vote, running 3.1 percentage points ahead of Thomas E. Dewey.[26]

Roosevelt's electoral success in the region reflected his ability to hold on to most of his party's earlier voters while attracting new support from Republicans, abstainers, and coming-of-age voters (table 10.9). In 1932 Roosevelt's appeal to old-line Democrats was stronger in the Mountain states than in the Pacific region, but in both areas he attracted about a quarter of those who had voted Republican or who had abstained in 1928. He also mobilized about a third of the coming-of-age voters in both areas.[27]

Four years later, FDR scored an even larger triumph in the West, polling 66 percent of the region's vote and running 34.3 percentage points ahead of his Republican opponent. He forged this landslide by retaining the

Table 10.9
Forging the Roosevelt Coalition[1]

	Democrat	Republican	Abstain	New Voter
1928 to 1932 Democrat[2]				
Mountain	93	24	24	30
Pacific	72	25	25	35
1932 to 1936 Democrat[2]				
Mountain	77	9	25	31
Pacific	80	13	22	39
1936 to 1940 Democrat[2]				
Mountain	87	0	28	17
Pacific	80	0	11	43
1940 to 1944 Democrat[2]				
Mountain	81	1	9	29
Pacific	86	0	0	36

[1] All entries are weighted means of regression estimates calculated for each state.
[2] Entries are percentages of the itemized category voting Democrat for president in 1932, 1936, 1940, or 1944.

support of over three-quarters of his 1932 voters, while adding about a quarter of that year's abstainers and a third of the new voters.[28]

This surge in voting support for FDR had a sizeable spillover affect that aided other Democratic candidates, thus helping to alter the region's competitive balance. But the Democrats were not immediately able to translate Roosevelt's personal popularity into a party coalition. Between 1932 and 1934, for example, about 12 percent of Roosevelt's voters switched to Republican congressional candidates and another 9 percent simply chose not to vote in the off-year election. And FDR's 1936 voters were no more loyal to his party: 8 percent of them cast Republican ballots in 1938, while 16 percent abstained.

Roosevelt again carried the West in 1940 and 1944, although his leads were considerably smaller than they had been in 1932 and 1936. In his final two races, FDR attracted virtually no crossover support from previous Republican voters, and even his appeal to abstainers waned by 1944. His victories in the region depended on mobilizing over 80 percent of his previous supporters, while continuing to outpoll his Republican opponents among new voters.[29]

While the political sources of Roosevelt's personal support remained pretty stable after 1936, that was not the case for the Democratic party. Only about half of those who voted for FDR's reelection in 1940 and 1944 cast Democratic ballots in the 1942 or 1946 congressional elections, and about a third of them opted not to vote at all in these off-year contests. As a result, the fortunes of the party's other candidates continued to lag behind that of its presidential nominee. For example, even though his support had fallen off a bit by 1944, Roosevelt still enjoyed a comfortable 11-point margin in the West, while his party's congressional candidates collectively led their combined Republican opposition by only 1.7 points, about the same margin they had polled in the 1942 congressional elections.

Since Roosevelt ran considerably ahead of his party's other candidates in the western states, we might reasonably expect to find that the social profile of his support was distinctive. We can test this likelihood by executing the same regression models for presidential support and congressional voting in off years. By comparing the regression coefficients across models, we will be able to determine whether, and along what dimensions, FDR mobilized a distinctive coalition.[30]

The president's voting coalition and the one his party's congressional candidates mobilized were quite similar in terms of their ethnic, religious, and locational characteristics.[31] Personal voter registration requirements did work to depress Democratic turnout by about 2.4 percentage points more in presidential than in off years, but this difference was not the most arresting contrast between the two sets of regression coefficients.[32] The major difference lay in the nature of the associations between voting support and the indices of economic prosperity (table 10.10).

The exact numbers differ slightly from one subarea of the West to the other, but the larger pattern is the same in both. In presidential years, Democratic turnout associated in a steeply inverse fashion with both measures of economic standing, and the economic indices associated in a statistically indeterminate way with abstention. This pattern of associations indicates that Democratic voting increased rather steeply as the economic standing of counties decreased. In off years, however, the pattern of associations is quite different: abstention increased at a sharper rate than the Democratic percentage as economic standing declined. In other words, Roosevelt seems to have been able to tap and mobilize voting support in poorer areas, but it was in exactly these same places that nonvoting increased and support for Democratic candidates declined in off-year contests. The presence of FDR at the top of the ticket apparently stimulated voters in low income areas to participate and to cast Democratic ballots, but sizeable proportions of the voters in these counties were unwilling to turn out for Democratic candidates in lower stimulus contests.

Party-cued behavior did increase somewhat in the West during the 1930s, of course; but the scope and depth of this revival were distinctly limited. Westerners' long-standing antipathy to identifying with parties or

Table 10.10
The Economic Base of Voting Support, 1932–1944

	1932–44 President			1930–42 Off Year		
	Democrat	Republican	Abstain	Democrat	Republican	Abstain
Mountain						
Economic status	-.69	.70	*-.02*	-.49	.93	-1.68
Farm wealth	-.65	*-.18*	*.13*	*-.12*	*.27*	-1.01
Pacific						
Economic status	-.50	.39	*.00*	-.68	*.17*	-1.40
Farm wealth	-.37	*.13*	*-.10*	*-.03*	*-.16*	-1.27

[1]Entries are unstandardized partial regression coefficients, and see Table 10.6 for the list of control variables. Coefficients *not significant* at .001 are italicized.

behaving like party loyalists partially explains this result. But there is still something of a paradox here, since westerners seemed especially supportive of the types of governmental solutions to issues of public concern that Democratic platforms and candidates usually espoused. More so than northerners, for example, they favored an activist government involving itself in the economy to regulate corporations, especially banks, insurance companies, railroads, and utilities. Indeed, small pluralities of westerners favored *public ownership* of banks and railroads, and 68 percent of the western populace favored government ownership of the electric power industry.[33] But Democratic party builders were not uniformly able to tap these sentiments and link them with FDR's popularity to develop and sustain a stable and winning electoral coalition.

Sharp economic downturns produce strong popular reactions against the political party in power, but they do not automatically create electoral majorities for the opposition. Accomplishing that requires that the party out of power identify itself with and mobilize a sufficient number of discontented voters. The Democrats in the 1930s achieved this goal in a few western states but not in others, so that the voting results for the region as a whole, or even for either of its subareas, failed to show the emergence of a new majority party. We can better understand this outcome, and the process of party redevelopment that occurred during the 1930s, by looking more closely at two states that represent opposite ends of the continuum—the neighboring states of Oregon and Washington in the Pacific Northwest.

From the turn of the century at least, these states had similar political histories. The Republicans were the dominant party in both, enjoying a slightly larger lead in Washington than in Oregon (see table 10.2). And in both states, the Democrats were weak, factionalized, and reduced to preaching the gospel of nonpartisanship in an effort to win elections.

Democratic candidates did win some contests in these states prior to the 1930s, but these were not party victories. Their successful candidates deemphasized their party connections during their campaigns, concentrating their rhetoric instead on economy and efficiency. And in office they behaved as nonpartisans, making no effort to strengthen the party organization or even to extend their personal popularity to other Democratic aspirants.[34]

The Democrats were especially forlorn and factionalized in both states during the 1920s. Oregon's Democrats battled each other over social and moral issues—prohibition, nativism, and religious fundamentalism—while the Republicans dominated the state's elections. Prohibition, labor conflicts, and battles among strong personalities for control over the party, all combined in Washington to reduce the Democrats to third-party status, behind the Farmer-Labor party. In both states, as one friendly commentator observed of Oregon's Democrats: "There exists no party, only the name, and the various factions are far enough apart to even spurn the label rather than unite."[35]

The depression and FDR's candidacies created a new and more favorable context for Democratic state organizations throughout the West. Washington's Democrats seized these new opportunities, identified their party and its candidates with the popular national administration, and began the difficult and slow task of building a party coalition. Oregon's Democrats, on the other hand, essentially repudiated their party's national leadership, losing their chance to develop majority support in the process.

The issue of hydroelectric power played the central role in producing this outcome in each state. For several decades, citizens and interest groups had agreed that the area needed to develop more hydroelectric power. They also agreed on the need for public funds—particularly federal money—to support these capital-intensive projects. And there was even agreement on the need for "cheap power." But beyond this general slogan, the consensus broke down. Determining *for whom*—that is, for which groups—the newly developed hydroelectric power should be cheap produced sharp and durable social cleavages.

Since the turn of the century, the Grange had led the movements for public power in both states, and each State Federation of Labor had joined these efforts early in the new century. These groups and their civic and political allies aimed at delivering "cheap power"—i.e., providing electricity at cost—to consumers. Opposition to this public power movement was led by private utility companies, urban chambers of commerce, and manufacturing interests. These groups were primarily concerned with developing and delivering "cheap power" for industrial purposes.

The agitation for public power became heated during the 1920s. High charges levied by the private power companies to extend their service lines into rural areas was one source of this growing public animosity. And the high rates that the private companies charged for the use of electric power was another. As more farms and homes came to use electricity, and as they came to depend upon it more to run equipment and appliances, the size of this aggrieved clientele increased.[36]

In Washington, Homer T. Bone, a Farmer-Labor representative in the state legislature, took advantage of the growing antagonism toward the private power companies to qualify an initiative for the 1924 general election. Bone's measure, which authorized the creation of public utility districts, reflected his views that power could be provided less expensively, that alternative sources should be established when private companies refused to extend service, and that public utilities could provide a "yardstick" against which to judge the service rates charged by private companies. Bone and his public-power allies, however, failed to allay the concerns of rural voters who feared domination by Seattle, Tacoma, and Spokane, urban centers with resources to establish extensive power systems. As a result, only 39 percent of the voters supported the initiative and it failed to pass.[37]

The publicity surrounding the 1929 Federal Trade Commission investigation of the utility industry, which showed extensive use of unethical practices to promote the companies and influence legislation, likely contributed to a shift in public opinion. And the depression, which reduced employment and income, probably made electricity users more aware of and hostile to the level of their utility costs. In any case, in 1930 the voters in both Washington and Oregon approved public-utility-district initiatives similar to the rejected 1924 measure.[38]

The terms and partisan consequences of the battle over public power changed with Roosevelt's election in 1932. Campaigning in the Pacific Northwest in that year, FDR committed himself to supporting an extensive Columbia River hydroelectric development proposal, and within a year the Public Works Administration began construction of the Bonneville and Grand Coulee Dams. The Granges and Federations of Labor in both states then began supporting a Columbia Valley Authority to provide for integrated development and administration of these projects and to guarantee federal distribution of power from the dams. Private power companies and their allies also supported federal development of the Columbia River Valley, but they opposed integrated development and favored assigning distinct activities to the jurisdictions of the Corps of Engineers and the Bureau of Reclamation.[39]

Washington's Democratic leaders consciously took advantage of these events and used the public power issue both to unite their party and to solidify its support base among the electorate. The data in table 10.11 chart the critical stages of this process.[40]

There was no relationship between partisan support and voting on the 1924 public-utility-district initiative. While the Democratic state convention had endorsed the measure, the party's candidates generally distanced themselves from the issue, and majorities of both parties voted against it. The initiative's smashing defeat did nothing to encourage Democrats to champion the cause of public power, and in 1930 the party's state platform concentrated on prohibition and avoided any reference to that year's initiative on the public-utility-district question. Support for public power in 1930 cut across party lines, as majorities of both parties' voters cast their ballots for it.[41]

After the passage of the 1930 initiative, leaders of the public-power

Table 10.11
Partisan Support for Public Utility Initiatives in Washington[1]

	Yes	No	Abstain
1924: Establish Public Utility Districts			
Democrat 1924	0	76	24
Republican 1924	30	54	16
1930: Establish Public Utility Districts			
Democrat 1930	50	27	23
Republican 1930	53	36	10
1940: Restrict Bond Sales by Public Utility Districts			
Democrat 1940	28	65	7
Republican 1940	55	45	0

[1] Entries are percentages of partisan voters for Congress choosing each itemized option.

wing of the Democratic party saw their opportunity. They used the summer months of 1931 to encourage the formation of grassroots Democratic Clubs throughout the state. These became the bases for the following year's pro-Roosevelt movement, which culminated in FDR's endorsement by the state convention in February. More importantly, the clubs worked to recruit advocates of public power as candidates for the 1932 state elections. As a result, the Democratic primary in that year involved a series of "lively contests between old and new Democrats." The most significant of these was the contest for the U.S. Senate nomination, which pitted Bone, the former Farmer-Labor reform leader, against Stephen F. Chadwick, a founder of the Washington state American Legion and the most visible leader of the party's conservative faction.[42]

Bone's movement into the Democratic party was itself a signal of how much that party had changed. And his contest with Chadwick made clear the issue distance between the "old" and "new" Democrats. Indeed, Chadwick, who lost the primary by over 51,000 votes, recognized the irreconcilable difference between his Jeffersonian outlook and Bone's commitment to an active and interventionist government. Refusing to endorse Bone's candidacy, Chadwick explained that:

> The successful Senatorial nominee of the Democratic party—is not a Democrat—his philosophy is not that of the Democracy. He does represent however a majority of the 37,000 radical unemployed of this state. What is to become of our institutions if men the caliber of Bone are permitted to enter Congress.[43]

The Bone-Chadwick primary in 1932 did not entirely extinguish conservative opposition to a redeveloped—and distinctly liberal—Democratic party. And not all of the candidates elected on the Democratic ballot in 1932 shared Bone's enthusiasm for public power. But the Roosevelt administration's later actions to encourage the development of public power, vocal support for its decisions by the state's most prominent Democrats, and opposition to them by Republicans, all combined to give Washington's Democrats an image of commitment to public power.

That image became even sharper during the 1940 campaign. The private power companies qualified an initiative for that year's ballot to require voters' approval for any bonds issued by public utility districts.[44] In this way, the "Let the People Vote League," which directed the initiative campaign, hoped to cripple the PUDs, since they could not operate without issuing revenue bonds. The Grange, the Washington State Federation of Labor, and the Public Utility Commissioners Association battled successfully to defeat the initiative, and so did the state's leading Democrats. Senator Bone was especially active, using his frank to distribute over 100,000 reprints from the *Congressional Record*. And in October he persuaded the Federal Power Commission to hold hearings in Seattle on the political activities of the private power companies. Five heads of utility companies testified, admitting that they sponsored the initiative and financed the "Let the People Vote League."[45]

These activities simply capped a decade-long attempt by the Democrats to identify their party with public power, and the voting returns testify to the success of this effort (table 10.11). Unlike 1924 or 1930, there was a clear partisan split on the 1940 initiative, with nearly two thirds of the Democratic voters opposing the measure to curtail the operations of the PUDs and a clear majority of Republicans supporting it.

During the 1930s, then, Washington's Democrats used the public power issue to redevelop their party. In the process, many of its previous leaders became inactive or abandoned the party—for example, Chadwick was the Republican nominee for the U.S. Senate in 1940. But by rebuilding their organization at the grassroots and identifying their candidates with a popular issue, Washington's Democrats built a party coalition.

Events unfolded differently in Oregon. There the public power issue did not take on partisan connotations during the 1930s. Votes on public utility initiatives showed increased opposition to public power by Republican supporters (table 10.12); but while Democratic voters gave proportionately more support to public power, on each occasion pluralities of them voted for the positions of the private power companies.[46] Since neither major party acted as a spokesperson for public power, its advocates had to turn to an independent organization, the Oregon Commonwealth Federation, to pursue their interests.

Table 10.12
Partisan Support for Public Utility Initiatives in Oregon[1]

	Yes	No	Abstain
1930: Establish Public Utility Districts			
Democrat 1930	43	45	12
Republican 1930	30	47	22
1930: Allow State to Develop Water Power and Hydroelectric Energy			
Democrat 1934	34	43	22
Republican 1934	27	63	10
1936: Allow State to Purchase Electricity from and Secure Building of Transmission Lines by the United States			
Democrat 1936	32	47	21
Republican 1936	5	94	0

[1] Entries are percentages of partisan voters for Congress choosing each itemized option.

Oregon's Democrats did not use the public power issue to redefine and rebuild their party. Instead, the issue became a key source of party schism, as those in control of the party organization rejected the Roosevelt administration's public power program, and especially those aspects of it endorsed by the Grange and State Federation of Labor.

The leaders of Oregon's Democrats in the 1930s had hoped to develop a majority coalition of farmers and laborers. The state central committee called a series of party meetings between 1930 and 1932 to plan a precinct-by-precinct reorganization of the party and established Young Democratic Leagues with chapters in every county of the state. And through 1932 the party's leaders and candidates were united in identifying themselves with Roosevelt and with his proposal for federal development of Oregon's water resources.[47]

This unity weakened, however, once the PWA began construction of the Bonneville project. It collapsed entirely when the state Grange qualified a public power initiative for the 1934 general election. This initiative, to which the Portland Chamber of Commerce led the opposition, divided both major parties, and each nominated for governor an advocate of the position of the private power companies. With the advocates of public power supporting an independent candidate in the general election, the Democratic nominee, Charles H. Martin, won the three-way race.

Politics without Parties

A retired army general, Martin had entered politics only a few years earlier as a registered Republican. Even in 1930, although still a Republican, he won a write-in campaign as the Democratic nominee for Congress in Portland's third congressional district. Following a successful reelection bid in 1932, he announced for governor in 1934 at the urging of Oswald West, who was the Democratic party's dominant personality in the 1920s and a lobbyist for private utility companies.

As governor, Martin became a center of controversy and a public relations disaster for the Democratic party. At one point he commended the suggestion that the state's aged and feeble-minded wards should be chloroformed, claiming it would save the state $300,000 on the next biennial budget if 900 or so of them were "put out of their misery." On another occasion the governor said that the able-bodied unemployed should receive no public assistance: "The need for the necessities of life will force these people to get some kind of work and to care for themselves." And on still other occasions, Martin attacked the attempts by labor leaders to win union recognition, belittling them as "pestiferous peewees" and advising local police officers to "beat hell out of 'em."[48]

Apart from statements indicating a lack of compassion, Martin's repudiation of FDR's public power policy destroyed Democratic unity. Describing himself as a "Hoover Democrat," Martin opposed the proposal for a CVA and the position of the Grange and the State Federation of Labor on the primary use of power produced at Bonneville. Apparently following West's lead, Martin believed that "Bonneville should not be allowed to infringe upon the marauding principles of privately owned utilities."[49]

Martin's posture on the public power issue put him at odds with his party's leadership in the state legislature, where the public power wing of the party was in control, and the Democratic governor had to rely on Republican votes for support. But Martin's conservative allies still controlled the Democratic party organization. The ensuing and overlapping battles between the governor and the party's legislative leadership over public power and between conservatives and liberals for control over the Democratic party apparatus produced hopeless factionalism.

This ongoing conflict among Democratic leaders obscured the party's public image and prevented it from using the public power issue as the basis for redefining the axis of party conflict. Thus, Oregon's Democrats were not able to link their efforts to build a majority coalition of farmers and laborers into the organizational infrastructure of the Grange and State Federation of Labor, as their counterparts in Washington had done so successfully. As a result, despite Roosevelt's personal popularity and a slow but steady increase in the proportion of registered voters calling themselves Democrats, the party was in such disarray by the early 1940s that one commentator advised his fellow Democrats to "fold the party up and call it a day."[50]

The political histories of Oregon and Washington diverged sharply after 1930 because their Democratic (and Republican) leaders reacted differently to the conditions created by the depression and New Deal. The two cases illustrate the important roles that local leaders play in building party organizations and defining the basis of partisan conflict. And they also draw attention to the importance of a state's earlier experiences. To build a party coalition in either state, Democratic leaders had to overcome a tradition of nonpartisanship. Leadership and ideological conflicts prevented them from doing so in Oregon. But even in Washington, where these problems were surmounted, the standing tradition still worked to dilute partisan sentiment, and the party coalition that emerged was less stable than its counterparts in most of the northern states.

While the depression ended Republican hegemony in the West, the Democrats' success was uneven and shortlived. World War II interrupted "politics as usual" and created a new economic and demographic environment for political activities. The war stimulated and diversified the economies of the western states, which in turn inaugurated migrations that changed their population compositions. Even strong, well-entrenched parties would have had difficulty coping with the scope and pace of these developments, and parties in most of the western states remained distinctly underdeveloped. Consequently, the post–World War II years, and especially those since the early 1960s, witnessed a revival of the pre-depression trends toward even lower levels of partisan constraint and responsibility (see tables 10.3 and 10.4).[51]

As party linkages resumed their decay, westerners were even more likely than earlier to behave as nonpartisans. By the late 1970s, all of the relevant indicators had reached historic highs. Over a quarter of the West's voters routinely switched their party choices from one presidential contest to the next, and only a slightly smaller proportion of them (22 percent) reported casting votes at each election that were inconsistent with their declared party identifications. And while "only" 25 percent indicated splitting their tickets between presidential and congressional candidates in the same year, an astounding 55 percent reported a comparable split between federal and state or local candidates.[52]

This "onward march of party decomposition" has two especially visible consequences. First, the size of the change from one election to the next contest of the same type has increased markedly. The average (or mean) change in the partisan lead between presidential elections was 8.4 percentage points during the period from 1940 through 1960; but from 1960 through 1984, the average has nearly doubled to 16 percentage points.

While prior to 1960 a lead change of as much as 10 points was unusual, since then only the 1980 to 1984 shift was below that level, and in three of the other five pairs the lead change was over twice that size.[53]

Second, increasingly weak party attachments help explain the emergence of a bifurcated pattern of election outcomes between presidential and off-year contests. With party cues mixed and confused and partisan sentiments weak in any case, voters make their choices on the basis of other identifications. The higher stimulus and personality-focused campaigns of presidential years draw more voters into the electorate, and since 1964 this new mobilization has had a clearly pro-Republican tilt in the western states. But when lower stimulus conditions prevail, an average of 18 percent of the Republican party's presidential voters have dropped out of the electorate in the following off-year election.[54] In the face of this dropout pattern, and without recruiting any new supporters, the more stable Democratic electorate has greater impact in off years. Combined with the broader national tendency toward insulation of incumbents, this accounts for seemingly stronger levels of Democratic support in off-year contests.

These symptoms of partisan decomposition reflect an unraveling of the association between economic standing and party support, a relationship that had characterized presidential voting between 1932 and 1944. The data in table 10.13 show an unmistakeable pattern: since the late 1940s, the economic measures reveal no evidence of partisan bias while nonvoting has tended to increase significantly in lower status and poorer areas.[55] And the steepness of the inverse association between abstention and the economic indicators has increased over time. In other words, not unlike the 1910s and 1920s, the economically defined constituency that Roosevelt attracted during the 1930s has become demobilized, politically inert and consequently unrepresented in the political systems of the western states.

Western Political Culture

What does this overview of eighty-four years of the West's electoral history suggest of the region's political culture? What does it reveal of those internalized expectations that underlay and shaped westerners' patterns of political behavior?[56]

We need to notice at least two major dimensions of western political culture. First, there is ample empirical evidence that antiparty, or at least nonpartisan, values have long been one of its important components. The origins of these values were diverse. For a small proportion of westerners, they reflected evangelical religious commitments. For larger numbers they

Table 10.13
Demobilizing an Economic Coalition, 1948 to 1984[1]

	Mountain			Pacific		
	Democrat	Republican	Abstain	Democrat	Republican	Abstain
1948–64 President						
Economic status	.09	.52	−1.14	*.13*	*−.10*	−1.16
Farm wealth	−.77	.22	−.99	.07	−.50	−1.10
1946–66 Off Year						
Economic status	*.01*	*.04*	−1.78	*−.10*	−.65	−1.57
Farm wealth	−.16	*−.03*	−1.05	*−.12*	.63	−1.04
1968–84 President						
Economic status	−.23	*.11*	−1.90	.43	*.02*	−1.75
Farm wealth	−.10	.53	−1.68	*−.06*	.60	−1.54
1970–82 Off Year						
Economic status	*.06*	−.71	−1.91	1.13	−.98	−2.43
Farm wealth	−.36	−.24	−1.81	*−.02*	.30	−1.90

[1] Entries are unstandardized partial regression coefficients, and see Table 10.6 for the list of control variables. Coefficients *not significant* at .001 are italicized.

arose from negative experiences with parties that operated as mechanisms of colonial control during the territorial period. And for both of these groups and still other citizens, antiparty outlooks developed as parties proved incapable of representing grassroots concerns. Weakly institutionalized parties operating as instruments of private interest groups especially drew the fire of civic associations and reformers. But whatever their specific sources and referents, antiparty values were broadly diffused among the western electorate.[57]

This explains much of the behavior of the empirical indicators. Because most citizens did not greatly value party regularity for its own sake, they picked and chose among candidates rather than followed party cues. This resulted in higher rates of split-ticket voting and party-vote switching than occurred in more partisanized contexts like the northern states. This type of selectivity at the individual level, in turn, produced comparatively large amounts of instability—that is, wide swings between elections—at the state and regional levels.

The absence of strong party commitments, or the spread of antiparty values, also had important consequences at the systemic level. Weak partisanship worked to skew the representational systems of most western states. Generally, eligible voters who are economically not well off and those with low levels of education can be expected to participate less regularly in politics than more affluent, better-educated citizens. Identification with political parties and grassroots actions by party organizations serve at least to boost the electoral turnout of these components of the population, thus offsetting their usual participation disadvantage. However, in the western states, where these attachments and activities were largely absent, better-off groups usually ended up comprising a disproportionate share of the active electorate. Under these conditions, the electoral process communicated to policymakers the concerns arising mainly from the middle and upper economic strata, while the interests of the electorally inactive remained largely invisible. This economically biased electoral participation allowed officeholders to define a political agenda that reflected mobilized and represented interests. The economic concerns of working-class citizens remained largely outside this agenda, because without institutions capable of penetrating to the grassroots, articulating their interests, and mobilizing them, these citizens had no way to play a role in defining the problems, let alone in developing solutions to them.[58]

The operation of most western state governments was affected by weak partisanship in another way. State governments are typically marked by a separation of powers among distinct branches, with shared party commitments often operating as the strongest—perhaps the only—inducement to cooperative action. But because party norms were weak among the western electorate, candidates for office often ignored party organizations and party cues. And when elected, such candidates behaved as independent entrepreneurs, showing at best only minimal party responsibility. Under these conditions, and even when the same party controlled all of its branches, the separate parts of state government did not work in tandem. The system appeared to be immobilized, and frustrated citizens and interest groups increasingly relied on other means of influencing policy, especially direct means like initiatives and referenda. Plebiscitarian democracy, sporadic manifestations of the general will, thus came to replace representative government through institutionalized and strong political parties capable of articulating modal public opinion and bringing its pressure to bear on specific issues.[59]

Electorates that did not value parties in the first place quite naturally responded to public attacks on the baleful influences of party. Because parties could neither command the allegiance of majorities of the electorate nor organize policy outputs at the legislative level, reformers found them irresistably tempting targets of attack. Their largely successful assault created a legal context that abetted individualism and factionalism and that worked to inhibit the development of stronger organizations when conditions changed, as they did in the 1930s.

Finally, an electoral politics without parties became a politics of personalities. Candidates did not tend to run as part of a team, but as independent operators creating their own campaign organizations, stressing their own qualifications and claims to office, and building their own electoral coalitions. Personality-focused campaigns became the norm, rather than party efforts or issue-driven movements. This placed a premium on charismatic candidates—like Theodore Roosevelt, Hiram Johnson, Franklin Roosevelt, and even Ronald Reagan—capable of attracting wide support even when voters were simultaneously rejecting their parties and programs.

The second major component of western political culture has been a sense of regional self-interest. This had displayed itself in distinctive ways at different periods of the West's political history. In the late-nineteenth and early-twentieth centuries, this regional outlook mirrored a strong, and rather defensive, self-image of colonialism. Westerners saw their states and territories as colonies of a not-very-benevolent eastern imperium, controlled by and exploited for the benefit of that region's dominant economic interests. Territorial governments directly controlled from Washington were only the most obvious signs of the West's subordinate status. Currency and credit systems that made the region's future growth and development dependent upon eastern bankers and shipping rates that discouraged manufacturing and encouraged the production of raw materials reminded even larger numbers of westerners of their region's exploitation.

When candidates articulated these concerns and represented western interests, voters responded appropriately, as they did when the Populists identified themselves with the West's depressed agricultural and mining interest during the 1890s.

This Populist impulse, or at least its anticolonial thrust, did not expire with the failure of Bryan's crusade in 1896. The battles during the following decades against the railroads, the banks, and corporations generally were examples of anticolonialism turned loose in politics. Westerners attacked these institutions both for their practices and for what they symbolized, and their control by outsiders—usually easterners—was a critical facet of that symbolism. The assault on these large-scale corporate enterprises, however, did not signal any commitment to a program of radicalism on the part of the western public. It was essentially a conservative thrust, aimed at promoting the economic self-interest of the West's citizens and preserving the sets of social expectations that underlay their understanding of the good life.[60]

At the same time, western congressmen and senators tried to increase their region's share of federal expenditures, especially by seeking funds for irrigation, reclamation, and power projects, as well as for constructing roads in rural areas. They aimed at harnessing the region's water resources and improving its production and distribution systems to promote economic development and growth. And, of course, by securing federal funds they also aimed at reducing their region's dependence upon eastern bankers and industrialists.

These efforts to promote economic change inevitably spawned conflict among competing groups of resource users in the West. Arizona opposed the construction of dams on the Colorado River during the 1930s, for example, because Californians were their chief beneficiaries. While northern and southern Californians united to resist the demands of Arizona and the other Colorado River states on issues of water resource development, they then battled each other over the intrastate distribution of the waters they won.[61]

But these internal conflicts did not detract from the larger community of interest that united the western states on issues of regional growth. Even while battling each other over vital issues of water distribution and use, westerners of all partisan and ideological stripes accepted the need for the federal government to play the primary role in funding the region's future development. And just as typically, western voters were willing to cross party lines to reward representatives and senators who delivered on their commitments to secure federal support for western projects.[62]

These efforts to increase federal funding finally paid off during the 1930s. New Deal programs had a pervasive impact on the West, and the federal government assumed an increasingly important role in the region's economy. And as public funds replaced private capital in promoting regional economic development, the referent of many westerners' anticolonial atittudes shifted. Washington began to supplant Wall Street as the focus of anticolonial sentiment and rhetoric.[63]

But colonialism itself began to fade as a self-image in the wake of World War II's impact on the economies and populations of the western states. Westerners became more optimistic, confident of the future, and sure that the boom times would continue. And their reactive and defensive anticolonialism gave way to an assertive sense of self-sufficiency.[64]

These changes in general outlook had significant implications for the region's political culture. They reshaped the internalized expectations that most westerners brought with them to political activity. During the 1930s, and more so than northerners, western citizens looked to Washington for solutions to the problems that affected their daily lives. They not only supported large federal outlays for regional development projects, they endorsed the federal government's social programs, including old-age pensions, relief expenditures, government aid for mothers at childbirth, and federal funding for medical care.[65]

Some traces of the West's enthusiasm for government solutions persisted through 1960. Until then the proportion of western survey respondents perceiving a government responsibility for helping people get jobs and low-cost medical care exceeded the percentage opting for individualist solutions (table 10.14).[66] Since then, however, northern and western attitudes have moved in opposite directions, with the latter becoming more wary of government's role and increasingly committed to individualist solutions.

This does not mean that westerners have become more conservative in any ideological sense.[67] Their electoral reactions have never been inflexibly determined by either ideological or partisan commitments. It means instead that changes in their region's relationships with the rest of the country have led them to redefine the proper role of government.

In the 1930s westerners generally accepted—indeed, encouraged—the federal government's role in funding regional development projects. But their view of government's role was even larger: they saw it as a positive instrument with responsibility to promote the general wellbeing of individual citizens. As the West's economy and population boomed, however, its collective regional image shifted from colonial dependency to self-sufficiency. In turn, this encouraged a sense of self-reliance at the individual level and a corresponding redefinition of the role of government. Increasing numbers of westerners came to see government as existing for strictly utilitarian purposes, to perform the functions demanded by the people who created it. It has no direct concern with questions of the "good society," or of the proper relationships of groups within society. Conse-

Table 10.14
Employment and Medical Care Government or Individual Responsibility?[1]

	West	North
1956	6.6	1.4
1958	5.3	1.5
1960	6.4	1.5
1964	−2.9	3.7
1968	−3.8	2.7
1972	−3.4	1.9
1974	−3.3	1.7
1976	−5.6	4.8
1978	−6.0	4.2
1980	−8.2	5.7
1982	−11.9	7.3
1984	−12.7	8.6

[1] Entries are the differences between the proportions of respondents choosing government or individual responsibility, with *negative* scores indicating a collective preference for individualist solutions. The percentages have been controlled for the effects of age, education, ideology, income, and urbanism.

quently, government should not act in these spheres but must confine itself to those areas, largely in the economic realm, which encourage individual initiative. Creating opportunities for self-reliant individuals to seize is the proper role of government. This outlook, which limits public involvement in private activities, places a premium on individualist solutions even to problems, like unemployment and medical care, that clearly have larger social implications.[68]

Viewed over time, the political behavior of the West and North seems to have converged. Both electorates, for example, are less partisan and more volatile in their behaviors than they were at the beginning of the century. And in this and other respects, the northern electorate seems to have become more like its western counterpart. But these similarities mask a continuing—even growing—difference in underlying attitudes and internalized expectations. The attitudinal profiles of the two electorates have come to diverge, especially over whether to pursue collective or individualist solutions to human problems. Of course, since this issue is at the heart of the post-1970s policy debate, the resolution of this clash of regional outlooks will have a great impact on the direction of national policy. But unlike the 1890s, or even earlier in this century, the West's greater economic resources and population make it more likely that the debate will be resolved on its terms.

Notes

The research underlying this essay derives from a larger project that has been supported by a grant from the General Research Program, National Endowment for the Humanities. The essay was written while the author was a Fellow of the Woodrow Wilson International Center for Scholars, The Smithsonian Institution.

1. There were actually 43 biennial elections between 1900 and 1984, but I have excluded the 1912 contest from this summary. In that year, the Democrats led the three-party field by 21 percentage points, but they trailed the combined Republican and Progressive vote total by 6.5 points. In 1924, despite another three-way split, the Democrats trailed the Republican vote by 37.7 percentage points in the region.

2. Roosevelt lost Colorado in 1940 and Colorado and Wyoming in 1944. Data for gubernatorial, Senate, and U.S. House elections are from Congressional Quarterly, *Guide to U.S. Elections* (Washington, D.C.: Congressional Quarterly, Inc., 1975). Data on the partisan division of seats in state legislatures were obtained from the Inter-University Consortium for Political and Social Research, University of Michigan, as well as all county-level voting and census data used in this essay.

3. The "North" includes the following states: Connecticut, Maine, Massachusetts, New Hampshire, Rhode Island, Vermont, New Jersey, New York, and Pennsylvania.

4. Since 1956 the changes between presidential elections have averaged 13.6 percentage points in the West and 20.7 in the North. The average, or mean, has been calculated in these cases by using the absolute size of the partisan leads and ignoring the signs associated with them. For more detail on this measure, see Paul Kleppner, "Searching for the Indiana Voter," *Indiana Magazine of History* 76 (December 1980): 362–65.

5. For a more complete explanation, see Kleppner, "Voters and Parties in the Western States, 1876–1900," *Western Historical Quarterly* 14 (January 1983): 54, n. 14. And for the mathematics involved in using regression procedures to estimate individual-level behavior from aggregate-level data, see Leo A. Goodman, "Ecological Regression and the Behavior of Individuals," *American Sociological Review* 18 (December 1953): 663–64; idem, "Some Alternatives to Ecological Correlation," *American Journal of Sociology* 64 (May 1959): 610–25; and Laura Irwin Langbein and Allan J. Lichtman, *Ecological Inference* (Beverly Hills, Calif.: Sage Publications, 1978).

6. For the general conception, see Philip E. Converse, "The Concept of a

Normal Vote," in Angus Campbell, et al., *Elections and the Political Order* (New York: John Wiley and Sons, 1966), 9–39. And the procedures used here to approximate Converse's concept with aggregate-level data follow Melvyn Hammerberg, *The Indiana Voter: The Historical Dynamics of Party Allegiance during the 1870's* (Chicago: University of Chicago Press, 1971), 155.

7. The concept and definitions are from Angus Campbell, "Surge and Decline: A Study of Electoral Change," Campbell, et al., *Elections and the Political Order*, 40–62.

8. In developing estimates of the size of the eligible electorate, I have taken into account state-by-state and year-by-year variations in the rules determining voter eligibility.

9. Except for the voter registration requirements, all data describing the social characteristics of the population were taken from the federal decennial censuses, reports on the statistics of churches or religious bodies, and the reports on wealth, debt, and taxation, and I made linear interpolations for the years between censuses. For descriptions of the census publications and their contents, see Henry J. Dubester, *Catalog of U.S. Census Publications* (Washington: U.S. Government Printing Office, 1950). The information on voter registration laws was compiled from state statutes in connection with other projects; see Paul Kleppner and Stephen C. Baker, "The Impact of Voter Registration Requirements on Electoral Turnout, 1900–16," *Journal of Political and Military Sociology* 8 (Fall 1980); 205–26; and Kleppner, *Continuity and Change in Electoral Politics, 1893–1928* (Westport, Conn.: Greenwood Press, 1987).

10. All changes in the laws governing voter eligibility and in boundaries of the counties were taken into account. Although it was not employed for that reason, the weighting procedure has the effect of eliminating problems that arise from having only a small number of counties in some states.

11. Each set of three equations has 68 regression coefficients, and there were 16 biennial elections between 1900 and 1930. This meant a total of 1,088 coefficients (or 68×16) for each regional grouping and for each state, or a grand total of 15,232 coefficients (or $1,088 \times 14$, for 11 states and 3 regional groupings).

12. For all of the regression analysis presented in this essay, I judged statistical significance at the .001 level. To make this call, I compared the weighted coefficient with its unweighted standard error. The use of the weighted standard error is inappropriate since the weighting procedure greatly increases the number of cases and virtually assures statistical significance. On the logical requirements of group behavior, see Lee Benson, "Group Cohesion and Social and Ideological Conflict: A Critique of Some Marxian and Tocquevillian Theories," *American Behavioral Scientist* 16 (May-June 1973): 741–67.

13. Each unstandardized partial regression coefficient indicates by how much the dependent variable increased (or decreased) for each percentage-point increase in the independent variable, net of the effects of the other independent variables. For example, in 1900, after taking into account the effects of the other variables, the Democratic share of the electorate *increased* by .17 percentage points for every 1 point increase in Catholic population density, and it *declined* by .19 for every percentage-point increase in Episcopalian density.

14. While the 1896 data are not presented here, it should be clear that Bryan could not have swept the West as he did if the 1900 pattern of regression coefficients had prevailed.

15. But the Irish coefficient was $-.57$ in 1906 and a statistically indeterminate .07 in 1910.

16. The Economic Status variable is the sum of the z scores of two variables: per capita wealth and the percentage of school-aged children attending school. The Farm Wealth index is the sum of the z scores of three variables: the number of improved acres per farm, the cash value of products per farm, and the cash value of machinery per farm. For the factor-analytic derivation of these indices, see Kleppner, *Continuity and Change*.

17. David Sarasohn, "The Election of 1916: Realigning the Rockies," *Western Historical Quarterly* 11 (July 1980): 288–90; Robert E. Burton, *Democrats of Oregon: The Pattern of Minority Politics, 1900–56* (Eugene: University of Oregon Press, 1970), 20–21; Richard Evans Fisch, "A History of the Democratic Party in the State of Washington, 1854–1956" (Ph.D. dissertation, University of Oregon, 1975), 72–78; and especially James Edward Wright, *The Politics of Populism: Dissent in Colorado* (New Haven: Yale University Press, 1970).

18. While the Democrats remained competitive in Nevada, New Mexico, and, to a lesser extent, Montana, the Republican leads in these states reflected the same combination of factors. Space constraints prevent describing the results here, but I have also analyzed gubernatorial voting in these states. Those patterns are generally the same as the ones marking congressional contests, with the exception of California's races where the local Progressives seem to have been more successful in mobilizing an economic coalition than elsewhere. For other relevant evidence, see Michael P. Rogin and John L. Shover, *Political Change in California: Critical Elections and Social Movements, 1890–1966* (Westport, Conn.: Greenwood Press, 1970), 35–89; and Alexander P. Saxton, "San Francisco Labor and the Populist and Progressive Insurgencies," *Pacific Historical Review* 34 (November 1965): 421–38.

19. For analysis of the political sources of Theodore Roosevelt's vote, see Kleppner, *Continuity and Change,* chapter 5, especially Table 25. At his lowest point in 1908, Bryan polled 43 percent of the vote, which represented 28.2 percent of the electorate. In 1912 Wilson received 41.8 percent of the vote, which was only 24.6 percent of the electorate.

20. Wilson's mobilization rates among these groups are not presented in Table 7, but they averaged about 3 percentage points below Roosevelt's. Taft's rates were considerably lower than either of these, of course. Among earlier abstainers and new voters in the Mountain and Pacific states, it was a two-way contest, with Theodore Roosevelt carving out a small but consistent lead over Wilson.

21. But 24 percent of Bryan's 1908 supporters did not vote in 1912. In the eight western states he carried, Wilson's highest percentage was 43.5 percent in Arizona, and he ran under 40 percent in Idaho, Montana, Nevada, Oregon, and Wyoming.

22. Coolidge received 53.7 percent of the West's total vote, with LaFollette running at 30.2 percent and Davis at 15.9 percent. But both Coolidge and

LaFollette were about 7 percentage points stronger in the Pacific states than in the Mountain region, while Davis ran about 14 points better in the latter area.

23. Kleppner, "Voters and Parties in the Western States," 49–68.

24. Respectively, the concepts and quotations are from Samuel J. Eldersveld, *Political Parties: A Behavioral Analysis* (Chicago: Rand-McNally, 1964), 1–13, 73–97; and Murray Edelman, *The Symbolic Uses of Politics* (Urbana: University of Illinois Press, 1964), 188.

25. The West's total population increased from 3.0 million to 11.8 million between 1890 and 1930, or by 292.9 percent. During the same interval, the number of western residents reporting the Midwest as their place of birth increased by 371.1 percent. For analysis and discussion of this change in one state, see Commonwealth Club of California, *The Population of California* (San Francisco: Parker Printing Company, 1946), 16–17, 43–46.

26. Truman lost only Oregon among the western states, but the Democrats lost the congressional vote in California, Oregon, and Wyoming.

27. Republicans mobilized about 13 percent of the new voters in each area; 8 percent of the abstainers in the Mountain states and 3 percent in the Pacific region. As might have been expected, Republicans attracted few Democratic crossover votes—only 2 percent in the Mountain area and none in the Pacific states.

28. In both areas, Republican recruitment among abstainers and new voters lagged well behind Roosevelt's levels. The Republicans attracted the support of less than 1 percent of the abstainers in the Mountain states and only 5 percent in the Pacific region, while enlisting 9 percent and 7 percent, respectively, of each area's new voters.

29. Between 1936 and 1940, Republicans mobilized 16 percent of the new voters in the Mountain states but only 1 percent in the Pacific region. Over the next four-year period, they mobilized about 24 percent in each of these areas.

30. Voting is systematically lower in off years than in presidential contests, but this will not pollute the comparisons since the models incorporate a control for total turnout.

31. That is, the regression coefficients associated with these variables within each subarea were about the same from presidential to off years.

32. In fact, the depressive effect of voter registration requirements on turnout in the 1930s was less in the West than in other parts of the country; see Kleppner, *Who Voted? The Dynamics of Electoral Turnout, 1870–1980* (New York: Praeger, 1982), 86–87.

33. These observations derive from a regional analysis of data from the following American Institute of Public Opinion surveys (Gallup Polls): #60 (7 December 1936); #66 (25 January 1937); #75 (22 March 1937); and #90 (5 July 1936). The original responses were obtained from the Roper Public Opinion Research Center, University of Connecticut.

34. Burton, *Democrats of Oregon*, 21, 25–27, 29, 35–46; Fisch, "History of Democratic Party in the State of Washington," 6, 169–73; Robert L. Cole, "The Democratic Party in Washington State, 1919–1933: Barometer of Social Change" (Ph.D. dissertation, University of Washington, 1972), 6–10, 64–83; and Robert

D. Saltvig, "The Progressive Movement in Washington" (Ph.D. dissertation, University of Washington, 1966), 298–402.

35. *Capital Journal* (Salem), September 8, 1927, quoted in Burton, *Democrats of Oregon*, 39, see 40–46, 56–58 for discussion of Democratic weakness in the 1920s. Also see Cole, "Democratic Party in Washington State," 26–31, 38–43, 122–23, 127.

36. Cole, "Democratic Party in Washington State," 231–32, 248; and also see Elliott Marple, "The Movement for Public Ownership of Power in Washington," *Journal of Land and Public Utility Economics* 7 (February 1931): 61–66.

37. Cole, "Democratic Party in Washington State," 104, 231–32. The text of the initiative and the county-level vote returns are in *Abstract of the Votes Polled in the State of Washington in the General Election of 1924* (Olympia: Secretary of State, 1924).

38. The texts of the measures and the county-level vote results are in *Abstract of the Votes Cast at the General Election [of 1930] in the State of Oregon* (Salem: Secretary of State, 1930); and *Abstract of the Votes Polled in the State of Washington in the General Election of 1930* (Olympia: Secretary of State, 1930).

39. Burton, *Democrats of Oregon*, 75; Cole, "Democratic Party in Washington State," 291; and Herman Carl Voeltz, "Proposals for a Columbia Valley Authority: A History of Political Controversy" (Ph.D. dissertation, University of Oregon, 1960), 17–18.

40. See notes 37 and 38 on the sources for the 1924 and 1930 votes; and for the 1940 measure, see *Abstract of the Votes Polled in the State of Washington in the General Election of 1940* (Olympia: Secretary of State, 1940). The regression estimates are weighted by the square root of the voting age population in the year of the election.

41. Cole, "Democratic Party in Washington State," 121–22, 235–39.

42. Cole, "Democratic Party in Washington State," 9–10, 269–70.

43. Quoted in Cole, "Democratic Party in Washington State," 286. Bone polled 54.6 percent in the four-person primary, while Chadwick finished second with 26.6 percent.

44. The measure stipulated that the total vote on the bond question had to exceed 50 percent of the total vote within the district at the previous biennial election, a turnout level that would have been difficult to satisfy at a general election and nearly impossible at a special election.

45. Fisch, "History of Democratic Party in the State of Washington," 266–68.

46. See note 38 for the 1930 measure; and for the later ones, see *Abstract of the Votes Cast at the General Election [of 1934] in the State of Oregon* (Salem: Secretary of State, 1934); and *Abstract of the Votes Cast at the General Election [of 1936] in the State of Oregon* (Salem: Secretary of State, 1936).

47. Burton, *Democrats of Oregon*, 62–64, 71.

48. For the quotations, see Burton, *Democrats of Oregon*, 70, 85; and Richard L. Neuberger, *Our Promised Land* (New York: Macmillan Company, 1938), 314–15.

49. For the quotations, see Burton, *Democrats of Oregon*, 82, 83, 78, respectively.

50. *Oregon Democrat,* June 10, 1942, 11, quoted in Burton, *Democrats of Oregon,* 65.

51. Gerald D. Nash, *The American West Transformed: The Impact of the Second World War* (Bloomington: Indiana University Press, 1985), 17–55; and for a view of the lack of partisan responsibility, see the reports on the western states in "The New Face of State Politics," *Congressional Quarterly* 41 (September 3, 1985): 1771–1871.

52. The data are means calculated over the 1976, 1980, and 1984 elections for western respondents in the Center for Political Studies, National Election Studies. The CPS/NES data were obtained from ICPSR, University of Michigan.

53. The quoted phrase is from Walter Dean Burnham, *Critical Elections and the Mainsprings of American Politics* (New York: W. W. Norton & Company, 1970), 91. The 1960–64, 1964–68, and 1968–72 shifts were all over 20 percentage points; and, excluding the 1980–84 change, the shifts since 1960 have averaged 19.1 percentage points.

54. This is the mean of the regression estimates from adjacent pairs of presidential and off-year elections between 1964–66 and 1980–82. The corresponding Democratic mean is 11 percent, but most of that is due to the 33 percent dropout rate between 1972 and 1974. Excluding the 1972–74 pair, the Democratic mean is only 6 percent.

55. Table 11.13 presents regression coefficients to facilitate comparisons with the data in Tables 11.6, 11.8, and 11.10. For the period since 1952, however, individual-level survey data are available in the National Election Studies, and I have also analyzed this body of evidence. Those results parallel the ecological findings: the low income group (bottom quarter of the population) gives more support to the Democrats than upper income earners, but much less than during the 1950s. Moreover, the income variable no longer has a statistically significant impact on voting choice in the West as it did during the 1952–60 period.

56. For definitions of political culture that emphasize these elements, see Harry Eckstein, "A Perspective on Comparative Politics, Past and Present," in Harry Eckstein and David E. Apter, eds., *Comparative Politics: A Reader,* (New York: The Free Press, 1963), 26; and Ronald P. Formisano, "Deferential-Participant Politics: The Early Republic's Political Culture, 1789–1840," *American Political Science Review* 68 (June 1974): 473–87. For other useful conceptions and insights, also see Donald J. Devine, *The Political Culture of the United States: The Influence of Member Values on Regime Maintenance* (Boston: Little, Brown, 1972), 14–18; and Daniel J. Elazar, *American Federalism: A View from the States,* 2d ed. (New York: Thomas Y. Crowell Company, 1972), 93–102.

57. On the religious sources of antipartyism, see especially Ronald P. Formisano, "Political Character, Antipartyism, and the Second Party System," *American Quarterly* 21 (Winter 1969): 683–709; and Kleppner, *The Third Electoral System, 1853–1892: Parties, Voters, and Political Cultures* (Chapel Hill: University of North Carolina Press, 1979), 293–96, 331–32. And for an overview of the other sources of antiparty outlooks among westerners, see Kleppner, "Voters and Parties in the Western States," 63–66.

58. Sidney Verba and Norman H. Nie, *Participation in America: Political*

Democracy and Social Equality (New York: Harper & Row, 1972), 106–14, 209–28; and Kleppner, *Who Voted?*, especially 4–7, 142–62.

59. V. O. Key, Jr., *American State Politics: An Introduction* (New York: Alfred A. Knopf, 1963), 34–41, 57–64; and Kleppner, "Voters and Parties in the Western States," 66–67.

60. Daniel J. Elazar, "Political Culture on the Plains," *Western Historical Quarterly* 11 (July 1980): 268.

61. Ray Everett, *Arizona History and Government* (Tempe: Center for Public Affairs, 1977), 75–78; Lawrence Clark Powell, *Arizona: A Bicentennial History* (New York: W. W. Norton & Company, 1976), 79–81; Elazar, *American Federalism*, 20–21; and, more generally, Dean E. Mann, *The Politics of Water in Arizona* (Tucson: University of Arizona Press, 1963).

62. Elazar, "Political Culture on the Plains," 274; Fred L. Israel, *Nevada's Key Pittman* (Lincoln: University of Nebraska Press, 1963), 59; and Roger T. Johnson, "Charles L. McNary and the Republican Party during Prosperity and Depression" (Ph.D. dissertation, University of Wisconsin, 1967), 15, 17, 30, 46–48, 93–94, 120, 138–39, 170–71.

63. Nash, *American West Transformed*, 5; Leonard J. Arrington, "The New Deal in the West: A Preliminary Statistical Inquiry," *Pacific Historical Review* 39 (August 1969): 311–27; and Richard Lowitt, *The New Deal in the West* (Bloomington: Indiana University Press, 1984), for a comprehensive treatment that also shows much of the unevenness of the New Deal's impact.

64. Nash, *American West Transformed*, 201–16.

65. AIPO surveys # 60 (7 December 1936); #74 (15 March 1937); #87 (14 June 1937); and #95 (9 July 1937). On all of these items, westerners were more supportive of governmental solutions than northerners or southerners.

66. The data in Table 10.14 are from a multiple classification analysis of responses in the Center for Political Studies, National Election Studies. For most years, the dependent variable used for the table was an additive scale of respondents' answers to two items: whether the government in Washington should help people get doctors and hospital care at low cost, and whether it should see to it that every person has a job and a good standard of living. When no question on medical care was asked (in 1958 and 1980–84), I used responses to the question on jobs. However, the pattern of change across time shown in Table 10.14 was not an artifact of using only one question from the final three surveys. Both the sizes of the negative scores for the West and the regional gap had turned upward prior to 1980.

67. The proportion of westerners identifying themselves as conservatives increased from 15 to 31 percent between 1964 and 1984, but in the North the increase was similar, from 14 to 33 percent. Moreover, in the North the 1984 proportion of conservatives was higher and the percentage of liberals lower than in the West. The data are from CPS, National Election Studies, 1964 and 1984.

68. This description accords with some (but not all) of the key features of Elazar's "individualistic political culture"; see Elazar, *American Federalism*, 94–96.

11

The West as Laboratory and Mirror of Reform

William D. Rowley

How the radical and reform traditions developed in western politics during the course of the twentieth century is a major concern of William Rowley's essay. Viewing the West as a land of economic opportunity, Rowley interprets its advocacy of reform as an effort to protect its gains against the exploitative forays of outside interests, particularly from the East. Since western settlers came from such diverse origins, reform movements in the region reflected a kaleidoscopic quality that Rowley finds a distinctive feature.

When many of the promises of the frontier West crumbled in the depression years of the 1890s, the panaceas of free silver, irrigation, and the single tax, and the indignations of Populism and industrial unionism appeared in western states. These outcries spoke to the growing contradictions of an industrializing society that denied much of the once-vaunted optimism of the western states. Demands for reform grew out of economic distress and struck a familiar note in American life that envisioned a more equitable society, open to individual opportunities promised by a now closed frontier.

The struggle for reform in the West took place within the political framework of national and state constitutions that eventually stamped governmental authority upon every remote section of the region. Underpinning the political structure of the West was its primary resource economy—mining, agriculture, and timber. Many Westerners saw their lives constricted by marginal economies whose interests seemed subservient to and plundered by the commands of the capital-rich East.[1] Where was justice in a system that seemed to condemn an entire geographical area to second-class citizenship, especially after the high drama of western expansion and conquest? Attempts to confront the seeming injustices of the economic system and build a mature economic base for the far-flung geographic areas of the West command center stage of the western reform picture from the beginning of the century through the end of World War II.

Opportunity for economic advancement beckoned Americans westward and provided a central theme in American history far into the twentieth century. The quest for betterment was largely an individualistic enterprise (with some notable communitarian exceptions) and in keeping with the private property ethics enshrined with the founding of the Republic and the writing of the Constitution. The emphasis upon individualism, however, did not preclude government at all levels from being a helpmate to private enterprise in canal, railroad, and bridge building.[2] So too did it reserve unto itself the power to regulate fees charged by private corporations performing public services for the community. While there was no mythical nineteenth-century world of pure laissez-faire capitalism, individuals in most ways, as well as corporations, were free to pursue opportunities for economic success and in the process risk the perdition of poverty.

Celebrants of economic liberalism and individualism see this freedom as central to any understanding of American history. Critics insist that Americans condemned themselves, for better or worse, to a competitive world of property accumulation or loss depending upon the good or ill fortune of the individual. An extreme view of Crevecoeur's "the American, this new man" was provided by Tocqueville when he wrote of a new bourgeoisie who "owe nothing to any man, they expect nothing from any man; they acquire the habit of always considering themselves as standing alone, and they are apt to imagine that their whole destiny is in their own hands."[3]

In the West lay what many envisioned, the boundless resources of an open-land frontier. Westward migration promoted a physical mobility that destabilized American communities. While Americans probably thought of themselves connected to community and family, the constant press of the market economy and looming-frontier opportunity tore at the fabric of community stability. Probably because community was so ever fleeting, Americans embarked on a drive to find it and, of course, economic satisfaction in the next place they came to.[4] Ultimately in the realities of American economic and social life this goal was illusory and romantic, especially in the face of a dawning urban and dynamic industrial America that made its presence felt even in the vast reaches of the American West.

There, sparse population, tyranny of vast distances, primary resource

The West as Laboratory and Mirror of Reform

economies, and an awareness of being outside the inner circles of national power all at various times produced a regional frustration. Still, the frustration never found successful expression in a regionwide protest movement. Populism tried. The Democratic party under William Jennings Bryan tried. Bryan's famous designation of the land northeast of the Mississippi River as the "enemy's country" attempted to evoke a regional consciousness that paired not only the West against the East but also a West-South alliance against the East.[5] The West was a scene of many proposed panaceas to correct the wrongs of society. Even Populism could fall into this category. Certainly free silver, the irrigation crusade, and Henry George's single tax qualify as cure-alls aimed at societal ills that seemed to surface and persist in the region.

The unrest associated with crusades and protests reinforced a conviction that the political system could be used to give these marginal economies and small states greater economic and political leverage in the nation. The epithet of "rotten borough," applied to many of the western states by the eastern press, had a particular sting, but the term also implied that if the western states had little population and weak economies, their one strength was that they were, justified or not, political entities with equal voices in the upper house of the Congress. Political clout offered the western states opportunities to make themselves heard, to gain advantages from the federal government, and possibly to tame the eastern corporations that dominated their primary resource economies.[6]

These tactics, however, involved problems. More often than not, corporations saw western U.S. Senate positions as easy pickings for their hireling politicians. The "good works" of these servants of power helped "to fix politically a form of internal colonialism upon western societies."[7] Corporate domination of politics became a special target of the first reform effort of the twentieth-century—Progressivism.

Progressivism was a broad-gauged social, economic, and political reform movement that found expression on the local and national levels. In the West not only did city and state governments feel the bite of Progressive reform, but also the crusade for conservation of natural resources captured the attention of the region. Theodore Roosevelt announced his brand of Progressivism in 1910 when he sketched the outline of a New Nationalism that saw the national government playing a major role in reforming the economic and political life of the nation. Even the western historian and contemporary Frederick Jackson Turner declared in the *American Historical Review* in 1911:

> On the other hand, we have the voice of the insurgent West, recently given utterance in the New Nationalism of ex-President Roosevelt, demanding

increase of federal authority to curb the special interests, the powerful industrial organizations, and the monopolies, for the sake of the conservation of our national resources and the preservation of American democracy.

In one sense Progressivism was a unifying force demonstrating that western states, towns, and cities were indeed a part of the greater national political culture, subject to the same aspirations and reform impulses afoot elsewhere in the nation. Sometimes reform took different forms that did not involve a search for social justice or even the noted quest for "status" that Richard Hofstadter suggested. Dominant business interests in western territories and states often sought measures to achieve economic stability through submission to regulatory commissions in return for the elimination of competition and the virtual granting of utility monopolies by government.[8] On the local level this view expressed the New Nationalism's acceptance of big business in alliance with government, if the greater good was being served by sanctioning natural monopolies. This apparent extension of privilege by government to the private sector ran contrary to Democratic party's and Woodrow Wilson's New Freedom brand of Progressivism that doctrinally rejected monopoly, public or private. But what the West stood in need of was services in irrigation development, electrical power, water sources for the cities, and transportation over great distances, not the purity of ideology that might defeat some of these projects because of the taint of monopoly or government involvement. If it worked for government to be involved along with the promotion of private monopoly, so be it. The important result was the accomplishment of the goal and the delivery of the service.

Progressivism touched every western state. While a diverse movement, Progressivism, unlike the reform movement of Populism preceding it, did not arise from conditions of economic distress but rather from conditions of growth and prosperity. As seen in table 11.1, western urban centers especially grew in the first decade of the twentieth century.

Usually three elements can be identified in this urban-oriented reform movement: (1) a desire to make government more responsive to the will of the people by implementing direct democracy procedures of referendum, initiative, recall, and direct primaries; (2) a drive to assert more governmental control and regulation over business in the public's interest and the denial of privilege; (3) a social uplift impulse that sought to protect the weaker members of society from the impersonal ravages of the economy assuming that society must play a role in protecting individuals from their weaknesses of character—drink, gambling, and prostitution.

Social uplift advocates drew support from newly enfranchised women voters and often critically judged immigrants and minorities by the moral

Table 11.1
*Urban Population Increase,
1900–1910*

	1900	1910
Seattle	80,671	237,194
Portland	90,426	207,214
Los Angeles	102,479	319,198
Reno	4,500	10,867
Denver	133,859	213,381
Kansas City	163,752	248,381
Albuquerque	6,238	11,020
Phoenix	5,544	11,134
Omaha	128,556	150,355

and social standards of white American Protestantism. Western reformers attacked the saloon (drink), prostitution, and gambling in western towns. The progressive upsurge was in part an attempt to deal with the dramatic population growth, the "new" immigration (eastern and southern Europe), and industrialization that was taking place in the country. In the western section of the nation it took on special meaning as the region struggled to modernize and move beyond its rude frontier stage of early development. Reformers regarded gambling houses, brothels, and the ever-present saloon as a temporary dysfunction of the passing frontier stage of society that must give way to order, progress, and moral enlightenment. The struggle for modernity in the West welcomed the support of women, labor, business, and churches.[9]

From pulpits came exhortations to follow the social gospel. Protestant ministers embraced the social gospel as they urged congregations to put their faith into action by seeking improvement in the social, economic, and political institutions of daily life. Ministers, newspaper editors, university presidents, lawyers, and doctors called for a reform of society and politics. Reform was necessary to preserve the system of constitutional government and free it from the corruptive influence of corporate wealth. Herein was contained a reaction against the captains of industry or as some termed them "the robber barons" of the nineteenth century.

As noted earlier Progressivism did not flow from a fountainhead of economic distress in the first decade of the century. In fact an economic upswing was in progress. At the turn of the century the revival of western mines, agriculture, timber industry, and a government commitment to arid land reclamation all helped paint a brighter economic future for the West. The harshness of the 1890s' depression, however, left a legacy of resentments against social injustices that the Progressives now addressed. A long, smouldering reform impulse, Progressivism converted "insurgency," "protest," and "panaceas" into sophisticated reform programs in the new century.[10] Some pragmatic western "boosters" saw the necessity of reforming western society and government to attract population, investment capital, and generally insure future growth. Local reformers argued that there would ultimately be more profit in beautiful and clean cities free from the vices that once characterized wide-open frontier towns. For example, in cosmopolitan San Francisco, the 1906 earthquake posed the challenge of rebuilding from the rubble. Reformers argued for planning that would promote parks, grand buildings, wide avenues, and noble statues. All of these endeavors would bring uplift and ennoble the spirit of the populace.[11]

Western Progressivism blended economic pragmatism with efforts toward social and spiritual uplift. A major effort to reinterpret Progressivism and soften its strain of economic protest against the conglomerates of wealth occurred when historians began seeing Progressive reform as having grown out of a crisis of status among middle-class professionals who saw their social and political values under attack.[12] According to this view, corporate wealth, the emerging labor movement, the influx of the new immigration and, in the West, the still persisting vestiges of frontierism—lawlessness, vice, improvident use of resources, and the lack of a society committed to social betterment—combined to threaten the positions of deference formerly held by white, Protestant, professional middle classes. Clearly there was much to reform and set right in western society for those imbued with such a reform commitment. The ruder elements of frontier society appearing in the cumulative settlement patterns of mining, ranching, and lumbering communities produced a nonfamily population structure. By the twentieth century and before in many western states, modern city and family values began to be asserted against the permissivism tolerated in the wide-open frontier or in comparably wide-open port cities. Indeed many towns of the mountains and plains were like port cities where miners, cowboys, ranchers, and railroad workers found entertainment and diversions in the same manner as sailors on holiday with high spirits and money to spend.

Both in the seaports (e.g. Seattle and San Francisco) and inland cities (e.g. Spokane and Reno) Progressive reformers sought to tame and discipline their society for the more serious responsibilities of building wholesome communities with families, schools, churches, and stable economic development. Perhaps, this quest better explains the true nature of western Progressivism as middle- and upper-middle class citizens struggled to gain control of communities and government to foster the kind of values and social programs they believed would promote the good society. This spirit meant advocating "at large" council elections instead of the "ward system" of city council representation. The "ward heelers," as the representatives from the various wards were sometimes derogatorily dubbed, often supported city political machines that winked at social vice, drew revenues from it, and enjoyed the support of working-class voters. In city after city from Seattle to Des Moines citizen reformers from the professional and business classes sought to smash political machines and wrest political control from what they regarded as the ruder and irresponsible working-class elements of the city. This trend might also explain the hostility of Progressives to the Industrial Workers of the World (IWW or Wobblies). Many Wobblies considered themselves within the reform tradition, but their appeal was to the down and out, to the proletariate of unorganized labor, and their view of the good society as "one big union" was sheer nonsense to the Progressive and far too radical.

On the other end of the economic and social spectrum, the possessors of great wealth and influence must, in the view of the Progressive, accept social obligations and governmental regulation by regulatory commissions. Sometimes this meant that municipal utilities should be owned by the cities under a program branded "municipal socialism." This program early marked off a battle ground between the advocates of public and private power, with public power interests generally winning in the Pacific Northwest and in the unlikely bastion of conservative economics—Los Angeles. Working classes and immigrants also had to accept discipline and restraints. Drinking, gambling, and prostitution presented targets for reform that often struck at the fabric of working-class social life. Not unpredictably, the skilled workers of organized labor allied in many instances with the middle class to achieve a wide spectrum of reform as they sought respectability and acceptance of craft unionism.[13]

Western Progressives faced challenges not only in cleaning up their "port" towns both inland and on the coast, but also in regulating and conserving the natural resources of the West. Most natural resources lay on and in the public lands that the federal government still possessed. Westerners, of course, wanted continued development and use of resources, but increasingly the urban West saw the necessity to protect watershed lands from overuse either in timber harvest or grazing. The integrity of urban water supplies and also irrigation water supplies were at stake in a growing battle over conservation that was part and parcel of the Progressive's desire to use resources efficiently.[14]

The creation of forest reserves and finally National Forests sharply focused the pro-and-con arguments over conservation in the West. Traditionally anticonservationists contended that National Forests meant closing access to western resources and slower economic development. Others, more in step with the economic efficiency thrust of Progressive reform, argued that conservation meant wise, regulated use of resources to avoid waste and insure the future of western economic opportunity. This was not simply a struggle of high-minded reform leaders representing the cause of the people against western resource exploiters. Historian Samuel Hays contends it was an effort to apply science, technology, efficiency, order, and system to the utilization of resources. It meant removing the decision-making process about resource use from the local level to the regional and national level and consigning it to trained experts.[15]

Conservationism was not met with unified western opposition. Strong support emerged in some of the western urban press, which argued that the use-regulations offered by national forests provided for stability and continuity in western resource use. Some western senators, with Nevada's Francis G. Newlands leading the way, supported conservation measures. These included the reservation of forest lands, the establishment of the U.S. Forest Service, the irrigation of western lands under the National Reclamation Act of 1902, the reservation of hydroelectric sites on rivers and streams. Here was the beginning of the bureaucratic regulation of western resources—a legacy of the Progressive period to the West. Although this brand of conservationism was highly utilitarian and still held to a commodity view of resources, it did introduce "a kind of scientifically oriented communalism that argued that certain lands, particularly the high mountain forests, should be held in trust for all members of society in order to protect water quality, timber supplies, and other resources."[16]

As in other manifestations of Progressivism, an elitism emerged in the conservation movement's administration of resources. To justify their regulation and restriction of western resource use, government agencies invoked science and scientific studies of resources by experts to reduce resource use to what they termed "a sustained yield." Calling upon experts meant a nondemocratic orientation of resource agencies just as the newly established business regulatory commissions employed the services of appointed experts in state government to oversee the affairs of corporations offering services to the public. These actions became one of the ironies of the Progressive period. In spite of Progressivism's emphasis upon more democracy in government, it endorsed elites to run many of the agencies of modern government. Nowhere is this irony more evident than in the conservation agencies established to administer many of the natural resources of the West.

The western reform agenda also included changes in political structures. City, state, and national governments felt these winds of change in movements toward direct democracy. At-large elections for city council members as well as experiments with commission and city manager forms of government became popular reforms to overcome the evils of the ward heelers and their political machines. On the state level the achievement of

The West as Laboratory and Mirror of Reform

referendum and initiative proposals in many instances substituted direct democracy for the representative democracy of the legislatures. Direct primary laws substituted primary elections for smoke-filled rooms at party conventions in selecting the party's slate of candidates. Also, recall provisions made elected officials subject to recall during their terms of office. At the national level the direct election of senators provided by the 17th Amendment to the U.S. Constitution in 1913 won overwhelming support in western legislatures. All of these direct democracy measures meant that individual voters must become more informed about the affairs of government. Oregon was a laboratory of reform. The Oregon System, as advocated by nationally known Oregon Progressive William S. U'Ren, transformed Oregon into a leading western progressive state exhibiting proudly the direct democracy measures of initiative and referendum. One observer remarked that prior to elections, "Oregon is turned into a university, where every whole community is being trained to a knowledge of politics."[17]

The amazing amount of energy invested in domestic political reform gradually lessened as Americans became concerned with the European war that broke out in 1914. Finally the American involvement with World War I in 1917 stalled the engines of reform. Public concerns turned to patriotic causes of the Great War to Save the World for Democracy. Western labor made gains in wages and better working conditions and farmers enjoyed high prices, but reform impulses faded to be replaced by nationalistic movements that crushed dissent against the war and spurred enthusiasm for it. The war virtually destroyed any of the political left that dared oppose it, and some of the most outspoken Progressives became uncompromising patriots when they endorsed measures to repress opposition to the war.

The West especially bade farewell to reform and witnessed the rise of repression. The year after the war, 1919, western legislatures passed a spate of antisyndicalist laws aimed at the IWW. In addition, the fear of radical labor produced general repression of the labor movement in the years after the war, and vigilante lynching incidents against IWW members. Widespread suspicion of immigrants called forth Americanization programs and demands for immigration restriction and new courses on American government and constitution in schools and colleges. Ultimately new national immigration laws in the early 1920s put in place a restricted immigration program based upon quotas for the population numbers already present in the United States and forbade Japanese immigration in response to pressure from California. The general cause of western labor suffered as well when the long-time closed shop city of

San Francisco—like its southern counterpart Los Angeles—became open shop after 1919.

The Republican presidential candidate's entreaties in 1920 for "a return to normalcy" replaced the enthusiasm for the reform of the Progressive period. Reaction and a narrow nationalism replaced reform in states where enthusiasms for reform had run highest. Oregon, whose reputation as a leading Progressive state was unmatched in the West, now became a front runner in reaction. Antisyndicalist laws, alien land laws, and most notably a measure to require public school education as well as frequent Ku Klux Klan rallies characterized Oregon in the postwar period as direct democracy procedures facilitated the passage of generally repressive legislation. One authority writes: "The Far West became less famous for reform than for repression as the people used direct legislation to discriminate against religious, racial, and political minorities."[18]

The much-touted prosperity of the "Roaring Twenties" did not come to many areas of the West, especially in agriculture. Some western reformers rallied around the cause of McNary-Haugenism (a scheme for the government to buy excess wheat production to raise the domestic price and to dump the surplus on foreign markets) only to have President Calvin Coolidge veto it several times. Western farm bloc Republicans broke with their party on this issue and continued a tradition of western insurgency begun during the Progressive period. These western senators were also dubbed "Sons of the Wild Jackass" for their independent stand.[19] Big western dam projects also caught the imagination of western reformers because they saw federal projects undermining the monopolies of private power interests. Both farm relief and dam projects were designed to transfer capital from the East to the West. Both went unrealized in the decade. In another arena, oil rich areas prospered when petroleum became the leading industry in California, but coal regions languished under the competition from the new fuel. A type of welfare capitalism prevailed in many of the primary industries, e.g. copper mining and lumber camps, with the growth of "company towns."

Although cases are made for the persistence of Progressivism in the 1920s, reformers in the West fought a holding action against the triumphant forces of corporate wealth, private power, and exhibited a faltering will to enforce prohibition and antivice legislation. Corporations working in western primary resources asserted their right to command loyalties by arguing that what was good for corporations was good for western states in which they operated.

In conservation the decade (marked by the Teapot Dome and Elk Hills oil scandals involving the infamous career of the Secretary of Interior Albert Fall) was a far cry from the previous era. Aesthetic conservation, however, made important forward strides with the establishment of additional national parks. Recreation in scenic areas of the West drew people with leisure time who came on new federally funded highways. The extension of highways into remote places touched off arguments among resource protectors on how to manage visitors to scenic lands. Mostly, the arguments centered upon whether to build roads and admit automobiles, and generally, America's love affair with the automobile won the day.[20]

The ensuing Great Depression brought a sudden reduction in these leisure pursuits when economic catastrophe settled upon the nation and the West. The crisis was of such magnitude that many questioned the survival of constitutional governments and democracy itself. Workers and farmers marched on various western state legislatures demanding debt moratoriums and relief. A general strike closed down the San Francisco bay region for four days in July 1934 as farm labor strife in California's central valley reached the level of class warfare. Could local governments preserve order and protect property and most of all restore hope and confidence? Clearly, only the federal government commanded sufficient resources and power to meet the enormous challenges of the collapse of the national and regional economies. Franklin D. Roosevelt's New Deal offered hope in the face of universal disaster. The New Deal portrayed itself as a reconstructor of a shattered economy, a healer, and a savior of the destitute. Yet it sought these goals conservatively and within the established economic and political systems—shoring up business, providing jobs for workers (but not without "means tests"), and seeking higher prices for farm goods within the free market system.

The New Deal emphasized action and experimentation. These were immediate, pragmatic concerns and quite unlike the broader moral and political reforms that gave Progressivism more of an ideological underpinning. New Dealers instituted programs that brought dollars and employment to local communities through the Civil Works Administration, the Works Projects Administration, the Public Works Administration, and the Civilian Conservation Corps. With the direct relief payments from the FERA (Federal Emergency Relief Administration) and the work of the other agencies, many came to believe that these actions saved the fabric of local life. Some western states like Colorado joined only reluctantly in these relief expenditures because most required a percentage of state matching funds.

The West had always looked to the federal government to save it from its special problems of geography and resource economy. As a deficit region, the West took far more in federal expenditures than it returned. The Depression increased the dependency upon government as the private economy failed. It also sparked old suspicions about federal power and influence over local affairs. By 1930 the longstanding western reclamation program had come under heavy criticism. Agricultural surpluses, high cost of reclamation projects, and budgetary restrictions also cast a cloud over the future of western reclamation projects. The New Deal invigorated the Bureau of Reclamation when it became an important vehicle for bringing more public works and expenditures to the western states and helping to make the region a higher per capita recipient of federal dollars than any other region during the period.[21]

Roosevelt's secretary of the interior, Harold L. Ickes, at first opposed new reclamation projects until he realized the potential hydroelectric value of dams in underwriting the urban development of the entire region. Many of the projects would be on line to meet the power needs of industry during World War II—Grand Coulee, Boulder, and Shasta. While the forces of private power generally triumphed in the 1920s, the concept of public power grew firmer and expanded during the Depression. As an example, the state of Nebraska, with the help of the federal government and especially the Rural Electrification Administration, set in motion a program that would make Nebraska the only public power state in the nation.[22]

Still, it is difficult to generalize about western states. In many, the Depression shattered the status quo that employer groups had enjoyed since the defeat of the closed shop and the imposition of the open shop on labor at the end of World War I. Now the possibility of important labor gains appeared, as did other reforms in the relationship of government with the economy. Although state governmental structures were similar, economies had grown increasingly diverse, geography was varied, and, most importantly, individual vagaries of political traditions in the states defied regional generalization. In some states bulwarks of propertied, conservative interest would be reinforced because many perceived the New Deal as a federal threat to established, respectable society. Many westerners who had turned to the Democratic party during the 1930s did so out of a sense of desperation, but they retained the feeling that it was not quite respectable to be voting for the party of the big city machines and southern aristocracy. In some states local power brokers grasped New Deal reforms to reshape and initiate new services for the purposes of building stronger state Democratic parties. New Mexico appeared to be a case in point with the local party using New Deal relief measures to build its patronage but at the same time showing little willingness to initiate state measures to deal with the crisis.[23]

Many states in the East and Midwest launched little New Deals, but few moved in this direction in the West. Although the New Deal nationally meant more involvement of government with citizens through taxation and spending programs, western state governments moved hesitantly in the direction of implementing "little New Deals" on the local level. "Not

The West as Laboratory and Mirror of Reform

one western state administration in the 1930s," maintains one historian, "came close to instituting a 'little New Deal' such as that in Herbert Lehman's New York, Frank Murphy's Michigan, Phillip La Follette's Wisconsin, or Floyd Olson's Minnesota."[24] Still, states like Colorado provided for an extensive old age pension system, California approved an income tax, and Washington state experimented with expanded welfare programs that conservative governors generally defeated.[25]

The historically impoverished state of Nevada used its sovereignty to fashion legislated industries and services that other states considered socially irresponsible. While making gambling, the six-week divorce, and the quickie marriage industry permanent fixtures of its economy during the Depression decade, Nevada also established a "One Sound State Policy" portraying it as a state that eschewed big spending New Deal programs, lived within its budget, and extolled limited government and low taxes. The objective was to attract people with large fortunes to settle with their money in Nevada. As "soak the rich" taxes passed other state legislatures, Nevada newspapers announced that "Oppressed Millionaires" should seek "refuge" in Nevada. The One Sound State legacy narrowed rather than expanded the scope of Nevada state government during the decade. In the 1930s, Nevada Senator Patrick McCarran emerged as a leading anti–New Deal Democrat and a principal member of the Conservative bloc in Congress that grew increasingly hostile to New Deal legislation after the court packing attempt by Roosevelt in 1937.

The New Deal found it must work with strong Democratic parties and personalities in the West, which viewed many of the new programs as "an alien operation."[26] Next to the South, no region resisted the plans of the federal government with more determination and so successfully undermined the authority of Washington bureaucrats.[27] While the Democratic party used hard times to forge an alliance with labor and unionism in the industrial East and upper Midwest, the undeveloped nature of much of the western economy precluded the growth of such solid bands of loyalty between workers and New Deal as grew up in more industrial sections of the nation, which were in part an outgrowth of a cultivated class consciousness. Alliances between the party and labor did occur, however, in the more industrial areas of the West—Puget Sound, Salt Lake City, San Francisco, and Denver, but not in the predominantly unindustrialized West.

This development contained a twist of irony. The New Deal began with a southern and western strategy, offering to the West, and the South as well, agricultural relief and regional hydroelectrical and irrigation programs. While these programs were welcomed and seen as a belated fulfillment of reform programs suggested in the 1920s, the West did not sell its loyalty to the Democratic party or the New Deal for these achievements. Even the western progressive Republican bloc joined a coalition against the New Deal.[28]

Marxists have argued that the failure of a working class revolution in the United States was linked to the presence of a frontier of opportunity in the West acting as a "safety valve" for discontent in the East. But this land of western opportunity was often a land of disappointment, with immature or marginal primary resource economies forever dependent on eastern markets. As the New Deal became more oriented toward the mature industrial economies of the East, upper Midwest, and to the special needs of the South, westerners found themselves unable to appreciate many of the New Deal social reforms designed to benefit landless working classes of an industrial society. As one authority writes:

> The New Deal alliance of the Solid South, city machines, labor, ethnic groups, and blacks represented the death of the western, small town, agrarian domination over political and social reform. The guarantor, welfare state had replaced the broker state. The old-style reform politics was dead.[29]

The West better understood relief and recovery measures that meant immediate dollars to western economies and capital improvements than it did the reform measures of the Wagner Labor Relations Act, which gave labor unions the means to organize, social security taxes, and unemployment insurance.

Some would be quick to point out that western reform, especially during the New Deal, was just another form of avarice dignified by its identification with a geographical region. But if this is so, the same can be said for national reform movements of which the western movements were often a mirror image, especially as the region moved into the twentieth century. Richard Hofstadter, the much-studied historian of reform on the national scene, detected an illiberal content in American reform and a shallowness rooted in "pragmatic opportunism" whose main quest was property acquisition. According to this view, American society's only notable reform triumph was the New Deal, and as one critic noted, it was a "stumbling chaotic exercise in political and economic self-preservation, unconnected to any coherent philosophy or moral vision. . . ."[30]

The West emerged from the Depression decade into the war-dominated 1940s with a suspicion that much of the New Deal had been largely an emergency experiment that had not entirely served the interests of Westerners. Looking back from the short perspective of 1944, Colorado's

The West as Laboratory and Mirror of Reform

Democratic governor during the New Deal, Edwin C. Johnson, condemned the entire undertaking: "As I see it, the New Deal has been the worst fraud ever perpetuated on the American people."[31]

Still, it was widely recognized that the New Deal brought relief measures, new public works programs related to water and hydroelectric development, as well as social security measures to protect against old-age poverty and to provide unemployment insurance. The New Deal also brought agencies from Washington to impose range-use regulations over the remaining public domain with the Taylor Grazing Act of 1934 and a new Indian reform movement including the passage of the Indian Reorganization Act in 1934 giving tribes legal powers that could be used aggressively against western resource users. The New Deal's various agricultural and range reform programs gave the federal government a decisive partnership in the economy of the rural West. But from the viewpoint of many westerners this partnership carried a heavy price—regulation of resource use on the public domain.

While the breakdown of the economy and the environmental catastrophes of drought and dust bowl combined to produce a regional hopelessness, the New Deal often predicated its rescue programs on limited expectations within a closed frontier of opportunity. Many New Dealers suggested that society's wealth was not infinite, but finite, and that society must learn to live within its material limitations. They could point to no limitless frontier that held vast wealth for everyone, but to a future of only modest provisions for all. If, then, American growth had reached its limits, as many New Deal economists suggested, the western states would never be allowed to grow to full potential. The economy had to move beyond a state of simply producing for adequate domestic consumption into a new growth era if the "vast, unused storehouse of wealth, awaiting the needs of a future America . . ." was to be used for the economic welfare of the people.[32]

The economics of limits is well illustrated in the early New Deal agricultural recovery methods, which emphasized prophylactic programs to shrink crop production to a declining domestic market. On the other hand the New Deal's investments in grand hydroelectric dams and other public works projects played to the West's traditional growth aspirations and its ever-present boosterism. Still, the decade assumed an "economy of scarcity," according to one contemporary observer, with the West "destined to remain for many years to come a vast, unused storehouse of wealth. . . ." On the horizon opportunity was close at hand. The outbreak of World War II unlocked the storehouse from which resources flowed forth to build weaponry and feed the world.[33]

As never before, World War II opened the doors of western opportunity. The restraints on government spending that had existed during the Depression (despite the Keynesian pump-priming efforts of the New Deal that brought charges of overspending and irresponsible deficits) fell by the wayside as the nation prepared for war and then entered into war after Pearl Harbor in December 1941. This two-ocean war brought the West into the struggle on an equal footing with the industrialized East. And from this struggle emerged a western economy and society farther along the road to industrialization than ever before. The pace of industrialization differed from state to state with California emerging the big winner, thankful to put refugees from the Dust Bowl to work in shipyards and airplane factories. But even interior cities received an economic stimulus from wartime spending that pushed them to the verge of an entirely different future from their ranch, railroad, and mining beginnings.

The new-found prosperity and economic maturity of the postwar years confirmed a faith in the economic system that had only been temporarily questioned during the darkest days of the New Deal when the region had swallowed with some discomfort government-sponsored "relief, recovery, and reform." Now western stock-producing groups enjoying the postwar prosperity chafed under the paternal presence of government on the public ranges. The new prosperity of these stock-raising groups after the removal of wartime price controls and a growing appetite for beef among urban Americans gave stock operators the motivation to campaign against federal ownership of western lands and bureaucratic regulations. Outside of agriculture, employer groups in western states joined forces with those pushing for the passage of the Taft-Hartley Labor Relations Act in 1947. The act, they claimed, was necessary to tame the arrogance that big labor had assumed during the war years. The act also defined the battle lines for pro- and antiunion forces in western states for years to come.

Clearly the pendulum moved away from reform toward conservative reaction. Many western states elected conservative Republicans to replace the few progressive reform-minded congressmen and senators. The reaction took the form of opposition to federal resource regulations, big dam projects that might compete with private power, and a suspicion of big labor in less industrialized western states. For example, an alliance of western and southern congressmen helped stymie domestic reform proposals as President Harry Truman tried to follow up the New Deal with his Fair Deal.[34] As the cold war gained momentum on the international scene, some spoke of a new red scare at home.

Would the reaction be similar to the repression following World War I that put an end to the prewar reform efforts? Such a reaction would mean an undoing of New Deal legislation and the destruction of labor's hard-won gains since 1935. Certainly many labor leaders viewed the Taft-Hartley Act in this light, especially with its provision to allow states to ban both union and closed shops. Antiunion forces in western states seized upon this provision. They placed so-called "Right to Work Laws" on general election ballots and pushed them through state legislatures. Often the struggle over "Right to Work" defined the battle lines of state politics throughout the 1950s. In addition Taft-Hartley banned communists from offices in union organizations. One of the prime targets of the communist hunters in these years was Harry Bridges, longtime leader of the Pacific Maritime Union in San Francisco.

Could a reform spirit emerge from the uncertain but promising postwar years? President Truman's presidential victory in 1948 showed that most of the nation, including most of the West, with the exception of Oregon and the Great Plains states north of Oklahoma, wished to retain the reforms of the New Deal. While the election of Republican candidate Thomas E. Dewey probably would not have dismantled New Deal reforms, that fear is exactly what President Truman successfully conveyed to the electorate. These were years of uncertainty about the economy: would it fall back into depression, or would it grow to meet the pent-up demands of a public starved for consumer goods by the war and the prewar hard times? Had Progressivism become a long-forgotten cause in the West, and was the spirit of the New Deal now a dim memory as millions scrambled to achieve the dreams interrupted by the Depression and postponed by the war?

Where would reform again emerge in the West? Would it rally around the forces of public power, the protection of natural resources from corporate greed, or would some see the federal government and its bureaucratic agencies as a great pariah that must be checked by a new peoples' crusade? But such crusades would be difficult to mount in the bureaucratized and corporatized mass society now present in most of the postwar West. Certainly new issues and even old issues couched in new terms would command the efforts of future reformers. Such issues as the environment, the pent-up demands of racial minorities, and women's issues would always be fought out against the background of the West's various stages of economic maturity and diversification, which differ from state to state.

Notes

1. An updated account of the "plundered province" thesis is to be found in William G. Robbins, "The 'Plundered Province' Thesis and Recent Historiography of the American West," *Pacific Historical Review* 55 (November 1986): 577–97.

2. Harry N. Scheiber, "Government and the Economy: Studies of the 'Commonwealth Policy' in Nineteenth-Century America," *Journal of Interdisciplinary History* 3 (Summer 1972): 135–51.

3. As quoted from Alexis de Tocqueville's *Democracy in America* in John Patrick Diggins, *The Lost Soul of American Politics: Virtue, Self-Interest, and the Foundations of Liberalism* (New York: Basic Books, 1984), 239.

4. Ruth E. Sutter, *The Next Place You Come To: A Historical Introduction of Communities in North America* (Englewood Cliffs, N.J.: Prentice-Hall, 1973).

5. Paolo E. Coletta, *William Jennings Bryan: Political Evangelist, 1860–1908* (Lincoln: University of Nebraska Press, 1969), 179.

6. A recent discussion of sectionalism in its modern setting is Richard Franklin Bensel, *Sectionalism and American Political Development: 1880–1980* (Madison: University of Wisconsin Press, 1984).

7. Kenneth N. Owens, "Patterns and Structure in Western Territorial Politics," *Western Historical Quarterly* 1 (October 1970): 391; Russell R. Elliott, *Servant of Power: A Political Biography of William M. Stewart* (Reno: University of Nevada Press, 1984).

8. Frederick Jackson Turner, "Social Forces in American History," *American Historical Review* 16 (January 1911): 223; Richard O. Davies, "Arizona's Recent Past: Opportunities for Research," *Arizona and the West* 9 (Autumn 1967): 247–50.

9. William Howard Moore, "Progressivism and the Social Gospel in Wyoming: The Antigambling Act of 1901 as a Test Case," *Western Historical Quarterly* 25 (July 1984): 301.

10. The idea that Progressivism was a culmination of long years of diverse protest is strongly supported in the work of David P. Thelen, *Robert M. LaFollette and the Insurgent Spirit* (Boston: Little, Brown and Company, 1976).

11. William D. Rowley, "Reno at the Cross Roads," *Halcyon: A Journal of the Humanities* 6 (1984): 26; Judd Kahn, *Imperial San Francisco: Politics and Planning in an American City, 1897–1906* (Lincoln: University of Nebraska Press, 1979).

12. Samuel P. Hays, *American Political History as Social Analysis* (Knoxville: University of Tennessee Press, 1980), 214–18.

13. George Mowry, *The California Progressives* (Berkeley: University of California Press, 1951); Richard Hofstadter, *Age of Reform: From Bryan to FDR* (New York: Alfred A. Knopf, 1955); Mansel G. Blackford, "Reform Politics in Seattle During the Progressive Era, 1902–1906," *Pacific Northwest Quarterly* 59 (October 1968): 181.

14. G. Michael McCarthy, *Hour of Trial: The Conservation Conflict in Colorado and the West, 1891–1907* (Norman: University of Oklahoma Press, 1977), 88; Gifford Pinchot, "Grazing in Forest Reserves," *The Forester* 7 (November 1901): 276–80.

15. Hays, *American Political History*, 235.

16. William deBuys, *Enchantment and Exploitation: The Life and Hard Times of a New Mexico Mountain Range* (Albuquerque: University of New Mexico Press, 1985), 9.

17. Frederick C. Howe, "Oregon the Most Complete Democracy in the World,"

The West as Laboratory and Mirror of Reform

Hampton's Magazine 36 (April 1911): 467, as quoted in Earl Pomeroy, *The Pacific Slope: A History of California, Oregon, Washington, Idaho, Utah, and Nevada* (New York: Alfred A. Knopf, 1966), 199.

18. Pomeroy, *The Pacific Slope*, 216.

19. Ronald L. Feinman, *Twilight of Progressivism: The Western Republican Senators and the New Deal* (Baltimore: The Johns Hopkins University Press, 1981), 1; Ray Tucker and Frederick R. Barkley, *Sons of the Wild Jackass* (Boston: L. C. Page & Co., 1932).

20. Alfred Runte, *The National Parks: The American Experience* (Lincoln: University of Nebraska Press, 1979), 156–61.

21. Donald C. Swain, "The Bureau of Reclamation and the New Deal, 1933–1940," *Pacific Northwest Quarterly* (July 1970): 137–46; Leonard J. Arrington, "The New Deal in the West: A Preliminary Statistical Inquiry," *Pacific Historical Review* 38 (August 1969): 311–16.

22. Robert E. Firth, *Public Power in Nebraska: A Report on State Ownership* (Lincoln: University of Nebraska Press, 1962).

23. William Pickens, "The New Deal in New Mexico," in John Braeman, Robert H. Bremner, David Brody, eds., *The New Deal: The State and Local Levels*, (Columbus: Ohio State University Press, 1975), 312.

24. James T. Patterson, "The New Deal in the West," *Pacific Historical Review* 38 (August 1969): 322.

25. Pomeroy, *The Pacific Slope*, 245–46.

26. Patterson, "The New Deal in the West," 324.

27. Patterson, "The New Deal in the West," 320.

28. Richard Lowitt, *The New Deal and the West* (Bloomington: Indiana University Press, 1984), 1–7; Feinman, *Twilight of Progressivism*, 143.

29. Feinman, *Twilight of Progressivism*, 207.

30. Richard Hofstadter, *Age of Reform*; Alan Brinkley, "Richard Hofstadter's *The Age of Reform*: A Reconsideration," *Reviews in American History* 13 (September 1985): 477.

31. James F. Wickens, "The New Deal in Colorado," *Pacific Historical Review* 38 (August 1969): 291.

32. Thomas C. Donnelly, ed., *Rocky Mountain Politics* (Albuquerque: University of New Mexico Press, 1940), 3.

33. Donnelly, *Rocky Mountain Politics*, 3.

34. Feinman, *Twilight of Progressivism Reform*, 208–9.

V

Culture of the Twentieth-Century West

During the nineteenth century many aspects of the West's cultural life were derived from the older regions as newcomers strove to replicate institutions and life styles that they had left behind. Within the context of national achievements in culture, the West did not rank very high. But as the West matured in the course of the twentieth century it developed an increasingly diverse array of cultural activities that in many instances made it an innovator or pacesetter for the nation. Fred Erisman traces these changes in the realm of western literary regionalism that fashioned a distinctive cultural genre in American literature. A similar trend is discerned by H. Wayne Morgan in the field of art although he notes that historians have yet to accord it its full significance. Both of these essays document the changing cultural image of the West—from imitator to innovator, from backwater to pacesetter, to the elaboration of a more sophisticated image that deserves fuller development in depth.

12

The Changing Face of Western Literary Regionalism

Fred Erisman

The merging of old and new—of European and American cultures—is clearly reflected in the development of western regional literature. That genre developed as a distinctive form only in the twentieth century, from European origins. Growing from these European roots, it gradually developed its own dynamics. The challenge that the experience of the peopling of the West presented to writers, Erisman notes, was to develop a distinctive image for the region's growth in the twentieth century. Although such an image should attest to the West's particular heritage, it should also be linked to broader trends reflecting the national experience. The challenge of fashioning an image for the West in the twentieth century belongs mainly to literary figures, Erisman notes, but that challenge still needs to be met.

Among the varied resources available to the researcher in American materials, none is so provocative—and so little exploited—as regional literature. The label *regional,* usually combined with *minor,* as in *minor regional* artist, carries an implicit sneer, for it has come to suggest in many minds a limited range of personal vision and a studied degree of artistic parochialism and antiquarianism that verges upon the precious. Behind the veneer of conventional attitudes, however, resides a body of material valuable to any scholar of the West, for in regional literature of any sort one finds matters of both general and specific historical significance—general in the degree to which the genre derives from European and native ancestries, and specific in the manner to which it speaks to the concerns of its time, its place, and its peoples.

The special value of western regional literature within the broader genre derives from its role as the most recent and the most inclusive of the

American regional literatures. Like those literatures, western regionalism derives initially from the regional impulse in general—that impulse seen in British and Continental literatures of the early to middle nineteenth century, as England, Germany, Italy, and other nations strove to assimilate the time's spreading nationalism, and reflected later in American materials of the mid-nineteenth century and after, as the same themes arose in the growing American nation. The particular elements of western regional writing, however, are native, for the genre is perhaps the most enduring legacy of Frederick Jackson Turner's frontier hypothesis of 1893, reflecting in its scope a vision of the all-encompassing, mythic grandeur of the American nation's steady, synthetic, accretive movement across the face of the continent.

At the heart of the hypothesis is the controlling metaphor of a people striving to come to grips—physical, emotional, spiritual, and aesthetic—with the demands of a distinctive but steadily evolving American experience. "The peculiarity of American institutions," Turner writes, "is, the fact that they have been compelled to adapt themselves to the changes of an expanding people—to the changes involved in crossing a continent, in winning a wilderness, and in developing at each area of this progress out of the primitive economic and political conditions of the frontier into the complexity of city life."[1] Compelling though Turner's evocation of environmental determinism remains, his statement of constant social change is the one that remains hauntingly in the mind of the modern reader.

A corresponding sequence of change underlies the growth of western regional literature and establishes its importance to students of western American culture. Janus-faced, even schizophrenic in the degree to which it encompasses past and present, the genre in its most fully developed form is almost wholly a creation of the twentieth century. Yet its origins are nineteenth-century. Like the people whose lives and endeavors it records, it is a genre that has "grown up with the West"; it reflects the interaction of past and present, culture and environment over the better part of two centuries, and it constitutes a compelling record of a people's response to time, to place, and to the lasting human need to organize the distinctive elements of experience in a way that links them to the more sweeping course of all human history.

From these sources, then, one can derive a preliminary definition of regional writing. A regional novel, Phyllis Bentley has argued with reference to British materials, "is the national novel carried to one degree further of subdivision; it is a novel which, concentrating on a particular part . . . of a nation, depicts the life of the region in such a way that the reader is conscious of the characteristics which are unique to [it]."[2] The essential part of the definition resides in the statement's beginning, for the regional novel must be seen as an offshoot of the *national* novel—that is, though it may focus upon the localized and distinctive elements of its chosen area, it nevertheless preserves a degree of national consciousness. The regional novel's action may take place within a tightly circumscribed time and place, but its frame of reference is the greater culture of which it is a part. The one referent gains from the other, and the dual content conveys a synergistic insight to the reader.

The principal components of British regionalism translate readily into the early stages of American regional writing. Even in the earliest stages, however, crucial changes in the genre take place, introduced first by the need to deal with the immense expanse of American landscape and second by the remarkable diversity—already well-established in the mid-nineteenth century—of the American populace. As Turner observes in his later "The Significance of the Section in American History" (1925),

> The American people were not passing into a monotonously uniform space. Rather, even in the colonial period, they were entering successive different geographic provinces; they were pouring their plastic pioneer life into geographic moulds. . . . Not a uniform surface, but a kind of checkerboard of differing environments, lay before them in their settlement. There would be the interplay of the migrating stocks and the new geographic provinces. The outcome would be a combination of the two factors, land and people, the creation of differing societies in the different sections.[3]

The early regional writers quickly perceived the distinctiveness of their geographic sections, and from their strivings to express this distinctiveness within the context of their culture comes American literary regionalism.

The first American literary region to emerge is, not surprisingly, New England and the Northeast. As early as the 1850s its authors began to explore the characteristic themes and tensions that had worked to define the region's early identity. One such theme is the Puritan past, present in works so different as Nathaniel Hawthorne's *The Scarlet Letter* (1850) and *The House of the Seven Gables* (1851) and George Santayana's *The Last Puritan* (1936). The Calvinistic presence is inseparable from New England, but responses to it, colored by changing times and society, differ; Hawthorne and Santayana, each in his own way, evoke that presence and reflect upon its sociocultural impact.

A second element is the presence of the sea, for the fortunes of the Northeast have long been linked to sea as transport, sea as livelihood, sea as a way of life. The sea, therefore, becomes as much a character of New England regionalism as the recurring human types. Its vastness and its silent power contribute to the impact of Herman Melville's *Moby Dick* (1851). Its tides and their influence upon the fisheries become an integral part of Thomas Bailey Aldrich's *The Story of a Bad Boy* (1870), as does the suddenness with which it can strike down a human. The expanded worldview and human vision that sea-borne commerce instills are central to Sarah Orne Jewett's *The Country of the Pointed Firs* (1896). All these works have other points to make, to be sure, but each acknowledges the contribution of the sea in shaping the New England vision.[4]

Perhaps the most distinctive of New England regional traits is its confrontation of age and change. Among the earliest of the developed regions in the United States, it was also one of the first to feel the effects of technological and socioeconomic change and a dwindling population. William Dean Howells's *The Rise of Silas Lapham* (1885), with its conflict between the "old families" of Boston and the city's *nouveau riche*, evokes one aspect of this theme, as does Henry James's *The Bostonians* (1886). Change, age, and the impact of a shifting society underlie Mary Wilkins Freeman's *A New England Nun* (1891) just as they do Jewett's *The Country of the Pointed Firs*, while James's *The Ambassadors* (1903) contrasts the New World's Puritan-based social values with the more humane perspectives of the Old. Taken together, therefore, all three motifs illustrate the synthetic interaction of people, place, and time within the confines of a geographic and cultural region.[5]

A similar gallery of distinctive traits appears in the next major region to gain literary expression, the South. Southern literature, like that of the Northeast, reflects the region's concern with its diverse populations and the effects of its distinctive past. Here, however, the past is largely that of the pre–Civil War era, and its evocation is colored by the presence of the plantation system and Negro slavery, while the population is a more multiethnic one than is found in New England writings. George Washington Cable's *Old Creole Days* (1879) and Kate Chopin's *Bayou Folk* (1894) dramatize the diverse racial mix of the South, while Joel Chandler Harris's *Uncle Remus, His Songs and His Sayings* (1881) and Thomas Nelson Page's *In Ole Virginia* (1887) speak to the peoples and circumstances of plantation life.

These same elements take on added breadth in the hands of more recent writers, who consider southern history and circumstances from the perspective of their mythic implications. The myth of the "Old South" is a powerfully formative one, and its presence shapes southern life and literature in many ways. One finds, for example, William Faulkner exploring the social evolution of the emerging modern South in *Sartoris* (1929), *The Sound and the Fury* (1929), and *Absalom, Absalom!* (1936), tracing the decline of the "old" families and the corresponding rise of the grasping Snopeses. Robert Penn Warren, in *All the King's Men* (1946), links the intrigues of a corrupt politician to the South's yearning for an unattainable ideal. Tennessee Williams's *A Streetcar Named Desire* (1947) uses the vitality of twentieth-century New Orleans to comment upon the futility of clinging to a vanished dream, while Truman Capote, in *Other Voices, Other Rooms* (1948), casts a tale of modern decadence and failure against a backdrop of the rotting dreams of the Old South. Whereas the Northeast views its history reflectively and retrospectively, the regionalism of the South uses its history as a way of contrasting past and present, the faded ideal and the inevitable reality.[6]

Diverse though the regional literatures of the Northeast and the South are, certain parallels exist. Both, for example, deal with relatively well-established social orders—though both societies undergo profound change, one established order evolves into another. The new order may be more or less attractive than the old, but it is nonetheless one that can be described, defined, and built upon. Both literatures, moreover, look in great part to the regions' pasts and their consequences. They reflect upon the ways in which communities have developed, how they have been touched by other communities and ideas, and how the social and emotional strains associated with these influences have brought about new communities. And both, finally, deal with regions in which distances are comprehensible and in which geographic diversity is minimal. Although the two areas differ in size, neither overwhelms its inhabitants—the distances of which the northeastern authors write are ones compatible with foot travel (the sea, in this instance, exists apart from the cohesive region), while those of the South are made manageable by horseback and carriage. The citizens of neither, therefore, have any difficulty in absorbing the region *as region* as a part of their culture.

This is not the case with the American West, and therein lies the region's challenge to the students of its literature and culture. From almost the very outset of American regional consciousness, the prevailing tendency has been to view the West as a coherent, homogeneous entity. Turner himself, in articulating his hypothesis in 1893, remarks that "American history has been in a large degree the history of the colonization of the Great West." Although he does acknowledge that "the farming frontier of the Mississippi Valley presents different conditions from the mining frontier of the Rocky Mountains," his concern is with the West as metaphor, the West as a magnetic attraction drawing the populace irresistibly toward the Pacific. Consciously or unconsciously, therefore, he reinforces a sense of "the West" as a single albeit enormous presence.[7]

The same comprehensive vision informs the work of Turner's followers. Hamlin Garland, for example, calling for realism and regional consciousness in *Crumbling Idols* (1894), poses the issue of literary and intellectual conflict between West and East, and at last gives the nod to the West. "It is my sincere conviction, taking the largest view," he writes, "that the interior is to be henceforth the real America. From these interior spaces of the South and West the most vivid and fearless and original utterance of the coming American democracy will come." In Garland's Romantic vision, it is enough that "West" is "non-East"; like a good Turnerian, he embraces the West comprehensively, discovering in its spaciousness a vitality not to be found elsewhere in the United States.[8]

Later studies echo Turner's all-encompassing vision. Henry Nash Smith, building his *Virgin Land: The American West as Symbol and Myth* (1950) upon Turner's hypotheses, announces that he is concerned with "the impact of the West, the vacant continent beyond the frontier, on the consciousness of Americans." Benjamin T. Spencer, tracing the origins and development of literary regionalism in "Regionalism in American Literature" (1951), suggests the possibility of some literary distinctiveness in the products of the Midwest and the Southwest, but nevertheless grounds his own vision of the West in an area beginning somewhere around the eastern boundary of Indiana and extending on to the Pacific. Both authors speak of geographical or cultural differentiations within the broader region (Smith, for example, separates the hunter's West from the farmer's), yet both speak sweepingly of the region as a whole.[9]

In the last third of the twentieth century, the focus of western studies shifts somewhat, as scholars, building upon *Virgin Land,* begin to consider the greater metaphoric elements of landscape and history. Yet even here the tendency to generalize and homogenize remains. Wallace Stegner, in his essay collection *The Sound of Mountain Water* (1969), speaks often of how the western experience as a whole colors its expression in historical works as well as in fiction. Stuart B. James's "Western American Space and the Human Imagination" (1970) combines mountains and prairie into "a country where the accoutrements of civilization, the supports of tradition and history, dissipate and are burned away; here men are able to carry with them into this stark and gigantic land only a few thin hoardings of culture; and the men themselves, stick-like Giacometti statues, move in emptiness beneath an unsheltering sky." Richard West Sellars, writing in "The Interrelationship of Literature, History, and Geography in Western Writing" (1973), goes even further. The literary West, for him, is "the West of the imagination, the West as a 'state of mind,' an abstraction involving such ideas as innocence, rebirth, and freedom. . . . [It is] the meeting point between myth and the more concrete reality of the western experience, the point where the Utopias and Edens begin to fade into contemporary social conditions and tensions."

The same comprehensive view of the West continues into the 1980s. Arrell Morgan Gibson, considering "The West as Region" (1980), observes that "one of the spectacular developments" in modern American life "has been the transformation of the West from a colonial outback to a mature, coequal region, regularly contesting its Eastern mentor for preeminence in national affairs." In calling for a reevaluation of the West's place in American life, however, he continues the synoptic vision, suggesting that the West be divided solely into the "Old West" (the area between the Thirteen Colonies and the westernmost rim of the Mississippi Valley) and the "New West," extending from the western borders of Missouri and Iowa to the California shore and on to Hawaii. And Fred Erisman, in "Literature and Place: Varieties of Regional Experience" (1981), considers how the West (as one of several other American regions) affects the ways in which its residents perceive it.[10]

That "the West" exists as an entity is undeniable. Like the regions that precede it, it reveals in its history a general, pervasive kind of experience that can be called "western," just as the history of the Northeast reflects a "New England experience," for example, or that of the South a "southern experience." (This generalized kind of history can, in some respects, be equated with "the frontier experience," but the varied western environment and the diverse circumstances of western settlement separate the western frontier experience from that of the earlier eastern settlements.) Yet it is an area vastly larger and more complex than those that precede it, and in that complexity lies its future significance for historians of regional literature.

The literary West can no longer be considered a single, uniform region. Its history within the twentieth century and the literature emanating from it make clear the existence of a number of subregions, each with distinctive environmental and cultural traits of its own, each possessing a discrete history of its own, and each reflecting at least some degree of that distinctiveness in the literature developing from it and about it. Gerald D. Nash's provocative *The American West in the Twentieth Century* (1973) identifies five such subregions: California, the Pacific Northwest, the Rocky Mountains, the Southwest, and the Plains. Raymond D. Gastil, in *Cultural Regions of the United States* (1975), proposes seven subregions; his definitions, however, based upon a more elaborate set of criteria than are Nash's, are oriented principally toward the concerns of social scientists rather than those of literary historians. Regardless of the definition that one accepts, though, the hypothesis that the West exists as a confederacy of regions makes possible an extension of Turner's hypotheses even as it provides an opportunity for new and informative analyses of the several regions' literatures.[11]

The importance of those analyses becomes clear when one considers the relationship of the subregions to the greater region. Each of the smaller locales possesses its own peculiar traits and circumstances. Yet each shares the "westernness" of the parent region and, through that, shares as well in the comprehensive qualities of the American nation. One might, indeed, visualize the West as an archery target—a series of concentric experiences extending from the largest (the national) to the smallest (the subregional).

Each ring of the target and each level of historical experience is identifiably discrete and can be examined in its own right, yet each is a component of the greater whole. It is in the relationships that they bear one to another that their significance lies.

Within the several subregions, the one so far least exploited is the Pacific Northwest, comprising Washington, Oregon, and the greater part of Idaho. The geographic components of the area attest to its distinctiveness: its mountains and forests color its environs as well as the society that has arisen within it, so that one cannot consider the region without acknowledging the pervasive presence of both. It is, moreover, unusual among the subregions of the West in having ample access to water throughout much of its area, so that its rivers, bays, and sounds contribute maritime elements to its identity. Despite this geographical distinctiveness, however, the area has yet to take on a distinctively *literary* regional identity.[12]

There are, to be sure, writers of stature associated with the area—Vardis Fisher, H. L. Davis, Ken Kesey, the poet Richard Hugo. Each of these, moreover, has striven in various ways to use the geographic locales of the area. Fisher's *Toilers of the Hills* (1928) and *Dark Bridwell* (1931) evoke the rigors of the harsh Idaho landscape, but remain largely works of personal exploration. H. L. Davis's *Honey in the Horn* (1935) takes its young antihero through the varied locales and peoples of its Oregon setting, yet rarely becomes more than a twentieth-century revival of nineteenth-century local color fiction. The later writers, Kesey and Hugo, bringing a more comprehensive national perspective to their works, come closer to evoking a sense of the region as region, yet they, too, have other points to make and reflect other influences. Kesey's *Sometimes A Great Notion* (1964) builds upon the region's logging industry to make a pointed comment about commercial bureaucracy and individual integrity, while Hugo's poems (for example, *Run of Jacks* [1961] and *The Death of the Kapowsin Tavern* [1965]) attest to the Northwest's growing environmental consciousness.[13]

Notable though these authors are, the work that to date most effectively evokes the Northwest's regional possibilities is David Rains Wallace's *The Klamath Knot* (1983). An essayist rather than a novelist, Wallace uses the geological and biological zones of the Klamath Mountains as springboards for musings about evolution, history, science, and the nature of the human race, producing a work that explores the full range of mankind's involvement with a place and a time. If, as Donna Gerstenberger has argued, "the inhabitation of the scene is part of the dynamic, the drama of the work and of the [regional] writer's subject," then Wallace's book, a northwestern analogue to *Walden,* serves well to suggest what may yet be done with the distinctive materials of the Northwest.[14]

To the east and south of the Northwest lies the Rocky Mountain subregion, an area as rich in materials for the regionalist as it is in works evoking its particular qualities. Like the Northwest, it is environmentally striking; the ruggedness of its mountain landscape is a fitting complement to the extremes of its climate. And, as in the Northwest, the setting gives rise to the occupations that characterize the area—hunting and trapping initially, mining later, oil exploration most recently. Here, in ways dramatically plain, one sees the truth of Lewis Mumford's observation that "the environment does not act directly upon man; it acts rather by conditioning the kinds of work and activity that are possible in a region. The place does not determine human institutions; but it sets certain conditions." These are all "extractive" undertakings, involving the one-way process of taking from the land while giving nothing in return, and they contribute to the people's characteristic vision of the region's life and culture.[15]

That vision appears strikingly in Wallace Stegner's *Angle of Repose* (1971), a richly complex novel that builds upon the tensions between a western mining engineer and his artistic, eastern-born wife. It is also an essential part of the six major novels of A. B. Guthrie, Jr. Although born in Indiana, Guthrie grew up in Montana, and in his principal writings has inseparably identified himself with the Mountain West. One group of books, the so-called "Dick Summers trilogy," embracing *The Big Sky* (1947), *The Way West* (1949), and *Fair Land, Fair Land* (1982), traces the early history of the area, from the first incursions of trappers, entrepreneurs, and mountain men to the wagon trains of the Oregon Trail. A second group, *These Thousand Hills* (1956), *Arfive* (1971), and *The Last Valley* (1975), records the development and urbanization of the area, bringing Guthrie's account from the later nineteenth century into the era of the 1950s.[16]

Throughout his six books, Guthrie is concerned with two principal themes: the cost of "progress" in human and environmental terms, and the irreversible impact of that progress upon the land. In this respect, therefore, he reflects the Turnerian elements of the regionalist's vision—he consciously invokes the particular environment of a time and place, then goes on to consider the ways in which that environment touches, and is touched by, the human society that encounters it. The land confronted by the mountain men is not that met by the townspeople of Arfive; certain physical features remain the same, to be sure, but the perspectives of one generation are not those of another. As each wave of settlement moves through the locale, it alters what the succeeding generation finds. The landscape endures, but as automobiles supplant horses, towns replace camps, and national concerns overlie local, the people's sense of place is altered irrevocably. Given the way in which that sense incorporates physical *and* cultural place, it is clear that the region does, indeed, have a discrete identity as a region and as a stimulus for its literary exploration.

As one moves into the midwestern subregion, the profound diversity of "the West" begins to emerge. This is the region of the Great Plains, characterized on the one hand by an almost featureless geographical spaciousness and on the other by an unusual mix of national cultures. Here one finds the open prairies that figure so prominently in O. E. Rölvaag's *Giants in the Earth* (1927), Laura Ingalls Wilder's *Little House on the Prairie* (1935), and Wallace Stegner's *The Big Rock Candy Mountain* (1943); the mix of Slavic, German, and Scandinavian cultures that permeates Willa Cather's *O Pioneers!* (1913) and Sinclair Lewis's *Main Street* (1920) as much as it does Rölvaag's novels; and the pervasive sense (seen variously in E. W. Howe's *The Story of a Country Town* [1883] and F. Scott Fitzgerald's *The Great Gatsby* [1925]) of a locale somehow standing apart from the later course of western advance. There can be no doubt that the Midwest possesses a distinctive identity.[17]

Contributing to the region's identity are several elements. One is the sweeping distances involved, for it is an area in which simple space is a significant factor. For Stuart James, the "unimaginable distances" of the prairies serve to reduce the human experience to its most elemental; the region's settlers "are thrown back upon themselves alone in the vast muteness of space. They see in the spiritual nothingness about them the forlorn condition of men." Madness and despair, therefore, become an integral part of midwestern regional writings, as individuals thrown upon their own resources find themselves unable to meet the challenge of space.[18]

Another is weather, for the Midwest is an area of startling climatic contrasts. Drought and floods, withering heat and paralyzing cold, devastating storms and oppressive calms are commonplaces in the region, and leave their mark on its literature. The Kansas cyclone that whisks Dorothy Gale to the Land of Oz is as much a part of the region's life as the drought-ridden farm she leaves behind, just as Laura Wilder's books record the devastations of a Dakota drought and a succession of blizzards.[19] The midwesterner's life is meshed inextricably with the patterns of the weather, creating a consciousness of and sensitivity to the climate that one finds in few other literatures.

A third element is linked to the weather, for the region is largely a farming one. Here, as in the case of the Rocky Mountains, the nature of the area's occupations becomes suggestive, for farming, unlike mining and trapping, involves a differing relationship between settler and locale. The farmer, like the trapper, is ultimately dependent upon natural resources, but becomes a contributor to the cycles of planting and harvesting rather than merely an extractor. Yet the power of nature remains a determining element, and the farmer ignores it at his peril. The inexorability of the natural cycles is clear in works like Howe's *Story of a Country Town* and

Hamlin Garland's *Main-Traveled Roads* (1891), giving to the regional farm novel its pervasive sense of a people at the mercy of forces larger than they.[20]

Throughout the literature of the Midwest one finds the synthetic interaction of culture and locale of which Turner speaks. The works deriving from the region reflect the distinctive circumstances faced by its settlers and its authors—space, climate, ethnic diversity, shifting definitions of and attitudes toward progress, political diversity, and the growth of the cities. In the works of this region, perhaps more clearly than in any of those considered earlier, one sees diverse peoples responding to natural circumstances, drawing upon their own cultural and personal resources to meet perceived needs, yet modifying those resources to suit the situations in which they find themselves.[21]

The diversity of the Midwest is paralleled by that of the Southwest, where still another confluence of environments and cultures occurs. It is here that one finds the sweeping landscapes that the cinema has trained us to think of as "western"—the deserts and cacti of Arizona, the volcanic monoliths of New Mexico and Utah. It is here that one finds the cultural mix traditionally associated with "the West"—Anglo, Spanish, Native American. And it is here that one finds the mythic occupations of "the West"—the vast cattle ranches of the Old West, the Texas oil developments, and the burgeoning cities of the New. Yet one finds other elements as well: the forests and farms of east Texas cannot be denied; the Mormons of Utah are as much a part of the region as the Catholics of New Mexico; the Germans of the Texas Hill Country must be considered alongside the Native American tribes of Oklahoma. Like the Midwest, it is a region distinguished by diversity of geography and population.

That diversity is reflected in its literature. O. Henry (William Sydney Porter) writes of the ranch life of the Spanish Southwest in *Heart of the West* (1907), as does Jack Schaefer in *Monte Walsh* (1963); both reflect the pervasive influence of Spanish culture and the changing nature of the cattle industry. Paul Horgan's concern in *Great River* (1954) is as much with cultural interaction (focusing upon the Anglo, Mexican, Spanish, and Native American peoples of the Southwest) as it is with the history of the Rio Grande. Larry McMurtry uses *Horseman, Pass By* (1961) and *Leaving Cheyenne* (1963) to relate rural–urban tensions in modern Texas, while Edward Abbey, in *Fire on the Mountain* (1962) and *The Monkey Wrench Gang* (1975), inveighs against the environmental cost of progress and what he sees as the relentless despoiling of the southwestern landscape by the greedy and indifferent forces of a burgeoning, bureaucratic society.

Diverse as the southwest's literature is, certain traits stand out. One is a degree of historical awareness, instilled perhaps by the region's cultural diversity and the relative lateness of its assimilation into national life. Unlike the literatures of older regions, that of the Southwest necessarily draws, as Larry Goodwyn points out, upon a peculiar mixture of frontier and nonfrontier elements. It therefore develops a dual vision of its materials that verges upon the self-conscious and frequently leads to a kind of cultural introspection that at times becomes near-chauvinistic. Related to this vision is a tendency to lay claim to particular and often highly localized kinds of distinctiveness. The collection of essays published as *The Texas Literary Tradition* (1983) is a case in point. Although it supplies a valuable overview of authors, works, and themes associated with Texas writing and struggles to arrive at a comprehensive judgment of the state of Texas writing in the late twentieth century, the book also reinforces what Elizabeth Hardwick in another context calls "the mark of the amateurish shining so brightly in the claim to local fame in the arts." Its efforts to establish a universal uniqueness for Texas literature often seem strained; it too frequently overlooks the state's ties with national culture at large, and Texas works at times seem acclaimed simply because they emanate from Texas. Its overall effect, therefore, is to emphasize the localism of Texas writing at the expense of the genre's undeniable regional ties.[22]

Yet the Southwest, like the Midwest, nevertheless demonstrates the workings of the Turnerian synthesis within its literature. The process is clearly illustrated by John Graves's *Goodbye to a River* (1960), an intensely personal account of a canoe trip along the Brazos River shortly before it is to be altered by a series of water-reclamation dams. Graves's book, cognate in many respects with Henry David Thoreau's *A Week on the Concord and Merrimack Rivers,* is a record of his own life-long association with the river, but he uses his memories as the starting points for discussions of "the history of a particular place and the people it has sheltered." That place and those people, like those of the Midwest, came together in a particular way over a particular time; what results is a distinctive, accretive culture shaped by the interaction of the people themselves, the values they brought with them, and the circumstances they encountered. Graves's boyhood and young manhood, recalled and observed by the adult that he has become, provide the specifics upon which he builds the general synthesis, and from both he derives a portrayal of a distinctive, discrete region.[23]

Few other subregions demonstrate the West's complex and contradictory nature so well as does California. Now the most populous of the American states, it is also the most intriguing and frustrating, for its combination of cultures, geography, and history makes it a diverse but telling demonstration of the Turnerian synthesis. As such, it has not lacked for interpreters. The philosopher, Josiah Royce, uses the state as touchstone to explore the national mind in his *California From the Conquest in 1846 to the Second Vigilance Committee in San Francisco; A Study of American Character* (1886). More recently, Franklin Walker focuses attention upon *A Literary History of Southern California* (1950), Frederick Bracher considers "California's Literary Regionalism" (1955), and Kevin Starr, in *Americans and the Californian Dream, 1850–1915* (1973) and *Inventing the Dream: California Through the Progressive Era* (1985) considers California's place in American national mythology.[24] All of these works attest to the fascination that California has held for writers and for critics, yet none entirely captures the state's diversity.

That diversity comprises many elements. One, not surprisingly, is the state's multiethnic nature, incorporating Asian, Hispanic, Anglo, and other cultures to a degree not found elsewhere in the United States. Awareness of this ethnic diversity appears early. Bret Harte won fame with his "Plain Language from Truthful James" (also known as "The Heathen Chinee") in 1870, and incorporated Chinese characters into many of the tales in *The Luck of Roaring Camp and Other Sketches* of the same year; Chinese characters also figure in Kate Douglas Wiggin's *A Summer in a Cañon* (1889). Frank Norris writes of the German colony in San Francisco in *McTeague* (1899); John Steinbeck builds *Tortilla Flat* (1935) upon the lives of the *paisanos* of Monterey; and William Saroyan's *My Name is Aram* (1940) invokes the Armenian culture of northern California. Other states, to be sure, have multiethnic populations, but California alone among the contiguous states has fused multiethnic diversity into a relatively cohesive, functioning society, and its literature reflects its distinctiveness.

A second element is occupational, for California is distinguished by a combination of the extractive and the cooperative, the urban and the agrarian. It is, for example, the state of the Gold Rush, a phenomenon memorably recorded in Bret Harte's "The Luck of Roaring Camp," "The Outcasts of Poker Flat," and other short stories included in his 1870 collection. Yet it is agricultural as well, as works so diverse as Frank Norris's *The Octopus* (1901), Steinbeck's *The Long Valley* (1938), and Gerald Haslam's *Okies* (1973) demonstrate. Norris's novel deals with the wheat farmers of the state while Steinbeck's and Haslam's are concerned with the truck farmers of the Great Central Valley, yet all make clear the part played by agriculture in the state's socioeconomic development. From that agriculture, moreover, comes another facet of California's occupational distinctiveness, its dependence upon the migrant worker and the mercantile complexity underlying the state's network of commercial farms. Haslam's work touches upon this, as does Steinbeck's *The Grapes of Wrath* (1939); however, it is Steinbeck's *In Dubious Battle* (1936) that best dramatizes the ambivalent place of the migrant worker in the California economy.

Also contributing to California's regional distinctiveness is a third element, its geography, for California writers are peculiarly sensitive to the state's varied ecology. California is a state oriented to the sea; the Pacific Ocean forms its western boundary and its ports contribute to its cultural and economic uniqueness. Yet it is also a state of scorching summers and desiccated deserts, fertile valleys, and rock-bound mountains, so that the California writer must accept a geography as complex and as varied as the culture. George R. Stewart captures this complexity well in *Storm* (1941) and *Fire* (1948), examining the varied impact upon the land of the phenomena of a Pacific storm and a forest fire. The seacoast and the coastal redwood forests underlie much of the poetry of Robinson Jeffers, as in *Thurso's Landing, and other Poems* (1932), while John Steinbeck goes on to incorporate virtually the entire ecology of the state into his works. *The Long Valley* (1938) movingly evokes the climate and fogs of the central state; *The Sea of Cortez* (1941), written with the biologist Ed Ricketts, records the philosophical as well as the biological implications of the Gulf of California; and *Cannery Row* (1945) uses the tide pools of the Monterey Peninsula as a backdrop for the musings of its biologist protagonist. All these works, however, achieve the same end: they demonstrate the physical distinctiveness of the state and the effects of that distinctiveness upon its peoples.[25]

The natural scene unquestionably plays a role in defining the California region; at the same time, however, the state's culture is equally affected by the presence and growth of the city. As a result, the presence of the city and the corresponding urban-rural tension become an inherent part of California regionalism. The city as significant element appears as early as Norris's *McTeague* (1899), which juxtaposes McTeague's mining past with the San Francisco in which he builds his dental practice. Jack London's *Martin Eden* (1909) continues the motif, using Eden's sea-faring past as a contrast to the city life that gradually envelops him. The ironies and hypocrisies of urban life inform Nathanael West's *The Day of the Locust* (1939), with its scathing portrait of the California film industry, while Dashiell Hammett's *The Maltese Falcon* (1930) and Raymond Chandler's *The Big Sleep* (1939) and *Farewell, My Lovely* (1940) explore life in San Francisco and Los Angeles, respectively, as seen from the individualistic perspective of the private detective. These works, like Joan Didion's later *Run River* (1963) and *Play It as It Lays* (1970), serve also to remind the reader of the bitter contrast between the ideal and the real that colors so much of California life. A place of variety, vitality, and potential, it nevertheless exerts upon its inhabitants an influence as inexorable as that of the

Midwest. It is a state in which fantasy and reality, beauty and ugliness, principle and hypocrisy coexist simultaneously, combining to give its life and literature their peculiar distinction.[26]

It seems clear that any effort to apply a single "regional" definition or methodology to the American West is doomed to failure. The region, as region, is simply too diverse and too complex for the traditional approaches as manifested in earlier studies of the regionalisms of the United States to accommodate. Indeed, Richard Maxwell Brown makes this dilemma clear in his "The New Regionalism in America, 1970–1981," as he reviews the course of regional studies through the middle 1950s, proclaims their inadequacy, and looks to the development of a "new" regionalism rooted in the technology and themes of the present.[27]

Persuasive though Brown's argument is, it falls short in at least one crucial respect—its rejection of the Turnerian hypothesis as one of the "ikons of American regionalism's past."[28] Turner's ideas, to be sure, have been subjected to extensive revision, and should not be accepted uncritically; nevertheless, the basic principle that Turner outlines, that of a distinctive and continuing interaction between the individual and the place, remains valid. There *are* specific attributes of a particular place; these attributes *do* impinge upon and affect the kind of life that develops in that place; and that life *is* further affected by the traits brought to the region by the persons inhabiting it. Yet Brown is emphatically correct in one respect, for the time has come to review Turnerism *and* regionalism within the context of a revised view of the American West.

Such a revision must begin with the acknowledgement that, within the West (as within any clearly delimited region), certain distinctive, defining traits will endure. These traits may derive from the characteristic ethnic and cultural mix of the area (the way, for example, in which Mormon culture affects the Utah subregion, or Hispanic culture flavors that of the Southwest). They may derive from the particular geographic and environmental configuration of the area (the juxtaposition of mountains and sea in the Northwest, for example, or the all-encompassing presence of the desert and its aridity in the Southwest). Whatever their nature, they provide the stable, ideological foundation upon which the region's conception of itself is built, becoming "keys to the understanding of [the region's] group experience, when examined in close conjunction with the records of everyday activity."[29] They are the intangible, unconscious bases from which development proceeds.

That development, of course, is "progress." Intellectual and conceptual as well as social and economic, progress comes to the subregion from within and without, in the form of new populations, new occupations, new values, and ways of life, all bringing tensions and change to the region. The result is an ongoing dialectic from which comes a regional synthesis. The fixed and traditional elements, Laurence R. Veysey writes, "provide a broad conceptual framework for the analysis of the subculture. They become Geiger counters, sensitively measuring specific actions and institutions. And if a gulf between belief and actual structure appears, such becomes a particular fact, a discrepancy to be accounted for in concrete terms, rather than an 'inevitable' consequence of a rigidly preconceived dichotomy."[30] But change plays a role as well, so that the West, with its continuing influx of new cultures impinging upon the deep-seated ideologies of the past, becomes a valuable testing-ground for the Turner hypothesis.

The very change of which Veysey speaks becomes the starting point for a second element to be considered in western regionalism—the inexorable disappearance of regional distinctiveness. As Jay A. Weinstein points out, "Four related national themes seem particularly well-reflected and well-differentiated in regional literature. These are inequality, race, social mobility, and geographic migration."[31] Within the United States, people move. Socioeconomic mobility is a basic element of the American Dream, present almost from the nation's origins (see Captain John Smith's *A Description of New England* [1616], or Benjamin Franklin's *Autobiography* [1790]), and coloring the lives of individuals ranging from Franklin himself to the fictional Jay Gatsby, born Jimmy Gatz of North Dakota. But physical mobility is also a basic element, as Turner recognized, and from that mobility comes further change, for it contributes to the decay of the particular and the distinctive in the nation's regions.

That change arises from three sources. One is mobility itself: with the advent of inexpensive, rapid, and comfortable means of transportation, the shifting of populations is accelerated. No longer do the unprecedented distances of the West pose a problem; indeed, cities hundreds of miles apart are in some respects closer in terms of "human time" than the more contiguous cities of Europe or the East. A second is the impact of nation-wide communications and the mass media. With the advent of satellite technology, instantaneous, national communication becomes a reality; thus, populations throughout the country, regardless of region or location, can (and do—witness the millions who simultaneously watch the Super Bowl or who saw the incessant replays of the space shuttle explosion) share in the same experience at the same time.[32] And the third is the spread of urbanization. Despite its vast areas of unsettled, even unlivable, territory, the West is an urbanized region: Los Angeles ranks among the most populous cities in the nation, while San Francisco and Seattle, Salt Lake City and Albuquerque, Minneapolis-St. Paul and Dallas-Fort Worth are major urban centers by any criterion. Each, certainly, reflects local elements (as in the weather-determined skyways of Minneapolis, for example, or the Chinatowns of Los Angeles and San Francisco), yet all share in the commonality of the urban experience and reflect already many of the sociopolitical concerns that are commonplaces in the East.

The final element essential to a revision of western regionalism is a reconsideration of the abstract concept of "place." Writers and critics alike must reflect against upon just what "the West" means—in terms historical, geographic, literary, and human. As they do this, it will be helpful to move away from the conception of the West as a homogeneous region, and consider it more closely in light of its varied and important subregions. The need for such a move is noted by Leonard Lutwack in *The Role of Place in Literature* as he remarks: "the more extensive the region and the wider its variety of places, the less precise is the line from environmental cause to literary result and the more we must call on other factors—local history and culture, dialect and folkways—to establish the regional quality of a body of literature."[33] Perceptive though Lutwack's point is, however, it needs clarification, for his heavy emphasis on localism as a guide to "regional quality" smacks of parochialism.

The solution, of course, is for writers to strive to retain a sense of the local, but to link it to the themes and elements that form the common thread of all human experience. As Wilson Clough points out, "Nor is the truly classic in literature ever solely regional in significance. Not the accidents of environment alone but human dilemmas appropriate to their given settings determine the depth of a literature."[34] In this observation is perhaps the final justification of Turner's argument, for Clough sets forth the extent to which both population and environment are participants in the process of regional definition.

The new regionalism for which Brown calls is needed—in literary and historical studies as well as in social and economic studies. The form it will take is difficult to say, but one thing is certain: it will take into account, like Turner before it, the human element of the regional experience. Clough's conception of the new western writer, that person explaining human dilemmas within a given setting, applies as well to the regional historian. What this individual must do is "take himself and his environment with a new seriousness, to examine afresh for weakness or for strength the pattern by which he and his fellow westerners appear to live, and to posit what that code might mean in any extended version over a larger segment of humanity. It is not so much a defense of his own inheritance that he needs as what other major writers have possessed, an enlarged awareness of what is his own and what is not his own."[35] To that end, the regional writer and the regional historian must strive to articulate a new vision of the particular nature of the American West, attesting to its specific and particular elements to be sure, but looking beyond them to the ways in which the life of the subregions expands our knowledge of life within the greater region and the nation. Only from the truly regional vision can come a full understanding of the evolving national synthesis, and when it comes, it will provide challenging new opportunities for students and scholars of the American experience.

Notes

1. Frederick Jackson Turner, "The Significance of the Frontier in American History," in Ray Allen Billington, ed., *Frontier and Section* (Englewood Cliffs: Prentice-Hall, 1961), 37. The backgrounds of western regional writing itself are discussed in Fred Erisman, " 'This is the place': A Regional Approach to Western Literature," *Cross Timbers Review* 1 (Autumn 1984): 41–49. See also F. W. Morgan, "Three Aspects of Regional Consciousness," *Sociological Review* 31 (January 1939): 68–88. The Romantic elements of western American regionalism are examined by Fred Erisman in "Western Regional Writers and the Uses of Place," *Journal of the West* 19 (January 1980): 36–44; also helpful is Sanford R. Marovitz, "Myth and Realism in Recent Criticism of the American Literary West," *Journal of American Studies* 15 (April 1981): 95–114.

2. Phyllis Bentley, *The English Regional Novel* (London: George Allen & Unwin, 1941), 7.

3. Frederick Jackson Turner, "The Significance of the Section in American History," *Frontier and Section*, 126–27. The interaction of people and place in selected literature of the American West is discussed in Fred Erisman, "Western Writers and the Literary Historian," *North Dakota Quarterly* 47 (Autumn 1979): 64–69.

4. For background on Aldrich, Jewett, and the New England context, see Charles S. Samuels, *Thomas Bailey Aldrich* (New York: Twayne, 1965), Richard Cary, *Sarah Orne Jewett* (New York: Twayne, 1962), and Lars Åhnebrink, *The Beginnings of Naturalism in American Fiction, 1891–1903* (Cambridge: Harvard University Press, 1950). Åhnebrink's work is also helpful in dealing with Hamlin Garland and Frank Norris.

5. A thoughtful consideration of change as an element in New England regionalism is Sister Mary R. Coyne, "New England Regionals in the Context of Historical Change" (Ph.D. diss., Case Western Reserve University, 1971).

6. Literary studies of the American South constitute an enormous body of writing, but a good general introduction is Louis D. Rubin, Jr., et al., eds., *The History of Southern Literature* (Baton Rouge: Louisiana State University Press, 1985). Special studies of particular value are Wilbur J. Cash, *The Mind of the South* (New York: Alfred A. Knopf, 1941); William R. Taylor, *Cavalier and Yankee: The Old South and American National Character* (New York: George Braziller, 1961); Charles E. Coate, "Regional Varieties of the American Literature," *Indian Journal of American Studies* 7 (January 1977): 8–27; and Carl N. Degler, *Place Over Time: The Continuity of Southern Literature* (Baton Rouge: Louisiana State University Press, 1977). A thorough although now somewhat

dated bibliography is Louis D. Rubin, Jr., ed., *A Bibliographical Guide to the Study of Southern Literature* (Baton Rouge: Louisiana State University Press, 1969). For one author's use of southern regional elements, see Fred Erisman, "The Romantic Regionalism of Harper Lee," *Alabama Review* 24 (April 1973): 122–36.

7. Turner, "Significance of the Frontier," 37, 43. An overview of the development of a distinctively western literary history appears in Fred Erisman, "Early Western Literary Scholars," in J. Golden Taylor and Thomas J. Lyon, et al., eds., *A Literary History of the American West* (Fort Worth: Texas Christian University Press, 1987), 303–16; also informative is Ben M. Vorpahl, "Roosevelt, Wister, Turner, and Remington," in the same volume, pp. 276–302.

8. Hamlin Garland, *Crumbling Idols*. [1894] (Cambridge: Harvard University Press, 1960), 134.

9. Henry Nash Smith, *Virgin Land: The American West As Symbol and Myth*. 20th Anniversary Edn. (Cambridge: Harvard University Press, 1970), 4; Benjamin T. Spencer, "Regionalism in American Literature," Merrill Jensen, ed., *Regionalism in America*, (Madison: University of Wisconsin Press, 1965), 219–60.

10. Wallace Stegner, *The Sound of Mountain Water* (Garden City, N.Y.: Doubleday, 1969); Stuart B. James, "Western American Space and the Human Imagination," *Western Humanities Review* 24 (Spring 1970): 149; Richard West Sellars, "The Interrelationship of Literature, History, and Geography in Western Writing," *Western Historical Quarterly* 4 (April 1973): 172; Arrell Morgan Gibson, "The West As Region," *Journal of American Culture* 3 (Summer 1980): 285–86; Fred Erisman, "Literature and Place: Varieties of Regional Experience," *Journal of Regional Cultures* 1 (Fall/Winter 1981): 144–53.

11. Gerald D. Nash, *The American West in the Twentieth Century* (Englewood Cliffs, N.J.: Prentice-Hall, 1973), vii–viii; Raymond D. Gastil, *Cultural Regions of the United States* (Seattle: University of Washington Press, 1975), 204–72.

12. Richard W. Etulain, "Comment," *Pacific Northwest Quarterly* 64 (October 1973): 157–59.

13. John R. Milton, *The Novel of the American West* (Lincoln: University of Nebraska Press, 1980), 135–50; Edwin R. Bingham, "Pacific Northwest Writing: Reaching for Regional Identity," in William G. Robbins, Robert J. Frank, and Richard E. Ross, eds., *Regionalism and the Pacific Northwest*, (Corvallis: Oregon State University Press, 1983), 151–74; Richard Maxwell Brown, "The New Regionalism in America, 1970–1981," *Regionalism and the Pacific Northwest*, 69–70. For details on the lives of authors mentioned, see Joseph M. Flora, *Vardis Fisher* (New York: Twayne, 1965); Paul T. Bryant, *H. L. Davis* (Boston: Twayne, 1978); Bruce Carnes, *Ken Kesey*. (Boise: Boise State University, 1974); and Donna Gerstenberger, *Richard Hugo*. (Boise: Boise State University, 1983).

14. Gerstenberger, *Richard Hugo*, 40; David Rains Wallace, *The Klamath Knot: Explorations of Myth and Evolution* (San Francisco: Sierra Club Books, 1983).

15. Lewis Mumford, "Regionalism and Irregionalism," *Sociological Review* 19 (October 1927): 285.

16. Essential to any study of Stegner and his work are Forrest G. Robinson and Margaret G. Robinson, *Wallace Stegner* (Boston: Twayne, 1977) and Wallace

Stegner and Richard W. Etulain, *Conversations with Wallace Stegner on Western History and Literature* (Salt Lake City: University of Utah Press, 1983). For Guthrie's career and achievements, see Thomas W. Ford, *A. B. Guthrie, Jr.* (Boston: Twayne, 1981); and Fred Erisman, "A. B. Guthrie, Jr.," in Fred Erisman and Richard W. Etulain, eds., *Fifty Western Writers*, (Westport, Conn.: Greenwood Press, 1982), 162–71.

17. See Calder M. Pickett, *Ed Howe: Country Town Philosopher* (Lawrence: University Press of Kansas, 1968); Paul Reigstad, *Rölvaag: His Life and Art* (Lincoln: University of Nebraska Press, 1972); and Barry Gross, "Back West: Time and Place in *The Great Gatsby*," *Western American Literature* 8 (Spring-Summer 1973): 3–13.

18. Stuart B. James, "Western American Space and the Human Imagination," 149–50. For illustrations of this theme, see also O. E. Rölvaag, *Giants in the Earth* (New York: Harper, 1927), and Laura Ingalls Wilder, *These Happy Golden Years* (New York: Harper, 1943). A good introduction to Wilder's life is Janet Spaeth, *Laura Ingalls Wilder* (Boston: Twayne, 1987). A consideration of the "Little House" books in a Turnerian context is Fred Erisman, "Laura Ingalls Wilder," in Jane M. Bingham, ed., *Writers for Children* (New York: Charles Scribner's Sons, 1988): 617–24.

19. The Great Plains exists as a genuine presence in such works as L. Frank Baum, *The Wonderful Wizard of Oz* [1900], ed. Michael Patrick Hearn (New York: Schocken Books, 1983); Laura Ingalls Wilder, *By The Shores of Silver Lake* (New York: Harper, 1939); and Laura Ingalls Wilder, *The Long Winter* (New York: Harper, 1940). A discussion of regional elements in these and other works for young readers appears in Fred Erisman, "Regionalism in American Children's Literature," in James H. Fraser, ed., *Society & Children's Literature* (Boston: David R. Godine, Publisher, 1978), 53–75. Also helpful is Erisman's "American Regional Juvenile Literature, 1870–1910: An Annotated Bibliography," *American Literary Realism* 6 (Spring 1973): 109–122.

20. Roy W. Meyer, *The Middle Western Farm Novel in the Twentieth Century* (Lincoln: University of Nebraska Press, 1965). See also Charles C. Walcutt, *American Literary Naturalism: A Divided Stream* (Minneapolis: University of Minnesota Press, 1956).

21. John Knoepfle, "Crossing the Midwest," in John Gordon Burke, ed., *Regional Perspectives* (Chicago: American Library Association, 1973), 78–174; Frederick C. Luebke, "Regionalism and the Great Plains: Problems of Concept and Method," *Western Historical Quarterly* 15 (January 1984): 19–38; Virginia Faulkner and Frederick C. Luebke, eds., *Vision and Refuge: Essays on the Literature of the Great Plains* (Lincoln: University of Nebraska Press, 1982).

22. Larry Goodwyn, "The Frontier Myth and Southwestern Literature," *Regional Perspectives*, 176–80; Elizabeth Hardwick, "Southern Literature: The Cultural Assumptions of Regionalism," in Philip Castille and William Osborne, eds., *Southern Literature in Transition* (Memphis: Memphis State University Press, 1983), 18; Don Graham, James W. Lee, and William T. Pilkington, eds., *The Texas Literary Tradition* (Austin: College of Liberal Arts, University of Texas, 1983). For bibliographical materials, see Mabel Major and T. M. Pearce, *Southwest Heritage*. 3rd ed. (Albuquerque: University of New Mexico Press, 1972), and

John Q. Anderson, et al., eds. *Southwestern American Literature: A Bibliography* (Chicago: Swallow Press, 1980).

23. Goodwyn, "The Frontier Myth," 190. A good starting point for any consideration of Graves is M. E. Bradford, "John Graves," in Erisman and Etulain, *Fifty Western Writers*, 142–51. See also Lou Rodenberger, "Man and the Land in John Graves' *Hard Scrabble*," *Cross Timbers Review* 1 (December 1984): 31–39.

24. Josiah Royce, *California from the Conquest in 1846 to the Second Vigilance Committee in San Francisco; A Study of American Character* [1886] (New York: Alfred A. Knopf, 1948); Franklin W. Walker, *A Literary History of Southern California* (Berkeley: University of California Press, 1950); Frederick Bracher, "California's Literary Regionalism," *American Quarterly* 7 (Fall 1955): 275–84; Kevin Starr, *Americans and the California Dream: 1850–1915* (New York: Oxford University Press, 1973); Starr, *Inventing the Dream: California Through the Progressive Era* (New York: Oxford University Press, 1985).

25. For discussions of Steinbeck and his work, see (among others) Richard Astro, *John Steinbeck and Edward F. Ricketts: The Shaping of a Novelist* (Minneapolis: University of Minnesota Press, 1973); Warren French, *John Steinbeck*. 2nd ed. (New York: Twayne, 1975); and Jackson J. Benson, *The True Adventures of John Steinbeck, Writer* (New York: Viking Press, 1984).

26. The contradictions of urban California are expressed well in David Fine, ed., *Los Angeles in Fiction: A Collection of Original Essays* (Albuquerque: University of New Mexico Press, 1984).

27. Richard Maxwell Brown, "The New Regionalism in America, 1970–1981," 37–96.

28. Brown, "The New Regionalism," 44; for a somewhat different perspective on the issue of regional identity in contemporary times, see Carl Abbott, "Frontiers and Sections: Cities and Regions in American Growth," *American Quarterly* 37 (Bibliography 1985): 395–410.

29. Laurence R. Veysey, "Myth and Reality in Approaching American Regionalism," *American Quarterly* 12 (Spring 1960): 42.

30. Veysey, "Myth and Reality," 43. For a discussion of this issue in a more extensive context, see Karl Mannheim, *Ideology and Utopia* (1936).

31. Jay A. Weinstein, "The Social Roots of Regionalism in American Literature," *Indian Journal of American Studies* 7 (January 1977): 4–5.

32. On the simultaneity of experience, see Daniel Boorstin, *The Image, or What Happened to the American Dream* (New York: Atheneum, 1962). A stimulating study of perceptions of space and time in *fin de siècle* Europe is Stephen Kern, *The Culture of Time and Space, 1880–1915* (Cambridge: Harvard University Press, 1983), for many of Kern's observations carry implications pertinent to the United States.

33. Leonard Lutwack, *The Role of Place in Literature* (Syracuse: Syracuse University Press, 1984), 138.

34. Wilson O. Clough, *The Necessary Earth: Nature and Solitude in American Literature* (Austin: University of Texas Press, 1964), 155.

35. Clough, *The Necessary Earth*, 165.

13

Main Currents in Twentieth-Century Western Art

H. Wayne Morgan

No less than writers, artists have played a major role as image makers of the West. As H. Wayne Morgan indicates in this essay, their role in the nineteenth century is well understood. In fact, they influenced not only the contemporaries of their own age, but succeeding generations in later years who no longer had a direct acquaintance with a frontier West that had long disappeared. Many Americans had an image of the West that had been drawn for them on canvas. But the role of art and artists in the twentieth-century West is still obscure. The changes in western life during the last one hundred years still need to be recorded and identified by artists—as they were for the nineteenth century—while scholars still have the mission of more fully assessing the impact of art on the cultural life of the West after 1890. Without a clearer understanding of this artistic dimension, the general image of the twentieth-century West will remain somewhat blurred.

When Horace Greeley advised young men to go west and grow up with the country, he had uppermost in mind the potential entrepreneur and settler. But he just as easily could have included the painter, for the region offered the brush and pencil opportunities equal to those that attracted the businessman. Artists were important in the settlement of the West, beginning with the white man's push over the mountains of Pennsylvania. They produced paintings that established an enduring set of images, such as that of George Caleb Bingham's *Emigration of Daniel Boone* (1851–52), which showed an idealized Boone striding toward the viewer in the midst of equally confident settlers armed with the implements of civilization. The woodsman clearing the land, the citizens of frontier hamlets in the Old Northwest and in the Missouri and Mississippi valleys, the rivermen of Bingham's *Fur Traders Descending the Missouri* (1845), and *Raftsmen Playing Cards* (1847), were vivid in the country's cultural imagination through such works.

Artists were among the first people into the country in the ongoing process of discovering and recording the West. They came in the van of military expeditions that mapped the national domain and encountered the Indians living on it. They accompanied both government and private expeditions that charted railroad routes. By the end of the century, the Santa Fe and other lines employed artists to depict and advertise the natural and human wonders along the tracks and beyond the romantic horizon that beckoned to tourists.[1] These artists recorded the dramatic landscape, its flora and fauna, rivers and lakes, and sought to capture its special qualities of atmosphere as well as appearances. The tradition of the artist as recorder, a historian in paint, endured well into the twentieth century. In 1940, the New Mexico painter Peter Hurd said that "the artist ... is the historian of the present, and it is only in linking the past with the present—viz., with his own lived experience, that he can make an enduring thing."[2]

These early painters and illustrators began to make the West and its life seem real through accurate and attractive visual images. They depicted life in army camps, among expeditionaries, and in the settlements scattered throughout the vast region. They were equally important in making the Indians seem real to many Americans. George Catlin recorded Indians with careful attention to their handicrafts, decorations, and persons, and depicted them as members of viable cultures. Richard H. Kern, an expeditionary artist in the Southwest before the Civil War, often depicted the ruins and relics of prior Indian civilizations, which gave current inhabitants an important history.[3] Painting and illustration thus gave Indian cultures complexity and variety before photography captured more realistic images in the latter part of the nineteenth century. These artists recorded the facts and types of Indian life, and also began to see them as artistic subjects worthy of formal treatment and interest.

A new generation of painters took a similar approach to the white civilization that began to dominate the trans-Mississippi region after the Civil War. The most famous of these was Frederic Remington, whose work captured national attention and marked him both as a significant formalist painter and a recorder of western life in a vivid illustrational style. Remington delineated aspects of frontier life that appealed to the American imagination. He focused on physical action and drama, whether in a cattle drive or in a skirmish between pony soldiers and Indians. His detailed canvases, often drawn for widely read popular magazines, made their stories and figures seem real. Few artists exceeded his ability to render motion, light and shadow effects, with a rich coloration that heightened the sense of the drama in western life. Above all, he combined romance and realism, myth and verity in ways that made his works seem comfortable yet challenging to Americans.

The eastern critic Royal Cortissoz, who was very knowledgeable about world art, appreciated these qualities in Remington's regionalism. "The joy of living gets into Mr. Remington's work," he noted in 1910.[4] Remington himself realized that he was recording a life and culture that was vanishing, however vivid it seemed to contemporaries. "I knew the railroad was coming—I saw men already swarming into the land," he wrote in 1905. "I knew the derby hat, the smoking chimneys, the cord-binder, and the thirty-day note were upon us in a restless surge. I knew the wild riders and the vacant land were about to vanish forever, and the more I considered the subject the bigger Forever loomed."[5]

Remington's contemporary Charles M. Russell had an equal popular impact, though he was a much less able painter. He took the West, its cowboy types, their labors and amusements seriously. He was Everyman as Artist, as self-made and successful as any eastern businessman, and spoke a democratic language in paint. His work seemed natural and effortless, easily accessible to the typical viewer. And while his canvases did not overtly call for reflection or analysis, they recorded a vanishing life that left enduring images in the national consciousness.[6]

This accumulating artistic vision of the West as a region with special qualities and viable cultures reached an expanding number of Americans in varied formats. Exhibitions of paintings impressed many viewers. But the images of western life were familiar to more people through handbills, magazine illustrations, and plates that enriched the texts of novels and travel books. The artist was as important as the writer in giving the West presence in American thought.[7]

Late-nineteenth-century painters were better trained and more reflective about the purposes of art than were many of the earlier artists who went west. The same was true of the growing art public, whose knowledge of and exposure to world art steadily expanded, even as both critics and patrons hoped to find special roles for American art and culture. In this context, the West had unusual appeals to some painters in the century that followed the Civil War.

Foremost among these was the power of the topography. Natural forms were so grand and unusual that they determined the reaction of both painter and patron. Mountains, canyons, river courses, lakes, and the horizon itself seemed over-scale, and offered potent subject matter for painters who worked in almost any style. New Mexico spoke with a clarified voice to the painter Ernest L. Blumenschein. "I realized I was getting my own impressions from nature, seeing it for the first time with my own eyes, uninfluenced by the art of any man."[8]

Light was an equally powerful influence. The clear air and broad vistas in many places created a sense of grandeur. The light in turn caused painters to adopt a higher, richer palette and to make the landforms even more impressive. Light combined with distance to alter traditional ideas about perspective and subject matter in designs. The dramatic weather made Peter Hurd recall the great art tradition. "The weather has been simply gorgeous—magnificent skies sweeping across infinite distances, shimmering mirages, thunderstorms that fly over the plains with the awful majesty of avenging angels in a renaissance painting. I had forgotten how truly marvelous it is. . . ."[9]

The scale of the West changed the artist's sense of man's relationship to nature and natural forces. Albert Bierstadt's huge canvases reflected the need to depict the complexities that followed from large scale and overwhelming natural forms. Many painters ignored or minimized the human figure. Thomas Moran and others made the landscape and natural processes the center of artistic attention. Still others attempted to depict man and his activities as part of much larger processes rather than as something central or special in the order of things.

Whatever their solutions to these problems of altered scale, coloration, and light effects, painters of enduring works such as Bierstadt or Moran sought first causes and large themes. Like their predecessors, they were recorders, interested in the land and its cultures. But they also hoped to capture a sense of the sublime that produced a feeling of unity and expanded imagination even while provoking awe in the midst of such grandeur.[10]

Painters steadily became aware of the role of culture in the landscape. The region had accommodated a host of civilizations, many now vanished, each of which left a layer of cultural deposit that influenced successors. The original Indian cultures yielded to Europeans, especially the Spanish, whose own civilization then absorbed that of the area they conquered. The American fell heir to these changes in language, customs, artifacts, architecture, and ways of thought. The man who brought modern civilization in a wagon or parlor car sooner or later had to reflect on the symbolism of the ancient Indian ruins and building sites, and the Spanish buildings where he lived, worked, or prayed.

This sense of layered civilization and cultural endurance was especially strong for artists in the Southwest. In many ways, this region played the role for American artists that North Africa and the Near East had played for earlier European Romanticists such as Eugène Delacroix. The land and people were dramatic, unusual, fit subjects for any painter. But both land and people also radiated a sense of cultural longevity that answered the need in many artists for order even as they pursued the temporal and picturesque. This kind of life and place offered the hope of expanded imagination, and of both continuity and variety in everyday life. Art, nature, and living might thus become one, or at least proceed in the same direction.

This feeling had a long life among artists. It lay at the heart of the experience and work of the celebrated Taos-Santa Fe school. Peter Hurd summed it up a generation later in the 1930s from his vantage point in Roswell, New Mexico. "People here do seem moved by the beauty of the country. Perhaps it is because the tempo is a bit slower here and there is time for observation and meditation," he wrote his skeptical father-in-law, the famous illustrator N. C. Wyeth, who lived in Pennsylvania. "Of course, one finds arid natures in many people—but there is also a deep resonant richness among the mountain folk [and] a simple mysticism, if one can combine the two words. I mean by this there is a continuous naive and child-like speculation on the phenomena of the world, physical and metaphysical, and on the universe."[11]

Indian life inevitably impressed both settlers and artists. The Indian cultures, of course, were as varied as those of Europe's nationalities. The arts and crafts of northwestern Indians commanded an audience among experts and some collectors, who prized their canoes, totems, masks and soapstone carvings. The Plains Indians were more generally familiar, and there was some interest in hide paintings, decorated teepees, and shell or bone jewelry. But popular attention soon focused on the southwestern Indian arts. Turquoise, silver, pottery and baskets, rugs and blankets all seemed part of the broad world tradition, however unusual. The discovery of ancient ruins, the settled life of the pueblos, and the increasing number of scientific reports of ethnographers and anthropologists combined to make this region seem both exotic and historic to whites. It was also easily accessible by railroad at the end of the century, then by car or tourbus. From the first, the Indian was central in the West's art tradition. He was *there* for white reaction, and had long related to nature while developing elaborate decorations and art forms based on both the appearance and the mysterious processes of nature.

The most impressive aspect of Indian art was its tendency to abstraction. Unlike whites, Indians sought essentials rather than realistic details. The Plains artist reduced battle experiences to simple figures and stylized horses. He often used nonrealistic colors, and exaggerated arms and legs to depict action. He might also telescope time, simultaneously showing the beginning, development, and end of a battle, in order to intensify the sense of action.[12] The elegant abstract designs on southwestern pottery represented stylized earth forms, flora and fauna, weather, and even dreams.[13] Early Navajo blankets employed stripes and bars to enhance the wearer's figure.[14] The tourists' demands for drama and variety that satisfied their stereotypes of the Indian and the West caused the Navajos and other weavers to adopt unusual designs and bright aniline dyes after the 1870s. But the inevitable reaction followed, and both traders and purchasers demanded a return to traditional work at the beginning of the twentieth century. The Navajos and others repeated this progression in jewelry. They learned metalworking from the Mexicans, and made silver jewelry, later set with stones and shells, for themselves, then for soldiers and traders, and finally for a tourist industry. Original simple abstract design yielded to ornate or detailed work, but then returned to essentials with what purchasers regarded as special Indian qualities.[15] The approach in painting, which all the crafts influenced, was similar. The materials and procedures in sandpainting, chipping or painting rock surfaces, working in hides or bark, all emphasized essentials over details. Indian artists painted kiva murals and other such works for religious or ceremonial purposes that emphasized flatness and mass rather than realism. The same process occurred in the decoration of shields and teepees.

On the whole, Indian artists and craftsmen were interested in designs that caught the character and roles of people, or the inherent power of nature. Displays of personal technique had their place, but chiefly to emphasize these ideas. Realism as whites knew it thus seemed nonessential or even trivial. The white assault on Indian life also reinforced tendencies to use traditional forms as a way of sustaining pride in tribal heritages. And such ideas and aims were unifying threads in Indian religion, cosmology, and daily life, as well as in arts and crafts. This desire for the condensed statement, and for symbolism and allegory paralled similar longstanding aims in western European art, even as it yielded to contemporary demands for realistic depiction of daily life. Anglo painters such as Ernest Blumenschein appreciated this quest for intensity and simplicity, which in turn produced a sense of power and continuity with the past. "The Indian understands these attributes far better than our own people, who are too often prone to order their art tempered with the ignorance that calls for photographic slavery to the details of nature."[16]

Improved transportation and advertising created a major tourist industry that affected western arts and crafts after 1900. Increasing numbers of easterners came west to see historic sites, ruins, and Indian markets. These Columbuses of the parlor car and tourbus were usually affluent middle class people, often as not women, with influence in their communities. They were happy to spread the gospel of western culture and to display arts and crafts from the great West.

Indian art and artifacts appealed to tourists and collectors. They bore evidence of the human hand and of individuality at a time when mass-produced, machine-made goods seemed inferior and inexpressive to art lovers. Their abstract designs were drawn from nature and seemed logical rather than bizarre amid the great national debate about modernism. The

Indian artist also dignified ordinary objects such as pottery, rugs, baskets, and jewelry. This appealed to the same sensibilities that liked oriental or Persian rugs because they were both beautiful and useful in daily living. Indian art steadily came to seem a natural and legitimate complement to the grand western art tradition, blending a sense of continuity and timelessness with the unusual appearance that appealed to both traditionalists and modernists.[17] The appreciation of Indian arts and crafts made the West seem more cultured and complex in the national mind.

No one understood this better than the Santa Fe Railroad and the Fred Harvey Company. The railroad realized that emphasis on exotic Indian life would increase business along its route. The directors contracted with the Harvey Company to provide passengers with restaurant and hotel facilities. The company tried to construct buildings that conformed to the region's history and Indian cultures. The architect Mary Coulter designed numerous facilities that blended into the natural terrain. She worked in rough, local stone, as in the observation tower on the south rim of the Grand Canyon, that resembled the local prehistoric Indian settlements. She also used the modernized pueblo style in hotel and shop design. This approach gained national attention and widespread use in the Southwest after the New Mexico state building, done in this manner, was the public favorite at the Panama California International Exposition of 1915–16. In the years that followed, John Gaw Meem employed this modernized pueblo mode throughout New Mexico in many private homes, and in major public buildings such as those for the University of New Mexico.[18]

The company also became a major supporter of Indian artists and craftsmen. It fostered the production of jewelry, pottery, rugs, and baskets, often with simplified designs that appealed to the modern tourist. These objects were essentially authentic, and the company and other traders also dealt in available older works. Hotels and stations at western stops had display and sales areas, likely as not with Indians working on artifacts of all kinds. Between 1894 and 1904, the sales of curios, crafts, and artworks along the Santa Fe line increased a thousand percent. The railroad also commissioned paintings of the scenery and people on its route, and had over five hundred by 1940. It issued an annual calendar with the works of major painters illustrating each month. The first of these in 1907 had a run of 300,000 copies, and the series became nationally famous.[19]

In its heyday, the Taos-Santa Fe school of painters was the subject of discussion in national art centers, and promoted both Indian subject matter and arts. John Sloan helped arrange a popular exhibition of Indian works in the 1919 annual show of the Society of Independent Artists in New York. Paintings dealing with New Mexico and its Indians were familiar to art lovers of most major cities by the 1920s. These developments also intensified interest in the arts among Indians. The Great Depression of the 1930s produced modest federal funding and helped create another generation of Indian painters and craftsmen after a period when their culture seemed to be waning. Government policy also aimed at developing arts and crafts for economic reasons.

The famous Taos–Santa Fe art colonies testified both to interest in the West and to the general development of American art appreciation. Such retreats for artists were common in the nineteenth century. France had many in its more exotic provinces such as Normandy and Brittany, as well as south of Paris. Cornish, New Hampshire, where many painters and sculptors spent their summers, was well known, and there were others in the East. But the artists who came to New Mexico differed from eastern counterparts. They tended to be permanent or long-term residents, shared common interests while remaining individualists, and were involved in local cultural and social affairs.

New Mexico captivated many painters. Its high, dry climate allowed them to work steadily the year around. The subtle vegetative covering, the changing colors of mountains and canyons, and cloud formations were all dramatic enough for pen or brush, but did not overwhelm the senses. The awesome majesty of the Rockies and higher elevations elsewhere that had so impressed earlier painters here yielded to a concern for subtlety and reduced scale. The clear atmosphere and brilliant light allowed artists to reproduce a wide range of effects.

The setting also was filled with the echoes of a colorful past. Indian, Hispanic, and Anglo cultures offered picturesque subjects, and created a sense of orderly progression and endurance in a period when many artists reacted against industrialization, standardization, and city life. The Indians might be indifferent to Anglo culture, but were seldom hostile, and there was active interchange between Anglo and Indian artists. Their settled pueblo life reinforced the sense of being in a culture that prized the arts as part of normal living, and that endured in the face of powerful changes. "It is the variety, the depth and breadth of it, rooted in eons of time which explains the secret of its infinite charm," one observer noted in 1916."[20]

The artists who began arriving in Taos in the 1890s, and later in Santa Fe, also had personal reasons for liking the area. Most were well-trained academic painters who had studied in Paris, Munich, or New York, but had wearied of formulistic approaches.[21] Other painters candidly escaped from the routine of studio work, or from fierce competition in the crowded New York art world.[22] In New Mexico, they created a setting in which they were important as artists. Fiestas, fairs, and holidays also allowed them to play out nonconformist roles in a colorful manner. And while several of the Taos–Santa Fe group did quite well financially, for many others this life softened the usual marginal financial situation. It was "more gracious, somehow, to be poor in an adobe house."[23]

The area also gradually developed several resources of major interest to painters. The University of New Mexico in Albuquerque had great collections of artifacts and artworks, as well as literary sources. The Museum of New Mexico and the School of American Research in Santa Fe collected native materials that pertained to archeology, anthropology, ethnography, and the arts. The restored Palace of the Governors and other buildings in Santa Fe became places in which to work and display, as well as to admire.

The results of these labors literally went out to the world. The Taos Society of Artists, formed in 1915, organized travelling art shows. The exhibitions went from Santa Fe to New York, then to Pittsburgh, Detroit, Chicago, Minneapolis, Kansas City, Denver, San Francisco, Los Angeles, and San Diego. Several were available in Honolulu, Shanghai, and Australian cities, and gained international attention.

Indians and their life formed the subjects of the most famous Taos paintings. In the reigning interpretation, Indian civilization was yielding to modern technological culture. The greatest of these painters, such as Joseph Henry Sharp and E. Irving Couse, infused their canvases with an elegiacal view of Indian culture. In general, they were interested in the gravity, dignity and exoticism of the people.[24] At the same time, they intended to depict these scenes accurately, and to record daily life, customs, dress and artifacts for posterity. Sharp was especially conscious of the need to make an accurate record, though he occasionally mixed artifacts from different tribes to enhance the design of a picture. Others, such as Walter Ufer, focused on contemporary life as well.[25] All would have agreed with Bert Phillips that Anglos had much to learn from these ancient cultures in the hurly-burly of modern life. "Why not expect something unusual from an intelligent people who have had only one book for thousands of years, which they have studied and upon which they have depended for their physical, mental and spiritual life—the book of nature?" he asked. "Their whole life is keyed to the rhythm of nature as evidenced by their sense of design in their blankets, pottery, baskets and in their music."[26]

Most of these painters were academic realists, who painted smoothly and elegantly, usually with rich colors, highlighting figures and other subjects with light and shadows. They infused their works with mystery and romanticism. Conscious of the long tradition of western art, they also spoke in allegory and symbols, in a realistic style, which helped make the Indian seem natural to viewers. The Indian father teaching a child to weave in Couse's *The Lesson* (ca. 1897) spoke of familial obligations and love everywhere. Sharp's *The Stoic* (1917), showing an Indian man drawing a heavy and painful burden as part of a test, referred to the lengthy western tradition of religious piety and ceremony. Bert Geer Phillips's *Indian Flute Player,* which showed an Indian man, playing a flute, while standing near a horse in a bucolic setting, resembled a great deal of symbolic European painting.

The portraits, scenes of communal dances and ceremonies, and landscapes with figures that these painters did all made Indians and regional painting seem part of the broad art tradition. The artists also depicted with great skill the special qualities of pueblo life, with its massed architecture as a dramatic backdrop to daily living. "There is almost an uncanny impressiveness to see the Indians at the close of the day standing about on the terraces against the walls reddened by the light," Andrew Dasburg reported to a friend in 1918, "shrouded in their blankets of black or white, looking as if they were the risen dead come out of their tombs to watch the setting sun."[27]

The Taos artists' most famous works dealt with such dramatic scenes, and with the character and symbolism of individuals. But over the years they depicted Indians in many activities, in tribal roles, performing household tasks, in farming or ranching, and as town dwellers or visitors. They also included many women and children as subjects. Many painters were landscapists, and also did genre, animal, and still-life works. Although they were primarily studio painters of the set-piece scene, they also worked outdoors. Victor Higgins was probably the best-known of the group to delineate light and brilliant colors in a suave, almost delicious manner.[28]

They paid similar attention to the lives and traditions of Hispanics, the other group that shaped the area. Hispanic culture had not fundamentally changed, and rested on the family, religion, and the earth that gave a meager living. As with Indians, this seemed to offer emotional satisfactions lacking in modern Anglo civilization, which followed broad concepts of change rather than stability.[29]

Hispanic culture appealed to artists in more specific ways. They studied its handicrafts, which like those of the Indians, enlivened daily life with color, unusual shapes, and even whimsy. The artists were especially taken with the *santos,* carved wooden figures of saints, and *reredos,* decorated altar screens, and other handmade scenes of religious life in clay, wood, or straw. These all seemed to be unmediated expressions of genuine individual beliefs.[30] The artists who believed that modern man must respond to the drama and gravity in Indian life also wanted to feel the intensity in these works.

Many painters in Taos–Santa Fe and elsewhere sought to capture the passing frontier of the cowboy. The photograph and motion picture spoke to a large audience, but there was still a market for book and magazine illustrations, as well as easel pictures. These artists wanted to be modern in employing vivid, flowing, brushwork, and traditional in using subject matter that dealt with myth and heroism. They depicted Indian and white skirmishes, ranch and town life, and the special qualities of vanishing types such as the cowpuncher, sheriff, and outlaw. W. Herbert Dunton hoped to create a legacy for these people who would soon pass into history.[31]

The Taos and Santa Fe painters won prominence just as the art world began to divide between traditionalists and modernists. For Americans, this celebrated conflict peaked with the Armory Show of 1913. The fierce debates involved differing opinions about both the appearance and cultural functions of the arts. Traditionalists, too often dismissed as mere academics, disliked what they saw as poor painting, design, and drawing in modernist work. It too often set out to shock rather than to communicate, in their view, with bold outlines and masses that did not delineate realistic subjects, brazen and noncomplementary colors, and unconventional subject matter. Traditionalists also disliked the untamed self-expression, or egotism as they styled it, in much modern work, which they feared made the artist seem angry or even irrational. This would separate the artist from the public, to art's loss.

The modernists in turn had wearied of the inherited tradition, and believed that the new century ushered in fresh perceptions of nature and the world that painting must express in new ways, however shocking. They were less interested in depicting observed reality than in delineating its essential structures and actions. Art should express sensations that lay behind appearances, which required a level of energy and expression that traditionalists found chaotic and destructive.

Modernism that involved abstraction, derived from European examples, did not influence western painters much until the 1920s. But many already had accepted at least some aspects of the currents of change flowing in American art. They desired a more vivid, exciting appearance for painting, with greater emphasis on depicting either action or the essential forms in appearance rather than on reproducing observed reality. The early American modernists, or independents around Robert Henri, had rejected academic formalism before the Armory Show. These painters, later styled the "Ashcan School," opted to treat unusual aspects of city life, to enhance the colors of their palettes, and to emphasize rich, loose surfaces at the expense of exact drawing.

In a broad sense, many of the Taos–Santa Fe painters were in step with some of these changes. They were realists, but had never hesitated to intensify their colors, use dramatic perspectives, or eliminate details. And somewhat like the New York independents, they had depicted the daily life they knew, often in loosely painted and evocative ways, while continuing to produce great works in the academic mode. They diverged from the modernists chiefly in remaining realistic, however broad their treatment.

The modernist tendency toward stronger expression of emotion and unusual depiction of reality found some champions among established western painters. Ernest L. Blumenschein cautioned against dismissing modernism. "No one artist can represent all the beauty of life," he wrote in 1914:

> Consequently, we have many schools, each accentuating its particular point of view. No man can honestly like them all. But because your taste leads you along certain lines, do not deny the virtues in any other healthy movement, provided, of course, you are convinced it is healthy. Be careful that you do not become over-refined, too elegant, too used to the pretty, to respond to the elemental truths when honestly and crudely presented in art.[32]

Other commentators thought that much of the modernist technique and credo fitted the experience of western artists. "Simplification in art, which with the Moderns is something of an abstract and intellectual problem, should become in our West the logical and inevitable thing, intuitive in process, and charged with emotional reality," Natalie Curtis, wife of the painter Paul Burlin, noted in 1917.[33] John Sloan, a frequent New Mexico visitor, reminded his New York students of the abstract power in the southwestern landscape.[34] Modernism did not win all these painters, but many of them went the logical step beyond traditional realism to render the region's natural forces, figures and drama expressively into basic abstract forms.

Nor did the modernists' fascination with "primitive" art and artifacts of Africa, Asia, and Oceana offend westerners, as it did academics in the East and in Europe. The western painters had devoted their careers to celebrating Indian cultures. They could readily accept the modernist idea that primitive works were more powerful and direct than the carefully studied, designed, and rendered art of the European tradition. They saw little artistic difference between an African mask and a North American Indian fetish or decorated bowl, or a Hispanic *santo*. Reflective modernists did approach the subject with a stronger interest in the theory of design than did western painters. And they sought to enfold these primitive elements into modern painting in general.[35]

By the 1920s, modernism was important in the art life of Santa Fe and Taos, and among western artists elsewhere. Its dynamism was hard to resist, as was its call for new subject matter, or freshly rendered familiar subject matter. The great works of Sharp, Couse, and other pioneers began to seem conventional and repetitive, through over-exposure if nothing else. As with all art movements or styles, success bred familiarity, which generated another cycle of taste. A procession of famous painters visited New Mexico, attempting to adapt modernist techniques to the ancient cultures and landscapes. Robert Henri, John Sloan, John Marin and others worked in their special styles.

Yet as modernism gained some headway among artists, it developed little broad appeal to the art public. The modernism that reduced reality to abstract forms tended to be about itself rather than observed nature. The more modernistic a painting became the more it resembled a style rather than a subject. B. J. O. Nordfeldt, for example, did many works that looked more like Cézanne paintings than like New Mexico subjects. John Marin's southwestern works resembled those he did in Maine. In seeking universal approaches to form, modernism weakened the distinctive appearances and emotional appeals of locales. On the whole, modernism evoked a style rather than a place.[36]

The most appealing of the moderns was probably Georgia O'Keeffe. As a young woman she had found the West compelling while teaching art at a college in the Texas panhandle. Later in New Mexico, she continued to simplify her works, seeking essentials, without losing a sense of communicable reality. She dealt in basic, symbolic forms in studies of pueblo churches, cattle skulls, clouds, or mountains. But these remained realistic enough to communicate symbolism and ideas. She retained a potent sense of design, suave drawing, and rich coloration that made her canvases compelling.[37]

The national art scene incorporated various aspects of modernism in the 1920s, and absorbed different trends in the turbulent decades that followed. The Great Depression of the 1930s affected every aspect of American life, including the arts. The economic collapse made the typical artist's existence even more precarious than usual, and curtailed the activities of museums and collectors. But it also compelled many artists and patrons to re-examine their cultural tastes and ambitions.

One result was a restatement of nationalistic themes in painting as a way of reassuring people that the country's cultural heritage was vital and ongoing, even under such a challenge as world depression. This broadly styled "Regionalism" was especially identified with midwestern painters such as John Steuart Curry, Grant Wood, and Thomas Hart Benton, who returned to the primordial authority of the land and the people and customs they nourished. This approach celebrated folk rituals, religion, and family life at a time when these signs of continuity were critical to people under economic stress. Curry's *Baptism in Kansas* (1928), which showed a congregation witnessing a new member's baptism in a cattle watering tank, testified to the enduring power of religion. Benton's *Cradling Wheat* (1938), with its flowing, stylized figures and landscape forms and vivid colors, symbolized the vitality and endurance of nature and harvest.

In the Southwest a talented group of painters in the Dallas area recorded their region's passage through the hard times of the thirties. They depicted ranchers and farmers struggling against drought and falling prices. The open landscape, with its dramatic vistas and light, also revealed the ill-effects of man's exploitation in this marginal region. But like other regionalists they infused their human types and the land with a sense of endurance. The painting was modernist in relying on thinly worked surfaces, strong outlines in drawings, unusual perspective, and flat, spare masses.[38]

In the West, artists had always focused on the special qualities of the land and people, but regionalism for the moment reinforced the idea of the individuality in each of the country's parts. The New Deal art programs devised to meet the economic emergency also sustained this regionalism. The various federal projects that employed artists, including Indians, such as those in the Works Progress Administration, the Treasury Department, and the Post Office, involved the use of local themes, persons, and history in murals and other decorations.[39]

World War II interrupted artistic developments, but the forty years after 1945 produced greater interaction than ever between painting in the West and that of the world and nation. The great artists of the Taos–Santa Fe tradition left no heirs of equal stature, and the authority of that particular approach declined. Postwar prosperity created new, eclectic art centers in the region's major cities. Interest in western art remained strong, but other styles inevitably gained attention and affected regional painting. There was also another wave of modernism, this time involving abstract or nonobjective painting, which influenced the appearance of the new work, and caused controversy among patrons about its merits.

These changes affected Indian art. Interest in handicrafts continued as the tourist industry expanded and demanded both traditional and new styles, especially in jewelry and rugs. Conventions established in the 1930s dominated painting. This generally involved symmetrical compositions, painting in flat masses of color without emphasizing naturalistic details, and using traditional subjects. Individual figure studies were usually done in outlined masses of watercolor, casein, or oil, with the aim of capturing essentials. Murals tended to be highly stylized, involving familiar symbolism, and done in controlled colors. Much of this work work was extremely elegant and subtle, but in due course became formulistic. Much was also purely decorative, lacking ideas, and was often simply pleasant. The Bambilike deer with large eyes, sleek coats, and cute feet gamboling in sanitized forests became a cliche of this kind of painting. Carefully executed but lifeless scenes of pueblo dances or other activities were standard fare among Indian artists. As always there were many exceptions, but the general trend by the 1950s was toward stagnation.[40]

Great art always depends on special individuals, but styles and expectations alter with social change. This was true at the beginning of the century, with the first incursion of modernist ideas into the American art world. It was true again beginning in the 1960s, when Indian painting received a series of shocks from new artists who examined their heritage in freshly realistic and expressive ways.

Perhaps the most discussed of these was Fritz Scholder, who was a California Mission Indian as well as German, French, and English in ethnic heritage. In the late 1960s, he began to attain both fame and notoriety for dramatic works that restated the appearance and content of Indian art. The typical Scholder canvas was done in a heroic, salon-sized scale. He ignored formal drawing or perspective, and boldly outlined the figures of chiefs, braves, and other Indians, and worked in heavy masses and noncomplementary colors. The figures had distorted proportions with blurred and exaggerated features, and seemed to be engaged in mysterious or threatening actions left to the viewer's imagination. A powerful sense of alienation and rage often suffused these works. Critics in the Indian community accused Scholder of depicting his subjects as savages, and of undermining the careful craftsmanship that had dominated their art for so long. They saw these works as crude and demeaning, unworthy of their concept of Indian nobility either in triumph or adversity.

Scholder came to this style after considerable study of European and American masters. He had obviously surveyed the work of Goya among earlier painters, and of Matisse and Picasso among the first moderns. His sense of scale owed much to the abstract expressionists. The most impressive contemporary influence was the English painter Francis Bacon, noted for his powerfully abstracted images of blurred figures caught in moments of mysterious distress. Scholder's richly painted, colorful surfaces also recalled the work of his teacher Wayne Thiebaud.[41] He could be humorous or ironic, posing an Indian in roughly delineated regalia, wearing sunglasses, eating an ice cream cone, or raising a Coors beer can.

These new levels of expression and irony reflected in part the larger social changes that had overtaken Indian life. Many Indians, including some artists, returned from wartime service with an expanded understanding of a world beyond their insulated reservations. By the 1960s, radio, television, education, and town life also brought fresh influences, for better and worse, into Indian life. Although Scholder did not consider himself exclusively, or even principally, an Indian painter, he realized that Indian art must adapt to social change and heightened intellectuality or become a mere curiosity.

Scholder really introduced mainstream modernism into Indian art, or into art about Indians. His strong outlines, oversized figures, and powerful colors reminded the viewer of the historical drama behind Indian subject matter. These techniques also bespoke a powerful sense of isolation, of suppressed anger and expansive drives. The bold stroke and large size restored grandeur to Indian painting. Scholder thus retained a strong feeling of the Indian's exceptional qualities and history, while using irony to comment on his continuing isolation from society and on the need to adapt to change while remaining self-conscious.

The Navajo painter R. C. Gorman had an equal though different impact on Indian art. In the late 1950s, he wearied of the abstraction that was becoming fashionable. He believed that the figurative tradition could express modern ideas without losing form, especially after seeing the works of the famed Mexican muralist José Clemente Orozco.[42] Gorman attained fame by the 1960s for his figure studies, chiefly of Indian women. These combined academic elegance with traditional native themes in a flowing line that often suggested many mysteries with a minimum of effort.[43]

His landscapes and studies of rock formations and canyons derived directly from historical approaches. "Real Indian art is not made on easels," he once said, "it's on rocks, as in Canyon de Chelly."[44] For all his modernism and suavity, Gorman was in the Indian tradition. He placed flat figures against monochromatic or delicately blended backgrounds. His early coloration was usually subtle, and he opted for essentials in order to create a mood of timelessness and grandeur. Gorman was not as controversial as Scholder because his work was not as expressionistic or anxious. He also became a familiar figure in fashionable circles, benefitting from a strong public demand for things Indian in the 1970s.

The varied ideas about form and content in Indian art continue, as they do in other art areas. But current Indian painters have greatly broadened their approach as a result of contact with mainstream culture, and the impact of dramatic individuals such as Gorman and Scholder. Innovative Indian art now deals with a wider range of subject matter than ever, encompassing portraits, landscapes, genre, even nude figures. It uses overt irony and even sarcasm, and includes a range of new ideas. The Indian artist also works in more media, including oil, pastel, pencil and charcoal, lithography, than did his predecessors.[45] Contemporary Indian art is weakest when it attempts to mimic abstraction and becomes purely decorative, with bright colors and little substance. Much of it also becomes cliched in introducing traditional symbols, such as the eagle or buffalo, or a stylized spirit into decorative or abstract designs. It is at its best when it restates timeless icons and ideas with either fine traditional drawing and composition, or strong individualistic expression.

Other modernist expressions took different forms elsewhere in the West. Modern West Coast art generally matured as variants of reigning national styles, but it retained many aspects of its locales, and had inventive individual artists. It was not always about the traditional West, yet was often western in both tone and subject matter. The Pacific Northwest produced a modernist painting connected to the Orient and local native cultures. Its contemplative, sometimes brooding aura fitted the area's foggy coasts and islands and forested shores. Mark Tobey and Morris Graves were the leading lights, and each created an enigmatic painting. Tobey developed a complex, mysterious abstraction based on interlocking sinuous lines in low-keyed colors. Graves dealt chiefly with animals and natural forms, often on a minute scale, that seemed to evoke a sense of nature's timeless processes. This tradition of contemplation and of cautious change remained strong in the area's arts, although by the 1960s and 1970s it boasted a range of modernist works.[46]

Developments were different farther south, where California was a special case in the arts as in most everything else. Many famous artists had painted the state's scenery in the nineteenth century, and a few local talents such as William Keith developed a landscape tradition based on Barbizon or impressionist models. There were colonies of both writers and artists in San Francisco, Carmel, and later in Los Angeles.

The painter and decorator Arthur Mathews, of the Bay area at the turn of the century, expressed a sense of being special and of having a great future that permeated the state's culture. A well trained academic who had studied in Paris, Mathews painted figures, usually female, in flowing lines, clothed in elegant drapery patterned with sumptuous colors. They were often set in lush landscapes, recalling the allegories of European painting, and symbolizing the exoticism so common in California. He was basically an outstanding figure painter, but also depicted the area's unusual landscape of coastal rocks, cypress tress, and low inland hills. He painted several murals for public buildings that drew on history to emphasize the state's romanticism. He and his wife made fine furniture, frames, and other household objects that integrated arts and crafts with painting and sculpture.[47]

Mathews and other academics did not survive the onslaught of modernism, but they spoke to the state's regard for the unusual and individualistic that would feed various strains of new art. California artists tended to be cautious in appraising the various modernist modes of the 1920s and 1930s, but modernism flowered in many guises after World War II. Its first early spokesman was Clyfford Still. His strange canvases, which began to attract notice in the late 1940s, affected many painters who desired to move beyond established modernist models. These large works, which usually consisted of overlapping areas of richly painted pigment with no apparent references to observed reality, radiated a powerful sense of mystery and grandeur. His desire for new expressions through paint alone that caused viewers to analyze their moods and ideas was a strong example for many younger people. Whatever his intentions, Still's canvases and the feelings they evoked resembled the large paintings of western scenery in the nineteenth century. The abstract as well as the realistic could provoke the sublime.

By the 1960s, interest in and production of new painting dominated the California scene, and the Los Angeles area produced various modernist styles that became the subject of local and national debate. There were the inevitable variations of the abstract, color field, and hard-edged painting that dominated the New York scene. But California also gave the first strong favorable response to the Pop art that challenged these modes. As the 1960s progressed, the Los Angeles art scene offered a proliferation of experimental, or bizarre, art that revealed the strength of the state's tolerance of individual expression. Much of this art employed objects drawn from daily life, used new media such as epoxy resins or plastics, or drew on advertising art to mock mainstream values or to celebrate the cliches that governed modern society. Much of it was simply brassy or outrageous, determined to attract attention. Still other artists worked in highly controlled, austere minimalist modes. Variety, shock, individualism were the watchwords, demonstrating in content and aim how much California's society had changed in a new western culture.[48]

The number of artists throughout the West increased dramatically in the 1970s and early 1980s. An economic boom in the region greatly increased demand for western art among both private collectors and corporations. The large house in Dallas and the huge office building in Phoenix each demanded works that proved the new West had not forgotten its heritage. This wide variety of art was naturally eclectic in style and subject matter. By any standards, its qualities varied greatly, always the case in an expanding market. Many painters attempted to revitalize traditional regional art with abstraction of various kinds, which became purely decorative and hardly distinguishable from similar work done elsewhere. Others opted for anecdote and nostalgia rather than genuine history in depicting life on the range, in the saloon, or in town. Painters of landscapes, animals, portraits, and other traditional subjects abounded. Yet few seemed to present the careful construction, evocative ideas, or beautifully wrought appearances of western painting prior to 1945.[49] Contemporary western painting as a whole needed greater thoughtfulness and more depth in execution than most of its practitioners seemed to use.

The central question confronting the painter of the West is a variation of one that affects everyone in the region: what distinctive aspects of the locale now merit cultural expression? In a time of rapid cultural homogenization in a world economy and society that demand standard rules of operation, can the appearance and spirit of a special West survive in art?

The answer, of course, depends upon events, but there is no inherent reason why western distinctiveness must pass. The landscape itself will always endure, and it retains the power to move artist and patron with scale, color, drama, and variety, the same qualities that so impressed earlier artists. Historical subject matter also survives, though in changing forms. The cowboy needs to be seen afresh. He is now as likely to oversee herds with an airplane as a horse. He drives cattle to market in trucks and tends fences with jeeps. He wears historical costume, visits town for amusement or relief, lives a life of both romance and loneliness, all of which invite artistic interpretation attuned to his continuing symbolism as well as surface appearances. The lawman now drives a fast car, has increased firepower, and talks on a radio, yet retains much of his historical glamor. Many Indians still live on reservations, but many others move to the city. The anxieties, and challenges in this clash of cultures certainly equal those in the first contacts of whites and Indians. How does the urban Indian, for instance, keep his sense of awe of nature, and of continuing traditions in city settings? Can he retain his historical appearances in the face of modern demands for conformity, especially in cities? These themes are as fit for the brush as the pen.

The West's dramatic past will always influence its artists, but should never be reduced to nostalgia or clever anecdote. The artist always has opportunities to delineate individual character in the midst of change. The ghost town is a perfect evocation of the ancient artistic theme *Et ego in Arcadia*, a reminder that other generations have passed this way and that all of life is uncertain. While not forgetting the past, art also needs to record the new West. The cities of the mountain and desert merit interpretation. Their skyscrapers and suburbs are part of a vital landscape. Wayne Thiebaud is a western as well as national artist in his rich, often detached interpretations of Bay Area city life. The same is true of Richard Diebenkorn, whose elegant abstractions are powerful statements about the sense of place and topography of the Santa Monica area.

Students of western art have an equally challenging mission. While the record of artistic and cultural achievement in the region grows each year, much remains to be done. There are no adequate biographies of many major figures, such as E. Irving Couse and Walter Ufer. The story of the Taos–Santa Fe colonies is well known. That of Carmel or San Francisco remains to be told in any detail. On a more complex level, scholars need to examine the relationship of dealers to the promotion of styles and the development of art publics. And what does this say of broader social change in the expanding West as it entered the mainstream of culture? The recent modernists in Los Angeles would be one good such case study. The role of archeologists, anthropologists, ethnographers, who were explorers and discoverers in their own ways, in drawing attention to Indian and Hispanic arts as well as the landscape needs telling. Formalist criticism has a role to play, but is secondary to the cultural historian's aim of seeing what styles express, how they develop and are spread, and why they provoke reactions.

For their part, western artists need to interpret traditional themes and subjects accurately, and with a full measure of attention to their enduring messages about continuity and beauty in life. They also need to adopt new subjects commensurate with the changes that have overtaken the West. Only thus can artists be what their predecessors were, recorders and interpreters of the best and most moving qualities of the region's life. The highway that crosses the desert or climbs the mountains bathed in color leads to new adventures, as did the cattle trail and wagon route.

Notes

1. The basic accounts of this complex process of discovery and mapping remain two books by William H. Goetzmann, *Army Exploration in the American West, 1803–1863* (New Haven: Yale University Press, 1957), and *Exploration and Empire: The Explorers and Scientists in the Winning of the American West* (New York: Knopf, 1966). The importance of artists in a relatively unknown area is discussed in Doris DuBose, "Art and Artists in Arizona, 1847–1912" (Master's thesis, Arizona State University, 1974). See also Richard A. Bartlett, *Great Surveys of the American West* (Norman: University of Oklahoma Press, 1962); and Robert Taft, *Artists and Illustrators of the Old West, 1850–1900* (New York: Scribner's, 1953).

2. Peter Hurd to Henriette Hurd, February 1, 1940, in Robert Metzger, ed., *My Land is the Southwest: Peter Hurd Letters and Journals* (College Station: Texas A & M University Press, 1983), 221.

3. See John C. Ewers, *George Catlin: Painter of Indians in the West* (Washington: Smithsonian Press, 1957), and Loyd Haberly, *Pursuit of the Horizon: A Life of George Catlin* (New York: Macmillan, 1948). See also *Karl Bodmer's America* (Lincoln: University of Nebraska Press, 1984). For Kern, see David J. Weber, *Richard H. Kern: Expeditionary Artist in the Far Southwest 1848–1853* (Albuquerque: University of New Mexico Press, 1985).

4. Royal Cortissoz, "Frederic Remington, A Painter of American Life," *Scribner's Magazine* 47 (February 1910): 192. See also Peggy and Harold Samuels,

Frederic Remington: A Biography (New York: Doubleday, 1982); and Ben M. Vorpahl, *Frederic Remington and the West: With the Eye of the Mind* (Austin: University of Texas Press, 1978).

5. "A Few Words from Mr. Remington," *Collier's* 34 (March 18, 1905): 16.

6. See Frederic G. Renner, *Charles M. Russell* (Austin: University of Texas Press, 1966). See also Brian Dippie, *"Paper Talk": Charlie Russell's American West* (New York: Alfred A. Knopf, 1979).

7. Patricia Trenton and Peter H. Hassrick, *The Rocky Mountains: A Vision for Artists in the Nineteenth Century* (Norman: University of Oklahoma Press, 1983), 244–45.

8. Quoted in Laura Bickerstaff, *Pioneer Artists of Taos*, rev. ed. (Denver: Old West Publishing Co., 1983), 31.

9. Hurd to Henriette Hurd, July 21, 1935, *My Land is the Southwest*, 142–43.

10. Barbara Novak, *Nature and Culture: American Landscape Painting 1825–1875* (New York: Oxford University Press, 1980), 137–56.

11. Hurd to N. C. Wyeth, March [?], 1933, *My Land is the Southwest*, 109–11.

12. Richard Conn, *Circles of the World: Traditional Art of the Plains Indians* (Denver: Denver Art Museum, 1982), 29–30.

13. Ruth L. Bunzell, *The Pueblo Potter: A Study of Creative Imagination in Primitive Art* (New York: Columbia University Press, 1929), 54–55.

14. Anthony Berlant and Mary Hunt Kahlenberg, *Walk in Beauty: The Navajo and Their Blankets* (Boston: New York Graphic Society, 1977), 63–64, 133, 148. For similar developments in an allied art, see Nancy J. Parezo, *Navajo Sandpainting: From Religious Act to Commercial Art* (Tucson: University of Arizona Press, 1983), esp. 20–21.

15. See Arthur Woodward, *Navajo Silver: A Brief History of Navajo Silversmithing* (Flagstaff, AZ: Northland Press, 1971), a reprint of the Museum of Northern Arizona Bulletin No. 14, 1938; John Adair, *The Navajo and Pueblo Silversmiths* (Norman: University of Oklahoma Press, 1944); Marjery Bedinger, *Indian Silver: Navajo and Pueblo Jewelers* (Albuquerque: University of New Mexico Press, 1973); and Larry Frank, *Indian Silver Jewelry of the Southwest, 1865–1930* (Boston: New York Graphic Society, 1978).

16. Alexandre Hogue, "Ernest L. Blumenschein," *Southwest Review* 13 (July 1928): 470. See also Jamake Highwater, *Song From the Earth: American Indian Painting* (Boston: New York Graphic Society, 1976), 62–63; Parezo, *Navajo Sandpainting*, 11–12; and Clara Lee Tanner, *Southwest Indian Painting*, 2nd ed. (Tucson: University of Arizona Press, 1973).

17. Robert Fay Schrader, *The Indian Arts and Crafts Board: An Aspect of New Deal Indian Policy* (Albuquerque: University of New Mexico Press, 1983), 7–13.

18. See Virginia L. Grattan, *Mary Coulter: Builder Upon the Red Earth* (Flagstaff, AZ: Northland Press, 1980); and Bainbridge Bunting, *John Gaw Meem: Southwestern Architect* (Albuquerque: University of New Mexico Press, 1983).

19. See Adair, *Navajo and Pueblo Silversmiths*, 27; Frank, *Indian Silver Jewelry of the Southwest*, 22; Schrader, *Indian Arts and Crafts Board*, 6–11; Keith L. Bryant, "The Atchison, Topeka and Santa Fe Railroad and the Development of the Taos and Santa Fe Art Colonies," *Western Historical Quarterly* 9 (October 1978); 437–53.

20. Paul A. F. Walter, "The Santa Fe–Taos Art Movement," *Art and Archeology* 4 (December 1916): 330. The best introductions to the colonies are Kay Aiken Reeve, *Santa Fe and Taos 1898–1942: An American Cultural Center* (El Paso: Texas Western Press, 1982), and Arrell Morgan Gibson, *The Santa Fe and Taos Colonies: Age of the Muses 1900–1942* (Norman: University of Oklahoma Press, 1983).

21. Van Deren Coke, *Taos and Santa Fe: The Artist's Environment, 1882–1942* (Albuquerque: University of New Mexico Press, 1963), 12–13.

22. Coke, *Nordfeldt the Painter* (Albuquerque: University of New Mexico Press, 1972), 53; Edna Robertson and Sarah Nestor, *Artists of the Canyons and Caminos* (Salt Lake City: Gibbs M. Smith, 1976), 78; Taft, *Artists and Illustrators of the Old West*, 247.

23. Robertson and Nestor, *Artists of the Canyons and Caminos*, 3.

24. Coke, *Nordfeldt the Painter*, 50.

25. Bickerstaff, *Pioneer Artists of Taos*, 128–29; Robertson and Nestor, *Artists of the Canyons and Caminos*, 22.

26. Bickerstaff, *Pioneer Artists of Taos*, 57. See also Ernest L. Blumenschein and Bert G. Phillips, "Appreciation of Indian Art," *El Palacio* 6 (May 1919): 178–79.

27. Coke, *Andrew Dasburg*, 48. See also D. Duane Cummins, *William Robinson Leigh: Western Artist* (Norman: University of Oklahoma Press, 1980), 88.

28. The best cross-section of Taos painting is in Patricia Janis Broder, *Taos: A Painter's Dream* (Boston: New York Graphic Society, 1980). See also Forrest Fenn, *The Beat of the Drum and the Whoop of the Dance: A Study of the Life and Work of Joseph Henry Sharp* (Santa Fe: Fenn Pub. Co., 1983); and the thoughtful essays in Charles C. Eldredge, Julie Schimmel, William H. Truettner, *Art in New Mexico, 1900–1945: Paths to Taos and Santa Fe* (New York: Abbeville Press, 1986).

29. Reeve, *Santa Fe and Taos*, 25–35; Broder, *Taos*, 222; Metzger, ed., *My Land is the Southwest*, 156, 168–69.

30. Coke, *Andrew Dasburg*, 46. See also Sharyn Rohlfsen Udall, *Modernist Painting in New Mexico 1913–1935* (Albuquerque: University of New Mexico Press, 1984), 37.

31. Coke, *Taos and Santa Fe*, 23. See also Julie Schimmel, *The Art and Life of W. Herbert Dunton* (Austin: University of Texas Press, 1984); Cummins, *William Robinson Leigh;* Mildred D. Ladner, *O. C. Seltzer: Painter of the Old West* (Norman: University of Oklahoma Press, 1979); James B. Horan, *The Life and Art of Charles Schreyvogel* (New York: Crown, 1969), for coverage of this genre.

32. Ernest L. Blumenschein, "The Painting of Tomorrow," *Century Magazine* 87 (April 1914): 850.

33. Quoted in Udall, *Modernist Painting in New Mexico*, 21.

34. John Sloan, *The Gist of Art* (New York: American Artists Group, 1944), 147.

35. See Gail Levin, "American Art," in William Rubin, ed., *'Primitivism' in 20th Century Art*, 2 vols. (New York: Museum of Modern Art, 1984), II: 453–73.

36. Coke, *Andrew Dasburg*, 54; Udall, *Modernist Painting in New Mexico*, 130–33; Coke, *Nordfeldt the Painter*, 62–63, 68–69.

37. See Laurie Lisle, *Portrait of an Artist: A Biography of Georgia O'Keeffe*

(New York: Seaview Books, 1980), and *Georgia O'Keeffe* (New York: Viking, 1976).

38. For background on depression art, see Richard D. McKinzie, *The New Deal for Artists* (Princeton: Princeton University Press, 1973). Charles C. Alexander, *Here the Country Lies: Nationalism and the Arts in Twentieth Century America* (Bloomington: Indiana University Press, 1980), is basic to understanding the theme. There is also interesting material in George H. Roeder, Jr., *Forum of Uncertainty: Confrontations With Modern Painting in Twentieth-Century American Thought* (Ann Arbor: UMI Research Press, 1980), esp. 115–85. The midwestern Regionalists can be sampled in Matthew Baigell, *Thomas Hart Benton* (New York: Abrams, 1974); Joseph H. Czestochowski, *John Steuart Curry and Grant Wood: A Portrait of Rural America* (Columbia: University of Missouri Press, 1981); Wanda M. Corn, *Grant Wood: The Regionalist Vision* (New Haven: Yale University Press, 1983); and James M. Dennis, *Grant Wood: A Study in American Art and Culture* (New York: Viking, 1975). The southwestern regionalists can be sampled in Rick Stewart, *Lone Star Regionalism: The Dallas Nine and Their Circle, 1928–1945* (Dallas: Dallas Museum of Art and the Texas Monthly Press, 1985), and Lea Rosson DeLong, *Nature's Forms/Nature's Forces: The Art of Alexandre Hogue* (Norman: University of Oklahoma Press, 1984).

39. See Peter Bermingham, *The New Deal in the Southwest: Arizona and New Mexico* (Tucson: University of Arizona Art Museum, n.d.). There is considerable information on post office murals in the region in Karen Ann Marling, *Wall to Wall America: A Cultural History of Post Office Murals in the Great Depression* (Minneapolis: University of Minnesota Press, 1982); and in Marlene Park and Gerald E. Markowitz, *Democratic Vistas: Post Offices and Public Art in the New Deal* (Philadelphia: Temple University Press, 1985).

40. See Tanner, *Southwest Indian Painting*, 431–46; *100 Years of Native American Painting* (Oklahoma City: Oklahoma Museum of Art, 1978); and J. J. Brody, *Indian Painters and White Patrons* (Albuquerque: University of New Mexico Press, 1971).

41. See Joshua C. Taylor, et al, *Fritz Scholder* (New York: Rizzoli, 1982); Rudy H. Turk, *Scholder/Indians* (Flagstaff, AZ: Northland Press, 1972); and *Two American Painters: Fritz Scholder and T. C. Cannon* (Washington: Smithsonian Press, 1972).

42. Stephen Parks, *R. C. Gorman: A Portrait* (Boston: New York Graphic Society, 1983), 33.

43. Highwater, *Song From the Earth*, 173–75.

44. Parks, *R. C. Gorman*, 38, 56–57, 60.

45. See Rennard Strickland, "The Changing World of Indian Painting and the Philbrook Art Center," in *Native American Art at Philbrook* (Tulsa: Philbrook Museum, 1980), 9–25; and the same author's "Where Have All the Blue Deer Gone? Depth and Diversity in Post-War Indian Painting," *American Indian Art Magazine* 10 (Spring 1985): 36–45. A useful cross-section of contemporary Indian modernists working in various media is Guy and Doris Monthan, *Art and Indian Individualists* (Flagstaff, AZ: Northland Press, 1975); and Edwin L. Wade, ed., *The Arts of the North American Indian: Native Traditions in Evolution* (New York: Hudson Hills Press, 1986).

46. See *Northwest Traditions* (Seattle: Seattle Art Museum, 1978); Bruce Guenther, *50 Northwest Artists* (San Francisco: Chronicle Books, 1983); and Peter Plagens, *Sunshine Muse: Contemporary Art on the West Coast* (New York: Praeger, 1974).

47. Harvey L. Jones, *Mathews: Masterpieces of the California Decorative Style* (Layton, Utah: Gibbs M. Smith and the Oakland Museum, 1985); see also Helen Laird, *Carl Oscar Borg and the Magic Region* (Layton, Utah: Gibbs M. Smith, 1985), 30–31, 49–51; Kevin Starr, *Americans and the California Dream, 1850–1915* (New York: Oxford, 1973), 239–306, and the same author's *Inventing the Dream: California Through the Progressive Era* (New York: Oxford, 1985), 64–127, 176–98.

48. Thomas Albright, *Art in the San Francisco Bay Area, 1945–1980* (Berkeley: University of California Press, 1985); and Plagens, *Sunshine Muse*, passim.

49. One of the best overviews of current western art is Peggy and Harold Samuels, *Contemporary Western Artists* (Houston: Southwest Art Pub. Co., 1982), and the same authors' *The Illustrated Biographical Encyclopedia of Artists of the American West* (New York: Doubleday, 1976). Two magazines are important in following current developments, *Southwest Art* (1971–), and the *American Indian Art Magazine* (1975–).

Epilogue
Sharpening the Image
Gerald D. Nash

As readers reflect on the diverse essays in this volume they are bound to confront some of the broader issues raised by the authors as these touch upon the developing image of the twentieth-century West. The whole is clearly larger than the parts, for collectively the essays suggest the outlines of an emerging image of the West during the last one hundred years. This Epilogue seeks to identify the distinctive characteristics of that image more explicitly, although it is obvious that it will need to be broadened and deepened in succeeding years. Whether this can be done by utilizing a single theme or hypothesis like the Turner Thesis is open to question since the academic environment of the later-twentieth century is quite unlike that of 1893 when Turner first announced his ideas. But the essays in this volume suggest a variety of approaches that can be used constructively in the effort to develop twentieth-century western history as a field and to fashion a sharper image of the region in the minds of Americans everywhere.

The image that Americans have of the West in the nineteenth century is clear—an image they share with many others around the world. It is of a sparsely populated wilderness peopled by trappers, mountain men, cowboys, and Indians. It is an image consistently fostered by the mass media, an image that is an essential part of the American myth, symbolizing the freedom and simplicity of a pre-industrial age. The perpetuation of that myth is not at all unique. In a rapidly changing society like the United States, successive generations have bemoaned the swift passing of the era in which they were born, with regret and nostalgia. So Thomas Jefferson bewailed the passing of the Enlightenment in his own lifetime. Southerners revelled in The Lost Cause after the Civil War, glorifying the antebellum period as a Golden Age forever gone. So at the turn of the century Theodore Roosevelt and a generation of writers about the West, and some Populists as well, bemoaned the passing of the frontier and America's agrarian society, along with its rich heritage.[1]

It was not at all surprising, therefore, that Americans in an urban industrial society such as emerged by the twentieth century looked back longingly to a supposedly simpler age, one like the nineteenth-century West, to which they could escape in their dreams. At first the image was embellished by scores of writers. Then came Hollywood, America's Dream Factory, and later still, radio and television, whose producers found it profitable to make those dreams even more vivid. The mass media fastened clear images of the American West in the nineteenth century in the minds, and psyches, of millions of Americans in the course of the twentieth century.

Myths are important to societies, for they play a crucial role, and certainly should not be disparaged. On the other hand, they should not be confused with reality. The West represented in the popular mind is a nineteenth-century West that is no more. It was a passing phase in the process of western development. Perhaps no other image can replace it, for it had a unique place in America's experience. But perpetuation of myths about the nineteenth-century West need not necessarily crowd out the reality of the twentieth-century West. The region's development in the century after 1890 was as much a part of the historical process as earlier Wests, requiring as well a sense of regional identity. The nineteenth-century model may be relevant to that period, but is less so for the twentieth century that witnessed momentous changes.

The image of the twentieth-century West in many ways contrasts with that of the region in the nineteenth century. It is, above all, an urban rather than a rural civilization with a heterogeneous, multicultural, and multiracial population. That differentiates it from the earlier age that was characterized by a more homogeneous society dominated by men of English or north European stock. The nineteenth-century West relied on a pre-industrial natural resources based economy, reflected by agriculture, cattle raising, and mining. In the twentieth century the West boasted a post-industrial, diversified economy. In addition to natural resources it included manufacturing, technological industries, information processing, military and science installations, and increasingly significant service industries. To most Americans the nineteenth-century West presented an image of virtually unlimited resources available to unfettered exploitation by individuals and corporations. The environment of the twentieth-century West is one beset by limitations, by fragility of ecological balance, and by the clear necessity for prudent management of remaining resources.

Epilogue

The nineteenth-century West was noted for a highly distinctive style of politics, stressing individualism and popular democracy. In the twentieth century the region had a far less distinctive style, reflecting very loose party and regional identity. The nineteenth-century West could claim no cultural life of its own, but reflected its eastern origins. The twentieth-century West established itself as a bold innovator in every phase of American cultural life, whether in high brow or popular culture. Thus, the image of the twentieth-century West differs from its nineteenth-century predecessor. It represents an urban, multicultural society, a diversified economy, a limited environment, a nondescriptive political outlook, and a dynamic pathbreaking trendsetter in American culture.

This changing image of the West in the twentieth century suggests the need for new cultural symbols. Instead of the rural, Anglo-Saxon cowboy of the nineteenth century, the typical twentieth-century western hero or heroine may be not only white, but also black, brown, yellow, or red, and the "he" may as likely be a "she." Instead of farmers, cattlemen, or miners, representative figures of the twentieth-century western economy may be corporate executives, scientists and engineers, government bureaucrats and military officials, and park rangers or tour guides. Instead of mountain men or fur trappers, the denizens of the western environment in the twentieth century are represented by professional foresters and land-management specialists, national park administrators, environmentalists, and back-packers. Instead of distinctive political personalities—whether in Congress, the county courthouse, or the local sheriff, the twentieth-century West had bland, media personalities who followed national trends and were disinclined to innovation. And the dance halls and saloons of the nineteenth-century culture of the West were hardly proper symbols for the region a hundred years later. Then, major art museums, concert halls, distinguished educational institutions, and great scientific laboratories came to be representative of the region. And its popular culture creations—such as Hollywood, Disneyland, and Las Vegas—set standards, for good or ill, not only for the United States but for the entire world.

Such is the image suggested by these essays. But their authors do more than to suggest an emerging image of the twentieth-century West. They also reflect a variety of approaches currently being utilized by historians in the study of the West. This, too, provides a contrast with the nineteenth century when one major approach—the Turner Thesis—dominated not only a generation of historians but Americans in all walks of life, and shaped their perception of the West.

But in 1988 it is perhaps questionable to expect an equivalent of the Turner Thesis to be formulated in the remaining years of the twentieth century. Not only has the historical profession undergone major changes in the years since 1893, but the complexities of western history after

1890—when the region became a more densely populated area—vastly increased. When Turner wrote his famous essay the number of professional historians in the United States was no more than 200. In fact, the number of specialists in American history was much smaller, so small that they did not organize their own professional organization—the Mississippi Valley Historical Association—until 1916. A century later the total body of professional historians exceeds 20,000 men and women, with at least half of them specializing in American history. Of this group, perhaps as many as 2,000 focus their main interests on the history of the American West.[2] In short, it was more feasible in Turner's time to secure a scholarly consensus in a profession that numbered no more than several dozen scholars specializing in the West. Most of them knew each other personally. Moreover, their social and cultural backgrounds were similar, and they shared values that provided a consensus.

By the later twentieth century the profession had changed dramatically. Sheer numbers often precluded personal contact except in small groups or scores of sub-specialities. Their means of communication were not so much the spoken word but the written page—whether through articles, books, or book reviews. Moreover, their social background had changed considerably. Instead of homogeneity and shared outlook, the profession was now characterized by enormous diversity—in race, sex, ethnicity, social class, ideology, and the absence of consensus or shared values. In such a professional environment it seemed highly unlikely that one, or even several historians, could fashion a consensus on a broad theory that would secure widespread acceptance, in academe or outside it, or that would find common ground amidst many thousands of devotees of western history, professionals or buffs.

In addition, the complexity of the field of western history in the later twentieth century, and also the increasing complexity of western development after 1890, impeded the formulation of a Turner-like theory a century later. In 1893 the field of American history was still in its infancy. Grand theories had a place in such a context—and in this incipient stage of the profession. But a century later historians had passed through decades of intense specialization, or as some might claim, over-specialization. And as they delved into small or minute aspects of their particular subjects, scholars became much more sensitive to complexities of which earlier generations had been unaware.

A kind of Gresham's Law thus developed. The more historians specialized during the twentieth century, the more difficult they found it to propagate broad theories or generalizations. It became easy to cite exceptions to virtually any hypothesis. Thus, generalization was stifled in favor of specialization. When, as in 1893, relatively few specialized studies existed, the urge to develop broad theories that could provide insights for

Epilogue

other scholars was greater. In short, the search for broad theory during the latter half of the twentieth century presented a very different challenge than that which existed a hundred years before.

At the same time the task of historians seeking to write about the history of the twentieth-century West became more difficult. Specialization had made them aware of subjects that had not even been developed a century earlier, whether psychohistory, popular culture, or gender and ethnic history. These now need to be considered in the treatment of most subjects. In addition, the West since 1890 has been a much more intensely developed region than it was before. No longer a virgin land, it witnessed more than a tenfold population increase with an increasingly diverse social structure and cultural fabric. The challenge of reconstructing this more intricate past thus became more formidable. And the problem of developing a theory to encompass an enormously wide range of variables was more difficult than a century before. In sum, the significant changes in the historical profession, in addition to the extraordinary development of the West in the one hundred years after 1890, provided a very different context than the one out of which Turner's hypothesis arose.

Within this changed intellectual environment a great variety of approaches to the study of the twentieth-century West developed, some of which are represented in this volume. These include the multicultural approach, of concepts dealing with subregions within the larger West.

Another approach of cultural historians has been the focus on the myths that comprise the West of the American imagination. Utilizing social psychology, they have analyzed the West in American myth and American thought, not only in the United States but in other countries as well. Henry Nash Smith, Richard Slotkin, John Cawelti, and Ray Billington have been among those who have pioneered this approach.[3]

Cultural historians like Richard Etulain have fashioned another approach by emphasizing the study of popular culture as a means of analyzing the history of the twentieth-century West. Whether in the Buffalo Bill Wild West shows in the 1880s and 1890s, the dime novels and "Westerns" of the succeeding generation, and radio, moving pictures, popular magazines, and television thereafter, the mass media have been a powerful means of fastening perceptions of the American West in the minds and hearts of the American public—and of millions of foreigners around the globe.[4] And as the pioneering work of art historians like H. Wayne Morgan illustrates, artists added a very influential dimension to the fashioning of such images.

The contributions of cultural historians to the emerging image of the twentieth-century West have been in embracing ethnic and gender history. Urban development and a primary focus on the growth of towns and cities have provided a major avenue for interpretation of the twentieth-century

West. Interdisciplinary social science methods applied to the historical evolution of the West have served to unravel new dimensions of the region's past. Fields such as demography, geography, cultural anthropology, sociology, economics, political science, and psychology have furnished theories and methods that illuminate major aspects of twentieth-century western history. To these, quantitative historians have added another unique dimension. In a different vein cultural historians have utilized their own special tools, including the use of literary criticism to gain new insights about the region's past. Moreover, their increasing interest in myth and symbolism has deepened our understanding of the significance of the western experience in American life over the years. Although still in its infancy in the study of the American West, the comparative approach has developed multicultural perspectives for identifying what is unique and what is typical in America's West as compared to similar areas elsewhere. And by midcentury some historians utilized ideological concepts such as Marxism to interpret the totality of the western experience in the twentieth century.

In the years after 1960 the multicultural approach gained increasing prominence. Its adherents viewed the mingling of peoples with distinct cultural identities as a major theme in western history. Initially historians developed it as a specialized subject, intent on clarifying the history of a particular ethnic, racial, or gender group. They were not really much interested in providing a broad or unified interpretation of the West. So the 1960s witnessed the development of black history in the West, Chicano history, Native American history, and the history of women in the region. In each case its practitioners believed that the history of their particular group provided a key to a better understanding of the West's development. Although concerned with only a segment of the area's population these historians consciously, or unconsciously, shared a common assumption. The United States was not really a melting pot in the twentieth century, they proclaimed, but a society characterized by ethnic, racial, or sexual diversity. Disparate groups, rather than homogeneity, characterized America's social structure in the twentieth century. This was as much a central element in the history of the West as of the United States.[5]

One contribution of the multicultural approach was to make previously invisible people in the settlement and development of the West visible. Women, blacks, Orientals, Chicanos, and Indians (within their own cultural environment rather than as adversaries of whites) had been largely absent from most accounts in western history before 1960. Now their history was presumed to be a central element in western history. That assumption paralleled a similar trend in southern history where scholars of the post–World War II generation claimed that black slavery constituted the central thread in the region's development. For the West, the

Epilogue

essays in this volume provide good examples of this approach. Anderson's work on women in the West, Romo on Mexican Americans, and Parman's on Indians are illustrative of diverse approaches that can be taken towards ethnic history—and its potential contributions to clarifying western studies.

Collectively—although these approaches seem disparate—these historians can be viewed as a group who offer a distinct perspective on the twentieth-century West. Of course the population of the West was always heterogeneous, but visibly more so after 1890. And given even greater diversity of the West's population in the future, according to projections of the United States Census, this approach will probably loom even larger in the next decade. In their studies so far, multicultural historians have made a contribution to development of an image for the twentieth-century West. That image focusses on the development of a pluralistic multicultural society that contrasts sharply with American perceptions of the nineteenth-century West. Then, according to the image, the West was a stridently male-dominated culture, primarily of homogeneous Anglo or western European stock. Women, blacks, Mexicans, Orientals or Indians played decidedly nonassertive, subservient, or subsidiary roles in such a society and were outside the mainstream. The emerging image of the twentieth-century West is quite different, however. It emphasizes the important part of women and minorities in western development and their assertiveness in maintaining their particular cultural distinctiveness while seeking to secure increasing influence within the dominant society.

Interdisciplinary studies provide an alternative approach to the history of the twentieth-century West, and among these the work of urban historians has been preeminent. Abbott's essay provides a fine example of this genre. As he emphasizes, the history of the twentieth-century West to a considerable extent is the history of its towns and cities. Even outlying ranches and sparsely populated areas of the region were affected by, or developed in relation to, neighboring urban centers. This urban dimension was largely ignored by Frederick Jackson Turner, although it must be admitted that its most important impact was not felt until the twentieth century.

The impact of urban historians on the emerging image of the twentieth-century West has already been considerable, and is likely to have a major impact in the coming decade. The studies that have appeared reveal a West dominated by towns and cities that set the pace for the life-styles of the entire region. As early as 1949 Carey McWilliams noted that in the West—in contrast to the more densely populated East—even small urban areas had an influence hardly commensurate with their size, and far beyond their own boundaries, often extending for hundreds of miles into sparsely populated places. A city such as Reno, Nevada, with no more than 25,000 people in 1940, nevertheless served as a major metropolitan center for the entire state, radiating its impact on much of Nevada.[6]

As yet not as fully developed as the urban approach is the effort to apply demographic theories to western development, as exemplified by Walter Nugent's essay. His emphasis on the importance of mobility in western growth is innovative, but also has roots in the work of previous historians who stressed it as a major theme in evolution of the region. Turner himself, of course, touched on the constant stream of moving settlers into the West as one important formative influence. But Turner was concerned more with movement *to* the region than with movement *within* it. Nor did he focus on the perception that developed in the twentieth century that the West was synonymous with freedom of movement. However, George W. Pierson, a Yale historian, emphasized what he termed as the "M" factor in western history, which he viewed as the key element to explain much of western history, particularly in the twentieth century.[7] Nugent's approach, however, provides a broader conceptual framework that encompasses the various elements of demographic changes more fully than his predecessors. Moreover, he utilizes the exciting studies of professional geographers during the last two decades whose work has direct relevance to historians of the twentieth-century West.

Within the interdisciplinary context, environmental historians, utilizing ecological approaches, have provided many useful insights and concepts for examining the twentieth-century West. Utilizing concepts drawn from environmental studies, they have renewed, and embellished, Turner's emphasis on the impact of natural environment on the region's social and cultural development after 1890. Such a consciousness was central not only to Turner, but to some of his contemporaries in the scholarly world who pioneered environmental history. The names of Ellsworth Huntington and Ellen Semple quickly spring to mind, and John Opie expands upon this tradition. Even if cultural and technological influences were of greater importance to the West in the twentieth century than in earlier eras, nevertheless historians still cannot ignore the impact of environmental factors, whether climate, topography, or valuable natural resources like water. As Opie indicates, the sweep of environmental history has been broad, encompassing not only economic, but also political, social, and cultural institutions.

The major contributions of environmental historians to the shaping of an image for the twentieth-century West have been to detail the impact of particular manifestations of environmental conditions. These include the climate of the Sunbelt, the availability of water in the semiarid regions, or the existence of wide, open spaces that attracted scientific and weapons research as well as manufacturing complexes. In addition, environmental historians have done much to increase national consciousness about the limitations of the western environment and its resources. The economic expansion of the region by the 1980s was no longer considered to be limitless, in view of the fragility of the western habitat. This contrasts sharply with the nineteenth century when environmental historians were influenced by the plenitude of resources with virtually limitless potentials. With a greater awareness of the complexities of western development in the twentieth century than earlier generations of historians the environmental history group has also shown itself to be less deterministic than those of Turner's generation.[8]

Although the work of quantitative historians has had considerable impact on the general fields of American economic, political, and social history during the last generation, as yet, as an approach, quantification has had relatively little impact on twentieth-century western history. But Paul Kleppner's essay provides an excellent illustration of the vast potentials of this technique in developing new subjects and new insights.

Moreover, Kleppner's piece makes a distinct contribution to the fashioning of a political image for the twentieth-century West. On the one hand, it provides an illustration of the extent to which national trends are reflected in the region's political culture. On the other, he reveals the uniqueness of western politics. In the twentieth century the West was still a young region compared to the older sections, and its political institutions as yet were far less stratified or institutionalized than those in the South and East. During the one hundred years since 1890 they were in flux, reflecting the very rapid movement of population into the West.

The social sciences have indeed been one of the most fruitful sources for providing approaches useful to the study of the twentieth-century West. Urban studies, demography, geography, sociological theories, cultural anthropology, and quantitative methods, among others, have done much to show the way in providing new data, new insights, and even new subject areas in western history. Their potential in the immediate future is enormous.

Not all who have written about the West in the past century have chosen to use social science concepts, however, for some have found ideological approaches more congenial. It could be argued, of course, that any approach contains ideological components. It could also be argued that many western historians have had an implicit bias in favor of a capitalist or mixed private and public enterprise system. But some writers dealing with the twentieth-century West have reflected a decidedly anticapitalist bias. Certain students of women's history have argued that the male suppression of women that they perceive is largely conditioned by an exploitative capitalist system. Journalists like Wiley and Gottlieb, in a crude approximation of New Left ideology of the 1970s, considered the twentieth-century West as an abject victim of corporate capitalism, a province exploited and plundered by large corporations. Herbert Marcuse's *One Dimensional Man* provided the framework for their jeremiad.[9] As Donald Pisani illustrates in his essay, a variation of neo-Marxist approaches was developed by the so-called Frankfurt school of political economy in Germany during the 1920s. Its adherents included William Neuman, Theodore Adorno, and Karl Wittfogel. All of these men favored social democracy but distrusted the all-powerful centralized state. Wittfogel developed this theory further after he immigrated to the United States in 1933 where for the next three decades he taught at the University of Washington. In his works he contended that in arid regions, government control of water resources was the key to development of every aspect of civilization. Although Wittfogel tried to illustrate his theme with reference to China, one of his disciples, Donald Worster, applied it to explain growth of the American West after 1890. In his *Rivers of Empire*, Worster claimed that the Bureau of Reclamation irresponsibly dammed over much of the West and sought centralized government control over its major water resources—to the great detriment of natural resources and people of the region.

The contributions of ideological historians to the image of the twentieth-century West have been varied. A major weakness of their approach has been that they have usually had a clear conception of their conclusions before beginning their research. Hence they seek only evidence that substantiates their particular view while deliberately neglecting or ignoring evidence that contradicts it. Still, ideological historians may sometimes have a focus on "the Big Picture," on worldwide and national trends of which the twentieth-century West is only a part. Thus, the approach can provide a broad context that is missing in the work of more narrow or highly specialized scholars. As for the image of the twentieth-century West, ideological historians have demonstrated that its history has not been totally unique, but that in some aspects of its development it shared characteristics common to other regions, or even other nations. Such an emphasis contrasts with the Turner thesis that viewed the West as an entirely unique historical phenomenon.

This theme—without a strong ideological bias—has been explicit in the work of those utilizing the comparative approach. Although efforts to deal with comparative frontiers in the West before 1890 were made by numerous scholars, few have attempted to use the approach applied to the twentieth-century West.[10] Howard Lamar is one of those very few, and his essay points to the broadened perceptions that the comparative approach can provide. Existing literature about the impact of the Great Depression on the American West has focused on a narrow, national context and viewed it as a unique occurrence. As Lamar demonstrates, however, American perceptions of the crisis, and the American historians who have written about it, were clearly conditioned by their cultural biases and preconceptions. The same issues, viewed from a Canadian perspective, reveal different values and assumptions. The comparative approach has distinctive contributions to make to the emerging image of the twentieth-century West. While not neglecting the uniqueness of the region, it emphasizes areas of commonality with other regions, and the importance of the population's system of values as a conditioning element.

The works of cultural historians have also made substantial contributions to the history of the region in the last century. These contributions have been diverse. Some have labored to analyze the literature of and about the region, in novels and short stories, and to analyze the perceptions that they reveal. Only in the last decade, however, have historians of literature attempted to analyze the historical development of such literary efforts, thus adding another perspective from which to view the West. Erisman's essay illustrates these efforts, particularly use of the regional concept that he views as a useful framework for analysis. To some extent it is a legacy of the Turner thesis that emphasized the influence of environment in producing constant social change. In its fullest form Erisman explores it as a twentieth-century concept that integrates past and present, culture and environment, to meet the "lasting human need to organize the distinctive elements of their experience in a way that links them to the more sweeping course of all human history." In the nineteenth century regional consciousness embraced the West as a coherent, homogeneous entity. But by the twentieth century it had become too diverse for such a perception, requiring more complex development. Students of American culture like Erisman and Etulain have done much to analyze the writers who described the transformation of the sparsely populated nineteenth-century West into the urban West more characteristic of the twentieth century. They have analyzed the sense of nostalgia for the old, for the passing of an era that lives on only in the imagination. They have brought out the sense of loss, the loss of innocence, of the coming of age of a virgin land. As for the image of the West after 1890, it is a region that may not be wholly unique, but one that developed into a pacesetter for the nation.

The approaches reflected by the essays in this volume are designed to be suggestive, not exhaustive, illustrative rather than definitive. By no means do they include all of the approaches currently being utilized by scholars in various disciplines who have shown some interest in the twentieth-century West. But they do illustrate increasing activity in this emerging field and contribute to a clearer image of the region. Such an image can serve the American people, the mass media, and Westerners themselves. But it will require the formulation of broad generalizations that will explain the complex interaction between the environment of the West and the culture and values of its occupants. Unlike the Turner thesis, the concepts that will be developed will focus not on a single but on diverse themes. Hopefully broad, integrative concepts can serve a variety of functions. They can relate the distinctive features of the western environment to the cultural impact of its people. They can identify the unique as well as derivative characteristics of the West as a region after 1890. They can explain the processes of change over time and can relate perceptions of the West with the context from which these spring. Moreover, they can integrate the history of the West with the history of the nation of which it is a part. Given such challenges, these concepts are likely to draw on various disciplines in the effort to achieve more integrative synthesis.

The time is ripe for augmenting our nineteenth-century model of the West with one that recognizes the significant changes that have transformed the region in the last one hundred years. A major purpose of this volume has been to suggest the elements of a clearer image of the West in the past century. Such an image, as the authors of the essays have suggested, includes that of an urban civilization characterized by great racial and ethnic diversity. In this respect the West was becoming increasingly similar to the rest of the nation and less distinctive than it had been in earlier stages of development. Yet the West's natural environment was still unique and imposed its own imperatives on the millions who settled it. Diminishing resources, attractive climates, open spaces, and a unique historical tradition—a tradition emphasizing freedom and mobility—continued to give the American West a distinctive mystique, even in the twentieth century. The essays in this book have highlighted the elements—in reality as well as myth—that can serve as ingredients for the development of a clearer image of the West and what it has become in the last one hundred years.

Notes

1. On Jefferson and the Jeffersonian heritage, see Merrill D. Peterson, *The Jefferson Image in the American Mind* (New York: Oxford University Press, 1960); on the Lost Cause, see William J. Cash, *The Mind of the South* (New York: Alfred A. Knopf, 1941), C. Vann Woodward, *The Burden of Southern History* (Baton Rouge: Louisiana State University Press, 1960), and George B. Tindall, "Mythology: A New Frontier in Southern History," in Frank Vandiver, ed., *The Idea of The South: Pursuit of a Central Theme* (Chicago: University of Chicago Press, 1964), 1–15; on Theodore Roosevelt, see G. Edward White, *The Eastern Establishment and the Western Experience: The West of Frederic Remington, Theodore Roosevelt, and Owen Wister* (New Haven: Yale University Press, 1968).

2. Statistics on membership are approximate, and fluctuate yearly. The figures noted are based on estimates by the Executive Secretary of the Organization of

Epilogue

American Historians in 1985. See Joan Hoff Wilson, "The Plight of a Mom and Pop Operation," *OAH Newsletter* 13 (May 1985): 2; a report on membership in the Western History Association is in *Western Historical Quarterly* 15 (January 1984): 111.

3. Henry Nash Smith, *Virgin Land: The American West as Symbol and Myth* (Cambridge, Mass.: Harvard University Press, 1950); Richard Slotkin, *The Fatal Environment: The Myth of the Frontier in the Age of Industrialization, 1800–1890* (New York: Atheneum, 1985); John G. Cawelti, *The Six-Gun Mystique* (Bowling Green: Bowling Green University Popular Press, [1971]); Ray Allen Billington, *Land of Savagery, Land of Promise: The European Image of the American Frontier in the Nineteenth Century* (New York: W. W. Norton, 1981).

4. See Richard W. Etulain, "Shifting Interpretations of Western American Cultural History," in Michael Malone, ed., *Historians and the American West* (Lincoln: University of Nebraska Press, 1983), 414–32, and by same author, "Frontier, Region, and Myth: Changing Interpretations of Western American Culture," *Journal of American Culture* 3 (Summer 1980): 268–84.

5. See Richard Polenberg, *One Nation Divisible: Class, Race, and Ethnicity in the United States Since 1938* (New York: Viking Press, 1980).

6. Ray West, ed., *Rocky Mountain Cities* (New York: W. W. Norton, 1949), 9–12.

7. Pierson developed the idea of the "M" factor in various articles including George W. Pierson, "The Frontier and American Institutions: A Criticism of the Turner Theory," *New England Quarterly* 15 (June 1942): 224–55, and "American Historians and the Frontier Hypothesis in 1941," *Wisconsin Magazine of History* 26 (September 1942): 36–60; (December 1942): 170–85.

8. Among Turner's contemporaries who emphasized environmental influences, see A. P. Brigham, *Geographic Influences in American History* (Boston: Ginn and Company, 1903), Ellen C. Semple, *American History and Its Geographic Conditions* (Boston: Houghton Mifflin, 1903), and Ellsworth Huntington, *The Red Man's Continent: A Chronicle* (New Haven: Yale University Press, 1919).

9. See, for example, Rosalinda M. Gonzalez, "Chicanas and Mexican Immigrant Families, 1920–1940: Women's Subordination and Family Exploitation," in Lois Scharf and Joan M. Jensen, eds., *Decades of Discontent: The Women's Movement, 1920–1940* (Westport: Greenwood Press, 1983), 59–84, and Sherna Gluck, "Socialist Feminism Between the Two World Wars: Insights from Oral History," in *ibid.*, 279–97; an excellent range of perspectives can be found in Susan Armitage and Elizabeth Jameson, eds., *The Women's West* (Norman: University of Oklahoma Press, 1987); Peter Wiley and Robert Gottlieb, *Empires in the Sun: The Rise of the New American West* (New York: G. P. Putnam's Sons, 1982).

10. W. Turrentine Jackson, "A Brief Message for the Young and/or Ambitious: Comparative Frontiers as a Field for Investigation," *Western Historical Quarterly* 11 (July 1980): 5–18; the University of Oklahoma published a Comparative Frontiers Newsletter in the 1970s that ceased publication in 1986; see also Jerome O. Steffen, ed., *The American West: New Perspectives, New Dimensions* (Norman: University of Oklahoma Press, 1979), and *Comparative Frontiers: Proposals for Studying the American West* (Norman: University of Oklahoma Press, 1980).

The Twentieth-Century American West

A SELECTIVE BIBLIOGRAPHY

Richard W. Etulain

This brief listing endeavors to provide students and scholars with a bibliography of more than 500 items dealing with the modern trans-Mississippi West. While most citations are unannotated, the compiler has tried to include only the most significant essays and books under each subject. Furthermore, in order to place major stress on recent publications, theses and dissertations, government documents, and personal memoirs have been omitted.

Users should realize that items about one topic may appear in two different categories. For example, most commentaries on urbanization are included under social history, but those stressing political or economic aspects of urbanization appear under those headings. Moreover, a majority of items on land and water are filed in economic history but others in the environmental and public policy sections. And classic interpretations by such historians as Frederick Jackson Turner, Walter Prescott Webb, and James Malin appear under general historiography even though their writings are also regional studies. Those users willing to examine several categories for overlapping entries will benefit most from this bibliography.

The checklist is divided into nine sections: (1) bibliographies and reference works; (2) regional and state histories; (3) general western historiography; (4) social history; (5) political history; (6) economic history; (7) environmental history; (8) public policy history; and (9) cultural history. Users wishing more extensive listings and checklists on other topics should consult the items listed in the first section, appropriate volumes in the second and third categories, and bibliographies in each issue of the *Western Historical* and *Journal of American History,* which include lists of recent essays and dissertations. The compiler, now preparing a book-length bibliography of historical publications dealing with the twentieth-century West, invites corrections and suggestions for important items omitted from this abbreviated list.

Bibliographies and Reference Works

Anderson, John Q., et al, eds. *Southwestern American Literature: A Bibliography.* Chicago: Swallow Press, 1980.

Billington, Ray Allen, with Martin Ridge. *Westward Expansion: A History of the American Frontier.* 5th ed. New York: Macmillan Company, 1982. First edition in 1949. The extensive bibliography contains some items on the twentieth century.

Davis, Richard C., ed. *Encyclopedia of American Forest and Conservation History.* 2 vols. New York: Macmillan Company, 1983.

Erisman, Fred, and Richard W. Etulain, eds. *Fifty Western Writers: A Bio-Bibliographical Sourcebook.* Westport, Conn.: Greenwood Press, 1982.

Etulain, Richard W. *A Bibliographical Guide to the Study of Western American Literature.* Lincoln: University of Nebraska Press, 1982.

Fahl, Ronald J. *North American Forest and Conservation History: A Bibliography.* Santa Barbara, Calif.: ABC-Clio Press, 1976.

Freidel, Frank, ed. *Harvard Guide to American History,* rev. ed. Cambridge, Mass.: Harvard University Press, 1974.

James, Edward T., Janet W. James, and Paul S. Boyer, eds. *Notable American Women, 1607–1950: A Biographical Dictionary.* 3 vols. Cambridge, Mass.: Harvard University Press, 1971.

Lamar, Howard R., ed. *The Reader's Encyclopedia of the American West.* New York: Thomas Y. Crowell Company, 1977: NY: Harper & Row, 1986.

"A List of Dissertations," *Western Historical Quarterly.* This listing of recent dissertations in western history appears each year in the July issue of the *Quarterly.*

Malone, Michael P., ed. *Historians and the American West.* Lincoln: University of Nebraska Press, 1983.

Meier, Matt S., comp. *Bibliography of Mexican American History.* Westport, Conn.: Greenwood Press, 1984.

Meier, Matt S., and Feliciano Rivera, eds. *Dictionary of Mexican American History.* Westport, Conn.: Greenwood Press, 1981.

Nichols, Roger L., ed. *American Frontier and Western Issues: A Historiographical Review.* Westport, Conn.: Greenwood Press, 1986.

Paul, Rodman W., and Richard W. Etulain, comps. *The Frontier and the American West.* Arlington Heights, Ill.: AHM Publishing Corporation, 1977.

Prucha, Francis Paul, ed. *A Bibliographical Guide to the History of Indian-White Relations.* Chicago: University of Chicago Press, 1977.

Prucha, Francis Paul, ed. *Indian-White Relations in the United States: A Bibliogra-*

Selective Bibliography

phy of Works Published 1975–1980. Lincoln: University of Nebraska Press, 1982.

"Recent Articles," *Western Historical Quarterly.* This listing of recent essays in western history appears in each issue of the journal.

Samuels, Peggy and Harold. *The Illustrated Biographical Encyclopedia of Artists of the American West.* Garden City, N.Y.: Doubleday, 1976.

Schlebecker, John T. *Bibliography of Books and Pamphlets on the History of Agriculture in the United States, 1607–1967.* Santa Barbara, Calif.: ABC-Clio Press, 1969.

Smith, Dwight. *Indians of the United States and Canada: A Bibliography.* Santa Barbara, Calif.: ABC-Clio Press, 1974.

Thernstrom, Stephan, ed. *Harvard Encyclopedia of American Ethnic Groups.* Cambridge, Mass.: Belknap Press of Harvard University Press, 1980.

Tuska, Jon, Vicki Piekarski, and Paul J. Blanding, eds. *The Frontier Experience: A Reader's Guide to the Life and Literature of the American West.* Jefferson, N.C.: McFarland and Company, 1984.

Vinson, James, and D. L. Kirkpatrick, eds. *Twentieth-Century Western Writers.* Detroit: Gale Research Company, 1982.

Winther, Oscar O., and Richard A. Van Orman, comps. *A Classified Bibliography of the Periodical Literature of the Trans-Mississippi West (1811–1967).* Bloomington: Indiana University Press, 1961, 1970; Westport, Conn.: Greenwood Press, 1972.

Regional and State Histories

Abbott, Carl. "Frontiers and Sections: Cities and Regions in American Growth." *American Quarterly* 37 (Bibliography 1985): 395–410.

Ashmore, Harry S. *Arkansas: A Bicentennial History.* New York: W. W. Norton and Company, 1978.

Athearn, Robert G. *High Country Empire: The High Plains and Rockies.* New York: McGraw-Hill Book Company, 1960.

Beal, Merrill D., and Merle W. Wells. *History of Idaho.* 3 vols. New York: Lewis Publishing Company, 1959.

Bean, Walton, and James J. Rawls. *California: An Interpretive History.* 4th ed. New York: McGraw-Hill Book Company, 1983.

Beck, Warren A. *New Mexico: A History of Four Centuries.* Norman: University of Oklahoma Press, 1962.

Bingham, Edwin R., and Glen A. Love, eds. *Northwest Perspectives: Essays on the Culture of the Pacific Northwest.* Seattle: University of Washington Press, 1979.

Blegen, Theodore C. *Minnesota: A History of the State,* rev. ed. Minneapolis: University of Minnesota Press, 1975.

Blouet, Brian W., and Frederick C. Luebke, eds. *The Great Plains: Environment and Culture.* Lincoln: University of Nebraska Press, 1979.

Brown, Richard Maxwell. "The New Regionalism in America, 1970–1981," in William G. Robbins, et al, eds. *Regionalism and the Pacific Northwest.* Corvallis: Oregon State University Press, 1983, 37–96.

Caughey, John W., with Norris Hundley, Jr., *California: History of a Remarkable State,* 4th ed. Englewood Cliffs, N.J.: Prentice-Hall, 1982.

Clark, Norman. *Washington: A Bicentennial History.* New York: W. W. Norton and Company, 1976.

Connor, Seymour V. *Texas: A History.* New York: Thomas Y. Crowell, 1971.

Davis, Kenneth S. *Kansas: A Bicentennial History.* New York: W. W. Norton and Company, 1976.

De Voto, Bernard. "The West: A Plundered Province." *Harper's Magazine* 159 (August 1934): 355–64.

De Voto, Bernard. "The West Against Itself." *Harper's Magazine* 194 (January 1947): 1–13.

Dodds, Gordon B. *The American Northwest: A History of Oregon and Washington.* Arlington Heights, Ill.: Forum Press, 1986.

Edwards, G. Thomas, and Carlos A. Schwantes, eds. *Experiences in a Promised Land: Essays in Pacific Northwest History.* Seattle: University of Washington Press, 1986.

Fireman, Bert M. *Arizona: Historic Land.* New York: Alfred A. Knopf, 1982.

Frantz, Joe B. *Texas: A Bicentennial History.* New York: W. W. Norton and Company, 1976.

Garreau, Joel. *The Nine Nations of North America.* Boston: Houghton Mifflin Company, 1981.

Gastil, Raymond D. *Cultural Regions of the United States.* Seattle: University of Washington Press, 1975.

Goodwyn, Frank. *Lone-Star Land: Twentieth-Century Texas in Perspective.* New York: Alfred A. Knopf, 1955.

Gressley, Gene M. *The Twentieth-Century American West: A Potpourri.* Columbia: University of Missouri Press, 1977.

Hollon, W. Eugene. *The Southwest: Old and New.* New York: Alfred A. Knopf, 1961.

Johansen, Dorothy O., and Charles M. Gates. *Empire of the Columbia: A History of the Pacific Northwest.* New York: Harper and Brothers, 1957; 2nd ed., 1967.

Knoles, George H., ed. *Essays & Assays: California History Reappraised.* San Francisco: California Historical Society, 1973.

Kraenzel, Carl Frederick. *The Great Plains in Transition.* Norman: University of Oklahoma Press, 1955.

Lamar, Howard R. "Persistent Frontier: The West in the Twentieth Century." *Western Historical Quarterly* 4 (January 1973): 5–25. Contains a useful bibliographical listing.

Lamm, Richard D., and Michael McCarthy. *The Angry West: A Vulnerable Land and Its Future.* Boston: Houghton Mifflin Company, 1982.

Larson, T. A. *History of Wyoming.* Lincoln: University of Nebraska Press, 1965; 2nd ed., rev., 1978.

Selective Bibliography

Limerick, Patricia Nelson. *The Legacy of Conquest: The Unbroken Past of the American West.* New York: W. W. Norton and Company, 1987. Contains useful bibliography.
Lowitt, Richard. *The New Deal and the West.* Bloomington: Indiana University Press, 1984.
Luebke, Frederick C. "Regionalism and the Great Plains: Problems of Concept and Method." *Western Historical Quarterly* 15 (January 1984): 19–38.
Luey, Beth, and Noel J. Stowe, eds. *Arizona at Seventy-Five: The Next Twenty-Five years.* Tempe and Tucson: Arizona State University Public History Program and the Arizona Historical Society, 1987.
McReynolds, Edwin C. *Missouri: A History of the Crossroads State.* Norman: University of Oklahoma Press, 1962.
McReynolds, Edwin C. *Oklahoma: A History of the Sooner State.* Norman: University of Oklahoma Press, 1954, 1972.
McWilliams, Carey. *Southern California Country: An Island on the Land.* New York: Duell, Sloan and Pearce, 1946.
Malone, Michael P., and Richard B. Roeder. *Montana: A History of Two Centuries.* Seattle: University of Washington, 1976.
Meinig, D. W. *Imperial Texas: An Interpretive Essay in Cultural Geography.* Austin: University of Texas Press, 1969.
Meinig, Donald W. "American Wests: Preface to a Geographical Interpretation." *Annals of the Association of American Geographers* 62 (June 1972): 159–84.
Meinig, D. W. *Southwest: Three Peoples in Geographical Change, 1600–1970.* New York: Oxford University Press, 1971.
Merk, Frederick. *History of the Westward Movement.* New York: Alfred A. Knopf, 1978.
Morgan, H. Wayne, and Anne Hodges Morgan. *Oklahoma: A Bicentennial History.* New York: W. W. Norton and Company, 1977.
Morgan, Neil. *Westward Tilt: The American West Today.* New York: Random House, 1961, 1963.
Nagel, Paul C. *Missouri: A Bicentennial History.* New York: W. W. Norton and Company, 1977.
Nash, Gerald D. *The American West in the Twentieth Century: A Short History of an Urban Oasis.* Englewood Cliffs, N.J.: Prentice Hall, 1973; Albuquerque: University of New Mexico Press, 1977.
Nash, Gerald D. *The American West Transformed: The Impact of the Second World War.* Bloomington: Indiana University Press, 1985.
Nash, Gerald D. "Mirror for the Future: The Historical Past of the Twentieth-Century West," in Thomas G. Alexander and John P. Bluth, eds. *The Twentieth Century American West.* Charles Redd Monographs in Western History No. 12 (Provo, Utah: Charles Redd Center for Western Studies, 1983), 1–27.
Nash, Gerald D. "The Twentieth-Century West." *Western Historical Quarterly* 13 (April 1982): 179–81.
Nash, Gerald D. "Where's the West?" *Historian* 49 (November 1986): 1–9.

Olson, James C. *History of Nebraska*. Lincoln: University of Nebraska Press, 1955; 2nd ed., 1966.

Peirce, Neal R. *The Great Plains States of America: People, Politics, and Power in the Nine Great Plains States*. New York: W. W. Norton and Company, 1973.

Peirce, Neal R. *The Mountain States of America: People, Politics, and Power in the Eight Rocky Mountain States*. New York: W. W. Norton and Company, 1972.

Peirce, Neal R. *The Pacific States of America: People, Politics, and Power in the Five Pacific Basin States*. New York: W. W. Norton and Company, 1972.

Peirce, Neal R., and Jerry Hagstrom. *The Book of America: Inside 50 States Today*. New York: W. W. Norton and Company, 1983.

Perrigo, Lynn. *The American Southwest: Its Peoples and Cultures*. New York: Holt, Rinehart and Winston, 1971.

Peterson, Charles S. *Utah: A Bicentennial History*. New York: W. W. Norton and Company, 1977.

Pomeroy, Earl. *The Pacific Slope: A History of California, Oregon, Washington, Idaho, Utah, and Nevada*. New York: Alfred A. Knopf, 1965; Seattle: University of Washington Press, 1973.

Richardson, Rupert Norval, et al. *Texas: The Lone Star State*. 4th ed. Englewood Cliffs, N.J.: Prentice-Hall, 1981.

Robbins, William G., Robert J. Frank, and Richard E. Ross, eds. *Regionalism and the Pacific Northwest*. Corvallis: Oregon State University Press, 1983.

Robinson, Elwyn B. *History of North Dakota*. Lincoln: University of Nebraska Press, 1966.

Rolle, Andrew F. *California: A History*. 4th ed. Arlington Heights, Ill.: Harlan Davidson, 1987.

Sage, Leland L. *A History of Iowa*. Ames: Iowa State University Press, 1974.

Sale, Kirkpatrick. *Power Shift: The Rise of the Southern Rim and Its Challenge to the Eastern Establishment*. New York: Random House, 1975.

Schell, Herbert S. *History of South Dakota*. Lincoln: University of Nebraska Press, 1961; 3rd ed., 1975.

Taylor, Joe Gray. *Louisiana: A Bicentennial History*. New York: W. W. Norton and Company, 1976.

Toole, K. Ross. *The Rape of the Great Plains: Northwestern America, Cattle and Coal*. Boston: Little, Brown and Company, 1976.

Toole, K. Ross. *Twentieth-Century Montana: A State of Extremes*. Norman: University of Oklahoma Press, 1972.

Ubbelohde, Carl, Maxine Benson, and Duane A. Smith. *A Colorado History*. Boulder: Pruett Publishing Company, 1972.

White, William Allen. *The Changing West: An Economic Theory about Our Golden Age*. New York: Macmillan Company, 1939.

Wiley, Peter, and Robert Gottlieb. *Empires in the Sun: The Rise of the New American West*. New York: G. P. Putnam's Sons, 1982.

Wilkins, Robert P., and Wynona H. Wilkins. *North Dakota: A Bicentennial History*. New York: W. W. Norton and Company, 1977.

Winther, Oscar Osburn. *The Great Northwest: A History*. New York: Alfred A. Knopf, 1947; 2nd ed., rev., 1950.

Selective Bibliography

General Western Historiography

August, Jack L., Jr. "The Future of Western History: The Third Wave." *Journal of Arizona History* 27 (Summer 1986): 229–44.

Bannon, John Francis. *Herbert Eugene Bolton: The Historian and the Man 1870–1953.* Tucson: University of Arizona Press, 1978.

Beckham, Stephen Dow. "John Walton Caughey: Historian and Civil Libertarian." *Pacific Historical Review* 56 (November 1987): 481–93.

Bell, Robert G. "James C. Malin and the Grasslands of North America." *Agricultural History* 46 (July 1972): 414–24.

Berge, Wendell. *Economic Freedom for the West.* Lincoln: University of Nebraska Press, 1946.

Billington, Ray Allen. *Frederick Jackson Turner: Historian, Scholar, Teacher.* New York: Oxford University Press, 1973.

Billington, Ray Allen. "Frederick Jackson Turner and the Closing Frontier," in Roger Daniels, ed. *Essays in Western History in Honor of T. A. Larson. University of Wyoming Publications* 37 (October 1971): 45–56.

Bogue, Allan G. "The Heirs of James C. Malin: A Grassland Historiography." *Great Plains Quarterly* 1 (Spring 1981): 105–31.

Brown, Richard Maxwell. "The New Regionalism in America, 1970–1981," in William G. Robbins et al., eds. *Regionalism and the Pacific Northwest.* Corvallis: Oregon State University Press, 1983, 37–96.

Caughey, John W. *The American West: Frontier and Region: Interpretations.* Eds. Norris Hundley, Jr., and John A. Schutz. Los Angeles: Ward Richie Press, 1969.

Caughey, John W. "The Insignificance of the Frontier in American History or 'Once Upon a Time There Was an American West.'" *Western Historical Quarterly* 5 (January 1974): 5–16.

Cronon, William. "Revisiting the Vanishing Frontier: The Legacy of Frederick Jackson Turner." *Western Historical Quarterly* 18 (April 1987): 157–76.

Etulain, Richard W. "Rodman Wilson Paul, Historical Perspectives of an Adopted Westerner." *Pacific Historical Review* 56 (November 1987): 527–44.

Fireman, Janet R. "Abraham Nasatir, Dean of Documents." *Pacific Historical Review* 56 (November 1987): 513–25.

"Five Historians of the American West." *Pacific Historical Review* 56 (November 1987). Special issue devoted to western historiography.

Furman, Necah Stewart. *Walter Prescott Webb: His Life and Impact.* Albuquerque: University of New Mexico Press, 1976.

Garnsey, Morris E. *America's New Frontier: The Mountain West.* New York: Alfred A. Knopf, 1950.

Gressley, Gene M. "Colonialism: A Western Complaint." *Pacific Northwest Quarterly* 54 (January 1963): 1–8.

Gressley, Gene M. "James G. Blaine, 'Alferd' E. Packer and Western Particularism." *Historian* 44 (May 1982): 364–81.

Gressley, Gene M. "Regionalism and the Twentieth-Century West," in Jerome O. Steffen, ed. *The American West: New Perspectives, New Dimensions.* Norman: University of Oklahoma Press, 1969, 197–234.

Gressley, Gene M. "The Turner Thesis—A Problem in Historiography." *Agricultural History* 32 (October 1958): 227–49.
Gressley, Gene M. "The West: Past, Present, and Future." *Western Historical Quarterly* 17 (January 1986): 5–23.
Gressley, Gene M. "Whither Western American History? Speculations on a Direction." *Pacific Historical Review* 53 (November 1984): 493–501.
Gressley, Gene M., ed. *The American West: A Reorientation.* Laramie: University of Wyoming Press, 1966.
Jackson, W. Turrentine. "A Brief Message for the Young and/or Ambitious: Comparative Frontiers as a Field for Investigation." *Western Historical Quarterly* 9 (January 1978): 5–18.
Jensen, Richard. "On Modernizing Frederick Jackson Turner: The Historiography of Regionalism." *Western Historical Quarterly* 11 (July 1980): 307–22.
Lamar, Howard R. "Earl Pomeroy, Historian's Historian." *Pacific Historical Review* 56 (November 1987): 547–60.
Lamar, Howard R. "Much to Celebrate: The Western History Association's Twenty-Fifth Birthday." *Western Historical Quarterly* 17 (October 1986): 397–416.
Lamar, Howard R. "Persistent Frontier: The West in the Twentieth Century." *Western Historical Quarterly* 4 (January 1973): 5–25.
Malin, James C. *Grassland Historical Studies: Natural Resources Utilization in a Background of Science and Technology. Vol. 1. Geology and Geography.* Lawrence, Kans.: privately printed, 1950.
Malin, James C. *The Grassland of North America: Prolegomena to Its History.* Lawrence, Kans.: privately printed, 1947. Reprint, *with addenda and postscript.* Gloucester, Mass.: Peter Smith, 1967.
Malin, James C. "Space and History: Reflections on the Closed-Space Doctrines of Turner and Mackinder and the Challenge of Those Ideas by the Air Age." *Agricultural History* 18 (April 1944): 65–74.
Mezerik, A. G. *The Revolt of the South and West.* New York: Duell, Sloan and Pearce, 1946.
Nash, Gerald D. "California and Its Historians: An Appraisal of the Histories of the State." *Pacific Historical Review* 50 (November 1981): 387–413.
Nugent, Walter. "Western History: Stocktakings and New Crops." *Reviews in American History* 13 (September 1985): 319–29.
Olin, Spencer C., Jr. "Toward a Synthesis of the Political and Social History of the American West." *Pacific Historical Review* 55 (November 1986): 599–611.
Parish, John Carl. *The Persistence of the Westward Movement and Other Essays.* Berkeley: University of California Press, 1943.
Paul, Rodman W. "Frederick Merk, Teacher and Scholar: A Tribute." *Western Historical Quarterly* 9 (April 1978): 141–48.
Paul, Rodman W., and Michael P. Malone, "Tradition and Challenge in Western Historiography." *Western Historical Quarterly* 16 (January 1985): 27–53.
Paxson, Frederic L. "A Generation of the Frontier Hypothesis: 1893–1932." *Pacific Historical Review* 4 (December 1935): 309–27.
Pomeroy, Earl. "Frederic L. Paxson and His Approach to History." *Mississippi Valley Historical Review* 39 (March 1953): 673–92.

Selective Bibliography

Pomeroy, Earl. "Toward a Reorientation of Western History: Continuity and Environment." *Mississippi Valley Historical Review* 41 (March 1955): 579–600.

Pomeroy, Earl. "What Remains of the West?" *Utah Historical Quarterly* 35 (Winter 1967): 37–55.

Putnam, Jackson K. "The Turner Thesis and the Westward Movement: A Reappraisal." *Western Historical Quarterly* 7 (October 1976): 377–404.

Ridge, Martin. "Ray Allen Billington (1903–1980)." *Western Historical Quarterly* 12 (July 1981): 245–50.

Ridge, Martin. "Ray Allen Billington, Western History, and American Exceptionalism." *Pacific Historical Review* 56 (November 1987): 495–511.

Robbins, William G. "The 'Plundered Province' Thesis and Recent Historiography of the American West." *Pacific Historical Review* 55 (November 1986): 577–97.

Scheiber, Harry N. "The Economic Historian as Realist and Keeper of the Democratic Ideals: Paul Wallace Gates's Studies of American Land Policy." *Journal of Economic History* 40 (September 1980): 585–93.

Steffen, Jerome O., ed. *The American West: New Perspectives, New Dimensions.* Norman: University of Oklahoma Press, 1979.

Stegner, Wallace. *The Uneasy Chair: A Biography of Bernard De Voto.* Garden City, N.Y.: Doubleday and Company, 1974.

Swierenga, Robert P., ed. *James C. Malin, History & Ecology: Studies of the Grassland.* Lincoln: University of Nebraska Press, 1984.

Terral, Rufus. *The Missouri Valley: Land of Drought, Flood, and Promises.* New Haven: Yale University Press, 1947.

Thomas, James H., ed. "Historians of the Southern Plains." *Great Plains Journal* 18 (1979). Includes eleven essays on leading regional historians.

Tobin, Gregory M. *The Making of a History: Walter Prescott Webb and "The Great Plains."* Austin: University of Texas Press, 1976.

Turner, Frederick Jackson. "Section and Nation." *Yale Review* 12 (October 1922): 1–21.

Turner, Frederick Jackson. "The Significance of the Section in American History." *Wisconsin Magazine of History* 13 (March 1925): 255–80.

Turner, Frederick Jackson. "The West—1876 and 1926: Its Progress in a Half-Century." *The World's Work* 52 (July 1926): 319–27.

Webb, Walter Prescott. *Divided We Stand: The Crisis of a Frontierless Democracy.* New York: Farrar and Rinehart, 1937.

Webb, Walter Prescott. *The Great Plains.* Boston: Ginn and Company, 1931.

West, Elliott. "Cowboys and Indians and Artists and Liars and Schoolmarms and Tom Mix: New Ways to Teach the American West," in Dennis Reinhartz and Stephen E. Maizlish, eds., *Essays on Walter Prescott Webb and the Teaching of History,* College Station: Texas A & M University Press, 1985, 36–60.

"Western State Historiography: A Status Report." *Pacific Historical Review* 50 (November 1981): 387–525. A collection of several essays.

Worster, Donald. "New West, True West: Interpreting the Region's History." *Western Historical Quarterly* 18 (April 1987): 141–56.

SOCIAL HISTORY: Ethnic Groups, Women and Family, Urbanization, Violence, Demography, and Community Studies

Acuña, Rodolfo. *Occupied America: A History of the Chicanos.* 2nd ed. New York: Harper and Row, 1981.
Anderson, Karen. *Wartime Women: Sex Roles, Family Relations, and the Status of Women During World War II.* Westport, Conn.: Greenwood Press, 1981.
Armitage, Susan. "Women and Men in Western History: A Stereoptical Vision." *Western Historical Quarterly* 16 (October 1985): 381–91.
Armitage, Susan, and Elizabeth Jameson, eds. *The Women's West.* Norman: University of Oklahoma Press, 1987.
Barr, Alwyn. *Black Texans: A History of Negroes in Texas, 1528–1971.* Austin: University of Texas Press, 1973.
Barrera, Mario. *Race and Class in the Southwest: A Theory of Racial Inequality.* Notre Dame: University of Notre Dame Press, 1979.
Bataille, Gretchen M., and Kathleen Mullen Sands. *American Indian Women: Telling Their Lives.* Lincoln: University of Nebraska Press, 1984.
Berkhofer, Robert F., Jr. "The Political Context of a New Indian History." *Pacific Historical Review* 40 (August 1971): 357–82.
Bernard, Richard M., and Bradley R. Rice, eds. *Sunbelt Cities: Politics and Growth since World War II.* Austin: University of Texas Press, 1983.
Blackwelder, Julia Kirk. *Women of the Depression: Caste and Culture in San Antonio, 1929–1939.* College Station: Texas A & M University Press, 1984.
Bonacich, Edna, and John Modell. *The Economic Basis of Ethnic Solidarity: A Study of Japanese Americans.* Berkeley: University of California Press, 1980.
Broussard, Albert S. "Organizing the Black Community in the San Francisco Bay Area, 1915–1930." *Arizona and the West* 23 (Winter 1981): 335–54.
Brown, A. Theodore, and Lyle W. Dorsett. *K. C.: A History of Kansas City, Missouri.* Boulder, Colo.: Pruett Publishing Company, 1978.
Camarillo, Albert. *Chicanos in a Changing Society: From Mexican Pueblos to American Barrios in Santa Barbara and Southern California, 1848–1930.* Cambridge, Mass.: Harvard University Press, 1979.
Campbell, D'Ann. "Was the West Different?: Values and Attitudes of Young Women in 1943." *Pacific Historical Review* 47 (August 1978): 453–64.
Cardoso, Lawrence A. *Mexican Emigration to the United States, 1897–1931: Socio-Economic Patterns.* Tucson: University of Arizona Press, 1980.
Clark, Norman. *Mill Town: A Social History of Everett, Washington.* Seattle: University of Washington Press, 1970.
Cronon, William, Howard R. Lamar, Katherine G. Morrisey, and Jay Gitlin. "Women and the West: Rethinking the Western History Survey Course." *Western Historical Quarterly* 17 (July 1986): 269–91.
Daniels, Roger. "American Historians and East Asian Immigrants." *Pacific Historical Review* 42 (November 1974): 449–72.
Daniels, Roger. *The Politics of Prejudice: The Anti-Japanese Movement in California and the Struggle for Japanese Exclusion.* Berkeley: University of California Press, 1962.

Selective Bibliography

Daniels, Roger, et al, eds. *Japanese Americans: From Relocation to Redress.* Salt Lake City: University of Utah Press, 1986.

DeGraaf, Lawrence B. "Recognition, Racism, and Reflections on the Writing of Western Black History." *Pacific Historical Review* 44 (February 1975): 22–51.

Deloria, Vine, Jr., ed. *American Indian Policy in the Twentieth Century.* Norman: University of Oklahoma Press, 1985.

Deutsch, Sarah. *No Separate Refuge: Culture, Class, and Gender on an Anglo-Hispanic Frontier in the American Southwest, 1880–1940.* New York: Oxford University Press, 1987.

Dippie, Brian W. *The Vanishing American: White Attitudes and U.S. Indian Policy.* Middletown, Conn.: Wesleyan University Press, 1982.

Douglass, William A., and Jon Bilbao. *Amerikanuak: Basques in the New World.* Reno: University of Nevada Press, 1975.

Fixico, Donald L. *Termination and Relocation: Federal Indian Policy, 1945–1960.* Albuquerque: University of New Mexico Press, 1986.

Fogelson, Robert M. *The Fragmented Metropolis: Los Angeles, 1850–1930.* Cambridge, Mass.: Harvard University Press, 1967.

Franklin, Jimmie Lewis. *Born Sober: Prohibition in Oklahoma, 1907–1939.* Norman: University of Oklahoma Press, 1971.

García, Mario T. *Desert Immigrants: The Mexicans of El Paso, 1880–1920.* New Haven: Yale University Press, 1971.

Gómez-Quiñones, Juan, and Luis Leobardo Arroyo. "On the State of Chicano History...." *Western Historical Quarterly* 7 (April 1976): 269–308.

Griswold del Castillo, Richard. *La Familia: Chicano Families in the Urban Southwest, 1848 to the Present.* Notre Dame: University of Notre Dame Press, 1984.

Hagan, William T. "Tribalism Rejuvenated: The Native American since the Era of Termination." *Western Historical Quarterly* 12 (January 1981): 5–16.

Horsman, Reginald. "Well-Trodden Paths and Fresh Byways: Recent Writing on Native American History," in Stanley I. Kutler and Stanley N. Katz, eds. *The Promise of American History: Progress and Prospects.* Baltimore: Johns Hopkins University Press, 1982.

Issel, William, and Robert W. Cherny. *San Francisco, 1865–1932: Politics, Power, and Urban Development.* Berkeley: University of California Press, 1986.

Iverson, Peter. *Carlos Montezuma and the Changing World of American Indians.* Albuquerque: University of New Mexico Press, 1982.

Iverson, Peter, ed. *The Plains Indians of the Twentieth Century.* Norman: University of Oklahoma Press, 1985.

Jensen, Joan M., and Darlis A. Miller. "The Gentle Tamers Revisited: New Approaches to the History of Women in the American West." *Pacific Historical Review* 49 (May 1980): 173–213.

Jensen, Joan M., and Gloria Ricci Lothrop. *California Women: A History.* San Francisco: Boyd and Fraser Publishing Company, 1987.

Jordan, Terry G. "A Century and a Half of Ethnic Change in Texas, 1836–1986." *Southwestern Historical Quarterly* 89 (April 1986): 385–422.

Josephy, Alvin, Jr. *Now That the Buffalo's Gone: A Study of Today's American Indians*. New York: Alfred A. Knopf, 1982.
Kelly, Lawrence C. *The Assault on Assimilation: John Collier and the Origins of Indian Policy Reform*. Albuquerque: University of New Mexico Press, 1983.
Kelly, Lawrence C. *The Navajo Indians and Federal Indian Policy, 1900–1935*. Tucson: University of Arizona Press, 1968.
Kitano, Harry H. L. *Japanese Americans: The Evolution of a Subculture*. 2nd ed. Englewood Cliffs, N.J.: Prentice-Hall, 1976.
Koppes, Clayton R. "From New Deal to Termination: Liberalism and Indian Policy, 1933–1953." *Pacific Historical Review* 46 (November 1977): 543–66.
Lotchin, Roger. "City and Sword in Metropolitan California, 1919–1941." *Urbanism Past and Present* 7 (Summer-Fall 1982): 1–16.
Lotchin, Roger W. "The City and the Sword: San Francisco and the Rise of the Metropolitan-Military Complex, 1919–1941." *Journal of American History* 65 (March 1979): 996–1020.
Lotchin, Roger W. "The Darwinian City: The Politics of Urbanization in San Francisco between the World Wars." *Pacific Historical Review* 48 (August 1979): 357–81.
Luckingham, Bradford. "The American Southwest: An Urban View." *Western Historical Quarterly* 15 (July 1984): 261–80.
Luckingham, Bradford. "The Urban Dimension of Western History," in Michael P. Malone, ed., *Historians and the American West* (Lincoln: University of Nebraska Press, 1983), 323–43.
Luckingham, Bradford. *The Urban Southwest: A Profile History of Albuquerque, El Paso, Phoenix, and Tucson*. El Paso: Texas Western Press, 1982.
Luebke, Frederick C. "Ethnic Group Settlement on the Great Plains." *Western Historical Quarterly* 8 (October 1977): 405–30.
Luebke, Frederick C. "Ethnic Minority Groups in the American West," in Michael P. Malone, ed., *Historians and the American West*. Lincoln: University of Nebraska Press, 1983, 387–413.
Luebke, Frederick C., ed. *Ethnicity on the Great Plains*. Lincoln: University of Nebraska Press for the Center for Great Plains Studies, 1980.
Lyman, Stanford. *The Asian in the West*. Reno: University of Nevada, 1970.
McComb, David. *Houston: The Bayou City*. Austin: University of Texas Press, 1969.
McWilliams, Carey. *North from Mexico: The Spanish-Speaking People of the United States*. Philadelphia: J. B. Lippincott, 1949; Westport, Conn.: Greenwood Press, 1968.
Matthiessen, Peter. *Sal Si Puedes: César Chávez and the New American Revolution*. New York: Random House, 1969.
Melendy, H. Brett. *Asians in America: Filipinos, Koreans and East Indians*. Boston: Twayne Publishers, 1977.
Mirande, Alfredo, and Evangelina Enriquez. *La Chicana: The Mexican-American Woman*. Chicago: University of Chicago Press, 1979.
Modell, John. *The Economics and Politics of Racial Accommodation: The Japanese of Los Angeles, 1900–1942*. Urbana: University of Illinois Press, 1977.

Selective Bibliography

Moses, L. G. *The Indian Man: A Biography of James Mooney*. Urbana: University of Illinois Press, 1984.

Moynihan, Ruth B. *Rebel for Rights: Abigail Scott Duniway*. New Haven, Conn.: Yale University Press, 1983.

Nash, Gerald D. "Planning for the Postwar City: The Urban West in World War II." *Arizona and the West* 27 (Summer 1985): 99–112.

Olson, James S., and Raymond Wilson. *Native Americans in the Twentieth Century*. Provo: Brigham Young University Press, 1984; Urbana: University of Illinois Press, 1984.

Parman, Donald L. *The Navajos and the New Deal*. New Haven: Yale University Press, 1976.

Philp, Kenneth R. *John Collier's Crusade for Indian Reform 1920–1954*. Tucson: University of Arizona Press, 1977.

Philp, Kenneth R. "Stride toward Freedom: The Relocation of Indians in Cities, 1952–1960." *Western Historical Quarterly* 16 (April 1985): 175–90.

Philp, Kenneth R. "Termination: A Legacy of the Indian New Deal." *Western Historical Quarterly* 14 (April 1983): 165–80.

Pomeroy, Earl. "The Urban Frontier of the Far West," in John G. Clark, ed., *The Frontier Challenge: Responses to the Trans-Mississippi West*. Lawrence: University Press of Kansas, 1971, 7–29.

Prucha, Francis Paul. "American Indian Policy in the Twentieth Century." *Western Historical Quarterly* 15 (January 1984): 5–18.

Prucha, Francis Paul. *The Churches and the Indian Schools, 1888–1912*. Lincoln: University of Nebraska Press, 1979.

Prucha, Frances Paul. *The Great Father: The United States Government and the American Indians*. 2 vols. Lincoln: University of Nebraska Press, 1984.

Rabinowitz, Howard N. "Growth Trends in the Albuquerque SMSA, 1940–1978." *Journal of the West* 18 (July 1979): 62–74.

Riley, Glenda. "Women of the Great Plains: Recent Developments in Research." *Great Plains Quarterly* 5 (Spring 1985): 81–92.

Romo, Ricardo. *East Los Angeles: History of a Barrio*. Austin: University of Texas Press, 1983.

Romo, Ricardo. "Work and Restlessness: Occupational and Spatial Mobility among Mexicanos in Los Angeles, 1918–1928." *Pacific Historical Review* 46 (May 1977): 157–80.

Rosenbaum, Robert J. *Mexicano Resistance in the Southwest: "The Sacred Right of Self-Preservation."* Austin: University of Texas Press, 1981.

Ruoff, A. LaVonne Brown. "American Indian Literatures: Introduction and Bibliography." *American Studies International* 24 (October 1986): 2–52.

Sale, Roger. *Seattle: Past to Present*. Seattle: University of Washington Press, 1976.

Saloutos, Theodore. "Cultural Persistence and Change: Greeks in the Great Plains and Rocky Mountain West, 1890–1970." *Pacific Historical Review* 49 (February 1980): 77–103.

Samek, Hana. *The Blackfeet Confederacy: A Comparative Study of Canadian and U.S. Indian Policy*. Albuquerque: University of New Mexico Press, 1987.

Spence, Mary Lee. "They Also Serve Who Wait." *Western Historical Quarterly* 14 (January 1983): 6–28. Waiters and waitresses in the West.

Szasz, Margaret Connell. *Education and the American Indian: The Road to Self-Determination Since 1928.* 2nd ed. Albuquerque: University of New Mexico Press, 1977.
Taylor, Graham D. *The New Deal and American Indian Tribalism: The Administration of the Indian Reorganization Act, 1934–45.* Lincoln: University of Nebraska Press, 1980.
Toll, William. *The Making of an Ethnic Middle Class: Portland Jewry over Four Generations.* Albany: State University of New York Press, 1982.
Underwood, June O. "Civilizing Kansas: Women's Organizations, 1880–1920." *Kansas History* 7 (Winter 1984–85): 291–306.
Underwood, June O. "Western Women and True Womenhood: Culture and Symbol in History and Literature." *Great Plains Quarterly* 5 (Spring 1985): 93–107.
Washburn, Wilcomb. "The Writing of American Indian History: A Status Report." *Pacific Historical Review* 40 (August 1971): 261–81.
White, Richard. "Race Relations in the American West." *American Quarterly* 38 (no. 3, 1986): 396–416.
White, Richard. *The Roots of Dependency: Subsistence, Environment and Social Change Among the Choctaws, Pawnees, and Navajos.* Lincoln: University of Nebraska Press, 1983.
Wilson, Raymond. *Ohiyesa: Charles Eastman, Santee Sioux.* Urbana: University of Illinois Press, 1983.

POLITICAL HISTORY: Politics, Reform, and Political Movements

Alexander, Charles C. *The Ku Klux Klan in the Southwest.* Lexington: University of Kentucky Press, 1965.
Ashby, LeRoy. *The Spearless Leader: Senator Borah and the Progressive Movement in the 1920's.* Urbana: University of Illinois Press, 1972.
Bates, J. Leonard. *The Origins of the Teapot Dome: Progressives, Parties and Petroleum, 1909–1921.* Urbana: University of Illinois Press, 1963.
Bean, Walton. *Boss Ruef's San Francisco: The Story of the Union Labor Party. Big Business, and the Graft Prosecution.* Berkeley: University of California Press, 1952.
Braeman, John, Robert H. Bremner, and David Brody, eds. *The New Deal: The State and Local Levels,* vol. 2. Columbus: Ohio State University Press, 1975.
Brennan, John. *Silver and the First New Deal.* Reno: University of Nevada Press, 1969.
Brodie, Fawn M. *Richard Nixon: The Shaping of His Character.* New York: W. W. Norton, 1981.
Brown, Eugene. *J. William Fulbright: Advice and Dissent.* Iowa City: University of Iowa Press, 1985.
Brown, Norman D. *Hood, Bonnet, and Little Brown Jug: Texas Politics, 1921–1928.* College Station: Texas A & M University Press, 1984.
Burbank, Garin. *When Farmers Voted Red: The Gospel of Socialism in the Oklahoma Countryside, 1910–1924.* Westport, Conn.: Greenwood Press, 1976.

Selective Bibliography

Burk, Robert F. *Dwight D. Eisenhower: Hero & Politician*. Boston: Twayne Publishers, 1986.

Burke, Robert E. *Olson's New Deal for California*. Berkeley: University of California Press, 1953.

Burton, Robert E. *Democrats of Oregon: The Pattern of Minority Politics, 1900-1956*. Eugene: University of Oregon Books, 1970.

Chan, Loren Briggs. *Sagebrush Statesman: Tasker L. Oddie of Nevada*. Reno: University of Nevada Press, 1973.

Cherny, Robert W. *Population, Progressivism, and the Transformation of Nebraska Politics, 1885-1915*. Lincoln: University of Nebraska Press, 1981.

Clark, Norman H. *The Dry Years: Prohibition and Social Change in Washington*. Seattle: University of Washington Press, 1965.

Coletta, Paolo E. *William Jennings Bryan, I: Political Evangelist, 1860-1908; William Jennings Bryan, II: Progressive Politician and Moral Statesman, 1909-1915; William Jennings Bryan, III: Political Puritan, 1915-1925*. Lincoln: University of Nebraska Press, 1964, 1969, 1969.

Conkin, Paul K. *Big Daddy from the Pedernales, Lyndon Baines Johnson*. Boston: Twayne Publishers, 1986.

Coombs, F. Alan. "Twentieth-Century Western Politics" in Michael P. Malone, ed. *Historians and the American West*. Lincoln: University of Nebraska Press, 1983, 300-22.

DeGrazia, Alfred. *The Western Public, 1952 and Beyond*. Stanford: Stanford University Press, 1954.

Donnelly, Thomas C., ed. *Rocky Mountain Politics*. Albuquerque: University of New Mexico Press, 1940.

Edwards, Jerome E. *Pat McCarran: Political Boss of Nevada*. Reno: University of Nevada Press, 1982.

Elazar, Daniel J. *Cities of the Prairie: The Metropolitan Frontier and American Politics*. New York: Basic Books, 1970.

Elazar, Daniel J. "Political Culture on the Plains." *Western Historical Quarterly* 11 (July 1980): 261-83.

Elliott, Russell R. *Servant of Power: A Political Biography of Senator William M. Stewart*. Reno: University of Nevada Press, 1983.

Feinman, Ronald L. *Twilight of Progressivism: The Western Republican Senators and the New Deal*. Baltimore: Johns Hopkins University Press, 1981.

Goble, Danney. *Progressive Oklahoma: The Making of a New Kind of State*. Norman: University of Oklahoma Press, 1980.

Gould, Lewis L. *Progressives and Prohibitionists: Texas Democrats in the Wilson Era*. Austin: University of Texas Press, 1973.

Green, George Norris. *The Establishment in Texas Politics: The Primitive Years, 1938-1957*. Westport, Conn.: Greenwood Press, 1979.

Green, James R. *Grass-Roots Socialism: Radical Movements in the Southwest 1895-1943*. Baton Rouge: Louisiana State University Press, 1978.

Henderson, Richard B. *Maury Maverick: A Political Biography*. Austin: University of Texas Press, 1970.

Holmes, Jack E. *Politics in New Mexico*. Albuquerque: University of New Mexico Press, 1967.

Israel, Fred L. *Nevada's Key Pittman.* Lincoln: University of Nebraska Press, 1963.
Johnson, Claudius O. *Borah of Idaho.* New York: Longmans, Green and Company, 1936; Seattle: University of Washington Press, 1967.
Jonas, Frank H., ed. *Politics in the American West.* Salt Lake City: University of Utah Press, 1969.
Jonas, Frank H., ed. *Western Politics.* Salt Lake City: University of Utah Press, 1961.
La Forte, Robert Sherman. *Leaders of Reform: Progressive Republicans in Kansas 1900–1916.* Lawrence: University Press of Kansas, 1974.
Lowitt, Richard. *George W. Norris: The Making of a Progressive, 1861–1912.* Syracuse, N.Y.: Syracuse University Press, 1963; *George W. Norris: The Persistence of a Progressive, 1913–1933.* Urbana: University of Illinois Press, 1971; *George W. Norris: The Triumph of a Progressive, 1933–1944.* Urbana: University of Illinois Press, 1978.
McCoy, Donald R. *Landon of Kansas.* Lincoln: University of Nebraska Press, 1966.
Malone, Michael P. *C. Ben Ross and the New Deal in Idaho.* Seattle: University of Washington Press, 1970.
Morlan, Robert L. *Political Prairie Fire: The Nonpartisan League, 1915–1922.* Minneapolis: University of Minnesota Press, 1955.
Mowry, George E. *The California Progressives.* Berkeley: University of California Press, 1951.
Murray, Keith A. "Issues and Personalities of Pacific Northwest Politics, 1889–1950." *Pacific Northwest Quarterly* 41 (July 1950): 213–33.
"The New Deal in the West." *Pacific Historical Review* 38 (August 1969). Special issue with several essays.
Nye, Russel B. *Midwestern Progressive Politics: A Historical Study of Its Origins and Development, 1870–1958.* East Lansing: Michigan State University Press, 1959.
Olien, Roger M. *From Token to Triumph: The Texas Republicans since 1920.* Dallas: Southern Methodist University Press, 1982.
Olin, Spencer C. *California's Prodigal Sons: Hiram Johnson and the Progressives, 1911–1912.* Berkeley: University of California Press, 1968.
Patterson, James T. "The New Deal and the States." *American Historical Review* 73 (October 1967): 70–84.
Peterson, F. Ross. *Prophet Without Honor: Glen H. Taylor and the Fight for American Liberalism.* Lexington: University Press of Kentucky, 1974.
"Politics in the West." *Journal of the West* 13 (October 1974). Special issue with several essays.
Putnam, Jackson K. *Modern California Politics 1917–1980.* Golden State Series. San Francisco: Boyd and Fraser Publishing Company, 1980.
Putnam, Jackson K. *Old-Age Politics in California: From Richardson to Reagan.* Stanford: Stanford University Press, 1970.
Rogin, Michael P., and John L. Shover. *Political Change in California: Critical Elections and Social Movements, 1890–1966.* Westport, Conn.: Greenwood Press, 1970.

Selective Bibliography

Ruetten, Richard T. "Senator Burton K. Wheeler and Insurgency in the 1920s," in Gene M. Gressley, ed., *The American West: A Reorientation*. Laramie: University of Wyoming Press, 1966, 111–31.
Saloutos, Theodore, and John D. Hicks. *Agricultural Discontent in the Middle West, 1900–1939*. Madison: University of Wisconsin Press, 1951.
Sarasohn, David. "The Election of 1916: Realigning the Rockies." *Western Historical Quarterly* 11 (July 1980): 285–305.
Scales, James R., and Danney Goble. *Oklahoma Politics: A History*. Norman: University of Oklahoma Press, 1982.
Schruben, Francis W. *Kansas in Turmoil, 1930–1936*. Columbia: University of Missouri Press, 1969.
Smith, A. Robert. *The Tiger in the Senate: The Biography of Wayne Morse*. Garden City, N.Y.: Doubleday and Company, 1962.
Tyson, Carl. "A Bibliographical Essay: Politics in the West." *Journal of the West* 13 (October 1974): 117–22.
Woodward, Robert C. "William S. U'Ren: A Progressive Era Personality." *Idaho Yesterdays* 4 (Summer 1960): 4–10.

ECONOMIC HISTORY: Agriculture and Ranching, Water and Land Policies, Labor, Mining, Lumbering, Transportation, and Business History

Abbott, Carl. *The New Urban America: Growth and Politics in Sunbelt Cities*. Chapel Hill: University of North Carolina Press, 1981.
Abbott, Carl. *Portland: Politics, Planning, and Growth in a Twentieth-Century City*. Lincoln: University of Nebraska Press, 1983.
Arrington, Leonard J. "The Sagebrush Resurrection: New Deal Expenditures in the Western States, 1933–1939." *Pacific Historical Review* 52 (February 1983): 1–16.
Brown, Ronald C. *Hard-Rock Miners: The Intermountain West, 1860–1920*. College Station: Texas A & M University Press, 1979.
Byrkit, James W. *Forging the Copper Collar: Arizona's Labor-Management War of 1901–1921*. Tucson: University of Arizona Press, 1982.
Clayton, James L. "Impact of the Cold War on the Economies of California and Utah, 1946–1965." *Pacific Historical Review* 36 (November 1967): 449–73.
Cox, Thomas R., et al. *This Well-Wooded Land: Americans and Their Forests from Colonial Times to the Present*. Lincoln: University of Nebraska Press, 1985.
Daniel, Cletus E. *Bitter Harvest: A History of California Farm-workers, 1870–1941*. Ithaca, N.Y.: Cornell University Press, 1981.
Dubofsky, Melvyn. *We Shall Be All: A History of the Industrial Workers of the World*. Chicago: Quadrangle Books, 1969.
Elliott, Russell R. *Nevada's Twentieth-Century Mining Boom: Tonopah, Goldfield, Ely*. Reno: University of Nevada Press, 1966.
Fell, James E., Jr. *Ores to Metal: The Rocky Mountain Smelting Industry*. Lincoln: University of Nebraska Press, 1979.
Fite, Gilbert C. *American Farmers: The New Minority*. Bloomington: Indiana University Press, 1981.

Foster, Mark S. "Prosperity's Prophet: Henry J. Kaiser and the Consumer/Suburban Culture, 1930–1950." *Western Historical Quarterly* 17 (April 1986): 165–84.
Frost, Richard H. *The Mooney Case*. Stanford: Stanford University Press, 1968.
Green, Donald E. *Land of the Underground Rain: Irrigation on the Texas High Plains, 1910–1970*. Austin: University of Texas Press, 1973.
Gressley, Gene M. "Regionalism and the Twentieth-Century West," in Jerome O. Steffen, ed. *The American West: New Perspectives, New Dimensions*. Norman: University of Oklahoma Press, 1979, 197–234.
Hayes, Lynton R. *Energy, Economic Growth, and Regionalism in the West*. Albuquerque: University of New Mexico Press, 1980.
Hoffman, Abraham. *Vision or Villainy: Origins of the Owens Valley-Los Angeles Water Controversy*. College Station: Texas A & M University Press, 1981.
Hofsommer, Don L. *The Southern Pacific, 1901–1985*. College Station: Texas A & M University Press, 1986.
Hundley, Norris, Jr. "The Dark and Bloody Ground of Indian Water Rights: Confusion Elevated to Principle." *Western Historical Quarterly* 9 (October 1978): 454–82.
Hundley, Norris, Jr. *Dividing the Waters: A Century of Controversy Between the United States and Mexico*. Berkeley: University of California Press, 1966.
Hundley, Norris, Jr. *Water and the West: The Colorado River Compact and the Politics of Water in the American West*. Berkeley: University of California Press, 1975.
Hundley, Norris, Jr. "The 'Winters' Decision and Indian Water Rights: A Mystery Reexamined." *Western Historical Quarterly* 13 (January 1982): 17–42.
Isern, Thomas D. *Custom Combining on the Great Plains: A History*. Norman: University of Oklahoma Press, 1981.
Jensen, Vernon H. *Heritage of Conflict: Labor Relations in the Nonferrous Metals Industry up to 1930*. Ithaca, N.Y.: Cornell University Press, 1950.
Jensen, Vernon. *Lumber and Labor*. New York: Farrar and Rinehart, 1945.
Jensen, Vernon H. *Nonferrous Metals Industry Unionism, 1932–1954: A Story of Leadership*. Ithaca, N.Y.: Cornell University Press, 1954.
Kahrl, William L. *Water and Power: The Conflict over Los Angeles' Water Supply in the Owens Valley*. Berkeley: University of California Press, 1982.
Lovin, Hugh T. " 'Duty of Water' in Idaho: A 'New West' Irrigation Controversy, 1890–1920." *Arizona and the West* 23 (Spring 1981): 5–28.
McGregor, Alexander Campbell. *Counting Sheep: From Open Range to Agribusiness on the Columbia Plateau*. Seattle: University of Washington Press, 1982.
Nash, Gerald D. "Oil in the West: Reflections on the Historiography of an Unexplored Field." *Pacific Historical Review* 39 (May 1970): 193–204.
Nash, Gerald D. "Stages of California's Economic Growth, 1870–1970: An Interpretation." *California Historical Quarterly* 51 (Winter 1972): 315–30.
Nash, Gerald D. *U.S. Oil Policy, 1890–1964: Business and Government in Twentieth Century America*. Pittsburgh: University of Pittsburgh Press, 1968.
Opie, John. *The Law of the Land: 200 Years of American Farmland Policy*. Lincoln: University of Nebraska Press, 1987.

Selective Bibliography

Pearce, William Martin. *The Matador Land and Cattle Company.* Norman: University of Oklahoma Press, 1964.

Pisani, Donald J. *From the Family Farm to Agribusiness: The Irrigation Crusade in California and the West, 1850–1931.* Berkeley: University of California Press, 1984.

Pisani, Donald J. "State vs. Nation: Federal Reclamation and Water Rights in the Progressive Era." *Pacific Historical Review* 51 (August 1982): 265–82.

Pisani, Donald J. "The Strange Death of the California-Nevada Compact: A Study in Interstate Water Negotiations." *Pacific Historical Review* 47 (November 1978): 637–58.

Reisner, Marc. *Cadillac Desert: The American West and Its Disappearing Water.* New York: Viking Penguin, 1986.

Reno, Philip. *Mother Earth, Father Sky, and Economic Development: Navaho Resources and Their Use.* Albuquerque: University of New Mexico Press, 1981.

Robbins, William G. *American Forestry: A History of National, State, and Private Cooperation.* Lincoln: University of Nebraska Press, 1985.

Robbins, William G. "Labor in the Pacific Slope Lumber Industry: A Twentieth-Century Perspective." *Journal of the West* 25 (April 1986): 8–13.

Robbins, William G., *Lumberjacks and Legislators: Political Economy of the U.S. Lumber Industry, 1890–1941.* College Station: Texas A & M. University Press, 1982.

Robbins, William G. "The Social Context of Forestry: The Pacific Northwest in the Twentieth Century." *Western Historical Quarterly* 16 (October 1985): 413–27.

Schlebecker, John T. *Cattle Raising on the Plains, 1900–1961.* Lincoln: University of Nebraska Press, 1963.

Schlebecker, John T. *Whereby We Thrive: A History of American Farming, 1607–1972.* Ames: Iowa State University Press, 1975.

Schwantes, Carlos A. "The Concept of the Wageworkers' Frontier: A Framework for Future Research." *Western Historical Quarterly* 18 (January 1987): 39–55.

Schwantes, Carlos A. *Radical Heritage: Labor, Socialism, and Reform in Washington and British Columbia, 1885–1917.* Seattle: University of Washington Press, 1979.

Sheffy, Lester Fields. *The Francklyn Land & Cattle Company: A Panhandle Enterprise, 1882–1952.* Austin: University of Texas Press, 1963.

Shideler, James H., ed. *Agriculture in the Development of the Far West.* Washington, D.C.: Agricultural History Society, 1975.

Skaggs, Jimmy M. *Prime Cut: Livestock Raising and Meatpacking in the United States, 1607–1983.* College Station: Texas A & M University Press, 1986.

Spence, Clark C. *Mining Engineers and the American West: The Lace-Boot Brigade, 1849–1933.* New Haven: Yale University Press, 1970.

Spence, Clark C. *The Rainmakers: American 'Pluviculture' to World War II.* Lincoln: University of Nebraska Press, 1980.

Tyler, Robert L. *Rebels of the Woods: The I.W.W. in the Pacific Northwest.* Eugene: University of Oregon Books, 1967.
Wessel, Thomas R., ed. *Agriculture in the Great Plains, 1876–1936.* Washington, D.C.: Agricultural History Society, 1977.
Williamson, Harold Francis. *The American Petroleum Industry.* 2 vols. Evanston, Ill.: Northwestern University Press, 1959, 1963.

ENVIRONMENTAL HISTORY: Conservation, Ecology, and National Parks

Bonnifield, Paul. *The Dust Bowl: Men, Dirt, and Depression.* Albuquerque: University of New Mexico Press, 1979.
Cohen, Michael P. *The Pathless Way: John Muir and American Wilderness.* Madison: University of Wisconsin Press, 1984.
deBuys, William. *Enchantment and Exploitation: The Life and Hard Times of a New Mexico Mountain Range.* Albuquerque: University of New Mexico Press, 1985.
Doughty, Robin W. *Wildlife and Man in Texas: Environmental Change and Conservation.* College Station: Texas A & M University Press, 1983.
Dunlap, Thomas R. "Values for Varmints: Predator Control and Environmental Ideas, 1920–1939." *Pacific Historical Review* 53 (May 1984): 141–61.
"Environmental History." *Pacific Historical Review* 41 (August 1972): 271–372. Special theme issue.
Flader, Susan L. *Thinking Like a Mountain: Aldo Leopold and the Evolution of an Ecological Attitude Toward Deer, Wolves, and Forests.* Columbia: University of Missouri Press, 1974.
Fox, Stephen. *John Muir and His Legacy: The American Conservation Movement.* Boston: Little, Brown and Company, 1981.
Hollon, W. Eugene. *The Great American Desert: Then and Now.* New York: Oxford University Press, 1966.
Hurt, R. Douglas. *The Dust Bowl: An Agricultural and Social History.* Chicago: Nelson-Hall, 1981.
Huth, Hans. *Nature and the American: Three Centuries of Changing Attitudes.* Berkeley: University of California Press, 1957.
Ise, John. *Our National Park Policy: A Critical History.* Baltimore: Johns Hopkins Press, 1961.
Lee, Lawrence B. "Environmental Implications of Government Reclamation in California." *Agricultural History* 49 (Fall 1975): 223–30.
Limerick, Patricia Nelson. *Desert Passages: Encounters with the American Deserts.* Albuquerque: University of New Mexico Press, 1985.
McCarthy, G. Michael. *Hour of Trial: The Conservation Conflict in Colorado and the West, 1891–1907.* Norman: University of Oklahoma Press, 1977.
Nash, Roderick. *Wilderness and the American Mind.* 3rd ed. New Haven: Yale University Press, 1982.
Opie, John. "The Environment and the Frontier," in Roger L. Nichols, ed. *American Frontier and Western Issues: A Historiographical Review.* Westport, Conn.: Greenwood Press, 1986, 7–25.

Selective Bibliography

Opie, John. "Environmental History: Pitfalls and Opportunities." *Environmental Review* 7 (Winter 1983): 8–16.

Opie, John. "Frontier History in Environmental Perspective," in Jerome O. Steffen, ed. *The American West: New Perspectives, New Dimensions.* Norman: University of Oklahoma Press, 1979, 9–34.

Petulla, Joseph M. *American Environmentalism: Values, Tactics, Priorities.* College Station: Texas A & M University Press, 1980.

Pyne, Stephen J. *Fire in America: A Cultural History of Wildland and Rural Fire.* Princeton: Princeton University Press, 1982.

Rakestraw, Lawrence. "Conservation Historiography: An Assessment." *Pacific Historical Review* 41 (August 1972): 271–88.

Righter, Robert. *Crucible for Conservation: The Creation of Teton National Park.* Boulder: Colorado Associated University Press, 1982.

Runte, Alfred. *National Parks: The American Experience.* Lincoln: University of Nebraska Press, 1979.

Schrepfer, Susan R. *The Fight to Save the Redwoods: A History of Environmental Reform, 1917–1978.* Madison: University of Wisconsin Press, 1983.

Stein, Walter J. *California and the Dust Bowl Migration.* Westport, Conn.: Greenwood Press, 1973.

Strong, Douglas H. *Tahoe: An Environmental History.* Lincoln: University of Nebraska Press, 1984.

Vecsey, Christopher T., and Robert W. Venables, eds. *American Indian Environments: Ecological Issues in Native American History.* Syracuse: Syracuse University Press, 1980.

White, Richard. "American Environmental History: The Development of a New Historical Field." *Pacific Historical Review* 54 (August 1985): 297–335.

White, Richard. *Land Use, Environment, and Social Change: The Shaping of Island County, Washington.* Seattle: University of Washington Press, 1980.

White, Richard. "Native Americans and the Environment," in W. R. Swagerty, ed. *Scholars and the Indian Experience.* Bloomington: Indiana University Press, 1984, 179–204.

Wild, Peter. *Pioneer Conservationists of Western America.* Missoula, Mont.: Mountain Press, 1979.

Worster, Donald. *Dust Bowl: The Southern Plains in the 1930s.* New York: Oxford University Press, 1979.

Worster, Donald. "History as Natural History: An Essay on Theory and Method." *Pacific Historical Review* 53 (February 1984): 1–19.

Worster, Donald E. *Nature's Economy: The Roots of Ecology.* San Francisco: Sierra Club Books, 1977.

Worster, Donald. *Rivers of Empire: Water, Aridity, and the Growth of the American West.* New York: Pantheon Books, 1986.

PUBLIC POLICY HISTORY: Governmental Policies, Reclamation, Military History

Blumell, Bruce D. *The Development of Public Assistance in the State of Washington During the Great Depression.* New York: Garland Publishing, 1984.

Clark, Ira G. *Water in New Mexico: A History of Its Management and Use.* Albuquerque: University of New Mexico Press, 1987. A mammoth 839-page study.

Franks, Kenny A. *Citizen Soldiers: Oklahoma's National Guard.* Norman: University of Oklahoma Press, 1984.

Gates, Paul W. "The Intermountain West Against Itself." *Arizona and the West* 27 (Autumn 1985): 205–36.

Gordon, Margaret S. *Employment Expansion and Population Growth: The California Experience, 1900–1950.* Berkeley: University of California Press, 1954.

Gunns, Albert F. *Civil Liberties in Crisis: The Pacific Northwest, 1917–1940.* New York: Garland Publishing Company, 1983.

Kunetka, James W. *City of Fire: Los Alamos and the Atomic Age, 1943–1945.* Albuquerque: University of New Mexico Press, 1979.

Lee, Lawrence B. "100 Years of Reclamation Historiography." *Pacific Historical Review* 47 (November 1978): 507–64.

Lee, Lawrence B. *Reclaiming the Arid West: An Historiography and Guide.* Santa Barbara, Calif.: American Bibliographical Center-Chio Press, 1980.

Libecap, Gary D. *Locking Up the Range: Federal Land Controls and Grazing.* Cambridge, Mass.: Ballinger Publishing Company, 1968.

Nash, Gerald D. "Bureaucracy and Reform in the West: Notes on the Influence of a Neglected Interest Group." *Western Historical Quarterly* 2 (July 1971): 295–305.

Nash, Gerald D. "The Influence of Labor on State Policy 1860–1920: The Experience of California." *California Historical Quarterly* 42 (September 1963): 241–57.

Nash, Gerald D. *State Government and Economic Development: A History of Administrative Policies in California, 1849–1933.* Berkeley: University of California Press, 1964.

Peffer, E. Louise. *The Closing of the Public Domain: Disposal and Reservation Policies, 1900–1950.* Stanford: Stanford University Press, 1951.

"Reclamation." *Pacific Historical Review* 47 (November 1978): 507–658. Special topic issue.

Richardson, Elmo R. *Dams, Parks, & Politics: Resource Development & Preservation in the Truman-Eisenhower Era.* Lexington: University Press of Kentucky, 1973.

Richardson, Elmo R. *The Politics of Conservation: Crusades and Controversies, 1897–1913.* Berkeley: University of California Press, 1962.

Rowley, William D. *U.S. Forest Service Grazing and Rangelands: A History.* College Station: Texas A & M University Press, 1985.

Steen, Harold K. *The U.S. Forest Service: A History.* Seattle: University of Washington Press, 1976.

Swain, Donald C. "The National Park Service and the New Deal, 1933–1940." *Pacific Historical Review* 41 (August 1972): 312–32.

Szasz, Ferenc Morton. *The Day the Run Rose Twice: The Story of the Trinity Site Nuclear Explosion, July 16, 1945.* Albuquerque: University of New Mexico Press, 1984.

Selective Bibliography

Twight, Ben W. *Organizational Values and Political Power: The Forest Service versus the Olympic National Park.* University Park: Pennsylvania State University Press, 1983.

Welsh, Michael. *A Mission in the Desert: Albuquerque District, 1935–1985.* Washington, D.C.: U.S. Corps of Engineers, 1985; *U.S. Army Corps of Engineers: Albuquerque District, 1935–1985.* Albuquerque: University of New Mexico Press, 1987.

CULTURAL HISTORY: Literature, the Arts, Religion, Education, and Popular Culture

Albright, Thomas. *Art in the San Francisco Bay Area, 1945–1980.* Berkeley: University of California Press, 1985.

Alexander, Thomas G. "Historiography and the New Mormon History: A Historian's Perspective." *Dialogue* 19 (Fall 1986): 25–49.

Alexander, Thomas G. *Mormonism in Transition: A History of the Latter-day Saints, 1890–1930.* Urbana: University of Illinois Press, 1986.

Aquila, Richard. "Images of the American West in Rock Music." *Western Historical Quarterly* 11 (October 1980): 415–32.

Arrington, Leonard J., and Davis Bitton. *The Mormon Experience: A History of the Latter-day Saints.* New York: Alfred A. Knopf, 1979.

Athearn, Robert G. *The Mythic West in Twentieth-Century America.* Lawrence: University Press of Kansas, 1986.

Baigell, Matthew. *Thomas Hart Benton.* New York: Abrams, 1974.

Banham, Rayner. *Los Angeles: The Architecture of the Four Ecologies.* New York: Harper and Row, 1971.

Benton, Thomas Hart. "American Regionalism: A Personal History of the Movement." *University of Kansas City Review* 18 (Autumn 1951): 41–75.

Berkhofer, Robert, Jr. *The White Man's Indian: Images of the American Indian from Columbus to the Present.* New York: Alfred A. Knopf, 1978.

Bingham, Edwin R. "American Wests Through Autobiography and Memoir." *Pacific Historical Review* 56 (February 1987): 1–24.

Bold, Christine. *Selling the Wild West: Popular Western Fiction, 1860–1960.* Bloomington: Indiana University Press, 1987.

Borne, Lawrence R. *Dude Ranching: A Complete History.* Albuquerque: University of New Mexico Press, 1983.

Broder, Patricia Janis. *The American West: The Modern Vision.* New York: Little, Brown and Company, 1984.

Broder, Patricia Janis. *Taos: A Painter's Dream.* Boston: New York Graphic Society, 1980.

Carstensen, Vernon. "Making Use of the Frontier and the American West." *Western Historical Quarterly* 13 (January 1982): 5–16.

Coe, Ralph T. *Lost and Found Traditions: Native American Art 1965–1985.* Seattle: University of Washington Press, 1986.

Coke, Van Deren. *Taos and Santa Fe: The Artist's Environment, 1882–1942.* Albuquerque: University of New Mexico Press, 1963.

Czestochowski, Joseph H. *John Steuart Curry and Grant Wood.* Columbia: University of Missouri Press, 1981.
Dennis, James M. *Grant Wood: A Study in American Art and Culture.* Columbia: University of Missouri Press, 1986.
Dunn, Dorothy. *American Indian Painting of the Southwest and Plains Areas.* Albuquerque: University of New Mexico Press, 1968.
Eldredge, Charles C., Julie Schimmel, and William H. Truettner. *Art in New Mexico, 1900–1945: Paths to Taos and Santa Fe.* New York: Abbeville Press, 1986.
Erisman, Fred. "Western Regional Writers and the Uses of Place." *Journal of the West* 19 (January 1980): 36–44.
Etulain, Richard W. "The American Literary West and Its Interpreters: The Rise of a New Historiography." *Pacific Historical Review* 45 (April 1976): 311–48.
Etulain, Richard W. "Frontier, Region, and Myth: Changing Interpretations of Western American Culture." *Journal of American Culture* 3 (Summer 1980): 268–84.
Etulain, Richard W. "Shifting Interpretations of Western American Cultural History," in Michael P. Malone, ed. *Historians and the American West.* Lincoln: University of Nebraska Press, 1983, 414–32.
Etulain, Richard W., ed. *The American Literary West.* Manhattan, Kans.: Sunflower University Press, 1980. Reprints *Journal of the West* (January 1980).
Etulain, Richard W., ed. *Western Films: A Brief History.* Manhattan, Kans.: Sunflower University Press, 1983. Reprints *Journal of the West* (October 1983).
Fenin, George N., and William K. Everson. *The Western: From Silents to the Seventies.* New York: Grossman, 1973.
Fredriksson, Kristine. *American Rodeo: From Buffalo Bill to Big Business.* College Station: Texas A & M University Press, 1985.
Gibson, Arrell Morgan. *The Santa Fe and Taos Colonies: Age of the Muses, 1900–1942.* Norman: University of Oklahoma Press, 1983.
Hendrick, Irving G. *California Education: A Brief History.* Golden State Series. San Francisco: Boyd and Fraser Publishing Company, 1980.
Higham, Charles. *The Art of the American Film.* Garden City, N.Y.: Anchor Press/Doubleday, 1973.
Lawrence, Elizabeth Atwood. *Rodeo: An Anthropological Look at the Wild and the Tame.* Knoxville: University of Tennessee Press, 1982.
Lenihan, John H. *Showdown: Confronting Modern America in the Western Film.* Urbana: University of Illinois Press, 1980.
McDonald, Archie P., ed. *Shooting Stars: Heroes and Heroines of Western Film.* Bloomington: Indiana University Press, 1987.
Malone, Bill C. *Country Music, USA,* rev. ed. Austin: University of Texas Press, 1985.
Marovitz, Sanford R. "Myth and Realism in Recent Criticism of the American Literary West." *Journal of American Studies* 15 (April 1981): 95–114.
Milton, John R. *The Novel of the American West.* Lincoln: University of Nebraska Press, 1980.

Selective Bibliography

Pomeroy, Earl. *In Search of the Golden West: The Tourist in Western America.* New York: Alfred A. Knopf, 1957.

Renner, Frederic G. *Charles M. Russell.* Austin: University of Texas Press, 1966.

Samuels, Peggy and Harold. *Contemporary Western Artists.* Houston: Southwest Art Publishing Company, 1982.

Savage, William W., Jr. *The Cowboy Hero: His Image In American History & Culture.* Norman: University of Oklahoma Press, 1979.

Savage, William W. *Singing Cowboys and All That Jazz: A Short History of Popular Music in Oklahoma.* Norman: University of Oklahoma Press, 1983.

Shipps, Jan. *Mormonism: The Story of a New Religious Tradition.* Urbana: University of Illinois Press, 1985.

Singleton, Gregory H. *Religion in the City of Angels: American Protestant Culture and Urbanization, Los Angeles, 1850–1930.* Ann Arbor, Mich.: UMI Research Press, 1979.

Sklar, Robert. *Movie-Made America: A Cultural History of American Movies.* New York: Random House, 1975.

Sonnichsen, C. L. *From Hopalong to Hud: Thoughts on Western Fiction.* College Station: Texas A & M University Press, 1978.

Starr, Kevin. *Americans and the California Dream 1850–1915.* New York: Oxford University Press, 1973.

Starr, Kevin. *Inventing the Dream: California through the Progressive Era.* New York: Oxford University Press, 1985.

Stegner, Wallace, and Richard W. Etulain. *Conversations with Wallace Stegner on Western History and Literature.* Salt Lake City: University of Utah Press, 1983.

Storey, John W. *Texas Baptist Leadership and Social Christianity, 1900–1980.* College Station: Texas A & M University Press, 1986.

Tatum, Stephen. *Inventing Billy the Kid: Visions of the Outlaw in America, 1881–1981.* Albuquerque: University of New Mexico Press, 1982.

Taylor, J. Golden, Thomas J. Lyon, et al, eds. *A Literary History of the American West.* Fort Worth: Texas Christian University Press, 1987.

Topping, Gary. "The Rise of the Western." *Journal of the West* 19 (January 1980): 29–35.

Tuska, Jon. *The American West in Film: Critical Approaches to the Western.* Westport, Conn.: Greenwood Press, 1985.

Twombly, Robert. *Frank Lloyd Wright: An Interpretive Biography.* New York: Harper and Row, 1973.

Underwood, Grant. "Re-visioning Mormon History." *Pacific Historical Review* 55 (August 1986): 403–26.

Underwood, Kathleen. "The Pace of Their Own Lives: Teacher Training and the Life Course of Western Women." *Pacific Historical Review* 55 (November 1986): 513–30.

Vaughn-Robertson, Courtney Ann. "Having a Purpose in Life: Western Women Teachers in the Twentieth Century." *Great Plains Quarterly* 5 (Spring 1985): 107–24.

Vaughn-Robertson, Courtney Ann. "Sometimes Independent but Never Equal—

Women Teachers, 1900–1950: The Oklahoma Example." *Pacific Historical Review* 53 (February 1984): 39–58.

Vorpahl, Ben M. *Frederic Remington and the West: With the Eye of the Mind.* Austin: University of Texas Press, 1978.

Walker, Franklin. *A Literary History of Southern California.* Berkeley: University of California Press, 1950.

Wollenberg, Charles. *All Deliberate Speed: Segregation and Exclusion in California Schools, 1855–1975.* Berkeley: University of California Press, 1975.

Wright, Will. *Six Guns and Society: A Structural Study of the Western.* Berkeley: University of California Press, 1975.

Young, Mary. "The West and American Cultural Identity: Old Themes and New Variations." *Western Historical Quarterly* 1 (April 1970): 137–60.

Contributors

Carl Abbott is Professor of Urban Studies and Planning at Portland State University, where he teaches courses on urban history and urban revitalization policy. Recent publications include a revised edition of *The New Urban America: Growth and Politics in Sunbelt Cities* (1987) and *Urban America in the Modern Age: 1920 to the Present* (1987).

Karen Anderson is Associate Professor of History at the University of Arizona, where she teaches recent U.S. and women's history. Her publications include *Wartime Women: Sex Roles, Family Relations, and the Status of Women During World War II* (1981) and numerous articles on women and work. She is currently completing a comparative study of minority group women in modern America.

Fred Erisman is Lorraine Sherley Professor of Literature and chairman of the English Department at Texas Christian University. A specialist in American Studies, he has published widely in the fields of regional literature, children's literature, and detective and suspense fiction. His most recent books are *Fifty Western Writers* (1982), coedited with Richard Etulain, and *Barnboken I USA* (Stockholm, 1986).

Richard W. Etulain is Professor of History at the University of New Mexico where he teaches courses in western historiography and cultural history. His most recent books are *Conversations with Wallace Stegner on Western History and Literature* (1983) and *Faith and Imagination* (1985).

He has recently coauthored with Michael P. Malone, *American West: A Twentieth-Century History* (1989).

Paul Kleppner is University Research Professor of History and Political Science and Director of the Social Science Research Institute at Northern Illinois University. His most recent books are *Who Voted? The Dynamics of Electoral Turnout, 1870–1980* (1982); *Chicago Divided: The Making of a Black Mayor* (1985); and *Continuity and Change in Electoral Politics, 1893–1928* (1987). He is currently working on a book on political culture and party development in the western states since 1900.

Howard R. Lamar is Sterling Professor of History at Yale University where he teaches graduate and undergraduate courses on the History of the Trans-Mississippi West as well as courses on comparative frontier history, Indian history, and family history. His publications include *Dakota Territory, 1861–1889: A Study of Frontier Politics* (1956), and *The Far Southwest, 1846–1912: A Territorial History* (1966). Among several edited works are his *The Reader's Encyclopedia of the American West* (1977) and, with Leonard Thompson, *The Frontier in History: North America and Southern Africa Compared* (1981). Since 1973 he has served as coeditor of *The Histories of the American Frontier Series*, founded by Ray Allen Billington.

H. Wayne Morgan is George Lynn Cross Research Professor of History at the University of Oklahoma, where he teaches courses in various aspects of the last hundred years of American history. He has written numerous books on the Gilded Age, including *Unity and Culture: The United States, 1877–1900* (1971), and *New Muses: Art in American Culture 1865–1920* (1977). He is currently doing research for a general history of the arts in the twentieth-century Southwest.

Gerald D. Nash is Presidential Professor of History at the University of New Mexico, where he teaches courses in U.S. and western twentieth-century history. Among his publications in these fields are *The American West in Twentieth Century* (1973), *The Great Depression and World War II* (1979), and *The American West Transformed: The Impact of World War II* (1985). He is currently completing a book on the economic impact of World War II on the American West.

Walter Nugent is Andrew V. Tackes Professor of History at the University of Notre Dame. He teaches American frontier and environmental history and the United States from 1860 to 1920. His recent publications include

Contributors

Structures of American Social History (1981), and he is working on the history of westward population shifts in the twentieth century.

John Opie is a professor of history at the New Jersey Institute of Technology in Newark. His books include *Americans and Environment: The Controversy over Ecology* (1971), *Energy and American Values* (1982), *The Law of the Land: 200 Years of American Farmland Policy* (1987), and a forthcoming history of the agricultural development of groundwater from the High Plains/Ogallala aquifer.

Donald L. Parman is Associate Professor at Purdue University where he teaches courses on Indians of the United States and the American West. He is author of *The Navajos and the New Deal* and several articles on twentieth-century Indian history. He is currently working on a study of Indians of the American West in the twentieth century.

Donald J. Pisani is Associate Professor of History at Texas A & M University, where he teaches courses in environmental, legal, and western American history. He is the author of *From the Family Farm to Agribusiness: The Irrigation Crusade in California and the West, 1850–1931* (1984) and many articles on the law, natural resources, and American economic development. He is currently completing a manuscript to be published in the *Histories of the American Frontier Series, How Water Won the West: Building a Dryland Empire, 1850–1940.*

William G. Robbins is Professor of History at Oregon State University and teaches western American history, Indian history, and environmental history. He is the author of *Lumberjacks and Legislators: Political Economy of the U.S. Lumber Industry* (1982) and *American Forestry: A History of National, State, and Private Cooperation* (1985).

Ricardo Romo, a San Antonio native, completed his undergraduate studies at the University of Texas at Austin and earned his doctorate in history at the University of California at Los Angeles. Professor Romo's essays have been published in Germany, Spain, France, and Mexico. He is the author of *East Los Angeles: History of a Barrio* (1983) and coauthor of *The Mexican American Experience: An Interdisciplinary Anthology* (1985). Professor Romo is currently serving as editor of *Ethnic Affairs* and teaches at UT-Austin.

William D. Rowley is Executive Secretary of the Western History Association and Professor of History at the University of Nevada-Reno where he teaches Nevada history, American West, and U.S. Environmental history. His books include *M. L. Wilson and the Campaign for the Domestic Allotment Plan* (1970) and *U.S. Forest Service Grazing and Rangelands: A History* (1985). He is currently completing a study of U.S. Senator Francis G. Newlands as a western and national Progressive.

Index

NOTE: Boldface numerals indicate full-chapter treatment of a subject.

Abbey, Edward, 210, 371
Abbott, Carl, xiii, 33, **71–98**, 100, 413, 447
Acuña, Rodolfo, 124
agriculture, 175–206, 212–13
Alaska, 65
Alberta, 192, 196, 197
American Council for Spanish-Speaking People (ACSSP), 134–35
American G. I. Forum, 133–35
Anderson, Karen, xiii, 25, 33, **99–122**, 413, 447
Arizona, 46, 55, 58, 64, 238–39
Arizona v. California, 280
art, **383–406**
Athearn, Robert G., 15–16
automobiles, 107

Benton, Thomas Hart, 395–96
bibliography, **421–46**
Bierstadt, Albert, 386
Billington, Ray Allen, 19, 411
Bingham, George Caleb, 383–84
blacks, 53, 63, 65, 412, 413
Blumenschein, Ernest L., 385, 394
Bone, Homer T., 318–21
Bonnifield, Paul, 187, 197
braceros, 132–34

British Columbia, 241–42, 245, 246, 247
Brown, Richard Maxwell, 375, 377
Bureau of Indian Affairs (BIA), 148, 150–52, 154–61
Burke Act of 1906, 150, 152

California, 80, 212, 312–13, 372–75, 399–400; demographic patterns in, 40–41, 43, 50–52, 60–61, 66–67; lumber industry in, 235–40, 245–49; water policies in, 261, 263, 268–69, 270, 271–72, 276–77
Canada, 173, 175–77, 189–99, 220–21, 241–42, 249–51, 417
Carmel (California), 399, 401
Carter, Jimmy, 265–66
Cather, Willa, 370
Caughey, John Walton, 13–14
Chadwick, Stephen F., 320–21
Chávez, César, 136–38
Chicanas, 110, 112–13
Chicanos. *See* Mexican Americans.
Collier, John, 153–61
colonialism, 12, 72, 186, 328, 330, 339–40
Colorado, 44–45, 55, 63

INDEX

Colorado River, 210, 214–16, 220, 329
comparative history, **175–206**, 416–17
Conservative Party, 195, 196
Co-operative Commonwealth Federation (CCF), 196, 197
counties (population), 56–57
Couse, E. Irving, 391, 394, 401
Cox, Thomas R., 235
Curry, John Steuart, 395–96

Davis, H. L., 368
Democratic party, 296–99, 301–2, 305–11, 313–26, 341–42, 350–53
demography. *See* populations.
Depression, 130–31, **173–206**, 242–43, 296, 349–50, 416–17
De Voto, Bernard, 9–12
dust bowls, 175–76, 184–87, 251

economic history, **173–206**
Emmons, Glenn L., 163–64
energy and environment, 215–16
environmental history, **207–92**
Erisman, Fred, xiv, 359, **361–81**, 417, 447
Etulain, Richard W., xiii, xiv, **1–31**, 411, 417, 447–48

Farmer-labor party, 317, 318, 320
Federal Power Commission (FPC), 277–78, 279
Fisher, Vardis, 368
Fitzgerald, F. Scott, 370
forestry. *See* lumbering.
Frankfurt school, 416

Garland, Hamlin, 365–66, 371
Garnsey, Morris E., 11
General Allotment (Dawes) Act of 1887, 149–51, 156
Georgia-Pacific Lumber Company, 246, 247–48
Gorman, R. C., 389
Gottlieb, Robert, 21–22, 88, 415–16
Graves, John, 372

Graves, Morris, 399
Great Plains, 181–89
Greeley, William B., 238
Gressley, Gene M., 18
Guthrie, A. B., Jr., 369
Guthrie, Woody, 215–16

Harte, Bret, 373
Haslam, Gerald, 373
Hawaii, 65
Henri, Robert, 393, 395
Hernandez v. State, 135
Hispanic culture, 390, 392. *Also see* Mexican Americans.
historiography, **1–31**
Hofstadter, Richard, 342, 352
Hollon, W. Eugene, 16–17, 211
Hollywood, 408, 409
Hugo, Richard, 368
Hurd, Peter, 384, 387
hydraulic empire, 262–63

Idaho, 48, 58–59, 240–41
Indian Claims Commission, 160
Indian Reorganization Act (IRA), 156–57
Indians, **147–72**, 224–25, 412–13; and art, 386–89, 396–98
Industrial Workers of the World (Wobblies), 345, 347
Internationalization, 82–84
irrigation, 257–92
irrigation districts, 268–72, 283

Jakle, John J., 218
Jeffers, Robinson, 374
Jensen, Joan, 100, 109
Jim Crow, 132–34

Kesey, Ken, 368
Klamath Indians, 162–63
Kleppner, Paul, xiii–xiv, 293, **295–338**, 415, 448
Kraenzel, Carl Frederick, 11–12

Lamar, Howard R., xiii, **173–206**, 416, 448

Index

Latino, 138–39
League of United Latin American Citizens (LULAC), 131–32, 134
Lemke, William, 178, 179–80
Liberal Party, 195, 196
Limerick, Patricia Nelson, 25
literature, **361–81**
Los Angeles, 52, 60–61, 73, 260
Lowitt, Richard, 23–24, 181, 187–88, 199
lumber industry, **233–56**

McWilliams, Carey, 12–13, 89, 123–24, 413
Malin, James C., 6–7
Malone, Michael P., 24
Manitoba, 191
Martin, Charles H., 322–23
Mathews, Arthur, 399
Merk, Frederick, 19–20
metropolitan. *See* urbanization.
Mexican Americans, **123–45**
Mexico, 126–29, 131, 220–21
Mezerik, A. G., 10
Miller, Darlis, 100
modernism, 388–89, 393–95
Montana, 43–44, 54, 62–63, 240–41
Moran, Thomas, 386
Morgan, H. Wayne, xiv, 359, **383–406**, 411, 448
Morgan, Neil, 21–22
Mormons, 63, 267, 271
Moynihan, Ruth Barnes, 108–9
mutual water companies, 266–67
Myer, Dillon S., 160

Nash, Gerald D., xiv, 2, 18–19, 23–24, 100, 211, 367, 448
natioinal parks, 218–19, 220, 221, 222
Native Americans. *See* Indians
Navajo Indians, 154, 158, 387–88
Nevada, 47–48, 58, 64, 351, 413–14
New Deal, 156–58, 159, 179–81, 185, 188, 303, 396; and western politics, 329–30, 349–55
New England, 363–64

Newlands Reclamation Act (1902), 126, 278, 346
New Mexico, 45–46, 55, 63–64, 238–39, 388–95
Nonpartisan League, 178, 181
Norris, Frank, 373, 374
North Dakota, 176–81
Nugent, Walter, xiii, 33, **35–70**, 414, 448–49

O'Keeffe, Georgia, 395
Opie, John, xiii, 207, **209–32**, 414, 449
Oregon, 49–50, 59–60, 65; lumbering industry in, 235–40, 242–43, 246–51; politics in, 317–18, 321–24

Pacific Northwest, 235–38, 240–41, 242–50, 368
Palliser, John, 189–91
Parish, John Carl, 5–6
Parman, Donald L., xiii, 34, **147–72**, 413, 449
Paxson, Frederic Logan, 4–5, 7
Peirce, Neal R., 22–23
Pelton Dam case, 276–78, 279–80
Phillips, Bert G., 391, 392
Pisani, Donald J., xiii, 207, 213, 219, **257–92**, 449
political culture, 325–32
political reform, **339–57**
politics, **293–357**
Pomeroy, Earl, 15, 17–18, 211, 222–23
populations, **33–70**
Populism, 295, 306, 341, 408
Potter, David, 99–100, 209, 217
Powell, John Wesley, 185, 188, 209–10, 214
Progressivism, 150–52, 221, 341–47, 348
prostitution, 112
public hydroelectric power, 318–21

Regionalism, 7–9, 188–89, 197–99, **361–81**, 395–96, 418

453

Reisner, Marc, 262–66
religion, 305, 306–7, 317, 325
Remington, Frederic, 384–85
Republican party, 295, 296–99, 301–2, 305–10, 312–17, 320–26, 348
Robbins, William G., xiii, 207, 217, **233–56**, 449
Robinson, Elwyn, 179, 180
Romo, Ricardo, xiii, 34, 123–45, 413, 449
Roosevelt, Franklin D., 179, 181, 296, 313–15, 318–20, 322–23, 349
Roosevelt, Theodore, 308–9, 310, 341–42
Rowley, William D., xiv, 293, **339–357**, 449–50
rural, 36–37, 40, 53
Russell, Charles M., 385

San Francisco, 51, 60
Saskatchewan, 192, 194–96, 197
Sauer, Carl O., 223–24
Scholder, Fritz, 396–98
Sells, Cato, 151–53
Sharp, Joseph Henry, 391–92, 394
Sloan, John, 389, 394, 395
Smith, Henry Nash, 16, 26, 366, 411
Social Credit Party, 196–97
South, as region, 364–65
South Dakota, 176–77
Stegner, Wallace, 366, 369, 370
Steinbeck, John, 373–74
Still, Clyfford, 399–400
Sunbelt, 86–87, 102, 106, 414

Taft-Hartley Act, 354–55
Taos-Santa Fe school of art, 387, 389–95
Tapia, Primo, 127–28
termination of Indian reservations, 161–63
Texas, 80, 131, 132–35, 371–72
Thiebaud, Wayne, 397, 401
Tobey, Mark, 399
tourism, 84–85, 217–19

Truman, Harry, 313, 354–55
Turner, Frederick Jackson, xii, xiii, 15, 19, 24, 36, 99, 222–23; and western historiography, 2–8, 407–17; and western literature, 363–64, 365–67, 375, 376–77
Tweton, D. Jerome, 177–78

Ufer, Walter, 391, 401
United Farmer Workers Union (UFW), 137
U.S. Bureau of Reclamation, 264–65, 269, 271, 273, 274, 275, 416
U.S. Corps of Engineers, 264–65, 275
urbanization, 37, 40, 53, **71–98**, 103, 111–13, 214–15
Utah, 46–47, 58, 63

Wallace, David Rains, 368
Washington, 48–49, 65; lumbering industry in, 235–38, 240, 242, 244–47, 249; politics in, 317, 318–21
water and water policy, 213–14, **257–92**
Webb, Walter Prescott, 5–10, 188, 199, 223
West Coast Lumberman's Association, 237, 238
western myth, xii, 408
Weyerhaeuser Lumber Company, 246, 248
White, Richard, 89, 157–58, 222
White, William Allen, 10
Wilder, Laura Ingalls, 370
Wiley, Peter, 21–22, 88, 415–16
Wilson, Woodrow, 309–10, 311
Wittfogel, Karl, 259, 262, 416
woman suffrage, 108, 109–10
women, **99–102**, 412, 413
Work, Hubert, 154–55
World War I, 126–28, 152
World War II, 71, 82, 132, 181, 244, 275, 353–54
Worster, Donald, 183, 185, 186, 199, 211, 213, 222, 251, 261–63, 416
Wyoming, 44, 54–55, 63

454